Bertil Ohlin

Bertil Ohlin
April 23, 1899–August 3, 1999
Painting by Fritiof Schüldt, 1964

Bertil Ohlin

A Centennial Celebration (1899–1999)

edited by
Ronald Findlay, Lars Jonung,
and Mats Lundahl

The MIT Press
Cambridge, Massachusetts
London, England

This book was set in Palatino on 3B2 by Asco Typesetters, Hong Kong.
Printed and bound in the United States of America.

Library of Congress Cataloging-in-Publication Data

Bertil Ohlin : a centennial celebration, 1899–1999 / edited by Ronald Findlay, Lars Jonung, and Mats Lundahl.
p. cm.
Includes bibliographical references and index.
ISBN 978-0-262-06228-2 (hc : alk. paper)
1. Ohlin, Bertil Gotthard, 1899– 2. Economists—Sweden—Biography.
3. Heckscher-Ohlin principle. I. Findlay, Ronald. II. Jonung, Lars. III. Lundahl, Mats, 1946–
HB116.5.O36 B472 2002
380.1′092—dc21
[B] 2002023022

ISBN13 978-0-262-51903-8 (pb.)

Contents

The Ohlin Lectures

1. Jagdish Bhagwati, *Protectionism* (1988)

2. Richard N. Cooper, *Economic Stabilization and Debt in Developing Countries* (1992)

3. Assar Lindbeck, *Unemployment and Macroeconomics* (1993)

4. Anne O. Krueger, *Political Economy of Policy Reform in Developing Countries* (1993)

5. Ronald Findlay, *Factor Proportions, Trade, and Growth* (1995)

6. Paul Krugman, *Development, Geography, and Economic Theory* (1995)

7. Deepak K. Lal, *Unintended Consequences: The Impact of Factor Endowments, Culture, and Politics on Long-Run Economic Performance* (1998)

8. Ronald W. Jones, *Globalization and the Theory of Input Trade* (2000)

9. W. Max Corden, *Too Sensational: On the Choice of Exchange Rate Regimes* (2002)

10. Ronald Findlay, Lars Jonung, and Mats Lundahl, editors, *Bertil Ohlin: A Centennial Celebration (1899–1999)* (2002)

Contributors

Benny Carlson
Lund University

Donald R. Davis
Columbia University

Antoni Estevadeordal
Inter-American Development Bank

Ronald Findlay
Columbia University

Harry Flam
Stockholm University

M. June Flanders
Tel Aviv University

Torsten Gårdlund
Lund University

Carl B. Hamilton
Stockholm School of Economics

Björn Hansson
Lund University

Rolf G. H. Henriksson
Stockholm University

Douglas A. Irwin
Dartmouth College

Ronald W. Jones
University of Rochester

Lars Jonung
Stockholm School of Economics

Paul Krugman
Princeton University

Mats Lundahl
Stockholm School of Economics

Karl-Gustaf Löfgren
Umeå University

Robert A. Mundell
Columbia University

Svante Nycander
Dagens Nyheter

Hellen Ohlin
SIDA, Bertil Ohlin's daughter

Tomas Ohlin
Linköping University
Bertil Ohlin's son

Kevin H. O'Rourke
Trinity College, Dublin

Paul A. Samuelson
Massachusetts Institute of Technology

Bo Sandelin
Gothenburg University

Alan M. Taylor
University of California, Davis

Niels-Henrik Topp
Copenhagen University

Eskil Wadensjö
Stockholm University

David E. Weinstein
Columbia University

Anne Wibble
† Ex Minister of Finance, Bertil Ohlin's daughter

Jeffrey G. Williamson
Harvard University

Anne Wibble, 1943–2000

Anne Wibble
October 13, 1943–March 14, 2000

Anne Wibble was born in 1943. She was the youngest of Evy and Bertil Ohlin's three children. At the time of her birth her father was member of Parliament (Liberal) and professor of economics at Stockholm School of Economics. A year later Bertil Ohlin became the leader of the Liberal Party and the Minister of Trade (while still a professor). After her matriculation examination, Anne Wibble studied at the Stockholm School of Economics and received her *civilekonomexamen* (M.Sc. in economics) in 1966. The next steps for her were a Masters degree at Stanford University, a *licenciatexamen* (M.Phil.) from Stockholm School of Economics, and a teaching position at that School. Before going to the United States, she married Jan Wibble, a political scientist working at Stockholm University. They have two daughters.

In 1985 Anne Wibble became member of Parliament for the Liberal Party. She was right away appointed shadow spokesperson on financial and economic affairs for the party. She soon established herself as one of the leading opposition politicians, not the least thanks to her strong background in economics, her soft and efficient debating style, and her sound, stable judgement. She was one of the architects behind the radical and very important Swedish tax reform of the early 1990s. In this way Anne Wibble fulfilled one of her father's major political ideas, viz. "It must pay to work," as Bertil Ohlin formulated the problem of high marginal taxes already in the 1950s.

As minister of finance in 1991 to 1994, Anne Wibble had to handle the deepest economic crisis in Sweden since the 1930s. The crisis was the result of a combination of the domestic demand driven inflationary boom of the late 1980s and the European arrangements for fixed exchange rates that collapsed in 1992. During this tough period her economic skills, clear liberal ideology, strong willpower, and exceptional capacity to work long hours became invaluable assets for the government. The strong upswing in the Swedish economy in the 1990s no doubt had its important foundations in the budget austerity program, the move to independence for the Swedish central bank, and the deregulations of markets (for telecom, electricity, transport, etc.) that began during her time in office. Anne Wibble was also deeply involved in the negotiations for Swedish EU membership, concluded in 1994.

In 1997 Anne Wibble left Parliament to take up the position as chief economist of the Swedish Federation of Industries. She died from cancer in March 2000.

As a person Anne Wibble was wise, generous with her time, helpful, absent-minded, analytical, economical, sometimes excessively loyal and unselfish, and always laid back and relaxed during her vacations. I know, since I worked with Anne Wibble first as a Liberal MP and finance minister Wibble's parliamentary representative in the Parliament's Finance Committee, later as the State Secretary in the Ministry of Finance, and finally I succeeded her in Parliament.

Of course, she was no saint. For example, in addition to all the positive characteristics mentioned above, she gradually could grow very irritated when people refused to be convinced by her facts and logical reasoning even after hours of haggling. She had a rare capacity to work long hours. When needed, she worked regularly till after midnight, but she could also "cancel sleep," as she phrased it, altogether and continue to work, drink coffee, and smoke throughout one or two nights a week.

As one of the very few women in her generation with a high academic degree in economics, Anne Wibble became Sweden's first female minister of finance. She became a role model and a source of inspiration for women with an interest in economics and politics. Among the young generation, of both sexes, she seems to be most remembered for her intellectual and credible leadership, characterized by an ability to listen and discuss with an open mind. That ability she no doubt inherited from her father but also acquired in the coffee and seminar rooms of the Stockholm School of Economics.

Carl B. Hamilton

Preface

The origin of this book is the conference *Bertil Ohlin: A Centennial Celebration (1899–1999)*, held at the Stockholm School of Economics on October 14–16, 1999. This conference could not have been carried out without the unselfish support of a number of individuals. Most important are, of course, the various authors, whose combined efforts have increased our knowledge of Bertil Ohlin's life, work and influence considerably. Peter Diamond read Paul Samuelson's contribution. Claes Berg, Arne Bigsten, Karolina Ekholm, Tore Ellingsen, Rikard Forslid, Klas Fregert, Carl B. Hamilton, Göte Hansson, Per-Olov Johansson, David Laidler, Lars Magnusson, Otto Steiger, Bo Södersten, Hans Tson Söderström, and Hans-Michael Trautwein all served as discussants of the chapters presented. Lars Bergman, Bengt Jönsson, Håkan Lindgren, Lars Ljungqvist, Ingemar Ståhl, and Jörgen Weibull chaired the various sessions.

Logistic service from the staff of the Stockholm School of Economics was ensured by its president, Claes-Robert Julander, who gave the undertaking his full and generous support. The hub of the conference organization was Pirjo Furtenbach, who undertook all the time-consuming work connected with such tasks as travel scheduling, hotel room bookings, reimbursements, meals, and everything else. Christina Lönnblad checked the English of a number of the contributions and in addition translated Ohlin's *licentiat* thesis into English.

Financial support was provided by the Kjell and Märta Beijer Foundation, the sponsor of the annual Bertil Ohlin Lectures at the Stockholm School of Economics, by the Prince Bertil Foundation and by the Central Bank of Sweden. To all these people and institutions go our heartfelt gratitude. Without their support there would have been no conference. We owe a special thanks to Bertil Ohlin's three children: Hellen, Tomas, and the late Anne Wibble, who supported the project throughout. Anne passed away before the work could be completed. We dedicate the present book to her memory.

Bertil Ohlin

1 Introduction

Ronald Findlay, Lars Jonung, and Mats Lundahl

Bertil Ohlin was undoubtedly the major single influence on the development of international economics in the twentieth century. He not only enriched and extended the factor proportions theory of comparative advantage first proposed by Eli Heckscher in 1919 into the imposing theoretical edifice that bears their joint name, but also was responsible for the revival and consistent reformulation of the "income-expenditure approach" to the theory of the balance of payments in his famous controversy with Keynes over the German reparations problem. There is no need for additional reasons to justify a volume devoted to the centenary of his birth in 1899.

There are, however, a few such reasons. Despite his fame and secure position in the history of economic thought, the details of Ohlin's life and work are not as well known outside Sweden as might be expected. One main reason is that his seminal contributions were made as long ago as the 1920s and early 1930s. After that he devoted most of his time to politics. Furthermore his major work was a long and discursive treatise that even many specialists in the field have not read, deriving their acquaintance with his ideas second-hand from the concise models formulated by Paul Samuelson, Ronald Jones, and others. His pioneering work in macroeconomics became an early victim of "the attractive Anglo-Saxon kind of unnecessary originality" that Gunnar Myrdal (1939:8) long ago complained about, to no avail. The emergence around 1980 of what was called the "new trade theory," emphasizing the role of increasing returns to scale and monopolistic competition, raises the question of the extent of Ohlin's awareness of these factors and their compatibility with the factor proportions view. Finally, the factor proportions approach has inspired much recent research on "global economic history" that needs to be examined and integrated with earlier literature. For these reasons the centenary of Bertil Ohlin's birth is a suitable occasion for a volume that will commemorate his many-sided life and work.

A Capsule Biography

Bertil Ohlin, born in 1899, was raised in Klippan, a village in the province of Skåne in southernmost Sweden. His family had a middle-class background with roots in the local farming community. His father was *landsfiskal*, district attorney.

After finishing high school in nearby Helsingborg at the tender age of 16, the young Ohlin continued to the University of Lund in the fall of 1915, beginning his studies of economics, statistics, and mathematics. He attended some classes of the aging Knut Wicksell, dealing with the financing of German agriculture—but as Ohlin (1972:46–47) noted in his autobiography, Wicksell did not appear very interested in the subject of his lectures. Ohlin did not make contact with Wicksell at this time.

Having obtained a university degree in two years, Ohlin left Lund for Stockholm to continue his studies at the Stockholm School of Economics, where he was allowed to attend the seminar in economics run by Eli Heckscher. Ohlin immediately impressed his elders. He was soon allowed to attend the meetings of the Political Economy Club, set up by Heckscher—at the suggestion of Wicksell's wife Anna—to give Knut Wicksell a platform after retiring from his chair in Lund and returning to Stockholm. The club served as a graduate seminar for its members.

Sweden could not offer any graduate teaching in economics worthy of the name at that time. Thus Ohlin went abroad, studying at Cambridge and Harvard in the early 1920s where he had fruitful contacts with Frank Taussig and Allyn Young. In 1922 Ohlin presented his *licentiat* thesis on interregional exchange where, for the first time, he set out the ideas of what was later termed the Heckscher-Ohlin model. Here Ohlin merged ideas from Gustav Cassel's general equilibrium theory and Eli Heckscher's work on international trade.

Two years later Ohlin defended his doctoral dissertation *Handelns teori* (The theory of trade) under Gustav Cassel at Stockholm University. It was written in Swedish—and thus not available to an international audience. Actually, however, Ohlin submitted a manuscript to the *Economic Journal* in the early 1920s that contained the basic ideas of his theory of international trade. Upon receiving the rejection letter, signed by the aging F. Y. Edgeworth, Ohlin found a note with a comment that unintentionally had slipped into the letter and which stated: "This amounts to nothing and should be refused. J. M. Keynes" (Ohlin 1975:107). Ohlin cherished this remark and kept the note for the rest of his life.

Ohlin never translated his dissertation into English. Instead, he began expanding it. In the process the size of the work grew between four and five times—but the original approach was maintained. When it finally appeared in English almost ten years later, in 1933, as *Interregional and International Trade*, the book was immediately recognized as a pathbreaking study. It became the foundation of the theory of international and interregional trade as well as of empirical work in international economics. It still holds this position—witnessing the profound impact of Ohlin's work. The Heckscher-Ohlin theorem—a term coined by Wolfgang Stolper and Paul Samuelson in 1941—laid the foundation for Ohlin's subsequent fame as an economist. This contribution was singled out in the citation for the prize in memory of Alfred Nobel that Ohlin was awarded in 1977. As an immediate result of his work on trade, Ohlin became a full professor at the University of Copenhagen in 1924 at the record young age of 25. He spent the rest of the 1920s in Denmark, maintaining frequent contacts with Sweden.

Ohlin obtained international recognition in 1929 in an exchange of views in the *Economic Journal* with John Maynard Keynes on the theory of capital transfers. The debate between the two dealt with the German reparation payments stipulated by the Versailles Treaty. Ohlin noted in his memoirs that it was valuable for his reputation and professional standing to challenge a famous economist like Keynes—and to prove him wrong.

Bertil Ohlin was appointed professor at the Stockholm School of Economics, returning to Sweden at the end of 1929 for the chair that was vacated by Eli Heckscher who by then had been given a personal chair in economic history. Following the Swedish tradition, Ohlin held this chair from 1930 until his retirement in 1965.

Upon his return, Ohlin moved away from international economics into the field of macroeconomics. The depression and the high unemployment in the early 1930s inspired the young generation of Swedish economists including Gunnar Myrdal, Erik Lindahl, Erik Lundberg, and Bertil Ohlin. Their goal was to find solutions to high unemployment and economic stagnation, the burning social question of the day.

In 1931 Ohlin prepared a study on the world depression for the League of Nations. As the depression grew deeper, Ohlin became keenly involved with the Committee on Unemployment. In a report published in 1934, *Penningpolitik, offentliga arbeten, subventioner och tullar som medel mot arbetslösheten. Bidrag till expansionens teori,* (Monetary policy, public works, subsidies and tariff policy as remedies for unemployment. Contributions to the theory of expansion) Ohlin presented a sequence analysis with Keynesian features. It included a multiplier and an accelerator analysis expressed verbally. Ohlin recommended more active policies to counteract the depression and reduce unemployment. Unfortunately for Ohlin and Swedish economics, the report was not translated into English. When Keynes's *General Theory* appeared—by invitation from Keynes as editor—Ohlin summarized the views of the younger generation of Swedish economists and contrasted them with those of Keynes in two articles in the *Economic Journal* in 1937. Here, he coined the term the Stockholm School (of economists) suggesting that it represented a school in its own right.

In the 1930s Ohlin turned into an extremely prolific writer of newspaper articles, columns, editorial articles, and comments, in particular in *Stockholms-Tidningen.* His contributions demonstrate how he evolved as an outspoken advocate of expansionary measures to counteract the depression. He moved away from Heckscher's classical or orthodox liberalism. This caused a rift between him and his former mentor as Ohlin argued for a modern form of liberalism with a more active role for government in economic and social affairs, which he termed *social liberalism.*

Gradually Ohlin moved into party politics as well. He became chairman of the Liberal Party youth organization in 1934, member of Parliament a few years later, leader of the Liberal Party in 1944, and member of the government of national unity that ruled Sweden in 1944–45, during World War II. In the elections of 1946 and 1948, the Liberals gained much ground, however, at the expense of the other nonsocialist parties. Ohlin emerged as the opposition candidate for the post of prime minister, without being able to overthrow the social democratic government. Between 1956 and 1958 Ohlin made another unsuccessful attempt to obtain the post of prime minister in the struggle over the pension system. He left the liberal leadership in 1967 and Parliament in 1970. In the 1970s he went back to doing some work in economics, writing about his views in the 1930s, publishing comments on current affairs, and arguing for a better education of the public on economic issues. He also published his memoirs in two volumes in 1972 and 1975. Bertil Ohlin died in 1979, two years after receiving the Nobel Prize.

Ohlin thus completed two brilliant careers, one as an economist and one as a politician. He spent a little more than a decade of his life, mainly the 1920s, on the theory of international trade, leaving a permanent mark on the subject. He spent approximately another five years, the first half of the 1930s, on the macroeconomic issues of the Great Depression, working on pre-Keynesian theories and policy recommendations.

He then devoted most of his activities to politics. His brand of liberalism was influential in the Swedish post–World War II period, making the policies of the ruling Social Democrats less socialistic. Ohlin's style in politics was "academic," raising the level of debate. He was influential in the process that gave Sweden a new constitution by 1970. Throughout his life, he was an active writer of newspaper contributions, publishing thousands of articles where he presented what he regarded as a "sound" economic analysis. He thought it important that the public have a good understanding of economic issues.

The purpose of this volume, emanating from the centennial of Bertil Ohlin's birth, is to give a portrait of the man, his life, his contributions to international economics and macroeconomics, his journalism, and his many years at the center of Swedish politics, with emphasis on Ohlin the economist, even though he spent most of his active life in politics.[1]

The Man

Three major documents dealing with Ohlin's life and career exist: his own two autobiographical volumes (Ohlin 1972, 1975) and Sven-Erik Larsson's (1998) recent biography. All three are in Swedish—unfortunately for most of the international audience—and in his preface Larsson (1998:9–10) furthermore states that as far as his own book is concerned, "the private person of Bertil Ohlin has received less attention than is customary in biographies." Instead Larsson concentrates on Ohlin the politician. Our first section, on Bertil Ohlin the man, is intended to provide a partial filling of this gap.

Bertil and Evy Ohlin had three children: Hellen, Tomas, and Anne. In chapter 1 they present a charming account of their childhood, their upbringing in Stockholm, the summers in the countryside, and the relationships to their father. In the 1930s and 1940s the Ohlin family led a rich social life. Bertil Ohlin was very much a public figure, and the Ohlin home was a frequent meeting place for journalists, liberal politicians, and academic economists.

Hellen Ohlin's story emphasizes her father's keen interest in all family matters, including those of his six brothers and sisters and his strong belief in the liberal cause and his loyalty to fellow liberals. Father and daughter had some disagreements, among others on gender issues. Hellen remarks that her father was emancipated in theory but not in practice.

Tomas Ohlin notes the difficulty of being the son of a well-known father. To him, there was too much politics at home. His response was to turn to sports and music. Tomas was given great freedom in forming his views and opinions, however. His father was not trying to influence him. Tomas chose to study technology and information sciences. Later in life, father and son shared an interest in the use of information technology to foster local democracy.

Anne, being the youngest, got more attention from her parents than Hellen or Tomas. Following the advice of her father, she studied at the Stockholm School of Economics, Sweden's leading business school. Eventually she developed a lively interest in economics, defending a *licentiat* thesis (cf. below) on fiscal policy for professor Erik Lundberg. Father and daughter carried out lengthy discussions on various economic issues.

Anne Wibble also followed in her father's footsteps in another way. She turned to politics working for the Liberal Party, but she began this career rather late in life. She was not a member of the Liberal youth movement, for example, only entering Parliament in 1985. Following the general election of 1991, the nonsocialist parties formed a coalition government, and Anne Wibble was appointed Minister of Finance. She was the first woman to occupy this post, holding it during the period 1991 to 1994.

The Stockholm School of Economics was the academic base for Bertil Ohlin. Leaving his chair in Copenhagen in 1929, he remained professor of economics at the school from that year until his retirement in 1965. The same year as Ohlin started teaching at the Stockholm School of Economics, 1930, Torsten Gårdlund began his studies there. In his account of Ohlin as friend and colleague, in chapter 3, he remembers Ohlin as a well-dressed young professor with a sporty outlook, lecturing on economics, a subject ranked as less important and less interesting for students in search of successful careers in business.

After graduating from the School in 1933, Gårdlund continued to study economics at the Stockholm University, eventually obtaining a doctorate in 1942. In 1947 he was back at the Stockholm School of Economics, now as a professor of economics and as a colleague to Bertil Ohlin. In the meantime Ohlin had become the leader of the Liberal Party and Gårdlund a liberal Social Democrat.

As colleagues in the coming years, Gårdlund and Ohlin maintained a friendly relationship, although they met infrequently. The reason was Ohlin's political commitments. He was the main leader of the opposition in Sweden and was writing newspaper columns regularly in addition to being a full professor. He was extremely busy, often arriving and leaving the school by taxi to attend to his lectures and teaching.[2]

Gårdlund describes the background to Ohlin's scientific career. Ohlin started in Lund but transferred to the Stockholm School of Economics. Gårdlund is convinced that Ohlin soon learned that he could not get a thorough and modern training in economics within Sweden and decided to go abroad, to Cambridge, England, and to Harvard. At Harvard Ohlin found what he was looking for: a first-rate program in economics. His one-year stay there set him off on his dissertation, toward international fame and recognition.

In chapter 4 Paul Samuelson offers "his" portrait of Bertil Ohlin, including a fresh look at some neglected aspects of Ohlin's 1933 magnum opus. The starting point is that it is self-evident that economists of all generations, including the youngest one, refer to Ohlin in the context of the theory of factor proportions based trade that carries his name: the great idea developed by him out of the 1919 Heckscher paper that would become a never-ending source of inspiration for later scientific work on trade.

With Erik Lindahl and Gunnar Myrdal, Ohlin belonged to what may be termed the second generation of modern Swedish economists, the first generation consisting of David Davidson, Knut Wicksell,

Gustav Cassel, and Eli Heckscher. Attending Heckscher's economics seminar at the Stockholm School of Economics, the young Ohlin quickly proved that he had a better grasp of the classical rotation problem of forestry than his teacher (cf. chapter 7). His next contribution was his seminal work on trade theory (the first version of which appears as chapter 9) which culminated in his monumental 1933 book on interregional and international trade, but before that his classical exchange with Keynes on the German reparations problem after World War I (cf. chapter 12) had taken place.

Considering the 1930s and the Great Depression, Samuelson describes Ohlin's claims on behalf of the so-called Stockholm School of economists to have grasped the fundamental ideas that were to be presented in the *General Theory* much in the same way as Abba Lerner once pointed out in his famous "Some Swedish Stepping Stones" (1940) that this "school" failed to produce a coherent theory that could serve as a foundation for future developments. From the mid-1930s Ohlin's scientific career came to a gradual halt as he entered politics: "Economics' loss," as Samuelson calls it. Despite his Herculean political burden, Ohlin managed to produce a significant contribution to the analysis of overfull employment after World War II.

The appendix to Samuelson's chapter deals with some buried gemstones in *Interregional and International Trade*, notably the endogenization of the input–output coefficients—a contribution that, if it had been noted by Abraham Wald at approximately the same date, would have provided a much better vehicle for his proof of the existence of a general equilibrium than Cassel's simplified version of Walras.

Ohlin's main academic contributions were made in the 1920s and early 1930s. How well have they fared in the eyes of latter-day economists? In chapter 5 Bo Sandelin takes a look at the "hard" evidence in the form of citations in journals covered by the Social Science Citations Index between 1973 and 1999. The results are somewhat surprising. First, as far as the time path is concerned, there is a "natural" peak in 1978 and 1979, because Ohlin got the Nobel Prize in 1977, but there is also an inexplicable low point in 1993, with a mere six citations—something that casts severe doubts on the coverage of the SSCI.

Second, in a comparative perspective—the Stockholm School economists and Wicksell—he comes in third. Myrdal was cited more than eight times and Wicksell more than twice as frequently. For the theoretically minded this may appear as a puzzle, since as Bo Södersten pointed out in recent newspaper article (1999), there is no theoretical insight that today is connected with the name of Myrdal, while Ohlin's position in this respect is outstanding. However, the answer is that Myrdal is frequently cited by noneconomists, particularly for *An American Dilemma*, *Asian Drama*, and other interdisciplinary works.

When it comes to the individual publications, *Interregional and International Trade* (1933) is the most frequently cited work, followed by the 1937 articles on the "Stockholm School" and the 1929 articles on the transfer problem. Over time these three works increasingly tend to obscure the rest of Ohlin's writings in the eyes of his fellow economists.

To economists, Bertil Ohlin is best known for his contributions to the theory of international trade. To Swedes, he is best known as the leader of the Swedish Liberal Party for more than twenty years. Under his leadership this party became the main opposition force to the ruling Social Democrats who held a hegemonic position in the Swedish parliament since the 1930s. Gradually he stood out as the main nonsocialist challenger to the post of prime minister. In chapter 6 Svante Nycander gives a thorough account of Ohlin as a liberal politician, his successes and failures. In the process he also gives a personal portrait of Ohlin.

In the book *Fri eller dirigerad ekonomi?* (Free or controlled economy?), published in 1936, Ohlin set out his own brand of "social" liberalism, opposed to the orthodox or classical variety. Basically he wanted a liberalism that was aware of social problems, based on an approach where the state provided primarily a framework for private sector decision making. The government should be active in economic matters: stabilizing the business cycle, fighting monopolies, and improving the conditions for long-run growth, but Ohlin strongly opposed socialism and the central planning ideas of the time. He was to remain faithful to these ideas for the rest of his life. Ohlin dealt with the whole spectrum of issues emanating in public debate, but his focus was on economic ones. He also had a strong international outlook with an Anglo-American orientation—stemming largely from his contacts as an economist.

During World War II, Sweden was run by a government of national unity with representatives from all the democratic parties.

Ohlin became minister of trade in this government in 1944. The following year it was dissolved. After the war, the Social Democrats adopted a party program with strong socialist elements. There was a severe ideological clash between them and the Liberals, culminating in the parliamentary election of 1948. Here Ohlin and his party were highly successful, and he was firmly established as the main contender to Tage Erlander, the prime minister and leader of the Social Democrats.

In 1951 the Social Democrats formed a coalition government with the Agrarian Party, downplaying the socialist ideology. Thus Ohlin's opponents in effect accepted parts of his critique, depriving him of some of his best arguments, and thereby reducing his chances of bringing about a change in power. His policies gained acceptance but at the expense of his own success as a politician. Ohlin had another chance to overthrow the Social Democrats during the struggle for a new pension system in 1957 to 1959. The government coalition broke down, but Ohlin did not manage to form a nonsocialist government. The Social Democrats remained in power. This was the biggest failure of his political career and in addition a harsh blow at the personal level.

In the latter part of the 1960s, Ohlin took an active part in the process of giving Sweden a new constitution, abolishing the bicameral system in favor of a single chamber. This reform improved the chances for a change in power in the 1970s. In the election of 1976, the nonsocialist parties managed to form a government. Ohlin's struggle had finally met with success. He himself had left parliament six years earlier at the age of 71, though he remained active in public debate for several years.

The Early Bertil Ohlin

An important period of Bertil Ohlin's life, and simultaneously one that is least known, dates from the beginning of his studies at the University of Lund in 1915 until his return to Stockholm as a professor in 1929. This is unfortunate, since it was during this period that his main economic ideas were formed: the conception of his contribution to foreign trade theory, his views on the transfer problem, his solution of the optimum rotation problem in the economics of forestry, and, as it seems, also his approach to macroeconomics.

During this period Ohlin studied in Lund and Stockholm (both at the Stockholm School of Economics and Stockholm University), at Cambridge, and at Harvard. He also spent five years as a professor at the University of Copenhagen. All these years he could devote wholeheartedly to studies and research in economics, but not too much is known about the intellectual and social environment in which Ohlin was working or his sources of inspiration. Our second section deals with these years.

The first chapter (chapter 7) in this section, by Karl-Gustaf Löfgren, analyzes Ohlin's rediscovery of what today is known as the Marshall-Faustmann-Pressler theorem in the economics of forestry. At the age of 18 Ohlin had arrived at the Stockholm School of Economics, after finishing his BA (*fil kand*) at Lund University, in economics, mathematics, and statistics. He was not supposed to join Eli Heckscher's economics seminar, since this was for second-year, not first-year, students. After some deliberation, Heckscher let him in—a decision founded on Ohlin's economics studies in Lund.

The first task assigned to Ohlin in the seminar was to comment on a paper on a classical problem in forestry economics: that of the optimal rotation period. Heckscher had published an article on the subject in 1912 where he had derived a solution that made the false analogy with wine storage. By maximizing the present value of all future cuttings, Ohlin derived the correct formula: that the time to cut a forest stand had come when the rate of change of its value was equal to the interest on the value of the stand plus the interest on the value of the land itself. What Heckscher had missed was the value of the land. His solution rested on the implicit assumption that land was not scarce and hence had no value.

Löfgren also demonstrates how Knut Wicksell, who knew wine storage well, in an unpublished manuscript had also—in a slightly different manner—independently arrived at the same correct solution as Ohlin. Whereas the latter maximized the net present value directly, Wicksell proceeded by maximizing the return to the land on which the forest owner has to pay an annual rent. As Löfgren shows, the two solutions are equivalent. The verdict of Löfgren is a win on points against Heckscher and a draw against Wicksell—at 18!

Ohlin's next feat would take place at the age of 23. This is the subject of the next three chapters, 8 to 10. In the first of these Rolf Henriksson explores the evolution of Ohlin's thinking and writings on trade theory and international monetary issues leading up to his *licentiat* thesis in 1922 and his doctoral dissertation in 1924. From where did Ohlin get his inspiration? Did it emanate from Eli Heckscher—as commonly asserted and manifested in the Heckscher-Ohlin approach—or from Gustav Cassel, Knut Wicksell, or independently from Ohlin himself? Could the influence run the other way around: Did young Ohlin have an impact on the views of his elders? Henriksson provides tentative answers to these questions.

The point of departure for Henriksson is Ohlin's account in his memoirs of his "Eureka": the moment when—seemingly as a bolt out of the blue—he conceived his central idea. In the first volume, Ohlin (1972:79) writes: "Above all ... I began writing on the foundations of a to some extent new approach to foreign trade theory for which I had got the inspiration during a walk on *Unter den Linden* in Berlin in 1920." However, he does not give much of a clue to the actual contents of his inspiration.

Trying to clarify the contents of Ohlin's Eureka, Henriksson explores the background to this event. He assesses to what extent it served as a point of departure for Ohlin's later contributions. The result appears to cast some doubt on the reliability of Ohlin's recollection. Henriksson argues that the seminal Heckscher paper of 1919—dealing with the effect of foreign trade on the distribution of income—was not part of the Eureka. The influence of Heckscher's pathbreaking paper on Ohlin's theoretical work should be dated to a point in time *after* Ohlin had begun his writing. In other words, the Heckscher conception of factor price equalization was not fundamental to the design of what Ohlin intended to do at the outset. Thus, contrary to the view advanced in recent research, Henriksson concludes that initially Ohlin was more strongly influenced by Cassel than by Heckscher.

The Eureka event still may serve as a point of departure for an overview of Ohlin's early work. Henriksson tells the story of the making of Ohlin as an economist. He also considers the relationship between the *licentiat* thesis and the doctoral dissertation. Following the retrieval of Ohlin's *licentiat* thesis—a result of Henriksson's archival research—it was noted that the thesis was different from the dissertation in being devoid of any analysis of the monetary side of the Heckscher-Ohlin trade equilibrium. This suggested that Ohlin's stay at Harvard in 1922 to 1923 had a decisive influence on the monetary part of his dissertation. However, Henriksson proposes that Ohlin might have drawn considerably on his own extensive research and writings on exchange rate theory and monetary dynamics in Sweden prior to his dissertation work at Harvard.

Chapter 9 is an English translation of Ohlin's dissertation for the degree of *licentiat* in economics. In the following chapter Harry Flam and June Flanders comment on the dissertation and connect it with later developments in *Handelns teori* and *Interregional and International Trade*.

A *licentiat* degree in Sweden in Ohlin's time was the first step on the road that would in the best case eventually lead to a Ph.D. and an academic career. The Ph.D. at the time was a serious affair. It involved a public defense of a printed and published book, where the author had to respond to the criticism offered by two opponents, one appointed by the faculty and one chosen by the author himself. Thereafter the floor would be left open for opposition *ex auditorio*.[3] The first opponent was responsible for criticizing the *grandes lignes* of the thesis and the second opponent concentrated more on the details. The defense would usually take the better part of the day, with a break for lunch, during which the author would not eat together with the opponent.

A graded mark would be awarded by the professors of the faculty, separately on the contents and on the defense of the work, and this mark would decide the author's academic future. The mark was given on the scale A, a, AB, Ba, B, and C, where C meant that the author failed. To ensure a continued life in academe, a grade of AB+ (docent cum laude) would have to be obtained. This entitled the author not only to a Ph.D. but also to the title of docent, without a salary.[4] A grade below that level often led to a teaching career as a lecturer in a high school, or some other career outside the university system.[5]

Compared to the Ph.D. ordeal, the *licentiat* degree was a relatively uncomplicated affair, both in terms of defense, which was an internal departmental matter (usually a matter simply between the professor and the author), size of the work, number of copies made, and the technique of production of the work. Typically only a handful of typed and carbon-copied versions of the *licentiat* thesis were made, and the level of originality was lower than in a doctoral dissertation, although standards varied considerably. Usually, obtaining a *licentiat* degree took between three and four years. Hardly any coursework was involved, but most of the activities took place in seminar form (the so-called higher seminar)—seminars that were very unstructured. The most important part was the writing of the thesis. (Obtaining a doctorate could take any number of years after that. Frequently doctoral dissertations turned out to be the output of a lifetime.)

Needless to say, Ohlin's *licentiat* thesis was among the more ambitious ones.[6] As Flam and Flanders explain in their comments, the idea that Ohlin had was to combine Heckscher's 1919 explanation of the origin and pattern of trade with Gustav Cassel's version of general equilibrium, in the setting of two economies that traded with each other. Already in the *licentiat* thesis Ohlin explained in clear terms both the Heckscher-Ohlin theorem and the factor price equalization theorem. This exposition constitutes the heart of the thesis, and of course its main contribution. The remainder (more than half of it) is devoted to a discussion of the effects of changes in some of the main assumptions: factor mobility across national borders, limited mobility of goods, limited divisibility of factors, and the creation through this of increasing returns.

In chapter 10 Flam and Flanders establish the connection between Ohlin's *licentiat* and Ph.D. dissertations, and to some extent, his 1933 book.[7] In both theses Ohlin argues that trade will tend to equalize factor prices between nations, but that in practice this would not occur. Differences between commodity prices will result in complete specialization and no factor price equalization. Flam and Flanders show how Ohlin failed to take factor substitution into account in both works.

The chapter on international capital mobility in *Handelns teori* has no counterpart in the *licentiat* thesis. According to Flam and Flanders, the addition in the later work appears to have come from Ohlin's exposure to international finance during his stay at Harvard in 1922 to 1923. Also from Harvard came the idea of what Flam and Flanders choose to call *transitional dynamics*, lacking in the earlier piece, namely the description of the adjustment over time of endogenous variables in the general equilibrium system, in response to exogenous shocks—a theme that would be expanded a great deal in *Interregional and International Trade*.

Still, given these and other differences, the important conclusion from the *licentiat* thesis is that already the first version of what would later constitute Bertil Ohlin's "trade trilogy" contained the core ideas of what would become his main contribution to economics—

the one that would eventually earn him the Nobel Prize in economic sciences, fifty-five years later.

In chapter 11, Niels-Henrik Topp examines Bertil Ohlin's five years as professor in economics at the University of Copenhagen in the latter half of the 1920s. Applying a Danish perspective, Topp traces the answers to a number of questions: Why did Ohlin go to Denmark? Was Ohlin's thinking on economic matters influenced by his sojourn in Copenhagen? Did Ohlin have an impact on the teaching of economics in Copenhagen and on Danish economic policies?

Ohlin arrived at a small department of only four professors. Among them, primarily Lauritz Birck influenced him. The two colleagues lived for some time in the same hotel, centrally located in Copenhagen, which facilitated communication. There was only minor or no interaction between Ohlin and the other two professors. The Copenhagen students expected much from Ohlin as teacher. He contributed to the introduction of the seminar system into the training of economists. However, Topp finds no evidence that the young and handsome Ohlin attracted additional students to economics, not even additional female students. With great energy Ohlin entered immediately into public debate in Denmark, making himself a well-known public figure in his new country. Topp focuses on his popular contributions in Danish to monetary policy and labor market issues.

Ohlin left his chair in Copenhagen at the end of 1929 when he accepted a post as professor at the Stockholm School of Economics. A Dane was appointed to the chair that was vacated. The choice of a native was supported by the argument that "the refreshing effect of having a foreigner depreciates by repetition." Topp views this wording as suggesting that Ohlin was not a complete success in Copenhagen. Ohlin retained, however, an interest in Danish affairs, publishing more than 160 articles in the Danish newspaper *Politiken* in the 1930s.

The Macroeconomics of Bertil Ohlin

Ohlin developed a keen interest in current economic affairs and economic policy very early. At the age of 20 he began to publish newspaper articles with his comments and interpretations of economic and political events. He followed the international debate closely, and participated in it himself, notably in his controversy with

Keynes over the transfer problem. Toward the end of the 1920s Ohlin was pulled into serious scientific work of the causes of unemployment and depression. During the following decade three major competing approaches to macroeconomics developed: the Austrian School, centered around the London School of Economics, with Friedrich von Hayek and Lionel Robbins, the Stockholm School, and the school surrounding Keynes in Cambridge. Eventually the Keynesian school prevailed. However, Ohlin himself viewed his work on macroeconomics as an important contribution. It was frustrating to him that it was not given the attention that he believed it deserved. A section on Ohlin's macroeconomic thought is thus highly warranted.

The contribution in chapter 12 by Robert Mundell re-examines the debate between Ohlin and Keynes on the transfer problem. Mundell provides a succinct summary of the German reparations question and its resolution, as well as a valuable survey of the contending "relative price" or "elasticities" approach to the balance of payments, associated with John Stuart Mill, Alfred Marshall, Frank Taussig, and Jacob Viner, and the "income-expenditure" approach that Ohlin revived and employed so effectively. He also provides new results based on a three-commodity Heckscher-Ohlin model and an application of his own "monetary" approach to the balance of payments to the transfer problem.

Mundell concludes that Ohlin was the clear winner of the debate with Keynes, who, just six years before the publication of the *General Theory*, still seemed not to have completed the "long struggle of escape" from "habitual modes of thought and expression" that he refers to in his preface to that volume. To continue with the prize-fighting metaphor, Ohlin can be credited not only with a win on points over Heckscher and a draw with Wicksell at the age of 18 but also with a technical knockout over Keynes by the time he was 30!

Swedish professors of economics have traditionally published articles in the daily press—a tradition begun by Wicksell, Davidson, Cassel, and Heckscher. Bertil Ohlin followed in their footsteps, becoming the most prolific economic journalist of them all in the twentieth century with a total of more than 2,300 contributions to the daily press. This impressive number of articles is partially explained by the fact that Ohlin started early as a journalist. Half of his contributions, appearing as articles, editorials, and comments, emerged in the 1920s and 1930s, before he moved finally into politics.

The Great Depression became the major intellectual challenge for the economics profession in Sweden, in particular, for the younger generation of economists. This generation, later to be regarded as the "Stockholm School" of economists, aimed at working out a "new" economics that could be used to counter the effects of the depression. Was Ohlin a pioneer or an orthodox thinker in the field of macroeconomics when turning to the general public? In order to answer this question, in chapter 13 Benny Carlson and Lars Jonung examine about 80 articles published by Ohlin in *Stockholms-Tidningen*, a Stockholm daily, from 1926 to 1935.

Ohlin was an eager but cautious commentator on current affairs. Initially he was quite optimistic, underestimating the extent of the depression, but later, as the situation worsened, he proposed a number of measures such as increased public works and public investments as well as an expansionary monetary policy to fight unemployment. Ohlin also reported positively on the expansionary policy proposals of British liberals, in particular on Keynes's views. By 1932 Ohlin had adopted a multiplier approach. He was strongly opposed to cuts in nominal wages and public expenditures. During the height of the depression, in 1933, Ohlin appeared to lose his optimism for a moment but it returned with the first signs of recovery. Summarizing his views, Ohlin the following year concluded that the depression was not the result of any inherent weakness of capitalism. The crisis policy pursued by the Swedish government was the proper response but its impact should not be exaggerated.

Bertil Ohlin invented the concept of the "Stockholm School" to characterize the analytical work of Swedish economists in the 1920s and 1930s—a term that caused some surprise among his fellow economists in Sweden. Some of them did not consider themselves members of any specific school. Ohlin launched the concept in the 1937 articles in the *Economic Journal*, comparing it with John Maynard Keynes's approach in *The General Theory*.

In chapter 14 Björn Hansson examines the differences and similarities between Bertil Ohlin and the other major members of the Stockholm School of economists, in particular, Gunnar Myrdal and Erik Lindahl. He first defines the approach of the Stockholm School as the study of change, that is, the study of dynamic processes, as the unifying theme, showing how Myrdal, Lindahl, Dag Hammarskjöld, and Erik Lundberg made original contributions to this field. All of them developed different approaches, both within micro- and macroeconomics. They worked with such notions as plans, anticipations, uncertainty, temporary equilibrium, disequilibrium, sequence analysis, the distinction between ex ante and ex post, struggling to bring the analysis of change into the center stage.

How was this theoretical work related to that of Ohlin? Hansson argues that Ohlin made hardly any contribution to the study of dynamic methods proper. Rather, he was critical of the approach of Lindahl and Myrdal. Hansson suggests that Ohlin's lack of interest in the theory of dynamic methods was due to his focus on the real world. Ohlin simply found no practical use for the theoretical and nonobservable concepts introduced by the other Stockholm School members.

Instead, Ohlin developed his own approach, stressing the role of autonomous changes in consumption as a driving force behind cyclical downturns in economic activity. Equilibrium could be restored via accompanying changes in output and real income. Here Ohlin moved the attention away from the capital market to the product market and from savings and investment to total demand and total supply, paving the way for a macroeconomic approach different from the framework of the other members of the Stockholm School.

What remains of the Stockholm School today?[8] It ceased to exist as an independent entity already in the 1940s and 1950s, though several of its ideas and concepts have been absorbed into mainstream economics. The work of Ohlin and his Swedish compatriots in the 1930s was thus a promising and original start, even if soon to be surpassed and incorporated into Keynesian macroeconomics.

Swedish economists have traditionally engaged themselves in public affairs, most notably in governmental expert committees. Ohlin was no exception. Already at the age of 20, he served for the first time on a governmental committee. And there was more to come. In chapter 15 Eskil Wadensjö presents an in-depth account of Ohlin's work for the Committee on Unemployment—set up in 1927 and ending its work in 1935. This Committee is regarded as a "classical" one in the history of Swedish economics and economic policy. A considerable number of economists were associated with it. The Committee was instrumental in framing stabilization policy views in Sweden, and Bertil Ohlin played an important role in it.

Ohlin was recruited in 1929 to contribute a report on the effects of tariffs on unemployment. He argued that cyclical—but not noncyclical—unemployment could be reduced by the use of tariffs and public work programs. Ohlin's assignment was also extended to deal with monetary policy measures. Wadensjö traces the development of his views on business cycle theories and on stabilization policies. Ohlin argued that the economists working for the Committee adhered to the Anglo-Saxon school of Keynes, Dennis Robertson, and Ralph Hawtrey. Wadensjö notes that Ohlin at this stage did not envisage a Stockholm School of economists. It is safe to conclude that it was Keynes's *General Theory* that inspired Ohlin to present the Stockholm or Swedish School as a separate approach in the 1937 article.

When Sweden left the gold standard in September 1931, price stabilization was announced as the goal of Swedish monetary policy—the first time that price stability was made the goal of a central bank. Wadensjö demonstrates that Ohlin in 1932, less than a year after this event, argued that minimization of unemployment, that is, full employment, should be the proper norm for stabilization policy. He was well ahead of his time.

Today Ohlin's supplement for the Committee where he proposed expansionary policy measures to fight unemployment is commonly regarded as a pathbreaking study where the new ideas, later to be part of the Stockholm School approach, were given a thorough presentation. However, within the Committee, Ohlin's supplement became the topic of controversy and opposition, led by Dag Hammarskjöld, at that time secretary of the Committee. A major effect of the critique was that Ohlin revised his views. The analysis of the multiplier effects was given a less prominent place. The relationship between Ohlin and the Committee soured and the personal relationship between Hammarskjöld and Ohlin turned frosty—a pattern that unfortunately was common among many economists in those days.

The Heckscher-Ohlin Theory of Trade

Bertil Ohlin's contribution to the theory of international trade is without any question his most important contribution to economics. Most economists know the Heckscher-Ohlin theorem not from the writings of Ohlin himself (or Heckscher) but from textbook representations. There is, however, a great deal more both in Ohlin's own works and in the factor proportions approach in general than what most of the profession may be aware of. Also the empirical relevance of the theory has been subject to debate for close to half a century. For these reasons we devote the fourth section of the book to Ohlin's views on trade and their standing in the contemporary paradigm.

In chapter 16 Ronald Jones examines the core of Bertil Ohlin's scientific contribution. As he explains, the title of his chapter is "Heckscher-Ohlin Models for the New Century," the emphasis being on the plural. All too often both adherents and critics of the factor proportions approach fall into the trap of treating it as a rigid monolith that stands or falls with a fixed set of assumptions. Jones demonstrates, however, that the approach is inherently a highly flexible one if used with sufficient imagination. The essential insights are that commodities differ in their factor requirements and countries in their availability of factor supplies. Combined with competitive (not necessarily perfectly so) markets, these assumptions lead to predictions about patterns of trade and their impact on factor prices. Within these boundaries we have extensive freedom to choose between alternative specifications of the structure and dimensions of the appropriate model to use for any particular problem. Thus, contrary to what many appear to believe, the factor proportions approach *is* consistent with nonidentical technologies, nonhomothetic tastes, variable factor supplies that can be both mobile and immobile between sectors and also with instances of increasing returns to scale.

Finally, Jones deals with criticisms against and alternatives to the Heckscher-Ohlin theory of trade: product cycle theories and "new" trade theory. He finds no contradiction in principle between product cycles à la Raymond Vernon and the Heckscher-Ohlin approach. What happens is simply that where in the product cycle a particular country will find itself at a given point in time is dictated by its current factor endowments. Nor is it impossible to reconcile intra-industry trade based on product differentiation and monopolistic competition with some of the main characteristics of the Heckscher-Ohlin approach. Thus, Jones concludes, the existence of imperfect competition and differentiated products does not invalidate the factor proportions approach to trade. Rather, new trade theory complements the Heckscher-Ohlin approach. Just as Ricardian models have been with us since 1817, he confidently predicts that Heckscher-Ohlin models will enjoy a half-life well beyond the new century.

The excitement associated with the development of the Heckscher-Ohlin model at the hands of Abba Lerner, Paul Samuelson, and others, led Wassily Leontief to apply his input–output tables to the calculation of the factor-content of U.S. foreign trade, resulting in the celebrated Leontief paradox, that U.S. imports appeared to be more capital-intensive than U.S. exports. Research on this question has been going on ever since.

A low point in the empirical relevance of the theory appeared to be the finding by Edward Leamer and co-authors in 1987 that factor abundance did no better than tossing a coin in predicting which country will be the net exporter of the services of a particular factor. Donald Davis and David Weinstein, in chapter 17, point out that this rejection of the factor proportions hypothesis is overturned when the tests are applied in a suitably restricted and modified way across countries or regions over which factor price equalization can plausibly be expected to hold and *not* the entire world. They go on to plead for a closer integration of theoretical and empirical research in the trade field, in particular, castigating the theorists for their egregious neglect of empirical findings that run counter to the implications of their favored models. They also point out that a new generation of researchers is rapidly rectifying the problem.

Heckscher and Ohlin themselves would presumably heartily have endorsed the program called for by Davis and Weinstein. They would also be gratified to note, as Davis and Weinstein point out, that factor endowment differences are widespread in the world, not only between developed and developing countries but even within the OECD itself. Despite whatever neoclassical growth theory might say about "convergence," differences in factor endowments continue to be as applicable today as when Heckscher and Ohlin first wrote on factor proportions as the fundamental explanation of the pattern of international trade.

The logical complement to the chapter by Ronald Jones is found in Paul Krugman's discussion, in chapter 18, of increasing returns and "economic geography." The question that Krugman attempts to answer is which of the ingredients of "new trade theory" were anticipated by Ohlin and which were not. He begins with a sketch of how increasing returns may be modeled in a trade context—outside of the monopolistic competition story that has become so popular in recent international trade theory. The story he tells instead is one of the integration of external economies with factor proportions. He demonstrates how in a world with two countries, two factors, and three products, production of the good displaying external economies may be concentrated in one country only and how this is likely to increase the purchasing power of both countries by saving on the resources needed to produce the good with increasing returns and by trading abundant resources for scarce in the exchange of commodities. With this story in place, Krugman proceeds to demonstrate that Ohlin was amazingly close to having worked out the same insight—an insight that Krugman states took five years and more than a little help from his friends to work out himself.

Why then, was the insight that increasing returns may cause international trade lost for about fifty years? In the first place Ohlin himself was to blame for understating their practical importance in an age when international trade was typically a matter of exchange of primary products for manufactures. By downplaying the role of increasing returns, Ohlin in turn prepared the field for Samuelson's formalization of the Heckscher-Ohlin theory—one that would dominate the textbooks for some decades to come and that left out increasing returns altogether.

Concerning new economic geography, those who want to argue that Ohlin was on the track have a harder time. Indeed, he made a number of observations that fit the latter-day economic geography models well, but writing in the Marshallian tradition he did not model them carefully. Also he did not pay much attention to the endogeneity of factor location, arguing that it was the given factor endowment that made for the location of industry, and not vice versa.

Last, Krugman deals with those pieces of modern trade theory that are not found in Ohlin at all. What he finds missing, in addition to rigor and precision in modeling technique, are a clear analysis of imperfect competition (not surprising since the 1933 treatise preceded the work of Edward Chamberlin and Joan Robinson), ideas associated with the rubric of "strategic trade policy," the distinction between equilibria and optima, and the idea that small differences in parameters can cause big changes in outcomes as a result of cumulative processes. Although this last point has been popularized by recent developments in nonlinear dynamics, it was intuitively appreciated long ago by Wicksell and Myrdal, and so it is a little surprising that Ohlin did not mention it. The final impression left by Krugman's chapter is a sense of the extent to which Ohlin's vision transcended the factor proportions approach itself to embrace the insights of the "new" trade theory and (to some extent) of the "new" economic geography as well.

One of the glories of the Heckscher-Ohlin model is that it enables us to link changes in relative commodity prices to factor prices and income distribution. The way is thus opened for the analysis of the effects of tariffs and other instruments of commercial policy on income distribution, through their alteration of the relation between world and domestic product price ratios. The Stolper-Samuelson theorem, that protection benefits the scarce factor, is only the most famous of these connections between product and factor prices. In chapter 19 Douglas Irwin examines a perennial problem of American economic history, the effect of tariffs on imports of manufactured goods on real wages.

Frank Taussig staunchly defended the classical position that an intersectorally mobile factor like labor could not be harmed by international trade and conversely could not be helped by a tariff. As Irwin shows, Ohlin himself was somewhat ambivalent on this question. He acknowledged in principle that a tariff on *labor-intensive* manufactured imports could raise real wages of American workers, but he did not subscribe to the two-good, two-factor view of his own model that was later to be embodied in the Stolper-Samuelson theorem. With capital, land, and labor in a more general model, it would not follow that labor would necessarily be helped by a tariff on labor-intensive manufactured imports. Irwin applies a special case of a three-factor model, due to Max Corden and Fred Gruen, to show that a tariff on labor-intensive manufactured imports would indeed raise real wages. This is because the real wage and the return to capital are determined by the relative product price of the two manufactured goods, independently of the demand and supply for the agricultural good to which land is a specific input, within the context of the Gruen-Corden model. We cannot of course say with any certainty how convinced Ohlin himself would have been by what is still a very special case of a full general equilibrium model. However, the continuing debate on trade and wages in the United States and elsewhere demonstrates how relevant the insights of Ohlin continue to be for contemporary concerns on trade, commercial policy, and income distribution.

The Heckscher-Ohlin Theory and Economic History

The usefulness of the Heckscher-Ohlin theory of international trade can be tested in many ways. Some of these we have already met: the formal tests, relying on econometric methods. Such tests do not, however, exhaust all the possibilities of making use of the factor proportions approach. On the contrary, in the last decade or so, factor proportions based methods have come to be used extensively in the examination of historical patterns of trade, migration, commercial policy, and income distribution. Such exercises serve at least two useful purposes. In the first place they help in ensuring that economic history does not become overly descriptive. Second, they provide an alternative way of checking the generality of the approach as such. All the contributions in this section of the volume are in this rapidly emerging tradition.

In chapter 20 Kevin O'Rourke and Jeffrey Williamson track the appearance of commodity-price convergence historically and examine the consequences for factor prices and income distribution, using the specific-factors version of the factor proportions model. They find that high transport costs prior to the early nineteenth century limited intercontinental trade to a few resource-intensive items such as spices and precious metals with a high ratio of value to bulk or weight. The 1815 to 1914 era, however, saw a remarkable reduction in transport costs, the convergence of commodity prices for major primary and manufactured products, and significant impact on domestic factor prices of global price trends.

A striking result in this chapter is that the ratio of the real wage to the rent of land in Britain prior to the 1820s is influenced mainly by changes in the land–labor ratio, while afterward it is strongly correlated with the relative product price of manufactured to primary products, indicating the impact of globalization on what was previously a mainly closed economy. O'Rourke and Williamson also look at the experience of other highly open economies in Europe, the Americas, and Asia, finding strong and ample evidence of the effect of an integrated world economy on domestic factor prices in all of these diverse cases. It is hard to imagine how there can be any further doubts about the empirical relevance of the Heckscher-Ohlin model, suitably interpreted, in the light of these abundant and striking historical results.

One of the perennial problems of the Heckscher-Ohlin theory of trade has been its alleged tendency to run counter to observed trade patterns—ever since the day of the celebrated article by Leontief. We have already met it in the Davis-Weinstein contribution to the present volume. Despite some recent advances, it may be argued that no complete empirical *Ehrenrettung* of the theory has yet been produced.

This finding provides the starting point for chapter 21, by Antoni Estevadeordal and Alan Taylor, who argue that Heckscher's and Ohlin's work should be tested with data from the period when it was first formulated, assuming that it was conceived against the background of the institutional reality of those days. Trade barriers were lower and factor endowments (not least land) differed widely across the globe. Against this it may be argued that transportation costs were higher, productivity differences were considerable, and factor mobility was very high—which may turn out to be critical when testing a model that assumes factor endowments to be given. Estevadeordal and Taylor test the predictions of the Heckscher-Ohlin theorem on a sample of 18 countries for the period around 1913, mainly European nations and some regions of recent settlement.

The results that they obtain are broadly similar to most of the studies on more recent data. The effects of differences in capital and labor endowments on trade are disappointingly small and insignificant but much more encouraging for the two natural resource factors, land and minerals. More refined tests to allow for differences in technology, tastes, and other variables could be undertaken for this period, and the chapter by Estevadeordal and Taylor points the way for these extensions.

The last chapter (chapter 22), by Ronald Findlay and Mats Lundahl, continues the effort to apply the factor proportions approach to economic history. Findlay and Lundahl use an augmented specific-factors model to examine the economic aspects of two significant events of European history: the Black Death of the fourteenth century and the discovery of silver in the Americas during the sixteenth. In the Findlay-Lundahl model, population and the labor force are made endogenous through the introduction of a Malthusian mechanism linking wages to fertility and mortality. Goods, which may be either consumed or invested, are produced together with commodity money—silver. A third commodity, Eastern luxuries, is imported from outside Europe and has to be paid for with silver.

Both the Black Death and the discovery of silver by the Spaniards in the New World are modeled as exogenous shocks to the general equilibrium system. The drastic reduction of the population during the pandemic over time produces a deflation of the price level in the situation where the survivors are richer per capita than before, the output of silver shrinks, and silver flows to the East as a result of the demand for luxuries. As the wage rate rises and the population starts growing back, however, the demand for commodities increases, the excess demand for silver is turned into an excess supply, and the model produces an inflationary phase.

This sequence is broadly consistent with the Great Bullion Famine of the fifteenth century and also provides a theoretical underpinning based on demographic factors to the Price Revolution of the sixteenth century—one that has nothing to do with American silver. The latter, however, also had an impact on the European price level. In terms of the model, the time path is one of inflation (the Price Revolution), followed by deflation, and an expansion of the European population as a result of the enlarged base of natural resources. The effects of the Black Death and the increased output of silver in Peru and Mexico partly overlapped in time, which allows Findlay and Lundahl to reconcile the demographic and monetary explanations of the Price Revolution with each other.

It is a tradition in Sweden that upon leaving their chair or reaching an even age like 50 or 60, professors get a *Festschrift* with contributions by fellows and friends in the academic profession. David Davidson, Knut Wicksell, Gustav Cassel, Eli Heckscher, Erik Lindahl, and Erik Lundberg were all recipients. Ohlin as well received a "semipolitical" book from the Liberal Party when he turned 60. Half of the contributions were by economists and the other half from fellow liberal politicians. We suggest that the present volume should be regarded as a belated posthumous "pure" academic *Festschrift* to Ohlin. He deserves one.

Notes

1. A full-fledged biography of Bertil Ohlin the politician is available: Larsson (1998), a book that to date has appeared only in Swedish. This biography constitutes a complement to the present volume.

2. The malice hints that the taxi was waiting while he lectured and that he examined students in taxis as well.

3. At times, a third "opponent" would appear out of the blue, usually a friend who did his best to make fun of the work and the author.

4. This is usually translated as associate professor. There were also salaried positions as *docent* that could be held for a maximum of three plus three years. They involved very little teaching and were intended as a preparation for an eventual chair.

5. In the first volume of his memoirs, Ohlin (1972:91–92) provides a short account of the defense of his Ph.D. The first opponent was Gösta Bagge, at the time professor of economics and social politics at Stockholm University (later member of Parliament

and between 1935 and 1944 the leader of the Conservative Party), but "it had also been arranged that Cassel would step in as an extra opponent and take over the critical elucidation of some parts" (1972:91). The second opponent was Curt Rothlieb, second chancery secretary [*kanslisekreterare*] in the Ministry of Agriculture, who himself had defended a thesis in economics a year earlier. Knut Wicksell also performed from the floor, offering a penetrating criticism, which, however, "hit the Walras-Cassel price system as much as my own extension of it to deal with the price conditions of several trading countries" (ibid.). Finally, Ohlin had persuaded his friend Johan Henrik Lehmann, a physician from Lund, to act as third opponent. The core of Lehmann's argument was that the dissertation lacked all originality, since it simply consisted of an application of the obscure financial transaction principles that Ohlin had practiced to finance his studies in Lund. The total duration of the defense was five and a half hours. Ohlin was awarded a grade "one step above the requirements for docent [i.e., a], and in addition A on the defense" (1972:92).

6. The expedition of Ohlin's *licentiat* thesis appears to have been swift. Ohlin left it to Cassel at the beginning of April 1922, and Cassel came back a couple of weeks later, and asked Ohlin when he wanted to undergo the oral examination that also formed part of the *licentiat* degree. Ohlin suggested a date at the end of May, but Cassel, who was going abroad and would not be back until after the end of the semester, told Ohlin to see him the following Sunday, "in order to talk about it." So Ohlin did. They talked for an hour and a half, "about a great deal of things," and then Cassel asked his student whether he carried his examination book. Ohlin, somewhat surprised, answered that he did not, since he had not expected any examination, whereupon Cassel told him to send it to him by mail so he could write in the mark (1972:92).

7. A more extensive discussion of the relation between *Handelns teori* and *Interregional and International Trade* is found in Flam's and Flanders' introduction to Heckscher and Ohlin (1991).

8. The Stockholm School is discussed with the wisdom of fifty years of hindsight in Jonung (1991).

References

Heckscher, Eli F., and Ohlin, Bertil. 1991. Harry Flam and M. June Flanders, eds., *Heckscher-Ohlin Trade Theory*. Cambridge: MIT Press.

Jonung, Lars, ed. 1991. *The Stockholm School of Economics Revisited. Historical Perspectives on Modern Economics*. Cambridge: Cambridge University Press.

Larsson, Sven-Erik. 1998. *Bertil Ohlin*. Stockholm: Atlantis.

Lerner, Abba P. 1940. Some Swedish stepping stones in economic theory. *The Canadian Journal of Economics and Political Science* 6:574–91.

Myrdal, Gunnar. 1939. *Monetary Equilibrium*. London: Hodge.

Ohlin, Bertil. 1972. *Bertil Ohlins memoarer: Ung man blir politiker*. Stockholm: Bonniers.

Ohlin, Bertil. 1975. *Bertil Ohlins memoarer 1940–1951: Socialistisk skördetid kom bort*. Stockholm: Bonniers.

Södersten, Bo. 1999. Ohlin framför Myrdal. *Sydsvenska Dagbladet*, 18 October 1999.

I The Man

2 A Portrait of Our Father

Hellen Ohlin, Tomas Ohlin,
and Anne Wibble

We have been asked to give a more personal picture of our father Bertil Ohlin than is available elsewhere. We have chosen to start with a joint presentation, and then to add some individual comments, reflecting our different relationships with our father.

Our father married relatively late in life, at the age of 32. He met the nine year younger Evy Kruse on a boat to Iceland to attend a Scandinavian student conference, where he had been invited to deliver the main lecture. They were actually related, their mothers being first cousins, but had not met before. The romance on board led to marriage when our mother had finished her B.A. in modern languages and political science at Uppsala University.

After some time, they settled in Stockholm. They rented a flat at Norr Mälarstrand by the lake, where they lived for almost 50 years. Their first child Hellen was born in March 1933, Tomas in August 1934, and Anne in October 1943. Our parents' marriage was a happy one. Mother was always well-informed about political events, and they discussed recent developments every night. Bertil's mother, who was very fond of our mother, once stated that father could not have found a better wife.

Our parents led an active social life during the thirties. Father was professor of economics at the Stockholm School of Economics (*Handelshögskolan*), and participated frequently in the public debate with lectures and newspaper articles. Economists, Swedish as well as international ones, politicians, journalists, other friends, and many relatives were frequent guests in our home. In accordance with the general social pattern of the 1930s, our parents employed a nurse for their children until Hellen was eight and Tomas seven years old. For a number of years mother worked part time in a Nordic association on a voluntary basis.

Summer vacations were spent in Torekov, on the southwest coast of Sweden, where the family rented a summerhouse every year until the end of the 1940s. In the winters the whole family would go skiing near Stockholm, and occasionally in the northern mountains. There were also occasional skating trips on Lake Mälaren. In 1937 our parents spent six months at University of in California, Berkeley. During that time Hellen and Tomas and the nurse stayed with our maternal grandparents in Gothenburg.

Close contact was kept with both father's and mother's families. Our family, aunts, and uncles and their children would meet at Christmas and also in the summer at father's parents' house in Klippan, in the south of Sweden, for a number of years. It was a big house with a large garden, where many young cousins could play. Anne was not yet born. Later, when our grandparents had died, meetings became less frequent, except with those relatives living in Stockholm. Father had a close relationship to his older brother Holger (senior vice president at L.M. Ericsson) and his wife Ba, and our family always went to their home for dinner on Christmas Day. Mother's sister Birgit and her husband Ivar Högbom (professor of economic geography and president of the Stockholm School of Economics) also lived close by in Stockholm and the families regularly spent Christmas Eve together, as well as other holidays.

Father's political career progressed. In 1944 he was elected chairman of the Liberal Party and became Minister of Trade for a year in the wartime coalition government. He had less and less time for his family, except for the summers in Torekov. A number of relatives and Stockholm friends also stayed there during the 1930s and 1940s. There was an active social life, including swimming, boating, tennis, picnics at the beach with wonderful newly baked sugar buns with vanilla filling, bicycle excursions for berry picking, as well as parties with crayfish and smoked eel and other dishes that seemed strange to us children. Our memories from this period are those of an easygoing life, with relaxed and happy parents. Seen from the outside, Anne was born in the worst of the war years, but from a family point of view, these years were quite harmonic.

The standard of living in the summerhouse in Torekov was not very high. There was no telephone, no refrigerator, and no bathroom. For many years there was no car. Even if political life at that time was less hectic than today, our father became more and more occupied, and more and more pressed for time. Although father had a high stress tolerance level, our parents decided that the distance to Torekov was too long, and the train journeys too time-consuming. Thus, in 1949, they bought a country house in the neighborhood of Stockholm. Father needed to rest more during his vacations. Mother probably missed the Torekov life more than he did, as she was a very social and popular person. At that time, they also bought a car, a Volvo PV444.

The upbringing of Anne, born in 1943, was to some extent different from that of Hellen and Tomas, thus reflecting the change of times. The family no longer had a nurse for the children, and there was no maid after 1952. Mother learned to cook very well, even if it must sometimes have been disappointing to cook for father who was rather conventional when it came to food. All his life he preferred traditional Swedish dishes. Our parents liked late evening sandwiches and beer in the kitchen, both of them sitting there for hours reading newspapers and books. A big black poodle called Hassan, a very friendly dog, entered the family in the early 1950s. By that time Hellen and Tomas had finished school and were almost grown up, and our parents thought that a dog would be good company for Anne. Mother and Anne were the ones mostly taking care of Hassan, even if father would occasionally take him for walks. Young economists would find themselves exposed to the very lively and friendly attention of the poodle during examinations at our home.

Father spent more time with his youngest daughter Anne than he had done with his older children. Every day when he was at home, he would tell a story after dinner, spontaneously invented, with little Anne on his lap. The stories grew with the child—starting with Lita, a small black girl, and later adding a troll called Klumpe and a cartwheel boy called Simsalabim, from way above the clouds. These stories were quite nice children's stories, and might very well have been published. The rest of the family would sit and make ironic comments, but father and Anne were totally absorbed and took no notice.

In the 1940s Swedish members of Parliament had miserable administrative facilities. For a long time father had no secretary, and mother was more or less his full-time assistant, typing and retyping manuscripts and keeping track of his whereabout and his callers. The telephone rang all the time. Father would often call home to ask for help to find texts or manuscripts from which he needed to quote, or half-ready texts supposedly lying on the huge desk in the living room. They were more often found on the bedroom floor! He was certainly not one for neat filing. It was an exciting environment, privileged in many ways. Our upbringing gave us access to newspapers and magazines, radio and TV, and many interesting people. Even in the summer, contacts with political life were rather intense. However, we children picked up fewer secrets than one might have expected.

Father was not in favor of gossip. What he heard in confidence was not revealed. He stressed that responsibility toward people who had given him private information, and such promises were always kept.

Father worked harder than many people and had a good income, but he and mother did not live a luxurious life. He saved rather than spent. However, he paid many of the expenses of his political life himself, travel for example. He was the donor of the family, and the family was large. To his children he was generous, but there was no excess. We often had less pocket money than our friends. He felt that his children should have no special advantages due to his position. However, our parents paid for our university education and provided us with financial resources for a start in life.

Father was concerned about health, following such issues in a scientific way. He took good care of his own health and was fortunate not to have many problems. He stayed in good physical shape most of the time. He liked to walk, and did so almost every day. When he was young, he played golf. He liked swimming in the summer, and skating and skiing in the winter. In his youth, father enrolled in a temperance organization, and all through his life he was deeply concerned about alcohol as a social problem. He was one of the first to calculate the cost of alcohol for society at large, and these figures were used in public campaigns against misuse of alcohol. He almost never touched strong liquor, limiting himself to ordinary beer. Later in life he discovered wine, and took an interest in wine qualities.

All through his life, he was considered an elegant and good-looking man. He was interested in dressing well, which was one of the few personal areas where he did spend some money. From the mid-1950s our parents developed an interest in art. They did not buy much, but most of their purchases were contemporary Swedish figurative paintings. Father was always careful in these purchases; both as concerns price and subject, he felt that art should not be too dominating.

Not everyone saw father's social talents. He was, for instance, almost always happy and relaxed in international meetings and parties. The speeches he made on such occasions were easygoing and humorous.

If father had little time for his children during long periods, this was very much compensated for by our mother. She was always there, and her person was central to us. Every day when we came home from school, we would find her at home often reading English or French novels. From the 1960s grandchildren started to arrive, seven in all. Father took great interest in these children, even though, due to increasingly bad hearing, he sometimes found it difficult to hear their young voices. If a grandchild was ill, he would call almost every day. He was concerned that they should do well at school. Some of them found his constant asking about school somewhat repetitious. He was a caring grandfather, reflecting his strong sense of family closeness.

Hellen's Story

I lived at home until graduating from high school at the age of nineteen, when I went to study social sciences at Uppsala University. Considering the disturbing political events going on all the time at home and the problems that would have implied for studying, it turned out to be a good idea. Actually it was a decision taken by my parents, without consulting me. The reason was the shortage of bedrooms in the flat.

To have a prominent father has certain implications. On the whole I had not inherited his precociousness. To have a father, who was actively interested in most intellectual issues was, however, a fantastic gift. I used to list topics for discussion every time I visited my parents during my university years to get his views. My father was always open to discussion, and I remember only one time when we had a serious disagreement. Despite his busy life he often picked up the fancies I had in life. To my surprise, I later found that he had quoted me to the strangest people. Long after I had lost interest in certain issues myself I might meet people who still knew about them through him. His view on my intellectual curiosity is shown by his nice acknowledgment—which I treasure—in the first book of his memoirs: "To Hellen, who has a great capacity to take an interest in the problems of today with the author's hope that a description of old times may also deserve a study."

He was clear in communicating his deep commitment to his political task, such as once when I was about twenty. He stressed the importance of keeping Sweden away from the planned economy model, which he saw as his mission in life. He had experienced enough praise in the economic community at a young age and felt that he needed no more.

Occasionally he would disagree with my opinions, for example, on developing country policies and women's issues and on some articles I wrote, but he never really questioned them, which might have been a way of providing the encouragement he felt I needed. I was a shy girl. In women's issues, he was emancipated in theory but certainly not in household practice.

He did not approve of my decisions to work during school and university summer vacations. With a good education, he claimed, you would always get an interesting job. In this case as well as in relation to my efforts in making my own dresses, he disagreed with the way I spent my time and calculated the money cost of activities other than studies. During many years, however, he himself spent considerable time getting elegant tailor-made suits and overcoats. A blue suit demanded a blue overcoat to match, as did a new brown suit.

Some writers have commented on father's inability to express his sympathy, to communicate with people. This is not the whole story. He had, for example, great concern for his family—and by that I mean the extended family. He kept in close contact with his six brothers and sisters and many cousins and other relatives. He would engage in long conversations with family members on recent developments and certainly kept track of most relatives.

He did, however, have problems providing help on more emotional issues. Personal subjects were taboo to our parents—reflecting the shyness of that generation. After my father's death, I learned from my mother that he had sympathized more than I realized with my feelings after a broken affair and had never managed to like the man concerned. A surprising and sweet reaction!

It has been pointed out that he seldom expressed any negative views on Liberal Party members. That may be the case. A type of loyalty perhaps. It was the same with family—liberals and relatives could do no wrong. On the other hand, this great tolerance was combined with a strong feeling for intelligence and intellectual clarity as important criteria for his evaluation of people.

With his Anglo-American interests he was actually tempted by the offer he once got from the prime minister, maybe in the sixties, to become Swedish ambassador in the United States, but since mother was not in favor, it was not seriously considered. The implications for the socialist government of his leaving Swedish politics no doubt influenced the offer as well as his own evaluation of it.

In later years he once said that he realized that he had underestimated the value of social contacts, for example, with political opponents. One example of this is his relationship with the Center Party leader Gunnar Hedlund. He was aware that Hedlund found it difficult to relate to him. Many years later, however, he and Hedlund became good friends, and the two retired politicians used to meet for dinner for political talks.

In the end of the sixties and seventies, after he had left active politics, he loosened up personally. Over the years I used to arrange parties for large groups of friends from different parts of society. My father loved these events and his easygoing style on those occasions would have surprised some of those who had only seen him in his previous role, when he was—maybe too much for his own good—locked in the chains of politics. My female friends certainly found him a charming man.

I want to end by quoting a statement on himself, which he had picked up and once mentioned, to me: "Bertil Ohlin can do anything but that is the only thing he can do." The implicit meaning was something he recognized.

Tomas's Story

It might have been somewhat more demanding for a boy than for a girl in my youth to be brought up as the son of a great father, even in an emancipated country like Sweden. Quite often, I felt that it was not clear to what extent I was recognized in my own capacity.

How did I experience him as a father? Was he dominating? The answer is no. To dominate was not in accordance with his principles. As a young boy, I was against taking part in any discussions on politics. Father did not interfere with this reaction from his son. During my school years and later I spent a lot of time with sports and music, which was my choice of opposition. Music was one of the few areas in which father took no interest—he mostly wanted to turn the gramophone off. For some time, I was more successful in jazz than in studies or politics, both at school and when beginning at the university

I inherited a respect for facts and knowledge from father. This was surely mostly a good thing, but for this young boy it also led to a reluctance to speak up in public. To me, father stressed that in public you should know what you want to say, say it, and then keep quiet.

My own closer personal contacts with him developed in my early childhood, but they became more intense later. When I had got a driving license, I often drove him and mother. He himself was not a good driver, analyzing all possible alternative traffic actions for too long before acting in the car, or in our small motorboat. When I was at the wheel, he used to tell me—"now, don't go too fast, we are in no hurry . . ." Actually most of the time he was in a hurry as he, for some reason, always ended up not having enough time. Mother was a much better driver, and was almost always at the wheel when I was not there.

How did his political views influence life at home? The answer is that there was never any pressure on us to share his liberal political ideology. His approach to us, as to everyone else, was to convince through reasoning and to show respect for other people's views. But surely, his values and priorities were, at least indirectly, influential at home.

In relation to his children's choice of academic studies, father left it to us to make our own decisions. He showed a deep interest, and there were many discussions, but he only gave advice. A university education was recommended, but the choice of field of study was left to us. He provided me with one specific piece of educational advice, though, and that was to take a course in typing, which I found helpful later in life.

I started at the university with mathematics, and later found myself in studies of technology and information sciences, fields that were distant from father's own scientific interests. But he had an open mind and had no problems extrapolating into my field. Actually, in his youth, he had studied mathematics for one term, and he always kept his respect for the natural sciences.

Father was an economist with a wide scientific imagination. It was interesting for me to follow his reaction to the rapid development of information science. Our contacts on such issues took place during many years. Already in his book *Fri eller dirigerad ekonomi* (Free or Controlled Economy), published in 1936, he referred to the importance of technology for development, and the need for society to support technological as well as social development. He even used the very words "the use of machines for development." This was before the first computer was constructed. As he died in 1979, he never experienced the development of the Internet.

In 1971, I had an interesting discussion with him about a manuscript of mine dealing with local democracy. My text suggested the use of (then unknown) personal computers for new types of democratic citizen participation. He criticized the text in many details, but added constructive comments, and ended with a positive statement about the possibility of increased use of local advisory citizen referendums—in words that I still remember clearly. He had been positive to efforts to promote such increased participation much earlier (documented in a book of his from 1956), but at that time there was no technology around to support local democracy.

He often took an active interest in my later work on several government commissions on information technology policies in Sweden. At times, we cooperated on the use of IT for public sector reform, and on the creation of liberal IT texts.

Father had a talent for languages. During the time of his studies of economic science, as a young man, he took a course in the Russian language, which, he claimed, helped him with contacts later in life. His English was excellent, with a British accent, and he was also comfortable with French. I remember when he came home after presiding at a big scientific conference for three days—was he not tired? Well, he said, a little, but if the proceedings had not been carried out in the French language, and if he had not been expected to sum it all up in French at the end, then it would have been an easier task.

I very seldom saw him simply relax and contemplate in general. Whenever possible, he brought a book, too many newspapers, or piles of scientific papers that were to be read and commented on. He kept few personal files, and his papers and letters were often in a mess. His large desk in the living room was always filled to and above its maximum. Before parties at home mother requested him to file some, but papers were then often hidden under his bed, with a long retrieval process.

Father received much praise in his life, but he also experienced bad luck in politics. However, he was not as hurt by such events as most of us would be; he almost seemed to treat them as the result of bad planning. He was a man for whom it was always natural to aim high.

Anne's Story

My mother once told me that she and father waited to see which way the Second World War would go before having a third child, but since I was born in October 1943, this must have been a later invention. Or else they were exceptionally clear-sighted! Anyway, arriving rather late in my parents' life, I had a slightly different upbringing. My parents had less help at home, so I saw more of them both. We have already mentioned the daily storytelling. At this time, father was chairman of the Liberal Party and had made a highly successful election in 1948. Obviously there must have been many days when he was not home for dinner, but when he was, there was always a story.

Around the time I started school, my parents bought our summerhouse in Bammarboda, about thirty miles north of Stockholm. Thereafter all summer holidays and many weekends were spent there swimming, rowing, planting, or cutting. Father had what he thought was a scientific approach toward cutting down a tree, and this usually meant a lot of inefficient work with partial cutting and the use of ropes. It might take hours to cut down one small tree. We went mushroom picking in the autumn, although father was very careful about what to bring home.

He liked to walk, and the dog Hassan and I sometimes went along. What I mostly remember are the frequent stops; whenever we met someone father knew he would stop and engage in a lengthy conversation. He was always genuinely interested in other people's points of view. It was not only courteous listening but also a true curiosity of how other people thought and reasoned. All his life he liked to argue and formulations such as "on the one hand" and "on the other hand" were frequent. He kept an open mind and a respect for what others thought, even though he might not agree. I have often thought that he could not have remained so active as leader of the opposition for so long if he had not had this genuine respect for and interest in the points of view of others.

In the winter there were walks in the city or skating trips on Lake Mälaren. Father had special skates for long trips. I did not, however, but when I got tired, he sometimes pulled me along with a stick. And at the end of every trip there was hot chocolate with whipped cream, loved by us both.

Family life had certain rules. Dinnertime was supposed to be at 6 pm but more often than not it was adjusted to suit his convenience. He wanted to rest for 15 minutes before dinner, and the meal had to be squeezed in between this resting time and the news on the radio. When TV became important in the late 1950s, a television set was moved into the dining room and ordinary dinner conversation suffered. His favorite comments concerned the lack of economic knowledge and the tendency toward socialist ideas among journalists.

After the disastrous elections in 1958, father needed time to "recharge his batteries" and arranged to be visiting professor at the University of Virginia in Charlottesville in the United States, and mother and I went with him. My parents went home after Christmas, but I stayed on as a boarder at high school. It was usually mother who wrote, but I also have some letters from father, mostly dealing with my progress in school. He made me take a year of Latin, which he said was useful for learning French. (It may have been for him, but it didn't work for me.) He also arranged for me to spend the Easter holidays with the Svennilsson family instead of at an empty boarding school (Ingvar Svennilsson was a colleague, professor of economics, visiting Yale at the time).

Neither my sister nor my brother had chosen to study economics, and as far as I know, our father did not mind. But when I left school with no decided preference, he suggested that I apply to the Stockholm School of Economics (*Handelshögskolan*). So I did, and it was one of the best pieces of advice he gave me. Economics turned out to be fascinating. In the beginning, however, most of his comments on my studies were concerned with the pace of studying, strange to him, with weekends off for partying. According to him, the five-day working week ought not to apply to university students. Doing well in one's studies was very important. Any argument based on facts got his respect, whereas sentences beginning with "I just think" was a sure way of getting nowhere. The only argument of that kind that I ever won was about the dog Hassan sleeping on my bed at night. Father was opposed to the idea for fear of germs, but Hassan and I did what we wanted anyway.

Later we had more serious discussions about current economic matters. This was in the mid-1960s, when economic growth in Sweden seemed to be autonomous and the business cycle to have been reduced to quite small variations in the growth rate. He put great stress on incentives and wealth-creating forces. Taxes, for instance, are not only for financing public expenditure, they also influence people's behavior, their will to work, to save, to study, and to take risks in entrepreneurial activity. He was fond of saying that if we had all been concerned only with the distribution of wealth instead of the creation of wealth, we might have been more equal but mainly equally poor. He also left me a strong feeling for private ownership and private savings, without which the market economy cannot function well. He was quite keen on anticyclical stabilization policy, and liked to talk about his discussions with Keynes in the 1930s on demand management policies. This would usually turn into more of a lecture than a discussion, and has not left me with any lasting belief in fine-tuning policies. I am quite sure that he would have agreed that what was appropriate in the 1930s might not work fifty years later in a different institutional framework.

One specific discussion is more fixed in my memory than others. It concerns the Wage Earners Fund discussion in Sweden, where the Liberal Party did some very curious thinking for some time in the late 1970s. Father strongly opposed the idea of this fund, which he saw as a means of introducing a planned economy in Sweden. He had retired from active politics at this time, and usually he would be careful not to call and give his points of view on current issues to people in the Liberal Party.

But this time his feelings were so strong that he called several people, as well as held forth at the dinner table whenever there were any listeners. At this time I had become somewhat active in the Liberal Party myself and he could not really understand why I did not manage to persuade everybody that he was right.

Father was exceptionally keen on education for everyone, not least for girls. A good education opened many doors, and a job and an income of one's own made a woman less dependent on her husband. To me, he gave a thirst for knowledge and a never-ending curiosity about the future, how other people reasoned, and innovations of different kinds. He was always interested in knowing more and always kept an open mind. Someone else might know better! I know that I speak for my sister and brother as well as myself when I say that we are proud to have had him as our father.

3 Bertil Ohlin as a Friend and Colleague

Torsten Gårdlund

In the 1950s Bertil Ohlin published two memoirs: the first excellent as a story and charming in tone, the second more a piece of personal political history. Recently a regular biography and, at the same time, a piece of serious research, 550 pages long, was published, written by Sven-Erik Larsson, a journalist friend of his.[1]

In his foreword Larsson explains that he has been unable to give a personal touch to his book, mainly due to lack of material: Bertil wrote only few letters and kept no diary. Because of this lack of material, I myself have had difficulties in creating a good picture of my former teacher and colleague. My intention is to start by presenting a few facts about Bertil's personality. Then I will present an aspect that the other contributions in this volume are not dealing with: Bertil's early scientific training in the meager environment of Swedish economics as it then appeared.

I first met—or rather saw—Bertil in the fall of 1930, which was his first year of teaching at the Stockholm School of Economics. That year I had finished high school at the age of nineteen. Having worked at a shipping agency in Stockholm during the summer holidays and having taken to the lively atmosphere of the freightage market, I had decided to continue my career in shipping. But before that I wanted to seek deeper wisdom at the Stockholm School of Economics.

The particular high school in Stockholm where I had spent the previous ten years, was founded at the beginning of the nineteenth century and its premises were shabby—as were most of its teachers. The Stockholm School of Economics turned out to be a revelation—not only in its elegant architecture and the quality of its teaching staff—but forgive my pretensions—also in the level of the students who were screened according to their previous school marks.

The Stockholm School of Economics was thus superior to my high school, not only in material ways but also in the intellectual standard and personal style of the teachers. Martin Fehr, professor of law and also president of the School, had made a brilliant academic career. He rapidly went to the head of the law writing bureau of the government, created a private solicitor's firm, and, on top of all, became an MP and one of the leaders of the Liberal Party. I hesitate to add that he had also found the time to become a reserve officer in the First Royal Lifeguard!

The professor of business economics, Oskar Sillén, had received his basic training in Germany. He brought the new technique of business accountancy to Sweden and moreover had created a personal accounting business, which came to audit a number of large Swedish industries. He looked very much like a managing director of a worldwide group of companies, somewhat heavy, precise, and taking no nonsense from the students.

Finally I come to Bertil Ohlin. Although recently appointed to a chair in economics in Copenhagen, at the age of twenty-five, Bertil was, of course, less known than the leading teachers just mentioned. In Stockholm he was taking over the chair in economics of Eli Heckscher, who was promoted to a research fellowship in economic history.

My memories are those of a youngster starting his studies in 1930—and thus are early impressions of outward traits. Most of the students looked up to Bertil Ohlin—in both senses of the word—when he spoke from the rostrum of the big lecture hall. He had an easy way of talking, but there was also a great deal of substance in what he said. He was well dressed and, in his early thirties, obviously in good shape. You could have met him on a tennis or golf court, on a sporting ground, or on a ski slope.

Bertil lectured without manuscript, and he invited his audience to freely ask questions. Sometimes in his public speaking, however, he showed a slight tendency toward superciliousness, of which he only later did become aware. In fact few students dared to ask questions during the lectures. He seems later to have created the same kind of reaction when speaking in Parliament or in the open-air debates with aggressive postwar socialists. When leading discussions among about twenty students in smallish classrooms during the seminars of the Stockholm School of Economics, he was very relaxed and friendly, however.

I would now like to bring up the question of how students generally looked upon the subject matter formerly taught by Heckscher and now by Ohlin. The answer is that a large number of the students did not take much interest. Such down-to-earth subjects as business economics and law ranked much higher, because they were of direct importance for their future careers in business.

Personally, I was captivated by the subjects that Heckscher and Ohlin taught. After my graduation from the Stockholm School of Economics in early 1933, I continued my studies at the economics department at Stockholm University. My earlier plans to continue in shipping were abandoned. In my new environment, the teacher I turned to was Professor Alf Johansson. Under his leadership I was, somewhat later, employed as one of the younger assistants in the teaching of price and distribution. These courses had grown out of a program developed by Alf Johansson and Tord Palander, a program of popular education directed toward members of the co-ops in Stockholm. As we now know from Bertil's memoirs, he ran a similar program, although at a slightly higher level.

As the years went by, I took up my own research, mainly in the field of modern economic history. In 1947 the economics chair of Sven Brisman at the Stockholm School of Economics became vacant, and I had the good luck to win it. Fifteen years after my graduation from the School, I had become one of Bertil's colleagues.

In the interval, we had not seen much of each other. But as, at the beginning of the war, I had been appointed to the editorship of the social democratic monthly review *Tiden*—and turned it into a general cultural review with reform orientation—we had, at any rate, followed and sympathized with each other's journalism. As he was a left-wing liberal and I a right-wing socialist, we could easily agree on politics. I might add that such high-ranking social democrats as Gustav Möller, Torsten Nilsson, and Gunnar Sträng, with whom I was closely in touch as an editor, had a high personal regard for Bertil Ohlin.

Our first arrangement as colleagues in 1947 was to divide the teaching according to our tastes and capacities. Bertil chose trade, money, and business cycles while I took price, distribution, and economic ideas.

I now come to the question, What sort of relationship did we have during the following twenty years? The answer is that our relation was friendly, agreeable, and rare. This also goes for his relations with other colleagues and for the staff of the School. Let me tell you some more about the rarity of our cooperation, which I of course now miss.

Bertil mainly used his very nice office for examinations. But on one occasion, which has become part of local history, he is said—probably untruly—to have examined a student in a running taxi. In later years he usually arrived at the School by taxi, and when he had finished his teaching, he left in the same way. These hectic transfers were certainly due to an extremely heavy burden of work.

His contract with one of the leading Stockholm papers called for two lengthier articles a week and one longer overview a month, which gave him as large a salary as the one from the School. He also had a contract with a leading paper in Denmark. Much work but little money came from his pioneering research and from the writing of popular texts. As an MP, he touched the normal compensation, but he seems to have lost money on the very demanding party work. He regularly came to the professorial meetings, which were held a few times each term. He took part in their essential discussions, but he was brief in his arguments and never criticized a colleague.

Even if I rarely saw him on the premises of the School, we occasionally met socially, normally in each other's homes. But this was not very often. After all, I was a dozen years younger and born in Stockholm, which meant that I already had a set of friends of my own age. Bertil had several close friends since his younger days and also a remarkably close contact with his parents and brother and sisters. So we had a friendly relation without being close friends. On the other hand, Bertil was very fond of what I would call qualified gossip. When I came back from shorter or longer jobs in developing countries or when I happened to clash with somebody—especially his good friend Ruben Rausing—Bertil used to ask me to come over for a chat.

Let me end this review of personal traits with a more general statement. I never heard Bertil utter a word of conceit, he never boasted. And he seldom spoke disparagingly about people.

In my account of how he learned the trade of economic science, let me first say that Bertil seems to have been unnecessarily modest and apt to refer his achievements to other people. Let us then see how his academic career began. His high school marks were not better than the average. He shone in mathematics, but as a Latinist, he did not have to treat very difficult problems. The atmosphere in his comparatively well-to-do and certainly enlightened home was no doubt conducive to higher studies. So it was quite natural that he decided to begin at the University of Lund, situated only a couple of hours from his home.

In Lund, he began to follow the instruction in mathematics, and he also visited the lectures given by the famous—or notorious—Professor Wicksell. But being at the end of his tenure, Wicksell had chosen a very boring subject for his lectures—something about agricultural policy in Germany—so Bertil instead began to follow the "rather elementary" lectures of Associate Professor Emil Sommarin.

The third subject of Bertil's choice was statistics, but no courses were given that term and the examination was entrusted to the teacher of political science. Both in economics and statistics, the examiner happened to be a nice and complacent person, and as a result Bertil got a pass that he himself regarded as "unwarranted." In mathematics, things were somewhat more difficult. Thanks to hard work and a number of private lessons, he was one of the few to pass the written part. But the oral part did not "go very well." As the examiner did not exactly know the requirements on a lower level, the pass was given after some hesitation.

In the spring of 1917, at the early age of eighteen, Bertil thus got his Bachelor of Arts—and was ready for more serious study at the Stockholm School of Economics. He had the following to say about his start at the School:

"Already in the first week of the fall 1917 Heckscher held a meeting to plan seminars for the second form. After my studies in Lund I regarded myself as qualified for this seminar and turned up for the meeting. When at the roll call Heckscher caught sight of me he asked: *"What are you doing here?"* I explained the situation. He looked as if he was to turn me out but he changed his mind and allowed me to stay."

I can well understand that Heckscher hesitated when Bertil mentioned the name of the professor in Lund who had given a mark over the pass standard. Sommarin certainly was an odd man to be appointed to a chair in economics. His basic training was in Nordic and Germanic languages up to the doctorate level. Later he had studied law and ended up as an historian, writing a thesis on labor conditions before 1720 in one particular Swedish ironworks. The reason why I bring in the name of this gentle and unimportant professor is

Table 3.1
Educational backgrounds of Ohlin's contemporaries in Swedish economies

	Name	Born in	Chair in economics	Previous training
Lund University	K. Wicksell	1851	1901–1916	Mathematics
	E. Sommarin	1874	1919–1939	History
Uppsala University	D. Davidson	1854	1889–1919	Bachelor of law
	F. Brock	1877	1921–1941	Bachelor of law
Stockholm University	G. Cassel	1866	1904–1935	Mathematics
	G. Bagge	1882	1921–1949	Economics
Gothenburg University	G. Steffen	1864	1903–1929	History
	G. Åkerman	1888	1931–1953	Bachelor of law
Stockholm School of Economics	E. Heckscher	1879	1909–1929	History
	S. Brisman	1881	1927–1946	History
Gothenburg Business School	G. Silverstolpe	1891	1928–1932	Economics
	E. Lindahl	1891	1932–1939	Bachelor of law

that he well represents the majority of the men appointed in economics during the years around World War I.

For this occasion I have done some research on the earlier training of the twelve economics professors appointed up to 1932 and who were still active when Bertil began his economic studies (table 3.1). Four out of these twelve had history as their academic basis, four had law, two had mathematics, and only two had economics.

One of the two professors, who had studied economics before his appointment, was Gösta Bagge. Heckscher had closely supervised his thesis on the supply and demand of labor. Bagge had also belonged to the conservative Heckscher junta around the charismatic history professor in Uppsala, Harald Hjärne. The other professor with a degree in economics was Gunnar Silverstolpe, a pupil of Cassel's, who was appointed to a chair at the Business School in Gothenburg—but disappeared after a few years, possibly into popular writing and good living.

About Bertil's early training in economics, two conclusions can be drawn from my figures. One is that for a gifted and purposeful young man, it must have been fairly easy to find a chair in this professorial world colonized by historians and lawyers. The other conclusion seems to be that it must have been difficult for a beginner to find a competent teacher to lead him through the labyrinths of theoretical economics.

After this detour, I will go back to specifics and ask the question: Was Eli Heckscher right as a teacher of this clever but relatively uninstructed pupil whom he had received from Lund? When trying to answer this question, I will somewhat weaken my case by mentioning that in his memoirs Bertil tells us that, during his year in Lund, he read books about four hours each working day. He might have read Wicksell's two volumes of recently published lectures in economics, perhaps he found and perused Alfred Marshall's *Principles of Economics*, which, by the way, was known to Heckscher. But in his fairly detailed memories about his year in Lund, Bertil speaks only about how he listened to elementary lectures, improved his cultural education, and devoted himself to entertainment and sports together with other students.

During the years 1917 to 1919 Bertil no doubt learned a good deal by following Heckscher's seminars—but less from Heckscher's lectures in general theory. Heckscher took a special interest in such fields as trade, foreign exchange, and international finance. After all, both his grandfather and father had been private bankers in Denmark and Sweden. His father had actually translated George J. Goschen's *Theory of Foreign Exchanges* into Swedish, a translation that saw several editions. Heckscher was not so versed in such essential fields of economics as price and distribution, something that I remember from my own time as his student. It also corresponds with Bertil's view as expressed in his autobiography. Moreover, when Bertil became Heckscher's successor about ten years later, Heckscher gave him his lecturing notes to read and comment on. In a letter to Heckscher, Bertil pointed to several weaknesses in the text but seems to have avoided further criticism of his older colleague.

In summary, Bertil had, in my opinion, comparatively little to learn from Heckscher, and he completed his study of economics by reading literature in the field. But Heckscher certainly had considerable influence on the orientation of Bertil's scientific interests and research.

To reach versatility in a subject, it is clearly not enough to have followed lectures and read textbooks. In running discussions with a brilliant philosopher-historian-economist like Heckscher, Bertil certainly had an important asset. When the select Economic Club in

Stockholm was established, Bertil soon became a member, and both Wicksell and Heckscher were leading members.

It is my impression—or rather my conviction—that in these early years, Bertil regretted that he had never had the chance to follow a first-rate course in economic analysis—as a whole or in parts treated by specialists. In the summer of 1922 he got the chance to take up such studies abroad, however. With the help of a fellowship from the American Foundation and a personal bank loan, he set out on a one-year journey to Cambridge, England, and Harvard.

Cambridge turned out to be more or less closed for the summer. After a month's rest, Bertil went on to Harvard, where he was received with open arms. So, after having settled down, he embarked on a study program including trade, international finance, economic thought, and, above all, economic theory. "The outstanding pedagogue F. W. Taussig" taught this last course. On November 22, 1922, Ohlin wrote to Heckscher: "Taussig's theoretical course is excellent and gives above all a thorough knowledge of classical and neoclassical economics, which suits me very well, as my earlier studies of these topics have been unsystematic." He also mentioned in the letter that the large American universities had a better teaching system than the Swedish ones. According to the American system at its best, courses were built around textbooks, review articles, and the like, which were discussed under the guidance of a highly competent professor who met with his class about three hours a week.

Bertil received his Master of Arts in June 1923 and thereafter started his return trip to Sweden. He stopped at Cambridge, which again was a closed place, the students being away on summer holidays. As the poet says: "Young and old come forth to play, on a sunshine holiday." But not Bertil Ohlin. He sat down somewhere in this agreeable half-empty town to work hard on his forthcoming book about foreign trade. The book was to become his main scientific contribution.

Note

1. The title of the book is *Bertil Ohlin. Ekonom och politiker* (Bertil Ohlin. Economist and Politician), Stockholm, 1998.

4 My Bertil Ohlin

Paul A. Samuelson

A Pearl of Analysis

Ask newly minted economics Ph.D.'s at century's end, "What do you associate with Ohlin's name?" Probably they would answer: "Ohlin explained geographical trade and specialization patterns as depending on *differences* in geographical *endowments* of factor inputs. Free trade causes a region to export goods intensive in its relatively abundant factor, in exchange for goods intensive in its scarce factor. That way trade raises in each place the return of each region's superabundant factor, tending to move real factor prices nearer to equality everywhere. Moving goods thus substitutes for moving factors themselves."

It is a beautiful insight, one only vaguely noticed in the classical Ricardian literature. Ohlin deserves praise for it, even after he acknowledged that in 1919 his teacher Eli Heckscher had glimpsed its essence, and acknowledged that he used his teacher Gustav Cassel's version of the Léon Walras general equilibrium to perfect and develop its analytics. When I, the pupil of Jacob Viner and Gottfried Haberler, arrived on the scene, we called this *the Ohlin* system.

Knowing no Swedish, Lloyd Metzler and I wisely urged the then-Danish couple Svend Laursen and Agnete Laursen (later Kalckar) to translate into English Heckscher's 1919 classic article. Inadvertently, and I would say somewhat unjustly, gradually Ohlin lost some kudos for his crucial role in "the Heckscher-Ohlin" breakthrough. Further, after 1948, Ohlin sometimes became the meat in a Heckscher-Ohlin-Samuelson sandwich. Robert K. Merton, the historian and sociologist of science, aptly calls this, "obliteration by incorporation." Eventually no one cites a precept of Isaac Newton or John Maynard Keynes because we are all inhaling and exhaling what those masters have breathed. On this occasion of remembering Ohlin—my Ohlin—

it is proper to emphasize that it was he who launched half a hundred dissertations and learned-journal articles. Lionel McKenzie could do the great crowning work on this topic before and after 1967 because 40 years earlier a precociously original young scholar performed the alchemy of turning two noble metals into an alloy of pure gold.

The Scholar as a Young Virtuoso

The history that perforce has to be lived forward cannot be adequately told any other way. Bertil Ohlin by fate was born precocious and by family opportunity and timing lived up to his potential. Sweden is a small country. Early in the century Scandinavia was a northern outpost of Europe with moderate GDP per capita. But for whatever reason where economists were concerned, Sweden was fat city—a veritable Vienna. In the first wave were (alphabetically) Gustav Cassel, David Davidson, Heckscher, and Knut Wicksell. From their loins sprung the crown princes: (chronologically) Bertil Ohlin, Gunnar Myrdal, Erik Lindahl, Erik Lundberg, and Ingvar Svennilson.

Ohlin's chief masters were Heckscher and Cassel. What best illustrates how precocious young Bertil really was is an attested story. The austere Heckscher was a learned economic historian as well as a subtle theorist. In politics he was "liberal"—which then meant, staunchly in favor of laissez faire. Four great contemporaries are not required to love each other equally, or at all.

In his seminar at the Stockholm Business School, Heckscher asserted the dictum: the rational age to chop down a tree is just when its *percentage* rate of growing wood has fallen to precise equality with the (instantaneous) rate of interest. Not a wild notion and one (I believe) also held by Fisher (yes, Irving) and Johann von Thünen. "'Tain't so," in effect said the teenage Ohlin. "When you chop down the tree, that makes room to plant a new tree. And where forest land is scarce enough to earn a market-clearing *positive* rent rate, you should chop the tree *before* Heckscher's specified age."

The Emperor of the Seminar stood his ground. Ohlin, sitting with four aces in his hand, would not give way. When asked by forestry experts to adjudicate the same issue some sixty years later, by use of dynamic Bellman nonlinear programming, Samuelson (1976) had to rule against the Heckscher view. (Harold Hotelling would have thought well of Ohlin had he been told this story; for, in Hotelling's [1925] classic maiden article on depreciation, he had not spoken about this subtlety—a subtlety long hidden in the 1849 writings of the German forestry expert Martin Faustmann.) What is remarkable is that despite little advanced training in mathematics, Ohlin could still exhibit his native mathematical talent.

Time of Crucial Change

Just after I began my Chicago undergraduate study in January 1932, Ohlin published his thick English tome on interregional and international trade. During the 1930 to 1933 years, Ohlin's was one of the many seminal works that went beyond the labor-only models of comparative advantage that had prevailed in the writings of David Ricardo, Robert Torrens, J. S. Mill, Hans von Mangoldt, Francis Edgeworth, and Frank Taussig. Notable contributors to this renaissance were Jacob Viner, Gottfried Haberler, Abba Lerner, Wassily Leontief, and James Meade. As we in the Anglo-Saxon world learned later, Ohlin's contributions had been largely independent of the others. Already in his 1924 Swedish dissertation, Ohlin had written out much of what was later in his 1933 English book.

When Ohlin and James Meade received their well-deserved, shared 1977 Nobel Prizes, I estimated that most of what Ohlin accomplished in the pure theory of international trade he had already accomplished by the age of twenty-five. Joseph Schumpeter sentimentalized—oversentimentalized—the importance for scientific originality of youth, the importance of one's sacred third decade of life. Certainly Ohlin's career fitted in with Schumpeter's conceit. (But what about the great Wicksell, who got a late start and died with his boots on, running fast?) My appendix will say more about the 1933 Ohlin classic book.

The Transfer Controversy

Actually Ohlin's first world notoriety, his hour of Andy Warhol celebrity, came around 1929 when as a little known chairholder in Copenhagen and Stockholm, he crossed swords with the great John Maynard Keynes on the transfer or reparations problem.

As part of his critique of the Versailles Treaty, Keynes uncharacteristically espoused the "orthodox view" on the transfer problem. This maintained that when Germany had to make unrequited reparation payments to England, two burdens would necessarily fall on her: (1) the *primary* burden of the excess goods she must export abroad and do without at home, plus (2) the *secondary* burden stemming from the induced drop in her terms of trade—her drop in real $\sum P_j \text{Exports}_j / \sum P_k \text{Imports}_k$—(allegedly) made necessary to effectuate transfer of the reparations. Twenty-nine-year-old Bertil said to 45-year-old Maynard (my paraphrase): "Not necessarily so. You have taken account of the loss-in-income effect on Germany, but left intact England's (Marshallian) reciprocal demand. *Both* nations will experience opposite directional income shifts, so there is no presumption that the payer's terms of trade need fall, rise, or stay the same."

There is a landscape in Provence that may not be the world's most beautiful—or even the best in France. But it is the best known one because so many painters have addressed it over the years. The transfer problem is like that. Viner's 1937 survey of its earlier literature shows that David Ricardo, J. S. Mill, Frank Taussig, Keynes, A. C. Pigou, Dennis Robertson, and a score of other luminaries, had failed to reach agreement on the transfer problem. For Haberler's Harvard seminar I devoted around 1937 a term paper to clearing up the analysis. My former teacher, Jacob Viner, turned it down for the *JPE*, forcing me years later, in 1952 to 1954, to devote two *Economic Journal* articles to the subject. Notable post-1935 authorities included James Meade, Ronald Jones, Martin Bronfenbrenner, and many others. (With several regions and many goods, ambiguities in outcomes multiply.)

If called on to adjudicate between Keynes and Ohlin, under oath as a friend of the court, I would have to find for Ohlin. The agnostic and eclectic verdict on indefinite algebraic signs of secondary burdens is the better conclusion. If Keynes had understood this, his best-selling *Economic Consequences of the Peace* (1919) would have been a less exciting book but not a less accurate one.

The "Stockholm School" as Independent Keynesians?

The Great Depression drew from the 53-year-old Keynes a new macro paradigm of effective demand. *The General Theory* (1936) was not without earlier anticipation: 1931 Richard Kahn, 1931 J. M. Clark, 1934 Michael Kalecki, 1935 Ragnar Frisch, and so on. Bertil Ohlin (1937) argued eloquently that what he called the Stockholm School had been Keynesian even before Keynes. Ohlin's generation early advocated and justified use by the Labor Party of fiscal stimulus to reduce unemployment and increase demand. (Even the conservative Cassel and Heckscher had favored activistic lean-against-the-wind monetary policy, which was in marked contrast to Austrians like Friedrich von Hayek and Ludwig von Mises who subscribed to their version of neo-Wicksellianism.)

My considered judgment is that several anticipations of Keynes did arrive at the multiplier version of *The General Theory*—$Y = C(Y) + I + G$, $dY/d(I + G) > 1$, and all that. But the *full* Keynes system of the LM-IS type was not needed to rationalize *deficit* fiscal spending, and perhaps Ohlin overreached in his claims for mid-1930s Swedish macroeconomics. Myrdal's contemporary works, like earlier ones of Wicksell, presented no theory of output as a whole, instead concentrating on the ups and downs of the price level as such. Wicksell was and remains a favorite economic hero of mine. Still it was unwarranted for Ohlin and others to attribute their stimulation programs to Wicksell's leadings. Only after more extensive acquaintanceship with Wicksell's total bibliography did I come to realize how much that radical Bohemian believed in Say's law of markets clearing and in the macro Pareto-optimality of the capitalistic system.

Thus, after World War I, Wicksell advocated a return to 1914 currency parity, stressing that equity-justice required this and minimizing the deadweight losses that would be created by the process of deflation. Conservative Cassel was more realistic. Grudgingly Wicksell learned how overly optimistic he had been, but death overtook him before he could arrive at a final judgment in the matter. History runs a cruel casino: in a career you are called on to make only a few key judgments, and on the neutrality of deflation, Knut seems to have backed the wrong horse. When writing his *Treatise on Money* (1930), Keynes sinned in neglecting Wicksell; for the 1936 *General Theory*, there was no similar sin, and the famous Keynes circus, I suspect, had not much to learn from the Swedish learned journals of the early 1930s.

The Scholar as Politician

Economists in Sweden were accorded much respect and wielded considerable political power. Somehow the Marxian virus that flourished in Bismarck's Germany and elsewhere never took firm root in Scandinavia's northern soils. Politics' gain was economics' loss when

Bertil Ohlin after 1938 became a parliamentarian and leader of the Liberal Party. (Heckscher and Cassel were conservatives; Myrdal, Dag Hammarskjöld, and many of the university professionals began as Labor stalwarts; but as is the way with critical scholars, successers in the younger Swedish generations became somewhat disillusioned with the workings out of Sweden's middle way.) When I first visited Stockholm in the fall 1948, Bertil Ohlin came as close to being voted prime minister as he was ever to do. For the purpose of the present memoir, what needs reminding is that even before Bertil was forty he became virtually a part-time scholar.

What energy Ohlin must have had: to lead a party, to debate in parliament, to write often for the daily press and the quarterly bank journals. As a selfish theorist, I must regret Ohlin's preoccupations with politics; as a humanitarian and citizen of the world, I know there is rejoicing in heaven when a gifted mind helps to elevate democracy. Arthur Okun offers a similar case. From 1949 to 1980 we in America knew him as the wisest of our generation. By deliberate choice Okun left Yale and full-time academic life. That was no Faustian bargain with the devil. It was a rational choice in terms of comparative advantage, and it must have been envy of the gods that killed off an Okun at so early an age and just when the mixed economy needed so urgently the rare wisdoms that he could muster.

Quick of mind and energetic of spirit, part-time Ohlin kept up with the dynamic trends of mainstream economics. I remember when he visited Columbia University in 1947 to help celebrate its bicentennial. On his way home, at Harvard, I heard him give one of the earliest analyses of the over-full-employment economy. Masters with absolute pitch know when to change their focus. While a brilliant generation of Oxbridge economists stayed mired in Model T Keynesianism of the Great Depression—remember only the British Radcliffe Committee of 1959—Ohlin had moved on to late-twentieth-century issues and challenges.

To be a virtuoso of fixed-point theorems, I do not need the virtues of judgment and eclecticism. Our house of economics has many mansions, and we can certainly use the innovations of impractical ivory-towered shut-ins. Indeed, evolving excesses in unrealistic doctrines will not be cured by the prosaic wisdoms of full-time sages. Always it takes a better theory to kill off an imperfect theory: from *within* the camp of academic research will come, eventually, the cleaning of the Augean Stables, rather than from a Hans Christian Andersen child or a Homeric sage.

The Bertil Ohlin I knew and admired added to the political economy of his teachers and contributed to the originality of his contemporaries and students. His was a fulfilled life.

Appendix: Gemstones in Ohlin's Great Book

Ohlin's 1933 classic was notable for several features. (1) In the spirit of Adam Smith, Frank Graham, and Allyn Young, Ohlin emphasized the importance for trade and location theory of *increasing returns to scale*. Such models deviate from the nice competitive models built on *constant* returns to scale. Such models become very difficult to analyze and to say new and elegant things about. At the end of this century Paul Krugman and other economists have had to return to Ohlin's courageous emphasis.[1]

(2) Ohlin tried to integrate *location* theory with economist's trade theory, a return toward von Thünen. Domestic (or untradable) goods interacted with easily tradable manufactures and raw materials. With technological improvements in transportation and communication, again paradoxically, trade may have now become more unified and production less balkanized.

(3) As I mentioned in my beginning, for reasons of theoretical elegance, increasingly Ohlin gained prominence for his theory (with Heckscher) to explain patterns of geographical specialization and trade in terms of differences in regions' proportionate factor endowments.

All this is simple general equilibrium filtered through Cassel's borrowings from Léon Walras. Ohlin applied Heckscher's 1919 factor-endowment insight to the Walras-Cassel constant-returns-to-scale model with *uniform* production functions everywhere in the world—a strategic oversimplification but not one that had been emphasized by earlier Ricardian trade theorists. Actually Ohlin generalized beyond Cassel's borrowing from 1889 second-edition Walras, with its *constant* (input/output) technical coefficients. These a_{ij} coefficients Ohlin makes be variable and endogenous cost-minimizing variables.

Ohlin writes the *prices* of n goods as $(p_1 \ldots p_n)$; their *quantities* he writes as $(D_1 \ldots D_n)$. For r primary factors of production, $r \lesseqgtr n$, he writes their total quantities as $(R_1 \ldots R_r)$, writes $(R_{11} \ldots R_{1n}; \ldots; R_{r1} \ldots R_{rn})$ for industries' factor inputs by industries, and writes $(q_1 \ldots q_r)$ for their factor prices. Clearly, he postulates a smooth neoclassical Clark-Solow technology connecting outputs to inputs; I write these for him as strongly concave and smooth, linear-homogeneous neoclassical production functions

$$D_1 = F^1(R_{11}, R_{12}, \ldots, R_{1r})$$

$$\vdots$$

$$D_n = F^n(R_{n1}, R_{n2}, \ldots, R_{nr}). \tag{1a}$$

For any $1 \le i \le n$, constant returns to scale implies that

$$1 = F^i\left(\frac{R_{i1}}{D_i}, \frac{R_{i2}}{D_i}, \ldots, \frac{R_{in}}{D_i}\right)$$

$$\equiv F^i(a_{i1}, a_{i2}, \ldots, a_{ir}), \tag{1b}$$

where the a's are Walras's technical coefficients of production, now *endogenous* unknowns. Unlike Cassel and early Walras who made the a's constant, Ohlin makes them infinitely substitutable in the J. B. Clark sense. Thus, for $r = 2$, instead of F^1 being $\mathrm{Min}(R_{11}/\bar{a}_{11}, R_{12}/\bar{a}_{12})$, it could be Cobb-Douglas $R_{11}^{1/4}R_{12}^{3/4}$ or could be $(\rho_1 R_{11}^{-1} + R_{12}^{-1})^{-1} + (\gamma_1 R_{11}^{1/2} + R_{12}^{1/2})^2$: strong Inada conditions specify that as $\partial F^1/\partial a_{ij} \to \infty$ as $a_{ij} \to 0$, and $\partial F^1/\partial a_{ij} \to 0$ as $a_{ij} \to \infty$.

Under autarky Ohlin specifies personal factor endowments to be exogenously given at $(\bar{R}_1^s\, \bar{R}_2^s \ldots \bar{R}_r^s)$ in his abbreviated mathematical appendix. Each of S persons, $s = 1, \ldots, S$ has endowments given at $(\bar{R}_1^s\, \bar{R}_2^s \ldots \bar{R}_r^s)$. Each gets an income to spend on consumption goods of $\sum_1^r q_j R_j^s = I^s$, just as the logician Gödel suggested to Wald later that they should do.

What Ohlin intuitively senses (but does not write out) is correct:

THEOREM There exists always a positive equilibrium for $(p_2^*/p_1^* \ldots p_n^*/p_1;\ q_1^*/p_1^* \ldots q_r^*/p_1^*;\ [I^1/p_1]^* \ldots [I^s/p_1]^*)$ and for $(D_1 \ldots D_n)^*$ satisfying the full equations

$$p_i^* = \mathrm{Min} \sum_{j=1}^{r} q_j R_{ij}, \qquad i = 1, \ldots n, \tag{2}$$

$$\sum_{i=1}^{n} R_{ij} = \bar{R}_j = \sum_{s=1}^{S} \bar{R}_j^S, \qquad j = 1, \ldots, r. \tag{3}$$

Also Ohlin adds Cassel-like consumer demands for goods in terms of income relations (which do *not* mention marginal utilities but which do behave like quasi-concave indifference contours):

$$D_i = f^i\left(p_1, \ldots, p_n; \sum_{j=1}^{r} \overline{R}_j^1 q_j, \ldots, \sum_{j=1}^{r} \overline{R}_j^S q_j\right), \qquad i = 1, \ldots, n, \tag{4}$$

$$\sum_{i=1}^{n} p_i D_i \equiv \sum_{s=1}^{S}\left(\sum_{j=1}^{r} \overline{R}_j^2 q_j\right) = \sum_{j=1}^{r} \overline{R}_j q_j, \qquad \text{Walras's law.} \tag{5}$$

The upshot is this. If Abraham Wald in the mid-1930s, instead of dealing with Cassel's and Schlesinger's imperfect version of Walras had dealt with Ohlin's 1933 extension, then he could immediately have proved the existence of one or more positive equilibria and could have proved (as Marshall knew in 1879) that multiple equilibria could easily occur. In this sense (of providing *sufficiency* conditions for a general equilibrium solution) Bertil Ohlin the non-mathematician was ahead of his time and of such mathematical stars as Abraham Wald, F. Zeuthen, H. Neisser, J. R. Hicks, and others. As Ohlin explicitly warns, his appendix does not grapple with intertemporal complexities of "capital and interest" theory. Rome was not built at one sitting! The modern reader can put in for Ohlin the Sraffa-Leontief input/output coefficients to bring the 1933 appendix fully up to date.

Note

1. In his 1931 preface, Ohlin strangely omits from his outlined claims his important advance into increasing returns. Paradoxically, modern "globalization" has vastly expanded the range of markets. Therefore the old competitive model in many ways seems somewhat more realistic than it used to be during the vogue of Joan Robinson's and Edward Chamberlin's imperfect competition. The U.S. Fortune 500 corporations probably enjoyed more oligopoly rents then (which they had to share with labor union employees) than they do today. As size of market grows with globalization and domestic integration, the early stages of increasing returns to scale exhaust themselves, making governmental trust-busting and regulation perhaps less important.

References

Cassel, Gustav. 1918. *Theoretische Sozialökonomie*. Leipzig: C. F. Winter. Translated as *Theory of Social Economy*, London: T. F. Unwin, 1923.

Clark, John M. 1931. *The Costs of the World War to the American People*. New Haven: Yale University Press; New York: H. Milford, Oxford University Press for the Carnegie Endowment for International Peace.

Faustmann, Martin. 1849. On the determination of the value which forest land and immature stands possess for forestry. English translation in M. Gane, ed., *Oxford In-*

stitute Paper 42, 1968 (entitled "Martin Faustmann and the Evolution of Discounted Cash Flow").

Frisch, Ragnar. 1935. Circulation planning: Proposal for a national organization of a commodity and service exchange. Parts I–II. *Econometrica* 2:258–336, 422–35.

Heckscher, Eli. 1919. Effects of foreign trade on distribution of income. *Ekonomisk Tidskrift*: 497–512. Translated in H. S. Ellis and L. Metzler, eds., AEA, *Readings in the Theory of International Trade*. Philadelphia: Blakiston, 1949, ch. 13, pp. 272–300.

Hicks, John. 1932. Marginal productivity and the principle of variation. *Economica* 12:79–88.

Hotelling, Harold. 1925. A general mathematical theory of depreciation. *Journal of the American Statistical Association* 20:340–53.

Kahn, Richard. 1931. The relation of home investment to unemployment. *Economic Journal*, 41:173–98. Reprinted in R. Kahn, *Selected Essays on Employment and Growth*. Cambridge: Cambridge University Press, 1972.

Kalecki, Michal. 1934, 1971. *Selected Essays on the Dynamics of the Capitalist Economy 1933–1970*. Cambridge: Cambridge University Press.

Keynes, John Maynard. 1919. *The Economic Consequences of the Peace*. New York: Harcourt Brace. Reprinted in *The Collected Writings of John Maynard Keynes*, vol. 2. London: Macmillan for the Royal Economic Society, 1971.

Keynes, John Maynard. 1929. The reparation problem. A rejoinder. *Economic Journal* 39:179–82.

Keynes, John Maynard. 1929. Mr. Keynes' views on the transfer problem. Reply. *Economic Journal* 39:404–408.

Keynes, John Maynard. 1930. *Treatise on Money: The Pure Theory of Money*, vol. 1. Reprinted in *The Collected Writings of John Maynard Keynes*, vol. 5. London: Macmillan for the Royal Economic Society, 1971.

Keynes, John Maynard. 1936. *The General Theory of Employment, Interest and Money*. Reprinted in *The Collected Writings of John Maynard Keynes*, vol. 7. London: Macmillan for the Royal Economic Society, 1973.

Marshall, Alfred. 1879. *The Pure Theory of Foreign Trade. The Pure Theory of Domestic Values*. Privately printed. Reprinted in *Scarce Works in Political Economy*, no. 1. London: London School of Economics, 1930.

McKenzie, Lionel. 1967. The inversion of cost functions: a counter-example. *International Economic Review* 8:271–78.

McKenzie, Lionel. 1967. Theorem and counter-example. *International Economic Review* 8:279–85.

Myrdal, Gunnar. 1939. *Monetary Equilibrium*. London: Hodge.

Neisser, Hans. 1932. Lohnhöhe und Beschèftigungsgrad im Marketgleichgewicht. *Weltwirtschaftliches Archiv* 36:413–55.

Ohlin, Bertil. 1924. *Handelns Teori*. Stockholm: Nordiska. Ph.D. Thesis. Translated into English as "Theory of Trade," in H. Flam and M. J. Flanders, eds., *Heckscher-Ohlin Trade Theory*. Cambridge: MIT Press, 1991.

Ohlin, Bertil. 1929. The reparation problem: A discussion. *Economic Journal* 39:172–78.

Ohlin, Bertil. 1933. *Interregional and International Trade*. Cambridge: Harvard University Press.

Ohlin, Bertil. 1937. Some notes on the Stockholm theory of savings and investment. Parts I–II. *Economic Journal* 47:53–69; 221–40.

Samuelson, Paul A. 1966, 1972. *The Collected Scientific Papers of Paul A. Samuelson*, vols. 2 and 3. Cambridge: MIT Press. For reference to factor price equalization, see chapters 67, 68, 69, 70, 74 and 75 in volume 2; and chapter 161 in volume 3.

Samuelson, Paul A. 1976. Economics of forestry in an evolving society. *Economic Inquiry* 14:466–92. Reproduced as chapter 218 in *The Collected Scientific Papers of Paul A. Samuelson*, vol. 4. Cambridge: MIT Press.

Schlesinger, Karl. 1934. Über die Produktionsgleichungen der ökonomischen Wertlehre. *Ergebnisse eines mathematischen Kolloquiums* 6:10–11.

Viner, Jacob. 1937. *Studies in the Theory of International Trade*. New York: Harper.

von Mises, Ludwig. 1912. *The Theory of Money and Credit*, 3rd English ed. Indianapolis: Liberty Classics, 1981.

Wald, Abraham. 1934. Über die eindeutige positive Lösbarkeit der neuen Produktionsgleichungen I. In K. Menger, ed., *Ergebnisse eines mathematischen Kolloquiums, 1933–34*. Translated by W. Baumol as "On the unique non-negative solvability of the new production equations, Part I." In W. Baumol and S. M. Goldfeld, eds., *Precursors in Mathematical Economics*. London School of Economics Series of Reprints of Scarce Works on Political Economy No. 19. London: London School of Economics, 1968.

Wald, Abraham. 1935. Über die Produktionsgleichungen der ökonomischen Wertlehre II. In K. Menger, ed., *Ergebnisse eines mathematischen Kolloquiums, 1934–35*. Translated by W. Baumol as "On the production equations of economic value theory, Part II." In W. Baumol and S. M. Goldfeld, eds., *Precursors in Mathematical Economics*. London School of Economics Series of Reprints of Scarce Works on Political Economy No 19. London: London School of Economics, 1968.

Wald, Abraham. 1936. Über einige Gleichungssysteme der mathematischen Ökonomie, *Zeitschrift für Nationalökonomie*. Translated by O. Eckstein as "On some systems of equations in mathematical economics." *Econometrica* 19:368–403.

Walras, Léon. 1889. *Eléments d'économie politique pure*. 2nd ed. Lausanne: F. Rouge; Paris: Guillaumin; Leipzig: Duncker & Humblot.

Walras, Léon. 1900. *Eléments d'économie politique pure*. 4th ed. Lausanne: F. Rouge; Paris: F. Pichon. Translated by W. Jaffe, as *Elements of Pure Economics*, 1954. Homewood, IL: Irwin; London: Allen & Unwin.

Wicksell, Knut. 1898. *Geldzins und Güterpreise bestimmenden Ursachen*. Jena: G. Fischer. Translated by R. F. Kahn as *Interest and Prices. A Study of the Causes Regulating the Value of Money*. London: Macmillan.

Zeuthen, Frederik Ludvig. 1932–33. Das Prinzip der Knappheit, technische Kombination und ökonomische Qualität. *Zeitschrift für Nationalökonomie* 4:1–24.

5 Ohlin Today: A Bibliometric Picture

Bo Sandelin

Introduction

There are many possible ways of looking at Bertil Ohlin today. I will present the image that appears when one looks at the frequency with which Ohlin is cited according to the Social Science Citation Index (SSCI).[1] This approach is not immune to criticism. Only citations in scientific journals are included. Therefore most of Ohlin's political writings are not counted because they are seldom cited in the SSCI journals. Furthermore most of the SSCI journals are in English, which means that non–English-language works are underrepresented among the works cited. Consequently such books as Ohlin's memoirs, which are well known in Sweden, are cited only a couple of times in the SSCI journals.

Another problem in counting citations is that when a theory or a theorem is well known, it is often mentioned without an explicit reference in a list of references, which means that it is not counted. This pertains to the Heckscher-Ohlin theory of international trade, which is often referred to without an indication of the source.

Another general question is whether citations always indicate influence. This is clearly not the case: one counterexample that has been given is that if citations always indicate influence, Lysenko would be a very important geneticist. We should bear in mind problems of this kind.

Nevertheless, I believe that the citations of Ohlin add interesting information. One of my findings is that there has been an increasing concentration in recent decades on three works, namely *Interregional and International Trade* (1933), the articles on the Stockholm School in the *Economic Journal* (1937), and the articles on the German reparations in the same journal in 1929.

Table 5.1
Number of citations from 1992 to May 1999

Bertil Ohlin	181
Gunnar Myrdal	1,515
Erik Lindahl	66
Erik Lundberg	100
Knut Wicksell	408

Ohlin and Other Swedes

The first question is how Ohlin compares with his Swedish colleagues and with Wicksell, from the previous generation. Table 5.1 shows the citations from 1992 to May 1999.[2]

Ohlin ranks in the middle. Myrdal and Wicksell are quoted more and Lindahl and Lundberg are quoted less then Ohlin. Myrdal's exceptional position depends in large part on the fact that he is much read and cited by scholars other than economists (see Sarafoglou and Sandelin 1992). Internationally, among social scientists, Ohlin is merely an economist who is limited in his contributions to the field of economics.

In figure 5.1, I show the variations, from year to year, in the number of citations of Ohlin according to the SSCI.[3] The peak in 1978, with 196 citations, can be explained by the fact that Ohlin received the Nobel Prize in 1977. This led to retrospective views of his contributions. Richard E. Caves wrote the traditional Nobel Prize review article on Ohlin in *The Scandinavian Journal of Economics* in 1978, which included a bibliography of 152 titles. The Nobel Prize effect evidently continued in 1979, when Ohlin got 142 citations. The year 1993 is Ohlin's nadir, with only 6 citations. It is not inconceivable that this extremely low number may reflect an error in the registration of citations.

Overall, no clear trend is discernible in the number of citations of Ohlin. There are large annual fluctuations. Taking into account the fact that the number of journals included in the SSCI (and whose reference lists are recorded) has increased considerably since 1973, one must conclude that the citations of Ohlin have decreased in proportion. This is no surprise. The same thing has happened for most economists of preceding generations. New research areas and new scholars divert attention from the older generations. Ohlin has, on the whole, been quite successful.

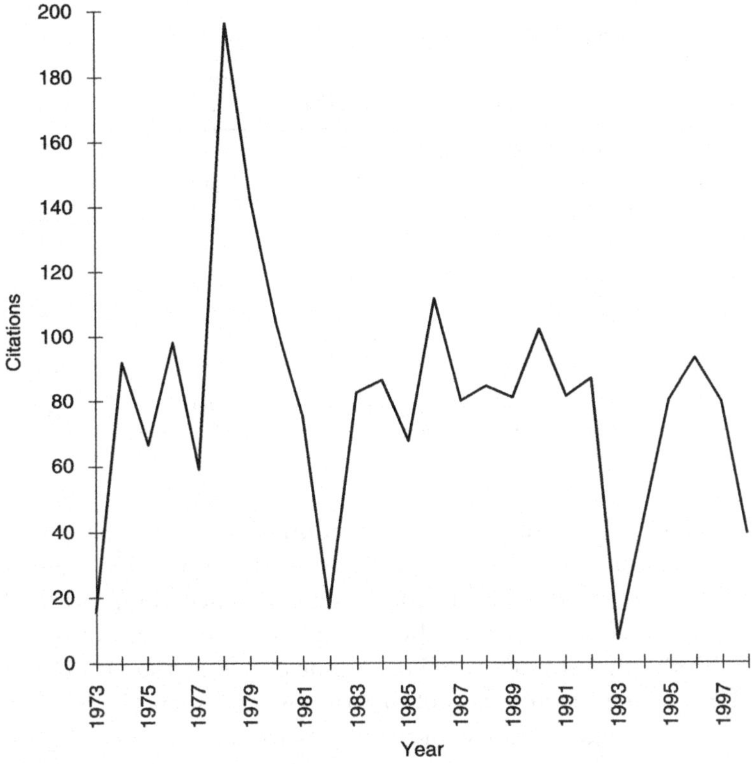

Figure 5.1
Number of citations of Ohlin's works, 1973 to 1998. Source: SSCI.

Which of Ohlin's Publications Are Cited Most?

The above-mentioned article by Caves (1978) ends with a bibliography compiled by Ohlin himself at the request of the editor. The subdivisions in the bibliography may indicate how Ohlin himself looked upon his contributions. The first category contains works on "international economic relations and related policy problems," and it consists of 49 titles, including Ohlin's dissertation *Handelns teori* (1924), *Interregional and International Trade* (1933), and his exchange with Keynes in 1929 on the transfer problem in connection with the German reparations. The 77 titles in the second category are on the "theory of money, economic fluctuations, and related policy problems," and they include the well-known 1937 article in the *Economic Journal* where Ohlin coined the expression "Stockholm School." The third group is on *miscellaneous* topics.

Table 5.2
Citations of Ohlin distributed by publications (in percent)

Publications	1973 to 1979	1980 to 1989	1990 to 1999
Interregional and International Trade	14	29	33
Economic Journal, 1937	16	19	27
Economic Journal, 1929	10	13	15
History of Political Economy, 1978	2	2	4
History of Political Economy, 1981	0	2	4
Weltwirtschaftliches Archiv, 1931	2	2	2
Handelns teori	1	2	1
Other	55	31	14
Total	100	100	100

Source: SSCI.

In his review Caves devotes his attention almost exclusively to Ohlin's contributions to international trade, and to how Heckscher's and Ohlin's trade model has been developed since their original articles. At the end of the article he mentions some other contributions by Ohlin within international economics, such as the articles on the transfer problem, factor market distortions, and social legislation and efficient exchange. Ohlin's contributions to macroeconomics are ignored.

However, if one looks at citations of Ohlin by other economists, one finds that his macroeconomic publications play an important role. Table 5.2 shows the number of citations of some of Ohlin's publications.

There is an interesting general tendency: the total number of citations is concentrated on a limited number of titles, and this tendency is increasing. One expression of this is the evolution of the proportion of citations going to "other" titles than the seven specified in table 5.2. In the 1970s, 55 percent of the citations belong to this group. In the 1980, the proportion is almost halved, and it is halved again in the 1990s.[4]

The tendency for public attention to concentrate on one or a few publications as time goes by is probably a general tendency and not unique to Ohlin's works. There may be various reasons for this. Famous authors from earlier periods are often cited without being read. It is probably a reasonable conjecture that most of the citations of, such as Adam Smith, are based on secondary sources. However, a quotation of a recognized founding figure lends confidence and the impression of being acquainted with the background of modern theory. The greater the distance in time between the founder and the present day, the more the founder's secondary writings are forgotten, while the most important works are remembered relatively more.

Furthermore it is seldom easy to determine at an early stage which publications will later be considered pathbreaking. When the most important contributions have been sifted out, their position is strengthened when it comes to the number of citations.

Three titles by Ohlin dominate references, receiving 40 percent of the citations in the 1970s, and 75 percent in the 1990s. *Interregional and International Trade* (1933) is Ohlin's internationally best-known book. Caves's (1978) presentation is worth quoting:

> On the appearance of *Interregional and International Trade* in 1933, the book was immediately recognized by reviewers as a major contribution. C. R. Whittlesey called it "by all odds the most important book on international economics that has appeared in recent years." "A signal contribution to the theory of international trade, and one which will interest every student of economic problems," wrote James W. Angell. The model soon became enshrined in textbooks, such as the first edition of Professor Ellsworth's well-known volume. Research extending and formalizing Ohlin's ideas began to appear a few years later. Since World War II probably a majority of papers published in the pure theory of international trade have employed the framework of this model.

Ohlin's articles in the *Economic Journal* in 1937 account for approximately the same number of citations as his trade book. In a lengthy article entitled "Some Notes on the Stockholm Theory of Savings and Investment," which was divided into two parts and published in the March and June issues of the journal, Ohlin presented what he considered a more or less common Stockholm view, and coined the term "Stockholm School."[5] The original article was followed by a brief comment by Keynes, to which Ohlin made a short rejoinder.[6]

Ohlin's point of departure in his lengthy article was the following:

> Owing to a coincidence of circumstances, already at an early stage of the depression Swedish economists came to deal with the problem of variations in employment, output and prices by means of a theoretical apparatus rather different from the price theory in economic textbooks. There are surprising similarities as well as striking differences between that apparatus and the conclusion reached in Sweden on the one hand and Mr. Keynes' "General Theory" on the other hand. Hoping that a discussion of two independent attacks on the same set of problems may throw some light on the latter, I

intend in this and the succeeding paper to make some observations on these two theories.

One may question whether there was such a common view among the Stocholm economists that the expression "Stockholm School" or "Stockholm theory" was justified. Erik Lundberg (1987), one of the alleged members of the Stockholm School who preferred to call himself a Keynesian, wrote in his last article:

> It is generally accepted, I think, that the Stockholm School was and is a *myth*. As early as in 1937, when Ohlin launched the concept in the *Economic Journal*, many of us economists in Stockholm protested and thought it was a curious idea. But the language dominates the thought. The concept was accepted and used (sparsely) even by ourselves. Even a myth has a real background; the myth can become at least as real as the reality.

As Lundberg indicates, the idea of a Stockholm School has taken root and spread, whether it is justified or not. In almost every article on the Stockholm School, Ohlin's 1937 article seems to be mentioned. This bibliographic circumstance is evidently the main reason why the article is the most cited of Ohlin's articles.

Ohlin's third most cited publications involve his contributions to the debate initiated by Keynes on the German reparations problem after the First World War. Ohlin's main contribution was his article "Transfer Difficulties, Real and Imagined," published in the June issue of the *Economic Journal* 1929. Keynes's reply resulted in a rejoinder by Ohlin in the September issue of the journal.

The rest of Ohlin's many publications include no title that bears comparison with those mentioned above in terms of citations. A few of them are listed in table 5.2.

The article in *History of Political Economy* 1978 has the title "On the Formulation of Monetary Theory." It is a translation of an article in Swedish ("Till frågan om penningteoriens uppläggning") published in the *Ekonomisk Tidskrift* in 1933, which in Patinkin's words "plays a crucial role in the perennial debate about the relationship between the 'Stockholm School' and Keynes' *General Theory*." It was followed by commentary articles by Otto Steiger, Hans Brems, Don Patinkin, and William P. Yohe.

History of Political Economy, no. 2 (1981), was a memorial issue dedicated to Bertil Ohlin, Clark Warburton, and William Jaffé. It included, among other things, four manuscripts by Ohlin on the monetary and employment theory of the 1930s, edited with introductions and comments by Otto Steiger. The first one was an article on which Ohlin was working at the time of his death, entitled "Some Observations on the Monetary Theory of the Period 1930–1936—Comments on Comments on my Monetary Theory." The second was "On Pre-war Keynesian and Stockholm Theories of Employment—Chiefly through Demand Management," the third was "A Comparison of the Development of Monetary Theory at Cambridge and in Sweden in 1928–1936," and the fourth was an installment of Ohlin's 1937 article that had never been published. Formally, the three latter articles are arranged as appendixes of the first one.

The article in *Weltwirtschaftliches Archiv* 1931 was on "Protection and Noncompeting Groups." *Handelns teori* from 1924 is Ohlin's doctoral thesis. Its content is essentially included in the 1933 book on *Interregional and International Trade*, but the fact that it was written in Swedish means, of course, that it is not often quoted in the journals included in the SSCI, most of which are English-language journals.

Conclusions

Compared with his Swedish contemporaries, Ohlin is still a frequently cited economist, surpassed in this respect only by Myrdal. There is an increasing tendency for these citations to concentrate on three publications: the book *Interregional and International Trade*, the articles on the Stockholm School in the *Economic Journal* in 1937, and the debate with Keynes on the German reparations problem in the *Economic Journal* in 1929. In the 1990s, 75 percent of the citations of Ohlin pertain to these publications.

Notes

1. The Social Science Citation Index is based on references in about 1,700 journals in the social sciences. In addition, references in relevant articles in 3,300 other scholarly journals are included. The index is constructed by the Institute for Scientific Information, ISI.

2. The source is Bibsys, a database that includes SSCI. Table 5.1 and figure 5.1 are based on different, and not quite consistent, versions of the SSCI.

3. The figure shows the total number of hits each year; that is, each publication by Ohlin is multiplied by the number of times it appears in a list of references.

4. The 1990s include citations registered before 7 August 1999.

5. The term "Stockholm School" appears only in passing in Ohlin's article. Instead, he repeatedly uses the expression "Stockholm theory," which is short for the "Stockholm theory of processes of contraction and expansion."

6. Citations of the rejoinder are included in the percentage numbers in table 5.2. The same is true for the 1929 articles.

References

Brems, Hans. 1978. What was new in Ohlin's 1933–34 macroeconomics?, *History of Political Economy* 10:398–412.

Caves, Richard E. 1978. Bertil Ohlin's Contribution to Economics. *Scandinavian Journal ef Economics* 80:86–99.

Lundberg, Erik. 1987. Minnen kring Stockholmsskolan. *Ekonomisk Debatt* 15:280–86.

Ohlin, Bertil. 1924. *Handelns teori*. Stockholm: Nordiska.

Ohlin, Bertil. 1929. Transfer difficulties, real and imagined. *Economic Journal* 39:172–79. Reprinted in Sandelin (1998).

Ohlin, Bertil. 1929. A rejoinder from Professor Ohlin. *Economic Journal* 39:400–404. Reprinted in Sandelin (1998).

Ohlin, Bertil. 1931. Protection and non-competing groups. *Weltwirtschaftliches Archiv* 33:30–45.

Ohlin, Bertil. 1933. *Interregional and International Trade*. Harvard University Press. Reprinted as volume 5 in Bo Sandelin, ed., *Swedish Economics*. London: Routledge, 1998.

Ohlin, Bertil. 1937. Some notes on the Stockholm theory of savings and investment. *Economic Journal* 47:53–69, 221–240. Reprinted in Sandelin (1998).

Ohlin, Bertil. 1937. Alternative theories of the rate of interest. Rejoinder. *Economic Journal* 47:423–27. Reprinted in Sandelin (1998).

Ohlin, Bertil. 1978. On the formulation of monetary theory. *History of Political Economy* 10:353–88. Reprinted in Sandelin (1998).

Ohlin, Bertil. 1981. Stockholm and Cambridge: Four papers on the monetary and employment theory of the 1930s. *History of Political Economy* 13:189–255.

Patinkin, Don. 1978. Some observations on Ohlin's 1933 article. *History of Political Economy* 10:413–18.

Sandelin, Bo, ed. 1998. *Swedish Economics*, vol. 1. *Introduction and Selected Essays*. London: Routledge.

Sarafoglou, Nikias, and Sandelin, Bo. 1992. Myrdal fortfarande mest citerad. *Ekonomisk Debatt* 20:229–32.

Steiger, Otto. 1978. Substantive changes in the final version of Ohlin's 1933 paper. *History of Political Economy* 10:389–97.

Steiger, Otto. 1978. Prelude to the theory of a monetary economy: Origins and signifiicance of Ohlin's 1933 approach. *History of Political Economy* 10:420–46.

Steiger, Otto. 1981. Bertil Ohlin, 1899–1979. *History of Political Economy* 13:179–88.

Yohe, William P. 1978. Ohlin's 1933 reformation of monetary theory. *History of Political Economy* 10:447–53.

6 Bertil Ohlin as a Liberal Politician

Svante Nycander

Bertil Ohlin received political impulses early in life, in the family home through his mother who was a liberal and an admirer of Karl Staaff.[1] As a young student he was on the left side of the political spectrum, in an environment in which there was no fixed dividing line between Social Democrats and Liberals (Ohlin 1972:16, 30, 49). In 1920, together with Herbert Tingsten, among others, he was elected to the committee of the Liberal Reformists Youth League. During the 1920s he wrote articles on economic policy questions in the Danish newspaper *Politiken* and also in *Stockholms-Tidningen*, a Swedish daily, where he had a permanent position as a leader-writer from 1931 to 1944 (Larsson 1998:114 et seq; Lindblad 1999).[2] His way of thinking brought him quite close to the Social Democratic Party (SDP). In a passage in his memoirs about his own attitude as the newly elected leader of the Liberal Party, he said, "If only the Social Democrats had not been socialists in basic political principle, I would have felt myself more in harmony with them than with any other party" (Ohlin 1975:91).

Not until the mid-1930s did Ohlin become more actively engaged in politics, though he had already felt the urge to become a politician much earlier. In a letter from Copenhagen in 1929 he said that he had long had the aim of returning to Stockholm. "In five or ten years, when I have put behind me a certain amount of work as an economist, it is very possible that I will devote myself to politics" (Larsson 1998:111). He was elected chairman of the Liberal Party Youth League at the end of 1934, became a member of the Riksdag (Parliament) in 1938 and leader of the Liberal Party and a member of the wartime four-party government of national unity after the general election in the fall of 1944. From the summer of 1945 until the spring of 1967 he led the Liberal Party in opposition. He left the Riksdag in 1970.

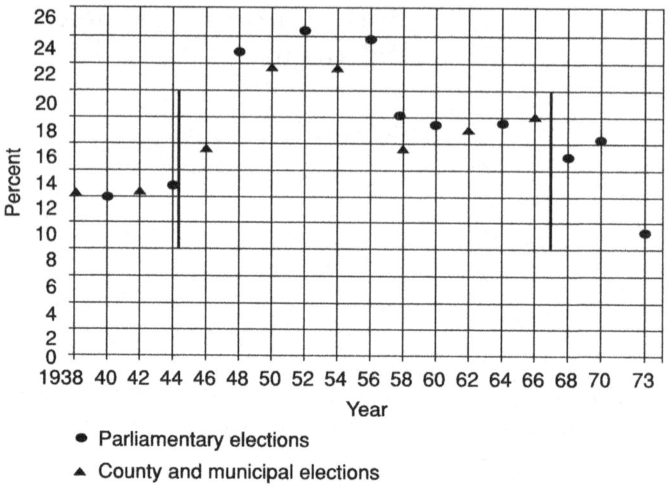

Figure 6.1
Bertil Ohlin's period as Liberal leader: Election results, 1938 to 1973, showing the Liberal Party's share of the votes. Ohlin's period as Liberal leader was from 1944 to 1967. All elections were held in September except for the supplementary parliamentary elections in June 1958. In the elections of 1964 and 1966, there were some common nonsocialist lists, and the Liberal Party was allotted one-third of the votes. From 1970, parliamentary elections and county and municipal elections took place at the same time.

The Swedish Political Landscape

Bertil Ohlin's importance to the Liberal Party is apparent if its electoral support during his time as its leader is compared with that in the periods immediately before and after (see figure 6.1). Thanks to his personality, the Party came to play a significant part in the postwar period. The Liberal Party was formed in 1934 through a merger between two liberal parties that had been divided since 1923 because of differences of opinion about prohibition. There were two traditions within the Party, one being rooted chiefly among academics and the urban middle classes, and the other among nonconformists and the antialcohol movement. Ohlin skillfully held these groups together and broadened the Party's electoral base, chiefly among salaried employees. When the Party was at its maximum it had approximately as many voters in the two major cities of Stockholm and Gothenburg as did the Social Democrats. However, the party organization was weak, and it had few members in relation to the number of voters it attracted. On the other hand, the liberal press was powerful, not to say dominant (Johanson 1984:143f).

The party against which all others had to measure their strength was the Social Democrats. At the 1940 general election, they received 53.8 percent of the votes cast. Their exceptional success was connected with the fact that in Sweden, the preconditions were favorable for the organization of the working class, both as regards trade unions and politically. After a liberal economic order had been introduced in the 1860s, there was no state regulation of trade union activity, collective agreements, or strikes until 1928. The trade unions were early organized on an industrial rather than craft basis, which gave them both breadth and strength. In 1906 the Swedish Confederation of Employers (SAF) recognized the workers' freedom of association and their right to negotiate collectively. An understanding on central questions between SAF and the Swedish Confederation of Trade Unions (LO) was incorporated in the Saltsjöbaden Agreement of 1938, which reinforced the legitimacy of the trade union movement. The Social Democratic Party, which had its roots in the trade unions, became a powerful factor in Sweden as early as the beginning of the 1900s (Westerståhl 1945:9f, 37f, 173f, 199f). The Party was in power from the fall of 1932 and came to be linked with the economic recovery after the Great Depression. A Swedish sociologist has correctly pointed out: "Fifty years later the 1930s still play a key role in any attempt to explain the position of social democracy and labor organizations in Sweden" (A. W. Johansson 1995:91).

There were thus structural reasons for the labor movement's strength in Sweden. At the beginning of the 1940s, many believed that the Social Democrats' dominance was as good as unshakable, which gave rise to the idea of a permanent all-party government of national unity as a means of enabling all groups in society to share in the exercise of political power. As prime minister until his death in 1946, those were the lines along which Per Albin Hansson thought, but his successor, Tage Erlander, did not agree (Ohlin 1972:349; Erlander 1973:252).

At the general election in 1944 the Social Democrats and Communists received a combined total of 56.9 percent of the votes cast. During Ohlin's time as party leader the socialist share of the vote fell below 50 percent only at the general elections of 1956 and 1958, in both cases to 49.6 percent, and at the local elections in 1966, when their share was 48.6 percent. In the upper chamber the Social Democrats were overrepresented because of the indirect method of election. A temporary fall in the number of votes cast for them was bridged over by the fact that the upper chamber was renewed slowly and in stages. The election results and the workings of the constitution prevented a change of government during Ohlin's active period, but the Liberal Party was the largest opposition party during the periods 1948 to 1958 and 1960 to 1967. Ohlin was the leading analyst and critic of government policy and the one who, time and again, led the effort to create a political alternative to Social Democracy.

The Postwar Program and the Narrowing Range of Views

Originally the Social Democratic Party was Marxist in its outlook. Its long-term aims remain radical, but its practical policies have, in most situations, been pragmatic and flexible. When Bertil Ohlin became leader of the Liberal Party, the SDP had just put forward a 27-point postwar program that largely set the agenda for political debate in the following years.

Ernst Wigforss, Minister of Finance and the party's leading ideologist, closely supported by, among others, Alva and Gunnar Myrdal, had conducted work on the program. Certain elements in the program came to figure prominently in subsequent debate:

The chief task before us is to coordinate economic activity in a planned management of the national economy

Individual interests are to be subordinated to the collective goals

All financial credit is to be allocated on the basis of social views in such a way that production develops in a planned fashion in accordance with need

With the same objective, a comprehensive state-owned commercial bank network will be set up

Insurance services are to be nationalized, partly in order to bring about the required rationalization, and partly to establish increased public control over the capital market. Investment activity will be conducted largely by a public co-operation agency, which will represent enterprise activity by the state, private interests and the cooperative movement.

State participation in the conduct of foreign trade will continue to be required even in the longer term. In some areas more favorable import conditions ought to be achievable, if the nation's purchasing requirements are channeled through one pair of hands.

Building plots and rented housing in towns will gradually be transferred into local authority ownership. The state-owned housing authorities should retain and develop their primary influence in decisions on housing construction.

In those cases where all production is dominated by one enterprise or combination of enterprises, or where competitive production may be regarded as uneconomic, the existing enterprises should be transferred into public ownership.

Social Democratic postwar planning comprised social and economic reforms across the whole field, completing what had been started during the 1930s. There was no attempt to conceal that the objective of the program was "a transformation of society in a socialist direction" (Labor movement's postwar program, 1944). A new SDP program in 1944 confirmed the socialist line of development in more general terms.

In the spring of 1933 the Social Democrats and the Agrarian Party initiated close cooperation, from 1936 in the form of a governing coalition. This collaboration over crisis policy, aiming at the stabilization of prices and incomes and increased employment, between parties representing the manual-laboring classes was of great symbolic significance and resulted in a lasting split on the nonsocialist side. Gunnar Hedlund, the leader of the Agrarian Party (later known as the Center Party) 1949 to 1971, was both politically and personally closer to the Social Democrats than to the Liberals or Conservatives, though he did not favor either economic planning or socialism. In opinion-forming and election campaigns the Center Party remained aloof from the ideological trial of strength between the Social Democrats and the nonsocialists.

In the years immediately before and after the end of the war anti-Nazism was a common overriding ideology throughout the Western world. With the cold war anti-Communism acquired a similar significance. The historian Alf W. Johansson has observed that what in Sweden came to be called the end of ideologies can be considered as an effect of the influence exerted by the two "dystopic ideologies" across the whole ideological field. Anti-Nazism tended to put a taboo on parts of traditional conservatism. "The Conservative Party abandoned its paternalistic attitude directed primarily at disciplining the lower classes, in favor of a readiness to accept socially remedial measures directed at creating a sense of economic security among the masses. In the same way as anti-Fascist ideology contributed to the "distortion" or conversion of the Conservatives into a more unambiguously liberal party, anti-communism contributed to a reinforcement of the liberal elements in Social Democracy. Indeed, one can even say that the Social Democrats' active adoption of anti-communism involved the injection into the party of an anti-socialist element" (A. W. Johansson 1995:227).

The range of views narrowed. With Jarl Hjalmarson as its leader in the period 1950 to 1961, the Conservative Party was significantly more penetrating in gaining a hearing for its social-conservative and liberal message. In the words of the historian Bo Stråth, "the Conservative Party's successes in the political debate can be seen against the background that it sought not only to define and provide an alternative to Social Democracy but also to come closer to it" (Stråth 1998:40).

The affinities of the wartime years, which had put their stamp on a generation, to some extent blunted the edge of the conflicts. At the Party Congress 1944, which confirmed the SDP's socialist direction, Per Albin Hansson advocated a continuing broad cooperation in government (Larsson 1998:182). For a long time both the Liberal Party and the Conservative Party also found it natural to see a new all-party government as a possible solution to political crises.

Such was the political landscape in which Bertil Ohlin had to stake out the Liberals' course. The most important dimension of conflict related to the trend towards socialism and the planned economy in accordance with the 27-point program. Ohlin, the man of the left, became the leader of the nonsocialist opposition to the governing Social Democrats.

Bertil Ohlin's Political Ideas

There was a manifest British influence on the young Ohlin's political thinking. He read John Stuart Mill and showed admiration for the Fabians, in particular, Sidney and Beatrice Webb. Keynes's "The End of Laissez-Faire" also impressed him. He commented favorably on the so-called Yellow Book ("Britain's Industrial Future"), which built on Keynes's ideas and also inspired Ernst Wigforss (Larsson 1998:113; Nilsson 1999:7).

In 1927 Ohlin published a radical article on liberalism at the parting of the ways. Time had passed laissez-faire liberalism by.

He advocated a system of death duties which, step by step, would transfer fortunes to the state as the inheritance passed on for the second, third, and fourth time. Long-term unemployment had revealed weaknesses in the private capitalist structure of society. "A planned organization that guarantees rationality and efficiency has become the solution of the day rather than the liberal society's laissez-faire policy" (Larsson 1998:112; Wennås 1984:84). That sentence contains several key words. Political and economic action carried out on a planned, rational, and effective basis was for Ohlin always worthy of praise. Even much later he would occasionally use the expression "economic planning" in a positive sense (Wennås 1984:98, 110). He was alien to a view of civilization that called into question industrialism, technical development, and rational organization, irrespective of whether the overtones were conservative or radical. In 1936 he wrote that modern industrial systems of production are "perhaps the most powerful tool of liberty of our age." It is "machines that are in the process of setting the mass of human-beings free in the deeper sense of the word," and we are only at the beginning of that process. This perspective of Ohlin's is significant, since an antimodernist view of civilization has been strongly preferred within the cultural elite in Sweden and has also significantly penetrated political opinion during the greater part of the twentieth century.

In discussions on economic policy Ohlin was irritated by criticism of planning. In his view, the important issue was whether economic life should be centrally controlled. He frequently justified measures to promote efficiency, on the ground that increased production was the means by which the standard of living of the poor might be radically improved (Ohlin 1936:8, 219f).

Economic policy debate can easily get bogged down in arguments about more equitable distribution and in demands for fuller exploitation of the available resources. As a man of the Left and a Keynesian, Ohlin was not opposed to either view, but he always attached higher priority to increased growth through greater productivity. He used to speak about the extent to which the standard of living could increase in twenty-five or thirty years if attention were paid to the forces improving welfare, and he was surprised at people's inability to see how much everybody would benefit from an increase in GDP. The need for a favorable environment for enterprise was therefore self-evident to him (Larsson 1998:112f; Ohlin 1936:8).[3]

In *A Free Economy versus Dirigisme* of 1936, Ohlin argued in favor of social liberalism, clearly differentiated from old-style liberalism and socialism.[4] He emphasized that in its main features, the policy he advocated accorded with the policy that was then being followed in Sweden, and constituted only "a reform and rationalization of it." A term frequently used in his book is "the organization of society," which refers both to public and private organization for various purposes. A major thesis is that the organization of society must be continually adapted to economic and technical changes, and the resulting shifts in the general way of thinking; all dogmatism is therefore to be avoided. The political perspective is determined by the understanding that society is always developing as a consequence of dynamic events in constant interaction with one another.

Ohlin defended a rather far-reaching interventionism, not only on the then-current business cycle and social policy arguments but also as a means of buttressing civic liberty. He drew the attention to the fact that economic depression creates an impression of a surplus of goods, which leads producers and other sellers to fix prices, limit production, and call for measures of support and protection against competition from imports. The consequence is an improvised and unplanned interventionism restricting freedom. The unemployed and others afflicted by the depression also demand measures against it. If the politicians respond that there are no measures that can be of assistance, and that one must be patient until the crisis is over, by itself, the advantage goes chiefly to "the Nazi and Communist agitators, who have no inhibitions about making promises and holding out prospects." In short, "old-style liberal passivity in times of crisis opens the way to dictatorship."

The growth of private cartels and monopolies was a question that greatly occupied Ohlin. Agreements regulating competition had become increasingly numerous in business life, and a new attitude of mind had arisen "which forbids unrestricted competition." Ohlin considered the recent tendency toward a more rigid organization of society to have significantly reduced mobility and adaptability in the economy. He analyzed the conflict of objectives as between mobility and the sense of security. He conceded that the risk of rigidity constituted a weakness of the social liberal organization of society, as compared with the old-style liberalism. It could not be taken for granted that the organization would adapt sufficiently in response to changes in the preconditions. In the social liberal society it was therefore necessary to be most keenly on the alert "lest rigid forms develop unnecessarily, where it would be possible to retain mobility." It was necessary to show vigilance on this in both the private and the public sector. State intervention in the form of, for example, the regulation of monopoly could make society "more liberal than if private organizations were left completely at liberty."

Ohlin was in the main positive about trades unions, on the argument that without these individual employees find themselves in a weak position in relation to their employers. He recalled that in the early 1930s he had protested against calls for wage reductions, and it is illuminating that in his book, he argued that the labor market organizations should enjoy greater influence at the central level. If the Swedish Confederation of Trade Unions were to be given greater power in relation to the individual unions, the risk of industrial conflict would probably diminish. In several places he criticized trade union action as shortsighted and protectionist. His ambivalence was obvious (Ohlin 1936:17, 147, 232f).

Ohlin asserted that the major social questions are in essence cultural and moral. "In the last resort the solutions to the major problems of society's organization, that is to say, of human co-existence, lie for the most part on the ethical and moral plane." In a section headed "Liberty is a question of upbringing" Ohlin concurred with Georges Clemenceau's maxim that "Liberty is the art of self-discipline." The defense of liberty demands that "honesty be preserved." Activity in private business life is a social service, "which should be conducted with thought for the general good." The more a spirit of social service permeates business life, the more the need for legislation and control falls away. Here, as elsewhere, he wrote, problems in the organization of society are in the main questions of upbringing. He was critical of certain phenomena in business life, for example, the trend toward nepotism in appointments to top management posts and what he called the dictatorship of the boards of directors (Ohlin 1936:49, 106, 222). Later he developed an idea about "trusteeship" which was close to what is today called "corporate citizenship."

The understanding that in many cases social questions are a matter of upbringing and ethics made it possible for Ohlin to attack problems and social evils without at the same time offering a solution in the form of political measures.

In the chapter "A Critique of Socialism" Ohlin quoted from the then-current Social Democratic Party program: "The following are to be transferred to public ownership: all natural resources, industrial enterprises, credit institutions, means of transport and communications channels necessary for the introduction of a planned national economy, state control of enterprises that remain in private ownership." He attacked notions that played a major part in the Social Democratic Party program and propaganda, among others, the belief that in the capitalist system production is "unplanned," that class struggle is inevitable, and that capitalist enterprises "exploit" the workers. Industrial workers in Sweden belong to the economic middle class, he wrote. There were other groups with greater needs who would benefit from a reduction in differences in income. Ohlin wrote of the importance of free price setting and of the harm caused by public monopolies and central control of business life. He drew the attention to the risk of measures of state compulsion against the labor force and the difficulty for a socialist society of generating sufficient savings. In characterizing the social liberal alternative to socialism and a centrally controlled and directed national economy he used the expression "framework economy" (*ramhushållning*); within a fixed framework, enterprises, consumers, and organizations should be free (Ohlin 1936:51f, 110f).

A Political Solo Artist

A Free Economy versus Dirigisme singled out areas in which reform was urgent and laid the foundation for a radical modernization of Liberal Party policy. Ohlin remained faithful to his 1936 ideas, often right down to detail and the manner in which they were formulated. In a letter written in the early 1970s, he stressed the continuity in his political advocacy: "For fifty years the central burden of my political work and my political attitude has been the necessity for a more active policy of economic management, monopoly control, and so forth, alongside a more ambitious policy to create a sense of economic security, the preconditions for which would improve, decade after decade, as a result of growth in the national income. In addition it was important to conduct policies in the industrial and commercial field that ensure that national income really did develop sufficiently favorably, even if some of the rate of progress could be sacrificed on the altar of other concerns, for example, the need to sustain a general sense of economic and social security" (Larsson 1998:154). This is a prosaic but accurate summary, if one considers his positive endeavors, but it leaves out Ohlin's critical and analytical work. As a politician, Ohlin soon became known for his wide knowledge and desire to take initiatives across the whole field, but economy and welfare always lay at the center of his political engagement. As a politician he wished to translate into reality ideas that he had developed as a social scientist.

Ohlin's interest in the demands for social reform soon moved into the foreground, while problems related to the organization of society slipped down the agenda. In the Liberal Party Youth League concern for "The Forgotten Sweden," that is, the part of the population that was worse off than industrial workers, became a leitmotif. Ohlin asserted that any significant reduction in overall taxation was incompatible with the reforms the Liberal Party should pursue, and he was highly critical of those with high incomes who complained about taxes. He wanted the Liberal Party to have "a vision of social and economic security," and in the run-up to the general election of 1936 he irritated the party leader, Gustaf Andersson i Rasjön, by departing from the approved party policy; the relationship between the two men was always sensitive (Larsson 1998:128f; Wennås 1984:94f). Ohlin's strategic aim was to transform the Liberal party into a strong and independent party of the center. As a member of the Riksdag from 1938 he was very active, with a broad range of interests and an unusual ability to attract attention (Larsson 1998:131).

Thanks to his extensive network of contacts and his experience, Ohlin was one of the most internationally oriented politicians in Sweden. He strongly opposed both Communism and Nazism and took up the cause of Jewish scientists who sought asylum in Sweden. During the 1930s he was engaged by a Canadian insurance company and a firm of brokers in Chicago to keep them informed about political and economic conditions in Europe (Larsson 1998:138). During the war years he took an interest in the minutiae of questions such as Sweden's military preparedness, trade relations, rules of engagement in the case of foreign overflights, war credits to Germany, ball-bearing exports, the structure of the armed forces, and so on. Often he was the only member of the Riksdag to formulate an alternative to the policy of the wartime government of national unity. He took a strong and active interest in support for Sweden's Nazi-occupied neighbors. In May 1943 he called upon the Swedish government to make a public declaration that Sweden's objective would not be to seek isolationism, whether Swedish or Nordic, but to prepare for participation in postwar reconstruction. He also belonged to the minority in the Riksdag who opposed restrictions on freedom of speech and of the press (Larsson 1998:156; Lindblad 1999). On the other hand, he supported the main line of Swedish foreign policy. In his memoirs he wrote that he considered foreign policy during the war to have been "in the main natural and skillful" and that he felt little sympathy for the moralizing ranters who criticized the concessions made to Germany as "compliancy" (Ohlin 1975:49).

However, his main contribution during the war concerned economic policy. In the wartime government of national unity, party ties were not so strong, and Ohlin could quite often perform as a solo artist. In the exceptional situation that obtained, he had no objection to import regulation, foreign exchange control, price controls, or large tax increases. On the contrary, he was one of the first to call for adjustments: his view in 1940 was that half the Swedish economy ought to be put on a war footing without delay (Larsson 1998:172).

It was also under Ohlin's influence that the Liberal Party in political practice distanced itself from the Conservatives during the war years and became a social reformist competitor of the Social Democrats (Lindblad 1999). The program published in the spring of 1944, entitled "Post-war Society" and partly written by Ohlin, was influenced by the Beveridge Plan in Britain and contained an ambitious social policy program, inter alia a recommendation for obligatory health insurance. Its proposals on agriculture were aimed at improving conditions for small farmers, which reflected the influence of Waldemar Svensson, who was of the same generation as Ohlin and for many years one of the most important men in the Liberal Party. Ohlin himself had much earlier argued in favor of targeted measures of support for smallholders, for example, subsidized feedstuffs, as an element in the policy for "the forgotten Sweden" (Ohlin 1936:167, 1975:80f).

He had a strong sense of which needs for reform and which electoral groups the Social Democrats tended to disregard. He took up the cause of women working in the home, and also of domestic servants (Wennås 1984:96), and maintained that work in the kitchen, which on the basis of the hours worked and the value added was Sweden's largest industry, ought to be supported by means of planned technical and organizational research and improved education. He annoyed feminists, including Alva Myrdal, by arguing that equality of status for women working in the home was of greater importance than the principle of equal pay for men and women, which he also supported (Ohlin 1975:85).

The election campaign in 1944 largely revolved around the socialist elements in the labor movement's postwar program. Some weeks after he had been elected Party chairman, Ohlin entered the government of national unity as Minister of Trade, where he became a colleague of Tage Erlander, previously the immediate deputy of Gustav Möller in the Ministry of Social Affairs. There was a strained relationship between them, probably the outcome of earlier contacts. In his memoirs, Erlander said that in Cabinet Ohlin embarked on long discussions about questions that others thought had been settled and asked lots of questions that civil servants were more competent to answer than were his Ministerial colleagues (Larsson 1998:190; Ohlin 1975:22f; Erlander 1973:201).

In the beginning of 1945 a strike broke out in the engineering industry and lasted for five months. Prompted by the Metalworkers Union, Tage Erlander proposed that striking metalworkers who took work in forestry should, like unemployed workers who had been assigned jobs in forestry, receive housing benefits out of unemployment funds. This proposal would require a change in the law and was opposed by Ohlin because such benefits would be in conflict with government neutrality in labor-market disputes.

Contrary to the views of the Center-Right members of the Cabinet, the government put forward a Bill in accordance with Erlander's proposal. In the view of the political scientist, Hilding Johansson, there followed "the sharpest political battles in the Riksdag during the wartime government of national unity." The payment of labor market benefits to strikers touched on a classic dividing line between Center-Right and Social Democratic policy, and it was hardly a matter of chance that the first major collision between Erlander and Ohlin occurred over that particular question. They both knew very well what was at issue, and they treated the case in detail in their memoirs. Erlander thought he had detected a resurrection of a Center-Right policy on unemployment which had been the cause of two changes of government in the 1920s (Erlander 1973:204f; Ohlin 1975:22f).[5]

Per Albin Hansson, the prime minister, hoped that the government of national unity might continue after the war. An argument that he put forward internally was that "it could be in the Social Democrats' interest to involve the other parties and thereby put a brake on their intended attacks on our pursuit of socialist objectives." The ruling view within the SDP was, however, that the government of national unity should be dissolved. On the nonsocialist side, opposition to continued co-operation in government seems to have been strongest within the Liberal Party. In a speech in June 1945 Ohlin said that if the SDP persisted in their socialist objectives, they should govern alone. In his memoirs he states that he would undoubtedly have advised the Liberal Party to remain in the government of national unity if only "Per Albin Hansson had offered continued delay on socialist measures which were a source of difference between the parties." According to him it was the SDP that broke up the government of national unity (Ohlin 1975:91, 128; Ruin 1968:130f).

Sven-Erik Larsson, Ohlin's biographer, maintains that the policy program presented to Ohlin by Hansson was so moderate that in itself, it hardly justified breaking up the government of national unity. According to Larsson, what disturbed Ohlin was the general direction taken by the SDP. He also saw the opportunity to "give the Liberal Party a boost by exploiting their position in opposition to launch a much stronger ideological attack than the one in 1944" (Larsson 1998:185).

In the SDP's debate about the government there were many who argued that the 27-point program must not be put in jeopardy (Ruin 1968:136). Ernst Wigforss has maintained that the SDP could have concentrated on less controversial matters and avoided bringing the question of socialism to the fore. "But we were also bent on conflict along the whole front. We had long had an interest in making clear what we meant by socialist policy" (Wigforss 1954:299).

Ohlin and the majority of leading Social Democrats thus found themselves in agreement that the labor movement's postwar program did not permit a continuation of the wartime cooperation. The government of national unity broke up at the turn of the month, June–July 1945.

The Battle against Socialism and the Planned Economy

The Liberal Party wanted to occupy an independent position between the two largest parties, the SDP and the Conservatives, but they were far from being able to control the balance. While the SDP had indeed suffered losses in the 1944 general election, the Communists had made gains, so that the socialist share of the vote was 56.9 percent, roughly unchanged over several elections. Had the Left been more successful in mobilizing their supporters, their share of the vote could have been even greater, because the majority of the stay-at-home voters were on the Left. According to Ohlin himself, during his first ten years as Party leader he thought there was little chance of a change in government, and instead, he endeavored to drive the SDP back far enough to ward off developments in a more socialist direction. In the longer term his objective was of course to form his own government, but he did not exclude cooperation in government with a more liberal SDP. The important thing was to break the domination by one party, which looked easier after the death of the popular national father-figure, Per Albin Hansson, in the fall of 1946 (Larsson 1998:209, 216, 238; Ohlin 1975:97).

The task of promoting the Liberal Party's character as an in-between party, with two ideological fronts, was made more difficult by there being a competitor with a similar ambition. Ohlin described the dilemma in his memoirs: "If the Liberal Party were very vigorously to oppose Social Democratic policy, it would be easy for the Agrarian Party to place itself, for a long time to come, alongside the Social Democrats and thereby, to some degree, become the balancing factor in the scales. My attitude on this problem could probably best be expressed as 'let's cross that bridge when we come to it'" (Ohlin 1972:348). The problem proved to be insoluble during Ohlin's time as Party leader. With Gunnar Hedlund as its leader from 1949, the Agrarian Party guarded its position as the party closest to the SDP and seemed little concerned by the unequal balance of strength between the two. First after Ohlin's departure, when the Agrarian Party/Center Party had come to the fore as a leading opposition party with an inescapable responsibility for the alternative government, it was possible for the non-Socialist Parties to unite in a common offensive with a view to bringing about a change of government.

The Social Democratic monthly *Tiden*, declared in an editorial in 1945 that the postwar period would be a time when the labor movement was to gather in the harvest. The expression "harvest-time" (*skördetid*) made its mark, and it was given a purely socialist meaning by its opponents: the policy of building the Swedish welfare state was to be replaced by doctrinaire socialism.

From the fall of 1945 until the election in September 1948, the campaign against Social Democratic plans to introduce socialism, which the Finance Minister, Ernst Wigforss, and the Minister of Trade 1945–47, Gunnar Myrdal, were regarded as spear-heading, was a recurrent theme in Ohlin's efforts to influence public opinion, and he established a reputation as an implacable opponent of the Social Democrats. The labor movement's postwar program had aroused broad opposition from business and industry, sections of the daily press and the whole of the conservative élite. In parallel with the campaign by the political parties was another, financed by business interests, which Per Albin Hansson dubbed "the PHM-campaign" from the Swedish acronym for "opposition to the planned economy." It was much shriller in tone than the political debate proper. Ohlin considered that the PHM campaign "implied colossal exaggerations" and was anxious to stick to soundly based arguments. His pedagogical skills and energy made him the Social Democrats' most troublesome critic.

There is a striking contrast between what Ohlin said in substance and the impression he made as a political speaker. He was almost always cautious and balanced in his argumentation, never called in question his opponent's motives, avoided generalizations, and took care not to lay himself open to justifiable objections. Where any other politician would say that business and industry should be decentralized, Ohlin said "in the main decentralized." Instead of freeing people from a sense of insecurity, he would "diminish different kinds of insecurity." He could hollow out his own statements with reservations to the extent that they almost became tautological. New sectors should not be made subject to state monopoly "unless there are particularly good reasons." Young people's conditions of life should be made more equal "in so far as that can be done without giving rise to other drawbacks that exceed the benefits." In controversial questions he could seem to have two opposite opinions. He adopted "a decidedly positive attitude to the essence of trade unionism, without denying that there are serious problems connected with it." At any given moment he thought about the conflicts of objectives that, as a politician, he had to manage. Sven-Erik Larsson somewhat ironically describes him as a master of the conduct of policies that were "not too little, not too much, but just right" (Ohlin 1936:149, 1999:34f; Larsson 1998:146).

Even so, as a speaker—though seldom as a political writer—Ohlin could display a sharp edge polemically, which gave an impression of aggressiveness. He was temperate in word, but his tone and obstinacy in the pursuit of his argument spoke another language. Ernst Wigforss, who respected Ohlin, wrote: "In his polemic he sometimes gives an impression of magisterial severity, in which no smiling hints that perhaps we are all sinners mitigates the judgments he delivers." Many people have testified to this side of Ohlin, including colleagues and others who shared his opinions. Gunnar Helén, who became leader of the Liberal party in 1969, wrote of "the arrogance he radiated" (Wigforss 1954:286; Helén 1991:173f).[6]

Ohlin's election as party leader inaugurated a generational change. Within six years all the parties had new leaders. Ohlin introduced a new political style, which was in contrast with the slow, avuncular manner the Swedish people had become accustomed to in their politicians. The new Party leaders, with the exception of the Communist, Hilding Hagberg, were academics; they were intellectually nimble polymaths, well honed politically. The young, energetic Ohlin was widely admired but also seemed provocative and attracted ill will. He was the first to break with the polite, respectful tone between the parties that had been observed during the war years.

The party in office was soon on the defensive about its socialist intentions and economic planning. Social Democratic historians have customarily toned down the plans for socialist measures and the conflict of ideas between socialism and social liberalism, but in 1945 there was every reason to take the 27-point program seriously. The regulated economy of the war years, which had been successful in the given conditions, had broken down some of the psychological opposition to central bureaucratic control and direction of business and industry. In the spring session of the Riksdag in 1945 the Social Democrats, inspired by Ernst Wigforss (Myrdal 1982:211), tabled motions proposing committees to inquire into policy on business and industry, manifestly linked with the calls for socialist measures. Nationalization of the trade in oil soon became a major question. Since the Communists backed the postwar program, there was a large majority in the Riksdag prepared for action on radical policies. As late as 1948, in a debate in the Concert Hall in Stockholm with the Communist leader, Sven Linderot, Tage Erlander went through every one of the 27 points to show that the program was still a valid statement of policy.[7]

The campaign against socialism and the planned economy was combined with an increasing effort to form anti-Communist opinion. The Communists had won over 10 percent of the vote in the general election in 1944, and a further percentage point in the local elections in 1946. The government's dependence on the Communists in the Riksdag was an obvious campaign theme for the Center-Right, often with the implicit accusation that the SDP was not fully reliable from the democratic point of view. This criticism became sharper as the conviction that socialism was incompatible with democracy grew ever stronger as a result of the influence of Friedrich von Hayek's book *The Road to Serfdom* and Herbert Tingsten's articles in *Dagens Nyheter*.[8]

In the major Riksdag debate on government policy in October 1946, a few weeks after Tage Erlander assumed office as prime minister, Ohlin put critical questions about the government's relationship with the Communists. He drew attention to the fact that in his youth, Erlander had been active in *Clarté*, an association "which had been a nursery for many Communists." Sven-Erik Larsson writes: "The Official Record of the Riksdag does not convey the aggressiveness with which Ohlin pressed Erlander. I sat on the press bench and have a strong recollection of the strained atmosphere during the debate and Erlander's palpable nervousness" (Larsson 1998:190f). The attack on the new and inexperienced prime minister was thought to be ungentlemanly and has since been reckoned one of the reasons why the personal relationship between these two figures in the foreground of Swedish politics always remained unfriendly (Helén 1991:143).

Ohlin's antisocialism related to public ownership, both at the national and the local government level, to public monopolies, and to central regulation. He did not allow the polemic to cross the border into a general condemnation of increased activity by the state. One of his main arguments against socialism was that the public agencies already had such wide-ranging tasks that attempts at central management of business and industry would overstrain the system. In areas where the government's responsibility was undisputed, he called for better planning.[9] He wanted a ten-year plan for social reforms, with the financing well thought out. In particular, he emphasized the common responsibility to maintain a high and constant level of employment, though he also cautioned that Social Democratic policy would lead to mandatory direction of labor. He quoted the SDP program adopted in 1944: "The workers' collective right of decision carries with it their collective responsibility, every citizen's obligation to accept the work and fullfil the tasks that are necessary for an effective organization of production" (Ohlin 1975:135f; Larsson 1998:189).

Disputes about Stabilization Policy and Welfare

The question of socialist measures gave an ideological color to the political battle, which was however mostly about imbalances and crisis phenomena during the conversion to a peacetime economy. Inflationary pressure arose, the Swedish krona was revalued in 1946, the foreign exchange reserves were depleted the following year, regulations and rationing were re-introduced, and some taxes were increased as others were reduced. These were problems that permitted Ohlin's skills to come into play. He gave early warning of the risk of inflation, but it is not easy to discern a coherent pattern in the positions he adopted. In the September 1946 election campaign his main demand, that the turnover tax should be abolished at the end of the year, was motivated more by politics than economics. In his memoirs he admits that the Liberal Party was much too late in calling for a flexible interest rate, in practice a higher rate as a means of reining in the economy. "It is so little fashionable to talk about interest policy," he wrote in a professional context in 1947. In Sweden the low rate of interest was dogma in which both the Social Democrats and the Agrarian Party placed blind faith (Ohlin 1975:174f; Larsson 1998:188).

The background to the problems was that the Minister of Finance, contrary to his professional economic advisers, long remained passive in face of the threat of inflation. Gunnar Myrdal, the Minister of Trade, later wrote "the plain truth is that in Cabinet I constantly, but in vain, opposed our then lax economic policy which was dictated by Ernst Wigforss. In the winter of 1947 it led to the need for an extremely drastic control of imports, followed by tight rationing" (Myrdal 1982:225). When Tage Erlander on two occasions tried to obtain broad backing for the economic stabilization policy, the mutual mistrust between him and Ohlin was too great, and no agreement could be reached. Ohlin was, on behalf of the Liberal Party, disinclined to assume political risks arising because of a situation which he, in common with Myrdal, considered the government to have brought about itself (Larsson 1998:211f; Ohlin 1975:168f, 191f).

The Liberal Party's electoral successes in 1946 and 1948 put Ohlin in an unrivaled position as the leading nonsocialist politician and bore witness to the effectiveness of the social liberal message. The socialist majority declined, and it was clear that there was no broad electoral support either for a planned economy or for measures of socialism in accordance with the 27-point program. But the SDP retained the initiative, and Ohlin contributed to the creation of a broad understanding about social reforms, nine-year compulsory education, re-equipment of schools and universities, and other measures placing demands on the taxpayers. A number of regulations from the crisis period remained, without being subject to serious public criticism from Ohlin; however, internally in the Liberal Party he expressed strong disapproval. This related to the agricultural regulation, on which the Party took up the cause of better conditions for small farmers, and to the fixing of rents in principle at the 1942 level, which made necessary an expensive public financing of new housing construction. In 1951, when the SDP and Agrarian Party went into coalition and agreed to put their differences aside, it was no longer very easy to see the differences of principle between the Liberal Party's social liberalism and the pragmatic reform policy for which the government stood.

The government coalition was based on an alliance of interests between workers and farmers. A recurrent theme in Ohlin's public declarations was that the Liberals were a party of ideas, who addressed themselves to liberal thinking electors in all social groups and who therefore ought to inspire greater confidence than the two governing "class parties." But as the liberals traditionally included a large number of farmers and were also trying to broaden their support among the workers, they had to be cautious when criticizing the dominance of special interests in the governing coalition; those interests also made themselves felt in the Liberal Party. Opponents used to speak of Ohlin's "general store"—the Liberal Party had some little thing to offer to each and all.

In connection with the inflation caused in 1951 by the Korean War, Ohlin put forward a proposal for a special tax on windfall gains. The idea came readily to him as he had already proposed such a tax at the outbreak of World War II (Nilsson 1999:9). But now he was Party leader, and his radical initiative gave rise to tensions in the Liberal Party and anger in the business community. Ohlin must have calculated that the proposal would drive a wedge into the newly formed coalition. The Agrarian Party could be expected to oppose the tax, as it would hit the forestry owners, whereas the SDP were under pressure from LO to tax windfall gains. But the Agrarian Party unexpectedly agreed to it. In the end the tax introduced was higher than that advocated by Ohlin and the Liberal Party. Hjalmarson attacked Ohlin in a Riksdag debate for his "astonishing party-tactical speculation and thoroughly disreputable political opportunism." The question gave Erlander the opening for scornful attacks on the Liberal Party in the 1952 election campaign (Larsson 1998:248f; Erlander 1974:293f).

In general, Ohlin was a good tactician. His cautious but well-directed actions contributed to a gradual reduction in the socialist share of the vote, to just under 50 percent in the 1956 general election. The governing coalition was creaking at the seams, and most observers believed that a change of regime was relatively close.

The Liberal Party seldom mounted outright opposition to government bills, which had often been prepared in parliamentary committees. To quote Sven-Erik Larsson: "The Party managed to create the impression of opposing them, by putting down a reservation on one point or another, and making a great song and dance about it. Even if the area under attack was small, the criticism could be enlarged in the debate. The Party wanted to be involved in important decisions, but at the same time, with an eye to elections, it tried to preserve a distinct profile on specific questions." The profile quite often consisted in calling for higher benefit payments. A constant Social Democratic criticism during the 1950s was that the Liberals always put in a higher bid, and wanted to borrow to finance tax reductions and increased expenditure (Larsson 1998:208; Erlander 1974:101).

Ohlin was scrupulous and careful in his formulations about the reduction of economic disparities, which has always been a central Social Democratic theme. He saw it as a benefit worth certain sacrifices, but equalization should not be pressed so far that welfare-creating forces were significantly damaged. He avoided the word "equality" but sometimes expressed his support for "equal footing." He opposed exaggerated calls for equality by advancing instead the idea of "equal opportunities" (Wennås 1984:122f).

Larsson maintains that Ohlin allowed himself to be guided by his economic expertise and his analytical skills chiefly when he was advancing long-term arguments. A recurrent theme was his criticism of high marginal effects in the tax and benefits systems. The Liberals found that their most effective electoral slogan, "It must pay to work," which they first launched in 1950, could be re-used time and again. Ohlin doggedly demanded that reform policy should be planned on a basis of many years so that the total costs could be kept within the framework of growth in the tax base. The norm he championed was that overall taxation should not grow as a proportion of GNP. In 1954 he pointed out that inflation had raised income tax by 30 percent in six years and called for a change in the system that would eliminate the effect of inflation on the level of taxation. Indexation of tax rates later became a permanent Liberal Party demand. Inflation was higher in Sweden than in neighboring countries, and it would be difficult to find any major statement by Ohlin during the 1950s and 1960s in which he did not castigate inflation policy. (Ohlin 1975:200; Nilsson 1999:9f).

He considered political decisions to be more rational if taken in a calm atmosphere of mutual understanding, and the constant recipe as regards economic stabilization policy was that the government should issue invitations to roundtable conferences with representatives of the interest organizations and politicians. His point was that burdens should be distributed simultaneously so that every individual group would more readily accept them (Larsson 1998:188f, 242; Ohlin 1999:149).

The Liberal Party did not regard itself as part of a Center-Right bloc. Ohlin defended himself against the outside world's tendency to see the leaders of the Liberals and Conservatives as horses of the same pair; for example, he avoided being photographed for the press side by side with Jarl Hjalmarson. He avoided making public comments on which party or parties the Liberals would be prepared to join with in government when the Social Democrats' monopoly on power was at last broken, and did not accept the Conservatives' thesis that the nonsocialist opposition should refrain from polemics among themselves. If the Conservatives put forward proposals, which the Liberals could not support, the Liberal Party must have the right to inform the electorate about the reasons for their attitude.

Ohlin's Ideological Position during the 1950s

By the mid-1950s the public perception of Ohlin had changed. Ten years of energetic polemics against the Social Democrats had rendered invisible the radical elements in his thinking. In his ideological speeches he now, as a rule, used the word "liberalism" rather than "social liberalism." When the Conservatives, in election after election, came out with promises of tax reductions and lower social security contributions, including deferment of universal sickness insurance, the Liberal Party was forced to give greater thought to the more conservative among its electoral supporters, who connected everything "social" with the Social Democrats. However, one could still meet the radical Ohlin in discussion among party colleagues and others who shared his opinions. On one occasion, he discussed the various ways in which capital gains being made by private landowners as a result of public investments in, for example, road building could be avoided. If anyone begins to talk about the rights of private ownership in the context of unearned increases in land values, he said, then you know that he's a Conservative.[10]

If one compares *A Free Economy versus Dirigisme* with the manuscript of a book he wrote in 1956, and which was published in 1999 under the title *Democracy, Economy and Liberty*, one can trace shifts in his way of thinking. In the former he wrote: "The assumption that there is a concordance between the private interest and the public interest is untenable." In the latter he maintained, in defending the market economy, that: "The private interests of individuals are thus, in general, largely in accordance with the public interest." (He made an exception in regard to monopoly situations.) In the one case he wanted to justify interventionism, in the other the freedom of the market (Ohlin 1936:49, 1975:167f, 1999:37).

In the 1956 book manuscript Ohlin considered that despite certain socialist elements in politics, Sweden "in the main has remained a social liberal society based on the right of private ownership." It was clear that the SDP had made a huge retreat in its practical policies.

(Ohlin 1999:52, 125.) Now his anxiety was that the dynamism of the economy could be damaged by an exaggerated readiness to regulate it and to re-distribute incomes with the consequent risk of, among other things, an inadequate savings ratio. He criticized the then common belief that technical and economic developments rendered both greater guidance and control by the state and a larger public sector more or less inevitable (Ohlin 1999:147f).

The best chapter in the book is the one about the relationship between democracy and various forms of private exercise of power outside the political sphere. Democracy, he writes, is a form of government in which the people can decide how society is to be governed "in all respects, political, economic, cultural, etc.," but it is fully compatible with democracy that the people do not exercise all that power but choose to allow enterprises and organizations to function independently under their own management. Ohlin effectively countered fallacies that were to play a considerable part in the discussion about collective ownership as a condition for democracy in the 1970s (Ohlin 1999:68f).

There was a particular reason why the book remained unfinished. Ohlin himself stated that he had been forced to abandon it due to the difficulty of elucidating, from a Liberal standpoint, the role in society of the organizations. He was faced with problems to which he had no ready solutions (Larsson 1998:201).

His own divided attitude toward trade unions can be found in a number of places in the book. Ohlin wrote that already in the nineteenth century many liberals saw the justification for trade union solidarity. The Swedish trade union movement had shown a wisdom and a balance that had contributed to labor market problems having been solved better here than in many other countries. The trade unions had "in many ways been of great benefit to the workers and to society in general, including their contribution to better preconditions for growth of production and the calm way in which society has developed." On the other hand, he was disturbed by the tendency toward corporatism, especially in situations with a socialist majority in the Riksdag, since the trade union movement was then tempted to try to extract legislation on matters where it had failed to gain a hearing in its negotiations with the employers (Ohlin 1999:33f, 88, 116).

Twenty years earlier Ohlin had written that the social liberal type of society, compared with old-style liberalism, contained a risk that things would get set in their mold. At the same time he saw that in so far as that had occurred in the 1930s, it was a consequence of the Depression and unemployment, and that state interventions to stabilize the economy were a necessary remedy. In the 1950s he observed how organizations representing the demands for welfare measures for large groups in society grew ever stronger when the economy was going well and, in their interplay with political power, posed a danger to flexibility. Ohlin struggled with these problems throughout his time as a politician. He did not only consider that different welfare objectives must be weighed against one another in different ways in different phases, but also that the political tools employed can have quite contrary effects depending on the situation and the spirit of the time. In the thirties, welfare measures could also make society more flexible, at other times they had the opposite effect. The fact that his projected book in 1956 became bogged down due to Ohlin's inability to find a satisfactory formula for the interest organizations' role in society indicates that he understood the seriousness of this future problem earlier than most people. In the mid-fifties the Swedish labor market model was at the beginning of its heyday, on its way to becoming an example to the rest of the world, but it later appeared that this model was in itself a potential threat to Sweden's capacity for adaptation and economic growth. The solution of that period became the problem of a later period.

The coalition years 1951 to 1957 were a time when everything stood in the balance. The SDP had, in practice, shelved its demands for socialist measures, and together with the Agrarian Party it was conducting a policy of pragmatic reform, not essentially different from that of other countries in Western Europe. The Liberal Party and, especially, the Conservative Party took up and reinforced nonsocialist opinion opposed both to high taxation and far-reaching income redistribution, and to the Social Democrats' long period in office as such. The fifties have been described, on the basis of a major analysis of reservations tabled in committees of the Riksdag, as a period of increased confrontation in comparison with years 1900 to 1949 and with the period after 1960 (Uddhammar 1993:431f).

Uddhammar's observation may seem surprising, since both the SDP and the Conservative Party had, in practice, abandoned their traditionally most controversial standpoints and had moved nearer the center in the fifties. The enlargement of the public sector, in line with Tage Erlander's ideas about "the strong society," had not yet diverged from the general trend in Western Europe. As a matter of principle, hardly anybody called in question the welfare state. The explanation for the fact that the level of confrontation nonetheless rose is probably that the struggle for power intensified when a change of regime was so clearly within the bounds of possibility. Such a very great deal was at stake for the principal players. The difference between a Social Democratic government and a Center-Right government was potentially very significant over a period of years. A change of government would have a different and more profound significance than in countries where changes of government were a more common occurrence.

The Great Dispute about Pensions

For two years, from the spring of 1957 to the spring of 1959, the Supplementary Pension scheme overshadowed everything else as a subject of contention in Swedish political life. The outcome was a great victory for the SDP and a crushing defeat for the Liberal Party and Bertil Ohlin. The consequence was a new "harvest-time" for the Social Democrats, with more profound effects on Swedish society.

Manual workers in the private sector and many salaried employees at the lower levels had virtually no old-age pensions or protection for their dependents, other than the standard State Old-Age Pension. Ohlin came forward very early, even before the war, with proposals for reform. In a draft resolution in the Party in 1946 he proposed the examination of a voluntary supplementary pension scheme for those in private employment, on the basis of a distributive system, that is to say, without creating special investment funds (Ohlin 1975:101f). (Therein lay a contradiction: a distributive scheme cannot be entirely voluntary, because it is more advantageous for the young to save privately for their pensions.) The question was examined several times in official committees. In a report in 1950 it was proposed that there should be a common pension system for all employees, in accordance with the distributive method. The proposal was also supported by the employers' representatives and demonstrated the broad unity which then existed in views about social insurance. Five years later a new proposal was presented, based on the same principles, but with the difference that there should be some fund creation. Now the employers rejected the idea. SAF had its own proposal for pensions arranged through collective agreements, based on the method of reserve premiums and decentralized administration of the fund.

The question was sensitive both for the Social Democrats and for the Liberals. Salaried employees and employees in the public sector with satisfactory occupational pensions saw a new comprehensive system as a threat. Pension funds dominated by the state could have considerable effects on the capital market. Ohlin made energetic efforts to induce SAF to make LO such an attractive proposal on pensions that no universal state supplementary pension system would be necessary, but the conflicts of interest proved insurmountable, particularly as regards fund management. The strategy adopted by the Social Democrats was to try to gain the salaried employees' support for an obligatory supplementary pension system according to the distributive method. The proposal that had been elaborated in negotiations in the committee of enquiry on a universal pension system envisaged that pensions should be calculated as a certain proportion of income during the 15 best years and that 30 years of pensionable income would be enough to qualify for a full pension. Both of these rules favored salaried employees with a long period of education and a rising salary curve throughout their career. The proposal also included protection for surviving dependents. A significant fund would be built up to compensate for the ending of private saving for pensions.

After bitter wrangling over procedural questions, a consultative referendum was arranged in October 1957 in which three competing proposals were put forward for consideration. The Social Democratic pension proposal received just under 46 percent of the votes. A joint Liberal and Conservative proposal to submit the question to negotiation between employers and trades unions received approximately 35 percent, while a proposal from the Center Party for a purely individual and voluntary pension arrangement received 15 percent. After the referendum the coalition split up, and the government tendered its resignation. The possibility of a Center-Right government, based on a majority in the lower chamber of the Riksdag, was examined but came to nothing. Tage Erlander formed a new Social Democratic minority government.

Ohlin elaborated a new proposal for a pension system according to the premium reserve method, based on legislation. Among other things, Ohlin emphasized that "every payment of a contribution should go to building up the pension." Negotiations with the government on a compromise led nowhere.

On June 1, 1958, supplementary elections to the Lower Chamber were held on the pensions question. In the electorate as a whole the Centre-Right retained a narrow majority, but many Liberal voters went over to the Conservatives and the Center Party, and the Liberal Party lost twenty seats. After a Liberal member of the Riksdag, a metalworker named Ture Königson, decided to abstain in the vote on the Social Democratic pension proposal, it was adopted in May 1959. In the Lower Chamber the majority was just one vote.

The day after the decision in the Riksdag, Tage Erlander wrote in his diary: "Ohlin's fate seems so hopelessly tragic that I have to call up my memories of all his earlier effrontery in order not to become altogether too sentimental. But it is seldom that fate has dealt a politician such a blow" (Larsson 1998:320).

The pensions system adopted, the Universal Supplementary Pension (known by its Swedish acronym ATP), was problematic in several ways. It was entirely based on benefits. The pension commitments were inflation-proofed and fixed by law; the balance between income and expenditure in the system was regulated solely by the contributions. There was no link between benefits and contributions at the individual level, which rendered the system open to manipulation: an individual could maximize the pension payments received by exploiting the 15 and 30 years rules. The ATP's collective character made it tempting for the Riksdag to increase pension payments in good times without making extra provision for financing, and then to confiscate earned rights to pensions in bad times. It was to be feared that the pension fund, whose size would become significant after a few years, might be used for socialist objectives.

Ohlin considered that in the long term the system was untenable from the economic standpoint. In a thoroughly prepared Riksdag motion, he set out all its arbitrary and unjust features. On the basis of the view that he and the Liberal Party took of society, their opposition to the ATP must be considered as well founded, and the fears that Ohlin expressed proved to be justified. After a few years the pensionable age was lowered from 67 to 65, the parents of small children who stayed in the home earned entitlements to pensions without paying contributions, many middle-aged employees took early pensions because of the state of the labor market, and so on. These concessions increased the costs of the scheme to the extent that it became necessary to withdraw already earned pension rights. Only in the 1990s, after endless trouble, did it prove possible to reform the ATP. The pension scheme now adopted resembles the proposal on which Ohlin fought the 1958 election. It is based on contributions, not on benefits. The principle is that every krona paid in as contribution results in an addition to the pension.

The pension fund that was connected with the ATP came to be used partly to buy shares, though not as an element in a socialist policy. The earlier fears about "fund socialism" were nonetheless justified. During the seventies LO induced the SDP to adopt a proposal for employee funds as an instrument for collectivizing ownership of a broad range of industrial and commercial enterprises. It was a frontal attack on the market economy and individual ownership.

Ohlin's failure in 1957 to 1959 unleashed criticism of his political leadership from a number of sources. Of immediate political importance was Herbert Tingsten's dissatisfaction over the Liberal Party's refusal to come to terms with a solution of the pension question on Social Democratic terms. The schism between Ohlin and the editor-in-chief of the leading liberal newspaper caused dismay in the Liberal Party.

In his biography Larsson writes: "In questions that were complicated in terms of public opinion Ohlin often had difficulty in distinguishing which factor would make the greatest impact in a given situation. In the pensions question the anxieties of those who lacked a guaranteed and satisfactory income in their old age had a weight in public opinion which Ohlin's analysis may have underestimated." Larsson concedes, however, that Ohlin's criticism of the pension proposal was justified. The ATP "was built on sand" (Larsson 1998:323, 340).

Would it have been possible for the Liberal Party to come to an acceptable settlement with the SDP, if Ohlin had set his sights on a compromise at an early stage? A major problem lay in the sharp conflict of interest between SAF and LO in the fund question. LO was wholly set on legislation to establish a distributive system with a relatively rapid buildup of pension rights; workers should not have to wait for a generation before they could enjoy a secure old age. The government had excluded the Liberal Party from the work of the committee examining the problem. The prospects of a settlement without the weaknesses that were subsequently built into the ATP cannot have seemed very good. If taking into account the explosive nature of conflicts of interest, between employers and wage-earners, between groups with organized pensions and those without them, and between the middle-aged and the young, it is not, even with hindsight, easy to plot a course of action that Ohlin could have followed with a reasonable chance of success. Of all the leading players he had the clearest knowledge of the long-term significance of the design of the pensions system. Within his party there was only a minority who wanted a settlement with the SDP on the pensions question. Sven-Erik Larsson's criticism does thus not seem quite justified.

Ohlin's Errors of Judgment during the Government Crisis in the Fall of 1957

The referendum led to the dissolution of the coalition government between the SDP and the Center Party, contrary to the wishes of Gunnar Hedlund. It was the only occasion during Ohlin's time as party leader when a change of regime could have occurred.

In the directly elected lower chamber there was a basis for a nonsocialist government. In the upper chamber there was a socialist majority, as when the two chambers voted together, which they did on economic questions. However, there was a parliamentary doctrine according to which the position in the lower chamber counted more when governments were being formed. If the three nonsocialist parties held together, King Gustaf Adolf would probably invite them to form a Center-Right government. How long it would survive was an open question. After the local elections in the fall of 1958, the new membership of the county council assemblies, which elected the upper chamber, might make it possible to overturn the socialist majority in the two chambers voting together.

The king summoned Ohlin and Hjalmarson for an exploratory discussion. In the first instance, both suggested that there should be an all-party government, which they knew the Social Democrats would reject. The king asked if Ohlin was prepared to examine the possibility of forming a government based on the three nonsocialist parties. Ohlin requested an opportunity to discuss this with Hjalmarson before replying. After a while the king returned with a prepared written communique in which he, strangely enough, announced that he had entrusted the task jointly to Ohlin and Hjalmarson. This dismayed Ohlin, but in Hjalmarson's presence he did not wish to protest.

Hjalmarson was the most enthusiastic to bring about a change of government. He was aware of Gunnar Hedlund's opposition to cooperation in a coalition with the Conservatives, and he was prepared to support either a minority government drawn from the Liberal Party and the Center Party, or a minority government of the Liberal Party alone. Ohlin considered a Liberal administration supported in the Riksdag by the Conservatives and the Center Party to be a possible interim solution.

Gunnar Hedlund informed Ohlin and Hjalmarson that the Center Party would not go direct from one coalition government to another. He pointed out that a nonsocialist government would have problems when the two chambers voted together. During the government crisis Hedlund maintained contact with the leadership of the SDP. In a final conversation with Ohlin and Hjalmarson, Hedlund also rejected alternative nonsocialist governments other than a three-party coalition. In the end Tage Erlander was invited by the king to form a purely Social Democratic minority government.

Ohlin made several serious errors during the government crisis. To advocate an all-party government was a sign of weakness; it indicated that the Liberals lacked the real will to carry out policies of their own. When he accepted that the king had jointly invited him and the Conservative leader to try to form a government, the perception spread that the Liberal Party and the Conservatives were the obvious components in a new government, despite the fact that the most realistic prospect was a nonsocialist government that did not include the Conservatives. Ohlin's desire not to appear motivated by considerations of prestige, or unfriendly, during the discussion with the king was allowed to weigh more than his understanding of what was politically right. The greatest mistake was that Ohlin did not put forward the idea of a coalition between the Liberal Party and the Center Party alone. Had that alternative been on the table in the public debate, it might have been difficult for Hedlund to reject it on behalf of the Center Party despite his personal skepticism.

Sven-Erik Larsson draws attention to the fact that Ohlin, acute analyst though he was, appeared so little determined to achieve a result. "He was restrained and cautious in manner, which in sensitive situations made him a poor and rarely successful negotiator." Larsson also points out that the inability of the nonsocialists to form an administration, when after two decades they had at last obtained a majority in the lower chamber, reinforced Tage Erlander's thesis that the nonsocialists were hopelessly divided (Larsson 1998, pp. 345–57).

The Long March to the Left

With the dispute about pensions, the Social Democrats' popularity curve turned upward. The elections in 1960 and 1962 confirmed their superiority and contributed to a gradual radicalization of the political climate. The lesson of the pension question seemed to be that opposition to welfare reforms was not only politically risky but also democratically and ideologically mistaken. In 1960 the Conservatives suffered a heavy defeat on their electoral program comprising reductions in welfare and the abolition of ATP. They fought an uphill battle throughout the 1960s. Instead the Center Party, no longer seen as representing only the farming and rural community, grew larger, attracting in particular small businessmen.

Ohlin showed greatness in his defeat over the pension question that had interrupted his exceptional success. He betrayed no bitterness and made no effort to explain things away, but retained his analytical and forward-looking attitude. He turned 60 in 1959 and could have retired having served 15 years as party leader, but he was determined to fight on and after 1960 he was once again the opposition leader setting the tone. Even if he seemed more relaxed, readier to listen, and more generous than before, he continued to attack Social Democratic policy energetically and inventively. He was not tempted by the halo of wisdom and the mild afterglow attaching to the elderly statesman who has put strife behind him. He remained popular among Liberal Party members. Within the inner circle of the party a move directed against his leadership foundered when the intended successor, Sven Wedén, refused to take part (Larsson 1998:397f).

For the group of Liberal politicians who entered the Riksdag in 1948 and 1952, it was natural to show external loyalty in taking their lead from Ohlin, and in general, they also did so internally. Around 1960 a new generation of Liberals made their debut. They did not have the same relation to him, and they made the Party's Youth League an independent power factor, often in opposition to the leadership. Their leading figure was Per Ahlmark, who was culturally radical and an anticommunist whose idol and source of inspiration was Herbert Tingsten. The opposition from the Young Liberals was an early and mild variant of the revolt against authority among the growing numbers of university students in the whole of the Western world in the 1960s. Few people in this circle were trained economists or had any connection with the business world. They took the increasing standard of living for granted, and their political interest mainly focused on other objectives, such as third world aid and solidarity with national liberation movements, questions of democracy, equality between the sexes, free abortion, the separation of church and state, and so on. Ohlin was justifiably afraid that the young Liberals, with their cultural radicalism, would drive away the nonconformists and prohibitionists who had long formed the stable core of the party. After a national petition in support of the teaching of Christianity in schools, a new party was formed in 1964, the Christian Democratic Assembly, which today is twice the size of the Liberal Party. At congresses of the Youth League Ohlin criticized their ideological one-sidedness and lack of contacts outside the student world. There were lively discussions of high quality, conducted without animosity. Among party colleagues and people who shared his views Ohlin was a brilliant debater, persuasive and charming (Larsson 1998:348f).

Economic growth during the fifties and sixties was rapid, and there was room for both increases in real take-home pay and steadily increasing taxes. The turnover tax was re-introduced in 1959, against the combined opposition of the nonsocialists, and the municipalities gradually raised local taxes. The needs of the public sector were coming more and more into the foreground, inter alia under the influence of John Kenneth Galbraith's *The Affluent Society*, which had a strong impact (Larsson 1998:425f). In the prevailing climate of values there was no effective counter to constantly rising public expenditure. In several sectors, for example, third world aid and family benefits as an element in the policy of equal opportunities for women, the Liberal Party promoted increased state contributions. "An End to the Queue Society!" was a Liberal Party slogan in the spirit of the times (Zetterberg 1984:312f; Drangel 1984:377).

For Ohlin it became more and more difficult to maintain that reforms must keep to a long-term plan and be held within the framework of the growth in resources. In the mid-1940s he already considered taxation to be too high, but he contributed to its near doubling during his time as Party leader (Larsson 1998:255). Nor did the Conservative Party offer very strong opposition to the growth of the public sector or its increased powers. "After the at times strong opposition in the fifties, the next two decades were characterized both by rapidly rising public commitments, and by very sporadic, feeble, or non-existent nonsocialist objections," writes Emil Uddhammar (Uddhammar 1993:441).

An economic downturn at the end of the fifties gave the starting-signal for the activation of labor market policy. The inspiration came from the trade union economists, Gösta Rehn and Rudolf Meidner, who saw in an active labor-market policy to encourage mobility as a means of maintaining full employment combined with price stability. The idea was also that labor mobility would facilitate the policy of wage-solidarity, that is to say, a continuing reduction in wage-differentials among different branches of industry, enterprises, and individuals.

Ohlin was the Liberal Party representative in an official committee, which studied labor market policy in the first half of the sixties. During the war years he had argued in favor of a similar policy, and in all essentials he supported the expansive, ambitious activity that developed during the sixties as a central component of economic policy. It may be regarded as an adaptation of his thesis in *Freedom of the Economy versus Dirigisme* that state intervention can be a means of increasing flexibility in the economy. In the long term, however, labor market policy became an illustration of his warning in the same book that the social liberal model of society contains the risk of inflexibilty. As time has gone by, this activity has increasingly acquired the character of a system of welfare benefits with a serious tendency to lock things in place, despite its objective of encouraging flexibility and facilitating structural change (Ohlin 1975:26f).

Ohlin never accepted the trade unions' wage-policy motives for the active labor market policy. He did not like the so-called Rehn-Meidner economic policy model, and that also made him unsympathetic toward the idea of wage-earner funds as a means of eliminating excessive profits arising as a result of the wage-solidarity policy.[11]

In the political game the Center Party was the joker in the pack. The alternative of a nonsocialist government was completely dependent on Gunnar Hedlund. In the 1960 election campaign both the Center Party and the Liberal party kept their distance from the Conservatives, and adopted certain common standpoints. In identically worded statements Ohlin and Hedlund laid down that the guidelines for a nonsocialist government must in the main come from the two parties in the center, and that voters need not to fear that they would lose their children's allowances and other welfare benefits. The Conservatives were isolated.

That was just an episode, but after the fall of 1962 the alliance of the center became an ever more important element in Swedish politics. The two parties gradually developed their cooperation, with common Riksdag motions and election campaign program material. Ohlin regarded this cooperation with the Center Party as strategically important, and he overcame the skepticism of many Liberals. Shortly before his resignation as Party leader he said in interviews that he hoped that, in time, the Liberal Party and the Center Party would together form a new party, which would be socially aware and liberal in its views (Wennås 1984:137). In the longer term the Center Party gained more from this cooperation than the Liberal Party: in the period 1968 to 1979 the Center Party was the largest nonsocialist party. The alliance of the center had a decisive political significance in 1976 to 1982, when the nonsocialist parties were in control.

Ohlin's Victory on Constitutional Reform

Since the beginning of the 1920s there had been universal suffrage, both for men and women, in elections to the Riksdag and to local government councils, but for the rest the constitution remained largely unchanged since the time before Sweden became a democracy. According to the constitution both Chambers of the Riksdag enjoyed equal rights. Members of the upper chamber were elected for a period of eight years, and one eighth of its seats came up for election each year through indirect elections from county assemblies (*Landsting*) and some municipal assemblies. Twelve years after a local election had taken place, its outcome still influenced the composition of the chamber, and the indirect method of election resulted in an over-representation of the larger parties. In the lower chamber a proportional electoral system was applied. General elections took place every two years, alternately to the lower chamber of the Riksdag and to the municipal councils and county assemblies. The manner of government was parliamentary in practice, without any formal basis in the written constitution.

The constitution was not a question in which Bertil Ohlin had shown any interest at first. Tage Erlander, on the other hand, had since his youth been a convinced supporter of the majority representation system ("first-past-the-post"), which would guarantee governments enjoying a strong position in parliament. He considered the twenties to have been a "pretty wretched" time because of party fragmentation and frequent changes of government. His ideological fathers on the constitutional question were two Liberal politicians: Louis de Geer, who had based the upper chamber on the municipalities, and Karl Staaff, who supported the majority representation system and parliamentarism on the British model (Erlander and Lagercrantz 1982:165f). As prime minister, Erlander had no interest in constitutional reform, however.

The upper chamber was an obvious obstacle to changes of government, but it was not until 1953 that the Liberal Party put forward a proposal for its being abolished. After motions had been proposed from different quarters about various constitutional reforms, the government set up a parliamentary committee under the chairmanship of Rickard Sandler, the former prime minister and foreign minister. Unlike the other parties, the Liberal Party had a clear understanding of what they wanted to achieve, namely a unicameral system with proportional representation, and that gave them an advantage in the debate. The government could not steer Rickard Sandler, and the committee's proposal in 1963 for a unicameral system faced the Social Democrats with a dilemma. Erlander's notion of majority representation was politically unrealistic. He would have preferred avoiding constitutional reform altogether, but the Social Democrats' arguments in favor of the status quo barely concealed their self-seeking nature. Among the Nordic countries only Sweden had a bicameral system. In order to retain as much as possible of the prevailing system Erlander demanded that the constitution should have a "municipal connection," that is to say, a link between local elections and the composition of the Riksdag.

The local elections in the fall of 1966 were a severe defeat for the Social Democrats. After the elections Tage Erlander, who wanted to see the back of a question that had become a political encumbrance, entered into negotiations on the constitution at a disadvantage. Having learned their lesson from their defeat on the pension question, the nonsocialist parties held together. In the spring of 1967 a broad agreement was reached on a unicameral system, strictly proportional representation ensured with the aid of "top-up" seats, a 4 percent threshold against small parties, a three-year parliament and simultaneous parliamentary and local elections. It was a great success for the Liberal Party and a vitamin injection for the whole of the nonsocialist opposition. At a stroke the chances of a change of government improved.

Ohlin was now 68 years old, and some of the Liberal Party wanted to see a change. In the spring of 1968 he retired as party leader, though still with the hope that he might be a member of a nonsocialist government if one could be formed after the elections the following year. That never came about, and it was not by chance that a decline now followed for the Liberal Party. Without Ohlin at the helm, the party lost voters, prestige, and influence (Larsson 1998:402f, 460).

Ohlin remained in the Riksdag until 1970. Even after that he still took part in public debate, inter alia with his book *Uncomfortable Facts* (1971).

A Politician with a Broad Perspective

Throughout his political career Ohlin distinguished himself by his breadth of perspective and his readiness to take up the most varied of questions. He continued to hold his chair at the Stockholm School of Economics, had good contacts in the business world, took an important part in discussion on foreign policy, was an assiduous critic of government and a driving force in Nordic co-operation. "Bertil Ohlin is the brightest star in the Swedish delegation to the Nordic Council—and in the whole Council as far as the economic debates are concerned," wrote the Social Democratic publicist, Alvar Alsterdal, in *Arbetet* in 1957 (Larsson 1998:299).

The international perspective was obvious for Ohlin and determined his assessment even in down-to-earth questions. As a member of the cabinet and a new Party leader in 1944, he publicly argued the case for Sweden to switch to driving on the right, which would have been an inexpensive reform at that time. The Minister of Finance, Ernst Wigforss, rejected the idea with support from, among others, Tage Erlander (Ohlin 1975:230).[12]

Before Denmark and Norway joined NATO in 1949, there were negotiations among the three Scandinavian countries about forming a defense union, an idea that Ohlin had early supported. Tage Erlander put his full weight behind this Nordic project, which was supported by Swedish public opinion. Ohlin took part in the negotiations as a member of Parliament and expressed his great appreciation of the commitment shown by Erlander. When this attempt failed, Sweden returned to her policy of neutrality with unanimous support from the political parties. This did not prevent numerous controversies over foreign policy between the strictly orthodox guardian of Swedish neutrality, the Foreign Minister Östen Undén, and the opposition leaders Ohlin and Hjalmarson, especially the latter. Ohlin's chief point was that Sweden should clearly register her ideological Western orientation and at the same time stick firmly to her policy of freedom from alliances in peace, with a view to neutrality in war. A dispute broke out in 1953 between Ohlin and Undén about the right of refugees to be politically active in Sweden. In practice, it related to refugees from the Baltic states, whose activities might be deemed to irritate the Soviet Union. Ohlin supported their right to freedom of speech and association (Nilsson 1999:23).

There was an old strand of opinion in the Liberal Party that was traditionally skeptical about heavy expenditure on defense. Ohlin was a convinced supporter of the defense effort, and for some years in the fifties he considered that Sweden ought to acquire nuclear weapons. There would have been a serious conflict within the Liberal Party had not the Social Democrats found a formula for putting the question off into the future that was acceptable to Ohlin. An agreement with the government in 1958, about increased defense expenditure and additional selective purchase taxes, aroused the Party's old negative attitude to defense, though only internally (Larsson 1998:297).

Ohlin was never in doubt about the importance of freer trade and increased integration, both as a means of increasing prosperity and as a contribution to liberal development. He remarked that there was a streak of isolationism in the realm of socialist thought. Freer trade was difficult to combine with national economic planning and a policy of regulation. He was critical of plans for a Western European customs union and reacted negatively to the federalist elements in the Treaty of Rome. He advocated a free trade area and early recognized both the opportunities and the problems that the new pattern of cooperation in Europe would create. He wanted to keep the door open for Swedish membership of the Common Market, but did not differ fundamentally from the cautious line adopted by the Swedish government (Larsson 1998:304; Nilsson 1999:18f).

Ohlin's pro-American attitude made it difficult for him to maintain contact with the currents of feeling among the younger generation during the Vietnam conflict. The Liberal Party was critical of the United States but did not compete with the Social Democrats and Olof Palme, Tage Erlander's successor and leader of the Social Democrats in 1969 to 1986, in trying to harness the Vietnam solidarity movement. Ohlin criticized Palme because his references to communist oppression were rather infrequent (Nilsson 1999:21).

The Social Scientist as Politician

Just after Tage Erlander succeeded Per Albin Hansson, it was remarked that there were no high expectations of him. That's no bad starting point, he replied. Ohlin's situation was the contrary. His merits as an economist and as a debater on public affairs were exceptional, and his brilliance and talent were undisputed. In the situation of conflict in which he found himself, all this was soon turned against him. His mistakes and shortcomings were exaggerated and accorded a more serious significance than would have been the case with a more commonplace politician. Among the Social Democrats a malicious portrait of him as being power-hungry emerged, constantly compromising his insights as an economist and lacking appeal for ordinary people.

As party leader he was obliged to develop a strategy aimed at election results, to hold together a heterogeneous party, and to be active in many questions that at root did not interest him, and all this in conditions that varied greatly from time to time. It is nonetheless striking how far his contributions bore the stamp of certain fundamental ideas and insights he had already developed as a young economist. There is a strong continuity, connected with the fact that he early saw social questions in a dynamic perspective and was ready to adapt policy to new and unforeseen situations. He had a vision of a social liberal society to which he remained faithful, combined with (to quote Sven-Erik Larsson) "better judgement and a sounder intuition for the effects of economic measures than perhaps anyone else in the Riksdag" (Larsson 1998:432).

Ohlin's platform as an opposition leader gave him the opportunity to exercise his pedagogical talent in front of big audiences. His eloquence also bore witness to his intellectual vitality and ability to develop lucid arguments. In those days, politics were less governed by the media, and leading party representatives had greater freedom to play the democratic role as adult educators. The debates between Ohlin and the most prominent Social Democrats—Ernst Wigforss, Tage Erlander, and Gunnar Sträng—were of a quality and substance that their successors seldom attain. Ohlin forced the government representatives to sharpen their arguments: it was no use trying to fob him off with empty phrases and slogans.

After 1948 the threat of an out-and-out socialist policy was thought to have died away, but Ohlin considered that the SDP still harbored strong socialist tendencies that could only be held in check by external pressure. He brought his last major speech in the Riksdag to a close with the following words: "The choice is between, on the one hand, a socialist development in an ever more collectivist direction and with tightly concentrated political power and, on the other hand, a social-liberal society with a strong emphasis on enabling both individuals and groups to influence their working lives and the society they live in." Many thought he was tilting at windmills, at "the specter of socialism." Even in his own ranks he met with a weary reaction, but only a few months after his resignation as leader of the Liberal Party, ideas of a planned economy and socialism were re-launched by Krister Wickman, the government's star economist, before an enthusiastic party congress, and in the seventies first LO and then the SDP went in for a large-scale collectivization of ownership in business and industry, through wage-earners investment funds. Socialism was still latent within the labor movement and the brakes could be put on it only by mobilizing strong opposition on the nonsocialist side, exactly as Ohlin thought.

The Liberal Party's clearly defined position, ranged in the frontline against the Social Democrats, gave it credibility among voters in the broad middle classes, and hence significant political freedom of movement. Ohlin avoided the dangers to which a party of the center exposes itself by joining a firm nonsocialist bloc. Under the umbrella of orthodoxy on the most central questions a new generation of Liberals could find an outlet for their interests and impulses in other areas of politics. But Ohlin did not succeed in bringing forward a leading group in the party who could continue his own contribution of criticism in the economic debate, combined with constant vigilance against any tendencies to socialism and collectivism. He neglected to affiliate to the party any qualified economist of the younger generation. It was not until the 1980s that the Liberal Party acquired an economist in a leading role—his daughter Anne Wibble, who became minister of finance in the Center-Right coalition government from 1991 to 1994 (Larsson 1998:451).

The decline of the party and of the trend of views represented by Ohlin, and the impression of inner reserve and impersonal correctness that he gave in public, have subsequently tended to cool the interest in his achievements. There has been a marked lack of generosity on the part of the majority of his political opponents. However, he has been widely and unhesitatingly admired in one respect in particular. Tage Erlander said the following of Ohlin in his memoirs: "He had a quality which I never ceased to admire—his ability to sustain his morale. He never gave up a battle. He met adversities but they never seemed to diminish his readiness to fight on" (Erlander 1973:341). Other leading politicians, such as Olof Palme and Carl Bildt, have found it difficult to endure even two short electoral periods in opposition. Ohlin stubbornly kept the opposition flag flying high for twenty-two years.

Notes

1. Karl Staaff was the leader of the Liberal party, prime minister from 1905 to 1906 and from 1911 to 1914.

2. Altogether, Ohlin wrote about 1195 articles in *Stockholms-Tidningen*; see Carlson et al. (2000).

3. Ohlin advocated increased productivity, rather than re-distribution, as the means of advancing the poor, as early as 1920 in his first known contribution to political debate (Wennås 1984:81).

4. The expression "social liberalism" had earlier been used by the social reformer G. H. von Koch and by E. H. Thörnberg in his depiction of popular movements (Lindblad 1999).

5. In the mid-1930s Ohlin argued in *Stockholms-Tidningen* for wage differentials that would make it easier for those with few qualifications to obtain jobs. That led Erlander, in a leading article in *Arbetet*, to describe Ohlin as "the most energetic champion of high finance" (Larsson 1998:190).

6. As a journalist covering cultural affairs at *Stockholms-Tidningen* at the end of the 1940s, Helén (1991) thought that "Ohlin wrote very badly," especially when he strayed outside the field of economics. Ohlin was no great stylist.

7. Personal recollection of the author, who was present.

8. Tingsten, a friend of Ohlin's since the early 1920s, was a professor of political science and the chief editor from 1946 to 1960 of Sweden's leading morning daily *Dagens Nyheter*.

9. Tage Erlander found Ohlin's attitude paradoxical. In his memoirs he said, in regard to research policy: "Here is a Social Democratic government that does not want to be involved in managing and planning one of our most important sectors, as many in the Riksdag demanded. In particular, the demand came from Bertil Ohlin and the Liberals" (Erlander and Lagercrantz 1982:93).

10. Personal recollection from a meeting in 1955 in the Liberal Party Youth League. Ohlin's interest in the question is apparent in Ohlin 1999, p. 179, where, among other things, he sees major public holdings of land as a solution.

11. Gösta Rehn and Rudolf Meidner were LO economists in the 1940s and 1950s. They advocated solidarity wage policies combined with anti-inflationary fiscal policies and an active labor market policy designed to promote flexibility.

12. Sweden switched to right-hand traffic in 1967, at a cost many times higher than it would have been in 1944, when there was no private car traffic.

References

Arbetarrörelsens efterkrigsprogram. De 27 punkterna med motivering. Stockholm 1945.

Arbetsmarknadspolitiken—vad kan vi lära för framtiden. Ett forskarseminarium. Svenska Arbetsgivareföreningen. 1995.

Carlson, Benny, Orrje, Helena, and Wadensjö, Eskil. 2000. *Ohlins artiklar*. Stockholm: SOFI.

Delander, Lennart. 1991. Thoursie, Ragnar och Wadensjö, Eskil. Arbetsförmedlingens historia. Göteborg.

Drangel, Louise. 1984. Folkpartiet och jämställdhetsfrågan. (Liberal ideologi och politik 1934–1984.) Falköping.

Erlander, Tage. 1940–1949. Nacka, 1973.

Erlander, Tage. 1949–1954. Nacka, 1974.

Erlander, Tage, and Lagercrantz, Arvid. 1960–talet. Samtal med Arvid Lagercrantz. Kristianstad, 1982.

Helén, Gunnar. 1991. Alltför många jag. Memoarer. Uddevalla.

Johansson, Alf W. 1987. Den svenska socialdemokratin och fascismen på trettiotalet. (Studier tillägnade Wilhelm M. Carlgren den 6 maj 1987.) Stockholm.

Johansson, Alf W. 1995. Herbert Tingsten och det kalla kriget. Stockholm.

Johanson, Gösta. 1984. Frisinnade och liberaler 1934–1984. (Liberal ideologi och politik 1934–1984). Falköping.

Larsson, Sven-Erik. 1998. Bertil Ohlin. Ekonom och politiker. Stockholm.

Lindblad, Hans. 1999. Bertil Ohlin—den ständige förnyaren. Stencil.

Myrdal, Gunnar. 1982. Hur styrs landet? Borås.

Nilsson, Olle. 1999. Bertil Ohlin, en liberal "i pagt med tiden." Stockholm.

Ohlin, Bertil. 1936. Fri eller dirigerad ekonomi, Uddevala.

Ohlin, Bertil. 1963. Liberal utmaning. Arboga.

Ohlin, Bertil. 1971. Obekväma fakta. Stockholm.

Ohlin, Bertil. 1972. Bertil Ohlins memoarer. Ung man blir politiker. Stockholm.

Ohlin, Bertil. 1975. Bertil Ohlins memoarer. Socialistisk skördetid kom bort. Stockholm.

Ohlin, Bertil. 1999. Demokratin, ekonomin och friheten. Stockholm.

Ruin, Olof. 1968. Mellan samlingsregering och tvåprtisystem. Stockholm.

Stråth, Bo. 1998. Mellan två fonder. LO och den svenska modellen. Uddevalla.

Uddhammar, Emil. 1993. Partierna och den stora staten. En analys av statsteorier och svensk politik under 1900-talet. Smedjebacken.

Wennås, Olof. 1984. Beril Ohlin om socialismen, liberalismen och folkpartiet. (Liberal ideologi och politik 1934–1984). Falköping.

Wigforss, Ernst. 1954. Minnen III. 1933–1949. Stockholm.

Zetterberg, Kent. 1984. Folkpartiet och biståndspolitiken 1945–1983. (Liberal ideologi och politik 1934–1984). Falköping.

II The Early Bertil Ohlin

7 Ohlin versus Heckscher and Wicksell on Forestry: One Win (Points) and One Draw

Karl-Gustaf Löfgren

Bertil Ohlin finished his *fil kand* exam at the Univeristy of Lund in the spring of 1917. He majored in economics, but he had also taken, despite his high school degree in humanities (*Latinlinjen*), what corresponds to two semesters of studies in both mathematics and statistics. He was 18 years old, and he decided to broaden his education by joining the two-year program at the Stockholm School of Economics.

The first week he showed up for Eli F. Heckscher's economics seminar for the second-year students. Ohlin had to fight a little to become a member of the seminar, since Heckscher probably found him too young. He was appointed as an opponent on a paper written by a master of forestry by the name of E. Lindeberg. The paper was about the optimal rotation period of an even-aged forest stand, and none of the other participants in the seminar were interested in discussing the paper.

The author advocated a solution to the rotation period, which was referred to as *Geldreinertragswirtschaft* by German foresters, and which corresponds to Jevons's wine-aging formula. Heckscher himself had suggested the same formula during the so-called Swedish profitability war in forestry.[1] The same kind of war had already taken place in Germany. It started in 1813, when König introduced an incorrect formula for the land value, and one can say that it ended after the papers by Faustmann (1849) and Pressler (1860), where the correct principles for the present-value maximization of the sum of an infinite number of rotations were developed. The Swedish war was waged at the yearly meetings of the Swedish Association of Forest Conservation, and started in 1907, when the colorful Swedish master of forestry Uno Wallmo presented his paper on "Sustained Yield Forestry." He advocated the maximization of the (net) sustained yield (*Waldreinertragswirtschaft*). This solution principle, like the wine-aging solution, results in too long a rotation period. It will, however, lead to the same rotation period as present-value maximization if the interest rate is zero.[2]

The wine-aging formula neglects the value of bare land, and Ohlin writes in his memoires, "that one should in, principle, account for the land value could easily be shown by differential calculus." Ohlin's "inaugural lecture" was published in *Ekonomisk Tidskrift* (now *Scandinavian Journal of Economics*), in a special issue in honor of Knut Wicksell.[3] Wicksell did not publish anything about the optimal rotation period in forestry during his career, but as shown by Wicksell (1987) and Hedlund et al. (1993), he worked on forestry as an example of a flow input point output technology.

In the rest of this chapter, I will compare the solution suggested by Ohlin to that put forward by Wicksell. Because of different capital-theoretical starting points, they work out the solution in different manners, but both arrive at the correct formula. Ohlin's solution method is more in line with Fisherian investment theory, maximizing present value under a given market interest rate, while Wicksell maximizes the rate of return under a given land rent.

A Brief Historical Note

Martin Faustmann (1849) and Max Robert Pressler (1860) have, until recently, been credited as the persons who were first to solve the optimal rotation problem in forestry. Faustmann did not solve the optimal rotation problem explicitly, but as Samuelson (1976) points out, there are indications that he knew how to determine the optimum. Pressler introduced the concept of *das Weiserprozent* (the indicator percent), which is equal to the rate of growth of the stand less the interest on the land value divided by the current value of the stand. The correct rule is to cut the stand when *das Weiserprozent* is equal to or less than the ruling interest rate, and keep the stand otherwise. The Faustmann-Pressler result was published in Swedish by Holmerz (1876). However, the Swedish "profitability war" showed that extremely few people had any fundamental insights. There were at least two obstacles. In the first place there was not, at the time, any theoretical explanation of why the maximization of the present value would constitute a correct investment criterion; that is to say, the investment with the greatest present value should be chosen, independently of the intertemporal preferences of the investor. Second, the derivation of the cutting rule, given the correct goal function, required either an extremely good economic intuition or knowledge of differential calculus.

In a recent paper by Scorgie and Kennedy (1996) it is shown that the ideas behind Jevon's wine-aging formula and the Faustmann-Pressler theorem are much older. The *Geldreinertragswirtschaft* formula was put forward by an English plantation owner, Richard Watson, already in 1794. Besides growing trees, he was the bishop of Lladaff. In an introductory paper addressed to the newly formed Board of Agriculture and Internal Improvement, he wrote the following, about the appropriate rule for when a forest stand should be cut: "If profit is considered, every tree of every kind ought to be cut down and sold, when the annual increase in the value of the tree, by its growth, is less than the annual interest of the money it would sell for." What is even more remarkable is that Watson's solution was augmented correctly by William Marshall (1808), an agriculturist who was an honorary member of the Board of Agriculture. Marshall reviewed the reports submitted to the Board and made comments where he deemed it appropriate. In a review of a report concerning agricultural improvement in the county of Westmoreland, Marshall corrected Watson's solution by adding in a footnote: "Together with the annual value of the land it grows upon—of more consideration than, perhaps, the interest of the money." He also refers to the opportunity cost of land twice more in his report.

Ohlin's Rediscovery of the Marshall-Faustmann-Pressler Theorem

What the young Ohlin implicitly assumes in his paper is that the capital market is perfect (i.e., you can lend or borrow any amount of money at the ruling interest rate), that the price of timber is known for the future, that forest land can be bought and sold in a perfect market, and that technical timber yields are known for the future. Following Ohlin, let

$pf(t)$ = the value of a forest stand of age t

$f(t)$ = the stock of timber in a stand of age t

p = the price of one unit of timber

r = the ruling interest rate

The rotation problem can now be formulated as the maximization of the present value from all future cuttings:

$$\max_t PV = \max_t\{pf(t)e^{-rt}(1 + e^{-rt} + e^{-r2t} = \cdots)\} = \max_t \frac{pf(t)}{e^{rt} - 1}. \tag{1}$$

Equation (1) is the land value that would be the result of a perfect market economy. It was an easy task for a two-semester student of mathematics at the University of Lund to derive the first-order condition for an interior solution. It can be written

$$pf'(t) = rpf(t) + \frac{rpf(t)}{e^{rt} - 1}, \tag{2}$$

and making use of the interpretation of (1), one arrives at the following theorem:

THEOREM A forest stand shall be cut down when the time rate of change in its value is equal to the interest on the value of the stand plus the interest on the value of the forest land.[4]

Needless to say, Ohlin became a permanent member of Heckscher's seminar after his demonstration of this argument, although Heckscher did not, according to Ohlin (1972), quite accept that he had been partly wrong. According to the great Swedish industrialist Ruben Rausing, a friend of Bertil Ohlin from his early high school years in Helsingborg and also a member of Heckscher's seminar, Heckscher knew very little mathematics, and as Rausing remembers it, Ohlin avoided mathematics during his discussion[5] of the paper.

It is worth mentioning that after the presentation of his paper, Ohlin was made aware, by David Davidsson, of the fact that his results were already known to the scientific community.[6] Ohlin, it seems, was the second person to use differential calculus to prove the theorem. The first was likely Knut Wicksell.

Wicksell on Forestry

In his *Lectures in Economics*, part 1, Wicksell discusses the concepts of capital and interest, and to understand the core meaning of capital, he decides to let the influence of time become very explicit by working with a flow input point output example. The example he chooses to discuss is wine aging, or, as he writes, "the planting of trees on *worthless* bare land" (author's translation of Wicksell 1911:203). In other words, he seems to be aware of the fact that valuable land slightly complicates the analysis. As is clear from Wicksell (1987), he had indeed worked out the case when bare land has a positive value. Here he writes, "forestry, on valuable land will serve as our example." He ignores labor input, and under this condition the annual land rent represents the forest owner's sole capital outlay, and the sole objective of the forest owner is to maximize the return on his capital. The rate of return, ρ, on an acre of forest land which can be rented at the rent R, can be written

$$\frac{pf(t)}{e^{\rho t}-1}=\frac{R}{\rho}$$

or

$$pf(t)=R(e^{\rho t}-1)\rho^{-1}, \tag{3}$$

which is were Wicksell starts. He then writes: "one condition for the maximum of ρ is"

$$\rho=\frac{pf'(t)-R}{pf(t)}. \tag{4}$$

When I first saw this equation I was teaching a graduate course in forest economics at Berkeley (back in 1987), and I remember that my first reaction was that even Wicksell went wrong on the rotation problem. Then, in the back of my mind I remembered Frisch's words: "Sometimes it happened that I thought that I finally had caught him in an inconsistency or in unclear thinking. Every time this happened, it turned out, however, that the error was mine" (Frisch 1952:654).

Substituting for R in (4), one immediately obtains equation (2), which is the correct condition for the optimal rotation period. In a perfect capital market, the interest rate is given, and the rent is given by the interest on the capital. Competitive bidding would result in a rent equal to

$$R^*=r\max_t\frac{pf(t)}{e^{rt}-1}, \tag{5}$$

which, since it maximizes the interest on the capital at a given interest rate, gives the same rotation period as the one that maximizes the value of the capital.

Putting $R=R^*$ in the Wicksellian constrained optimization problem means that this problem is solved by an internal rate of return equal to the market interest rate. Further the Wicksellian optimal rotation period will, in this case, coincide with the Marshall-Faustmann-Pressler rotation period. It is not completely clear from the manuscript that Wicksell understood how the rent would be determined in a perfect market, but given Frisch's experience it is a "gimme."

Concluding Comments

It is interesting to know that three of Sweden's most famous economists did theoretical work on the classical rotation problem in forestry. Only two of them got it completely right. Heckscher is, given the number of great economists who have neglected the value of land, excused. The choice of the wine-aging solution for forestry is also rather suggestive, and perhaps, in practice, does not make much of a difference.

It is not unlikely that it was Heckscher's inability, or unwillingness, to use mathematics that led him wrong. Wicksell is the only one of the three who relied heavily on mathematics in all his writings. Ohlin used math in chapter 3 of his thesis *Handelns teori* (The theory of trade) but very sporadically in his later writings. Heckscher avoided mathematics completely and relied on his extremely good economic intuition. It is clear from what they accomplished that all three of them had a talent for analytical thinking.

However, it was Bertil Ohlin who was the most precocious. To match Wicksell and outperform Heckscher at 18 makes him worth the, often misused, epithet talented.

Acknowledgments

The author acknowledges comments from Thomas Aronsson, Umeå University, Per-Olov Johansson, Stockholm School of Economics, and Martin L. Weitzman, Harvard University. The usual disclaimer applies.

Notes

1. See Heckscher (1912).
2. See Samuelson (1976), and Johansson and Löfgren (1985).
3. Not David Davidson as Ohlin asserts in his memoires.

4. This principle is called *Bodenreinertragswirtschaft* by the German forest economists.

5. These facts are known to me from a personal letter from Ruben Rausing to Mrs. Evy Ohlin. I am grateful to Mrs. Ohlin who has sent me a copy of Rausing's letter.

6. See Ohlin (1972).

References

Faustmann, M. 1849. Berechnung des Werthes, welchen Waldboden, sowie noch nicht haubare Holzbeständen für die Waldwirtschaft besitzen. *Allgemeine Forst- and Jagdzeitung* 15:441–55.

Frisch, R. 1952. Frisch on Wicksell. In H. W. Spiegel, ed., *The Development of Economic Thought*. New York: Wiley.

Heckscher, E. F. 1912. Skogsbrukets räntabilitet. *Ekonomisk Tidskrift* 13:139ff, 253ff.

Hedlund-Nyström, T., L. Jonung, K. G. Löfgren, and B. Sandelin. 1993. Wicksell on Forestry. In L. Jonung, ed. *Swedish Economic Thought*. London: Routledge.

Holmerz, C. G. 1876. *Studier i skogstaxation del 1*. Stockholm: Norstedts.

Johansson, P. O., and K. G. Löfgren. 1985. *The Economics of Forestry and Natural Resources*. London: Blackwell.

Marshall, W. 1808. A review of the reports to the Board of Agriculture: From the Northern Department of England. London: Longman, Hurst, Rees, Orme.

Ohlin, B. 1921. Till frågan om skogarnas omloppstid, *Ekonomisk Tidskrift* 22:89–113.

Ohlin, B. 1972. *Ung man blir politiker*. Stockholm: Bonniers.

Ohlin, B. 1924. *Handelns Teori*. Stockholm: Stockholms Högskola.

Pressler, M. R. 1860. Aus die Holzzuwachlehre. *Allgemeine Forst- und Jagdzeitung* 36:173–91.

Samuelson, P. A. 1976. Economics of forestry in an evolving society. *Economic Inquiry* 14:466–92.

Scorgie, M., and J. Kennedy. 1996. Who discovered the Faustmann condition? *History of Political Economy* 28:77–80.

Watson, R. 1794. *Preliminary Observations. General View of the Agriculture of the County of Westmoreland, with Observations on the Means of Its Improvement*, ed. A Pringle. Edinburgh: Chapman.

Wicksell, K. 1911. *Föreläsningar i Nationalekonomi del 1*. Lund: Gleerups.

Wicksell, K. 1987. Ett opublicerat manuskript av Knut Wicksell. *Ekonomiska Samfundets Tidskrift* 3:123–36.

The papers by Faustmann (1849), Pressler (1860), Ohlin (1921), and Samuelson (1976) are all available in English versions in *Journal of Forest Economics, 1, No 1 1995*, Umeå Forest University Press. A copy of the letter (1979) from Ruben Rausing to Mrs. Evy Ohlin is available from the author.

8

Eureka unter den Linden: A Reinterpretation of Ohlin's Early Contributions to the Heckscher-Ohlin Theme

Rolf G. H. Henriksson

So far attention has centered mostly on Ohlin's accomplishments in his licentiate thesis (Ohlin 1922b) and his doctoral dissertation (Ohlin 1924) as concerns his contribution to the Heckscher-Ohlin model. The present chapter has a wider objective in extending the view to include also Ohlin's thinking prior to these writings. Although the chapter reports an important finding regarding Ohlin's dependence on Heckscher in the thesis, this is premised on an even more important finding about his earlier work. The basic continuity in Ohlin's thinking is underscored, but the generic origins of his later theoretical achievements are shown to be the outcome of a much more complex thought process than has been understood. Ohlin's early thinking was centered on a theme that was quite different from the theme he dealt with in his thesis. This chapter's findings on the genesis of the Ohlin approach turn out to be important not only for assessing his contributions to the Heckscher-Ohlin theory but also for assessing his post dissertation work.

The presentation evolves from a critical examination of what must be considered a misleading wording in his memoirs (Ohlin 1972). In these memoirs Ohlin singled out an event that is said to be his Eureka experience. This was the crucial point in his thinking when he arrived at the core conception of his later contribution to trade theory. In a close reading of Ohlin's own contemporary account, especially in his correspondence with Heckscher, the chapter refutes the prevalent misinterpretation of that event and focuses on what its actual content was. In closing, the chapter offers an appraisal of the significance of the findings in opening a wider perspective on Ohlin's work.

Interpreting the Eureka

In recalling his Eureka moment in his memoirs, Ohlin relates how in early 1920, about a year before he started the writing of his licentiate thesis, he had an idea that became the alleged linchpin of his later contribution to trade theory:

> Above all . . . I began (in 1921) writing on the foundations of a to some extent new approach in foreign trade theory to which I had been inspired during a walk on Unter den Linden in Berlin in 1920. (Ohlin 1972:79)[1]

Those of us steeped in traditional international trade theory according to Heckscher and Ohlin nowadays know of Ohlin's explicit acknowledgment in the introduction to his dissertation (Ohlin 1924) and so have generally accepted the view that Ohlin's contribution in his thesis and dissertation was a fusion of Cassel's and Heckscher's approaches. Ohlin's statement quoted above has therefore been interpreted with the presumption that what Ohlin had in mind in Berlin 1920 was the merger of ideas he refers to in the acknowledgment of 1924. This interpretation of Ohlin's Eureka has appeared especially convincing as Ohlin had reviewed Cassel's (1918) magnum opus in the spring of 1919 (Ohlin 1919) and had also read Heckscher's paper that appeared in early 1920 (Heckscher 1919, 1920). Further the interpretation seems to be supported by the analytical design of Ohlin's licentiate thesis of 1922. Unlike the dissertation, this thesis (Ohlin 1922b), which antedates the doctoral dissertation (Ohlin [1924] 1991) by two years, is almost solely concerned with the central issues of the Heckscher-Ohlin theory.[2] Ohlin's mind-set shortly before the departure to Berlin would thus appear as uniquely prepared for such a fusion of ideas as is commonly attributed to him.

However, all this is a debatable interpretation of Ohlin's Eureka. Although Ohlin, in the introduction to his doctoral dissertation, recognizes the influence of Heckscher's contribution, he only admits it to have been subconscious. In referring back to his thesis of 1922 Ohlin says:

> The origin of this research was an attempt to extend Cassel's system of equations of price determination in *one* market to that of several trading countries. Although the point of departure is totally different, the results of that attempt (presented in chapter III) exhibit important similarities to Heckscher's treatment in "The Effect of Foreign Trade on the Distribution of Income," published one year earlier in *Ekonomisk Tidskrift*, 1920. There is no

doubt that the author was unconsciously influenced by Heckscher's paper, both at this and at later stages of the work. The influence of this pathbreaking paper, both conscious and unconscious, has surely been particularly decisive in the development of the material in chapters I–III. (Ohlin 1924; see Flam and Flanders translation 1991:76)

While Cassel's explicit influence on the design that guided Ohlin's work from the start in 1921 may be incontestable as a conscious influence, Heckscher's ideas could not have been part of that design at the outset. The strong tribute Ohlin pays Heckscher in this quote hides this important point. Ohlin's wordings must largely be understood as an attempt to make up for his failure to refer sufficiently to Heckscher's work in the text of his 1922 thesis.[3]

Evidence Regarding Ohlin's Dependence on Heckscher

The correspondences of Ohlin and Heckscher offer some insight into the nature of Ohlin's dependence on Heckscher. To be sure, Heckscher was quite pleased with Ohlin's thesis of 1922. He expressed great appreciation of Ohlin's performance in a letter to Per Jacobsson by the following words:

I consider Ohlin to be the leading economist of the next generation.... His thesis dealt largely with the same topic as my paper in the Davidson festschrift but considerably more systematically and successfully. (Heckscher to Jacobsson, July 7, 1922, author's translation)

Privately to Ohlin, however, Heckscher had offered some negative reactions. On reading the first version of Ohlin's 1922 thesis, Heckscher complained about Ohlin's failure to refer to his work in an appropriate manner. This can be inferred from a letter written in the fall of 1923, in which Ohlin responds to this complaint. The letter relates to Heckscher's comment on the first draft of Ohlin's dissertation completed in 1924. The following excerpt from the letter renders Ohlin's words in as literal a translation as possible:

... I gladly seize the opportunity to explain what I consider to be the relationship between my paper and yours. I have long felt a need to make such a clarification, more precisely ever since I saw your very justified note in the margin of my licentiate paper: "Why is not my paper cited?" ... As I had recently read Cassel for the second time, I decided to take his equation system relating to one country and extend the reasoning to cover two countries, i.e., give a mathematical illustration of the price formation mechanism in the exchange between two countries. Thus I arrived at the equation systems that are reproduced in my licentiate thesis and my present manuscript.... "Trade cannot arise if relative commodity prices are the same": That far I had come at the beginning of August 1921 without having seen your paper since the spring of 1920, when I read it carefully twice. As I now set out to explore what the proposition above implied with respect to factor prices, I remembered your paper ... (and that you had found two cases, 1) relative factor prices are equal and 2) something about the proportions (of factors of production) in different commodities of which I did not have a clear memory). It took me a week or so before I got hold of your paper (I was on leave in Klippan[4]); meanwhile I continued the purely mathematical analysis of my equations and when your paper arrived found that our results did not agree with each other (as regards case 2). Concerning the causes of trade or rather the conditions for its absence, an analysis of the equations could not possibly yield more than one result. Although I was no doubt greatly assisted by my partly subconscious knowledge of your results, I hold that I had reached my results from a completely different point of departure. To say that I had taken your results and changed them a little is surely not to describe the development correctly. (Ohlin to Heckscher, November 22–24, 1923, author's translation)

Besides the invaluable light this letter sheds on the relationship between Ohlin and Heckscher at the time, it clarifies for us the extent of dependence of Ohlin's thesis on Heckscher's work. The letter specifically indicates that Heckscher's approach influenced Ohlin's work only after that work had already been pursued independently for some time.

Further Evidence on the Background to Ohlin's Thesis

The letter also provides the following background information on the licentiate thesis in June 1921:

Let me start from the beginning. I intended at the outset, spring 1921, again to write on the theory of exchange rates, but found that I had to go more deeply and take up the theory of international trade. (Ohlin to Heckscher, November 22–24, 1923, author's translation)

Returning later to the little intriguing word "again," we will begin with the main message. From our knowledge of the content of Ohlin's licentiate thesis, we can surmise that "at the outset," or before settling for the thesis theme as we know it, Ohlin contemplated such a seemingly different topic as the theory of the exchange rate. There is no exchange rate theory in the thesis of 1922, and it only plays a marginal role as in the dissertation of 1924.

Naturally we cannot rule out that Ohlin might have intended to descend beneath the veil of money and monetary conceptions as a completely different topic. But the impression one gets from Ohlin's wording is that the change in focus from a theory of exchange rate to a pure theory of trade was not as radical a change as between two entirely separate alternatives. Ohlin's ambition to probe more "deeply" indicates that he was concerned with a more in-depth exploration of the determinants of the exchange rate. Thus for Ohlin his explication of the theory of international trade was a natural extension of the task of explaining the exchange rate. Evidence that Ohlin had not lost sight of the monetary goal can be gathered from the following excerpt from Ohlin's application for travel funds in early 1922, which was shortly before the completion of his licentiate thesis. Ohlin was here already presenting his plans for the doctoral dissertation on which he intended to start immediately after the thesis:

> I am presently at work on a dissertation dealing with the theory of international trade and foreign exchange rates. In dealing with this, studies of the intervention of recent years in the area of trade and exchange rates of different countries is of the greatest importance. I therefore hope to be able to begin a six month study tour to Switzerland, France and England at the end of May this year. After having collected the necessary material I intend—if the economic side can be arranged—during a stay of 6–12 months in England (probably Cambridge) or possibly the United States (in that case probably Harvard University)—to work out the above mentioned dissertation as a specimen for the doctoral degree in philosophy and pursue studies in general. I have not yet any detailed study plan. That should appropriately be set up after the arrival. (Ohlin's application to the Royal Academy of Sciences, January 30, 1922, author's translation)

This piece of information establishes that in a very late phase of his work on the licentiate thesis, Ohlin was still attentive to the exchange rate issue, though not as a purely theoretical problem. Ohlin might deliberately have emphasized the empirical part of his plans in order to enhance his chances for a grant. But it is more likely that he considered the theoretical exchange rate problem to offer less of a challenge than before. This conclusion Ohlin had probably reached already in the spring of 1921 when his thesis work was refocused from exchange rate theory to the real theory of international trade. Nevertheless, closer scrutiny of this switch is needed.

Ohlin's Earlier Contribution to the Theory of Exchange Rate

In the fall of 1920 Ohlin had worked out an impressive diagrammatic analysis of the determination of the exchange rate. He then had it published in *Ekonomisk Tidskrift* as his first printed contribution to economic theory (Ohlin 1921a).[5] Ohlin was no doubt proud of this accomplishment, but during a study tour abroad he soon discovered that his results had been anticipated by John Stuart Mill. In a letter to Heckscher from Grenoble in France, May 1921, he reports the following on his studies:

> But the third book by Stuart Mill (*Principles*) was a pleasant surprise. I became especially interested in the chapter on international values as it contains a theory of exchange rates including among other things, the basic idea I have tried to express in my little paper. Had I not known that I had never held that book in my hand, I would have been tempted to believe that I had subconsciously copied his presentation, but as I had last year read neither Ricardo (except for the first five chapters) nor Stuart Mill, that is evidently impossible. The reading of §1–5 of the chapter on international values and the erroneous (as far as I can see) §6–8 made me think anew on the theory of exchange rates and I began to consider if I ought not return to my idea of spring last year to write the licentiate thesis on that. (Ohlin to Heckscher, May 15, 1921, author's translation)

The little paper Ohlin so modestly refers to in the quote is the publication in *Ekonomisk Tidskrift* mentioned above (Ohlin 1921a). The quote confirms the previously noted fact in the letter of fall 1923 that Ohlin as late as the spring of 1921 had planned on the theory of exchange rate as his thesis topic. The reasons for his decision to discard that topic can only be inferred. Despite what the quote brings out, Ohlin's discovery that Mill had dealt with the problem, as it appears quite preemptively, could not have been so "pleasant" a surprise. One may easily deduce his finding out about Mill's contribution to be the main reason for abandoning the theme for his thesis. Clearly, Ohlin was not satisfied with being merely original independently of earlier work, he wanted to make a contribution in the sense of being the first. Apparently, in viewing his diagram model as a merely expository device, he could not claim it as a substantive achievement beyond Mill.

Today many scholars might consider Ohlin to have thrown away a gold nugget. Mill's formulation of the theory of exchange rate has long been eulogized. Chipman (1965) remarks on Mill's law of international values or reciprocal demand that in "its astonishing simplicity it must stand as one of the great achievements of the human intellect."[6]

It is possible that Ohlin failed to see the scientific potential of his diagram model because he was not sufficiently familiar with the literature on the Millian theme. Already Marshall's and Edgeworth's works had set a rather geometric agendum for the tasks that were waiting to be dealt with (Gram 1987). Indeed, if Ohlin had known about these latter works, he might have been even more discouraged. Still, although Ohlin naturally recognized Mill's priority, it is hard to understand why, with some elaboration, he could not have turned his 1921 paper into a thesis.[7]

Ohlin's Thoughts on Productivity Changes and Exchange Rate Changes

The most important point in the 1921 letter quoted above is made by the little word "anew." Like the little word "again" noted in the previously quoted 1923 letter, the word "anew" refers back to the spring of 1920. Thus neither word lends any support to "the received view" of the Eureka. On the contrary, they both suggest that the content of that event in Berlin concerned the determination of exchange rate rather than the pure theory of trade.

But these words further indicate that in the interim after the Eureka, Ohlin had an alternative to the general exchange rate topic in mind. The possibility that this alternative topic was the Cassel-Heckscher fusion in Ohlin's thesis can, however, be ruled out. It was rather a third possible theme for a thesis. Ohlin diffusely states in the same letter that at the time he had considered a thesis idea that would be a query into the relationships between exchange rate changes and productivity changes. The reason he gives for abandoning that particular theme seems to be a gentlemanly respect for the priority rights of a colleague in exploiting an idea. The text in the letter that informs us reads as follows:

> I would also like to take up the question concerning the connection between the exchange rate and the productivity deterioration as it seems evident to me that the increase in the economic productivity of Swedish industrial life under certain preconditions that may now exist and existed last year (with free monetary standard) would tend to decrease our price level, while it might increase prices under a gold standard. However, I think it is

unpleasant to block the way for Silverstolpe who is dealing with these questions. Surely, we began at about the same time (my draft where the reasoning on productivity is developed dates from that time) but he has been working on them continuously and has therefore, in a sense, the right of way. However, a topic like the exchange rate may perhaps be seen as "commune bonum" or at least as "commune."[8] (Ohlin to Heckscher, May 15, 1921, author's translation)

Of course, Ohlin could have abandoned his "productivity" approach for other reasons on which it would be interesting to have more information. What the letter brings out nevertheless is how important real world developments were to Ohlin's thinking about the exchange rate.

Summary Perspectives on the Central Findings

From the thought-provoking information offered in Ohlin's and Heckscher's correspondence referred to in this chapter, two central findings have been established about Ohlin's early work.

The first concerns the content of the Eureka moment. The close-up view of the evolution of Ohlin's early thinking has presented a compelling case for a revisionist interpretation. There is no support for "the received view" that the Eureka was an embryonic anticipation of Ohlin's later inserting of Heckscher's theory of trade within a Casselian general equilibrium framing. Ohlin's letter from Grenoble in the spring of 1921 has shown convincingly that the Eureka in the spring of 1920 concerned the theory of exchange rate. Although the new view of the Eureka raises questions as to how the Eureka came about, these are matters that do not affect this new view, and attending to them would take us too far afield from the present account. Those questions are pursued at some length in Henriksson (2001).

The second central finding concerns what might be called the priority issue. The chapter accepts, in the main, the predominant view that the role of Ohlin as a contributor to Heckscher-Ohlin theory is a subordinate one. Heckscher is undeniably the lead performer in the Heckscher-Ohlin hiatus, since his seminal contribution of 1919 antedates Ohlin's writings by two years and his priority status is further reinforced by the fact that he had been Ohlin's teacher at the Stockholm School of Economics and remained a close mentor to him even after Ohlin's graduation in 1919 (Ohlin 1972:99).

Ohlin himself never opposed the received view of Heckscher's basic priority relating to the Heckscher-Ohlin theory, but already in his dissertation of 1924 he made a claim to have arrived at the Heckscher findings somewhat independently of Heckscher, and furthermore he considered his contribution partly as a criticism of the Heckscher results. By attempting to clarify some of the assumptions that limited the validity of Heckscher's theory, Ohlin expressed the need for a complementary approach, which together with the Heckscher-Ohlin conception would amount to a more general theory.

Already in his dissertation (Ohlin 1924), but with more emphasis in his later magnum opus (Ohlin 1933), Ohlin showed that such a more general theory of trade would also include the monetary dimension. This latter aspect of his contribution became more attended to after his Nobel award in 1977, but unfortunately, Ohlin himself delayed this recognition through the noted misleading formulations in his memoirs about the content of the Eureka. In recent years the understanding that Ohlin's monetary thinking actually antedated his work in trade theory has been further hampered by the discovery of Ohlin's licentiate thesis. This manuscript was retrieved for wider reading only after Ohlin's death in 1979, and it has no doubt contributed to the prevailing faulty understanding of the Eureka. When compared with the dissertation, the exclusive focus in the thesis on the central issues of the later Heckscher-Ohlin model has served to strengthen the view that Ohlin's attention to the monetary aspects of the theory of trade was a later development, with the period at Harvard from 1922 to 1923 seen as providing the crucial impetus.

The findings reported in this chapter suggest a contrary interpretation of the difference between the thesis and the dissertation. Ohlin's concern with exchange rate issues assumed in his dissertation a broader and empirical objective that cast the monetary net more widely to catch all facets of the balance of payment, in particular, capital movements. Admittedly Ohlin's studies at Harvard are important in imputing a monetary dimension to his earlier analysis in the thesis, but the inclination in this direction would have been "pre-set" through his earlier studies in Sweden. What he learned at Harvard no doubt enabled him to approach the theory of the exchange rate with a fresh view, but on the whole Ohlin had both his monetary theory and the exchange rate theory rather well worked out before arriving at Harvard. Thus the difference between the thesis and the dissertation cannot be attributed only to Ohlin's stay at

Harvard. Clearly, Ohlin's inclusion of a monetary and balance of payment analysis in the dissertation must fundamentally have drawn on his extensive research and writings on exchange rate theory and monetary dynamics in Sweden prior to his thesis work presented in 1922.[9]

Although an important finding in the chapter is that Ohlin's contribution to the Heckscher-Ohlin model should be assessed more generously, more important is the evidence of Ohlin's independent early work on the exchange rate problem. Even after his discovery of the work by J. S. Mill which made him turn to the deeper issues of pure trade theory, Ohlin seems not to have completely abandoned the exchange rate theme. While Ohlin no longer saw that theme as a feasible thesis topic, the exchange rate issue that he had followed up after the Eureka in Berlin was retained as possibly the ultimate "explanandum" not only for his thesis and dissertation work but also for his later work in trade theory. Ohlin's early attention to and penetration of the foreign exchange problem is itself a notable achievement that has so far been neglected in his analytical record. Yet the main significance of the discovery of Ohlin's early monetary thinking and writing is that here lies a key to better understanding of his later work.

To restate by way of conclusion, in contextualizing the Eureka moment, we are presented not only with the intentions behind Ohlin's subsequent thesis and dissertation, thereby a window on his alleged dependence on Heckscher. We can look afresh at his post-dissertation work. The result complements Flanders's (1989) and Flam's (1993) reappraisal of Ohlin's work in international economics. In a wider perspective this result might even encourage a reappraisal of Ohlin's stage-setting role for the so-called Stockholm School position in the Keynesian macroeconomic discourse as it appears that the divergent pieces of information on Ohlin's entire work have started to fall into place.

Notes

This chapter has benefited from comments by Dan Nyberg. It is a revised version of my presentation at the Ohlin centennial symposium. I am very grateful for comments on the original draft by my discussant Göte Hansson and for the views and reactions of the editors, Lars Jonung and Mats Lundahl. Discussions with Torsten Gårdlund, David Laidler, and other participants in the symposium have been very helpful as have also later discussions with Rikard Forslid on recent advances in trade theory. As the chapter reports on archival work conducted in the 1970s and early 1980s, I would like to acknowledge financial support from the Jacob Wallenberg Fund. I also acknowledge the assistance from Hans Tson Söderström in making important source material available. I owe a note of special gratitude to my late friend Staffan Högberg who helped me locate Heckscher's copy of Ohlin's licentiate thesis. The thesis has since then been translated into English by Christina Lönnblad with a preface by Harry Flam and is published in the present volume.

1. This section of Ohlin's memoirs has been translated into English in *The Stockholm School Remembered* edited by Lars Jonung (in preparation). "Unter den Linden" was the name of Berlin's parade street at the time. A linden tree is, more prosaically, a basswood or a lime tree.

2. In the recent discourse on the making of Ohlin's contributions to trade theory, such an interpretation has been advanced by Flam and Flanders (this volume, chapter 10)

3. One must here consider the time constraint imposed on Ohlin in preparing the dissertation. After he left Harvard in the summer of 1923 to spend the remainder of his studies abroad in the United Kingdom working on his dissertation, Ohlin was afflicted by an incapacitating eye illness. This delayed him in the final revising and polishing of the manuscript for several months, although he was able to meet the original deadline in order to qualify for a suddenly vacant chair in Copenhagen for which Heckscher urged him to apply. As reported in his memoirs, Ohlin completed his dissertation work in the record period of eight weeks (Ohlin 1972:93).

4. Ohlin was on leave from his military service and stayed at his parents' home in Klippan.

5. In this his first published theoretical paper, Ohlin deals with the theory of the exchange rate along classical as well as Marshallian lines. He explores the problem within a diagrammatic reciprocal demand model, which also incorporates freights and transport costs, emphasized by Wicksell (1919) in particular. This appears to be an original achievement as Ohlin gives no references to the possible sources of the diagrams in his exposition. His only point of discourse with the scientific frontier on the issue is a polemic against a contribution by Pigou (1920).

6. This is cited in the *New Palgraves* article on Offer Curves by Harvey Gram (1987).

7. One reason for Ohlin's failure to pursue any work on Mill's equation of international demand could be that Edgeworth (1894) failed to elevate Mill to the standing Chipman (1965) allots to him. Edgeworth traced the reciprocal demand analysis to Marshall's (1879) offer curve formalization of Mill. Quite likely, Ohlin had not read Edgeworth. Marshall's more widely circulated version of his offer curve analysis did not appear until 1923. Further Edgeworth's works did not become widely known in Sweden until after the publication of his collected works (Edgeworth 1924), which were noted by Wicksell (1925). In 1920 Ohlin seems to have had no easy access to the Mill theme in the literature.

8. Shortly before Silverstolpe had published a paper in *Ekonomisk Tidskrift* where, in elaborating on Ricardo's (1817) theory of foreign exchange rate, he especially dealt with the issues that had come into focus after the suspension of the gold standard (Silverstolpe 1920). In this paper Silverstolpe had stated his intentions to deal more profoundly with the effect of differential productivity developments in two countries on the exchange rate between them. However, these intentions were never followed up.

References

Cassel, G. 1918. *Theoretische Sozialökonomie*. Leipzig: Winter.

Chipman, J. S. 1965. A survey of the theory of international trade I. *Econometrica* 33:477–519.

Edgeworth, F. Y. 1894. The theory of international values. *Economic Journal* 4:35–50, 424–43, 606–38.

Edgeworth, F. Y. 1924. *Papers Relating to Political Economy*, 3 vols. London: Macmillan.

Flam, H., and J. Flanders, eds. 1991. *Heckscher-Ohlin Trade Theory, with a Foreword by Paul A. Samuelson*. Cambridge: MIT Press.

Flam, H. 1993. Bertil Ohlin's contribution's to international economics. In Lars Jonung, ed., *Swedish Economic Thought Explorations and Advances*. London: Routledge, pp. 143–55.

Flanders, M. June. 1989. *International Monetary Economics 1870–1960: Between the Classical and the New Classical*. Cambridge: Cambridge University Press.

Gram, H. 1987. Offer curves. In *New Palgraves*, vol. 3. London: Macmillan, pp. 694–96.

Heckscher, E. F. 1919. Utrikeshandelns verkan på inkomstfördelningen. *Ekonomisk Tidskrift* 21:497–512. Festschrift issue titled *Nationalekonomiska Studier tillägnade professor David Davidson*.

Heckscher, E. F. 1920. Utrikeshandelns verkan på inkomstfördelningen. This is a separate print of Heckscher E. F. (1919).

Heckscher, E. F. 1922. Letter to Per Jacobsson, July 7.

Henriksson, R. G. H. 2001. New findings concerning Ohlin's early contributions to the Heckscher-Ohlin theme. Mimeo.

Jonung, L. ed. (in preparation). *The Stockholm School Remembered*.

Marshall, A. 1923. *Money, Credit and Commerce. Reprints of Economic Classics* New York: Augustus M. Kelley, 1960.

Marshal, A. [1879] 1930. *The Pure Theory of Foreign Trade: The Pure Theory of Domestic Values* (Series of Reprints of Scarce Tracts in Economics and Political Science No. 1).

Mill, J. S. [1848] 1909. *Principles of Political Economy*. Edited with an introduction by W. J. Ashley. London: Longman's, Green.

Ohlin, B. 1919. Ett nationalekonomiskt standardverk. Review of Cassel's *Theoretische Socialökonomie. Svenska Dagbladet*, May 28.

Ohlin, B. 1921a. Växelkursernas jämviktsläge. *Ekonomisk Tidskrift* 23:29–37.

Ohlin, B. 1921b. Letter to Heckscher, May 13.

Ohlin, B. 1922a. Application letter to KVA, January 30.

Ohlin, B. 1922b. Det interregionala bytets teori. Licentiate thesis.

Ohlin, B. 1923. Letter to Heckscher, November 22–24.

Ohlin, B. 1924. *Handelns teori*. Stockholm: Centraltryckeriet.

Ohlin, B. 1933. *Interregional and International Trade* Cambridge: Harvard University Press.

Ohlin, B. 1972. *Bertil Ohlins memoarer, Ung man blir politiker*. Stockholm: Bonniers.

Ohlin, B. [1924] 1991. The theory of trade. In H. Flam and J. Flanders, *Heckscher-Ohlin Trade Theory* MIT Press Cambridge, Massachusetts, London, England pp. 75–214.

Pigou, A. C. 1920. Some problems of foreign exchange. *Economic Journal* 30:460–72.

Ricardo, D. [1817] 1819. *The Principles of Political Economy and Taxation*, 3rd ed. London: Dent and Dutton.

Silverstolpe, G. 1920. Ricardo och växelkursteorin. *Ekonomisk Tidskrift* 22:281–95.

Wicksell, K. 1919. Växelkursernas gåta. *Ekonomisk Tidskrift* 21:87–103.

Wicksell, K. 1925. Matematisk nationalekonomi. *Ekonomisk Tidskrift* 27:103–25.

9 The Theory of Interregional Exchange

Bertil Ohlin
translated by Christina Lönnblad

Preface by Harry Flam

About the beginning of his work on international economics, Bertil Ohlin wrote in his memoirs: "I started [in 1921] to write on the foundations of an approach to international trade theory that was to some extent new and for which I received the inspiration during a stroll on [the popular promenade] Unter den Linden in Berlin in 1920."

Ohlin became a world-famous economist on the strength of his monograph Interregional and International Trade, *published by Harvard University Press in 1933. But before that he wrote a dissertation for the degree of licentiate, finished in the spring of 1922, and a doctoral dissertation, published in 1924. Both were in Swedish.*

The doctoral dissertation, entitled The Theory of Trade, *was translated into English and published in 1991, together with a new and full translation of Eli Heckscher's pathbreaking article* The Effect of Foreign Trade on the Distribution of Income. *The volume containing Ohlin's dissertation and Heckscher's article is called* Heckscher-Ohlin Trade Theory *and was translated, edited and introduced by M. June Flanders and myself.*

The turn has now come to Ohlin's licentiate thesis. This work, the earliest by Ohlin on trade theory, deserves to be known to an English-speaking audience. It contains Ohlin's short version of the Heckscher-Ohlin model, together with extensions and modifications that were to be dealt with more extensively in the doctoral dissertation, and even more in the monograph. The translation was made by Christina Lönnblad. She has been faithful to Ohlin's somewhat involved style of writing.

Introduction

In most presentations of economic theory, the theory of international exchange, with its classical origins, stands out uniquely from the general theory of price formation, whose origins are very different. This is quite natural because the former is based on the assumption that the values of goods are proportional to the quantity of labor used—an assumption that has been completely abandoned in the general theory of price formation in order to treat all factors of production equally.

This dualism constitutes an obstacle to constructing a consistent economic system. International exchange should not hold a unique position in such a system; it should be treated as a special case of general exchange, although certainly distinctive in some respects. It thus seems natural to build a general theory of exchange between different regions, based on the general principles of price formation. This theory will thus be valid for regions of any size; that is, for individuals as well as for regions and countries. The theory of international trade will then be a complementary study of exchange between a particular type of regions, that is, countries.

The present thesis is an attempt to solve the first part of the problem, that is, to present the general theory of interregional exchange. It is presented as a direct extension of the general theory of price formation, in accordance with the views above. The study of the latter part of the problem—that is, investigating the exchange between certain specific regions, above all, but not only, countries—has not even been carried out tentatively, and furthermore it would require more space than has been considered appropriate in the present thesis.

I The Problem

The general theory of price formation shows how the prices of goods and factors of production are determined to create a balance between supply and demand. The factors of production are directed toward the production of the goods that, with the given income distribution, give the maximum satisfaction of wants.[1] In this theory, where the fundamental nature of the causality is explained, goods as well as factors of production are assumed to be perfectly mobile. The question of the location of production is certainly of secondary importance and will thus not be dealt with here.

Under this assumption the theory of exchange is relatively simple. An individual endowed with certain factors of production carries out the tasks for which he is best suited, that is, for which he receives the highest compensation, and exchanges them for the other tasks he requires with other individuals. The increase in productivity due to division of labor is allocated among the different individuals and constitutes the gains from division of labor and exchange.

As mentioned, price formation directs all factors of production to the utilization where they will command the highest price. It is thus obvious that one factor of production will command a higher price than another. Furthermore there is nothing strange about the fact that although factor A would obtain a higher price in a certain employment than factor B, factor B is still the factor used. This is due to the fact that A commands an even higher price in another employment.

If the limited mobility of goods and factors of production is included in the argument, the question of interregional exchange arises, besides this purely individual exchange. The location of production is then no longer arbitrary and without effect on productivity, but is dependent on the local distribution of factors of production as well as the mobility and divisibility of these and the goods.[2] Since natural resources are immobile and other factors of production can only be moved from one place to another relatively slowly, the supply of factors of production remains different in different areas. Furthermore, due to the limited divisibility of factors of production, the scale of production becomes an important factor in determining the production costs. The producing unit with the lowest costs requires production at a large scale and distribution of the products over a corresponding area. For these two reasons, division of labor will take place between different areas, since different industries are concentrated in different areas. The costs of transporting the goods tend to counteract this division of labor and, thus, also the ensuing exchange, but they cannot completely prevent it. Nevertheless, they do affect the division of labor and the terms of trade.

What are thus the effects of exchange between local units, that is, regions, resulting from the above-mentioned factors?

Exchange between individuals is either physical or legal. Individual exchange is the only kind of exchange. Individuals can, however, be grouped in many different ways, which makes it possible to study their exchange both with individuals *within* the same group and individuals from other groups. If the study is limited to the latter case, the different individuals in each group can be put in the background, and each group can then be considered a complete unit in itself. Exchange between the groups will then take place.

Such groupings can be made in different ways. Within the theory of distribution, for example, three groups are formed, workers, landowners, and capitalists, and the rules for the conditions for exchange among labor, land, and capital are studied.

For these reasons a local division and a study of the conditions for exchange among these locally limited groups, regions, are of particular interest. This can be done in different ways, however. Since the main aim is to modify the theory of price formation in general, due to the immobility of different factors, it seems desirable to make this study as general as possible and not limit it to certain types of regions. When the importance of the nature and effects of the factors studied has been established in the various cases, the general theory of interregional exchange is slightly adapted to the situation in each particular case.

The main reason for dividing a country into different regions is the uneven distribution of the factors of production. Certain factors of production are more abundant in one part of the country, others in another. The fact that this immobility remains is, in turn, due to the limited mobility of the factors of production. This immobility varies a great deal between different factors; from perfect immobility to almost perfect mobility. In general, however, limited mobility is sufficient for differences to remain unchanged, if the periods considered are not too long, although the mobility will vary with the selection of regions. For the basic treatment of price formation and exchange of goods, it is most convenient to begin by assuming that the factors of production cannot move from one region to another, that is, by assuming perfect interregional immobility[3] and then, if an adjustment seems necessary, adjust the results with regard to the effects of the more or less high degree of interregional mobility, which might exist in one case or the other.

Studying price formation and exchange in a country with such regions will thus, as indicated, be equal to determining the *causes* for locating production in one region or the other and the *effects* of this choice. When the limited mobility and divisibility of factors of production, on the one hand, and the limited mobility[4] of goods, on the other, are the final determining factors for location, as will be illustrated later, the pure theory of price formation is modified with regard to the effects of limited mobility and divisibility.

This modification will probably be gradual, and for this reason the assumption that the goods and the factors of production are perfectly mobile is, at first, maintained. When the effects of the interregional immobility of the factors of production have been studied under this assumption, and the results have been modified with regard to the mobility of certain factors of production, the obstacles to the mobility of the goods are given due consideration. Finally the impact of the limited divisibility of the factors of production on the price formation mechanism, that is, the increasing and decreasing returns, is studied.

II The Theory of Interregional Exchange under Simplified Assumptions

A. Conditions for Interregional Exchange of Goods

According to the outline presented in the previous chapter, the aim is now to study the price formation mechanism in an isolated area consisting of regions between which the factors of production are immobile. There are two different ways in which to proceed. One is to begin with price formation in an area with perfect mobility and analyze the changes caused by the fact that factors of production cannot be transferred from one region to another. The other is to begin with two isolated areas with perfect mobility within each area and analyze the consequences of contacts between these areas when goods, but not factors of production, can move freely from one area to the other. In both cases the pure theory of price formation is assumed and the desired modification of this theory is achieved. The latter method is preferable, however, for a detailed study of the exchange of goods and its preconditions and effects. Under certain circumstances it is the starting point of the exchange of goods that causes certain changes, and for this reason the study *immediately* supplies the desired information.

Two isolated areas, between which autarky is removed for some reason, constitute the starting point of the following analysis. These two areas are assumed to have their own independent monetary systems.[5]

When a connection has been established, there exists a certain exchange rate between the two currencies.

This exchange rate must be such that if exchange of goods takes place, the imports of each region must exactly equal its exports. If the imports of either of the regions exceed its exports, the former can then not be entirely covered by the claims of the latter; the demand for "foreign" currency thus exceeds the supply and the value of the foreign currency increases. Exports are thus stimulated and imports are discouraged, until there is a balance in the exchange of goods. When this balance and a fixed exchange rate between the currencies have been established, all prices of goods in both areas will be equal.[6] The types of goods that would have commanded a higher price if produced "domestically" are imported while, once more, the types of goods that would have commanded a higher price if produced in the other region are exported to that region.

Exchange of goods can only take place due to such a difference in prices. When this difference has been removed through exchange, no *new* exchange will occur, while the ongoing exchange still continues to the extent required for price equalization.

At the moment before the connection is established, there is no question of a difference in *absolute* prices of goods, since each region has its own monetary unit with no exchange rate for the monetary unit in the other region. The condition for exchange of goods to occur will then be a difference in the *relative* prices of goods. This is not only a *necessary*, but also a *sufficient*, condition. If the relative prices are different, all prices of goods will be lower in region A than in region B or all prices lower in region B than in A or some prices lower in A and some in B, notwithstanding the exchange rate that was at first assumed between the currencies. In the first case, the goods will flow from A to B, without B being able to pay for them by exports to A. In other words, there will be a demand for A's currency in B, in order to import goods from A. In A, there is no demand for B's goods, however, and accordingly there will be no supply of A's currency. Under these circumstances the value of A's currency must increase in relation to B's currency. Thus all prices of goods from A will increase, *expressed in B's currency*, and the prices of goods from B will decrease, *expressed in A's currency*. It will thus be profitable to import certain goods from B to A, since only some goods, and not all as in the previous examples, can be imported from A to B. Equilibrium occurs when the exchange rate between the two currencies has reached the point where imports and exports are equal.

The effects would be analogous if all prices of goods were lower in B than in A. In the third case, when some prices are lower in A and some in B, imports as well as exports will occur, according to the exchange rate established at the starting point. If A's imports exceed its exports, the demand for B's currency will exceed the supply and its price will increase. The same applies if B's imports exceed its exports. Equilibrium will occur only when an exchange rate has been established, thereby establishing an equilibrium between imports and exports.

A difference in relative prices thus necessarily entails a difference in absolute prices, so that some prices will be lower in A and some in B, and exchange of goods will take place.

Using the term production costs instead of prices—which equal the costs, since these cover remuneration to all factors of production—this can be expressed as follows: the effects of a difference in comparative costs are that some goods can be produced at a lower cost in one region than in the other, while the opposite applies to other goods. Thus exchange will occur, and each region can concentrate its production on the goods it can produce at the lowest cost.

It now remains to be shown that exchange of goods cannot occur if comparative costs and prices in both isolated regions are equal. Whatever exchange rate is assumed between the two independent currencies, *all* costs and prices of goods must be lower in A than in B or lower in B than in A, or equal in A and B. In the former case, the value of the currency in A increases in relation to the currency in B; in the latter case, the currency in B increases in relation to the currency in A. The exchange rate reaches the point where all costs and prices of goods in A equal all prices of goods in B, without exchange of goods having occurred. According to the assumption of equality of comparative costs, some costs cannot be lower in A and some in B. *Different comparative costs thus constitute the necessary and sufficient condition*[7] *for interregional exchange.*

It then follows that one region cannot be competitively superior to another in the production of *all* goods. A difference in comparative costs creates an exchange rate between the monetary units in the two regions, which makes the costs for some goods higher in one region and for others in the other region. A completely different issue is that using other terms of costs as a yardstick, for example, the amount of labor used,[8] might yield the result that a country is superior in all kinds of production but that exchange of goods is still profitable. The paradox of this reasoning is removed if one considers that the yardstick of exchange is not the quantity of labor put into a good but rather the price of the good expressed in terms of money, where the price expressed in the currency of one country is converted into the currency of the other country according to the exchange rate.

Take, for example, Ricardo's classical example: Portugal can produce one unit of wine in 80 working days and one unit of cloth in 90 working days. The corresponding figures for England are 120 and 100. Portugal can thus produce both types of goods "at a lower cost" than England. Nevertheless, Ricardo shows that the production of wine in Portugal and of cloth in England will increase total production and thus be profitable.

Note that if Portugal can produce these types of goods with less labor than England, this is either due to the fact that labor in Portugal is of superior quality or that there is a relatively more abundant supply of other factors of production, for example, a favorable climate and fertile land, which can partly substitute for labor. In both cases the marginal productivity of labor can be considered as higher in Portugal, which means that wages are higher in Portugal,[9] since Ricardo does not consider compensation to other factors of production or considers it to be proportional to compensation to labor. The number of working days is thus not a way of expressing production costs, and accordingly not a way of expressing competitiveness either. The main point is thus that the higher wage level in Portugal makes it more expensive to produce cloth there than in England.

There must thus be a difference in relative costs and prices of goods, *expressed in terms of money*, for exchange to occur. This might also occur if the relative costs, estimated on basis of quantity of labor, are equal. Assume, for example, that two types of goods require an equal amount of labor, but that the one good requires much capital and little land, while the other requires little capital and much land. If capital rent is low in region A and high in B, while the opposite applies to land rent, the costs will be lower in A for the first and lower in B for the second good, and exchange of goods will occur.

This leads to the question of the reason for the differences in comparative costs and prices of goods, an issue hardly dealt with in most studies.[10]

The costs of producing a good depend both on the quantities required of the different types of factors of production and their prices. What is, then, the meaning of a difference in relative costs, with regard to these two factors?

The answer to this question is probably most easily found by a mathematical formulation. The quantities of different factors of production required for producing a good are denoted by a_{ij} in region A and α_{ij} in region B. The prices of the factors of production are denoted by q_1 and g_i, and the prices of the goods by p_i and v_i, respectively.[11] The following equations then show that the price of each good in each country equals the production cost of this type of good:*

A	B
$a_{11}q_1 + a_{12}q_2 + \cdots + a_{1r}q_r = p_i;$	$a_{11}g_1 + \alpha_{12}g_2 + \cdots + \alpha_{1r}g_r = v_1;$
$a_{21}q_1 + a_{22}q_2 + \cdots + a_{2r}q_r = p_2;$	$\alpha_{21}g_1 + \alpha_{22}g_2 + \cdots + \alpha_{2r}g_r = v_2;$
$\ldots\ldots\ldots\ldots\ldots\ldots$	$\ldots\ldots\ldots\ldots\ldots\ldots$
$a_{n1}q_1 + a_{n2}q_2 + \cdots + a_{nr}q_r = p_n;$	$\alpha_{n1}g_1 + \alpha_{n2}g_2 + \cdots + \alpha_{nr}g_r = v_n.$

(1)

If autarky is removed, exchange will occur, provided that the relative prices of the goods are not equal, that is, provided that the following condition does not hold:

$$p_1 : p_2 : \ldots : p_n = v_1 : v_2 : \ldots : v_n. \tag{2}$$

This will be the case, however, and exchange can thus not occur, if

$$q_1 : q_2 : \ldots : q_r = g_1 : g_2 : \ldots : g_r; \tag{3}$$

that is, if the relative prices of the factors of production are equal, for if condition (3) is fulfilled, $a_{ij} = \alpha_{ij}$ $(i = 1, 2, \ldots, n;\ j = 1, 2, \ldots, r)$ holds. The different a and α, that is, the technical coefficients, give the possible proportions in combinations of the factors of production; they are thus both dependent on certain technical conditions and the relative prices of the factors of production. If the latter are equal in two regions, the technical coefficients must be equal, since the technical conditions, which are related to the technical characteristics of the goods and the factors of production, are equal everywhere.[12]

Condition (3) can also be written

$$q_1 = lg_1;\ q_2 = lg_2; \ldots;\ q_r = lg_r, \tag{4}$$

*Translator's note: Notation is as in the original, including subscripts.

where *1* is an arbitrarily positive quantity. When $a_{ij} = \alpha_{ij}$,

$$p_1 = lv_1;\ p_2 = lv_2; \ldots;\ p_n = lv_n. \tag{5}$$

Since (5) is the same condition as (2), it appears that equality between the relative prices of the factors of production means equality between the relative prices of the goods, and thus no exchange will occur.

When a connection has been established between the two regions, the absolute prices of goods must be equal. The exchange rate will thus be l.

Condition (2), that the relative prices of the goods should be equal, can be fulfilled in another way than by (3), that is, if the following conditions are satisfied:

$$\begin{aligned}
&a_{11} : a_{12} : \ldots : a_{1r} = \\
&= a_{21} : a_{22} : \ldots : a_{2r} = \\
&= \ldots\ldots\ldots\ldots\ldots\ldots = \\
&= a_{n1} : a_{n2} : \ldots : a_{nr} = \\
&= \alpha_{11} : \alpha_{12} : \ldots : \alpha_{1r} = \\
&= \alpha_{21} : \alpha_{22} : \ldots : \alpha_{2r} = \\
&= \ldots\ldots\ldots\ldots\ldots\ldots = \\
&= \alpha_{n1} : \alpha_{n2} : \ldots : \alpha_{nr}.
\end{aligned} \tag{6}$$

If all types of goods contain the same proportions of all factors of production in *both* regions, exchange cannot take place, since the relative prices will then be equal.

It turns out, however, that (6) is not a new condition for failure of exchange to take place; it cannot be satisfied unless (3) is fulfilled. If the relative prices of the factors of production in both regions are different, they cannot possibly be combined in the same way in production in both regions. The factors of production that are relatively scarce in A will thus be used sparingly in A and be replaced by the less scarce ones to the largest possible extent. The opposite applies to B. Such possibilities for substitution might always exist, although to different extents. Only if the relative prices of the factors of production are equal in both regions can (6) be fulfilled. But then this condition will not be necessary. As shown above, the relative prices of the goods will then be equal, notwithstanding the proportions of the different factors of production in different types of goods.

There are, however, several ways of fulfilling (2). The different a and q, α and g, can of course take on such values that (2) is fulfilled "by accident," without their assuming any *regular* relationship with each other.

Condition (3), that is, that the relative prices of the factors of production should be equal in both regions, is therefore a *sufficient but not a necessary condition* for equalization between the relative costs and thus also for the nonoccurrence of exchange.[13] Reversed, we get the following phrase: *a difference in the relative prices of the factors of production constitute a necessary, but not a sufficient, condition for interregional exchange.*

In accordance with the classical procedure, two isolated regions have so far constituted the starting point. Being isolated, each region must be assumed to have its own individual monetary unit. It is clear, however, that the result will basically be the same if two regions with a common monetary system, for example, two parts of the same country, are considered. Under what circumstances might exchange of goods between two such regions not occur? Only if the *absolute* prices of goods are equal without exchange, that is, if the production costs for all goods are equal in both regions. If exchange of goods takes place, however, this shows[14] that the costs are lower in one region or the other, as would have been the price of the goods had no exchange occurred. The case where a difference in absolute costs also means a difference in relative costs only differs from the case just studied in that a difference in relative costs due to the common monetary unit is *directly* expressed by some costs being lower in A and others in B, while in the previous case this difference is only expressed by the exchange rate. There is thus only a formal difference in the conditions for exchange of goods, which means that the previous wording of the condition for interregional exchange, that is, different comparative costs, also applies to this case, and the *meaning of this condition* remains unchanged.

B. The Mechanisms and Effects of Interregional Exchange of Goods

If the above holds, this means that the difference in the relative scarcity of factors of production is the cause[15] of the difference in comparative costs and thereby of interregional exchange, although the comparative costs might remain the same, even when differences of the first kind exist. In practice, it might reasonably be assumed that the relative scarcity of factors of production leads to differences in comparative costs and thus to exchange of goods. In practice, the relative prices of the factors of production are consequently not only a necessary but also a *sufficient* condition for interregional exchange.[16]

As has already been shown, the principle of this exchange is that each region produces and exports the goods it can produce at a lower cost than others, and imports the other goods. The costs of production, and thus the *absolute* prices, will be decisive. Under the influence of the forces creating an equilibrium in trade, prices are controlled in such a way that exports will take place and cover the costs of imports, as has been shown in the previous section.

The reason why the production costs for certain goods are lower in one region than in another is part of the above-mentioned condition for interregional exchange, that is, the difference in the relative scarcity of factors of production. Since there is a relatively good supply of certain factors of production in A and their prices thus are low, the goods requiring a relatively large share of these factors of production can be produced at a low cost in that region compared to the types of goods requiring a relatively larger share of the more scarce factors of production. In B, where the former factors of production are more scarce and the latter less scarce than in A, the relation between the costs of different goods will be completely different. A will produce the goods for which it has a relatively large supply of suitable factors of production, and so will B.

A sparsely populated region, with much fertile land and a favorable climate, will export agricultural products and import industrial products from a region with a relatively rich supply of capital and technical skills.

Exports will then mainly consist of goods where the abundant factors of production are used in large quantities and the other factors in small quantities only, while imports consist of the types of goods requiring large quantities of the latter factors of production and factors of production not available in the region at all. The exchange of goods is thus an exchange of factors of production, in the sense that goods "containing" the relatively scarce factors of production are imported and goods "containing" less scarce factors of production are exported. It might be said that less scarce factors of production are exchanged for more scarce ones. The result is thus that the scarcity of factors of production is generally equalized.

The factors of production are assumed to be immobile between regions, and no transmission and direct equalization of the scarcity can thus occur. The mobility of the goods will thus, to a certain extent, replace the mobility of the factors of production, since exchange of goods leads to an equalization of the scarcity of factors of production, from the point of view of all traders.

There is thus a tendency that all regions get exactly the relative scarcity that would have existed, had there been no obstacle to the mobility of factors of production. *In other words, interregional exchange tends to create a uniform price structure of the factors of production.*

As shown above, different relative prices of factors of production are a necessary condition for different relative prices of goods before autarky is eliminated, and thus also for interregional exchange. Since exchange of goods tends to equalize these differences, it also tends to remove its own reason of existence. It must not be assumed, however, that exchange of goods goes on for a period of time, until equalization occurs, and then ceases altogether. The previous difference in the relative scarcity of factors of production would then almost immediately recur. The result is instead that exchange of goods will take place to the extent required for equalizing the relative scarcity of factors of production, and then *remain the same.* No *new* exchange of goods will occur after the equalization—since there are no conditions for such an exchange—but the existing exchange will persist.

If goods as well as factors of production were perfectly mobile, the entire world would constitute an economic unit in the real sense of the word, and the total supply of different factors of production would determine their relative scarcity. As mentioned, a free exchange of goods tends to give the same result, and might indeed do so, under certain conditions. What are these conditions, or conversely, what generally prevents this tendency from being fully realized?

It is difficult to find a general answer to this question. On the most profound level there is probably a certain disproportion in the distribution of the factors of production and their use in production, and thus the same results cannot be obtained as if the factors of production were mobile, notwithstanding the location of production.

The exchange of goods can only create a situation where one type of good will be produced here and another there, that is, that each good is produced in that or those places where the most favorable of the existent combinations of factors of production is to be found. Had the factors of production been mobile, however, an even more favorable combination could have been created in many cases, due consideration given to the worldwide scarcity of these factors of production. Because of the exchange of goods, the utilization of the factors of production that would have occurred at perfect mobility is not achieved.[17] A certain factor of production will be more scarce in one region, and less scarce in another.

Assume that the production of a good, such as wine, requires land[18] of a certain quality as well as a certain labor skill. A region fulfilling the condition of labor skill might only have a limited supply of land of the desired quality, while another region, lacking suitable labor, has an abundant supply of such land. The entire world demand for that good must then be produced in the first region. This might only be possible through an intensive, capital and labor squandering, cultivation of land. Land will be extremely scarce and will command a high land rent, while land in the other region will be of insignificant or zero economic value, depending on how it can be used for other purposes.[19]

If labor had been mobile, all land of the desired quality would have been used, and thus capital and labor would have been saved and land rent would have been equalized in both regions.

When the supply of the different factors of production is such that all factors of production would not be fully utilized if prices were uniform, notwithstanding how production is distributed between different regions, there will be a necessary shift in prices. The prices of the factors of production, which would, to a certain extent, have been unemployed in A, will fall and thus will be utilized to a greater extent, while the prices of other factors of production, which would have been unemployed in B, will fall in B. The relative prices in A and B will thus differ.[20] This phenomenon of disproportion counteracts, but cannot entirely remove, the tendency of the exchange of goods to equalize the relative scarcity of factors of production, that is, to create uniform prices of the factors of production, unaffected by local distribution. This tendency results from the economy's "tendency toward maximum satisfaction." Free competition within an isolated region tends to produce the production patterns and the consumption best suited to the nature and intensity of the wants, by leading to uniform prices of factors of production and goods, and it also tends to have the same effect in a number of regions mutually exchanging goods. In the latter case this tendency is counteracted by the above-mentioned phenomenon of disproportion, however. The smaller its effect, that is, the more uniform are prices, the more complete is the adaptation to wants and the larger is the extent to which the tendency to maximum fulfillment of wants is realized. Accordingly, the profits of the traders are determined by the extent to which a free exchange of goods can create an equilibrium among prices of goods in different regions and the extent to which it can reduce, if not entirely remove, the differences in the prices of factors of production.

The difference in the relative scarcity of factors of production in different regions creates an uneconomic production pattern. In a certain region, a certain factor of production should be used very sparingly, and everything be done to replace it with other factors of production, which are less scarce in that region. In another region, the latter factors might be relatively scarce and can only be utilized very sparingly. Certain factors might be abundant in one region and thus be utilized as such, while the other region might lack these very factors, and the other way round.

If there is a rich supply of labor in one region, A, and its price is thus relatively low, and land rent is relatively high, while there is a surplus of land and land rent is thus low and wages high in another region, B, the marginal productivity of labor must be relatively low in A but high in B, while the opposite applies to the marginal productivity of land. Wages and land rent thus equal the marginal productivity of labor and land. If part of the labor could be transferred from A to B, the production in the former region would obviously be subject to a relatively small decrease in relation to the increase in the latter. The result would be high marginal productivity instead of low. Wages would increase in A and decrease in B, thus tending toward the same level, and land rent would fall in A and increase in B, and thus also tend toward the same level in both regions. An equalization of the relative prices of land and labor would then result. As long as this equalization is not complete, there might still be a profit, but with complete equalization, it will have reached its maximum; that is, production will have been adjusted to wants, as far as is possible with an uneven distribution of income.

If the factors of production are immobile, and labor can thus not be transferred from A to B, the result will still be the same, provided that the requisite equalization of the relative prices of factors of production can be obtained by exchange of goods. This is the case, at least to a certain extent, since exchange of goods means an exchange of less scarce factors of production for more scarce ones, in both regions. The result will thus be the same in both cases: since the relative prices of the factors of production have been equalized in both regions and have reached the position determined by world supply and world demand, their combination will be the same as it would have been, had the factors of production been mobile. The only difference is that in the latter case it would have been equally advantageous to produce any type of goods anywhere, while the location of production is now determined by the location of the factors of production.

The more uniform is the price structure of the factors of production, the higher is the extent to which "the tendency toward maximum satisfaction" is realized through international trade.

Under these circumstances the profits from international trade cannot be exactly estimated. The value of the total production in each country before and after the exchange of goods has been established could, of course, be statistically determined and the figures obtained reduced according to the change in the value of the currency, as expressed in price index calculations. Changes in production and consumption due to changes in the relative prices of goods, and possibly the supply of entirely new goods, make the inherent logical weakness, or insustainability, of the calculations of the price index particularly obvious in this case. It is thus likely that such estimates would not be a good illustration of the actual profit.

There is even less likelihood of obtaining the desired result by using a central concept of classical theory, that is, terms of trade, thereby meaning the terms of trade between domestic and foreign goods, which is further illustrated by Bastable's example.[21] One unit of "productive power" in country A can produce 10 units of good x or 20 units of good y, while one unit in B can produce $10x$ or $15y$. According to the law of comparative costs, A will only produce good y and B good x. What are then the terms of trade between x and y? These will be somewhere between $10x = 15y$ and $10x = 20y$, that is, the limits given by the comparative costs: to be precise, at the point where A's demand for x exactly equals B's demand for y and the balance of trade is in equilibrium. Specialization increases total production from $20x + 30y$ to $20x + 35y$ and the profit is thus $5y$.

There is a major weakness in this reasoning about terms of trade, however. It is not suitable if, as required, the fact that exports as well as imports consist of a large number of different types of goods is taken into account. In analogy to price indexes, one might, of course, create quantity indexes and then obtain a figure for the quantity of exports and another for the quantity of imports. A comparison between these figures would thus show the terms of trade in interregional trade, which must be considered separately from the terms of trade which would have existed without trade. The same difficulties as when constructing a price index would then appear, however: prices as well as quantities of goods would have changed, and entirely new types of goods might also have been included. But there is also another difficulty, which should be mentioned already at this stage, that is, that not all types of goods will be subject to interregional trade when the assumption of the absence of transport costs and other such costs is removed. The effect of interregional trade on their production and on price formation will then not affect the terms of trade. Under these circumstances this condition does not seem at all suitable for shedding light on the question of the size of profits. The general reasoning about uniform prices and "the tendency toward maximum satisfaction" will have to suffice.

If the size of profits cannot be estimated, it is obviously just as impossible to determine how the profits are to be divided between traders. It is as impossible to determine the proportions in one case as in the other. It is, however, worth studying in what *direction*, advantageous or disadvantageous, changes in the conditions for trade affect different regions. The study of these questions should be postponed, however, and be made in a more general context, investigating the effects in different cases, once the simplifying assumptions regarding the mobility of factors of production, transport costs, and other such factors, have been removed. All problems, for whose solution abstracting conditions are not absolutely necessary, should be studied under conditions as close to reality as possible, in all respects.

In summary, this part of the study concerning the conditions, mechanisms, and effects of interregional exchange gives the following results:

Conditions: It can be derived from the law of comparative costs that the relative prices of the factors of production being different in both regions is a necessary, and in practice, also a sufficient, condition for interregional exchange.

Mechanisms and effects: Interregional exchange tends to equalize the relative scarcity of factors of production, that is, achieve a uniform price structure of the factors of production. Thus it tends to remove its own reason of existence. This tendency is usually not fully realized, however, since these factors are disproportionate. When the tendency has been realized, to the extent permitted by the obstacles, trade remains unchanged but no *new* trade occurs.

The tendency toward a uniform price structure means a tendency toward maximum satisfaction of preferences.

A general comparison between the price formation mechanism in two isolated regions and two regions exchanging goods will probably give a more general picture of the causality of interregional exchange. Due to the exchange, these two mechanisms become one only, where each factor is connected to all other factors in both regions. Any kind of change in the economy of one region can thus affect its exchange with the other region. Due to the mutual interdependence between all factors, the effects will spread to all parts of the price formation mechanism. Keeping this context in mind is important for studying several of the theories of international trade, for example, when assessing the attempts to give the goods that are actually part of the exchange a unique position in determining the equilibrium for foreign trade and the exchange rates.

This mutual interdependence, and the effects of exchange of goods on the price formation mechanism in two regions previously isolated from each other, can be most simply and most easily illustrated by equations.[22]

So far the reasoning has been based on the assumption that there can exist two regions only. It is, however, clear that the conditions for interregional exchange as well as its mechanisms and effects will remain exactly the same if an arbitrary number of regions are considered. No recapitulation of the reasoning should be required under this assumption. It should only be noted that if the factors of production in two isolated regions, A and B, command the same relative prices, while their prices differ in region C, exchange will take place between A and C and B and C when a connection has been established. Thus the scarcity of factors of production in both A and B is subject to a change, as shown above. It might thus be the case that the change in A differs from the one in B, that the relative prices of the factors of production in A and B will differ, and that exchange between these will also occur.

Another simplifying assumption, made above, is that the factors of production are completely mobile within each region. Naturally this is an abstraction. Land and natural objects are immobile and other factors of production are not even perfectly mobile within fairly small regions. The location of production *within* regions is thus a problem of the same kind as the distribution between regions. This is natural as the division into regions is entirely random, and the present problem concerns the general location of production and exchange. The abstraction makes the essential feature of exchange seem far more simple than would otherwise have been possible. Furthermore it is not difficult to abandon the arbitrary division into regions after having studied the limited mobility of goods and the limited divisibility of factors of production, and give a general picture of the location of production and exchange without abstract assumptions. This abstraction entails another advantage, however, besides serving as a bridge to presenting reality in its entire complex context. When the general results reached by the study of interregional exchange can be applied to trade among specific regions, above all, countries, the location of production within the country is of secondary importance. The distribution of production among countries and the exchange among these will then be the most interesting question. Thus the assumption of perfect mobility within the country is the most rewarding one, since it best illustrates the main questions.

For these reasons the assumption of perfect mobility of factors of production *within* regions is maintained for the time being. Only when it is time to present a general picture of the location of production and exchange, as it appears at the final stage of the general theory of interregional exchange, will this assumption be removed.

The third simplified assumption made above is the interregional immobility of the factors of production. For several of these factors, such as labor and capital, this immobility is far from perfect, however. It must therefore be shown to what extent the interregional mobility of factors of production affects the results obtained under the assumption of immobility.

III Modifications due to the Interregional Mobility of Factors of Production

To investigate the general causality, it is convenient to start by considering a small or large number of variable factors as constant. On this basis, one would create an equilibrium and investigate the effects of variations in these factors on the nature of causality and then *modify* the earlier presentation with due consideration to these variations. The presentation can then be completed with an illustration of the *shift*[23] in this modified system through changes in the determining factors.

This method which is, for example, used to a great extent within mechanics and astronomy was used in economics when constructing the general theory of price formation. It is, however, quite common not to proceed further than the first part of the study and be satisfied with a static theory. The same method has been used in this study. The assumption of the interregional immobility of factors of production does mean that the supply of factors of production is assumed to be constant. The extent to which the nature of the causality is subject to change when certain factors of production are actually transferred from one region to another then remains to be studied. The third step, that is, illustrating the shift in the entire system, will only be taken at a later stage.

Consider two regions where the relative scarcity of factors of production would be very different if there were no exchange of goods. This difference is reduced by the exchange of goods but cannot be entirely removed. If the factors of production are partly mobile and drawn to the location where they will get the highest compensation, some of the relatively abundant factors in A will eventually move to B, and the other way round. Thus there is a certain tendency to equalize the relative scarcity. A region with a high interest rate and low wages exports labor to and imports capital from a region with a low interest rate and high wages. There is thus, eventually, a change in the conditions for interregional exchange, its extent, and the entire price formation mechanism. Above, this change was called the shift in the system.

A completely different question is whether the ongoing exchange at a certain point in time will be different than it would have been with interregionally immobile factors of production. In other words, will their mobility affect the nature of causality? Will production and exchange at a certain point in time be affected by the fact that a certain inflow and outflow of factors of production are possible?

The reply to this question naturally depends on whether people consider present or potential changes in the relative scarcity of factors of production in their economic behavior. If the mobility of labor is first considered—land and natural resources are, of course, perfectly immobile—it will probably be found that it has a very small effect on interregional exchange. When determining the sales price of his goods, a producer considers the prices of the different factors of production, including labor, as they are at present, and hardly considers future changes in wages, in relation to the prices of other factors of production, which might be incurred by ongoing immigration. Ongoing immigration has no considerable effect on production and price formation, at present, although it causes a gradual and, in the long run, perhaps considerable shift. The nature of the causality will thus, to a large extent, be the same as explained under the assumption of immobile factors of production. The *current*, and not the future, distribution of labor constitutes part of the determinants of prices.

The above applies to labor in general, without considering its various qualities. The impact of mobility becomes more considerable if the large differences in the qualifications of labor are considered. A country with an abundant supply of unqualified labor can have a scarcity of more qualified kinds of labor, that is, people with technical and organizational skills. Even a relatively small immigration of such individuals can have considerable effects on the structure of the economy. Numerous examples can be found in certain parts of Africa where the colored population dominates in numbers but would be unable to run its present industries without its white leaders.

Thus the mobility of labor is often of major importance for the economy of a country, mainly due to the possibility of obtaining certain absent qualities. The conclusion to the above reasoning on the effects of the general mobility of labor remains more or less the same. There is a shift in the equilibrium, but hardly a more considerable change in the nature of causality. The imports of a country depend on the extent to which the demand for goods is actually satisfied by domestic production and not on the prospects of one type of good or another being produced if the missing labor were imported. It might, of course, be assumed that importers would decrease their stocks if they knew that a factory to be run by foreign engineers and foremen was under construction. A decrease in their demand might then tend to reduce the price abroad, which means that prices will be affected not only by the current but also by the future distribution of labor. In general, such effects should be quite insignificant. Only after a certain period of time will the immigration of labor have a more considerable effect on production. It is probably very rare to discount the effects of immigration *before* immigration has taken place. Price formation is mainly determined by the actual supply of labor, and not by expected changes.

It might thus be assumed that labor mobility does create a gradual shift in the entire equilibrium but no considerable change in the nature of causality, which, on the contrary, is more or less as illustrated under the assumption of interregional immobility.* In a way, the same is true of capital. On the one hand, this is due to the fact that capital rent is often approximately the same in all parts of a region with a common monetary and banking system, and for this reason, no major transfer from one part to another occurs. On the other hand, the obstacles to the mobility of capital between different countries are so high that the transfer of capital cannot considerably affect the capital resources of a country in the short run, despite the different interest rate levels. There is thus a gradual shift in the equilibrium, but no change in the nature of causality. *From one point of view*, it might thus generally be said that the mobility of capital and the mobility of labor do not considerably modify the presentation above of the causality of interregional exchange.

This reasoning is incomplete, however, since one important factor is ignored. Capital movements hold a unique position in relation to the movements of other factors of production, in the sense that they affect the "balance of payments" and thus, in a unique way, the entire equilibrium. *The condition that imports and exports of goods should be in equilibrium no longer applies.* A relatively insignificant capital movement in relation to total capital resources will thus considerably affect the equilibrium. A country with continuous capital inflow imports more goods than it exports. The foreign goods can be paid for not only with exports of domestic goods but also with borrowed money. The prices of goods in the country will then, to a large extent, depend on capital imports. If no such imports exist, prices must

*Translator's note: "mobility" in the original.

be such that imports entirely balance exports. Borrowing abroad creates another equilibrium, where a larger or smaller number of the domestic goods command higher prices, thereby decreasing the competitiveness with foreign countries. Thus imports will increase and exports decrease. At this new equilibrium the deficit in the trade balance will be exactly covered by capital imports.

The change in the prices of goods is only one side of the shift in the general equilibrium caused by borrowing. The prices and the utilization of the factors of production are also affected. Certain industries decrease, others increase; changes in income and the prices of goods will also lead to a restructuring of consumption. What has so far been said about the mobility of the factors of production has not required any substantial change in the presentation of the construction of the price formation mechanism, but in this case the situation is different. Capital movements constitute a factor in the trade balance. The causality is thus entirely different than it would have been, had capital movements not been possible.

So much for the nature of causality. The question of a shift in the equilibrium will only be studied later, in a different context. It should be observed, however, that at the same rate as capital movements change, there is a corresponding shift in the entire equilibrium. Since borrowings can change considerably and very often, these shifts might not only be numerous but also significant, which constitutes a difference from the cases studied so far. Neither the mobility of labor nor that of the organizational factors will produce anything but slow shifts, and this also applies to the effect of capital movements, through the supply of factors of production.

The considerable effect of capital movements is due to the fact that they might be large relative to the imports and exports of a region. Very considerable changes in the equilibrium would thus be required to create an equilibrium in the entire balance of payments, in the absence of capital imports or exports.

Summarizing the study of the effects of the interregional mobility of the factors of production on the price formation mechanism, it appears that because of the mobility of capital, a new factor is introduced into the balance of payments, which will determine the equilibrium together with the factors previously studied. However, the effects of mobility on the supply of different factors of production and thus, on the production pattern, do create a continuous shift in the mechanism but no important changes in the way it works.

IV Modifications due to the Limited Mobility of Goods

The pure theory of price formation builds on the assumption of perfect mobility, not only of factors of production but also of goods. Having studied the mobility of the former in the two previous chapters and having paved the way for the removal of all simplifying assumptions on this issue, the next step is to modify the presentation by considering the consequences of the obstacles to the mobility of the goods. Transport costs are among the most important of these obstacles. Their importance varies with the value of the goods per unit of weight and volume. Items such as fine instruments, watch-springs, and jewelry can be transported around the world for less than one percent of their market value, while transport costs for heavy and bulky articles, such as bricks, come close to or, at times, even exceed production costs, even when transported fairly short distances. Most types of goods fall in between these two extreme cases.

Besides transport costs, different kinds of trade costs[24] also constitute barriers to the mobility of goods. With a common name, these could be denoted as the mobility costs of the goods. Because of these costs one can no longer assume a single price for each type of good, but different prices depending on the distance between the place of consumption and the place of production. A difference in absolute costs[25] no longer suffices to induce an exchange between two areas. A good might be produced at a lower cost in one of these areas than in the other; if the difference is less than the mobility costs, the other area will still produce the article in question itself. No exchange will then occur.

Like the prices of goods, these mobility costs are variables determined by prices. They mainly consist of such costs as wages, costs of coal, and costs of constructing means of transport, and can be broken down into their components, that is, the quantity of each factor of production. In the price formation system, they hold a position completely analogous to the position of the price of goods. They affect the mechanisms and effects of the exchange of goods in the following way: the tendency to equalize the relative scarcity of factors of production, that is, to achieve uniform prices of the factors of production, is weakened, that is, cannot be realized to the same extent as previously assumed. Since the mobility costs prevent exchange of goods in the cases where these exceed the price difference, they thus also prevent the equalization of prices this exchange of goods would otherwise create. When an equilibrium has been established, there will still be a considerable difference in the prices of production factors in different areas. There is another reason for this difference: mobility costs are now also added to the effects of disproportionate factor supplies still at work even with perfectly mobile goods.

The fact that the tendency to establish uniform prices of goods and factors of production is indirectly and directly obstructed means a loss to the world economy. It is inherent in the meaning of the actual word "mobility costs" that they involve a sacrifice. Furthermore the difference in the prices of the factors of production means an uneconomical use of these factors. Both these inconveniences incur a decrease in the profits from the exchange of goods, in comparison to trade at *perfect* mobility of goods. There will still be a profit, however, and it will be larger, the more uniform are the price structure of goods and factors of production, that is, the lower are the mobility costs.

V Modifications due to the Limited Divisibility of Factors of Production

So far it has been shown that the difference in the supply of factors of production constitutes one reason for exchange between individuals as well as between groups of individuals, so-called regions. This difference, which is only marginally reduced by the mobility of factors of production, or in other words, the difference in the relative scarcity of factors of production, creates division of labor and exchange.

The question is then whether this is the only reason for exchange. If the factors of production were perfectly mobile, so that each difference in their relative scarcity could be equalized by transfers, would no division of labor then occur? Would each country, each region, each area, each individual, procure for himself the goods and services he requires?

The answer must be negative. Division of labor is also due to another factor, that is, increasing profits. Even if the relative scarcity of factors of production were exactly the same in two regions, there would still be division of labor; if each area were to produce all goods it required, this would suppose production on a very small scale.[26] If producing on a small scale, several factors of production would not be fully utilized, however, that is, in those cases where the smallest possible unit is relatively large or relatively less efficient than a larger unit. Since production on a small scale is thus more expensive than production on a larger scale, the latter becomes more profitable. This is usually called the law of increasing returns, and means that there will be one type of production in one area and another type of production in another, and that products will then be exchanged.

This is not only a question of the impact of the law of increasing returns, which means that a firm of a certain size is most suitable financially and, thus, that only a certain number of firms is required; these firms could be spread all over the world, and each firm would satisfy its wants in its respective region. An even more considerable division of labor between different regions is due to the fact that two firms or more that are closely located are often financially superior to those alone in their area, even if their size is the same. Firms that are closely located learn from each other and find it easier to follow technological and organizational progress. Improvements made by one producer stimulate the other in a completely different way if they work on each other's doorsteps than in different parts of the country. They find out about and make use of each other's improvements, for example. A concentration of industries in a certain region thus often leads to an increase in economic efficiency. If so desired, this could be denoted as the limited divisibility of the organizational factors.

Basically all phenomena of increasing and decreasing returns are due to the limited divisibility of factors of production.[27] The increasing returns are due to the fact that some indivisible factors of production, of which the firm previously had too rich a supply, are more efficiently used when the scale of production is increased. A tendency to decreasing returns, on the other hand, occurs when an increase in production from one point to another necessitates an acquisition of indivisible factors of production that cannot be completely utilized.

Assume that four factors of production, A, B, C, and D, are used to produce a certain good. A is fully utilized at the production rate of 1,000 units of goods a day, B at 500, and C at 200, while D is perfectly divisible so that the quantity of this good used in production can be freely adjusted to the extent of the production. Furthermore assume that a unit of A costs 1,000 kronor, a unit of B 500 kronor, a

Table 9.1
Production costs for different sizes of firms

Production units	A	B	C	D	Total	Cost per unit
200	1,000	500	200	200	1,900	8.50
300	1,000	500	400	300	2,200	7.33
400	1,000	500	400	400	2,300	5.75
500	1,000	500	600	500	2,600	5.20
600	1,000	1,000	600	600	3,200	5.33
700	1,000	1,000	800	700	3,500	5.00
800	1,000	1,000	800	800	3,600	4.50
1,000	1,000	1,000	1,000	1,000	4,000	4.00
1,100	2,000	1,500	1,200	1,100	5,800	5.27
1,500	2,000	1,500	1,600	1,500	6,600	4.40
2,000	2,000	2,000	2,000	2,000	8,000	4.00
2,100	3,000	2,500	2,200	2,100	9,800	4.67

unit of C 200 kronor, and a unit of D 1 krona, all costs estimated on a daily basis. The costs of production at different sizes of firms are shown in table 9.1.

There is thus alternatively an increase and a decrease in the average costs. The optimum is reached at the scale of production allowing a full utilization of all factors of production. A twofold, a threefold increase, and so on, of this optimum entails no change in the average costs. An increase in production from 500 to 600 units and from 1,000 to 1,100 units incurs increasing costs, that is, decreasing returns, however. In practice, there are no absolute limits to the capacity of one unit of a factor of production. A certain overutilization of a steam engine, for example, is usually possible, so that production might increase from 1,000 units to 1,050 or even 1,100 units, without the need to acquire either a new unit of A or a new unit of B. Although such an overutilization has certain disadvantages, for example, a more extensive use of D (labor) per unit, the average cost might still be as low as for the production of 1,000 units—for example, 1,000(A) + 1,000(B) + 1,200(C) + 1,200(D) = 4,400; 4 kronor per unit. The optimum is thus not a point but rather a range on the scale of production.

Such an overutilization does, however, have its limits. When producing 1,500 units, the production costs are 4.40 per unit, that is, above the optimum. At an increase from 1,000 to 1,500 units, a decrease in returns should be expected. When production increases from 600 to 1,000 units, or from 1,600 to 2,000 units, however, there is a decrease in the average cost.

According to this reasoning, there is an indefinite number of optima, that is, at the production of 1,000*t* units, where *t* is a completely random integer. In practice, however, only a limited number of certain factors of production, above all those related to the management of the firm, can be used in the same firm. There can, for example, be no more than one managing director, which constitutes a barrier to giant factories.[28] The efficiency of one individual manager decreases when production exceeds a certain limit. Even if the "margin of indeterminateness" is unusually large in this case, that is, a great deal of "overutilization" is possible, productivity will still decrease. The utilization of certain factors of production is thus less efficient. An optimum occurs at the point, or rather in the range, where the average best utilization of the factors of production is obtained. The tendency to a more efficient use when production increases is here met and balanced by the tendency to a less efficient use of certain factors.

A special case of limited divisibility occurs when a smaller unit of a certain factor of production can be obtained, but is relatively less efficient than a larger such unit. A steam engine of 1,000 hp does not consume 10 times more coal than a machine of 100 hp. If 1,000 hp had been the smallest possible unit from a technical viewpoint, there would have been pure limited divisibility. This limit is now somewhat obscured since a smaller unit, although less efficient, is technically possible. The disadvantage of only producing 100 hp is thus smaller than if one had to keep a machine with a capacity of 1,000 hp, but it still exists. In this case we are also dealing with limited divisibility. It is of a different kind but with essentially the same effects as in the case just dealt with.

It is clear, however, that such a simplified reasoning as above does not completely correspond to reality. Within most industries the number of firms is much larger than would be required at the most favorable size of firms. Since an extension of production in all firms operating below the optimum would result in decreasing average costs, one might ask why they continue at a smaller scale of production instead of reducing the price and increasing production. It must then be observed that such a process would not be quick and painless and assumes a considerable effort to conquer new markets.[29] Moreover all firms have equal opportunities. If one firm started selling at its marginal cost, the others would be obliged to do the same, and there would be a devastating competition for an unforseeable period of time. For this reason producers generally prefer not to start any "uncontrolled" competition, for example, by selling at their marginal cost on certain markets or temporarily reducing all prices to this level in order to reach an optimum, but will instead maintain a relatively uniform price, covering average costs. The firms that have reached their optimum and thus produce at lower average costs have less reason than others to expand production under these circumstances; they will be satisfied with obtaining a somewhat better return, that is, trade profit.

There seems to be a growing tendency toward such a policy. The aim of the firms to reach an optimum still remains, however. The above-mentioned and other similar tendencies act as checks to this development and are not forces turning it in another direction. Due to the swift changes in all areas of the economy, caused by population growth, technical progress, and changes in wants, for example, there will never be a situation resembling an equilibrium where all firms have reached their optimum.

What are then the consequences of this concentration of production, induced by increasing returns, even if it is not as extensive as might be assumed a priori? In other words, what are the effects of this division of labor and this exchange among different areas or regions? Apparently there are no other effects than that the inconveniences caused by the limited divisibility of the factors of production are diminished or eliminated. When producing on a small scale, a large number of factors of production were not fully utilized. Due to the concentration of production, production on a large scale, and exchange of goods, these indivisible factors of production are also fully or at least almost fully utilized.[30]

The closer one is to an optimum, the more complete is utilization. The increase in exchange thus means that production is concentrated in a small number of areas, each with a relatively large-scale production. The factors of production are thus better utilized and there are fewer disadvantages due to limited *divisibility*. This tendency of exchange to remove the disadvantages of the limited *divisibility* of factors of production exactly equals the tendency to remove the disadvantages resulting from their *limited* mobility dealt with earlier, since it entails a uniform price structure of these factors for their most efficient use. There is thus a tendency for exchange to create a situation where the utilization of the factors of production remains the same, or rather, as efficient, as if perfect divisibility and mobility did exist. The gain is then that the most inefficient use of the factors of production is prevented or reduced.

Just as exchange cannot create a completely uniform price structure, because of a certain disproportion in the distribution of the factors of production and their utilization in production, that is, just as the effects of limited mobility cannot be entirely removed, another phenomenon of disproportion will counteract the tendency to eliminate the effects of limited divisibility.

The optimum size of a firm is thus not the point where all factors of production are fully utilized but the point where the overall utilization is the best possible. If all factors were fully utilized, the scale of production would often be so large that it would be uneconomical for other reasons.[31] At the optimum the advantages of extending production, and thus obtaining a better utilization of certain factors of production, will be counterbalanced by the disadvantages of mass production, such as less efficient management, more expensive control, and the employees having less power of initiative.

Even if all firms were at an optimum, this would not necessarily entail a full utilization of the factors of production but would only mean that the disadvantages of limited *divisibility* were minimized. As already mentioned, if an on-the-spot picture of the economy were presented, it would show that a number of firms fall below the optimum. One of the reasons for this has already been mentioned. Whatever these reasons might be, however, the actual existence of such firms means that division of labor and exchange has not been carried so far that optimum utilization occurs. Besides the phenomenon of disproportion just mentioned, this is another circumstance that counteracts the tendency of exchange to remove the effects of limited divisibility. There is, however, also another obstacle.

In order not to complicate the reasoning more than necessary, the mobility costs of the goods have not been accounted for so far in this chapter, although they clearly constitute an obstacle to the division of labor and exchange. The optimum size of a firm does not only depend on the pure costs of production, it exists at the point where an increase in production incurs new costs, which together with the transport costs exactly cover the highest price to be obtained on a possible new market. Assume, for example, that 1 million units are produced at the average cost of 4 kronor and that an increase in production of 100,000 units would incur costs of 350,000 kronor. Returns are then increasing, that is, the average costs are falling. Nevertheless, this expansion of production will incur a loss if the highest price the goods can command on the new market, without inviting competition, is 4.50 kronor and transport costs are 1.15 kronor per unit. The cost price on this market is thus $3.50 + 1.25 = 4.75$. The optimum is thus a production of 1 million units, despite the fact that the average production costs would fall if production were expanded. This real optimum apparently exists at the point where the advantage of decreasing production costs are equalized by the disadvantage of increasing transport costs, or rather, at the point where the prices on possible new markets less transport costs begin to fall below the additional costs for an increase in production.

If sales of a product from one region to another are to take place, the increase in costs in the export region together with transport costs must thus fall below the production costs in the other region. This condition might very well be fulfilled, even if the relative prices of the factors of production are equal. Assume that A can produce good *a* as well as good *b* at the price of 1 krona per unit, and so can B. Furthermore assume that if A also produces the good for B, the additional costs will only amount to 0.75 kronor per unit, and the good can thus be sold to B at that price. In the same way, B can sell good *b* to A at the price of 0.75 kronor. As long as transport costs fall below 0.25 kronor, it is not profitable for A to produce good *b* or for B to produce good *a*; instead, division of labor and exchange will take place.

The *precondition* for exchange is thus that a more efficient use of the nondivisible factors of production more than outweighs the disadvantages of transporting the goods. The *function* of the exchange is thus to obtain a more efficient use of the factors of production, to which transport costs constitute an obstacle.

It has already been noted that divisions of labor and exchange are not as extensive as would have been required by the prospects of falling costs due to expanded production; that is, many firms operate much below the optimum. This will now be somewhat further illustrated in connection with the mobility costs of the goods.

Reaching the optimum production of a good, for which the transport costs vary considerably with the distance,[32] means, according to the result above, that the producers apply price discrimination. When deciding whether a certain sale to a new market is to take place, only the marginal costs must be considered, that is, the increase in total costs that a required increase in production would incur. For various reasons—one of which has already been mentioned[33]—many firms apply uniform prices,[34] approximately corresponding to the average costs of an average firm.[35] The best firms, that is, those that are close to the optimum, are thus profitable, while the least successful incur a loss; assuming "normal" business cycles.

Failing to use price discrimination means that the concentration of production and exchange is not taken as far as required by the above-mentioned conditions.[36] Even if a certain quantity of a certain type of good can be produced at the additional cost of, for example, 3 kronor per unit, the transport costs to a "new" market are 1 krona and the price on this market 4.50 kronor per unit, sales to that market will generally not take place, as long as the average costs of the firm are 4 kronor and can only be reduced to 3.90 kronor per unit through the expansion. Failing to use price discrimination thus works as a check on the firm's tendency toward the optimum.

A summary of the results of chapter V is that increasing returns, and the resulting exchange of goods, are due to the limited divisibility of factors of production. They might also occur even if the relative prices of the factors of production in two regions are the same. A full utilization of the nondivisible factors of production is made possible by the exchange of goods. Full utilization seldom occurs, however.

1. The mobility costs of the goods prevent all kinds of exchange, unless the profits from a more efficient use of the factors of production are higher than the mobility costs.

2. Not even if the mobility costs of the goods were removed would *all* factors of production be fully utilized in a firm; a certain disproportion in their composition cannot be avoided, as long as the firms cannot be expanded to any extent.

3. Not all firms reach their optimum size, on account of the two factors stated above.[37]

VI The Theory of Interregional Exchange without Simplified Assumptions: Summary

It is now time to address the issue of the conditions and effects of interregional exchange, on the basis of the previous observations, without any simplifying assumptions; that is, to try to present a picture of the price formation mechanism, the way it works with limited mobility and divisibility of factors of production and with limited mobility of goods.

The studies have shown that there might be two reasons for exchange: the relative scarcity of factors of production, on the one hand, and increasing returns, on the other, which in turn are connected to the limited divisibility of factors of production. The exchange that then takes place tends to equalize the relative scarcity of factors of production and make a more complete utilization of the indivisible factors of production possible, in other words, creates a more economic utilization of the factors of production. The tendency is to obtain as efficient a use as if these had been perfectly mobile and divisible. To the same extent that this tendency is realized, the difference in the relative scarcity of factors of production will decrease and disappear, and the degree to which they are utilized will increase and become the largest possible, since the industries will approach and attain the optimum. The exchange thus removes its own causes. Realizing this tendency makes all *new* exchange impossible, while the ongoing exchange continues.

The tendency cannot be fully realized, however, partly due to certain phenomena of disproportion, and partly to obstacles to the mobility of goods, mainly transport costs. In addition the equilibrium that would appear through the hindrance of this tendency by these two obstacles does not exist in practice. If one switches from a purely static approach and also considers dynamic factors, it is found that the attempts of the economy to reach this equilibrium will never be fully realized, because of continuous changes in the determining factors. Division of labor and exchange do not attain either the direction or the extent that would give the highest economic efficiency.

The factors studied here—even if disregarding the dynamic factor—depend on a modification of the price formation theory, building on the assumption of perfect mobility and divisibility. In this theory the total supply of factors of production, the technical conditions,[38] and the hierarchy of wants of the population can be considered as the only factors determining price formation. Price formation in the isolated economic unit that the world constitutes does not have such a simple structure.

The different supply of factors of production in different areas, their limited mobility and divisibility, and the limited mobility of goods[39] are factors determining a specific location of production.

They are thus part of the determinants of the price formation system. Due to their existence, the prices of goods as well as of factors of production are completely different than would otherwise be the case. As is apparent from this study, exchange does mean that there is a tendency to create the same price structure as if perfect mobility and divisibility did exist. For various reasons this tendency cannot be fully realized. These factors will thus have a considerable effect on the price structure.

Besides the total quantity of the factors of production, their local distribution is important. The technical conditions must be understood in another and more comprehensive context, which also includes the limited divisibility of factors of production and the suitability of land for transportation. For each possible state of these factors and the hierarchy of wants of the population, there is a specific production pattern: the location of production as well as the prices of the factors of production and the goods are determined, that is, the entire price formation system is determined.

Acknowledgments

The translator thanks Harry Flam and June Flanders for useful comments on the translation.

Notes

1. Given wants must be assumed and the study deals with their maximum coverage. The hierarchy of wants is, from this point of view, given by the distribution of incomes, and it is thus not the best hierarchy of wants from any point of view but a certain (in any way) fixed hierarchy of wants. As soon as there is also a choice between different hierarchies of wants, we enter the area of ethical values and lose the required fixed starting points for the theoretical economy under discussion. The author's point of view is based on an unconscious hedonism which is moreover ... and ... [undecipherable].

2. This issue is treated more extensively in chapters III to V.

3. From the point of view of exchange, such a region will then, in certain ways, be equivalent to an individual in the pure theory of price formation. It has certain productive forces that will be attracted to the utilization where they command the highest price, without *leaving the region*. Nor can an individual's productive forces be moved outside himself. His tasks, however, that is, the results of his productive forces, can be transported, just as the goods of a region can be sent to other regions. An important difference, however, is that the individual, but not the region, can be moved in its entity.

4. Expressed as difficulties in transportation, particularly transport costs.

5. Two isolated areas can, naturally, not be assumed to have a common monetary system [sic].

6. The condition is the absence of transport costs for the goods.

7. The condition for the entire chapter II is that the factors of production are perfectly divisible, that there are thus no increasing returns, and that the goods are perfectly mobile.

8. Or similar units of quantity for productive forces.

9. Higher real wages in Portugal and equal prices of goods in both countries must mean higher wages in Portugal.

10. See Heckscher, "The Effect of Foreign Trade on the Distribution of Income." *Ekonomisk Tidskrift* 1919.

11. Cf. Cassel, *Theoretische Sozialökonomie.*

12. See appendix 3 [appendix is missing].

13. In the paper referred to, Heckscher has come to the conclusion that exchange of goods will not occur if all goods use the same proportions of factors of production in both regions. From the above, this is wrong, for it must apply to all goods in *both* regions. See equation (6). Because of this mistake, the fact that the condition "different relative scarcities of factors of production" in itself contains the latter condition concerning the proportions of the factors of production in the goods, has been overlooked. Moreover the mistake seems quite serious, since H. like Bastable, Pierson, and others, uses the unit productive force as a yardstick when first studying foreign trade. This means that the factors of production are assumed to constitute fixed proportions of all goods in each country, although not equal proportions in *both* countries. Foreign trade is thus studied under an assumption which, according to H. himself, in itself precludes all kinds of foreign trade.

14. Under the assumptions of chapter II.

15. By "cause" is meant necessary *and sufficient* condition. The wording of the text should not be a source of misunderstandings.

16. When the transport costs of the goods and the increasing returns are not considered.

17. For further discussion of this issue, see appendix 4 [appendix is missing].

18. The term "land" here covers general natural conditions, such as climate.

19. Cf. Heckscher.

20. This question is discussed in more detail in appendix 4 [appendix is missing].

21. *Theory of International Trade*, London 1903.

22. See appendixes 3 and 4 [appendixes missing].

23. Which, accordingly, does not affect the nature of the causality.

24. Costs of sales and purchases.

25. Reduced according to the exchange rate, if the monetary units are different.

26. Note the borderline case, where each *individual* produces all his own goods. The production of each good is then small. His numerous occupations prevent him from acquiring skills equaling those of a specialist; this means a certain indivisibility in an individual's productive forces, since specialization, that is, production on a larger scale, makes these more efficient.

27. The expression "decreasing returns" is at times used for two different phenomena, the one discussed in the text, and the fact that an increase in certain factors of production, for example, labor and capital, when the utilization of other factors of production remains constant, leads to a decrease in returns per quantity of labor and capital; cf. Bagge, *Ek*[onomisk] *Ts* [Tidskrift], 1920.

28. What is studied here is the extent of the production in a single firm, technically speaking, not a trust, a cartel, or something of the kind.

29. Cf. Marshall, *Industry and Trade*, according to which "marketing costs" are of increasing importance.

30. It is the *static* price formation theory and the effects of the limited divisibility on this theory that are studied here, although it has been considered that a dynamic factor should be included in the reasoning. No account is taken of such dynamic phenomena as regular or irregular variations in demand, however, that prevent a full utilization of indivisible factors of production.

31. Cf. the above concerning obstacles to giant firms.

32. For a number of goods it is of little or no importance if they are transported 20 or 1,000 kilometers. Packing and shipment costs are in no way related to distance. An increase in other costs might be insignificant, expressed as a percentage.

33. Another reason is that implementing price discrimination is, in practice, very difficult.

34. There are exceptions, of course, for example, within power producing firms. Price discrimination in sales to other countries will be studied in the next chapter.

35. Cf. Marshall's "representative firm."

36. See above.

37. This dynamic factor is included already at this stage so that the argument does not rest on excessively unrealistic conditions.

38. See appendix 3 [appendix is missing].

39. That is, the properties of commodities and geography with respect to [the facility of] transport.

10

The Young Ohlin on the Theory of Interregional and International Trade

Harry Flam and M. June Flanders

Bertil Ohlin's international fame as an economist rests to a large extent on his 1933 monograph *Interregional and International Trade* (Ohlin 1933). The monograph marked the definitive break with the Ricardian and early neoclassical theory of international trade. Eli Heckscher's contribution of 1919 did not become known to a wider audience until his article was published in English in 1949 (Heckscher 1949, 1991).

But *Interregional and International Trade* was not Ohlin's first formulation of the neoclassical theory of international trade; it was his third. His first attempt is his licentiate thesis of 1922 and the second his doctoral dissertation published in 1924. The latter was published in English in 1991 under the title *The Theory of Trade* (Heckscher and Ohlin 1991). The licentiate thesis, entitled *The Theory of Interregional Exchange*, has remained untranslated until very recently (Ohlin 1999).

We will trace the development of Ohlin's thinking on international trade by comparing the three works. Special emphasis will be placed on *The Theory of Interregional Exchange* since it is the first and practically unknown. We have discussed and compared *The Theory of Trade* and *Interregional and International Trade* elsewhere (Flam and Flanders 1991).

Origins of Ohlin's Ideas

The beginning of his work in international economics is described by Ohlin in his memoirs by the following sentence: "I started [in 1921] to write on the foundations of an approach to international trade theory that was to some extent new and for which I received the inspiration during a stroll on [the popular promenade] Unter den Linden in Berlin in 1920."

The inspiration did not fall from a lime tree. Ohlin graduated from the University of Lund in 1917, where he had spent two years studying economics, mathematics and statistics. From Lund he went on to the Stockholm School of Economics, then a college mostly for practical training of businessmen. He enrolled in Eli Heckscher's seminar in economics in the fall of 1917. We do not know whether and to what extent Ohlin was exposed to trade theory in the seminar. Heckscher published *The Continental System: An Economic Interpretation* in 1918, a study of Napoleon's blockade of England and its relation to the mercantilist system. Heckscher could have talked about this work in the seminar, but we can be fairly safe in saying that Heckscher had not thought out his new trade theory until well into 1919, since this was inspired by Wicksell's review in 1919 of Heckscher's collection of papers *Swedish Production Problems.* Heckscher's seminal article was published later in 1919. We can, however, safely assume that Ohlin read the article, since Heckscher was his mentor, had introduced him into the Economics Club, a forum for academic economists in Stockholm, and given him a job upon his graduation from the Stockholm School of Economics in 1919. This was a position as a staff economist on a government commission dealing with tariffs and trade treaties of which he himself was a member.

Thus Ohlin had been exposed to Heckscher's ideas about trade when he moved on to graduate studies in economics at Stockholm College (later Stockholm University) in the fall of 1920. His professor there was Gustav Cassel. Cassel was a public figure both in Europe and the United States after the war, as a proponent of re-establishing the gold standard based on his concept of purchasing power parity. He was also well known among economists for his *Theoretische Sozialökonomie*, the centerpiece of which was a system of equations describing general equilibrium, very much like the early Walrasian system with fixed coefficients.

The idea that came to Ohlin during his walk in Berlin was to combine Cassel and Heckscher. Cassel had neoclassical general equilibrium for a single economy, Heckscher a neoclassical theory of international trade. Ohlin's idea was to extend Cassel's paradigm to international equilibrium with two trading economies, where the reasons for trade and the trade pattern were those given by Heckscher.

The Theory of Interregional Exchange

The Theory of Interregional Exchange is composed of six chapters and consists of only 52 typewritten pages in the original. The core is chapter II, which gives the conditions for interregional exchange, to wit differences in factor endowments that lead to differences in comparative costs, and then discusses the effects of interregional exchange. Chapters III to V extend the model to include respectively interregional factor mobility, limited goods mobility, and economies of scale due to indivisibilities of factors of production. Chapter I and VI are a short introduction and summary.

II The Theory of Interregional Exchange under Simplified Assumptions

After having established that differences in comparative costs (prices) constitute a necessary and sufficient condition for interregional exchange, Ohlin goes on to explain the reasons for such differences, "an issue hardly dealt with in most studies," and here he refers to Heckscher's article without comment. The explanation is carried out by "mathematical reasoning," that is, in terms of the equilibrium conditions that cost equals price for every good. But the explanation leads nowhere; all Ohlin says is that differences in relative factor prices are a necessary but not sufficient condition for differences in comparative costs. The nonsufficiency arises from the possibility that the technical input–output coefficients accidentally just neutralize the differences in relative factor prices. It is only after this discussion of the conditions for interregional exchange that Ohlin states, without any reference to his general equilibrium conditions, that the reason for differences in comparative costs is differences in the relative scarcity of factors of production. In practice, he now says, this is also a sufficient condition for interregional exchange.

On pages fourteen to fifteen in *The Theory of Interregional Exchange* Ohlin gives a clear and succinct explanation both of the Heckscher-Ohlin and the factor price equalization theorems:

> The reason that the production costs for certain goods are lower in one region than in another is ... the difference in the relative scarcity of factors of production. Since there is a relatively good supply of certain factors of

production in A and their prices thus are low, the goods requiring a relatively large share of these factors of production can be produced at a low cost in that region compared to the types of goods requiring a relatively larger share of the more scarce factors of production. ... Exports will then mainly consist of goods where the abundant factors of production are used in large quantities and the other factors in small quantities only, while imports consist of the types of goods requiring large quantities of the latter factors of production and factors of production not available in the region at all. The exchange of goods is thus an exchange of factors of production, in the sense that goods "containing" the relatively scarce factors are imported and goods "containing" less scarce factors of production are exported. ... The result is thus that the scarcity of factors of production is generally equalized.... There is thus a tendency that all regions get exactly the relative scarcity that would have existed, had there been no obstacle to the mobility of factors of production. *In other words, interregional exchange tends to create a uniform price structure of the factors of production.* (Italics by Ohlin)

III Modifications Due to the Interregional Mobility of Factors of Production

In the rest of *The Theory of Interregional Exchange* Ohlin analyzes the effects of making the model more realistic. This was a prime concern to him; on page twenty he writes: "All problems, for the solution of which abstracting conditions are not absolutely necessary, should be studied under conditions as close to reality as possible, in all respects."

Lifting the assumption that factors are immobile between regions would not alter the workings of the trade model qualitatively, according to Ohlin. Factors of production would be drawn to the region with the highest compensation. But this would in practice lead only to *gradual* changes in prices and resource allocation. The short-run effects would be small. This would be true also in the case where large movements of factors were foreseen: "Price formation is mainly determined by the actual supply of labor and not by expected changes." It is not until *International Trade* that he formulates the idea that the crucial magnitude is the difference in the price of a factor between regions compared to the annuity cost of transferring the required amount of the factor from one region to another. (This correct concern about the present value of future flow is reminiscent of his contribution to the forestry debate about the optimal rotation period in forestry; see Flam and Flanders 1991.) The only instance where factor movements across regions could have a significant and rapid effect was in the case of financial capital, that is, foreign borrowing and lending. Financial capital movements were unique, according to Ohlin, in that they affected the balance of payments, the exchange rate, and thereby the entire equilibrium. Ohlin probably had the large capital flows of the late nineteenth century in mind. We return to this point below.

IV Modification Due to the Limited Mobility of Goods

Ohlin devotes just one and a half pages to the limited mobility of goods, that is, to the effects of transportation and other costs of interregional trade. He notes that these could be sufficiently high to prevent exports of goods produced at lower cost than in the importing region. In any event, they served to diminish trade and prevent equalization across regions of goods prices and therefore of factor prices. This would, Ohlin argued, lead to a loss in welfare equal to the mobility costs themselves plus the resulting inefficient resource allocation.

V Modification Due to the Limited Divisibility of Factors of Production

Far more space and far more importance is given by Ohlin to economies of scale and their effects on trade, with many ramifications and side discussions. In the restatement of the theory in the conclusion, it has essentially equal weight with factor proportions in causing trade. Ohlin starts his analysis by asking if trade would cease if relative factor supplies were equal between regions. His immediate answer is no; specialization would take place between regions due to increasing returns to scale (and, presumably, limited factor supplies in any one region) and give rise to trade. Specialization would be strengthened by externalities: "Firms that are closely located learn from each other and find it easier to follow technological and organizational progress." The gain from exploitation of increasing returns would be a more efficient use of resources, although Ohlin adds, true to his penchant for realism, that in practice not all firms can reach an optimum size. A major reason for this, in his view, is the fact that in practice there will be more than one indivisible factor so it may be physically (mathematically) impossible to operate where average output is maximized for each factor of production. Increasing returns would also contribute to factor price equalization, to the extent that factors were used efficiently everywhere. But just as trade could not effect factor price equalization completely in practice "due to a certain disproportion in the distribution of the factors of production and their utilization," increasing returns could not completely overcome the limited divisibility of factors and effect complete factor price equalization because of "another phenomenon of disproportion [that] will counteract the tendency to remove the effects of limited divisibility." By "another phenomenon of disproportion" Ohlin meant that increasing returns could not be utilized to the full extent for every factor everywhere.

But most of the chapter is devoted to an explanation of how increasing returns come about through the limited divisibility of some factors; considerable space is taken up by a numerical example showing how average cost can be increasing and decreasing over some range of output. Ultimately an optimum is reached where the disadvantages of mass production, such as "less efficient management, more expensive control, and the employees having less initiative," balance the advantages of extending production. To add more realism, Ohlin throws in transportation costs to show that they could protect smaller-scale from larger-scale producers and that efficiency requires producers to use marginal cost pricing and price discrimination between locations based on costs of transportation.

The Theory of Interregional Exchange and *The Theory of Trade* Compared

Apart from being several times as long, *The Theory of Trade* contains some new elements compared to *The Theory of Interregional Exchange*. The most important are, first, a long chapter on international monetary economics, and, second, several chapters of verbal comparative statics exercises, or, as Ohlin saw it, transitional dynamics. There are also a short chapter on "interlocal" trade (perfect labor and capital mobility within a region and zero mobility between regions) and a chapter with a critical discussion of classical trade theory. But the basic outline is the same: first an analysis of the cause and effects of trade under simplifying assumptions, and then a repeated analysis where the assumptions about zero trade costs, perfect factor mobility, and constant returns are replaced one at a time by more realistic assumptions.

Both the discussion and the presentation of classical trade theory are much more highly developed and thoroughly explored in *The Theory of Trade* than in *The Theory of Interregional Exchange*, and much more still in *Interregional and International Trade*. This steady development may have been due, inter alia, to the Harvard influence. In *The Theory of Interregional Exchange*, the classical theory is presented tersely with little discussion, in terms of Ricardian wine and cloth, with consideration only of labor costs, since Ricardo does not consider compensation to other factors of production or considers it to be proportional to compensation to labor. Ohlin, however, wishes to discuss the question of the reason for the differences in comparative costs and prices of goods; an issue hardly dealt with in most studies. It is at this point that he cites the Heckscher paper. In *International and Interregional Trade* he devotes several long appendixes to discussions of classical and neoclassical theories of comparative cost.

Factor Price Equalization

In *The Theory of Trade* as in *The Theory of Interregional Exchange*, Ohlin concludes that trade will serve to make factor prices more equal between trade partners. But he is also convinced that complete factor price equalization is unattainable in practice as well as in theory. To prove his assertion, he employs Cassel's general equilibrium system, extended to a world consisting of two countries instead of one and with flexible coefficients technology. Ohlin describes the transition from autarky equilibrium to trading equilibrium in the following way. Assume that both countries produce the same set of goods in autarky. Apply some arbitrary exchange rate to make autarky prices commensurable. There is a nice, rather classical, discussion of how exchange rates must be brought by trade and exchange to such commensurability. Then some goods will be found to be produced at a lower cost in A than in B, and the rest will be cheaper in B. From this he concludes that A will specialize in the production of the goods that are cheaper there, and B in the others. The equilibrium exchange rate, which ensures trade balance, determines the exact division of the autarky set of goods between A and B. Given complete specialization, factor prices cannot be equalized, except by chance.

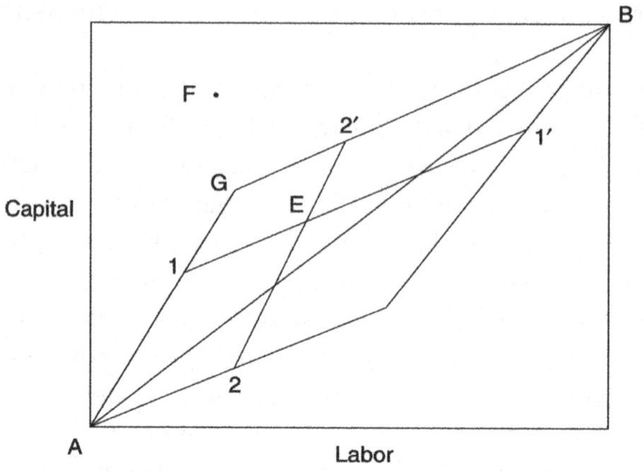

Figure 10.1

Ohlin's reasoning can be illustrated with the help of an Edgeworth box diagram (figure 10.1). The sides of the box measure the world supplies of the two factors, called labor and capital. Factor price equalization occurs when the world supply of factors is divided between country A and B inside the parallelogram in the box. For example, factor allocation *E* leads to factor price equalization and production of goods 1 and 2 in *both* countries. The slope of the rays from A and B shows the proportions in which capital and labor are used in the production of goods 1 and 2, and their length the quantities produced. Note that the rays from A and B respectively have the same slope for goods 1 and 2 respectively, indicating identical technology and factor price equalization.

Ohlin's view is that differences in goods prices under free trade must lead to complete and immediate specialization. He does realize that factor prices will become more equal, since abundant factors are exported and scarce factors imported. But he fails to take into account that the factor price changes in conjunction with substitution between factors in production will equalize production costs and make production of both goods in both countries competitive. What will happen in each country is that the price of the abundant factor will rise and the price of the scarce factor fall. Less of the abundant factor and more of the scarce factor will be used in each sector. An equilibrium is reached when factor prices and factor intensities in the respective sectors are equal, and hence also costs of production. The less intensive use of the abundant factor and more intensive use of the scarce factor tends to create an excess supply of the former and excess demand for the latter. But factors remain fully employed by expansion of the sector intensive in the abundant factor and contraction of the sector intensive in the scarce factor.

Ohlin's neglect of factor substitution in the framework of factor price equalization is puzzling, since he was aware of it and its consequences for the factor and goods markets. The following quote is from *The Theory of Trade* (p. 112):

If there is increased demand for a commodity that requires much land, for example, wheat, and decreased demand for a commodity requiring much capital, such as fine cloth, the rise in the production of the former and the decline in output of the latter lead to an increase in land rents and a decrease in the rental on capital. It then becomes profitable to use more capital and less land in all production, including that of totally different products. This will free some land which can be transfered to wheat production.

In terms of the box diagram, Ohlin would be right about complete specialization if the two countries were endowed with factors as shown by *F*. The factor endowments are too different to allow production of both goods in both countries. The extreme allocation of factors that allows factor price equalization is at *G*, where the production of the good intensive in the abundant factor is expanded so much in each country that it just employs all of the available factor supplies; production of the other good has just ceased. At *F* the abundant factor is used more intensively in each country to maintain full employment. This is possible only if the abundant factor becomes relatively cheaper. Hence factor prices can no longer be equal.

There are several passages in *The Theory of Interregional Exchange* that show that Ohlin was thinking in terms of complete specialization for traded goods. For example, on page nine he writes: "[T]he effects of a difference in comparative costs are that some goods can be produced at a lower cost in one region than in the other, while the opposite applies to other goods. Thus exchange will occur and each region can concentrate its production to the goods it can produce at the lowest cost." On page seventeen he writes:

Assume that the production of a good, wine, for example, requires land of a certain quality as well as a certain labor skill. A region fulfilling the condition of labor skill might only have a limited supply of land of the desired quality, while another region, which lacks suitable labor, has an abundant supply of such land. The entire world demand for that good must then be produced in the first region.

This does not mean that Ohlin thought countries would produce no goods in common. In the chapter on trade costs, he points out that such costs could make goods nontraded, and consequently allow production of the same good in different countries. And in the chapter on increasing returns to scale, he also points out that transportation costs prevent complete specialization.

It seems that Ohlin's belief in factor price *non*equalization was the result of his concern for realism in economics. He seems to have accepted on some level that factor price equalization was a theoretical possibility, not just an accidental fluke, but was so strongly influenced by the reality of nonequalization that he attempted nevertheless in *The Theory of Trade* to prove its theoretical impossibility. The following quote from *The Theory of Interregional Exchange* (page sixteen) is telling:

> If goods as well as factors of production were perfectly mobile, the entire world would constitute an economic unit in the real sense of the word, and the total supply of different factors of production would determine their relative scarcity. As mentioned, a free exchange of goods tends to give the same result *and might also do so, under certain conditions*. What are these conditions, or the other way around, what generally prevents this tendency from being fully realized?
>
> It is difficult to find a general answer to this question. On the most profound level, *there is probably a certain disproportion in the distribution of the factors of production and their use in production* that prevents the same outcome as when the factors of production were mobile, whatever the location of production. The exchange of goods can only create a situation where one type of good will be produced here and another there, that is, that each good is produced in that or those places where the most favorable of the existent combinations of factors is to be found. (Italics added)

In *The Theory of Trade* Ohlin is more elaborate and more precise on the conditions that would allow factor price equalization:

> It is difficult to give a precise meaning to the conditions for complete equalization of the prices of factors of production. The closest one could come, it seems, would be that there must be a specific relationship between (1) the technical characteristics of the goods and the factors of production, including the limited divisibility of the latter, (2) the supply of the factors of production, (3) the nature of demand. This relation must be such that at certain prices of the factors, common to all regions, there is a particular combination of industries in each region that uses the factors in precisely the same proportions as they are supplied. As will be explored in greater detail in the following chapter, this condition can be satisfied only if there is an appropriate relationship between the three elements stated above, which must be

considered to be given in the price determination problem. Unfortunately, it is impossible to assess the likelihood of this occurring, and there is therefore no justification for assuming that it will. A purely mathematical analysis shows that it is far more probable that particular constants will not fulfill the required conditions than that they will do so. Under such conditions the conclusion is that the tendency of interregional trade to effect a uniform price structure will not be fully realized.

It is clear from the passage cited on the conditions for factor price equalization that Ohlin was on the right track, but his mathematical treatment of the problem led him to conclude that the probability of the right combination of quantities and parameters was very low.

It should be added in conclusion on this point that the mathematical proof of nonequalization appears in both the 1933 and 1967 editions of *Interregional and International Trade.*

An important reason for the nonequalization of factor prices, however, can be found in the indivisibility phenomenon. In *The Theory of Trade*, chapter II, he argues that trade tends to equalize factor prices, but this will be incomplete, in general, because of indivisibilities of factors (economies of scale). That is, here the emphasis is on indivisibility as a barrier to factor price equalization, not just as a cause of trade. Ohlin's reasoning is somewhat contradictory when discussing the effects of indivisibility on factor price equalization. On one hand, he argues that exploitation of increasing returns will lead to a more intensive utilization of indivisible factors of production, and thereby to a tendency to factor price equalization. On the other hand, he argues that in the absence of transportation costs, increasing returns will be exploited to the full, leading to specialization in production between regions and, presumably, to unequal factor prices.

International Monetary Economics

The Theory of Interregional Exchange contains no international monetary economics, while *The Theory of Trade* contains a long chapter on capital mobility in which Ohlin deals with fixed and flexible exchange rates, the gold standard, money supply, the price level, and balance of payments adjustments, among other things. Also there is a shorter chapter on international differences in price levels.

Here one can detect the influence on Ohlin of his stay at Harvard during the academic year 1922–23. At Harvard he took a course in international finance and came into contact with Taussig's students in international economics, especially John H. Williams and Jacob Viner. Viner let Ohlin read the manuscript of *Canada's Balance of International Indebtedness 1900–13*, published in 1924. Some of what Ohlin learned from his reading is reproduced in *The Theory of Trade*, published the same year.

Perhaps the most interesting part of Ohlin's treatment of international financial flows is his analysis of the effects of international borrowing and lending on the terms of trade. The question discussed by Ohlin is whether Canada's relatively large international net borrowing in the beginning of the twentieth century had caused an improvement in her terms of trade. If all goods were traded, no change in the terms of trade would occur. The borrowing was tantamount to a shift in "buying power" from the lending countries to Canada. The lending countries would demand less of domestically produced and Canadian goods, but this fall in demand would be replaced by equal increases in Canadian demand for domestic and foreign goods. Implicit is the assumption of identical and homothetic demands in Canada and among her trading partners. But in reality some goods were not traded. In Canada, the increased demand for nontraded goods would raise factor prices in the nontraded sector, and this would spill over into the traded goods sector, raising costs and prices. The reverse would take place abroad. Thus the Canadian terms of trade would improve. The adjustment to international capital flows therefore normally consisted both of changes in spending and of changes in the terms of trade, which in turn would cause changes in the pattern of production (making the nontraded sector in Canada expand relatively to the traded sector).

The analysis of the effects of international capital flows is interesting because it is clearly influenced by Taussig, Viner, and Williams (who wrote his dissertation on the Argentinian experience of borrowing under flexible exchange rates), and prepares Ohlin for his interchange with Keynes in the *Economic Journal* in 1929 on the transfer problem. Ohlin himself attributes to Wicksell's influence the underlying awareness of the importance of matching aggregate supply and demand in analyzing the transfer problem. This was precisely what helped him show that Keynes's analysis was incomplete. Keynes had argued that for Germany to be able to pay reparations to England after World War I, it would have to create a trade surplus. This would necessarily worsen its terms of trade and impose an additional burden to the transfer. Ohlin's point was that the transfer of buying power from Germany to England would not change the terms of trade if the decreases in demand for German exportables and imports from England in Germany were exactly offset by increases in demand for German goods and English exportables in England. In any case, the deterioration in Germany's terms of trade would be considerably less than in Keynes's model.

And yet, without the monetary analysis, the discussion of the transfer of capital and the difference between it and the transfer of any other factor in *The Theory of Interregional Exchange* is very succinct and elegant. In one of the few passages relevant to countries rather than regions in general, he argues that capital is like labor in being mobile between regions, but the obstacles to the mobility of capital between different countries are so high that the transfer of capital cannot considerably affect the capital resources of a country in the short run, despite the different interest levels. But a capital flow that is small relative to the capital stock of a country may be large relative to the trade flows. The need to equate prices of goods in the two countries converts into another equilibrium where a larger or smaller number of the domestic goods fetch higher prices, so as to achieve a new equilibrium, in which the deficit in the trade balance will be exactly covered by capital imports. He goes on to describe changes in prices and utilization of factors of production as some industries increase and others decline, and how changes in income and prices of goods will also incur a restructuring of consumption. Since capital flows are important and volatile, shifts in the entire equilibrium may not only be numerous and frequent but also significant and hence different in their effects from flows of either labor or the organizational factors, which affect the equilibrium only slowly.

Transitional Dynamics

Perhaps the greatest influence of the Harvard group is seen in what we choose to call transitional dynamics. That the economic system is dynamic and should be treated as such was important to Ohlin, as is quite evident in *The Theory of Trade* and *Interregional and International Trade*. Nothing of that can be found in *The Theory of Interregional Exchange*. The lack of dynamics in classical theory was of great concern to Williams, who discussed it with Ohlin. Williams apparently influenced Ohlin strongly on this point. One may only guess that Ohlin appreciated dynamics not only for its own sake but also because it helped him to differentiate his product from classical theory.

The Theory of Trade is divided into three parts. The second part is by far the longest, and contains much transitional dynamics. By that is meant that Ohlin introduces an exogenous change, for example, a shift in demand or a change in factor endowments, and then describes the various adjustments to the change over time. Ohlin did not believe in equilibrium or steady state except as a theoretical construct. In his view, the economy is forever adjusting to various shocks. He just focused on one shock and analyzed its consequences ceteris paribus.

Chapter IX, entitled "The Mobility of Capital," contains the best examples of Ohlin's transitional dynamics exercises. He starts out the section analyzing the effects of a capital inflow (p. 128) in the following way:

> Borrowing implies a transfer of buying power, which enables the borrowing region to buy a larger share of world output than before, while other regions buy less. If there were no transport costs, changing the location of consumption for some goods would have no effect on production. Only if the borrowing region demanded goods other than those that the rest of the world ceased to produce would there be a change in the composition of total demand and eventually also a change in the pattern of production.

Normally the borrowing region will be producing nontraded goods and the increase in demand for both nontraded and tradable goods will raise the relative price of the former, since their supply is less elastic. The increase in demand for exportables and imports, and lending countries' decreased demand for the borrowing country's exports will create an import surplus. This will help to maintain equilibrium in the balance of payments. In the next round of adjustments, demand is shifted from nontraded to tradable goods because of the relative price increase of the former. The import surplus is increased further, helping to maintain the balance of payments. There are also adjustments on the supply side: resources are moved from the tradable to the nontraded sector. Imports are then replacing production of importables, so the import surplus is increased even more. Equilibrium in the balance of payments can be maintained if the import surplus precisely matches the capital imports. In the third round of adjustments, factor supplies will change in response to changes in factor prices. Specifically, factors used intensively in the nontraded sector will recieve higher rewards and their supply will increase. This will, however, take some years, since it may involve changes in occupational choice and capital investments. Finally, the terms of trade may change as a result of the capital inflow. Ohlin maintains the assumption that the borrowing country is small on world markets and therefore has little influence on export and import prices. But in rare cases the small country may be large on the market for its exports and can shift higher production costs onto foreign consumers, so the terms of trade improve.

The general case of a capital inflow is then illustrated by two particular cases, those of Canada and Argentina. Here the account is borrowed from Viner, on Canada, and Williams, on Argentina.

Transitional dynamics of this kind was introduced in *The Theory of Trade* and very much expanded in *Interregional and International Trade*, together with many more empirical examples and much more detail.

Finally

When he wrote his licentiate thesis, Bertil Ohlin, at 23, had the core (not only the seed) of what was to become his more fully articulated theory of trade and payments. In the three monographs that constitute the body of his work in trade theory, he built, developed, and added, but never changed, the main arguments. (We have concentrated here primarily on the passage from *The Theory of Interregional Exchange* to *The Theory of Trade*, having discussed elsewhere the development from *The Theory of Trade* to *Interregional and International Trade*.[1]) What came later, as we have noted, was the highly important monetary and macro ramifications of the theory, clearly stimulated by the Harvard experience. However, his brief but incisive early discussion in *The Theory of Interregional Exchange* of the difference between the mobility of capital and that of other factors of production can be considered the beginnings of his research agenda on this subject. He did not have to go to Harvard to understand that capital is not simply mobile, that it has to be transferred, and that this has important repercussions on the other factors of production and on trade and output.

As well as the macro analysis, the licentiate thesis lacked the relatively detailed criticism of the classical school that, like the monetary analysis, was developed considerably in *The Theory of Trade* and expanded and extended in *Interregional and International Trade*. But the core of his trade theory, the emphasis on the importance of factor endowments and factor intensities in production, is there in the licentiate thesis, albeit tempered by his almost equal stress on economies of scale. These he gave less prominence in later works, and they were, of course, eschewed by trade theorists of the Heckscher-Ohlin persuasion until the last two decades and the emergence of the "new trade theory." Why Ohlin dropped the emphasis on the economies of scale is somewhat of a puzzle on which one can only speculate.

In the short period intervening between *The Theory of Interregional Exchange* and *The Theory of Trade*, from the licentiate to the doctorate, Ohlin seems to have been influenced by, and attracted to, even more than previously, the work of his teacher Cassel (and to have continued to drift from Heckscher). Thus he proudly displays general equilibrium as expressed in Cassel's *Theoretische Sozialökonomie*, much more heavily emphasized in *The Theory of Trade* than in *The Theory of Interregional Exchange*. He also develops more fully his objections to classical and early neoclassical trade theory and has more detailed and specific arguments with them.

What did not change was his basic approach, his style, the heart of the idea, the passion for realism and for detail, and the insistence on empirical relevance.

Ohlin was competent mathematically, and he highly valued, as we have noted, what he occasionally called the "Lausanne method," but most of his analysis, in this and later works, is verbal. His desire to carry out general equilibrium analysis was combined with an unwillingness to abstract for long from reality and lack of ability (or desire) to simplify and pare reality. (This was done subsequently by several of the people sitting in this room.) Here he deviated considerably from the style and inclinations of his teachers. Heckscher's paper is archetypical simple verbal general equilibrium analysis, though as passionately committed as Ohlin's work to empirical relevance, and even more so to policy issues. Cassel's work is either formal general equilibrium or, as in the monetary works on purchasing power parity, straightforward, monocausal, and simple. Ohlin could not walk down the strait and narrow path without stopping to smell the roses, making countless detours into the woods, though always coming back. As a result, following him, though difficult, is always exciting.

Note

1. The difference in the titles of the three works is interesting and instructive. In all three of them he took pains to emphasize the distinction between international, interregional, and interlocal trade while at the same time switching the discussion interchangeably between them. The distinction had mainly to do with factor mobility and transportation costs, and it was important to Ohlin, who was much preoccupied with the locational significance of trade theory.

References

Cassel, Gustav. 1918. *Theoretische Sozialökonomie.* Leipzig: Winter.

Flam, Harry, and M. June Flanders. 1991. Introduction. In Bertil Ohlin and Eli Heckscher, *Heckscher-Ohlin Trade Theory.* Cambridge: MIT Press.

Heckscher, Eli. 1918 [1949, 1991]. The Effect of Foreign Trade on the Distribution of Income. In Bertil Ohlin and Eli Heckscher. *Heckscher-Ohlin Trade Theory.* Cambridge: MIT Press.

Ohlin, Bertil. 1933. *Interregional and International Trade.* Cambridge: Harvard University Press.

Ohlin, Bertil. 1924 [1991]. The Theory of Trade. In Bertil Ohlin and Eli Heckscher, *Heckscher-Ohlin Trade Theory.* Cambridge: MIT Press.

Ohlin, Bertil. 1922 [1999]. *The Theory of Interregional Exchange.* Seminar paper 675. Institute for International Economic Studies. Stockholm University.

11 Bertil Ohlin in Copenhagen

Niels-Henrik Topp

Introduction

In December 1924 Bertil Ohlin became professor of economics at the University of Copenhagen, at the age of 25. During his five-year stay Ohlin worked on several of the contributions to economics that were to make him famous. This chapter traces the interactions between Ohlin and his colleagues and students in Denmark.

The first question to be raised is, How did Ohlin come to Copenhagen? Ohlin himself has written extensively on this event in his autobiography, but there is also an interesting Danish perspective to the story. The second question is, What was Ohlin's relationship with his colleagues and students? Did the new surroundings have any effect on his work, and how did he himself influence the economics faculty and teaching?

Finally, Ohlin's major contributions to the Danish theoretical and political debate are investigated. Ohlin participated extensively in the public debate, but the question is, Did such a change in the economic policy then follow as the one he and other members of the Stockholm School contributed to in Sweden in the 1930s?

How did Ohlin Get to Copenhagen?

The chair of economics and statistics at the University became vacant when Professor Harald Westergaard reached the age of retirement in April 1923. Although this hardly came as a surprise to the University, no successor had been nominated, and the position had not even been publicly advertised. To aggravate the problem, two out of the three remaining professors at the Department were on leave that spring term. Lauritz V. Birck was on a commission on bank failures, and Jens Warming was in the United States to make a government inquiry of the Volstead Act. The teaching staff was therefore reduced to one full professor, Axel Nielsen, and two part-time lecturers.[1]

In these circumstances the students naturally became concerned when it was reported that Professor Nielsen was to be a trustee in the Danish National Bank (the Central Bank). To overcome the urgent problem of the teaching load, Westergaard was granted the right to continue his teaching until February 1924. Furthermore the Swede, Professor Eli F. Heckscher, lectured on mercantilism and the theory of foreign trade during part of the spring term of 1923, and conducted weekly seminars in economics. Finally, Frederik Zeuthen, the chief economist at the Danish Ministry of Social Affairs at that time, took care of Birck's teaching load and lectured on the theory of value in 1922 and 1923.[2]

To the students' dismay, no action was taken until October 1923 when it was reported that the Faculty of Law and Economics planned to convert the chair into two readerships and hire Hans Cl. Nybølle in theoretical statistics and Zeuthen in economics. This time the students intervened and addressed a public statement to the Dane, K. A. Wieth-Knudsen, professor of economics at the Norwegian Technical High School in Trondheim, and urged him to seek the position in Denmark:[3]

> Since we the undersigned students of economics have received the impression from the Professor's personal, didactic, and scientific merits that your becoming a professor at the University would benefit our Faculty and science as well as the education of the students, and since moreover we consider the Professor to be the best qualified for the position and, consequently, the one we should prefer to have attached to the Faculty, we hereby venture to call upon the Professor to apply for the vacant position, while expressing our hopes that those with whom the decision rests may take into consideration the sentiments of the students that are expressed by this address.

The statement was signed by no less than 89 students of economics out of a total student body of 158. However, the students' expectations were not met. In late 1923 the position was announced to be open for application, and the deadline was fixed at January 5, 1924. At the same time members of the Faculty made inquiries to their Nordic colleagues in order to increase the number of foreign candidates. Shortly before Christmas Heckscher drew Ohlin's attention to the possibility and hinted that though the outcome was uncertain, he saw no reason why Ohlin should not apply. Ohlin had published several articles on monetary theory in the Swedish Journal *Ekonomisk Tidskrift* and three minor volumes for a Swedish trade commission, and together with his doctoral thesis, which he was about to finish, this might suffice to make him qualified (see Ohlin 1972:92).

Ohlin's rivals for the chair were Erik Lindahl from Lund, the Norwegian economist Kristian Schönheyder, and Edvard Philip Mackeprang and Svend Røgind from Denmark. The 33-year-old Lindahl held a position as lecturer at the University of Lund and his thesis on taxation had been published five years before. Both Schönheyder and Mackeprang (50 and 47 years old) had never held a permanent position at a University despite the fact that both of them had defended a thesis and frequently issued new publications. Schönheyder's thesis from 1909 dealt with the theory of capital, whereas Mackeprang's thesis from the same year on price theory contains the first estimation of demand functions.[4] The last combatant, Røgind, held a position as part-time lecturer at the Technical University of Copenhagen. At the age of 37, he had published some articles on taxation but no major research work.

The five applications were screened by a committee of the four professors of the Department—Westergaard, Birck, Nielsen, and Warming. The committee's report was delivered shortly after and it stated:

> On the basis of the available information the Committee considers that the scholarly merits of all the best qualified applicants are such that it is not obvious which of them should be nominated for the vacant professorship. The Committee therefore recommends that a competition is held and that all applicants are allowed to participate. (Translated from *The Yearbook of the University of Copenhagen*, 1924–25:16)

On March 19, His Majesty signed a royal decree forming a new committee, which included the Dean of the Faculty (K. Berlin from the Department of Law), Heckscher, Nielsen, and Birck, all nominated by the University, and three persons nominated by the Ministry of Education, Professor Westergaard, the Norwegian Professor Thorvald Aarum, and the former senior civil servant Cordt Trap, who had for a long period of time been officially appointed external examiner to the program in economics.

The rules for the competition allowed new applicants within fourteen days, and thus the door was left open to Wieth-Knudsen. However, he renounced and did not apply for the position this time either. Neither did Zeuthen, although rumors had long made him a likely candidate since he had acted as substitute for Birck the previous years. As no new competitors turned up, the five applicants were asked to write a paper on the topic: "The Effects of a Reduction in the Working Hours on the Methods and Scale of Production and on Welfare in General." The topic was announced in May, and the papers were to be presented within three months in printed, but not published, form.[5] Even though it is common for University committees to drag their heels, it is somewhat surprising that it took two months to agree on a topic. The committee might have taken into consideration that one of the applicants was quite busy right to the end of May, when he was to defend his own thesis.

The second part of the competition consisted of two lectures by each applicant. The topics of the first, freely chosen lecture were quite interesting. Lindahl and Ohlin lectured on mainstream topics—"The Interest on Capital" and "Monetary Theory"—while Mackeprang's and Schönheyder's topics were "The Development in Mathematical Economics" and "The Method of Exact Sciences and Its Application in Economics." For the second lecture all applicants got 48 hours to prepare a lecture on "The Economic Consequences of Establishing Production on the Basis of the Employees' Organization (Guild-Socialism)."

The competition took place in September and was widely reported in the newspapers. Røgind had withdrawn from the competition in July, but the remaining four applicants all got positive assessments from the committee:

> ... With regard to all participants in the competition the appointment committee would like to express its recognition of their scholarly works prior to the competition and of their participation in the same. However, the committee do after all undoubtedly consider Doctor of Law Erik Lindahl and Doctor of Philosophy Bertil Ohlin to be the best qualified. The entire committee have agreed that these applicants are almost equal, and several members of the committee have had their doubts about whom to prefer. It has not been possible to reach a unanimous agreement on the nomination and [the committee] has divided into a majority of five and a minority of two. The majority which consist of the undersigned Axel Nielsen, Heckscher, Birck, Cordt Trap, and Berlin nominate Lecturer Bertil Ohlin, while the minority consisting of the undersigned Th. Aarum and Harald Westergaard nominate Lecturer Erik Lindahl. (Translated from *The Yearbook of the University of Copenhagen*, 1924–25:18–19)

Based on the committee's report, the Ministry of Education appointed Ohlin to the chair of economics from December 1, 1924. Ohlin was only appointed a temporary professor, the definite appointment was to be postponed until he had been naturalized as a Danish subject. The official announcement came on October 21, 1925, and as a compensation for the delay to the young professor, the announcement stated the appointment took effect already from May 1, 1925.

Ohlin's Colleagues

Ohlin came to a small Department with only four full-time professors and the retiring Professor Westergaard. Westergaard, who had held the chair for 37 years, was a well-known statistician. He had been a leading European demographic researcher from the 1880s to the late 1920s with extensive international publications on mortality in different social classes. Westergaard still remained active after his retirement. He wrote his famous *Contribution to the History of Statistics* at the age of 79, and 15 titles were published after his eightieth birthday. Alongside his work at the University, he was on numerous committees for ecclesiastical, temperance, and social reform societies. In this regard he shared a common interest with another professor at the Department, Warming; see Kærgård and Davidsen (1998:349–51).

According to Ohlin, Birck was the Danish economist who had the greatest influence on him. Birck was 53 years old and had been a member of the Faculty for 17 years when Ohlin came to Copenhagen. The close contact with Birck was established right from the beginning. In his autobiography Ohlin writes: "Birck lived with his wife at the Hotel "Kongen af Danmark" where he had two or three rooms. When I came to Copenhagen I took his advice and moved into the same hotel in January 1925 to get the time to look for something more permanent. Birck rarely went to bed before six o'clock in the morning, and consequently I was engaged in a good deal of stimulating nightly conversations" (Ohlin 1972:121).

It is difficult to think of a more suitable person to introduce Ohlin to the Danish society. Birck's position as the leading Danish economist in the 1920s was undisputed and his theoretical contributions were closely related to the marginal revolution. His major works on the theory of marginal value and production were influenced by

Jevons, Menger, Wiser, and Böhm-Bawerk, but foremost by Marshall. The influence from the British economists was striking, "... even a number of technical terms were taken directly from the English language and became part of the Danish economists' vocabulary until Ohlin taught them to speak Swedish" (Zeuthen 1944:97).

Birck's book on the theory of marginal value from the turn of the century is today acknowledged for having placed "the marginal concept" as the firm foundation of Danish economic science and teaching at the University. On the other hand, it would be justified to say that Birck never made any major contribution to economics. No "Birck theorem" has survived, and as a scientist his merits were chiefly those of serving as a mediator of the international development in economic theory.[6] Internationally he had close contacts with the London School of Economics, which he visited frequently, and two of his major books were translated into English.[7]

However, as a participant in the public debate, Birck's influence was far-reaching. His fame as a remorseless inspector of the dark side of the capitalist economy was established when, as a Conservative member of the Danish Parliament, he participated in the campaign in 1908 against the Danish Minister of Justice, Peter Adler Alberti, who in the end had to turn himself in for having committed large-scale forgery. During the war he served as a member of the committee in charge of price controls, which made him a much disliked person in the Danish business community. When Ohlin came to Copenhagen, Birck had just finished serving on a committee investigating the failure of the largest bank in Denmark and Scandinavia.

A general distrust in a free capitalist economy was at the center of many of Birck's writings. He was in favor of government regulations to cope with the problems of monopolies. In this regard he was more in line with the left wing, though he did not share their belief in central planning. However, he remained pessimistic about the possibility of establishing a mixed economy, because governments remained weak compared with the business community. His faith in the ability of governments to be in control of the economy diminished due to experiences during and after the war. He blamed the reckless fiscal policy and the extensive increase in public debt for the demolition of the European economies. In Denmark this policy went hand in hand with a monetary policy, which, according to Birck, was led by the paralyzed and ignorant managers of the Central Bank (Zeuthen 1944:110).

In his autobiography Ohlin attributes his increasing consciousness of the defects of the economic system to Birck, which made Ohlin firmly convinced of the need of government control with monopolies and cartels.[8] The impact was not just recognized with hindsight. In 1935 Ohlin had a disagreement with Heckscher, who felt that Ohlin had diverted too much from the neoclassical approach to economic problems, and in a letter Ohlin pointed out to Heckscher:

> To a certain degree your disillusion may be due to an inability to comprehend the personal development I underwent from 1925 to 1929 under the influence of, a.o. [among others], Birck. In 1930 you expected me to pick up the thread of the B.O. of 1924 and interpreted the change in me as spinelessness. (Translated from Larsson 1998:105)

Birck's impact relates to his view of the economic system and the need for government intervention, whereas Ohlin was critical of Birck's achievements as a theoretical economist. Ohlin published a frank review of Birck's book on the theory of production from 1927, in which he pointed out the lack of rigor in the presentation and the inconsistencies with Birck's earlier works (see Ohlin 1928:71–73). Shortly after he left Copenhagen, Ohlin wrote an article for the newspaper *Politiken* in which he highly praised Gunnar Myrdal's new book *Vetenskap och Politik*, 1930. Ohlin joined Myrdal in his criticism of the theory of marginal value and singled out Birck as its most prominent, contemporary spokesman in the Nordic countries. Birck, however, was in good company this time as Ohlin (1930b) pointed out that the same criticism could be addressed to Wicksell, Marshall, and Warming. Second, Ohlin stated that if "the quasi-psychological arguments were eliminated, books like Birck's *Theory of Value* would give a far more satisfactory and fundamental explanation of the formation of prices."[9]

The teaching in macroeconomic or monetary theory was taken care of by Nielsen. He was 44 years old but had already been a professor for 14 years. Like Birck, he had a high profile in the public debate due to his harsh criticism of the way monetary policy was conducted during and after the war. Today Nielsen is primarily remembered for his criticism of the Keynesian approach, and when he retired in 1951, his views were seen as clearly outdated. It was not the Keynesian framework per se that made him reject the *General Theory* but rather the air of irresponsible monetary policy.

Boserup has argued that Nielsen's teaching in monetary theory and banking before the *General Theory* was on a par with the standard on either side of the Atlantic. "Nielsen's older masters were Fisher, Hawtrey, and Wicksell. Waiting at the end of his labyrinths were younger ones like Lindahl and Albert Hahn—the German forerunner of Keynes. That was the best and most advanced available at the time."[10] Ohlin has only made very brief comments on Nielsen, but they seem to have been very much in line regarding the principles of monetary policy. When Ohlin entered the debate on the Danish monetary policy, he raised his voice in favor of the views of Nielsen and Birck. Similarly references to Ohlin can be found in Nielsen's works on monetary policy. Controversies were more likely to occur in the 1930s when Ohlin and the Stockholm School departed from the straight and narrow path.

The fourth professor at the Department of Economics in 1925 was the 51-year-old Warming. He had been teaching applied statistics at the University since 1906, but the position was converted to a chair only in 1919. Warming's name was established by his publication of large-scale statistical descriptions of the Danish economy. A detailed knowledge of the Danish economy was—and still remains—an important part of the education of future Danish civil servants. However, as indicated by Boserup, his contributions to theory were not appreciated. Even his closest colleagues failed to identify the substance behind his bizarre style, and his old-fashioned and deeply religious manners served as an obstacle to the next generation of Danish economists.[11]

The esteem for Warming has changed considerably over the last 30 years, and he is now recognized to claim priority in several areas. He explained the identification problem in econometrics already in 1906—about 20 years before the well-known American publications. The arguments in his 1911 article on the rent of a fishing ground are identical with the results of Gordon's classical article on fisheries economics from 1954. Finally, he worked very precisely with the multiplier theorem in the 1920s, before Kahn, Keynes, and even Ohlin. While the two first contributions remained restricted to a Scandinavian audience, Warming's account of the multiplier and the interaction between savings and investment was published both in Danish and English (Kærgård, Andersen, and Topp 1998:331–38).

The portrait given by Ohlin fits in well with the Danish accounts of Warming. In his autobiography, he writes:

> The teaching of applied statistics was taken care of by Professor Jens Warming, who was just as much an economist as a statistician. However, as an economist he was met with some reserve by my fellow economists, Birck and Axel Nielsen. Admittedly, Warming showed an inclination for oversimplification which easily raised doubts about his scientific standard. However, this was a mistake. He published a couple of extensive articles in journals that attracted some interest internationally. The lesson I learned from his case was that you must not judge the potential of a scholar on the basis of his ability to converse and a possible lack of brilliance and quickness. (Translated from Ohlin 1972:125)

The lack of rigor in Warming's theoretical publications and his rather nonclassical approach ought to have made him an easy target for Ohlin's sharp comments in the 1920s. But strangely enough Ohlin commented publicly on Warming's macroeconomic ideas only once, that is, in 1932. Warming for his part often referred to Ohlin and undoubtedly ranked him highly, though he did not always agree on Ohlin's policy recommendations (Topp 1992).

The incident where Ohlin made a comment on Warming occurred in his dispute with Johan Åkerman in the Swedish journal *Det ekonomiska Läget*. Åkerman (1932) had singled out Warming, Ohlin, and Ernst Wigforss as the spokesmen of inflationary policy and proponents of a "theory of purchasing power." Åkerman's basic argument was that consumption had to be reduced to make resources available for investments. Ohlin was allowed to make a rejoinder in the journal, in which he rejected Åkerman's criticism and took a stand in favor of Warming's position that savings and investments took place simultaneously (Ohlin 1932).

There are also indications of direct contact between Warming and Ohlin after his return to Sweden. On September 12, 1933, Warming entered into his diary that he felt embarrassed for having turned down a request from Ohlin. Warming notes that he was "too old to react with such a short notice, previously more flexible" (Davidsen 1999:6). The diary only gives a brief account and gives no indication of the contents of Ohlin's request. It can therefore only be stated that Ohlin's confidence in Warming existed at least in some specific area.[12]

In his biography Sven Erik Larsson (1998:55) states that Ohlin was not particularly impressed by the Danish economists. Unfortunately, no direct references are made to this statement, and it is difficult to accept when reviewing Ohlin's autobiography and other publications. It is quite obvious that apart from Westergaard, the Faculty did not have any high profile scholars in this decade. However, the three Danish professors were not totally absent in the international debate, as indicated in table 11.1. A comparative assessment would probably rank the Danish Faculty in line with the Norwegian in the 1920s. On the other hand, the Danes lagged far behind the Swedes. As pointed out by Birck in 1923, "No country has so many distinguished economists as Sweden: Wicksell, Silverstolpe, Cassel, Eli Heckscher, Sommarin, Brock, Gösta Bagge, Åkermann, Rohtlieb, Lindman, etc. etc."[13]

Ohlin and the Students

Ohlin came to the Faculty at a time when it was generally agreed that the course of study in economics needed reform. It was evident to the students that Copenhagen lagged behind the American universities in the teaching of economics. The teaching methods were outdated, mainly lectures were offered, and the object of the courses was primarily to give the students an overview within economics, statistics, political history, and law. There were few opportunities for in-depth studies of specific economic topics, and the Faculty had no scholarships for funding young researchers (Friis 1924). The course program had been created by Westergaard with a strong emphasis on theoretical and applied statistics and the study of law, which was considered essential to future civil servants.[14] The result was a course program that was indeed considered to be one of the most difficult to pass at the University but whose curriculum was not focused on economics. As pointed out by Heckscher in a letter from 1923 to Ohlin, the task of the new professor was "no less than to establish the foundation of a research-based teaching in economics in a neighboring country that in so many other areas has a level of research equal to the Swedish" (Ohlin 1972:92–93).

It is evident from reading an article in a student chronicle that the students met Ohlin with great expectations. His training at Harvard University and Cambridge University was considered a great advantage, and the article expressed the hope that Ohlin might work together with the students in reforming the course program.[15] Ohlin himself was aware of the requirements of changes in the teaching. In

Table 11.1
Publications in native or foreign languages, 1920 to 1939

	Birck		Nielsen		Warming		Ohlin	
Period	Danish	Foreign	Danish	Foreign	Danish	Foreign	Danish + Swedish	Foreign + index
1920–1924	16	2	4	0	10	3	1 + 10	0 + 0
1925–1929	15	8	12	4	9	0	10 + 4	9 + 11
1930–1934	16	0	13	8	19	5	3 + 14	13 + 5
1935–1939	—	—	4	2	13	3	1 + 2	13 + 4

Sources: Ohlin's publications are computed on the basis of the bibliography in *Scandinavian Journal of Economics* 1978, pp. 93–99, and *The Danish National Bibliography*.
Note: Ohlin's publications in foreign languages include the articles in Svenska Handelsbankens Index. Warming published extensively on non-economic subjects, mostly religious matters and the temperance movement. These articles and books have not been included in the calculation. The four economists' articles in newspapers have not been included.

an interview shortly after becoming professor, he set out his views on teaching:[16]

> Indeed, the teaching here [in Denmark] is carried out solely in the form of lectures. They have certainly been kept in Sweden, too, but not as a mere presentation of the existing curriculum. A lecture must be an incentive to independent reflection and attach importance to the collaboration between the student and the teacher. Currently, this collaboration is also improved by seminars, which I for my part intend to start already on Wednesday.
>
> ... When ... a subject is discussed thoroughly under guidance [in a seminar], a practice is acquired in analyzing problems in economic terms.... In short, I think the object of this university method can be expressed like this: the aim is not to teach the subject but to teach how to handle the subject.... It is going to be interesting to get down to teaching Danish students, who are after all able to express themselves far more easily than the Swedish.

The seminars in economics were introduced on a voluntary basis, but they became quite successful and were given by Ohlin every term during his stay.[17] The integration of the seminars in the academic courses is acknowledged as one of Ohlin's main impacts on teaching, and when a reform was carried through in 1929, seminars became a compulsory part of the program in economics (Winding Pedersen 1976:267). The second part of Ohlin's teaching load was to lecture for one hour three to four times a week to the students of economics and some terms to the law students. Ohlin alternated with Birck in giving lectures at introductory and advanced levels. In 1928 Ohlin lectured on international trade and tariffs for the first time, and during the next few years the topics were economic theory on the basis of Birck, Cassel, and Marshall. Even his approach to lecturing astonished the students when he asked them not to take notes but instead to use the time to consider thoroughly the economic problems. Winding Pedersen has given a record of Ohlin's teaching in the late 1920s:[18]

> He preferred to organize the teaching of economic theory as discussions that were highly stimulating. When in charge he could outline the principal contents of a complicated topic with brilliant clarity like nobody else. It happened, however, that he appeared to be a bit poorly prepared. Then it was assumed that the young Professor had once more been to a nightclub.

In Ohlin's own recollection of his teaching he remarks, "I learnt as much from the students and those who had recently been students as from my colleagues," and he singled out a handful of Danish economists, who later became professors at Danish universities (Ohlin 1972:126, 1977). In this group, however, only Carl Iversen can be pictured as a disciple of Ohlin. Jørgen Pedersen and Jørgen Dich dealt extensively with unemployment and macroeconomic problems in the 1930s, but it was rather from a Keynesian or Marxist perspective, and they were both critical of the achievements of the Stockholm School. To Hans Winding Pedersen and Thorkil Kristensen business economics became the area of research. The latter might have been influenced by Ohlin who in his last address to the Danish Economic Association dealt with the importance of research-based education in business economics and frequently discussed the cooperation between scientists and the business community (Ohlin 1930a).

In retrospect, Ohlin acknowledged that the Swedes could learn a great deal from the Danish teaching system. In particular, he drew attention to the seminars in applied statistics that gave the Danish students a far better understanding of the integration of statistical material and economic theory than the Swedish students obtained (Ohlin 1972:125). However, there were flaws in the education of economists, and Ohlin took part in the renewal of the course program, which took place in the late 1920s. Apart from the introduction of compulsory seminars in economics the important changes were to increase the curriculum in economics at the expense of the study of law, and to substitute economic history for political history. Finally, business economics became part of the undergraduate curriculum, and a thesis was added to the graduate study. In this respect the course program of economics was in far better shape when Ohlin left Copenhagen, and it might be said that Ohlin had contributed to the fulfillment of the task Heckscher had outlined in 1923.[19]

In the Danish university system all oral examinations are carried out by the professor and an officially appointed external examiner. Therefore we are able to get an impression of Ohlin's method of carrying out examinations from the memoirs of the head of the Danish Department of Statistics, Adolf Jensen. He singled out two aspects which he found to be characteristic of Ohlin's examination practice. First of all, he recalled that in his examinations Ohlin, just like Birck, occasionally rose to superior levels, and second, that Ohlin used two different methods of examination:

> Professor Ohlin had his own practical way of presenting the subject that he wanted to discuss. He might start an examination by asking, "Have you read the morning papers today?" and as the candidate had, of course, not had the energy to read papers on the very day of his examination, the Professor would continue by giving a review of an article of economic interest saying, "Let's look a little bit closer at the substance of this argument." When examining undergraduates, Ohlin liked to ask several very short questions. It is a method, probably taken over from American universities, which appears to be quite useful with students who have only taken an introductory course. There is, however, a danger that the examinee becomes wearied of jumping several times from one subject to another and is thereby knocked off balance. (Translated from Jensen 1946:195)

Ohlin's record of being a tough examiner who would put a poser to a candidate and swing his pocket watch to and fro waiting for an answer is also part of the story. However, it was mainly a problem for the law students (Larsson 1998:514).

Does Supply Create Its Own Demand?

The appearance of a new professor of economics who became heavily involved in the public debate once more drew attention to the Department, and it is natural to ask to what extent it improved the public rating of the Department. Did it make a difference at all?

If the number of Faculty members is taken as an indicator of the University's and the Ministry of Education's appreciation of the Department, there was little change during Ohlin's stay in Copenhagen. In 1925 he tried to get funding for establishing a research institute with the specific aim of studying business cycles, but his ideas evoked no response (Ohlin 1972:127).

To evaluate the Department's esteem in the public opinion, the Danish system of free admission to the University might serve as a crude indicator. The stir created by the appointment of the young professor and his eagerness to participate in the economic debate would have been expected to have attracted an increasing number of students within a short period of time. In reality, the intake of new students of economics became depressingly low from September 1924, and there was no sign of recovery until September 1928 when the admission suddenly increased by 50 percent and surpassed the level of the early twenties.

The decline in the mid-twenties cannot be attributed to a reduction of the general intake at the University. The Department of Law, which was the closest competitor also experienced a decline, but far less significant. The decline in the number of students in economics is indeed hard to understand. The public debate on economic matters was intense, and the return to the gold standard and the problems following the massive bank failures played important roles in politics. However, the first Danish Labor government also took office in 1924, and the explanation might simply have been that students hesitated to study at the Faculty of Law and Economics because the career as a civil servant had become uncertain under the new ruling.

The rapid increase in the intake of students in economics in the late 1920s seems to have been at the expense of the law studies, and this might be taken as an indicator of a somewhat delayed "Ohlin-effect." Throughout Ohlin's stay in Copenhagen the newspapers frequently made references to the effect of Ohlin's appearance on the female students. The theme was introduced right from the start when Birck in his welcome address pointed out that it had been with some degree of reluctance that he had cast his vote in favor of Ohlin, because Birck would now no longer be the most handsome man at the Faculty![20] The number of female students of economics, however, remained stable at 26 to 28 percent of all female students within the Faculty of Law and Economics during the period 1925 to 1930, a level in line with the general level in the interwar period.[21] The fluctuation came within the body of male students where the economists' share dropped from 15 in 1925 to 11 percent in 1927. The conclusion must be that if the recovery from 1928 can be attributed to Ohlin, it was rather in his capacity as an economist than as a young bachelor. Or to put it more bluntly, it is difficult to find evidence that Ohlin attracted female students to economics.

Contributions to the Danish Economic Debate

Ohlin's residence in Copenhagen is today mainly remembered for his famous exchange with Keynes on the German reparation problem in 1929 and for his struggle to rewrite and expand the English version of his thesis on international trade. Both subjects will be dealt with extensively elsewhere in this book, and since they have no direct connection to Denmark, I will not comment on them.

This does not mean that there were no spillover effects, however. The discussion on the reparation problem was treated extensively in the Danish newspapers by Ohlin, Nielsen, and foremost by

Iversen.[22] Likewise we know from Ohlin's preface that Iversen was involved in the revision of the book on international trade, a statement repeated in Ohlin's Nobel autobiography: "several colleagues, and, particularly, Iversen, made useful, more or less critical observations about the manuscript." The influence was reciprocal. During Ohlin's stay in Copenhagen Iversen himself became heavily involved in the research area and later wrote his thesis on the theory of international capital movements.[23]

It has to be taken into account that by using this line of demarcation, Ohlin's important theoretical contributions are excluded. The remaining publications primarily deal with economic policy. Few treasures are to be found, and only one is frequently mentioned in the history of economic thought. The subjects of these publications were primarily monetary policy and the labor market, which were also at the center of his daily comments.[24]

Ohlin and the Danish Monetary Policy, 1914 to 1927

The conduct of the Danish monetary policy during and after the war had led to an acrimonious conflict between the Danish National Bank (the Central Bank) and the leading economists at the University, a debate corresponding to the debate carried out in Sweden (Haavisto and Jonung 1995). Like the Swedes, the Danish economists had a strong position and they were able to convince the public opinion that the managers of the Bank had no knowledge of contemporary monetary theory (Nielsen 1930).

During the war the National Bank had pursued a policy of accommodation with the purpose of stabilizing production and employment rather than the price level. After the suspension of the gold convertibility in August 1916 the Bank had purchased gold and foreign currency from Danish exporters, and during the next years, substantial credits were granted to foreign countries and the government. The massive expansion in credits by the National Bank and the private banks led to an increase in demand, and the National Bank made little effort to combat inflation but maintained a low discount rate at 5 percent from 1915 to 1919. Throughout the war Nielsen and Birck urged the National Bank to commit itself to price stability and use the discount rate as an instrument to reduce demand. The National Bank, however, defended its position by pointing out that a strong consideration for the Danish economy had

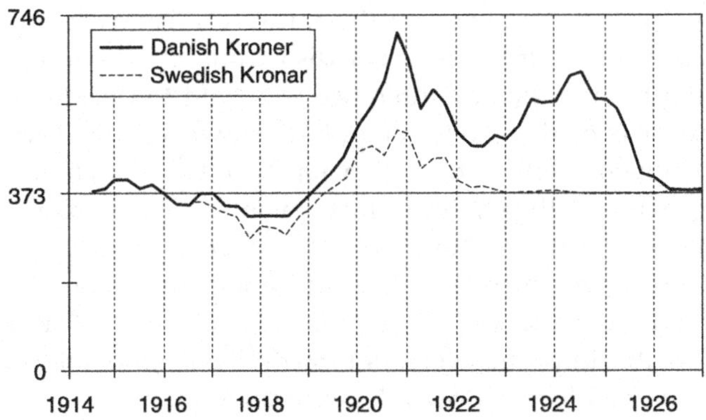

Figure 11.1
The Swedish and Danish rate of exchange in dollars, quarterly data for 1914 to 1927.
Sources: Olsen and Hoffmeyer (1968) and *Danish Statistical Yearbook, 1914–1920.*

priority over price stability, and that the malaise of high prices was subordinate to economic policy.[25]

The criticism of the policy of the National Bank escalated during the postwar period 1919 to 1920, when the combination of monetary overhang and peace optimism led to an increase in the Danish wholesale price index of 33 percent while the dollar rate, which had been close to par in December 1918, had fallen dramatically to 52 percent of the gold parity by October 1920, see figure 11.1. Throughout this period little was done to cope with inflationary pressure. The discount rate was increased twice, but no attempts were made to decrease the money supply and the credit to the public. The stabilization of the economic activity continued to be the overall ambition of the National Bank, and when the postwar recession caused Danish unemployment to rise, the discount rate was reduced several times during the next years.

During the next four years, the Danish exchange rate fluctuated heavily despite several attempts to introduce a stabilization policy. At first the attempts seemed to be successful, and by mid-1922 the exchange rate came close to 80 percent of the gold parity. However, during the next year the rate steadily decreased to 66 percent of the gold parity by the end of 1923.[26] The main issues in the Danish debate throughout this period continued to be whether a monetary policy could stand alone or, as the National Bank insisted, whether broad measures must be taken to make the stabilization work.

The effort to establish a consensus on the future Danish exchange rate policy in 1923 turned out to be rather disastrous. At the initiative of the National Bank a major conference was held to decide on the measures and goals of the economic policy. However, no clear-cut answers were given, neither to which parity Denmark should choose in the future, nor to the choice of instruments.[27] The outcome of the conference was that the National Bank raised an international loan to stabilize the currency. The additional recommendations, which implied a contraction of the monetary and fiscal policy and restrictions on the imports, were not carried out, and within months, speculations had forced down the exchange rate.

It was only in mid-1924, when the first Danish Labor government was formed, that coordinated measures were taken, which in the end led to Denmark's return to the gold standard. Under the chairmanship of the new prime minister, Thorvald Stauning, a small parliamentary committee was formed in July 1924 to make a new attempt to establish the guidelines for the exchange rate policy. At this point the influential businessman H. N. Andersen recommended to the prime minister that an expert with special knowledge of the currency problems in the Baltic countries should be attached to the committee. The proposal was prevented by the Minister of Finance, Carl Valdemar Bramsnæs, who resented the interference of the business community, and instead Ohlin was asked to prepare a report on the Stabilization Problem in Central Europe.[28]

Ohlin's report contains a detailed record of the stabilization policies in the Baltic countries, Czechoslovakia and Poland. His overall conclusions were in line with the position taken by the leading Swedish and Danish economists, and he summarized his investigation by arguing that:

> On the basis of the experiences of the countries being investigated, it is conspicuous that it is a common feature to all of them, that stabilization of the currency has only been accomplished by means of a notably forcible credit squeeze.... It is only when the capital market is restored by a reduction in government borrowing and by a curtailment of business credits, that it has been possible to impede inflation and the depreciation of the currency. (Translated from Ohlin 1924:31)

Ohlin's statement that monetary policy was at the center of the stabilization of the currency was close to the argument put forth by Nielsen in the Danish debate. Ohlin further stated that an adjustment of the internal price level was necessary to obtain a lasting stability on the balance of payment. Regarding the prospect of a stabilization of the currency by means of a restrictive monetary and fiscal policy, Ohlin was optimistic: "The predominant impression ... is that a stabilization is not as difficult to carry through as is often expected" (Ohlin 1924:35).

Ohlin's report was only completed in November 1924, and at this point the committee had already made up their minds that the Danish currency should return steadily to the gold standard. The importance attributed to the investigation of the new professor can be seen from the fact that the report was published as a supplement to the committee's white paper together with the official statement by the National Bank.

Ohlin's 1924 report was basically the work of an impartial expert who did not directly take sides in the ongoing Danish dispute about the currency problem. In his address to the Danish Economic Association in February 1927, however, Ohlin did not hesitate to point directly to the policy of the National Bank as being the main cause of the development. He acknowledged that the managers of the Bank had been under pressure from the government, the private banks, and the business community, but Ohlin did not conceal from the audience that he had little sympathy for the arguments put forth by the managers and the economists who had supported the policy of the Bank. As always in the public debate, Ohlin was very outspoken in his criticism as he went through the individual arguments of his fellow economists. Ohlin had no doubt that it was in the power of the National Bank to hamper inflation, whether it originated in internal or external factors, and he showed no appreciation of the argument that the National Bank had to adapt to the political environment and make concessions in order to safeguard the economic activity. In his final remarks Ohlin pointed out:

> All in all I will conclude that no lasting and weighty arguments have been adduced that contradict the conception: 1) That the crux of the currency problem is the monetary policy of the Central Bank. 2) That the balance of payments and the trade balance no less than the Danish price level depend on the amount of buying power that is made available. 3) And consequently that both the internal and external value of the Danish currency is adjustable by means of the monetary policy of the National Bank. It is this standpoint that has been maintained all the time by the leading men of the economic profession, in this country first and foremost by the two professors of economics Axel Nielsen and Birck and Director [of the Factory Inspection] Lindberg.

> The objection that, with some success, was previously raised against this standpoint, indicating that it attached too much importance to the money aspect and too little to the production aspect—to the prosperity of business life—comes to nothing when the experiences of recent years are taken into account. (Translated from Ohlin 1927a:139–40)

It would have been interesting to know the reaction of the managers of the National Bank to Ohlin's severe criticism in 1927 as well as to his report in 1924 and his comments on the Danish monetary policy in the daily press. An inspection of the files of the National Bank, however, shows no indication that Ohlin's writings caused much alarm. Except for a newspaper article by Ohlin dealing with the prospects of a revival of the Currency Union between Denmark and Sweden, the files contain no direct references to Ohlin.

Ohlin's contribution to the Danish monetary debate in the 1920s was primarily to enforce the position taken by his colleagues at the University in the public debate: that price stability was essential to the economy and that the monetary policy should be directed to this aim. Second, Ohlin increased the self-esteem of the economic profession. The development, Ohlin stated, had shown that the economists were right in their advice. Though it had become clear that the monetary theory had to be elaborated further, the basic theory had served well as a guideline through a period of unrest, which was indeed a great triumph for economic science. On many occasions Ohlin had experienced how private businessmen and bank managers looked down on the economic profession. In these instances, Ohlin said in his address, it was a comfort to him that even Copernicus was ridiculed for a long time (Ohlin 1927a:141).

Professor Ohlin, the Popular Henchman of Sweated Labor[29]

The decision taken in November 1924 of Denmark's return to the gold standard implied a process that was planned to take place over several years, thereby leaving room for the required adjustments in wages and prices. The 1924 agreement among the political parties neither established a specific timetable nor did it state whether Denmark should return to the old parity. The follow-up agreement between the government and the National Bank was no less clear. It only established that the currency was not allowed to decline again and set limits which would lead to a rise in the Danish currency from 66 percent in 1924 to 70 percent of the old parity within two years.

It was a modest declaration of intent that indicates that Danish politicians had learned their lesson from the experience in 1923. However, in contrast to the previous experiments, the new currency policy was now based on a tightening of the economic policy. The contractions of the monetary and fiscal policy that were carried out in 1925, and the confidence abroad about the new economic policy, led to an immediate appreciation of the Danish currency, and within one year the rate was close to the old gold parity. The adjustment in prices and wages only came slowly, and the rates of unemployment among the insured wage earners increased rapidly from 15 to 21 percent. During the next years the wage levels came into the focus of the Danish economic debate, and Ohlin participated intensively in both Danish economic journals and newspapers (Ohlin 1972:130).

In his first address to the Danish Economic Association in March 1925, Ohlin argued that the government should abstain from direct regulation of monopolies, except in a few very obvious cases. Free trade did not only mean freedom to compete but also freedom to collaborate. In general, the government ought to restrict itself to the increase of competition by making new entries possible or to providing information to the public on the effects of monopolies and combines. According to Ohlin, the labor market ought to be treated in a similar manner. The government was not in a position to control the wage level, but it might be possible to increase competition by increasing mobility and supply in trades with shortages. It was to be left to the unemployed members of the trade unions to overcome the tendencies to high wages (Ohlin 1925a:192–95).

Ohlin did not stick to this rather unproblematic attitude to the functioning of the labor market for long. In January 1927 he published an article on the Danish wage level and unemployment, which was to be his only self-contained Danish theoretical article. Ohlin set out by lining up a neoclassical framework on the relationship between real wage and (marginal) productivity of labor, pointing out that wages above the normal level would lead to unemployment, because of a decrease in the international competitiveness of Danish trades. However, the result was not restricted to an open economy; even in a closed economy an increase in real wages would lead to unemployment by substituting labor for capital.

> To me it is therefore quite obvious that a substantial increase in wages in general must give rise to unemployment. To my knowledge this position has been taken by all economists who have investigated the problem closely. During the intense debate in Sweden, this position was maintained by Brisman, Cassel, Heckscher, and Åkerman. (Translated from Ohlin 1927b:3–4)

Ohlin made two qualifications to this general theoretical statement. First, he acknowledged the difficulties in estimating the equilibrium wage level. A preliminary study of the development in wages and productivity in Denmark and Sweden indicated that Danish wages were too high. However, a closer inspection was needed to make it an established fact, and therefore Ohlin called for the setup of a detailed and impartial investigation of the wage levels in Denmark and abroad. Second, Ohlin briefly indicated that part of the Danish unemployment was due to the unrest in Europe and the ongoing Danish deflation, which might have an effect for some time. However, to Ohlin it was vital not to fight shy of the effects of the wage level when discussing the unemployment problem:

> There is no point in maintaining wages at all costs at a level which is incompatible with the productivity.... It causes unemployment. It is not to the advantage of the working class, since the unemployed do not get a high relief from the public; maybe they get nothing at all. On the contrary, it harms the Danish economy, which in the *long run* will harm the working class too. (Translated from Ohlin 1927b:6)

Ohlin had little success in his request for a detailed study of the Danish wage level, nor did his newspaper articles on unemployment have much impact on economic policy.

In October 1927 Ohlin made another attempt to influence the public debate by publishing a pamphlet: *Start up Production Again*. Ohlin's basic argument was that the Danish unemployment consisted of two elements: unemployment due to the business cycle and long-run unemployment due to the wage level. The latter, Ohlin had labeled "the natural unemployment" in a newspaper article. In contrast to his previous article, Ohlin now stated that the high Danish wage level was not the main cause of unemployment; the stagnant state of business was mainly psychological and stemmed from the lack of future prospects. To overcome the crisis, new measures had to be taken, and Ohlin suggested a temporary 15 percent reduction in wages for one year and a half. By making the reduction only temporary, he expected it to serve as a strong impulse generating growth in the economy, whereas the fact that the wages would return to a level above the equilibrium was a minor problem. His basic argument for this is quite interesting:

> When the aim is to overcome a crisis quickly, the attention must be directed toward the immediate effects of the measures taken into consideration. This is "the short-run effects," to use an economic term. It is of little importance what results these measures will bring about in the long run, since the purpose is only to overcome a *temporary* crisis. There is a profound truth in Keynes's phrase: "In the long run we are all dead." (Ohlin 1927c:11–12)

The temporary reduction of the wage level was to be supplemented by an increase in money supply and the abolition of rent control to stimulate building activities. In his account of the proposals Ohlin described the multiplying effects of an initial outlay and referred to the positive effects of public works during a depression. Right from the start he compared the development of a depression with "the snowball effect," and later, when discussing the construction and house-building industry, which accounted for one quarter of the unemployment, Ohlin pointed out:

> The importance of [the building industry] ... is greater than indicated by these figures. If the building workers could get jobs, this would also affect their demands for other goods and give employment to bakers, tailors, shoemakers, etc. The unemployment among these workers would diminish. (Translated from Ohlin 1927c:36)

It is on the basis of this section that Hegeland (1961:219) has argued that Ohlin was "fully aware of the subsequent *and* multiplying effects of some initial outlays." The argument has later been incorporated in Steiger's (1971) analysis of the early development of the Stockholm School. However, it is doubtful whether the quotation contains new arguments distinguishing Ohlin from his contemporaries. It is difficult to imagine any contemporary economist who would not ascribe to this statement a sensible partial description of what was going on when unemployment existed.

There are indications that in reality, Ohlin did not take an interest in the multiplier theory at that time. A discussion of the multiplier is absent in the section on tariffs in the book, despite the fact that in the 1920s the Danes Julius Wulff and Fr. Johannsen had reintroduced a multiplier based on an import leakage to demonstrate the positive impact on the national income of a protection of the Danish manufacturing industry.[30] If Ohlin had attached any importance to the multiplier, it would have been natural for him—as it was for Warming (1924, 1928)—to have made a closer inspection of the theoretical and empirical validity of the calculations of the multiplier.[31]

Except for a few references in Warming's publications, there are no indications that Ohlin's book or his other Danish publications had any lasting effects on the political debate on economic issues. The recommendation of a temporary reduction in wages must have been unacceptable to the Labor party and the trade unions, which also goes for the Danish Employers' Confederation and the right-wing parties who demanded a permanent reduction in wages. Finally, Ohlin's recommendation was published at a time when prospects improved on the world market and wages started to rise in Germany, which made the adoption of drastic measures less obvious.

Nevertheless, a review by Warming from 1927 is quite interesting because it demonstrates a world of difference in the views of the two economists on the usefulness of adjustments of the wage level as a means of economic policy. The attitude of the review was sympathetic, and Warming acknowledged that within three years, Ohlin had acquired a considerable insight into the Danish society. Warming, however, strongly opposed Ohlin's recommendation. He accepted Ohlin's statement that "natural unemployment" had increased after the war, though he was not convinced by the empirical evidence put forth that the Danish wage level was indeed too high. Regardless of this, Warming disagreed fundamentally with Ohlin on the policy of wages: "My basic notion of the business cycles leads to conclusions that are quite opposite to the recommendation. In my opinion *stable wages will bring about stability in the business cycles* ..." (Warming 1927:189). This point of view is a common feature of Warming's publications in the 1920s. During the Depression of the 1930s Warming did on several occasions particularly make a strong case against including a wage policy in the short-term economic policy, however. In 1933 Warming observed that there was an increasing understanding of this view and that among others, Keynes, and later Ohlin, now favored a stabilization of wages and a restoration of the price level.[32]

Conclusions

Nothing fades away as quickly as the fame of retiring professors. It must be a comfort to the old ones that this is the common lot even to young movers.

When Ohlin left for Sweden, he received a telegram from his students in which they expressed their gratitude for his teaching and pointed out that he personally had meant a great deal to them. Ohlin's publications remained an integral part of the curriculum throughout the next decades, but it was due to their theoretical merits and not Ohlin's connection to Denmark. The official Danish recognition came in 1946 when Ohlin received an honorary doctorate at the University of Aarhus, where two of his former students, Jørgen Pedersen and Thorkil Kristensen, had become professors. Today Ohlin's name is still well known to all students for his theoretical contributions. However, hardly any—and that includes the members of the Faculty—associate these achievements with his stay in Copenhagen.

If one were to ask whether appointing the young Swede as professor in Copenhagen was a success, the answer would unquestionably be positive, taken into account that Ohlin was in contact with a number of Danish economists who later made a career at universities, and that he left his mark on the reform of the studies in economics in 1929. However, it was not a complete success, which can be seen from Birck's and Warming's statement about Gustaf Åkermann, who applied to become Ohlin's successor together with Zeuthen, Pedersen, Iversen, and Wieth-Knudsen:[33]

> Professor Åkermann is an excellent theorist. But since a knowledge of Danish affairs greatly lightens the workload connected with the teaching, which also includes applied economics, the Danish applicants naturally have an advantage, which only a substantial lead in other areas would be able to counterbalance. It is true that it has been very refreshing to have had a Swede among us for the past 5 years; but exactly because we just have had a foreigner, we do not consider it fair to promising Danes to take another one, and the refreshing effect of having a foreigner depreciates by repetition.

After returning to Sweden, Ohlin kept in contact with Denmark by continuing to publish articles in Danish newspapers. During the 1930s Ohlin published 162 articles in *Politiken*. It surpassed the number of contributions from most Danish professors of economics, though Ohlin lagged far behind Pedersen, who published 300 articles during the decade. In 1933 he published his review of Keynes's *Means to Prosperity*, and his arguments on economic policy and the esteem of the Swedish economists backed the Danish economists who tried to gain a hearing for an expansionary fiscal policy to overcome the unemployment problem.[34] But neither Ohlin nor his Danish fellow combatants were able to convince the politicians who could not abandon old conventions. When a newspaper made an inquiry in 1934 on whether Danish economists at the University were able to give useful advice on economic policy, the result was distressing. A politician pointed out that as a layman he often lacked a clear and comprehensible discussion of the present-day problems by the economists, and he added: "the *Danish* economist whom I appreciate the most in this respect and from whom I have frequently found real guidance is undoubtedly the *Swede*, Professor Gustav Cassel."

Notes

1. Carl Valdemar Bramsnæs taught policy of social security and Henrik Petersen lectured on agricultural policy. Bramsnæs was Minister of Finance from April 1924 to December 1926 and had a second term from April 1929 to May 1933.

2. *Studium*, 11/4 and 18/4, 1923. *Studium* was a students' chronicle at the University of Copenhagen.

3. Translated from Wieth-Knudsen (1930:75). Wieth-Knudsen had been awarded the University's gold medal for young scholars in 1901, and in 1908 he defended his doctoral dissertation on the Malthusian theory of population.

4. Mackeprang's pioneering works on econometrics have been investigated by Kærgård (1984).

Andvig has given an account of the life and contributions of Schönheyder, pointing out that Schönheyder was highly regarded by Birck, who later praised him as an original scholar. Birck also explained why it was so difficult for Schönheyder to get a permanent position: "Dr. Schönheyder has a special position among the Nordic economists; he is not 'all round' and cannot be used as a maid-of-all-work in University housekeeping" (Andvig 1984:20).

5. Lindahl's and Ohlin's papers have been reviewed by Sundström (1993:72–74). Both Lindahl and Ohlin were optimistic about the possibility that the negative effects would be offset by an increase in productivity.

6. Winding Pedersen (1976:250). "Professor Birck's exposition possesses many merits. Without adding much on his own account, he sets out clearly and accurately all the most elaborate developments and refined intricacies of the marginal conception," H. D. Henderson: "Review of L. V. Birck: *The Theory of Marginal Value*, London 1922," *Economic Journal*, 1922, 128:527.

7. Apart from *The Theory of Value*, 1922, Birck published *The Scourge of Europe, the Public Debt Described, Explained and Historically Depicted*. London, 1926, and New York, 1927.

8. Ohlin (1972:122–123) and Larsson (1998:56–57).

9. Myrdal's attitude toward Birck resembles the one expressed by Ohlin. In his postscript to *Value in Social Theory*, Myrdal points out that his book *Vetenskap och Politik* was a reaction toward the intellectual hegemony of the older generation of econo-

mists. "Professor Laurits V. Birck, . . . , [1] whom in his last years I came to know and who honored me with his friendship was well aware of this and used to call me jokingly parricide."

[Myrdal's footnote 1]: Birck had himself written an important and original exposition of the neoclassical value theory . . . 1902, and remained, with all his nonconformist adventures in social and economic criticism, which earned him the right to be called the political conscience of Denmark, a faithfully orthodox utilitarian" (Myrdal 1962:239).

10. Boserup (1980:432–33). A reappraisal of Axel Nielsen's monetary theory can be found in Andersen and Nielsen (1976).

11. Boserup (1980:430) and Gelting (1964:315).

12. The contact between Warming and Ohlin took place when Ohlin had just been exposed to Hammerskjöld's very critical examination of the preliminary draft of Ohlin's supplement to the Report of the Swedish Committee of Unemployment. Hammerskjöld's negative attitude concerns the analysis of expansionary effects of public works and Ohlin's description of the multiplier effects of public works, which was labeled "unrealistic"; see Wadensjö (2000:9). This naturally leads us to question whether Ohlin's inquiry concerned the multiplier? Did Ohlin try to persuade Warming to take part in the dispute with Hammerskjöld? A search for the correspondence in the files of the Swedish National Archives has been in vain, and the problems remain unsolved.

13. Birck, "Professor Gustav Cassel," *Studium*, 1923, September 3, p. 3. However, the praise of the Swedes was not wholehearted. Birck once proposed a toast to E. Sommerin of Lund "the only Swedish economist who is not world-famous." Zeuthen recounts that apart from one whom he appreciated very much, Birck thought it was a mistake that all Swedish economists were famous (Boserup 1980:430; Zeuthen 1944:120).

14. The bias in the study can be seen from the fact that the department was called "Statistisk Laboratorium" (the statistical laboratory) and the degree was named after the German title *Staatswissenschaft*.

15. *Studium*, 1/10, 1924.

16. Translated from *Studium*, 11/2, 1925.

17. Ohlin's seminars took place every Thursday at 7:30 to 9:00 pm. As indicated earlier, the seminars were actually introduced by Heckscher in 1923, and they were carried on in the spring term of 1924 by Nielsen.

18. Translated from Winding Pedersen (1976:267). The "night club" remark is part of Ohlin's legacy in Denmark. However, one must take into account that Ohlin mostly taught in the afternoon and never before 10 am.

19. It is difficult to assess Ohlin's direct impact on the reform. Ohlin was absent from the meeting in 1925 where Birck, Nielsen, and the students outlined the reform, but he took part at the committee stage. Ohlin also acted as a supervisor, together with Nielsen, on Iversen's translation of Ely's textbook on economics from 1927 into Danish. The book was used for introductory teaching right to the 1940s.

20. Nielsen (1944:175). "It was quite refreshing to hear his sonorous voice again in an auditorium at Frue Plads. Sun-tanned and as slim as when he won the vacant

professorship after Westergaard in the twenties—one understands the deep sighs of the Danish female students when Professor Ohlin went back to Stockholm." Report on Carl Iversen's public defense of his dissertation, *Dagens Nyheder* 26/4, 1935.

The same story was reported in another newspaper, although in a short version: "Ohlin ... as tanned by the spring sun in the mountains as a Greek athlete (again quite slim)," *Politiken* 26/4, 1935.

21. The ratio increased to 34 percent in 1926 because of a one-year drop in the number of female law students.

22. The assessment is based on the scrapbooks of Nielsen and Iversen and the list of Ohlin's Danish newspaper articles.

23. Iversen, *Aspects of the Theory of International Capital Movements.* Copenhagen 1935.

24. Ohlin wrote 84 articles in the newspaper *Politiken* from 1925 to 1929.

25. The position of the National Bank has been defended from a Keynesian perspective by Erling Olsen, who argued that by intense public relations, the Bank was trying to make a hearing for a combination of an incomes policy and a fiscal and monetary contraction (Olsen and Hoffmeyer 1968:54–78).

26. The prospect of carrying on a monetary contraction that could have depressed the price level was hindered by the Danish banking crises. A number of mostly minor Danish banks had failed in 1921, but in 1922 the situation became aggravated and even major banks were hit including "Landmandsbanken," the largest bank in Scandinavia. The National Bank serving as lender of last resort took part in the reconstruction of several banks but hesitated to take measures that could further aggravate the banking crisis (Hansen 1996:314–27).

27. The dispute not only involved the proper choice of means but also the choice of the future parity. The viewpoints of the University professors diverged regarding the future parity. Westergaard and Nielsen argued that Denmark had a moral obligation to return to the old parity, while Birck and Warming favored a stabilization at a lower rate in order to avoid a new period of deflation.

28. Bramsnæs (1965:138). Bramsnæs, however, does not mention Ohlin in his record of the episode.

29. "Professor Ohlin, Løntrykkeriets populare Vaabendrager." The heading is a quotation from an article in a socialist journal, which lumps Ohlin together with all the enemies of the working class. The author undoubtedly revised his views when, within the next decade, he became head of the Department of Taxes. Knud Korst, "Hadet til Maskinen" (The hatred of the machine), *Clarté* 1927(5):97–101.

30. Ohlin's 1927 book has a reference to Fr. Johannsen's newspaper article "Tidens Krav" from 1927 which contains the multiplier formula: $A + \frac{3}{5}A + (\frac{3}{5})2A + (\frac{3}{5})3A \cdots = 2\frac{1}{2}A$ (the marginal propensity to import is $\frac{3}{5}$).

However, Ohlin (1927c:47) refers to Johannsen only in a discussion of how prices are fixed within the manufacturing industry, and it has no connection to the discussion of the multiplying effects, Topp (1981, 1992).

31. See Garside and Topp (2001). Carlson and Jonung's (2000) investigation of Ohlin's articles in Swedish daily papers indicates that his attitude toward macroeconomic policy was quite conventional in the late 1920s.

32. See Warming (1931, 1933:101) and Kærgård, Andersen, and Topp (1998).

33. Translated from *The Yearbook of the University of Copenhagen 1930/31*, p. 51. The third member of the committee (Professor Nielsen) endorsed the statement on Åkermann and preferred that Iversen got the chair due to his high standards in both research and teaching. Birck and Warming, however, nominated Zeuthen, who got the position in the end after a competition.

34. Ohlin, "Vejen ud af Krisen" (The way out of the slump), *Politiken* 4/4, 1933.

References

Åkerman, Johan. 1932. Prisstegringens Problem (The problem of the rise in prices). *Det ekonomiska läget* (4):1–34.

Andersen, B. N., and P. E. Nielsen. 1976. Axel Nielsen. *Danske Økonomer*. Copenhagen: Samfundsvidenskabeligt Forlag, pp. 319–32.

Andvig, J. C. 1984. Kristian Gottlieb Fredrik Schønheyder (1874–1953)—den første modelbygger i norsk sosialøkonomi? (Schønheyder—The first Norwegian to construct economic models?) *Sosialøkonomen* 38:16–22.

Boserup, M. 1980. The international transmission of ideas: A small-country case study. *History of Political Economy* 12:420–33.

Bramsnæs, C. V. 1965. *Erindringer* (Memoirs). Copenhagen.

Davidsen, T. 1999. Statistiker mod sin vilje: Uddrag af Jens Warmings dagbøger. (Statistician contrary to his desire: Extracts from Jens Warming's diaries). *Fund og forskning i Det kongelige Biblioteks samlinger*. 38:153–200.

Friis, F. T. B. 1924. Nationaløkonomisk Studium i De forenede Stater—og Herhjemme (The study of economics in the states and at home). *Nationaløkonomisk Tidsskrift* 32:386–98.

Garside, W. R., and N.-H. Topp. 2001. The fate of nascent Keynesianism: Denmark in the 1930s. *History of Political Economy* 33: 717–41.

Gelting, J. 1964. Jens Warming. *Nationaløkonomisk Tidsskrift* 102:1–8.

Haavisto, T., and L. Jonung. 1995. Off gold and back again: Finnish and Swedish monetary policies 1914–1925. In C. H. Feinstein, ed., *Banking, Currency, and Finance in Europe between the Wars*. Oxford: Clarendon Press, pp. 237–66.

Hansen, P. H. 1996. *På glidebanen til den bitre ende. Dansk bankvæsen i krise, 1920–33* (Banking and financial crises in Denmark, 1920–1933). Odense: Odense Universitetsforlag.

Hegeland, H. 1961. On the genesis of the multiplier theory. In H. Hegeland ed., *Money, Growth and Other Essays in Economics in Honour of Johan Åkermann*. Lund: Gleerup, pp. 211–33.

Jensen, A. 1946. *Erindringer* (Memoirs). Copenhagen.

Johannsen, Fr. 1927. Tidens Krav (The challenge of the time). *Berlingske Tidende*, March 23–25.

Kærgård, N. 1984. The earliest history of econometrics: Some neglected Danish contributions. *History of Political Economy* 14:437–44.

Kærgård, N., and T. Davidsen. 1998. Harald Westergaard: From young pioneer to established authority. In W. J. Samuels, ed., *European Economists of the Early 20th Century*, vol. 1. Cheltenham, England: Edward Elgar, pp. 349–365.

Kærgård, N., P. Andersen, and N.-H. Topp. 1998. The Danish economist Jens Warming—An odd genius. In W. J. Samuels, ed., *European Economists of the Early 20th Century*, vol. 1. Cheltenham, England: Edward Elgar, pp. 331–48.

Larsson, S. E. 1998. *Bertil Ohlin. Ekonom och politiker* (Bertil Ohlin: economist and politician). Stockholm: Atlantis.

Myrdal, G. 1930. *Vetenskab och Politik i Nationalekonomin* (The political element in the development of economic theory). Stockholm.

Myrdal, G. 1962. *Value in Social Theory*. London: Routledge.

Nielsen. A. 1930. *Bankpolitik* (The theory of banking). Copenhagen: Westermann.

Nielsen. A., ed. 1944. *Bogen om Birck* (The book on Birck). Copenhagen: Hagerup.

Ohlin, B. 1924. Stabiliseringsproblemet i Mellan-Europa efter världskriget. (The stabilization problem in Central Europe after the World War). *Supplement til Beretning fra Valutaraadet afgivet* (Supplement to the report of the Parlimentary Commitee on the Danish currency). *5 November 1924*. Copenhagen.

Ohlin, B. 1925a. Samhällets ställning till arbets och varumonopolen (The attitude of society to monopolies in the markets for goods and labor). *Nationaløkonomisk Tidsskrift* 63:185–96.

Ohlin, B. 1925b. Åttatimmarsdagens ekonomiska verkningar (The economic effects of the eight-hour day). *Ekonomisk Tidskrift* 27:65–94.

Ohlin, B. 1927a. Den danske Kronan efter 1914 (Danish currency after 1914). *Nationaløkonomisk Tidsskrift* 65:121–42.

Ohlin, B. 1927b. Arbejdsløn og Arbejdsløshed (Wage and unemployment). *Socialt Tidsskrift* (3):1–6.

Ohlin, B. 1927c. *Sæt Produktionen i Gang* (Start up production again). Copenhagen: Aschehoug.

Ohlin, B. 1927d. Det nationalekonomiska forskningsarbetets Inriktning (The organization of economic research). *Nationaløkonomisk Tidsskrift* 65:36–45.

Ohlin, B. 1927e. Kort översigt över nationalekonomien i Sverige (A short survey of Swedish economics). *Nationaløkonomisk Tidsskrift* 65:448–56.

Ohlin, B. 1927f. Några samfundsekonomiska synpunkter på radhusbebyggelsen (An economic perspective on terraced housing). *Kritisk Revy* 1:35–36.

Ohlin, B. 1928. Anmeldelse af L. V. Birck: *Den økonomiske virksomhed* (Book review of L. V. Birck: *The Economic Activity*). *Nationaløkonomisk Tidsskrift* 66:65–80.

Ohlin, B. 1929. Anmeldelse af Fr. Zeuthen: *Den økonomiske fordeling* (Book review of Fr. Zeuthen: *Economic Distribution*). *Nationaløkonomisk Tidsskrift* 67:62–88, 149–69.

Ohlin, B. 1930a. Teori og Praktik i det ekonomiska Livet (Theory and practice in economic life). *Nationaløkonomisk Tidsskrift* 68:81–91.

Ohlin, B. 1930b. Er nationaløkonomi videnskab? (Is economics pure science?). *Politiken* December 8. Reprinted in *Det Frie Blad* (10):407–409.

Ohlin, B. 1931. Den internationale pengepolitik og dens indvirkning på konjunkturudviklingen (The international monetary policy and its impact on the business cycles). *Tilskueren* 48:179–99.

Ohlin, B. 1932. Presstegrings problem (The problem of the rise of prices: Rejoinder). *Det ekonomiska Läget* (4):21–32.

Ohlin, B. 1937. Book review of C. Iversen: *Aspect of the Theory of International Capital Mobility*. *Nationaløkonomisk Tidsskrift* 75:283–89.

Ohlin, B. 1941. Anmeldelse af H. Winding Pedersen: *Samfundsøkonomiens Grundtræk* (Book review of H. Winding Pedersen: *A Survey of the Danish Economy*). *Nationaløkonomisk Tidsskrift* 79:386–89.

Ohlin, B. 1972. *Bertil Ohlin's memoarer. Ung man blir politiker* (Ohlin's memoirs: A young man becomes a politician). Stockholm: Bonnier.

Ohlin. B. 1977. *Nobel-Biography*. www.nobel.se/laureates/economy-1977-1-bio.

Ohlin, B., and F. Vedsø. 1927. Den rette Arbejdsløn (The Appropriate Wage Level). *Socialt Tidsskrift* 3:94–98.

Olsen, E., and E. Hoffmeyer. 1968. *Dansk Pengehistorie* (Danish monetary history). Copenhagen: Danmarks Nationalbank.

Steenstrup, C. F. 1925. Anmeldelse af Bertil Ohlin: Handlens teori (Review of Bertil Ohlin: *The Theory of Trade*). *Nationaløkonomisk Tidsskrift* 63:56–57.

Steiger, O. 1971. *Studien zur Entstehung der Neuen Wirtschaftslehre in Schweden*. Berlin: Duncker and Humbolt.

Sundström, M. 1993. The Swedish economists, the labor movement and the 8-hour day. In L. Jonung, ed., *Swedish Economic Thought*. London: Routledge, pp. 66–81.

Topp, N.-H. 1981. A nineteenth-century multiplier and its fate: Julius Wulff and the multiplier theory in Denmark 1896–1932. *History of Political Economy* 13:824–45.

Topp, N.-H. 1992. Warming om Ohlin og Ohlin om Warming (Warming's comments on Ohlin and Ohlin's comments on Warming). Institute of Political Science. University of Copenhagen, Discussion Paper 10.

Warming, J. 1924. *Valutaspørgsmaalet* (The problem of the exchange rate). Copenhagen: Gad.

Warming, J. 1927. En Krisepjece. (A pamphlet about the crisis). *Polyteknisk Tidsskrift* pp. 186–190.

Warming, J. 1928. Beskæftigelsesproblemet. (The problem of employment). *Gads danske Magasin* 22:609–721.

Warming, J. 1929. *Danmarks Erhvervs-og Samfundsliv* (Denmark's economic and social life). Copenhagen: Gad.

Warming, J. 1931. A theory of prices and wages. *International Labor Review* 24:24–54.

Warming, J. 1932. International difficulties arising out of the financing of public works during depression. *Economic Journal* 42:211–24.

Warming, J. 1933. Den økonomiske Usikkerhed og Likvid Kapital (Uncertainties in economic life and liquid capital). *Nationaløkonomisk Tidsskrift* 71:89–126, 221–51, and 337–58.

Wieth-Knudsen. K. A. 1930. *Mit Videnskabelige Livs Drama* (The drama of my life as a scientist). Copenhagen: Hagerup.

Winding Pedersen, H. 1976. L. V. Birck. *Danske økonomer*. Copenhagen: Hagerup, pp. 249–278.

Zeuthen, F. 1944. Birck som Videnskabsmand (Birck as a scientist). In A. Nielsen, ed., *Bogen om Birck*. Copenhagen: Hagerup, pp. 91–124.

III

The Macroeconomics of Bertil Ohlin

12 Keynes and Ohlin on the Transfer Problem

Robert A. Mundell

Both Keynes and Ohlin were nurtured on classical economic theory. But the age difference between them was fundamental. Keynes was trained as an economist when the international system was dominated by the gold standard, a system that flourished until the start of World War I, when Keynes was already thirty. By contrast, Ohlin's formative years as an economist occurred in a world in which currency instability was the order of the day. This difference in the education of the two economists must be kept in mind in evaluating the positions they took in the transfer debate in the late 1920s. Keynes was rooted in the world of Cambridge orthodoxy, Ohlin in the more open spirit of Scandinavian rootlessness.

The Reparations Bill

"To the victor goes the spoils," and it was natural that the Allies, having decided to saddle Germany with sole war guilt, would seek reparations. The war, however, had left devastation, fiscal insolvency, and economic collapse all over Europe. The situation in Germany was the worst. Stripped of her African and Asian colonies, of Alsace-Lorraine, and part of her Eastern provinces, and prostrate from the economic destruction of the war, Germany was no longer the Kaiser's strutting empire of 1914. Among the victors, France was in the forefront of those anxious not only to "make Germany pay" but to use reparations as a whip to keep Germany subservient for the rest of the century. There was even talk of a "Carthaginian Peace," recalling the Roman policy in 146 BC that wiped out all that remained of Carthage's once-mighty civilization, a project that reemerged during World War II as the Morgenthau Plan.

That Germany should pay reparations was universally agreed by the victors. But how much? One precedent was the settlement in 1871, in which Bismarck stipulated a figure of five billion francs, approximately $1 billion, as the French reparation. But this moderate precedent was not considered very relevant in 1919. First, Bismarck's settlement of the war, paying attention to the postwar relations between the countries, required the cession of Alsace and Lorraine, a bitter enough pill for France without compounding it with a harsh reparations settlement. The reparations bill was decidedly below France's capacity to pay, and in the event France paid the indemnity ahead of schedule. Second, after decades of growth, the German economy, with its larger population and rapid growth, had outstripped France's in 1914, not to speak of 1870. Third, the World War I devastation, particularly in northern France, over a four-year period was on a completely different scale than that from the seven-month war of 1870 to 1871: the war took place entirely in the country of the loser.[1] Fourth, France and Britain had incurred huge debts to the United States, and reparations from Germany would be needed to cover at least part of these debts. Finally, the political incentives for British Prime Minister David Lloyd George as well as French President Georges Clemenceau were all directed at satisfying the extremist branches of the electorate that were clamoring for a huge settlement. The public had much less to say about events in 1871 than fifty years later.

Keynes, at the Treasury throughout the war, had been asked to look at the reparations question as early as 1917. An early figure that he thought feasible was something like $6 billion but later came to believe that $10 billion, if on the high side, might be feasible. The final figure would obviously have to take into account the fall in the value of money expressed either in dollars or gold during and after the war. As it turned out U.S. prices had doubled by 1920 but, after the severe postwar deflation of 1921, were still about 40 percent above the prewar price level.

The Reparations Commission set up at the Treaty of Versailles[2] "bickered throughout 1920 over the total sum to be demanded of Germany and its distribution among the Allies. At the Spa Conference (July 1920), France won 52 percent of German payments, Britain 22 percent, Italy 10, and Belgium 8.[3] At the conferences of Hythe, Boulogne, and Brussels, France presented a total bill of 230,000,000,000 gold marks, although the British warned that this was far beyond Germany's capacity to pay. But when German foreign minister Walter Simons offered a mere 30,000,000,000 marks (Paris Conference, February 1921), French Premier Aristide Briand and Lloyd George made a show of force, seizing in March the Ruhr river ports of Düsseldorf, Duisburg, and Ruhrort, taking over the Rhenish customs offices, and declaring a 50 percent levy on German exports."

Finally, on May 5, 1921, the London conference presented Berlin with a bill for 132,000,000,000 gold marks (about $33 billion), to be paid in annuities of 2,000,000,000 plus 26 percent ad valorem of German exports. The Germans protested adamantly that this was "an injustice without equal."[4] Chancellor Konstantin Fehrenbach resigned rather than accept this new "Diktat," and his successor, Joseph Wirth, acquiesced only under threat of occupation of the Ruhr.

The "fulfillment" tactic adopted by Wirth and his foreign minister, Walther Rathenau, was to make a show of good faith to demonstrate that the reparations bill was truly beyond Germany's capacity. They were aided in this by the continuing deterioration of the paper mark. The prewar value of the mark was about 4.2 to the dollar. By the end of 1919 it reached 63, and after the first payment of 1,000,000,000 marks under the London plan, the mark fell to 262 to the dollar.[5]

To appreciate the burden of the bill, the sum has to be put into a familiar perspective. One approach is to compare it with Germany's GDP at the time. An average estimate is 40 billion gold marks, so the total reparations bill represented 330 percent of Germany's current GDP. This can be compared to France's reparation debt to Germany in 1871 of 5 billion francs, equal to 23 percent of Fritz Machlup's estimate of France's 1871 GDP of 22.2 billion francs.[6] Germany's burden (ratio to GDP), compared to France's 1870 burden, would be 14.3 times larger than the reparations bills charged to France.[7]

Another approach is to calculate the gold equivalents. At a price of $20.67 an ounce, $33 billion represented 1,596,516.6 ounces of gold. This is three times the world stock of monetary gold in the 1920s and almost 50 percent more than the stock of gold in central banks and international monetary institutions today. At current prices around $300 an ounce, it corresponds to $479 billion today, which would be somewhat more than a quarter of a much different Germany's present-day GDP. But looking at it from the standpoint of 330 percent of Germany's GDP in the 1920s, the burden for present-day Germany would be closer to $7 trillion!

Germany was not, of course, required to pay the bill all at once. The debts were divided into three classes of bonds and only A and B bonds, totaling 50 billion marks, had to be serviced. As far as the initial 50 billion gold mark payment was concerned, the debt service totaled 3 billion gold marks (6 percent of 50 billion gold marks) or 7.5 percent of GDP. To this figure must be added an additional 1 billion gold marks per year for occupation costs and settlement of Germany's prewar debts, bringing the total to perhaps 10 percent of GDP.[8] Could Germany effect an export surplus equal to 10 percent of GDP?

Britain had transferred abroad eight percent of GDP through foreign lending in 1911 to 1913.[9] In common with reparations payments, lending requires an export surplus. But it differs from reparations in that it does not involve a reduction in wealth. A country that lends abroad does so voluntarily and receives in exchange a buildup of foreign assets. When Britain was investing 8 percent of its GDP abroad, it was doing so with the full knowledge that it was building up its net assets and net creditor position in the world economy. Germany's position in the 1920s was quite the opposite; she had given back Alsace and Lorraine, her foreign possessions were quite gone, she had just suffered devastating personal and material losses in the Great War, and after fulfilling the first round of her obligations, she had only to look forward to the dismal task of getting started on the much larger debt of 182,000,000,000 C mark bonds to follow.

Experience with Reparations

Could Germany pay the reparations? As a matter of history, the question has never been settled. Faced with an apparently impossible reparations debt, that was at the same time open ended—the more Germany paid, the more of the second tiers of it would be judged collectible—Germany resorted to passive resistance. Confronted with budgetary difficulties, the government resorted to inflation, which had the budgetary convenience of whittling away the huge public debt burden. In June of 1921 prices were 13.7 times the prewar level, and a year later they were 70 times that level. By the end of the year prices had again risen twenty-fold. But now a new factor came into play that was to turn the rapid inflation into hyperinflation and completely destroy the mark. Because Germany had fallen behind in its reparation payments, the French and Belgians, in January 1923, occupied the Ruhr, with the intention of forcing German industry to provide compensation for the French and Belgian losses. "Rather than accede quietly to the humiliation of occupation, the German government urged workers and employers to close down the factories. Idle workers were paid for the next months with a currency inflating so rapidly that printers gave up trying to print numbers on bills. By mid-1923 the German mark was losing value by the minute. A loaf of bread that cost 20,000 marks in the morning would cost 5,000,000 marks by nightfall. Restaurant prices went up while customers were eating. Workers were paid twice a day. On November 15, when the collapse came, it took 4.2 trillion German marks to buy a single American dollar."[10]

The hyperinflation virtually wiped out middle-class savings in Germany, most of which had been invested in bonds. Disenchanted voters turned to the far left or right, and German society became polarized. At the peak of the inflation, in November 1923, the leader of the small National Socialist German Workers' Party, Adolf Hitler, allied himself with other right-wing groups in an attempt to stage a coup in Munich, with the intention of using Bavaria as a base (taking his cue from Benito Mussolini) for a nationalist march on Berlin. Just at that time, however, the government ended its passive resistance in exchange for an end to the occupation of the Ruhr and a rescheduling of the reparation payments it owed to Allies.[11]

On the initiative of the British and U.S. governments,[12] a "committee of experts, presided over by a U.S. financier, Charles G. Dawes, produced a report on the question of German reparations for presumed liability for World War I. The report was accepted by the Allies and by Germany on Aug. 16, 1924. No attempt was made to determine the total amount of reparations to be paid, but payments were to begin at 1,000,000,000 gold marks in the first year and rise to 2,500,000,000 by 1928. The plan provided for the reorganization of the Reichsbank and for an initial loan of 800,000,000 marks to Germany."

The Dawes Plan seemed to work so well that by 1929 it was believed that the stringent controls over Germany could be removed and total reparations fixed. This was done by the Young Plan, and it was discussion of this plan that gave rise to Keynes's decision to publish his article on the "transfer problem" in the *Economic Journal* (of which he was editor). The sequel was as follows: "A new committee, chaired by the American Owen D. Young, met in Paris on Feb. 11, 1929, to revise the Dawes Plan of 1924. Its report (June 7, 1929) was accepted with minor changes and went into effect on Sept. 1, 1930. It reduced the amount due from Germany to 121,000,000,000 Reichsmarks in 59 annuities, set up the Bank for International Settlements to handle the transfer of funds, and ended foreign controls on German economic life."

Just at this auspicious moment, however, the plot turned sour. Raw material prices were falling and the world depression was in the offing. The cause of the depression needs to be understood. As already noted, the dollar price level was at least 35 percent above its 1913 level, with real gold reserves correspondingly lower. When, therefore, first Germany in 1924, and then Britain in 1925 and France in 1927, restored the gold standard (more precisely, the gold exchange standard), the new gold requirements—which were actually increased by the requirement that reparations be paid in gold—put pressure on the gold base of the system and led the way to conversions of foreign exchange reserves and a general scramble for gold.

The great deflation was part of a pattern that had recurred frequently in the past. When countries shifted away from gold, the value of gold, as typically at the outbreak of war, depreciates in real terms, leading to inflation in those countries still adhering to the standard; when countries shifted onto gold, as frequently after a war, gold appreciates and there is deflation in gold countries. In the eighteenth century this pattern was manifest after the East India Company put India on the silver standard, leading to deflationary perturbations that could still be felt in the nineteenth century. After the French Revolution and during the Napoleonic wars, countries went off specie and gold depreciated; after the end of the Napoleonic wars, countries went back to specie and there was deflation; after the Franco-Prussian war, countries shifted from silver to gold standards leading to the appreciation of gold and the depreciation of silver. The inflation during World War I and deflation following were simply following a well-established pattern in monetary history.

The weakening western European economy brought down the Creditanstaldt in Vienna, the largest bank in Central Europe, and the crisis spread to Germany. President Herbert Hoover of the United States proposed a one-year moratorium on reparations and war-debt payments, but even though the moratorium was adopted, it was a case of too little too late. In the wake of the crisis Britain left gold and thus escaped the worst of the deflation. But this option was more difficult for Germany; when Franz von Papen, who had been appointed chancellor in June 1932, considered devaluation, the trade unions threatened to raise wages proportionately. The German hyperinflation a decade earlier had wrung money illusion out of the German psyche. Hence Germany's descent into deflation, mass unemployment, and Hitlerism.

One of von Papen's few achievements (the way had already been prepared by his predecessor, Heinrich Brüning) in his otherwise disastrous Chancellorship was in getting Germany's reparations largely canceled. In June–July 1932, the Lausanne conference, attended by representatives of the creditor powers (Great Britain, France, Belgium, and Italy) and of Germany, agreed, on July 9, 1932, that the conditions of world economic crisis made the continued reparation payments impossible. Germany, however, was to deliver to the Bank for International Settlements, set up in 1929, 5 percent redeemable bonds to the value of three billion Reichsmarks. The creditor governments canceled war debts among themselves but made a "gentleman's agreement" that the Lausanne Protocol would not be ratified until they had reached a satisfactory agreement with respect to their own war debts to the United States. Although the agreement was never ratified, the Lausanne Protocol in effect put an end to reparations from Germany. Adolf Hitler came to power the next year, and within a few years all important obligations under the Treaty of Versailles—political as well as economic—were repudiated.

What was the bottom line from the reparations experience? Was Germany able to pay any reparations? In a technical sense, the answer is yes. From the implementation of the Dawes Plan in 1924 until 1931, Germany's reduced obligations were kept current. But over this period Germany was a capital importer and borrowed more than twice what it paid in reparations. Because these debts were also repudiated by the Hitler government, it can be said that Germany paid negative reparations and that the rest of the world paid reparations to Germany![13]

From the standpoint of his argument that Germany could not pay reparations, Keynes might have been pleased with the outcome. He seemed reluctant to admit Ohlin's point in his reply to Ohlin in the *Economic Journal* but later, after reparations had been effectively canceled, he wrote to the younger man: "As to your point that reparations cause a shift in the demand curve of the receiving country irrespective of any rise in the price level of that country, I do not think I disagree with you."[14] Hardly a resounding capitulation! But if Keynes took any intellectual pride in the failure of reparations, he could not by any stretch of the imagination view it as a vindication of his intellectual position. If Germany did not on balance pay reparations, the fact that the rest of the world in effect paid reparations to Germany undermines his contention that unilateral payments cannot be effected.[15]

The payment schedules outlined in the Dawes Plan was entirely feasible had prosperity continued. The failure of the more moderate reparations bill was due more to the great blunder of the 1920s—the return to the gold standard at the old parities before price levels had been readjusted downward—than to any inherent difficulties with paying indemnities.

Keynes's Position on the Theory and Practice

In the 1920s Keynes was the hero of those who opposed the Versailles Treaty. As an insider coming out, he wrote his brilliant *Economic Consequences of the Peace* to expose what he considered the sham of the Versailles conference, the clay feet of Woodrow Wilson, Clemenceau, and Lloyd George, and the hype that had exaggerated beyond all sense of economic reality the amount of reparations that could be extracted from the German economy.[16]

Keynes's *Economic Consequences of the Peace* had been an instant best-seller; it created a worldwide sensation, particularly in the United States. Keynes had been accused of using privileged information from his position at the Treasury during and after the War, but he was able to defend himself by showing that the relevant information was already in the public domain. To be sure, his vivid sketches of Wilson, Lloyd George, and Clemenceau benefited from his close-up view of them at Versailles. But what distinguished him from his contemporaries was his mastery of applied macroeconomics and sense of proportion. Long before he paved the way for a formal theory of the subject, he had proved himself to be a first-rate applied macroeconomist.[17]

Keynes maintained his position that the reparations bill was too high for Germany throughout the 1920s. Two years after the *Con-*

sequences, he published a sequel, *A Revision of the Treaty*, which, if it lacked the electric prose and dancing personalities of the first, has not deserved its total neglect by the economics profession. As a work in applied economics it is a better book than its predecessor. In both books Keynes was careful to argue that Germany had been treated unfairly between the Armistice and the Treaty, and that the indemnities charged to Germany were too high by an order of magnitude. There is not, however, any suggestion that a smaller reparations bill could not be paid.

The debate inaugurated by Keynes in his article, "The German Transfer Problem" began as follows:

> The Dawes Committee divided the problem of the payment of German Reparations into two parts—into the Budgetary Problem of extracting the necessary sums of money out of the pockets of the German people and paying them to the account of the Agent-General, and the Transfer Problem of converting the German money so received into foreign currency.
>
> As time has gone on, opinion has become even more sharply divided than it was on the question whether this dichotomy has theoretical and practical significance. The view has been widely expressed that the Transfer Problem is of quite secondary importance and that, so long as the Budgetary Problem is solved, the Transfer Problem will, in the main, solve itself. The following note is directed to a theoretical discussion of this issue.

Here Keynes apparently accepts the Dawes Committee division of the problem into a *budgetary* problem and a *transfer* problem. Yet right at the beginning, there is a puzzle. The definition of the "transfer problem" as that "of converting the German money so received into foreign currency" completely trivializes it. If, for example, the payer and payee had the same currency, there would, according to this definition, be no transfer problem! Remember also that Germany and her four reparation creditors had returned to the gold standard.

Everything Keynes writes in the rest of his article implies that the transfer problem goes much deeper than a mere problem of converting one currency into another. It has a side to it that would be just as real if all participants used the same currency. The transfer problem as it is conceived in the modern literature—and as both Keynes and Ohlin actually conceived it in their essays—was the problem of finding the new equilibrium pattern of production, consumption, trade balances, and prices that would be compatible with the financial transfer in real terms.

Keynes now gives his interpretation of what the controversy is about:

> Those who think that the Transfer Problem is secondary argue thus. The German people receives its income in return for its current output of goods and services. If an appropriate part of this income is sequestrated, there will be no buyers for a corresponding amount of goods, which will therefore be available (in addition to what would be available otherwise) to expand exports or in diminution of imports. Since not all the consumption of goods and services, which the German people are compelled to forgo, is suitable for export, there will have to be a certain amount of change-over in the character of production. There is, however, no reason to suppose that ordinary economic forces will not bring this about within a reasonable space of time. Thus—according to this school—the real question is, how much cash can the Government raise by sound financial methods and pay over to the Agent-General. Once this is settled, we can be sure that a way will be found of looking after the Transfer Problem.

This analysis misses the important factor, which Ohlin would be quick to add, that the transfer will be associated with an increase in foreign spending and the demand for imports. Keynes throughout ignores this factor making the same mistake as his mentor, Alfred Marshall, who, in his 1923 book, *Money, Credit and Commerce*, erred in shifting only one of the offer curves.

But let us continue with Keynes's line of thought where he sets up the extreme cases where the two lines of reasoning might be correct:

> Now I do not doubt that there are sets of premisses from which this conclusion follows. For example, there is one very simple set from which it obviously follows. For let us suppose that the German factors of production produce nothing but exports and consume nothing but imports; in this case it is evident that there is only a Budgetary Problem and no Transfer Problem;—or rather the Transfer Problem is removed from the shoulders of Germany and becomes a problem as between the recipients of reparation and the countries from which Germany previously drew her imports.

As subsequent analysis made clear, the criterion for no need for a change in the terms of trade arising from a transfer, in the context of a two-good model, was that the sum of the marginal propensities to import be zero. Keynes here has discovered the special case where the marginal propensity to import of the paying country is unity and there is no "transfer problem."

Keynes goes on to suppose the opposite case, where Germany is more like Russia exporting only caviar and platinum, and he comes up with a different answer:

> But, on the other hand, if we suppose that Germany is already exporting all the goods which she has facilities for producing on any terms on which the rest of the world will buy them—suppose, for example, that, not so unlike Russia today, her exports are limited to caviar and platinum, of which the output cannot be increased—then the Transfer Problem is paramount and, indeed, insoluble.

Keynes allows himself here to be trapped into a basic error by his failure to allow for the increase in foreign demand. Obviously, with domestic export supply elastic and an increase in foreign demand, the same quantity of exports will exchange for a much larger quantity of imports, greatly reducing the cost of the reparations program. Keynes arrives at his absurd result only because he (like Marshall) has neglected the reduction in domestic demand for exportables as well as the increase in purchasing power of the receiving countries.

Keynes goes on to consider the case where platinum and caviar can increase in supply but against this he sets the condition that it meets an inelastic demand:

> Or, again, let us suppose that, whilst, as before, Germany's exports are limited to caviare and platinum, she is, this time, in a position to increase their output, but unfortunately the demand of the rest of the world for these articles has an elasticity of less than unity. In this case the more she exports, the smaller will be the aggregate proceeds. Again the Transfer Problem will be a hopeless business.

The same mistake. Here, because of the inelasticity of demand, the reduction in domestic demand for exportables would not be of much help, but had he allowed for an increase in foreign demand and a positive marginal propensity to import, export proceeds would increase.

He now sets up the issue—incorrectly by modern eyes—as an empirical question that turns on the following:

> The first question to consider is, therefore, a question of fact—whereabouts between the two extremes exemplified above is present-day Germany situation. In other words, our first question is, whether there exists an ideal distribution of Germany's factors of production as between different uses which, if it could be arranged, would solve the Transfer Problem?

Keynes's complete neglect of the potential increase in foreign demand is puzzling in view of the passage that opens the following section:

> If £1 is taken from you and given to me and I choose to increase my consumption of precisely the same goods as those of which you are compelled to diminish yours, there is no Transfer Problem....

This passage provides the clue to a correct solution of the problem. It summarizes succinctly a special case of seamless transfer in the box-diagram two-country models of Meade and Samuelson. It acknowledges that the payer will reduce, and the payee increase, overall spending, and that in the special case where the marginal propensities to spend in the two participants cancel, there will be no need for a change in prices.

But immediately following this passage, Keynes shows either that he failed to understand what he had written or is hoodwinking his readers:

> ... Those who minimise the question of transfer seem sometimes to imply that the above is a fair representation of the present facts. To the extent that high taxation causes German consumers to buy less foreign goods, it is a fair representation. But clearly only a proportion of their abstention from consuming will be in respect of foreign goods, and, so far as one can judge at present, not a very large proportion....

After the ray of light, he now makes the same mistake in neglecting demand increases in the payee. But even supposing that these foreign income effects can be neglected, he undercuts his argument above, that the adjustment works by reducing home demand, for he goes on to say:

> ... Moreover, the German balance of trade already has most of the benefit of this, inasmuch as individual Germans are already paying enough, or nearly enough, taxes to solve the Budgetary Problem, and are, therefore, already reducing their personal consumption to the requisite extent.

Keynes also seemed not to be aware—what Ohlin would emphasize forcefully—that Germany was the recipient of huge capital inflows that in fact implied a reverse transfer!

Ohlin's Critique

Keynes's article appeared as the lead article in *The Economic Journal* in its March 1929 issue. Ohlin promptly read it and sent a critique of it to Keynes. After an exchange of correspondence that resulted in a clarification of what Ohlin meant by "buying power,"[18] Ohlin's essay was published, along with a rejoinder from Keynes, in the June issue.

Ohlin begins his critique, "Transfer Difficulties, Real and Imagined," as follows:

Mr. Keynes' article on "The German Transfer Problem" in the March number of this journal represents a forceful summing-up of the arguments of those economists who maintain that a transfer of the annuities fixed in the Dawes plan is beyond practical possibilities. His reasoning ignores, however, one very important side of the problem. In attempting to set forth why consideration of this neglected element must modify the practical conclusions I intend to imitate as far as it is within my power the brevity and clarity of Mr. Keynes' most elegant treatment.

Let me begin with a quotation: "If £1 is taken from you and given to me and I choose to increase my consumption of precisely the same goods as those of which you are compelled to diminish yours, there is no Transfer Problem. Those who minimise the question of transfer seem sometimes to imply that the above is a fair representation of present facts. To the extent that high taxation causes German consumers to buy less foreign goods, it is a fair representation. But clearly only a proportion of their abstention from consuming will be in respect of foreign goods, and, as far as one can judge at present, not a very large proportion. (p. 2)

This is the first part of a trend of reasoning which seems to me to be of fundamental importance in any discussion of international capital movements. It is a pity that Mr. Keynes has not followed it up, but has even failed to draw the consequences of the part of it he has stated in this passage.

He continues:

Moreover, the German balance of trade already has most of the benefit of this.... Evidently, no account is taken of the fact that, if Keynes has given me £1 and I have returned £2 to him, the effect on our trade balances must be the reverse of what it would be, if only the first transaction had taken place. Germany has paid half a dozen milliards of marks in reparation payments, but has borrowed twice has much. Thus, the German trade balance has not had the "benefit" of a reduction in total buying power, but the "disadvantage" of an increase to the amount with which borrowings have exceeded reparation payments. This increased buying power must have tended to swell imports and reduce exports.

Ohlin now goes on to show that Keynes, in his applied analysis of the German balance of payments, fails to take into account the impact of the transfer on total spending.

This fact, that the total buying power has been increased, not reduced—and that consequently experience tells nothing concerning the efficiency of a transfer of buying power in creating a German export surplus—is ignored also in the following passage, which forms the starting point for the whole reasoning in the first of Mr. Keynes's paper:

Now what prevents Germany from having a greater volume of exports at the present time? Is it that the export trades cannot attract more labour at the present level of remuneration? Or is it that they cannot sell an increased output at a profit unless they can first reduce their costs of production? The available facts seem to indicate that the first, namely, inadequate supplies of labour at present rates of remuneration, plays little or no part, and that the second is the real explanation. That is to say, the solution of the Transfer Problem requires a reduction of the German gold-costs of production relatively to such costs elsewhere. (Ohlin 1929:4)

Nothing is said about the influence of the German borrowings, which—being greater than the reparation payments—seem to me to be the real explanation why the excess of imports into Germany is what it is. They also largely explain why Germany's productive resources have to such an extent been used for production of capital goods for the home market and have not increased output and marketing of export goods.

These borrowings, in so far as they have exceeded the reparation payments, have not only increased the buying power in Germany and thus its importation for foreign goods; they have also reduced the buying power in the lending countries and, thus, their importation of German goods. It is true that the direct influence in this latter direction may not have been very great—as indicated in the first of the passages I have quoted—but indirect effects cannot be ignored.[19]

Ohlin now proceeds to consider the nature of these indirect effects of a transfer of purchasing power and sets up his model:

A and B are two countries with normal employment for their factors of production. A borrows a large sum of money from B this year and the same sum during each of the following years. This transfer of buying power directly increases A's demand for foreign goods while it reduces B's. Thus A's imports grow and its exports fall off.

"If the sum borrowed is 100 mill. marks a year, the excess of imports in A brought about in this direct manner may be 20 mill. marks. For in large countries only a small part of demand turns directly to foreign goods or to export goods. The rest, 80 mill. marks, increases the demand in A for home market goods.

Evidently Mr. Keynes and the school of economists who share his view think that this is the end of these 80 mill. marks. As they do not directly increase the excess of imports, they can have no effect whatever on the balance of trade. They can be left out of the reasoning altogether.

I venture to suggest that, on the contrary, this amount of borrowed buying power deserves special attention. It sets in motion a mechanism which indirectly calls forth an excess of imports in A of about the same magnitude. Just as the loss of this buying power indirectly creates an export surplus in B; or, rather, these changes in buying power bring about at the same time an excess of imports in A and of exports in B.

The increased demand for home market goods in A will lead to an increased output of these goods. In a progressive country this means that labour and capital, that would otherwise have passed to export industries and industries producing goods which compete directly with import goods, now go to the home market industries instead. Output of these "import-competing" goods and of export goods increases less than it would otherwise have done. Thus, there is a relative decline in exports and increase of imports and an excess of imports is created.

A corresponding adjustment takes place in B. Home market industries grow less as a result of reduced demand for their products, and the labour and capital turns in greater proportion to export industries and industries manufacturing goods which compete directly with imported goods. The outcome is an excess of exports. B finds a widened market for its goods in A as a result of the adaptation which takes place in that country. Thus, the readjustment of production is the consequence of the change in buying power in the two countries.

The monetary mechanism which brings about the change varies with the organisation of the monetary system. In all cases of fixed foreign exchanges, however, there is an increase in monetary buying power in A and a decrease in B, which may be much larger that the 80 or 100 mill. marks. A secondary "inflation" and "deflation" may be necessary to bring about the adaptation of production and trade quickly enough. The more sudden the readjustment has to be, the greater this inflation in A and deflation in B, and the greater the changes in sectional price levels that are called forth.

The character of these price changes must be discussed briefly. Home market prices tend to rise in A and fall in B, relative to prices of export and import goods and prices of the goods which compete with import goods. The readjustment of production is partly, but partly only, the consequence of this change in "sectional price levels." [Production has a tendency to expand in the same way as demand, i.e., as the development of "markets," even without the stimulus of considerable price changes.]

It is not necessary that A's export prices should rise and B's fall. Thus, B need not offer its goods on cheaper terms of exchange to induce A to take a greater quantity of them. Indirectly, however, it is probable that a certain shift of the terms of exchange will take place. The increased buying power in A will to some extent affect also the prices of its export goods and its "import-competing" goods in an upward direction, while the corresponding classes of goods tend to become cheaper in B. In that way the readjustment of the balance of trade is made easier.

This is a magnificent passage. We may discuss Ohlin's solution of the transfer problem in the following way: He takes into account three categories of goods in both A, the payee, and B, the payer: domestic or nontraded goods, exportables, and importables. A borrows a large sum of money from B that recurs during each of the following years. To finance the loan, B reduces its spending by (say) the amount of the loan, and in the disbursement of the loan, A increases its spending by (say) the amount of the loan. B therefore (in the absence of inferior goods) reduces its spending on importables and exportables, thus reducing imports and releasing exportables for exports, directly worsening the balance of trade. Analogously A increases its spending on the three categories of goods, increasing imports and reducing exportables available for export. Spending changes in both countries operate directly to improve B's and worsen A's balance of trade.

Ohlin recognizes, however, that even though these changes work in the right direction to effect the required real transfer, they may not improve it by enough. This is because of the bias in spending toward domestic goods, which, say, is 80 percent of total spending. A transfer of 100 million marks might therefore bring about at the maximum only 20 percent of the required transfer. If, for example, domestic goods accounted for 80 percent of spending in both countries, spending changed in each country by the full amount of the transfer. If A increased its spending on international goods in the same proportion that B reduced its spending on those goods, there would be no disequilibrium in the markets for international goods but only 20 percent of the transfer would have been effected in real terms. How do changes in domestic spending help?

Ohlin argues that the indirect effects of the transfer will lead to very important further increases in the balance of trade. Keynes ignores the fact that the (assumed) 80 percent of the transfer spent on domestic goods will have a further impact on the balance of trade. In B, the payer, the reduction in demand for domestic goods reduces production and releases resources used in these industries, making them available for increased production of import-competing goods and exportables. Simultaneously, in the payee, the increased expenditure on domestic goods will draw resources from the international goods industries and thus reduce the supplies of exports and import-competing goods—and thus increase imports. Both these effects work to further improve B's and worsen A's balance of trade.

Would price changes be involved in these shifts of production and demand? Ohlin thinks there probably would be price changes. But it is not necessarily, as Keynes thinks, a fall in the payer's export prices relative to import prices, that is, a change in the terms of trade.[20] The dominant effect will certainly be that the prices of domestic goods relative to its international goods will rise in the payee and fall in the payer, and to the extent to which this occurs, the transfer of resources in the right direction—from domestic to international in the payer and from international to domestic in the payee—will be expedited.

Following this discussion, Ohlin widens his target to attack what he calls "classical barter theory":

> Note that these price changes are quite different from those assumed by the classical barter theory, which seems to underly Mr. Keynes' analysis. Mill and after him Edgeworth, Taussig and many of their followers would say that B must offer its goods on cheaper terms of exchange in order to induce A to buy more. Thus, the primary price change is one between the prices of import and export goods in both countries, not between prices of these international goods and of home market goods, as explained above. This erroneous conclusion is reached because of the fact that the shift in buying power is ignored, except in so far as it directly affects demand for international goods. It is left out of account that the demand conditions—the demand curves in an analysis à la Edgeworth in the *Economic Journal* of 1894—are changed not only by 20 but also by the 80 mill. marks.[21]

The remainder of Ohlin's article addresses itself to extraneous issues such as the assumption of unemployment, the success of "transfer" as represented by the capital movement to Germany, the problem of protection that would make transfer from Germany more difficult, the possibilities of deliveries in kind that he thinks would be easy if not confronted by the opposition of "powerful American and British export industries," but none of these remarks strengthen or weaken Ohlin's fundamental criticism of Keynes.

Keynes's Rejoinder, Ohlin's Rejoinder to the Rejoinder, and Keynes's Reply

Keynes made an immediate rejoinder to Ohlin. Briefly, he claimed that there are two ways in which Germany's trade balance could be changed: a reduction in German gold wages, and a reduction in real wages. But Ohlin, Keynes asserts, claims there is a third development, involving, say, a reduction in German borrowing, which would reduce German demand and improve the balance. Strangely enough he never mentions the increase in foreign spending that would also improve Germany's balance, an omission that renders his rebuttal valueless.

In his rejoinder to the rejoinder, published in the September issue of the journal, along with an important comment by Jacques Rueff (1929) on Keynes's March article, Ohlin notes that Keynes rejects the theory of the transfer of purchasing power, and Ohlin takes pains to prove that it is valid. He closes with the following:

> In conclusion, therefore, I must uphold my contention that reactions on the demand side play their very important part in the mechanism of international capital movements just as well as reactions on the supply side. In my opinion, there has been a tendency to overlook the former and to concentrate attention on the latter, with the consequence that a too sceptical view of the possibilities of such movements on a large scale has been taken. Anyhow, the clearing up of the theoretical difficulties involved is a matter of considerable practical importance not only for the handling of the reparation payments, but also for central banking policy in the future.

In his reply (which follows his reply to Rueff), Keynes admits that he "attributed to changes in demand conditions very little practical importance in the particular instances before us. But now he gives us a clue into his new thinking:

> If Germany was in a position to export large quantities of gold or if foreign balances in Germany were acceptable to foreign Central Banks as a substitute for gold in their reserves, then it would be a different matter. For if Germany could set the ball rolling by exporting sufficiently large quantities of gold to have an appreciable effect on world prices, this, I agree, might help the situation by changing demand conditions. But I was assuming that what Germany could do along these lines would be, in fact, quite negligible. Professor Ohlin's analogy of capital movements between two districts with the same currency system would only apply if Germany were in a position to export enough gold to make a measurable difference to demand conditions in the rest of the world.
>
> This is where the difference of opinion between Professor Ohlin and myself comes to a head. He argues (in his §3) that even if gold does not flow on a significant scale, credit will nevertheless expand in the reparation-receiving countries. But why? Of course if B (Germany) can pay A (the reparation-receiving countries) in foreign bills expressed in the currency of a third country, there is no difficulty. But this is begging the whole question. The problem arises precisely because, on our hypothesis, Germany has no such foreign bills. Germany can only acquire such bills if she has already sold the necessary exports; so that these bills cannot be part of the mechanism which is to establish the situation which will permit her to sell the exports. I can make nothing useful of Professor Ohlin's §3.
>
> Finally let me remind him that even in so far as Germany can affect demand conditions in the reparation-receiving countries by exporting to them gold or its equivalent in foreign bills, this puts her at no advantage com-

pared with all the rest of the world other than the reparation-receiving countries. There is the whole of the rest of the world in purchasing from which the receiving countries can employ their increased buying power. So we are, even in this case (which I cannot admit to be quantitatively important), brought back to the (to my way of thinking) crucial question of the extent of the elasticity of the world-demand for German exports. Professor Ohlin has not expressed any opinion about the extent of this elasticity or whether he thinks it important. Yet—on the assumption that Germany will have to increase her exports of finished goods by more than 40 percent to pay reparations without borrowing—this is to me the kernel of the whole problem.

As regards the final paragraph his §4, I agree with him that a reduction in German incomes other than wage-incomes would be equally effective, provided the incomes in question are the earnings of a factor of production, so that a reduction in them lowers the costs of the German entrepreneurs. But this proviso takes away practical significance from his observation; for there is not much likelihood of rates in Germany being lower than elsewhere.

Keynes here shifts grounds to other issues, without conceding the importance of Ohlin's points even if they have theoretical relevance. Important here is the shift from a real to a monetary model. There are overtones of the need for "cash-in-advance" to get the shifts of demand going. An important point here is that the very existence of the reparations payments requires additional liquidity. We might say it was an additional factor bringing on the deflation of the early 1930s. The issues are important and relevant, but they are tossed out at the end of the debate and never entered the literature of the interwar period (except partially in the Viner-Robertson controversy of the middle 1930s).

Later Developments

What made readers of Keynes's 1929 article sit up and take notice was not the argument that Germany's reparations bill was too high but rather his astonishing argument that *whatever the reparations bill* the transfer could not be effected if the elasticity of demand for Germany's exports were less than unity. It will for a long time go down as one of the great puzzles of the history of economic thought why Keynes let himself fall victim to such an absurd position! The editor of the *Economic Journal*—Keynes himself—should have had it properly refereed!

Keynes's model completely ignored income and expenditure effects.[22] The only way, he argued, that (say) Germany could increase its exports surplus was to lower the prices of German goods relative to the prices of the goods of the rest of the world. In other words, Germany's terms of trade had to turn against her. This meant that in real terms Germany would have to pay more than the transfer by an amount equal to the income cost of the change in the terms of trade. But even then, the policy may not work, because if the elasticity of demand for German exports were less than unity, lowering their prices would bring less rather than more export proceeds and the price-lowering policy would be counterproductive.

The error in this reasoning, which Ohlin spotted quickly, is almost too well known to spend much time on. Keynes's argument is incorrect even on its own grounds. If, after all, the elasticity of demand for German exports were *less* than unity, the transfer could even more easily be effected by *raising*, not lowering, export prices, with the terms of trade moving in Germany's favor and easing the transfer burden. But this is a debating point, not a serious argument. The model itself is indefensible.

A major objection to Keynes's model, raised by Ohlin, is his ignoring of expenditure effects. But before turning to that objection, it is necessary to point out that his model is incorrect even with respect to relative prices. It is not the foreign elasticity of demand for Germany's exports that is relevant to the change in the trade balance but the global elasticity of demand for Germany's goods that is relevant. A sufficient condition for a fall in the relative prices of Germany's goods to improve the trade balance—in a two-good model—is that the *global* elasticity (defined to be normally positive) of demand for Germany's good be positive.[23] This condition can also be expressed as the sum of the elasticities of demand for imports in the two countries, reduced by unity, an expression that is sometimes called the "elasticity of the trade balance." In a case where the marginal propensities to import at home and abroad are each zero—the case where income effects do not affect the trade balance—Germany's balance of trade can be improved or worsened by a fall or a rise in the terms of trade according to whether the elasticities of demand for imports are in excess or fall short of unity.

The problem of transfer, as already discussed, was broken down into two parts: a budgetary problem and a transfer problem. The budgetary problem was for Germany to reduce its spending through taxation by the amount of the annual transfer payment, and for the receiving countries to increase their spending by a corresponding amount equal to the transfer receipts. Thus Germany's spending would be reduced below its income by the amount of the transfer payment, and the recipient countries' spending would be increased beyond its income by the same amount.

Keynes's position implicitly assumes that the marginal propensities to import in the two countries are equal to zero and that, therefore, the marginal propensities to spend are equal to unity. In this case the trade balance, relying on the expenditure changes at constant prices, is unchanged. The whole burden of adjustment therefore depends on the effectiveness of relative price changes in correcting the disequilibrium.

Against this position, Ohlin interposed the action of expenditure effects. At unchanged prices, the spending changes would reduce the demand for exportable goods in Germany, and also the demand for imports. At the same time the receipts of the transfer proceeds would increase expenditure in the rest of the world and thereby increase the demand for imports and, because they also increase the demand for exportables, reduce exports. Is that the end of the problem? No. It is also necessary to ascertain whether the goods for which demand has decreased in Germany are the goods for which demand will increase in the rest of the world. If they are not, any excess demand will result in either changes in relative prices or, in the case of constant costs, compensating changes in production.

But that's all there is to it! Because Keynes neglected the expenditure effects, he thought that Germany would have to lower its prices drastically in order to generate an export surplus. In the exchange with Keynes[24] in the *Economic Journal* at the end of the 1920s, Ohlin showed that on the contrary, the transfer could be made without any changes in the terms of trade. Keynes much later, in a half-hearted way, perhaps bolstered by the fact that the entire reparations episode had been proved a fiasco, admitted his mistake. The field of the battle of logic lay with Ohlin!

The great puzzle for economists is how Keynes came to adopt such an extreme—and even absurd—position. Throughout history unilateral transfers had been made. A typical conclusion of an armistice or treaty was the imposition of a tribute on the vanquished. Keynes, at least in the 1930s, was seeped in economic and particularly monetary history. How he could adopt such an absurd position will remain one of the great mysteries in the history of economic thought!

The Transfer Problem in History

Had a minor economist adopted the position Keynes took, it would not have been necessary or interesting to inquire more deeply into his mind. But the fact that Keynes is widely acknowledged as one of the great economists of the twentieth century, and possibly one of the five great economists of all time, it is necessary to inquire how a first-rate economist made such a second-rate mistake. To survey this question, it is necessary to investigate the prevailing paradigm at the time Keynes was writing.

Keynes's problem had its roots in the classical theory of adjustment. From the time that Hume wrote, in 1752, his magnificent essay on the balance of trade, economists came to believe that international adjustment was governed by the "price-specie-flow" mechanism. The mechanism as it came to be explained started out with a deficit in one country and a surplus in "the" other country. The deficit country would lose gold, the surplus country gain it, and prices would accordingly adjust downward in the deficit country and upward in the surplus country. The shift in relative prices would transfer demand from the surplus to the deficit country and bring on a correction of the disequilibrium.

This description was at best an incomplete, and at worst an incorrect, description of the adjustment process. Hume started with a disturbance to equilibrium caused by a "miraculous" increase or decrease in the quantity of money. Starting from a position of equilibrium, an increase (say) in the money supply creates a disequilibrium in the form of an excess supply of money. With exasperating ambiguity, Hume never tells us whether this increases expenditure and raises prices or worsens the balance of payments directly, without price changes. These two versions of the adjustment process dominated the literature of the nineteenth century and the first half of the twentieth century and reverberated in the background of the transfer problem.

The case that Hume was aware of adjustment without the need for changes in relative prices rests on his emphatic exposition of what later came to be called the "law of one price" by which law prices abroad could not differ, at least for international goods, from prices at home. If we emphasize this interpretation, we have to say that an increase in money raises expenditure and worsens the balance of trade (and payments) without the need for price changes. But Hume was not explicit about the absence of need for changes in relative prices in his exposition, and this created an ambiguity that confused the literature on the adjustment process for the next two centuries!

The theory of adjustment is relevant because it also relates to the motivation for expenditure changes. In Keynes's model the balance of trade is affected only by relative prices, so obviously unrequited transfers and expenditure changes can have no effect on the trade balance. In the same way one interpretation of the theory of adjustment is that the trade balance depends only on relative prices and is not affected directly by changes in the money supply. The mistake in the theory of international adjustment derives from the erroneous application of the closed economy model of money and prices—where it is applicable—to the open economy model where it does not apply.

It is a fair observation that the theory of capital transfers was only incidental to the great controversies with which the classical economists were concerned, including the bullion and currency controversies. No member of the classical school—not even John Stuart Mill—generalized on the subject. Mill's "supposed generalization represented merely a one-page addendum to the chapter on the "Distribution of the Precious Metals through the Commercial World."[25]

John Eliot Cairnes characterized Mill's discussion as inadequate. "But he suggested only the addition of the conventional foreign-exchange mechanism described by George Joachim Goschen. Cairnes's critique was accepted as merely an elucidation of the obvious implications in Mill's remarks, which were mistaken for a complete conclusion on the transfer process.... The textbook cliché is exemplified by Frank W. Taussig:

> Continuing now the analysis of the change of operation under a specie regime, it is obvious that the increase in remittances from London to New York will cause a demand for New York exchange in London. New York exchange will rise in London, sterling exchange will fall in New York. But in this situation—both countries on a gold basis—the fluctuations in foreign exchange will necessary be confined within the gold points. Specie will flow from London to New York. Then will follows that *train of consequences familiar to the reader of Ricardo and Mill.* Prices will fall in Great Britain and will rise in the United States. With the fall of English prices the export of commodities from England will be stimulated, and more of them will go the United States. With the rise of American prices exports from the United States will be discouraged, and imports correspondingly stimulated. These

> diverging movements—a general fall of prices and money incomes in Britain, and a general rise of prices and money in the United States—will continue until an excess of commodity exports from Great Britain develops to such an extent as to meet the obligation which the English [lenders] have assumed for making remittances to the United States. Then the money value of the excess of exports from Great Britain will be precisely equal to the remittances to be made from London to New York. The English balance of trade will be "favorable"; the American balance of trade "unfavorable." The balance of international *payments* will be completely adjusted; exchange in London and New York will again be at par.[26]

The issue with respect to transfers can be posed as follows: Are changes in relative prices necessarily associated with a change in the trade balance induced by unilateral transfers? The subject can most easily be addressed in two parts: first, that applying to barter and, second, that applying to the international monetary economy. The first problem is to see how changes in transfers and the balance of trade affect changes in the terms of trade and/or the real exchange rate. The second problem is to determine how transfer affects the balance of payments (under fixed exchange rates) and the exchange rate (when it is flexible and, say, the money supply is constant).

Even in the barter theory we get two camps, the difference between which only became generally known after the Keynes-Ohlin-Rueff debate on the transfer problem. The debate that emerged therein pitted what is best called the income-expenditure approach against the relative prices approach, with Wheatley, Ricardo, Longfield, Bastable, Nicholson, Wicksell, and Ohlin on the one side and Mill, Taussig, Viner, and Keynes on the other.[27] The Mill school argued that the generation of a balance-of-trade surplus required a fall in relative prices of the transferring country, whereas the income-expenditure school denied that changes in relative prices were an essential ingredient in the adjustment process. As the more refined mathematical models of Pigou, Meade, Samuelson, and others subsequently showed, the income-expenditure school was vindicated.

The income-expenditure school got the better of the argument as far as the effect of transfer on the terms of trade is concerned. Viner conceded the point, but Keynes was a different matter.

A revision of the literature became necessary to give credit to those classical writers who had fully incorporated expenditure effects into the analysis. Within the framework of the theory of exchange, a transfer of purchasing power produces expenditure effects that worsen the balance of trade of the receiving country and improve that of the paying country. The redistribution of world expenditure from the paying to the receiving country could leave global excess demand unchanged (if the expenditure effects cancel), or it could result in an excess demand for one country's goods, leaving room for changes in relative prices. The essential factor in the adjustment mechanism is the shift in expenditures relative to incomes in the two countries, the relative price changes being incidental to the process.

Mill and Marshall had investigated the stability question of whether a change in relative prices (in the context of their barter model this meant a change in the terms of trade) would shift excess demand onto the good whose relative price has fallen. Marshall deduced that it depended on whether an elasticity criterion—the sum of the elasticities of demand[28] for imports minus unity—was positive or negative. There is no a priori guarantee that such a criterion will be satisfied. Economists in the postwar period came to be divided into two camps—elasticity optimists and elasticity pessimists, with the former stressing the advantages of relying upon the price mechanism and the latter the need for direct controls. Nevertheless, it is usually assumed in trade theory analysis that the stability conditions are met or, if they are not, that an unstable equilibrium point, which must be flanked by stable equilibria, would quickly be dislodged to one of the stable equilibria.

Assuming that the underlying stability condition is satisfied, the direction of change in the terms of trade is determined by the way in which the transfer of purchasing power affects relative expenditure on the two products. This reduces to a comparison of the marginal propensities to spend or, alternatively and equivalently, the relative income elasticities of demand. If, for example, the receiving country has a high propensity to spend on import goods, whereas the paying country has a low marginal propensity to spend on its own export goods, the transfer will create an excess demand for the paying country's good and therefore an excess supply of the receiving country's good. The transfer on balance at constant terms of trade will therefore shift demand onto the goods of the paying country, improving its terms of trade and of course worsening the terms of trade of the receiving country, on the assumption that the initial equilibrium is stable.

How much would the terms of trade have to change? The answer to this question depends on the size of the gap between supply and demand at constant relative prices and the effectiveness of relative prices in eliminating excess demands, which depends on the elasticities. Because the elasticities fully incorporate supply effects,[29] the supply conditions play a role in determining the extent of any necessary changes in relative prices. The higher are the elasticities, the more effective any given change in relative prices will be in eliminating a given excess demand. It should therefore be noted that even if the rearrangement of world demand creates excess demand, supplies might adjust to prevent changes in relative prices if one country were incompletely specialized and produced both goods at constant costs.[30]

The development of the complete criterion for the effect of a transfer on the terms of trade was first given in Meade (1951). The simplest way to analyze the subject mathematically is to differentiate the balance-of-payments equilibrium equation $B(P, T) = T$ by T, with the result that $dP/dT = (1 - B_T)/B_P = (1 - m_a - m_b)/B_P$ where B_P can be translated into the usual elasticity conditions multiplied by the level of imports. A key contribution of this generalization is that it demonstrates what should have been obvious at the outset, that adjustment to a transfer would never involve a change in relative prices if one of the countries, or the world economy in general, were a large country relative to the home country such that the terms-of-trade elasticity of its offer curve is infinite.

Ohlin, of course, took account of nontraded or domestic goods, as did some earlier writers. The discussions of the 1920s had been initially couched in the framework of a two-good two-country model with primary focus on the terms of trade. But writers of both schools, going as far back as Cantillon and Hume, and including Ricardo, Taussig, Keynes, and Ohlin, had given some consideration to domestic (nontraded) goods. The existence of domestic goods brought into consideration not only the terms of trade but also the ratios of the prices of domestic and import goods and the ratios of the prices of domestic goods and export prices in each country. One convenient definition of the real exchange rate is the ratio of the prices of home-produced goods at home and abroad. For a small country, in which the terms of trade are constant, the real exchange rate is sometimes defined as the ratio of the price of domestic (nontraded) and international (traded) goods.

The introduction of domestic goods into the transfer debate seemed to qualify the victory of the income-expenditure school somewhat, giving the Mill-Taussig school a second line of defense. Changes in relative price levels can take place even if the terms of trade are constant. In his little treatise *Capital Imports and the Terms of Trade*, Roland Wilson (1931) repeated Ohlin's arguments and argued that an income transfer would shift demand onto domestic goods in the receiving country and away from domestic goods in the paying country. The effect on the relative prices would then depend on cost conditions. Under the assumption of increasing (opportunity) costs, the price level will tend to rise in the receiving country and fall in the paying country.

Increasing costs, of course, represent only one possibility. If opportunity costs between domestic and international goods are constant, no change in the real exchange rate will result. And if there are decreasing costs, the relative price of domestic goods would tend to move in the opposite direction from that postulated by the Mill-Taussig school. The result will depend on the conditions of supply.

An interesting case involving domestic goods that lends some support to Mill's conclusion, that the terms of trade of the paying country worsen as a result of transfer, has been analyzed by John Chipman (1974, sec. D, thm. 4).[31] If each country produces export and domestic goods (but no import-competing goods), there will be a tendency for the terms of trade to change in the Millian direction. This conclusion follows because resources are shifted from export to domestic industries in the receiving country, and in the opposite direction in the paying country, restricting the supply of exports in the receiving country and augmenting the supply of exports in the paying country. Note that in this case it is the relative price of domestic and export goods that will be constant in both countries, but the relative price of domestic and import goods will rise in the receiving country and fall in the paying country; the real exchange rate will thus also improve along with the terms of trade in the receiving country and fall in the paying country.

Chipman's result depends partly on the supposition that there are no import-competing goods in the two countries. To complete the analysis, it is worth considering the results from a two-factor three-commodity Heckscher-Ohlin model under conditions that permit factor price equalization in the two countries.[32] In this case it can be shown that a transfer may have no effect on relative prices despite the increase in the output of domestic goods in the receiving country and the decrease in the output of domestic goods in the paying country. Let us consider first the condition of a receiving country that faces fixed terms of trade, given by the rest of the world. This fixes factor prices in the import and export industries of the receiving country and therefore costs of production in the domestic goods industries. The receiving country's increase in expenditure (financed by the financial transfer) on import and export goods can be supplied by a decrease in its trade balance, but the increase in spending on domestic goods (assuming no inferior goods) must be supplied internally, by a shift of labor and capital out of the export and import-competing goods industries. It is possible to reduce the productions of the two international goods in exactly that proportion needed to release the needed factors—along the Rybczynski theorem lines—required to produce the additional domestic goods at constant factor prices. The conclusion does not, however, depend on the small country assumption provided that expenditure effects cancel. If marginal tastes for commodities are the same in the two countries, there will be no change in the global demand for factors and therefore no change in relative factor or commodity prices. But even if expenditure effects cancel, there is no presumption (given as always incomplete specialization) that the real exchange rate will change in the Millian direction.

Transfers, Gold Flow, and the Exchange Rate

Now consider the equilibrium after unilateral transfers in a monetary economy. Consider first the case where there is a single money—call it gold—in the world economy so that changes in monetary conditions will be reflected in the balance of payments rather than exchange rates. In the absence of transfers, equilibrium will prevail when the trade balances and the excess demands for gold are zero. Now let the equilibrium be disturbed by a unilateral transfer. How will this affect the balance of payments of the two countries? Will gold move to the receiving or the paying country?[33]

The answer to this question derives from the monetary approach to the balance of payments: money will flow to the country in which the transfer creates an excess demand for money. Of course, the demands for money in the two countries will depend partly on how demand shifts affect price levels. Money will normally flow to the country in which the price level increases. But there are also important independent effects that do not depend on changes in price levels. To isolate these effects, let us suppose that expenditure effects cancel.

The direction of change in the excess demand for money will depend on the arguments—apart from prices—in the demand-for-money function. To the extent that liquidity requirements depend on transactions, there will be an increase in demand for money in both countries to satisfy the additional transactions involved in arranging the transfer.[34] The extra transactions will therefore imply that domestic expenditure in the receiving country will rise by less, and in the paying country fall by more, than the transfer itself until the additional monetary requirements are met. If the stock of monetary gold in the world is constant, the increased world demand for money will result in a once-for-all decline in the world price level in order to raise the real value of the world gold stock to that required by the higher level of transactions.

Over and above this once-for-all transactions effect affecting both countries, there will be a differential effect on the two countries in view of their different positions after the transfer. The movement of gold between the two countries will depend on how the demand for money is affected by the increase in expenditure (absorption) in the receiving country and the decrease in the paying country.[35] If, as seems natural, the demand for money in the two countries depends partly on expenditure, the receiving country will require more, and the paying country less gold. To accumulate the additional liquidity, inhabitants (including the government) in the receiving country will increase spending by less than the transfer, thus improving the balance of payments and attracting gold, and similarly the paying country will for a time decrease its expenditure by less than the transfer, generating a balance of payments deficit until the lower equilibrium quantity of money is established.

The three individual types of effects of a transfer on the demand for money must be summed to determine the direction of the gold flow. The changes in the demand for money in the two countries arising from expenditure shifts must by superimposed on the pure transactions effect of the transfer discussed earlier; both effects operate to increase the demand for money in the receiving country, but they have opposing tendencies in the paying country. To these two effects must then be added any other effects resulting from altered patterns of demand that induce changes in price levels. To the extent that there is a presumption that the real exchange rate of the receiving country rises as a result of the transfer, the price effect will combine with the other two effects to increase unambiguously the demand for money and therefore the balance of payments of the receiving country. The transfer will in this case result in a flow of gold from the paying country to the receiving country in addition to a deflationary effect in the world as a whole in the absence of any increase in the global money supply.

An alternative monetary assumption is that exchange rates are fixed but that the central bank has some flexibility in its credit policy. Consider therefore two countries with gold-convertible currencies but whose central bank assets are composed not only of gold but of government or private-sector assets. Because it raises the level of transactions, the transfer will now, as before, increase the demand for money. Now, however, the central banks in the two countries could prevent world deflation by open market operations in government or private securities. Changes in the demand for money could be induced by an increase in the receiving country and a decrease in the paying country of spending. To preserve balance of payments equilibrium at fixed exchange rates, making a gold flow unnecessary, the central bank in the receiving country could expand credit, and the central bank in the paying country could contract credit. In these cases, in contrast, the ratio of gold to total monetary liabilities of the central bank would be correspondingly altered.

Let us next consider the alternative monetary assumptions where the authorities hold the money supply constant and allow flexibility of the exchange rates. According to the monetary approach to the exchange rate, the transfer will create an appreciation or depreciation of the exchange rate in those circumstances where, under a common money or fixed exchange rates, the balance of payments would move into surplus or deficit. Given the requirement of purchasing power parity as an equilibrium condition, an appreciation of a country's currency implies either a fall in the domestic price of tradable goods in the appreciating country or an increase in the price of tradable goods in the other currency.

As a result of a transfer—with fixed money supplies and flexible exchange rates—there will be, as before, a transactions effect that increases the demand for money in both countries, leading, to some degree, to worldwide deflation. Superimposed on this tendency will be an excess demand for money in the receiving country and an excess supply of money in the paying country due to the redistribution of world expenditure; this leads to appreciation of the currency of the receiving country and a depreciation of the currency of the paying country. Both effects therefore work to create some deflation in the receiving country, but there are opposing tendencies in the paying country. Changes in relative prices induced by the rearrangement of world demand will have additional effects. To the extent that the prices of home-produced goods rise in the receiving country and fall in the paying country, the appreciation of the currency of the receiving country will be reinforced.

Conclusions

What can be said on balance about the controversy? First, Keynes, who had been seeped in the subject of German reparations for more than a decade, deserves credit for developing a model for economists that could provide a starting point for more serious analysis. The Keynes model, which rested on the mistakes of the Taussig-Viner school, was naive, but it provoked others, especially Ohlin, but also Rueff and others, into building a more correct model of the adjustment process. Ohlin's work was especially prescient for his time. Although there had been a long history of the transfer discussion, including the correct treatment of expenditure effects, it was Ohlin who set the modern literature on the right track and paved the way for more formal mathematical analysis of the issues involved.

It should be said, however, that the issue is not dead. Much remains to be done in developing a complete model of the adjustment process involving not just import goods, export goods, and domestic goods but also gold, bank money, and securities. The problem will probably never die out because the transfer problem will survive as an opportunity for testing the application of new theoretical techniques and incorporating the theory of transfers explicitly into the theory of general economic equilibrium.

Notes

1. That this devastation was colossal is underlined by the fact that even today the area has not completely recovered. In the department of the Somme, the site of one of the bloodiest battles of World War I, when, on July 1, 1916, whole regiments of Allied soldiers went "over the top" only to be mowed down by German machine-gun fire. As

I learned on a recent trip to the area in September 1999, shells and grenades still rise to the surface of the fields, and 90 tons of these dormant time bombs are collected and destroyed every year!

2. The following sections are taken from the *Enc. Brit.* (CD-Rom 1999).

3. The United States decided to forgo any claim to reparations it might have submitted.

4. The *Encyclopedia* account continues: "Historians have differed sharply as to whether the obligations were within the capacity of the German economy. But the May 1921 schedule was less harsh than it seemed, for the bill was divided into three series—A bonds totaling 12,000,000,000 marks, B bonds for 38,000,000,000, and the unlikely C bonds in the amount of 82,000,000,000. The latter would not even be issued until the first two series were paid and existed as much to balance against the Allies' debts to the United States as actually to be paid by Germany." This judgment, however, ignores the oppressive disincentive effect of "conditional" reparations and thus fails to appreciate the incentives for the hyperinflation that followed. If Germany was successful in paying the A bonds, the B bonds would follow as the night the day, and if she succeeded in paying the B bonds, so would the C bonds. Germany therefore had every incentive to demonstrate its inability to pay the A bonds, and the hyperinflation was the best way to do it!

5. The *Encyclopedia* account goes on as follows: "The French argued that the inflation was purposeful, designed to feign bankruptcy while allowing Berlin to liquidate its internal debt and German industrialists like Hugo Stinnes and Fritz Thyssen to borrow, expand, and dump exports on the world market. Recent research suggests, however, that the government did not fully understand the causes of the inflation even though it recognized its social utility in stimulating employment and permitting social expenditures. Of course, the reparations bill, while not the cause of inflation, was a strong disincentive to stabilization for Berlin could hardly plead bankruptcy if it boasted a strong currency, a balanced budget, and a healthy balance of payments. And insofar as the German government was dependent on those who benefitted most from inflation—the industrialists—it was incapable of implementing austerity measures. This financial tangle might have been avoided by a program of reparations-in-kind whereby German firms delivered raw and finished goods directly to the Allies. The Seydoux Plan of 1920 and the Wiesbaden Accords of 1921 embraced such a mechanism, but the Ruhr magnates, delighted that the French might "choke on their iron" in the absence of German coal, and the British, fearful of any continental cartel, together torpedoed reparations-in-kind. By December 1921, Berlin was granted a moratorium."

I find this discussion wholly unconvincing. Germany had already made huge transfers of her navy and mercantile fleet to the Allies, and in addition most of the property owned by Germans in Alsace-Lorraine and her colonies. Payments in kind are no panacea. If valued at pre-transfer prices, they would not be fulfilling the letter of the reparations commitment, and if at post-transfer prices, they would not by any easier to dispose of than through money payments. See the discussion in Samuelson (1952).

6. See Eichengreen (1992:131). For Machlup's estimate, see Machlup (1964:379).

7. The immediate debt of 50 billion gold marks represented 125 percent of Germany's 1921 GDP, which would be 5.4 times the total French reparations bill.

8. See Eichengreen (1992:132).

9. Ibid.

10. *Enc. Brit.* (1999).

11. Ibid.

12. For the following and the next paragraph, see "Dawes Plan" and "Young Plan" in *Enc. Brit. CD-Rom ed.* (1999).

13. For an explicit analysis of the relation between loans to Germany and reparations, see Schuker (1988).

14. This is quoted in Dimand (1988:124) from Patinkin and Leith (1978:162).

15. The issue, however, is not so clear-cut. At least ex ante the transfers to Germany in the 1920s were loans and not "unrequited" transfers, though they were subsequently repudiated.

16. Keynes's passion for his cause may have been partly because he had, as he described it himself a decade later in his little book, *Two Memoirs*, fallen in love with Melchior, the German representative on the Reparations Commission. They spent several days together talking about reparations in the railway coach at Trier and Keynes kept in touch with him later, meeting again on a trip to Berlin in 1927.

17. This is not to say that Keynes had an adequate global economic model. In the 1920s he was still an "Edwardian" vexing at the new reality that the United States had taken over from Britain as top economic power. His role as a British nationalist was, as he saw it, to protect his country from the instability of prices now associated with the United States.

18. Ohlin (1929:172f). The footnote, added after correspondence with Keynes, related to the meaning of "buying power":

In a country, which neither borrows from nor lends to other countries and which maintains equilibrium on its capital market, "buying power" is identical with "aggregate of money earnings." Foreign borrowing, however, increases and loans reduce buying power. Similarly, inflationary credit policy increases and deflationary policy reduces it. In the former case new buying power is created by the banks; in the latter, money which is earned and saved is not lent by the banks to others,—it vanishes and buying power falls off.

19. Ohlin (1929:173).

20. Ohlin does believe, however, that while it is not necessary, it is likely that there will be a change in the terms of trade against the payer: "The increased buying power in A will to some extent affect also the prices of its export goods and its "import-competing" goods in an upward direction, while the corresponding classes of goods tend to become cheaper in B. . . ." He gets this result because he implicitly assumes that import-competing goods and imports are imperfect substitutes.

21. In the next two paragraphs Ohlin discusses Keynes' assumption about the need to lower export prices:

If the mechanism I have endeavoured to indicate briefly above corresponds to reality, evidently a sufficient adjustment of the balance of trade may take place without any considerable reduction in B's export prices or increase in A's. It seems, therefore, very misleading to represent the increase in B's exports as due entirely to a reduction in its export prices.

Of course, a discussion of the elasticity of demand for B's export goods, which tacitly assumes demand conditions to be unchanged, must reach the conclusion that considerable increases in the value of its exports are impossible. As Mr. Keynes points out: "if a reduction in price of 10 percent stimulates the volume of trade by 20 percent, this does not increase the value of the exports by 20 percent, but only by 8 percent ($1.20 \times 90 = 108$)" (p. 5). An increase by 20 percent as a result of a 10 percent price reduction may appear as a very great elasticity of demand, and yet the value of exports grows only by 8 percent. How violent, then, must the price reduction be, if export values are to increase by 40 percent as in the German case, when the borrowings have ceased and reparations have to be paid by means of an export surplus.

22. Keynes, following the Cunliffe Report and the incorrect theory championed by Frank Taussig and Jacob Viner, ignored income-expenditure effects in his model of the transfer controversy despite the fact that earlier economists, including men of such stature as Ricardo, Wheatley, Bastable, Nicholson, and Wicksell, had explicitly taken them into account and provided a correct analysis of related problems.

23. See, for example, Mundell (1960).

24. See Keynes (1929), Ohlin (1929), and Rueff (1929) for the main articles.

25. Mason (1956:493).

26. Quoted in Mason (1956:493–94).

27. See Mundell (1989a, and especially 1989b) for a recent review of the literature on this subject and for detailed references. An excellent review of the literature up to 1937 is offered by Viner (1937).

28. This assumes that trade is initially balanced; a slight adjustment is required where this is not the case.

29. The elasticity of import demand, for example, is a weighted average of the elasticities of demand and supply of the product, the weights being, respectively, the ratios of demand and imports and supply and imports. For a complete development of these relations see, for example, Mundell (1961), and Mundell (1968).

30. Constant costs and incomplete specialization imply that the elasticity of demand for imports is infinite. Meade (1951) produced the first algebraic formula for the change in the terms of trade, explicitly integrating expenditure and price effects. Note that because expenditure propensities and price elasticities are related by the Johnson-Slutzky condition, import propensities high enough (greater than one-half on the average) to shift demand onto the goods of the paying country (the anti-Mill direction) are sufficient to ensure that the elasticities of demand are large enough (greater than one-half on the average) to ensure stability of exchange equilibrium. See Mundell (1960, 1968).

31. Chipman's analysis was also presented at the 1988 meeting of the Eastern Economic Association in Baltimore.

32. This paragraph was part of my comment on Chipman's Baltimore presentation.

33. Jacob Viner addressed this question in his *Studies* (1937), analyzing the issue on the assumption that what he called the "final-purchases velocity" of money was constant. Viner's analysis resulted in an exchange with Dennis Robertson (1938). Robertson arguing that it was more natural to assume that the income velocity of money

was constant. In the ensuing debate a compromise position was arrived at, with Viner conceding that the money balances required to service the increase in expenditure in the receiving country would be, while still positive, less than that required to service expenditure from income produced at home, with the result that gold would still flow in the direction of the receiving country—changes in prices being abstracted from—but by a smaller amount than he had initially concluded. Robertson, however, held to his view that the receiving country would not require more money to service the additional expenditure made possible by tax reductions than was previously required to service the payment of taxes that the inward transfer made unnecessary.

A correct analysis of the issue requires splitting the demand for money balances into sectoral demands by consumers, producers, and governments. Because production in both countries is assumed to be constant, there would not ordinarily be a change in producer's money balances. But the money requirements of consumers would rise in the receiving country and fall in the paying country on account of the expenditure shifts. Government spending, however, would rise in both the receiving and the paying countries in view of the transactions associated with the disbursement of the proceeds through (say) an income subsidy in the payee and the raising of the proceeds by (say) taxation in the payer.

34. I have noted this transactions effect in Mundell (1989a). As mentioned in the preceding note, a precise treatment of the increased transactions demands would require splitting national demands into household, producer, and government sectors.

35. An alternative formulation would make the demand for money a function of wealth. Insofar as we are restricting our analysis to unilateral transfers, wealth, and therefore the demand for money, is lower in the paying country and higher in the receiving country, resulting in a balance of payments surplus in, and a flow of gold to the receiving country.

This formulation would have to be modified in the case of capital movements. Unlike unilateral transfers, capital movements do not imply a change in wealth. They represent a geographical redistribution of wealth. The purchasing power (absorption) of the borrowing country is increased, and of the paying country is reduced, by the capital transfer, but the GNPs, which take into account international interest payments, are only slightly affected (by the extra rent associated with differences in rates of return). On these grounds, therefore, the intertemporal pattern of consumption would not theoretically be affected by borrowing; most of borrowed money should therefore be devoted to the formation of physical or human capital. This implies that the product mix of marginal expenditure effects will be influenced by the proportion of the transfer that is unilateral and the proportion that is merely a loan.

References

Chipman, J. S. 1974. The transfer problem once again. In G. Horwich and P. A. Samuecson, eds., *Trade, Stability and Macroeconomics*. New York: Academic Press.

Dimand, R. W. 1988. *The Origins of the Keynesian Revolution*. Stanford, CA: Stanford University Press.

Eichengreen, B. 1992. *Golden Fetters: The Gold Standard and the Great Depression*, 1919–1939. Oxford: Oxford University Press.

Encyclopedia Brittanica. CD Rom Edition, 1999.

Keynes, J. M. 1929. The German transfer problem. *Economic Journal* 39:1–7, 179–82, 404–408.

Machlup, F. 1964. *International Payments, Debts and Gold*. New York: Scribners.

Marshall, A. 1923. *Money, Credit and Commence*. London: Macmillan.

Mason, W. E. 1956. The stereotypes of classical transfer theory. *Journal of Political Economy* 64(6):492–506.

Meade, J. E. 1951. *The Theory of international Economic Policy. The Balance of Payments: Mathematical Supplement*, vol. 1. Oxford: Oxford University Press.

Mundell, R. A. 1960. The Pure Theory of International Trade. *American Economic Review*, volume 50, March 1960, pp. 67–110.

Mundell, R. A. 1968. *International Economics*. New York: Macmillan.

Mundell, R. A. 1989a. Latin American debt and the transfer problem. In P. Brock, M. Connolly, and C. Gonzalez-Vega, eds., *Latin American Debt and Adjustment*. New York: Proeger.

Mundell, R. A. 1989b. The dollar and the policy mix: 1989. *Rivista di Politica Economica* 79(12):57–78.

Ohlin, R. 1929. The reparations problem: A discussion. *Economic Journal* 39:172–78, 400–404.

Patinkin, D., and C. Leith. 1978. *Keynes, Cambridge and the General Theory*. Toronto: University of Toronto Press.

Robertson, D. H. 1938. Indemnity payments and gold movements. *Quarterly Journal of Economics* 53 (February): 312–14, 317.

Rueff, J. 1929. Mr. Keynes' views on the transfer problem. *Economic Journal* 39:388–99.

Samuelson, P. A. 1952. The transfer problem and transport costs. I. *Economic Journal* 62(246):278–304.

Samuelson, P. A. 1954. The transfer problem and transport costs. II. *Economic Journal* 64(254):264–90.

Schuker, S. A. 1988. *American "Reparations" to Germany 1919–1933: Implications for the third world debt crisis. Princeton Studies in International Finance*, 61. Princeton: Princeton University Press.

Viner, J. 1937. *Studies in the Theory of International Trade*. New York: Harper.

Viner, J. 1938. A reply to Robertson. *Quarterly Journal of Economics* 53 (February): 314–17.

Wilson, R. 1931. *Capital Imports and the Terms of Trade*. Melbourne: Melbourne University Press.

13

Ohlin on the Great Depression: The Popular Message in the Daily Press

Benny Carlson and Lars Jonung

Introduction

In Sweden the economics profession has by tradition held a strong position in public debate. The first generation of "modern" economists created the basis for this position—a generation including Knut Wicksell, Gustav Cassel, and Eli Heckscher. They combined their scientific work with considerable journalistic activities and wrote prolifically in the daily press as indicated in table 13.1.[1] Cassel was the most active journalist and professor of them all with an output of more than 1,500 articles in *Svenska Dagbladet,* a Stockholm daily.[2]

Bertil Ohlin chose to follow this journalistic model. At an early stage he began his career as a writer of articles, editorials, and comments in the daily press. He was probably the most prominent journalist of them all; if not as regards style at least in numbers, with more than 2,300 articles in daily papers, half of which appeared in the 1920s and the 1930s, before he made the transition from science to politics.

An (almost) complete list of a Ohlin's contributions to the daily press has recently been compiled.[3] However, these writings have not yet been subject to any systematic investigation. In this chapter we take a first step by examining a selection—about 80 articles—written by Ohlin on issues related to the depression of the 1930s and published in the period 1926 to 1935. We are of the opinion that these articles make it possible to trace closely the development of his macroeconomic thinking, almost on a week-by-week basis. We expect it to be fairly easy to map his views, since newspaper articles on economic matters, aimed at the general public, ought to be characterized by simplicity and clarity.

Table 13.1
Number of articles in the daily press published by Wicksell, Cassel, Heckscher, Ohlin and Myrdal

Authors	Number of articles
Knut Wicksell	450 (approx.)
Gustav Cassel	1,506 (in *Svenska Dagbladet*)
Eli Heckscher	300 (approx.)
Bertil Ohlin	2,300 (approx.)
Gunnar Myrdal	50 (approx.)

Sources: Jonung (1992) and Carlson, Orrje, and Wadensjö (2000).

We concentrate on the depression in the early 1930s, since it exercised a deep impact on the thinking of Swedish economists, especially on Ohlin's generation.[4] The deep depression, accompanied by high unemployment and political unrest, served as a powerful incentive and challenge to bring forth new theories and policy proposals. According to prevailing views—fostered by Ohlin himself as well—Ohlin was a pioneer within the "new economics" that emerged in the 1930s in Sweden, eventually termed the Stockholm School of economics. The aim of our study is to add to the understanding of this process.

Research on Ohlin's work within the Stockholm School focuses on two contributions: Ohlin's article in *Ekonomisk Tidskrift* in 1933 "Till frågan om penningteoriens uppläggning"[5] (On the formulation of monetary theory), and his report in 1934 to the Committee on unemployment *Penningpolitik, offentliga arbeten, subventioner och tullar som medel mot arbetslöshet* (Monetary policy, public works, subsidies, and tariffs as remedies for unemployment). Ohlin's development in a longer perspective—from the mid-1920s to these works from 1933 and 1934—is analyzed by Karl-Gustav Landgren (1960) and Otto Steiger (1971).[6] They have both, and notably Steiger, taken an interest in Ohlin's articles in the daily press.[7] Furthermore in his memoirs Ohlin tried to buttress his position as a pioneer in the new economics by referring to his articles in the daily press.[8]

Our aim is to widen the basis for evaluating Ohlin's development by studying his writings in *Stockholms-Tidningen (ST)*. Ohlin gradually began to contribute to this paper in 1925, published more regularly in 1926, and in the next few years the rate was 10 to 20 articles annually. In the fall of 1931 his connection with the paper became more permanent. He became a regular contributor of editorials and

At the Klampenborg horse race track in the 1920s with the well-known dancer and actress Lillebil Ibsen and her husband, movie director Tancred Ibsen

At the Stockholm School of Economics, 1930

With Keynes on a boat trip in Antwerp, 1935

The Ohlin family in their home at Norr Mälarstrand, 1946. *Left to right:* Hellen, Anne, Evy, Bertil, Tomas

Bertil Ohlin in the late 1940s

With Social Democrat Prime Minister Tage Erlander before a debate during the election campaign, 1952

The party leader in 1963

Bertil Ohlin in 1972

Receiving the Nobel memorial prize in economics together with James Meade, 1977

The last photo, taken August 2, 1979, the day before he died articles to the business section. During the rest of the 1930s he published approximately 70 articles a year. By 1960 he had published about 1,200 articles in *Stockholms-Tidningen*.

We concentrate on Ohlin's writings on the depression and the crisis policy in the 1930s. The study covers a ten-year period (from 1926 to early 1935)[9] and thus the discussion of the great depression from its premonitory signs to its aftermath. We follow Ohlin's analyses of unemployment in the late 1920s, of the crisis on the U.S. stock exchange in 1929, of the financial crisis in 1931, as well as his attempts to understand the causes and consequences of the depression of the 1930s, and his policy proposals during the dramatic period of 1932 to 1933, and his retrospective analyses during the recovery of 1934 to 1935.

We organize the material chronologically around a broad question: What were Ohlin's views of the crisis, its causes, and the possible means to fight the depression? In particular, we are looking for the controversial issues looming in the Swedish debate on crisis policy: What are the causes of unemployment? Are they insufficient demand, unutilized savings (i.e. hoarding), too high wages? What policy measures should be taken against unemployment? Are these wage cuts, expansionary monetary policy, expansionary fiscal policy with mainly public works financed by borrowing? How then should wages be set for public works? Will such work crowd out activities in private industry (crowding-out effects), or rather increase overall economic activity (through multiplier effects)? We expect Ohlin's articles to illustrate the evolution of his views on these issues and to help us to identify important turning points in his thinking.

1926–28: Orthodox Views

In the fall of 1926 Ohlin explained in *ST* that scarcity of capital was an important reason for the prevailing unemployment.[10]

> The demand for labor actually emanates from capital. . . . If its supply could be increased by savings and then create larger capital investments in the industry, the situation on the labor-market would improve.

He clearly dissociated himself from an explanation based on the role of savings and demand:

> One often meets the view that by saving, people decrease the demand for goods and thus create unemployment. . . . This is a mistake. The savings are put into savings associations and banks, for example, which then lend these

to people wishing to invest in capital for production purposes; say, to purchase machinery. If the money had not been saved, it would have been used for purchasing additional shoes, clothes, or luxury goods, for example. The decision to save does thus only mean that the demand is *shifted* from consumption goods to what might be called production goods. Savings mean, from an economic perspective, that demand changes directions—from certain kinds of goods to others—not that there is a decrease in its total size. Savings do thus not reduce the number of job openings. On the contrary, by contributing to an increase in the capital of the country, one will increase them in the long run.

Here Ohlin took almost the same position as Cassel. Unemployment is not due to the fact that savings reduce demand but rather that limited savings have a negative effect on capital formation.

In a couple of articles written at the beginning of 1927, Ohlin discussed Swedish unemployment policy. He emphasized the importance of wages in relief work being lower than the wages of unskilled labor on the open market and cash allowances being lower than the wages for relief work, in order to maintain the mobility of labor.[11]

In that way it was clearly better for the unemployed to obtain relief work than to only draw cash allowances. But no one would be subject to the temptation to stay in relief work longer than necessary, when an opportunity to obtain work in the private industry should turn up. The creation of a permanent *kronoarbetskår* [i.e., a type of public works] is thus avoided.

Ohlin's view was entirely conventional, in line with that of leading economists such as Gustav Cassel, Eli Heckscher, and Gösta Bagge. Concerning the causes for unemployment, Ohlin defended views that could be described as mainstream in the 1920s. The causes were to be found in the limited mobility of labor and the limited flexibility of wages.[12] "Unemployment is mainly a problem of adjustment and everything that has a preservative effect and creates friction tends to make it permanent. . . ." Ohlin found it "very likely that industrial workers—particularly in certain professions—draw such high wages that it is impossible for them all to find employment." He declared that the main problem with the unemployment policy was that the government might have to "intervene with public support, but it cannot be denied that the larger is the extent to which this occurs, the more profitable it becomes for the working class to maintain a wage level exceeding the normal one."

Unemployment was also due to "the general European crisis." "The fact that it is impossible to distinguish between these two kinds of unemployment is what, above all, makes a rational unemployment policy difficult." He consequently suggested the appointment of an unemployment commission in order to determine the causes of unemployment.[13]

For the government to be able to increase the number of job openings, several conditions must be fulfilled. Taxes financing public relief work must reduce the taxpayers' consumption but not their savings. Thus an increase in public capital formation must not cause reduced private capital formation. Public works must quickly create products ready for consumption. The products must be sold "without creating disturbances and difficulties in other areas."

> The conclusion is that by increasing capital formation—to the extent that taxes enforce reductions in consumption—and by putting capital into production in the short run, the government is able to reduce unemployment.

Ohlin dealt with increased public savings during recessions ("in bad times") in an article in the fall of 1927.[14] He turned against the procedure of cutting public spending "with a ruler." One must distinguish between public expenditures for consumption and public expenditures for production, and cut the former but not the latter. In the former category, he included expenditures on items such as defense and culture, and in the latter, research and education. He did admit, however, that such a division could not be made "objectively" but only on basis of value judgements.

In the summer of 1928 Ohlin discussed the view that low wages and limited purchasing power were causes of unemployment:[15]

> The purchasing power of the working class is said to be too low. If it is only increased by higher wages, the demand for products will increase, the industry can sell more and the unemployed become employed.... Nothing would have been more convenient than if this theory would have been correct. Imagine to be able at once to increase the standard of living for the employed and create work for those without employment! An ideal method, for sure. Unfortunately, reality seldom or never offers such easy and convenient solutions to difficult problems.... If a country pays higher wages than before without increasing its production, this does mean an increase in the workers' purchasing power, but also that the *profits* of the owners of the firms *decrease* to the same extent. There will be no increase in the total purchasing power.

Such an increase could either take place through an increase in production or by the central bank increasing the nominal purchasing power in the country by granting more credit.

If industry were in a recession and the increased purchasing power and demand were to act as powerful stimuli, the wheels would begin to turn somewhat more quickly, and there would thus be an increase in the production of goods. The increase in purchasing power then corresponds to the increase in the supply of goods, and everything turns out well. But if there is no sharp increase in the latter, the result can only be *inflation*.

In a period of stagnation, one might consider a cautious increase in the granting of credit, but not under normal circumstances.

Thus it would be very dangerous to start trying to fight the semipermanent unemployment in the European industrial countries in the postwar period with an inflationary credit policy.

According to Ohlin, "not a single well-known economist had proclaimed himself to be in favor of the purchasing power theory."[16] He thought that the "equilibrium wage" for industrial workers in Sweden was well above the actual level of the prewar period but did not find a downward adjustment of wages to be necessary:

Such a downward adjustment by 5 to 10 percent and a corresponding increase within a few years would create considerable social conflicts and losses. Thus it is far better to maintain industrial peace, and because of increasing efficiency, industry will gradually "adjust to" the high wages. To the extent that this is actually the case, unemployment will decrease. . . .

In December 1928 Ohlin discussed Johan Åkerman's analysis of the economic situation under the headline "Business cycle prophecies."[17] Åkerman, who characterized the economic situation in the United States as very unstable, pointed at the wild speculation on the U.S. stock market and warned against a serious crisis. Ohlin waved these fears aside:

First of all, as concerns the prospects in the United States, there seems to me to be little or no reason to expect a depressive development in the year of 1929. . . . It is certainly true that a minor drawback within production and trade can follow from a collapse at the stock exchange; as far as I am concerned, however, I do not think that the effects will be very profound.

1929–30: No Fear of Depression

In the spring of 1929 Ohlin commented on the election program against unemployment of Lloyd George and the English liberals, whose aim was to set up a larger number of public works financed by borrowing.[18] According to Ohlin, the conservative criticism against the program, that it would draw capital from the private industry and reduce employment in that area, meant shooting over the mark. The same kind of criticism could, for example, be directed against a private car producer expanding his production.

If one admits that that new private incentives reduce unemployment, it is difficult to understand why public ones would not.... It should be observed that starting production does not only increase the number of goods to be sold, but also the purchasing power available for buying them; national income, that is the total purchasing power, is only the production volume seen from another point of view.

There were two problems, however. First, one had to produce the goods that people wanted to buy with their growing purchasing power—one solution to this problem was to begin national road constructions. "These cannot create an overproduction of goods that cannot be sold." Second, production could not be increased until purchasing power had grown—the simplest way of solving this problem was to increase the credit volume, for example, by lowering the rate of interest or by an increased government demand for credit. An increase in the volume of credits might, however, result in higher prices, and thus in higher imports and lower exports.

In a country such as Britain, this was remedied by reducing capital exports abroad.... It now becomes clear that the other method for increasing the volume of credits, that is, a reduction of the discount rate, cannot be realized. If the discount rate were lowered in London, capital exports would increase, instead of decrease.

A month later Ohlin commented on the brochure *Can Lloyd George Do It?* by J. M. Keynes and H. D. Henderson.[19] Once more, he brushed aside the crowding-out argument of the British government. He explained that Keynes and Henderson did not consider public works to be efficient measures against unemployment at all times. In the current economic situation in Britain, they might work, however. Ohlin's conclusion was fairly cautious:

Only experience can show whether this [liberal plan] is valid. Thus it would be extremely interesting if the elections brought Lloyd George into power and this major experiment on unemployment policy was carried out.

At the end of September 1929, Ohlin still had no feeling for the coming crisis. "There are some signs that a business cycle turning point, although possibly a very minor one, will affect America next year."[20] Two months later, after the great collapse of the stock market, he was still an optimist.[21] The stock market crisis might be connected to a general business cycle downturn. "There is, however, no reason to expect a general economic crisis in the United States," at least not within the next six months. Accordingly, Ohlin did not believe in a European crisis either—"on the whole, there seems to be more cause for optimism than pessimism in Europe." At the beginning of 1930, Ohlin was more than sure:

> There is no sign that it [the stock market crisis] will have an important impact on the world's economic situation for more than a few months.... One is fully entitled to expect economic development in the next few years to be worthy of the name of economic progress.[22]

In the fall of 1930, when the depression was on its way, even in Sweden, this all changed:[23]

> Our industry must expect a difficult winter, even if there is reason to expect the beginnings of a change for the better already in the spring. Even in this favorable case, a considerable part of 1931 will be characterized by a certain depression.

The question now was what kind of action the government and the municipal authorities should take to check unemployment. Ohlin argued:

> It is most likely that a more extensive public economic activity during the first stages of a recession can have a beneficial effect on production and on the labor market, even if unemployment will not be reduced to the same extent—the private sector will probably be somewhat reduced—as the increase in the number of workers in public works.

At this point in time, Ohlin did not foster any ideas of multiplier effects from public expenditures but rather ideas of limited crowding out effects.

Fall of 1931: Stabilization of Consumer Prices

Sweden was forced to abandon the gold standard in September 1931, a week after Great Britain had taken the same step. Upon leaving gold, the government announced that the domestic purchasing power of the *krona* should be preserved "using all means available."

In taking this step, Sweden became the first country to officially adopt price stabilization as the goal of its monetary policy. Following the introduction of the paper standard, a lively debate among Swedish economists on monetary issues arose. One issue concerned the choice of price index to be stabilized: the consumer price index or the wholesale price index? Another issue dealt with the proper level at which the price index should be held constant. One school maintained that the price level should first be raised through expansionary policies to the level preceding the deflation of the depression; another argued that prices should be kept at the prevailing level without any prior reflationary steps.[24]

Ohlin took part in this exchange of views starting in the fourth quarter of 1931. In 1931 he published no articles in *ST* until October because of an eye disorder. In December 1931 Ohlin presented his guidelines for Swedish monetary policy in the coming year of 1932 in a prominent article.[25] He stated that the *Riksbank* should prevent the cost of living index from rising above the level of 1930 as well as prevent an increase in wholesale prices and foreign exchange rates that might threaten to increase the cost of living above that level. However, an upward adjustment of wholesale prices was recommended so that production could be maintained without wage cuts.

At the same point in time, Ohlin commented upon the monetary program Eli Heckscher had proposed in his book *Sveriges penningpolitik* (Monetary policy in Sweden).[26] Ohlin thought that "basically all economists in Stockholm have more or less the same view of the present situation," and "at present, there is also quite considerable agreement between Professor Heckscher and myself, and a large number of other economists in Stockholm, as to what actions should be taken in the present situation." There was, however, far from complete unanimity. Heckscher wanted to keep the average wholesale price level constant, which, according to Ohlin, would require "very considerable wage cuts," and increase unemployment. Ohlin characterized Heckscher's program as "semideflationary" and maintained that it would require a tight policy by the *Riksbank*, which would aggravate the recession. Ohlin recommended instead a minor increase in wholesale prices:

If this course of action is taken, the price level will be somewhat higher next year than if Heckscher's program is carried out. Instead of reducing the relatively immobile price factors, first of all wages, which his course of action requires if a considerable increase in unemployment is to be avoided, there would be a relative increase in the more mobile price factors, that is, in wholesale prices.

The article demonstrates that no major difference existed between the old and young economists at this early stage of the depression. The gulf was to widen in the years to come.

In a subsequent review of Gunnar Myrdal's book *Sveriges väg genom penningkrisen* (Sweden's way through the monetary crisis)—published roughly at the same time as Heckscher's volume—Ohlin stressed that Myrdal, as Ohlin himself, recommended an increase in wholesale prices as long as this did not cause any considerable rise in the cost of living.[27] Less than a week into the year of 1932, Ohlin once more considered the main alternatives for monetary policy: stable wholesale prices or a stable cost of living, and gave the latter precedence.[28] To those fearing that rising wholesale prices would result in inflation, he explained that

the goal of monetary policy is to avoid inflation as well as deflation.... The aim should be to create the kind of stability within the monetary system that will create the highest possible stability within economic life.

In his review of the government budget proposal in January 1932, a pleased Ohlin noted that the government

supported the view that the purchasing power of the *krona* in the hands of the consumers, that is the cost of living and not the price level in wholesale trade, should be stabilized.... This monetary program is, in my opinion, a very satisfactory one.[29]

The proposal in the budget for public works as a measure against unemployment at the total sum of 125 million *kronor* was also praised.[30] Ohlin found it to be

subject to doubt, to what extent an increase in taxes for financing public works creates an increase in the number of job openings.... The situation is different for the kinds of government work that are financed by borrowing. In times of depression, the private industry reduces its capital investments and the government is, within certain limits, very likely to be able to increase its investments without creating any further reductions in private investments. In that way, unemployment can be reduced in an efficient way.

Ohlin did, however, complain that the liberal Minister of Finance, Felix Hamrin, had reduced the subsidies to public utilities—which gave the impression of "a certain dualism in the views of the Minister of Finance."

Spring of 1932: Job Redistribution and a Budget Fund

In February 1932 Ohlin wanted to go "one step further" in the debate on public works.[31] He explained that it is

> not a question of the general appropriateness of an expansion of public capital investment. The issue is only the distribution of public works between good and bad times. In my opinion, this means that public constructions and public works found suitable after balancing their costs and benefits should, to a certain extent, be concentrated to periods of depression.

The issue was in no way the squandering of public capital. On the contrary, the constructions would normally be cheaper and the interest on the loans lower if carried out in bad times. "Future taxes for interests and repayments by installments, will thus rather be lower, if this program is followed, than would otherwise be the case."

The only serious objection to such a policy Ohlin thought he had encountered was the opinion that the capital borrowed by the government and the municipal authorities would otherwise have been available to the private industry. There was one weak point in this reasoning, however: "How can we know that there is always 'someone else' who is willing to invest the capital that is not being used elsewhere?" In practice, there was "a next to certainty" that in periods of depression, there were savings that were not invested. "What does then happen to these savings? They are simply used to cover the losses made by many firms, when turnover and prices fall." Here Ohlin described a negative or positive process of a cumulative character, destroying or creating savings:

> If there is no initiative or incentives to invest capital in buildings, machinery, and other kinds of fixed capital, the number of orders given to firms producing such capital will decrease. Accordingly, there are losses, devouring savings made in other areas. If, on the contrary, there are new initiatives and an increase in capital investments in a period of depression—by public institutions or private manufacturers—there will be an increase in the demand for wood, iron, stone, cement, etc., and workers become employed. Deficits decrease in many firms, and costs for subsidies to the unemployed are reduced. Savings that would otherwise have been used to cover these losses and costs become available on the market for loans.

Ohlin's proposal of countercyclical redistribution of public works was not a radical one. Similar measures had been advocated by Gustav Cassel (1902) and other economists since then.

Concerning the policy of the *Riksbank*, Ohlin considered it to be too restrictive:[32]

The result is a deflationary pressure on the economy. I consider a neutral monetary policy to be a policy not trying to compensate for increases in wholesale and retail prices incurred by increasing exchange rates by pushing down the prices of goods and services on the home market.

The *Riksbank* had claimed to pursue such a policy, but in practice, it had put a check on the increase in the price level. According to Ohlin, the level of the discount rate of the *Riksbank*—within certain limits—did not have any major effect on the volume of credits in bad times and a substantial decrease of the discount rate would thus not necessarily create a considerable credit expansion. It could, however, bring about a decrease in the interest level and thus a relief for borrowers-producers. Ohlin suggested that if there turned out "to be serious inflationary tendencies, one could always return to a more restrictive monetary policy."[33]

The Kreuger crash in the spring of 1932 would, according to Ohlin's judgment in March 1932, not have any major consequences for the Swedish economy. He recommended "business as usual."[34] A month later, in April 1932, his views turned more pessimistic, however: Sweden had "once more been caught in the downturn of the world business cycle and there were no signs of a change in the next few months."[35] "To restrict the volume of public works, for example, at this point in time, would be a misunderstanding of the well-founded demands for thrift and would deepen the crisis." On the one hand, strict demands should be made on the workers' productivity.

On the other hand, activities that are *really required and productive* should not be postponed.... The *Riksbank* cannot pursue a solely negative policy, since foreign business cycles as well as a domestic crisis and depression psychosis work together to get the deflationary process going, which conflicts with our official monetary program.

The great danger was exactly that the crisis psychosis would prevent the official stabilization program for monetary policy from being implemented.[36]

So far the *Riksbank* has kept somewhat to the deflationary side of this program. Now purposeful measures are required, particularly against the tendencies toward a panic concerning liquidity, if we are to avoid being pressed further into a deflationary process, thereby worsening the crisis.[37]

If Sweden did not follow the deflationary development in the rest of the world, it would sooner or later be faced with the choice of tightening credit policy and strengthening the recession or limiting imports "in other ways."[38] Tariffs might thus become necessary, but one had to make sure that they did not remain after the crisis. "Protectionist attempts at fishing in shallow waters should be clearly rejected."

In June 1932 Ohlin returned to the question of the countercyclical government budget.[39] He found it

strange that it is generally considered evident that the budget is to be designed in the same way in bad times as in good ones. The requirement of a formal balance of tax revenues and public expenditures does, in practice, lead to taxes being raised considerably in bad times, when they are experienced as heaviest, while they are lowered in good times, when business firms and private citizens could more easily carry heavier taxes.

One should not hesitate "to use a budget regulation fund in the present crisis, which is the most severe experienced by the world in modern times." Such a fund would even create sounder public finances:

In bad times there are many restrictive forces, above all the decrease in income, that prevent waste. It is in good times that decisions are made about unnecessary expenditure. The constraint to create a considerable budgetary regulation fund at such periods would reduce the sense of having plenty of money in the public treasury and thus counteract this tendency to squander.

A month later Ohlin argued:

If government finances are to remain sound, one cannot, in bad times, rely on funded assets to a larger extent than what corresponds to the growth of public wealth in good times.... In a situation of crisis the *current* public expenditure must be cut in order to prevent higher taxes and to maintain the credit standing of the government and thus make it possible to finance public works with borrowed money at a reasonable interest.[40]

At this stage of the Depression Ohlin had not developed any preferences for economic planning. This is evident from an editorial featuring Arthur Salter's book *Recovery*.[41] Here Ohlin argued that capitalism cannot be blamed for the crisis: "The attempt to present the world crisis as the bankruptcy of private capitalism, when it is in fact due to war and nationalism must ... be considered off the mark."

Fall of 1932: The Multiplier Approach

In August 1932 Ohlin seemed to be seeing a ray of light in the darkness:

> While we have, so far in 1932, had every reason to expect a continuous business cycle downturn, it does not seem unlikely that there will be a business cycle turning point after another period of low interests.[42]

In the same month Ohlin discussed a book by Salter, Keynes, et al., which was published in Swedish as *Den ekonomiska världskrisen och utvägen ur den* (*The World's Economic Crisis and the Way of Escape*), in a prominent article on "Hur krisen botas" (How the crisis is to be remedied).[43] Ohlin mainly dwelled on Keynes's contribution, which he described as a "brilliant description" of the financial crisis in 1931.

> Keynes complains, and rightly so, about the extent to which the thesis that in all circumstances only savings are of importance has been preached.... Slogans such as the crisis is solved by "work and thrift" is the height of foolishness.

Ohlin continued by giving the following account of Keynes's ideas:

> No one has the right to assume that an increase in prices, and thus a business cycle upturn, will start by itself. Interest rates will decrease, but this is no guarantee that businessmen will be tempted to make considerable new investments in buildings and machinery, etc. And without such an increase in production in the capital goods industry, there will be no business cycle upturn. Thus it is very likely that the first push [*stöt*] must be given (or be strengthened) by "direct government intervention in order to promote and support new investments."

In the present situation the issue was whether lower interest rates would start up investments.[44]

> The determining factor for business cycle conditions is that there has not yet been any sign of an increase in the production of capital goods.... The major question is if this reduction in the rate of interest, and the psychological change that has just taken place, can increase real investment.

Early in October 1932 Ohlin commented upon the ambitions of the new social democratic government, formed after the election of September 1932, to launch public works on a larger scale.[45]

This part of the government statement should be greeted with satisfaction. It shows that leading members of government understand the necessity of public works as part of an active business cycle policy.

Ohlin objected to critics who claimed such work to be a waste of public funds:

It is evident that this is a case of pure confusion of terms. The largest possible thrift would otherwise mean that all public works were canceled. And since the private industry should then most likely also save, the production of fixed capital should be canceled in this area as well.

The whole issue was the "appropriateness of a certain concentration of public works to periods of depression." Here Ohlin was proposing redistributive works and not "expansionist works."

If public utilities and other public authorities drew up a directory of capital investments that should normally be made within a three- or four-year period and then advanced the startup of a project of, for example, 50 million *kronor* to 1933 that would otherwise have started up two years later, the additional cost will be limited to two years of interest on 50 million *kronor*, that is, three million *kronor*. At the same time one would find use for the constructions earlier than would otherwise have been the case, and they could probably be made at a lower cost.

The additional cost of advancing work would thus, in Ohlin's example, be three million *kronor*:

For this relatively trivial sum, there is thus the possibility of producing fixed capital for 50 million *kronor*, which means that job opportunities are created at a value most likely exceeding this sum. The direct wages might only amount to half or a third of this sum, but in return, firms favored by orders can increase their different kinds of purchases; that is, they are "encouraged to increased activity." Furthermore the previously unemployed now have a demand for consumption goods and thus increase the number of job opportunities within industry and trade. The public cost for these unemployed disappears, and there is thus a saving for the taxpayers which certainly exceeds the above 3 million *kronor*.

As far as we have seen, this is the first time that Ohlin presented a line of argument based on a multiplier approach in the columns of *ST*. Ohlin did also take the opportunity once more to reject the argument that the government would then attract capital that would otherwise have been invested in the private industry.

> This is not the case in reality. In a severe depression such as the present one, private firms only want to make insignificant investments. Thus firms whose sales require such investments in machinery, etc., get to sell very little, and their losses devour a considerable part of the general public's current savings. These are thus not converted into fixed capital.

From this reasoning Ohlin drew the following conclusion:

> Basically it is evident that a sound financial situation requires that the productive forces are used to the largest possible extent. Thus the government should increase public works in bad times. Savings on unemployment expenses, to which can be added increased tax returns due to production being maintained, will by far exceed the temporary increase in interest payments. Thus concern for government finances should create an increase in public works in 1933. Finally, it is not a question of government finances but of those of the country. Then the reasons for such an increase become even more overwhelming.

A few weeks later Ohlin made it crystal clear that he was advocating redistributive work, declaring "that this does *not* mean an *increase* in the number of public works in the long run. It is only a question of a different *distribution* of these works between good and bad times."[46]

He repeated that an allocation of public works to bad times would mean borrowing at a lower rate of interest, lower prices on raw materials, and lower wages. Wages in the building and construction sector were a tricky question. Wages in the building trade had, for a long time, been varying considerably between times of prosperity and times of recession.

> In the last few years the public authorities have, naturally in cities with a social democratic majority, shown a more pronounced tendency to support the attempts of the trade unions concerned to also keep the wage level of times of prosperity in a depression.

This would be inappropriate for several reasons. First of all, it would mean that these groups of workers were privileged compared to others. Second, one of the forces that might initiate a business cycle upturn would disappear.

> It is cost reductions of this kind for capital investments at the end of the depression, which usually induce private firms and private persons to start investing. It is thus clear that a concentration of public works to bad times

> must not be made in such a way that the wages of the labor groups concerned become fixed.... The funds available for public works should, of course, be used to create the largest number of job opportunities possible. It would then be absurd to pay the top wages of times of prosperity for such work.

In order not to be accused of proposing a general wage cut, Ohlin clarified: "On several occasions in the last two years, I have publicly taken a definite stand against major wage cuts in industry. The conditions within the areas of building and construction work are, however, very special."

In November 1932 Ohlin described the general atmosphere in the economy in most countries to be "calm" and even somewhat optimistic.[47] "The psychological change during the summer has thus turned out to be more than a temporary gust." At the same time he once more discussed—referring to such economists as Keynes, Stamp, Layton, and Salter—the role of savings.

> Savings have two sides, a *negative* side, consisting of a failure to buy goods for current consumption, and a *positive* side, where saved funds are used for buying some permanent commodity, either a factor of production or a durable article of consumption. The negative side without the positive one must minimize sales and increase unemployment.

In a "reply to the prophets adhering to the gospel of doing nothing," Ohlin repeated his conviction that public works must be concentrated to bad times.[48] He used three arguments: First, costs (interest, prices of material, and wages) were lower in bad times. Second, the government and the municipal authorities would have lower expenses for unemployment and poor relief and possibly higher tax revenues due to increased economic activity. Third, "a certain net charge" of public finances would be worthwhile, if this was a means of obtaining lower unemployment, an increase in production and higher national income. "Let Misters Manchester Liberals give this point some thought!"[49]

At Christmas 1932 Ohlin initiated a discussion of Cassel's argument that an extension of credit (i.e., a more expansionary monetary policy) would make it possible to increase production and employment.[50]

> It is such an increase in the granting of credits and in the velocity of circulation of the means of payment that the supporters of public works wish to obtain, in order to counteract the tendencies to stagnation in the economy.

Thus he thought that "there was total agreement on the, in practice, decisive point: job opportunities can increase through public initiatives without decreasing the number of jobs in the private sector, but this can only be achieved if the credit (monetary) policy of the country does not create any obstacles." Certainly credit policy should mainly be used to create conditions as favorable as possible for increasing production in the private sector. Further reductions of the discount rate of the *Riksbank* could unfortunately hardly be of any consequence.

What the *Riksbank* can do is, first of all, to assist in keeping down the interest on bonds and ensuring a considerable money supply. These are the classical means, normally used by Bank of England and other central banks in order to supply the commercial banks with liquid capital and thus increase their willingness to give credit. There is no reason why the *Riksbank* should not pursue the same policy.

If the *Riksbank* did not take such actions in 1933, there was a risk that government borrowing would reduce capital available in the private sector, and thus the creation of job opportunities in the public sector would crowd out job opportunities in the private sector.

It must thus be completely clear to the government and parliament that if, by deciding on a certain increase in public works, they adopt an expansionary policy, they must not only say A but also B. In other words, they must see to it that the *Riksbank* pursues a credit policy that is in harmony with the rest of the economic policy.

Spring of 1933: The Push Must Come from the Government

In the budget for 1933, Ernst Wigforss, the Minister of Finance, announced borrowings of approximately 160 million *kronor* for public works in order reduce unemployment. Ohlin only stated that such a policy, in the present situation, can no doubt "within certain areas exert a favorable influence on the economic situation."[51] Furthermore he thought that the Swedish balance of payments would allow an expansion of public works and credits.[52]

In the debate about wages for public works, which flared up in parliament, Ohlin sided with the former Minister of Health and Social Affairs Sam Larsson's proposal for a compromise.[53] Everyone seemed ready to accept an acceleration of the investments made by the public utilities, for example, in electrifying the state railways, without requiring that this should be done at a lower wage than that of the open labor market. The question was whether the remaining works were to be of the old kind (at lower wages) or the new kind (at "normal" market wages) or a mixture of these two kinds of employment. The nonsocialists wanted the old kind only; the social democrats wanted the new kind only. Ohlin, himself, thus supported a compromise with a mixture of these two kinds of employment. He warned against the fact that a concentration to the new kind of works would only create unease in the economy.[54]

At the beginning of 1933 Ohlin also showed his dissatisfaction with the *Riksbank* having failed to achieve a recovery of wholesale prices.[55] On the contrary, a deflationary tendency had asserted itself. "It is of the utmost importance that a stop is put to the present deflation." In the American case, a reflationary policy increasing the price level on goods was required.[56] Ohlin hoped that Roosevelt would enter on "the path of controlled reflation," that other countries would join the United States so that an international increase in the price level could be achieved and create the necessary conditions for a business cycle upturn. This was something entirely different than allowing an increase in prices from an equilibrium.

It is foolish to enter so much air into a sufficiently filled tire that it finally bursts, but that does not mean that one should refrain from inflating a soft car tire so that it is in good working order.

In April 1933 Ohlin commented on a series of articles on "The Means to Prosperity" published by Keynes in the *Times*.[57] As usual, when writing about Keynes, Ohlin was enthusiastic. "That Keynes' authority is increasing is not surprising. His forecasts have come true with an amazing accurateness." For Keynes, "as for all other sensible people," the starting point of all crisis discussions was the fact that the world price level must increase if a catastrophe was to be avoided. Above all, the liquid assets in the world should be increased by the international bank in Basle issuing a couple of million dollars in gold certificates. This was a necessary but not a sufficient condition for a business cycle upturn. Lack of money was not the main problem but the limited interest in spending it. "When the private sector ... is in such backwater as at present, it is not easy to see from which direction a strong private demand for articles of production is to come." Keynes's solution to this problem was an increase in public demand in the financially leading countries and Ohlin could but agree:

Personally, I have, for a long time, defended the view that the most important achievement of the conference on the world economy [in London] would be an international agreement on a simultaneous and considerable increase in job opportunities in the public sector.... An increase in prices requires an increase in demand. Then, one must not trust a first, sufficient, push to come from consumers or private firms, it must be made through demand from the Government and the municipal authorities.

According to Ohlin,

there was thus no other possibility than to see to it that, once favorable psychological conditions have been created, a sharp increase in public demand or the demand created by public initiatives is immediately established in the largest possible number of countries, so that one goes beyond the dead point.

Ohlin could also refer to Keynes's line of argument based on the multiplier approach: "If two workers are employed, at least one worker thereby gains employment in the private sector, and unemployment benefits for three people are saved." Subsidizing private investments might be even more favorable for the government:

From the point of view of public finances, subsidizing private capital investments in the near future would be pure profit. In comparison with public investments, the expenditure and the risks of the government and the municipal authorities are limited, while at least unemployment benefits are saved and there is an increase in tax returns.

Ohlin argued against the "orthodox" recommendation to reduce production costs during a crisis so that they reach a reasonable proportion to prices by stating that this meant "closing one's eyes to the fact that the expenses of one person constitute the income of another and that it is thus impossible to reduce expenses without also lowering incomes, which will thus lead to a continued fall in prices."

Debating the characteristics of the crisis of the 1930s, Ohlin suggested:

The strength of the present depression is, to a great extent, due to the fact that an agricultural crisis and a recession in the industry have occurred simultaneously, as in the 1870s but in contrast to 1900 and 1907. When this happens, the industrial crisis enhances the agricultural crisis and the latter intensifies the former.[58]

In this controversy Ohlin dissociated himself from any idea of general wage cuts, since these would decrease purchasing power and foster deflation.[59]

When the Finance Minister appointed a committee of experts to consider Sweden's exchange rate policy in the spring of 1933, Ohlin seized the opportunity to give monetary policy advice.[60]

In my opinion, the *Riksbank*, at present, has very limited possibilities to affect the interest and credit conditions by a discount rate policy and by purchasing government stock and securities so that an increase in prices is achieved, if the foreign exchange rates are fixed.

He wished it to be left unsaid whether a major increase in wholesale prices could be created without a considerable depreciation in the value of the *krona* for other countries. A minor increase in prices, in line with Cassel's suggestion, would be possible, however.

It should be remembered, however, that an increase in prices is not a goal in itself. The main purpose is to prevent the unnatural reduction in demand which incurs an increase in unemployment, which is the core of deflation.

Summer of 1933: A Completely New Situation

In the summer of 1933 Ohlin devoted several articles to Roosevelt's New Deal. He noted that the public works financed by borrowing that were being planned in the United States were more extensive, per capita, than their Swedish equivalents.[61] And he explained that after what had happened in America, "it can no longer be claimed that an active economic policy might not create an increase in prices."[62] The goal in the United States was reflation and not inflation, however.[63] In this context he criticized

the unfounded "theory of underconsumption" that considers crises to be due to the fact that consumers' purchasing power, in particular, that of industrial workers, does not grow at the same rate as production and thus considers rises in wages to be the cure for depressions.

The theory had become popular among the American public, which might partly explain why Roosevelt mainly tried to increase the demand for consumption goods by increasing the wages of industrial workers and the prices of agricultural products.[64] According to Ohlin the most natural way would be to stimulate demand through public works and inflation, without increasing wages, that is, costs, as a first measure.

Early in the summer of 1933 Ohlin observed that there was an upturn in the world business cycle and that the reasons for this were not only to be found on the psychological level.[65] "It is more likely that during the depression, a demand for *replacements* has accumulated, which now pushes its way forward." Stocks had been reduced, repairs postponed, machinery and tools had been worn out, and at a certain point, replacement acquisition must begin. Thus there was an increase in demand and confidence returned.

At the same time Ohlin continued to appeal for an agreement on a reflationary monetary policy among the largest number of countries possible.[66]

> The only requirement is that all these countries individually adopt an expansionary economic policy by using methods determined by domestic conditions in each country, for example, an active central bank policy, public works, subsidies for increasing building activities, and other kinds of private production.

It appeared from several articles at the end of the summer of 1933 that Ohlin considered the situation to be so desperate that he chose to recommend further government intervention and "economic planning."

> Last year [1932] it became increasingly clearer that if it [the depression] were to continue for another year, the existing construction of society would be shaken to its foundations and most likely collapse. In increasingly wider circles, one began to question the rationality of the fundamental institution on which society had so far been constructed, for example, individual ownership of factors of production, which resulted in half of these or more not being used at all.[67]

> Is it then not obvious that the revolutionary development and the crisis have brought us into completely new situations and brought us up against new problems, economic, political and cultural ones, but above all, psychological ones?[68]

Fall of 1933: A Trend toward Reinvestment

In the fall of 1933 Ohlin once again discussed the view that there was no such thing as unutilized savings and that investments in one area must mean a decrease in investments in another.[69] "All kinds of expansion would thus be impossible." Of what did the unutilized savings then consist?

> It would probably be natural to thus denote the savings from current income, savings which do not create any demand for goods and services, that

is, create no real capital formation. The issue is what actually happens to these savings, since they are apparently *not* accumulated in banks. Basically, the answer is simple. The income of one member of society is the expense of another.... If part of the consumers' income is thus saved and part of these savings does not lead to demand and purchase, the income of the business enterprises that is due to sales will, in certain areas, be lower than their expenses, that is, there will be *losses*. These losses obviously "devour" the savings not used for demand. They are thus the heart of the matter. The "unutilized" savings disappear since the limited demand creates losses in the industry.

When viewing the year 1933 in retrospect, Ohlin found that Roosevelt's economic policy and the "trend of reinvestment" dominated the picture. There was no doubt that reinvestment "after nearly four years of depression has finally taken off seriously," nor that "the violent American expansion last spring contributed to increasing the tendencies toward a business cycle upturn in other countries."[70] On the eve of 1934, he drew parallels to the optimism at the beginning of 1931.[71] But this time, the optimism was better founded, for several reasons: industrial production had increased, reinvestment had begun, optimism had grown. The interest level had fallen. Many nonviable firms had disappeared.

1934: Time to Reduce Public Works

When Ernst Wigforss's second budget was presented in early 1934, Ohlin began to express some uncertainty about continued expenditures on public works.[72]

Even to those who, on grounds of principle, take a standpoint close to that of the finance minister on these issues, the question arises, however, how long such a policy with considerable job opportunities financed by borrowing can continue. It is a typical crisis policy and builds on the assumption that an intense recession will be reduced after a few years and disappear. It is not, however, a suitable weapon against a more long-term crisis, determined by the world's economic structure. Just as natural as it is to apply less strict principles for balancing government finances in a temporary recession, from the point of view of the stabilization policy, just as dangerous would it be to subject government finances to a growing strain in the long run.

These comments demonstrate that Ohlin, at the end of the crisis, just as he had done before, advocated redistributive works and not a permanent increase in public expenditures on work programs.

In another comment, Ohlin reduced the importance of the actions of the social democratic government as well as the advice of the economists for the design of fiscal policy during the crisis.[73]

A defense of the current fiscal policy, aimed at maintaining the purchasing power through borrowing due to an acute crisis—which, in an extreme depression, is the natural policy if aiming at avoiding the fatal spiral of recession with reductions in costs, prices, and income—is thus in no way similar to defending the present government. The same policy would obviously have been carried out in 1933, even if it had not been the fiscal program of the present government, but the program of the nonsocialists that had been implemented. In fact this policy has been brought on by sheer necessity, such as it has appeared to the common sense when unbiased by fiscal "orthodoxy." The fundamental explanation, drawn up by a number of economists, has been of minor importance. In fact no feasible alternative fiscal policy has been presented in the political discussion in Sweden.

Ohlin now asked for restrictions on public works financed by borrowing in the coming fiscal year and emphasized that (from his countercyclical approach) *"such a reduction in borrowing would not mean a change in fiscal policy but, on the contrary, express its consistency."*

In a review of Myrdal's *Finanspolitikens ekonomiska verkningar* (The economic effects of fiscal policy)—"a pioneering work in the international literature"—Ohlin made one objection only, namely that "the importance of the balance of payments as a limiting factor for an economic "expansionary policy" is exaggerated. . . ."[74]

When viewing the monetary policy of the *Riksbank* during the crisis in retrospect, Ohlin pointed out that in order to avoid a recession, the Bank had bought gold and currency for more than half a billion *kronor*.[75] Every assertion that the monetary policy pursued by the *Riksbank* had no influence on the business cycle worth mentioning was thus absurd.

Even if it has not succeeded in achieving the desired recovery in wholesale prices, it has been of great importance by preventing a general fall in prices and by creating a sense of security through the knowledge that a recession will not be accepted.

The business cycle upturn in 1934 was so strong that Ohlin seemed taken by surprise. "The economic recovery in Sweden in the last twelve months has been so swift, that not until the past few weeks has it become entirely clear that we are no longer in a state of depression," he observed at the beginning of the summer of 1934.[76] Sweden was neither in a boom nor in a depression but in an "average business cycle," and most indications showed that it would remain there in the next six months.

According to Ohlin, this recovery brought to the fore "the demand for a considerable reduction in job opportunities in the public sector at an earlier stage than would have been expected a year ago."[77] It did not, however, seem as if job opportunities were to be reduced at all. "The demand for an adjustment to the fluctuations of the business cycle—one of the main principles of rational fiscal policy—has thus not been fulfilled." Ohlin gave the following message to those maintaining that unemployment was still considerable: fiscal policy concentrates on the future. "To require a boom to have been established even before the policy motivated by the depression has been wound up, is unreasonable." A more "normal" level of unemployment should not be fought by "violent government borrowing."

> If borrowing for nonprofitable constructions were to continue, as long as there is still considerable unemployment, that is, eight or nine years out of ten, government finances would soon be ruined. The only sound principle is that the exceptional borrowing of periods of depression is repaid in good times, while in more normal business cycles, the budget is balanced in the usual way without such borrowing, despite the fact that there is certain unemployment.

Ohlin also explained that "a new economic policy" was required in the sense of "straightening out the fairly hasty economic-political measures that had come into existence fairly quickly during the crisis and adapt them to the requirements in a longer perspective."[78] He stressed the difference between state socialism and economic planning and preferred talking about a "framework policy" (*ramhushållning*). The discussion about unutilized savings could also be put aside due to the business cycle upturn. "To create conditions for substantial savings will, obviously, be an important part of economic policy in the future."[79]

State Socialism, No Thanks!

How was "the riddle of business cycle fluctuations" then to be explained? According to Ohlin, the entire business cycle and not only a part of it—for example the depression phase—must be explained.[80] The fundamental view, which was accepted by all "economists of importance," was that "the business cycle is first of all a variation in the production of capital goods." Thus "all simple theories of underconsumption could be rejected." "In reality it is demand for investment purposes—and not consumer demand—that first changes, and in such a way that a business cycle turning point is reached." Ohlin argued that the goal of economic policy should be to raise production and employment: "It should be evident that the *goal* of an expansionary policy is to increase production and employment and that the increase in prices is only a *means*. . . ." In this context Ohlin referred to Wilhelm Röpke's book *Konjunktur och kriser* (*Krise und Konjunktur*) and made the following statement: "One must liberate oneself from 'the price level complex' and devote most of one's attention to the volume of production, income and demand."[81]

What role did economic policy play for this swift recovery? Like many other economists, Ohlin pointed at an increase in the demand for Swedish export goods, the depreciation of the Swedish *krona*, to the beginning of the "replacement acquisition" postponed during the crisis, and the fall of interest rates.[82] As concerns public works, only a small part of the sum granted had been used before the spring of 1934. "These job opportunities in the public works on the open market can thus not have had any important impact on the recovery that had already taken place." Larger amounts had been used during Hamrin's last fiscal year as well as Wigforss's first one to finance "reserve work" and similar kinds of work.

> An objective observer could probably not deny that the purchasing power created by the government since the fall of 1932 has had a great impact on the business cycle. The sums concerned are approximately equal to the increase in the demand for Swedish products from abroad. On the other hand, it is clear that since a number of other factors, besides these two, have been of importance for the upswing, the fiscal policy of the government cannot have had any determining impact. It might rather be considered as fairly equal to three or four other favorable circumstances.

It was not in Ohlin's liking to make "uncontrolled capitalism" responsible for the crisis, as some social democrats did.[83] His conclusion from the great depression was that government economic policy "apparently has a certain function."

> Whether a system of an entirely different kind would be better or worse is an unknown fact. . . . The practical and navigable way goes in a completely different direction and is not that far from the much decried crisis policy. It is a question of creating such a framework for economic activity—and adapting it to changes, for example, in our relationship to the industry in other countries—that tendencies to the development of a crisis are counteracted

and checked in time. Within the given framework, free initiative will then manifest itself without oppressive control.... Typical examples of measures of such "framework character" are tariff policy and monetary policy. Particularly, the latter must be enhanced by direct government influence on the size of total reinvestment in the country.... Measures of this kind are directly aimed at maintaining production, that is, by using the possibilities for production without endowing the industry with a bureaucratic straitjacket.

In his comment to the government budget in January 1935, Ohlin was basically satisfied with the budget being balanced. Now, however, a surplus was required for beginning to repay the borrowing during the years of crisis.[84] The warnings against rising expenditures and the ruin of government finances that had been issued in the years of the crisis had not come true.

When the crisis policy was now being wound up and transformed "into more permanent long-term measures," the dividing lines of three different views that tried to manifest themselves became clear according to Ohlin:[85]

First, there was the old liberal, passive attitude, which wants the government to keep out of economic activity.... View number two—active social liberalism—states that the role of the government in the economy depends on the circumstances and cannot be the same at present as in the nineteenth century.

The third view was state socialism, largely "a result of Karl Marx's speculations" and according to which Government should simply take care of the economy. Ohlin advocated the second view and his objection to the third was as follows:

From the social democratic point of view, one generally tries too hard to create a long-term state socialism, for example by considerable monopolization, as an extension of the stabilization policy and the crisis policy that have been successfully pursued in the last few years. These are, however, two different issues. Stabilization policy should not be used as a state socialistic policy of monopoly and control.

Summary

In the years of high unemployment and before the beginning of the crisis, that is, during 1926 to 1928, Ohlin did take—at least in the columns of *Stockholms-Tidningen*—an "orthodox" view: unemployment was not due to limited purchasing power. Unemployment was partly due to high wages (and thus high costs) and limited mobility of labor. It was not due to excessive savings but, on the contrary, to insufficient savings and capital formation. In 1928 Ohlin stated that an expansionary monetary policy might increase the monetary purchasing power and make the wheels turn more quickly. Such a policy would be dangerous in a situation with "semipermanent" unemployment, however. He was opposed to wage cuts since these would result in strikes—it would be better if industry could grow into its too large "wage suit" by increase in productivity.

In the spring of 1929 the British liberals entered the elections on a program proposing public works financed by borrowing in order to reduce unemployment. Ohlin was positive. He agreed that public works in combination with an expansionary credit policy would not necessarily result in crowding-out effects, but he warned against possible inflationary effects.

Ohlin was an optimist who, on several occasions, questioned the signs of an approaching economic crisis. At the beginning of 1930, several months after the crash on Wall Street, he still believed in good times. In the fall of 1930 he saw "a certain depression" coming and thought that an increase in public sector activities might reduce unemployment, even if they were to create certain crowding-out effects. At the end of 1931 he began to advocate an expansionary monetary policy asking for an increase in wholesale prices.

At the beginning of 1932 Ohlin wanted to advance the debate on public works "one step further." This step was about advocating a shift of permanent public works from good to bad times as well as suggesting that government borrowing would be less expensive during a recession. This measure was, however, no more remarkable than that it had already been proposed by Gustav Cassel (1902) and by many of the "old economists" since then like Gösta Bagge. Ohlin now began to talk about unutilized savings that were used to cover the losses of the firms. He continued to advocate an expansionary credit policy but doubted that the reductions of the discount rate would have any considerable effects.

In the autumn of 1932 he discussed a contribution made by Keynes. To believe public thrift (that is reduced government expenditures) to be the way out of the crisis was "the height of foolishness." Ohlin continued to advocate redistributive works and defended these with arguments based on a multiplier approach. He did not, however, suggest wages in public works to be adjusted to market conditions in building and construction work where market wages were high.

In his comment to Keynes's articles in the *Times* in 1933, Ohlin agreed with the request for an international agreement on investments in public works. He also referred to Keynes's line of argument based on the multiplier approach. He rejected all demands for wage cuts by arguing that they would reduce income. At the same time he rejected the theory of underconsumption since increases in wages in order to increase demand would, at the same time, also increase production costs. In summary, Ohlin did not want to fight the depression through wage policy but through public works and an expansionary monetary policy.

Ohlin maintained his optimism for a long time. He often saw glimpses of light in the darkness of the depression. But in the summer of 1933 his belief in the future was eroding. He feared that the present system would "be shaken to its foundations" and began to talk about the need for "organization," government intervention, and economic planning. At the end of 1933 his optimism returned due to a "trend of reinvestment." At the beginning of 1934 he showed some hesitancy toward continued investments in public works, and a year later he demanded a budget showing a surplus in order to pay back the borrowing from the period of crisis. During the period 1932 to 1935 he was consistent in his views on public works: they should be redistributed from booms to recessions in order to reduce the unemployment caused by the business cycle, but they could not be used against structural unemployment.

When in 1934 Ohlin looked back at the depression, he drew at least three decisive conclusions. The crisis was not due to capitalism—but it had brought up the need for a new economic policy, "a framework policy" (*ramhushållning*). The purchasing power "created" by government was one of several factors behind the recovery. The crisis policy pursued had been the only one possible, and the theoretical views of the economists had not played any major part in the process.

We have tried to focus on and select a few issues connected to the causes for and the measures against depression and unemployment. However, many arguments revolve around each other over time. Our hope to find a simple and clear message has, to some extent, evaporated while shifting through Ohlin's *ST* articles. We summarize

Table 13.2
Evolution of Ohlin's views on the causes of the depression in *Stockholms-Tidningen*, 1926 to 1934

	Causes of the depression		
Year	Insufficient demand	Unutilized savings	High wages
1926	Savings do *not* decrease demand and employment; on the contrary, insufficient savings reduce investments and thereby employment		
1927	Total purchasing power = total production		High wages cause unemployment
1928	Low wages, low purchasing power do *not* cause unemployment		
1929			
1930			
1931			
1932		In periods of depression there are probably unutilized savings	
		Savings in depression "height of foolishness"	High wages in the building sector prevent recovery
		Savings not invested increase unemployment	
1933	Theory of under-consumption not valid	Unutilized savings incur losses "devouring" savings	
1934	Falling demand for investments triggers crises	Discussion of unutilized savings can be put aside	

his views in tables 13.2 to 13.4 in order to give an overview of the evolution of his thinking.

Concluding Comments

Opinions diverge among researchers of Ohlin's development as a "new" economist from the mid-1920s to the mid-1930s. Landgren considered Ohlin to be fairly "skeptical and pursuing a wait-and-see policy" toward the new economics until 1933 when "the real break-through" in his views on public works occurred under the influence of Keynes.[86] Steiger, on the contrary, regarded Ohlin as an intrepid pioneer within the area of the "new" economics. The picture that

Table 13.3
Evolution of Ohlin's views on measures against the depression in *Stockholms-Tidningen*, 1926 to 1934

	Policy measures		
Year	Wage reductions	Expansionary monetary policy	Expansionary fiscal policy
1926			
1927			Taxes reducing consumption can increase capital formation and employment
1928	Wages too high but wage cuts lead to strikes	Increased granting of credits = increased monetary purchasing power can lead to increase in production; but, no measure against permanent unemployment	
1929		Increased credit volume increases purchasing power = scope for production in public sector	Increased production in public sector increases purchasing power
1930			Increased public activities can increase production and employment
1931	Wage cuts increase unemployment	A certain increase in prices, stable cost of living	
1932		Neither inflation nor deflation; stability	Public works financed by borrowing can reduce unemployment
			Redistributive works and nothing else
		Measures against deflation	Public works must be productive
			Redistribution of public expenditure gives a sounder economy
			Public works a necessity in an active stabilization policy
	No general wage cut, apart from the building sector	Public works can reduce unemployment if they go hand in hand with expansionary credit policy	

Table 13.3 (continued)

	Policy measures		
Year	Wage reductions	Expansionary monetary policy	Expansionary fiscal policy
1933	Wage reduction = reduced purchasing power	Increase in prices to maintain demand	The government must produce the first push
1934			Time to reduce public works Public works: one of several factors behind the recovery

Table 13.4
Evolution of Ohlin's views on public works in *Stockholms-Tidningen*, 1926 to 1934

	Public works		
Year	Wages	Crowding-out effects	Multiplier effects
1926			
1927	Important that wages in relief works are lower than on the market	Public capital formation can reduce private capital formation	
1928			
1929		Public initiatives do not crowd out other activities more than do private initiatives	
1930		Certain crowding-out effects	
1931			
1932		Crowding out does not necessarily occur in times of depression	
		Public investments create new savings	Wages in public sector have spreading effects
		Expansionary credit policy necessary to prevent crowding out	
1933	Certain kinds of works at market wages, others at lower wages		Two jobs in the public sector create a third in the private one
1934			

Ohlin has given of himself in his memoirs rather goes in the latter direction.

Our chronicle of Ohlin's articles in *ST* makes it difficult to determine whether we should talk about an ongoing pioneering achievement or a cautious progress toward a fairly late breakthrough. On the one hand, there is undeniably a gradual progress in Ohlin's writings between 1928 and 1933: the view that increased monetary purchasing power can increase production in 1928, that public works can increase purchasing power and the questioning of the crowding-out argument in 1929, that there are most likely unutilized savings in periods of depression at the beginning of 1932, an "acceptance without compromise"[87] of public works and for the first time (according to our findings) a line of argument based on the multiplier approach in the fall of 1932.

On the other hand, Ohlin does in no way appear to be an assaulting radical prior to 1933. He is fairly optimistic in his belief in a swiftly passing crisis, fairly orthodox in his crisis explanation, fairly careful in his recommendations on government intervention—he advocates redistribution of public works as a measure against unemployment caused by a cyclical downturn but takes a firm stand against more expansionist programs against structural unemployment.[88] Why does Ohlin appear to be so "late" in proposing expansionary policies? Steiger (1971, 1978) suggests that Ohlin was a latecomer to the field of monetary economics. First, he had to absorb the works of Erik Lindahl and Gunnar Myrdal before developing his theory of expansion.

It seems to be a matter of taste whether to talk about continuity or a breakthrough in Ohlin's development in the pages of *ST*. If talking about a break in his development, this should be dated to the Keynes-inspired article in the spring of 1933 or to the short-lived fear of a crack in the social order in the summer of 1933.

The general impression of caution and restraint in Ohlin's popular articles in *ST* is confirmed by Ohlin himself. In his memoirs, he explains, after an account of his "advanced" views in 1931: "As a political editorial writer in *Stockholms-Tidningen* the following winter I naturally expressed myself with more caution. . . ." As concerns his comment on the first budget of the new government in 1933, he writes that it "was favorable toward the expansionary trait, although expressed in the somewhat restrictive way that I used in my editorials."[89] If Ohlin, as the writer of memoirs, is to be believed;

Ohlin, the editorial writer and the economic journalist, was more conservative than Ohlin the scientist!

Acknowledgments

Christina Lönnblad has translated the original Swedish version into English. David Laidler, Otto Steiger, and Eskil Wadensjö have improved our analysis. We have received generous support from the Tore Browaldh Foundation for compiling the newspaper articles by Bertil Ohlin.

Notes

1. See also Carlson and Jonung (1996) for the output in the daily press by leading Swedish economists.

2. Cassel's articles are listed in Carlson and Jonung (1989).

3. See the register of Ohlin's articles compiled by Carlson, Orrje and Wadensjö (2000).

4. The older generation of Cassel and Heckscher was more skeptical toward the new ideas of the young economists. See Carlson (1993).

5. See, for example, the issue of *History of Political Economy (HOPE)*, 1978, where the translation of Ohlin's article from 1933 is published and discussed. The *HOPE* articles are also found in Blaug (1992).

6. See also Wadensjö (1991) and Wadensjö, chapter 15 in this volume, on Ohlin's work for the committee on unemployment.

7. Landgren (1960:159–60, 199–202) takes an interest in some articles in *Stockholms-Tidningen*, 1933. Steiger (1971:186–99) and (1976:349–52) follows Ohlin's development in the years 1927 to 1935 using, among other works, a dozen articles in *Stockholms-Tidningen* as well.

8. Ohlin (1972:207) mentions that he studied unemployment and its remedies in about eighty articles in *ST* and the Danish newspaper *Politiken*. In his memoirs, he deals with the Stockholm School and unemployment policy in three chapters (XIII, XV, XVI) and refers to about ten articles in *ST*.

9. To our present knowledge, Ohlin wrote at least 332 articles in *ST* during the period 1926 to 1934. Out of these (on basis of the headlines) we chose to examine 140 articles, and narrowed the selection to the 80 articles we refer to here.

10. "Sparandet och Sveriges ekonomiska utveckling" (Savings and the economic development of Sweden), October 31, 1926.

11. "Svensk arbetslöshetspolitik" (Swedish unemployment policy), January 26, 1927.

12. "Olika principer för arbetslöshetspolitiken" (Different principles for unemployment policy), January 27, 1927.

13. "Böra arbetslöshetens orsaker undersökas?" (Should the causes of unemployment be investigated?), February 7, 1927.

14. "Missriktad sparsamhet" (Misdirected thrift), November 18, 1927.

15. "Låga löner orsak till arbetslöshet" (Low wages causing unemployment), June 29, 1928.

16. "Löner, arbetstid och arbetslöshet" (Wages, working hours, and unemployment), September 21, 1928.

17. "Konjunkturprofetior" (Business cycle prophecies), December 14, 1928. See also "Konjunkturprofetior än en gång" (Business cycle prophecies once more), December 31, 1928.

18. "Lloyd George och arbetslösheten" (Lloyd George and unemployment), April 18, 1929.

19. "Valet och arbetslösheten i England" (Election and unemployment in Britain), May 26, 1929.

20. "Ränteparadoxen" (The interest paradox), September 30, 1929.

21. "Börskrisen och konjunkturerna" (The stock market crisis and business cycles), November 25, 1929.

22. "Ekonomiska framtidsperspektiv" (Future economic perspectives), January 2, 1930.

23. "Positiv arbetslöshetspolitik" (Positive unemployment policy), October 28, 1930.

24. The 1931 program of price stabilization and the views of the economics profession are studied by Jonung (1979) and Berg and Jonung (1999).

25. "Riktlinjerna för vår penningpolitik" (Guidelines for our monetary policy), December 8, 1931.

26. "Professor Heckschers penningprogram" (Professor Heckscher's monetary program), December 10, 1931.

27. "Dagens ekonomiska problem" (Today's economic problem), December 22, 1931

28. "Dagens stora fråga" (The major question of the day), January 5, 1932.

29. "Regeringens penningprogram" (The government's monetary program), January 14, 1932.

30. "Arbetslöshet och statsarbeten" (Unemployment and public works), January 16, 1932.

31. "Konjunkturpolitik. Offentliga arbeten i goda och dåliga tider" (Stabilization policy. Public works in good and bad times), February 12, 1932.

32. "Riksbanken bör lätta på kreditrestriktionerna" (The *Riksbank* should ease the credit restrictions), February 27, 1932.

33. "Ränteläget" (The level of the rate of interest rate), March 1, 1932.

34. "Sverige och Kreugerkoncernens kris" (Sweden and the crisis of the Kreuger enterprises), March 17, 1932. See also "Tragedien" (The tragedy), April 6, 1932.

35. "Kris och konjunktur" (Crisis and business cycles), April 10, 1932.

36. "Den stora faran" (The great danger), April 24, 1932. See also "Ansvaret och framtiden" (The responsibility and the future), May 3; "Klara linjer" (Clear guidelines), May 4; and "Direktivens innebörd" (The meaning of the guidelines), May 8, 1932.

37. The expression "liquidity panic," which means that everyone wants to keep their assets in cash, had, according to Ohlin, been coined by Sven Brisman in connection with the banking crisis in the United States. See Ohlin, "Likviditetskrisen i Förenta staterna" (The liquidity crisis in the United States), April 2, 1932. This term closely resembles Keynes's use of "liquidity preference."

38. "Krisen och tullpolitiken" (The crisis and the tariff policy), April 22, 1932.

39. "Hr Hamrins bekymmer" (Mr Hamrin's worries), June 21, 1932.

40. "Ett minimikrav" (A minimun requirement), July 5, 1932.

41. "Kris och planhushållning" (Crisis and economic planning), July 12, 1932.

42. "Kommer prisstegringen?" (Will there be an increase in prices?), August 4, 1932.

43. "Hur krisen botas" (How the crisis is to be remedied), August 7, 1932.

44. "Världskonjunkturerna vid vändpunkten?" (The turning point of the world business cycles), September 6, 1932.

45. "Ökade offentliga arbeten" (An increase in public works), October 2, 1932.

46. "Löner och offentliga arbeten" (Wages and public works), October 21, 1932.

47. "Konjunkturreflektioner" (Reflections on business cycles), November 15, 1932.

48. "Finanspolitiken under krisen. Svar till händerna-i-kors-evangeliets profeter" (Fiscal policy during the crisis. Reply to the prophets adhering to the gospel of doing nothing), November 20, 1932.

49. This article resulted in a skirmish with Marcus Wallenberg who feared that Ohlin's reasoning might lead the general public astray by making them think that the crisis could be shortened by "handing out money in any way." See "Vägen ut ur krisen. Ett inlägg av häradshövding Marcus Wallenberg" (The way out of the crisis. A contribution by Marcus Wallenberg, District Judge), November 21, 1932.

50. "Riksbanken och arbetstillfällena" (The *Riksbank* and the job opportunities), December 27, 1932.

51. "En krisbudget" (A crisis budget), January 12, 1933.

52. "Budget och betalningsbalans" (The budget and the balance of payments), January 18, 1933.

53. "Sam Larssons kompromisslinje" (Sam Larsson's line of compromise), January 20, 1933.

54. "Konjunktur och förtroende" (Business cycles and confidence), February 19, 1933.

55. "Deflationen bör hejdas" (Deflation should be stopped), February 3, 1933.

56. "Prisstegring hjälper" (An increase in prices would help), March 16, 1933.

57. "Väg ur depressionen. Keynes får instämmande från *Times*" (The way out of the depression. The *Times* agrees with Keynes), April 2, 1933.

58. "Jordbrukskris, världsdepression och anpassning. Svar till riksdagsman Carlström och dr Adrian Molin" (Agricultural crisis, world depression and adaptation. Reply to Parliamentary Member Carlström and Dr. Adrian Molin), April 9, 1933.

59. "Jordbrukets och industrins prislägen. Ännu ett replikskifte mellan dr Molin och professor Ohlin" (Price levels in agriculture and industry. Another exchange between Dr. Molin and Professor Ohlin), April 11, 1933, and "Jordbrukskrisen och krisen i industrien. Nytt replikskifte mellan riksdagsman Oscar Carlström och professor Bertil Ohlin" (The agricultural crisis and the crisis in the industry. New exchange of views between Parliamentary Member Oscar Carlström and Professor Bertil Ohlin), April 19, 1933.

60. "Ett penningpolitiskt råd" (Some monetary policy advice), April 23, 1933.

61. "Roosevelts ekonomiska politik" (Roosevelt's economic policy), June 2, 1933.

62. "Londonkonferensens uppgift" (The task of the London conference), June 11, 1933.

63. "Amerikas experiment. Det är med prisstegring som med vin: verkan beror på kvantiteten" (The American Experiment. Increases in prices are like wine: The effects depend on quantity), July 20, 1933.

64. "Roosevelts prövotid. Den psykologiska omsvängningen" (Roosevelt's trial period. The sudden psychological change), August 20, 1933. See also "Roosevelts industripolitik" (Roosevelt's industrial policy), July 19, 1934: "It is a fact that a raise in wages have a double effect, in that it does not only increase the purchasing power of the workers but also the costs of production of the industry and the price of goods."

65. "Konjunkturförbättringen" (The business cycle upturn), June 15, 1933. See also "Konjunkturläget" (The business cycle conditions), July 1, 1933.

66. "Roosevelts överraskning" (Roosevelt's surprise), June 27, 1933.

67. "Ordnad revolution hellre än kommunistisk. Männen kring Amerikas nye president presenteras" (An organized revolution rather than a communist one. A presentation of the men around America's new president), July 30, 1933.

68. "Den revolutionära verkligheten" (Revolutionary reality), August 5, 1933.

69. "Oanvända sparmedel" (Unutilized savings), November 16, 1933.

70. "Världskonjunkturen. Återblick på 1933" (The world business cycle. Retrospect of 1933), December 31, 1933.

71. "Världskonjunkturen 1934. Försök till prognos" (The world business cycle 1934. An attempt at making a prognosis), January 3, 1934.

72. "Hr Wigforss' andra budget" (Mr Wigforss's second budget), January 12, 1934.

73. "Bör finanspolitiken omläggas?" (Should fiscal policy be changed?), April 26, 1934. See also "Lånepolitik och löner" (Borrowing and wages), April 28, 1934.

74. "Finanser och finanspolitik. Två aktuella böcker" (Public finances and fiscal policy. Two recent books), May 7, 1934.

75. "Penningpolitisk rörelsefrihet" (The freedom of monetary policy), May 30, 1934.

76. "Svenska konjunkturutsikter för närmaste halvåret" (Prospects for the Swedish business cycle in the next six months), June 14, 1934.

77. "Budgeten och framtiden" (The budget and the future), June 16, 1934.

78. "En ny ekonomisk politik?" (A new economic policy?), June 25, 1934.

79. "Sysselsättning, sparande och löner" (Employment, savings and wages), August 8, 1934.

80. "Konjunkturväxlingarnas gåta" (The riddle of business cycle fluctuations), August 17, 1934.

81. Ohlin rated Wilhelm Röpke's book very highly: "In the entire international literature on business cycles, I know of none that within such a limited space ... gives such a good and trustworthy survey of our main knowledge of business cycles."

82. "Krispolitik och konjunktur" (Crisis policy and business cycles), August 21, 1934.

83. "Socialism och krispolitik" (Socialism and crisis policy), August 26, 1934.

84. "Den finansiella krispolitikens avslutning" (The termination of the crisis policy), January 12, 1935.

85. "Fronten mot statssocialismen" (The front against state socialism), January 20, 1935.

86. Landgren (1960:158, 160).

87. "Acceptance without compromise" is the wording used by Steiger (1971:189) to describe Ohlin's view on public works in the article "Ökade offentliga arbeten" (An increase in public works), October 2, 1932.

88. In his memoirs Ohlin (1972:209, 222–23) considers, on several occasions, the expansionary measures against structural unemployment proposed by Keynes and the British liberals at the end of the 1920s. He writes, for example, that these suggestions "were lost" in the unemployment policy of the 1930's, but says nothing about his own warnings against such measures.

89. Ohlin (1972:213).

References

Berg, C., and L. Jonung. 1999. Pioneering price level targeting: The Swedish experience 1931–1937. *Journal of Monetary Economics* 43(3):525–51.

Blaug, M. 1992. *Pioneers in Economics. Bertil Ohlin (1899–1979)*. Aldershot, England: Edward Elgar.

Carlson, B. 1993. The long retreat: Gustav Cassel and Eli Heckscher on the "new economics" of the 1930s. In L. Jonung, ed., *Swedish Economic Thought: Explorations and Advances*. London: Routledge, ch. 10.

Carlson, B., and L. Jonung. 1989. Gustav Cassels artiklar i Svenska Dagbladet. Register 1903–1944 (Gustav Cassel's articles in *Svenska Dagbladet*. Register 1903–1944). *Meddelande från Ekonomisk-historiska institutionen*. Lund: Lunds universitet.

Carlson, B., and L. Jonung. 1996. Hur såg de stora nationalekonomerna på sin roll i samhällsdebatten? (How did the great Swedish economists consider their role in the public debate?). In L. Jonung, ed., *Ekonomerna i debatten—gör de någon nytta?* Otta: Ekerlids, ch. 4.

Carlson, B., H. Orrje, and E. Wadensjö. 2000. *Ohlins artiklar. Register över Bertil Ohlins artiklar i skandinaviska tidningar och tidskrifter* (Ohlin's articles. Register of Bertil Ohlin's articles in Scandinavian newspapers and magazines). Stockholm: Swedish Institute for Social Research.

Cassel, G. 1902. *Socialpolitik.* Stockholm: Gebers.

Jonung, L. 1979. Knut Wicksell's norm of price stabilization and Swedish monetary policy in the 1930s. *Journal of Monetary Economics* 5:459–96.

Jonung, L. 1992. Economics the Swedish way, 1889–1989. In L. Engwall, ed., *Economics in Sweden: An Evaluation of Swedish Research in Economics.* London: Routledge.

Landgren, K.-G. 1960. *Den "nya ekonomien" i Sverige. J M Keynes, E Wigforss, B Ohlin och utvecklingen 1927–39* (The "new economics" in Sweden: J. M. Keynes, E. Wigforss, and B. Ohlin, and the development of 1927–39). Stockholm: Almqvist & Wiksell.

Ohlin, B. 1972. *Ung man blir politiker* (A young man becomes a politician). Stockholm: Bonniers.

Steiger, O. 1971. *Studien zur Entstehung der neuen Wirtschaftslehre in Schweden. Eine Anti-kritik.* Berlin: Duncker & Humblot.

Steiger, O. 1976. Bertil Ohlin and the origins of the Keynesian revolution. *History of Political Economy* 8(3):341–66.

Steiger, O. 1978. Prelude to the theory of monetary economy: Origins and significance of Ohlin's 1933 approach to monetary theory. *History of Political Economy* 10(3):420–46.

Stockholms-Tidningen, 1926–1935.

Wadensjö, E. 1991. The Committee on Unemployment and the Stockholm School. In L. Jonung, ed., *The Stockholm School of Economics Revisited.* Cambridge: Cambridge University Press, ch. 3.

14

Bertil Ohlin and the Stockholm School: Autonomous Changes in Consumption Demand; Ohlin, 1932 to 1934

Björn Hansson

Introduction

The existence of a "Stockholm School" was noted for the first time in Bertil Ohlin's famous article "Some Notes on the Stockholm Theory of Savings and Investments," in *Economic Journal,* 1937. Ohlin in this article did not only discussed the Swedish contributions to economic theory but also compared them to Keynes's findings in *The General Theory.* Interest in the development of economic theory among Swedish economists after Wicksell was certainly sharpened by this article. This interest was already partially due to the Wicksellian flavor of Keynes's *Treatise on Money,* which was followed up by the translation into English of Wicksell's *Interest and Prices* and *Lectures.*[1] It is easy to imagine that most of Ohlin's contemporaries considered him to be a central member of the Stockholm School.

In 1933 Ohlin summarized his own contribution to the Swedish debate from this period in the following way:

> The author attempts to construct a simple and more practical apparatus than that of neo-Wicksellian theory. It is necessary to clarify the ambiguities in current definitions of income, saving, and investment before we can apply statistical data. The description given by Wicksell, Lindahl and Hayek of the cumulative process is based on the assumption of a spontaneous lowering of the rate of interest and of the stickiness of wages and the demand for consumption-goods; but a rise in prices need not necessarily involve an increase in the demand for and relative price of production-goods. The relevance of the Austrian theory of capital and of the time-structure of prices to monetary theory is stressed, for the exchange structure and timesequence of prices is at the core of monetary problems. Finally, the neo-Wicksellian account of the equilibrium rate of interest and price-formation is stated to be inadequate. (Ohlin's report to "Recent Periodicals and New Books" in the *Economic Journal* December 1933, pp. 732–33).

Here the macrotheoretical issues are at the forefront, and Ohlin just mentions that some of the definitions of saving and investment were obscure.

In order to discuss Bertil Ohlin's relation to the Stockholm School, it is first necessary to give an idea what is meant by this school. In my view, a distinctive Stockholm School, including Gunnar Myrdal, Erik Lindahl, Erik Lundberg, Dag Hammarskjöld, Alf Johansson, and Bertil Ohlin, existed between 1927 and 1937. A "school" is here defined as an interrelated development of a common theme among these economists. The leitmotif defining the school is the explicit attention to and the development of a dynamic method.[2] Their development of a dynamic method is an original contribution. Although some elements of their work were discovered independently elsewhere, for example, intertemporal equilibrium, there is no evidence that other contemporary economists influenced the Swedes in any significant way, once the school had started to develop.

Ohlin's views on dynamic methods play a subordinate role in his analysis. In fact it will be argued that Ohlin made no significant contribution to the development of a dynamic method and that his main contribution instead lies within macroeconomic theory.

This chapter will focus on Ohlin's article "On the Formulation of Monetary Theory" published in *Ekonomisk Tidskrift*, 1933. The manuscript was sent to the editor David Davidson at the end of May 1933 (Landgren 1960:165), but Steiger has shown that an almost identical draft of the article already existed in the fall of 1932 (Steiger 1976:353). During the winter of 1932 to 1933, this draft was circulated "among some of Ohlin's colleagues in Sweden, notably Lindahl, Myrdal and Hammarskjöld" (ibid.). Ohlin's report to the Unemployment Committee (Ohlin 1934) was published in April 1934 (Landgren 1960:198n. 4). However, judging from Hammarskjöld's memorandum from August 1933, the report, or at least the theoretical parts, must have existed in a fairly final shape by the summer of 1933. The report will only be referred to in this article when it gives a more distinct version of Ohlin's ideas or shows a new development, since it contains an introductory part that is very similar to the article in *Ekonomisk Tidskrift*, apart from an inclusion of ex ante and ex post. The report is best characterized as an application to economic policy of the ideas from "On the Formulation."

The Dynamic Method of the Stockholm School

I would like to give a brief overview of the development of dynamic methods. It is possible to divide the period under consideration into four separate stages, where each stage is characterized by a specific dynamic method. The first stage is represented by Myrdal's dissertation, *Prisbildningsproblemet och föränderligheten*, 1927 (The Problem of Price Formation and Change), which shows how anticipations of an uncertain future constitute an independent part of the data that are supposed to determine a long-run equilibrium position. The crucial factor for the further development of the Stockholm School was the treatment of expectations and uncertainty as part of the theoretical core, and their being placed on the same level as preferences, technical conditions, and given resources.

Lindahl's construction of intertemporal equilibrium in 1929, "Prisbildningsproblemet från kapitalteoretisk synpunkt" (The place of capital in the theory of price), constitutes the second stage. This concept grew out of a critique of comparative static method used in handling dynamic problems, and its aim was to describe the process between two equilibrium positions. It seems that one reason why Lindahl gave up this method was that he realized that it could not treat imperfect foresight in a meaningful way. This weakness provided the rationale for the next stage, namely temporary equilibrium in *Penningpolitikens medel* (The Rate of Interest and the Price Level) of 1930, whose objective was to analyze cumulative processes. The development of dynamic methods then became intertwined with Wicksell's theory for the saving-investment mechanism, that is, the indirect relation between saving and investment via changes in the general price level. However, it will be shown that temporary equilibrium cannot really give a proper analysis of this mechanism since it is an equilibrium approach. Indeed, intertemporal as well as temporary equilibria are essentially equilibrium approaches. They refer to situations where the plans are consistent over several periods or one period, which allows them to be formally represented by a system of simultaneous equations. Both Lundberg and Myrdal criticized the equilibrium approach because simultaneity does not explain what happens in the links between consecutive periods, namely how events in one period determine outcomes in future periods. Thus Lindahl did not really portray a process over time.

The last stage came in 1937 with Lundberg's disequilibrium sequence analysis, in *Studies in the Theory of Economic Expansion*, but this concept is the result of a long and protracted development. Myrdal was once again the one to push the development in the right direction with the publication of *Monetary Equilibrium* (Swedish ed. 1932; German ed. 1933). This book laid the foundation for the disequilibrium approach with ex ante and ex post modeling, which made it possible to analyze a situation where the ex ante plans were incongruent while the ex post analysis showed which factors made up the ex post equality.

Hammarskjöld constructed some important elements for sequence analysis in "Utkast till en algebraisk metod för dynamisk prisanalys" (Draft for an algebraic method of dynamic pricing analysis) in 1932. His idea of windfall profit as a link between periods gave the first, though incomplete, formal sketch of sequence analysis. The discussion of the unit period where the length was coupled with the realization of unchanged plans later became a standard assumption within the Stockholm School.

Lindahl finally returned on the scene with two unpublished works from late 1934 and early 1935, respectively, "A Note on the Dynamic Pricing Problem" and "Introduction to the Theory of Price Movements in a closed Community." Building on Myrdal and Hammarskjöld, Lindahl formulated the first proper algebraic expression of a single period analysis, which exhibits how incongruent ex ante plans lead to determinate ex post results. Lindahl also discussed the problems in the building of a sequence analysis, but his own construction is an equilibrium sequence analysis, assuming that there is equilibrium in each period. In this regard Lundberg went beyond Lindahl, since his sequence analysis builds on disequilibrium within the separate periods. However, Lundberg's analysis is still an equilibrium process in the sense of the behavior being routine, which is represented by the assumption of constant response functions over the process.

The next section will show in some detail that Ohlin's work in 1932 to 1934 was no direct contribution to the development of a dynamic method. His insistence that a disturbance could emanate from an autonomous change in consumption, and did not have to come from the capital market as was generally assumed by Myrdal and Lindahl, furthered the macroeconomic analysis. Ohlin also stressed that those changes in output and real income could be part of the equilibrating mechanism between saving and investment.

Ohlin's Dynamic Method

This section shows Ohlin's own method is also a critique of the dynamic methods used by Lindahl and Myrdal. Ohlin's critique shows an inadequate understanding of these methods, in particular, the role of an equilibrium condition in an ex ante analysis. His total rejection of equilibrium, even as a reference point, appears in his discussion of the equilibrating mechanism and its relation to the principle of effective demand (Hansson 1982:75–81). But Ohlin's critique is also due to his concentration on finding concepts that could be used for an analysis of statistical data (see the introductory quotation). In this context, ex ante plans and related concepts are considered unsuitable for this purpose. In fact, since Ohlin deemed Lindahl and Myrdal's concepts unfit for practical analysis, he may have lacked the interest in really trying to understand their methods. However, we will see that Ohlin later accepted the use of ex ante plans in macroeconomic analysis.

Ohlin's overall objective is "to describe price changes over time" (Ohlin 1933d:359) via an analysis of the relation between total demand and total supply. This induces him to ask the following type of questions:

> Under which conditions, one may ask, will the system maintain a certain stability characterized by specific relations between the situation at one time and that at a later time? Under which conditions will the price system be moving upward or downward? (ibid.)

These questions seem to be related to the cumulative process and therefore to be in line with, for example, the problems analyzed by Myrdal in *Monetary Equilibrium.* It will be shown below, that Ohlin had, however, some additional ideas on the active forces behind a price change.

The dynamic method used by Ohlin to analyze the development of demand and supply (in particular, the former) is a peculiar mixture of ex post and ex ante:

> Along with a description of changes in supply, a description of the generation of demand for various goods must lie at the heart of every analysis of

price changes.... Such a demand analysis must be based upon an investigation of the composition of gross revenue reasoning *backwards* in time, as well as upon an investigation of prevailing notions of profitability computed forward in time. That is the only way to explain changes in demand. Quite simply, the task is to record transactions period by period, relating them to one another, thus illuminating why they came into existence. (Ohlin 1933c:358–59)

This method does not have a purely ex post character like Hammarskjöld's analysis (Hansson 1982:161–63), which only describes the outcome of the period. Ohlin also tries to explain what has been going on during the period by looking at the ex ante plans at the beginning of the period. However, the ex ante factors, for example, the prevailing notions of profitability, are estimated at the end of the period, which means that it is an ex post reconstruction of the ex ante plans. It is important to understand why Ohlin chose this method, since he certainly considered profit anticipations to play a crucial role (Hansson 1982:367, 385).

Using an ex post method was a conscious choice on Ohlin's part, but he only gives a few hints as to why he preferred his own method to Myrdal's ex ante analysis. First, he seems to argue that the notion of future plans is too vague and indeterminate and therefore that "a 'deep analysis' ... [would] imply a very misleading rationalization of human beings' conceptual world" (Ohlin 1934:43, 1933d:358n. 4, 377n. 26). Steiger makes the following interpretation of Ohlin's statement:

Ohlin, in his monetary approach, not only included expectations about future events but also stressed the fact that these anticipations were uncertain or as he expressed it, "indefinite," i.e., changeable and therefore capable of influencing the present economic outcome. (Steiger 1978:444; cf. Ohlin 1933:esp. nn. 4 and 26)

This seems to imply that Ohlin was criticizing the probabilistic approach of Lindahl and Myrdal. Thus Ohlin's ideas would be similar to the ones in *General Theory* (Steiger 1978:429). But I would argue that Ohlin's use of the word "indefinite" is equivalent to the words "vague" or "hazy," in the sense that individuals do not make specific plans for coming periods, which is his reason for not using an ex ante approach.

Second, even if individuals did form definite plans for the coming period, Ohlin could still not see "how such magnitudes, existing only in the human mind, could possibly lend themselves to statistical observation" (Ohlin 1933d:388). This is obviously true, since these "magnitudes" cannot be observed. Their importance to Ohlin is because one of his main aims is to construct an apparatus that has "a form easier to handle and lending itself to an analysis of statistical data available, among other places, in business accounting" (Ohlin 1933d:383n. 30; cf. p. 386). Hence *Ohlin's critique of Myrdal and Lindahl is mainly due to practical considerations.*

Ohlin's practical purpose and his critique of unobservable magnitudes are eloquently exemplified in his characterization of Lindahl's and Myrdal's concept of income as not only "mystical" but also "inapplicable in any statistical analysis" (Ohlin 1933d:383; cf. 1933d:76). However, Ohlin must to a certain extent face the same type of problem within his own method, since he attempts to investigate "prevailing notions of profitability computed forward in time" (1933c:359), unless he finds it easier to estimate these ex ante notions at the end of the period.

Despite this critique of what he calls the "neo-Wicksellian approach," Ohlin ends his discussion on the problem of the stability of the price system, which is the subject of his analysis, with the following idea, explicitly equated with "the core of Myrdal's formulation of monetary theory" (1933d:362n. 10):

> [O]ne must allow for planned investment and consumption demand as well as for available factor supply, for such plans could indicate pending price changes. The question is to what extent a certain state of the price system carries in it the seed of more or less violent and significant changes to come. (Ohlin 1933d:362)

Ohlin has also understood that in Myrdal's analysis, savings could differ from investment because they are plans "*ahead* in time" (1933d:359n. 7). However, *it seems that Ohlin has not understood one of the crucial advantages of the ex ante analysis, namely that equality between planned investment and planned savings is an equilibrium condition.* Indeed, without this, there would be no reason for examining monetary equilibrium. Instead, Ohlin speaks of the equilibrium implied by "ordinary price theory" (1933d:357) as referring to the *identity* between bought and sold quantities (cf. sect. 4:3). Hence in his own ex post method Myrdal's problem with a capital market equilibrium "simply does not arise" (Ohlin 1939d:354; cf. p. 379), since saving is always (ex post) equal to investment. This confusion between an ex post equality, a book-keeping identity that always holds, and an ex ante equality, a conditional relation, is the main drawback in Ohlin's analysis, and once more crops up in his analysis of the equilibrating mechanism.

Ohlin did not understand that the equilibrium condition, including his own addition of the consumption goods sector, that the plans for total demand are equal to the plans for total supply, is an answer to the question posed at the beginning of this section, namely how the system can maintain a certain stability over a period of time. Hence he did not see the great advantage of an ex ante analysis, at least from a theoretical point of view.

We may conclude that in 1933 to 1934 Ohlin had not yet grasped the advantage of an ex ante analysis for theoretical purposes, which may have "great practical usefulness" (see the quotation below). Thus he could reject it solely on practical grounds.

Ohlin must later have changed his mind, since it is evident in his article *Economic Journal*, 1937, that he has accepted the existence of plans based on expectations for the future, where the plans spell out the actions to be undertaken (Ohlin 1937a:61–62). Incidentally Ohlin much later gives one of the best accounts for why the concept of a plan must be precise in a theoretical analysis:

> Many may feel that all this talk in quantitatively precise terms of "planned savings" and "planned investment," and so on, is rather artificial. . . . In the theory it is necessary to assume a certain quantitative precision instead of vague ideas. Otherwise, a theoretical tool of great practical usefulness would not be at our disposal. (Ohlin 1949:117)

"What Happens First" and the "Case-by-Case" Approach

In this section I will take a closer look at some of Ohlin's more fruitful ideas concerning a dynamic method. These ideas are, once again, linked to the practical interest in a direct analysis of all possible causes for changes in prices and quantities. Ohlin is not interested in the construction of dynamic methods, nor does he understand that even a practical analysis may benefit from applying different notions of dynamic methods.

We have already seen that Ohlin attempts to describe price changes over time which involve a sequence, and that in analyzing such conditions, he has found "the timing of the various changes to be of obvious significance" (Ohlin 1933d:368). The idea of the importance of timing leads to the following central proposition:

[T]he effects of a given primary change will differ widely if the secondary reactions occur in one time sequence rather than another. (Ohlin 1933d:369, 1934:19, 21)

Hence, everything depends on "what happens first" (Ohlin 1933b:477), in the sense that the outcome of the process, triggered by "a given primary change," depends on the sequence of the concomitant reactions or changes.

In order to convey the meaning of "what happens first" see the following example of a general wage cut:

In a depression imagine a general wage cut of 10 percent in all industries, immediately reducing labor's consumption demand. If at the same time firms impressed with the improved profitability prospects expand their investment demand by the same amount, aggregate demand will not fall. Then average profitability will indeed improve and may indirectly stimulate investment demand. On the other hand, if no immediate tendency to expand firm investment demand arises, the wage cut reduces total consumption demand by as much as the cut in wage costs. Prices will tend downward, and profitability will deteriorate. (Ohlin 1933d:368–69; cf. Ohlin 1934:20)

In this case the outcome will depend on the speed at which the wage cut influences the demand for investment. Examples of this kind help explain why Ohlin rejected attempts "to offer simple rules for the relative magnitude of price movements" (1933d:375). Thus "what happens first" shows that the speed of reaction of various factors to a primary change, which is akin to Lundberg's velocities of adjustment (Hansson 1982:95–97), will determine the sequence of changes. Ohlin is, in a descriptive way, thinking of something like a disequilibrium sequence analysis, but he makes no attempt to construct such a dynamic method.

The importance of the notion "what happens first," and the concomitant difficulties for any generalization concerning the sequence of changes in prices and quantities, explain why Ohlin adopts a so-called case-by-case approach (Ohlin 1933d:381, 383, 384). However, Ohlin gives no clear and concise description of this approach until his debate with Lindahl in 1941 to 1942, where he defends his approach against Lindahl's attempts to develop a general dynamic approach in "The Dynamic Approach" of 1939. In this context, Ohlin describes his own procedure, which he considers to be analogous to Lundberg's model sequences (Ohlin 1941a:172), as follows:

[T]o construct a series of typical cases, where the economic development can be described and predicted on the basis of certain assumptions concerning the speed of reaction and the strength of the tendencies. (Ohlin 1941a:171; cf. Ohlin 1941b:331)

I would hold that Ohlin's critique does not really attack the core of Lindahl's dynamic method. In fact Ohlin himself provides the proper answer, since he portrays Lindahl's method as "a conceptual system, so general that it could applied for studying all different typical cases" (Ohlin 1941a:172; cf. Lindahl 1941:237, 1942:43–44; Ohlin 1941b:329–30).

We can draw the following conclusions concerning Ohlin's dynamic method and his critique of Lindahl and Myrdal. The case-by-case approach and "what happens first" were mainly used by Ohlin to criticize the neo-Wicksellian explanation of price changes, which is a problem pertaining to macroeconomic theory. But these notions do not disprove the usefulness of dynamic methods as developed by Lindahl and Myrdal before 1933 and 1934. In fact they imply a certain method, namely a disequilibrium sequence analysis like Lundberg's model sequences, that is a development of Lindahl's and Myrdal's early methods and a variant of Lindahl's "conceptual scheme" mentioned above. Ohlin is therefore confusing a critique of a certain neo-Wicksellian macrotheoretical proposition with a critique of the dynamic methods used in establishing this proposition.

A Critique of the "Neo-Wicksellians" or an Autonomous Change in the Demand for Consumption Goods

In this section I will study Ohlin's critique and extension of neo-Wicksellian macro theory. It will be seen that Ohlin's critique of Wicksell and his followers contains implicit assumptions on method. Once again, I will find that Ohlin's strivings for an ex post analysis of actual situations heavily influence his contribution.

Ohlin wants to give a *general* answer to "the question of the driving force behind price movements" (Ohlin 1933d:384). His explanation is basically a restatement of an old Wicksellian idea:

[R]ising prices in general imply that the demand for goods and services is rising more rapidly than the quantities supplied. One possibility is that so many entrepreneurs find immediate real investment profitable that investment is growing.... Another possibility is that demand for consumers' goods is rising. The necessary and sufficient condition for a process of rising prices is that the sum of those two kinds of demand is rising relative to output. (Ohlin 1933d:373–74; cf. 385–86)

Hence "the driving force" is made up of two forces: one coming from investment and the other from consumption. Therefore an explanation of price changes must look at the factors influencing the demand and supply of consumption goods and investment goods, respectively (Ohlin 1933d:358, 367, 385, 386).[3]

It is then not surprising that Ohlin finds the idea that the disequilibrium in the capital market represents the driving force, that is, what he considers to be the hallmark of the "neo-Wicksellian" approach, as too narrow an explanation. This is particularly so when he can construct examples where a disequilibrium in the consumer goods market is the only factor behind a price movement or at least the initiating force (Ohlin 1933d:368, 374, 380).

If the real world can show a variety of factors influencing the general price level and Ohlin strives to find all the possible factors behind price changes, then the following is obviously true:

[I]t serves no good purpose to press the analysis of several kinds of demand changes into the straitjacket of seeing everything in terms of the relation between a "normal" rate and the actual money rate. (Ohlin 1933a:368)

It is true that Wicksell almost exclusively explained price changes by his ideas on the "normal" rate, even if he started to consider other possibilities in his last years (Wicksell 1925:201). But when we reach Lindahl and Myrdal, it becomes obvious that they analyzed changes in saving that *first* reacted to the prices of consumer goods and thereby triggered off the cumulative process (Hansson 1982:75–81, 141–44). Later Lindahl also showed that an autonomous change in demand for consumption goods still appears as a disturbance of the equilibrium condition that savings should be equal to investments ex ante (Hansson 1982:210–11).

Ohlin's explicit treatment of *autonomous* changes in consumption is thus his specific extension of neo-Wicksellian macrotheory. This also seems to have been Ohlin's own evaluation of his contribution to the development of the Stockholm School:

Maybe it was no news in a purely logical sense when in the years of the Great Depression I pointed out intensively that a process of inflation could be possible despite equilibrium in the capital market. But I myself conceived it as a news, because the Swedish discussion to such a high degree concentrated on the assumption that all primary changes were shift of investments. (Letter from Ohlin to Steiger, 2 September 1972, as quoted in Steiger 1976:356n. 22)[4]

Ohlin's extension of the Wicksellian approach is certainly relevant, but his critique of Lindahl and Myrdal contains a methodological snag. Ohlin analyses an *actual* situation *ex post*. In that case, explaining a price movement that has taken place just by "referring to the relative amount of credit" (Steiger 1976:386) does not make sense, since other factors might also have been active; that is, a concrete analysis is necessary. However, Myrdal and Lindahl generally pursued an ex ante analysis of the effects of a ceteris paribus change in the money rate, or the real rate, on the price level. Hence Lindahl and Myrdal are certainly correct as long as they pursue an ex ante analysis on a theoretical level, and it seems that Ohlin has not really bothered to understand their method. Ohlin's critique shows that their macro theory had its limits, however, since "[one] merely succeeds in calling attention to the fact that a change in credit policy may produce a change in demand and price movements" (Ohlin 1933d:386).

The Equilibrating Mechanism

This section is mainly a study of Ohlin's analysis of the equilibrating mechanism, which is then compared with Myrdal and Lindahl's analyses of this phenomenon. It is first shown that Ohlin included quantity changes in his equilibrating mechanism and the extent to which Lindahl and Myrdal had already developed this idea. I then proceed to an explicit analysis of this mechanism. The next step is to find the equilibrium notion behind Ohlin's equilibrating mechanism, and to state my view of the nature of Ohlin's contribution and its relation to the Keynesian revolution. Finally, there will be an opportunity to look at some other interpretations of this relation. These interpretations have different views of the nature of Ohlin's contribution from the one taken in this essay, and by implication, also of the fundamental characteristic of the Stockholm School, and the Keynesian revolution, respectively.

Quantity Changes

Ohlin analyzes a case where the saving intentions are reduced during a process of falling prices, which will have the following ex post consequences:

> Rising consumption demand does not at all mean falling net saving, which equals new real investment. On the contrary, aggregate demand and gross income will be rising *more* rapidly than consumption demand. Consequently gross saving will be rising while negative incomes are falling. Net saving then will be rising for a twofold reason. (Ohlin 1933d:380)

Income changes will thus lead to higher savings ex post. But it is not explicit whether the income changes only consist of price changes or a mixture of price and quantity changes. However, in other examples, Ohlin assumes some spare capacity at the beginning of his analysis (Ohlin 1933d:368, 370, 375),[5] and then it is obviously "expanding output," which makes an increase in net savings possible ex post even if consumption has risen.[6] In a case with idle capacity, increased income and output accordingly stem from the following factors:

> [M]ore labor is employed, raising the total wage bill; for another, business income is up, both because of better utilization of durable capital goods and natural resources and because of a tendency of prices to rise. (Ohlin 1933d:370; cf. p. 372)

Ohlin has thus, more than Lindahl and Myrdal, stressed the importance of taking increased production into consideration as part of the equalization mechanism.

However, in an analysis from more or less the same period, Myrdal explicitly mentions income changes due to increased production. The starting point is a situation with unused resources, such as in the trough of a depression. We will look at Myrdal's comments concerning the credit market:

> [I]t is on the one hand obvious, that the increased production and consumption require disposition of capital. But at the same time the income of all social classes is increased, with the result, that an increased amount of capital disposition in the form of new savings is also brought about in a sufficient amount. (Myrdal 1933c:23; cf. p. 25)[7]

Myrdal considers this to be the normal state of affairs during the recovery from a depression (1933c:24). Lindahl, who had studied a draft of this memorandum, puts forth the same ideas in a speech from November 1932:

> [T]he capital which is absorbed by the public works is financed by the increase in societal production, which is the direct or indirect result of these works.... It appears probable that this condition is fulfilled when there ... is a large unused capacity in the private firms. In such a case the increased production could be so big that the accompanied increase in the national income could give rise to the saving which is necessary for the financing of the public works (Lindahl 1932:136–37).

Myrdal and Lindahl's ideas should therefore be compared with Ohlin's statements in *On the Formulation*.

Hence it is very difficult to find out who was the first to expound these ideas. From the correspondence between Lindahl and Myrdal, we can see that Myrdal's appendix already existed as a draft at the beginning of November 1932, since Lindahl asks Myrdal to send him the memorandum, which he had already seen (Lindahl to Myrdal, 12 November 1932; Myrdal to Lindahl, 14 November 1932). However, we do not know how extensive this draft was. Indeed, there is no way of telling how they influence each other. Ohlin, on the other hand, although he was present when Lindahl delivered his speech and supported Lindahl's thesis, probably precedes both Lindahl and Myrdal, since he had already put forth the same ideas in very sketchy form in August 1932 (cf. note 5).

An Example of the Equilibrating Mechanism

The most *formal* account of the equilibrating mechanism is to be found in *Monetary Policy* (Ohlin 1934:27). Here Ohlin draws a straightforward analogy between the supply and demand analysis for one good and the same analysis for all goods. In his example the income expectations remain unchanged as well as the will to save, which means fixed plans for consumption and savings.

A decrease in the rate of interest will now lead to an increase in planned investment, which is like an outward shift in the total demand curve, and as a result "volume of production, realized demand, measured in money, and perhaps prices will rise more or less." If the supply curve is assumed to be completely elastic because of spare capacity, it is obvious that an increase in investment leads to the same increase in real income ($dI = P(QI - Q)$). Consequently Ohlin draws the following conclusion:

> [T]he increase of investment purchases implies that at the end of the period, the incomes show themselves to be bigger than what was formerly expected [*PQ* was expected], i.e., they have given a "surplus." As the consumption purchases have been unchanged, this increase in income has been saved. The saving [realized] has increased due to the decrease in the rate of interest. (Ohlin 1934:27–28)

Hence the whole increase in income is saved, and is equal to the increase in investment.[8]

In this type of analysis we would have exactly the same effects on prices and quantities if the demand curve shifted out because of higher income expectations. Planned demand for consumption goods would then increase, even if planned investment were equal to planned savings (Ohlin 1934:27). This is a formal proof of the aggregate demand approach being superior to the analysis of Myrdal et al., who mainly looked at the ex ante balance between savings and investments. But as we have already mentioned, it only implies that we must add the plans for demand and supply of consumption goods to Myrdal's formulation of monetary equilibrium.

We will now look at some minor methodological implications of this analysis.

In the preceding example the entire increase in income is saved as a windfall, or as "residual income" as it is called by Ohlin (1934:28n. 1). This is similar to Myrdal's analysis, and this increase will only affect the plans for the next period as shown by Hammarskjöld (Hansson 1982:VII:3). However, Ohlin adds that during such a process "even the income expectations will increase during the period and thereby the consumption purchase" (Ohlin 1934:28), Even in this case certain income changes will appear as windfall. This is characteristic of Ohlin's failure to consider the intricacies of period analysis, which had just been developed by Hammarskjöld. In Hammarskjöld's analysis, the plans are fixed for the current period so that, even if expectations change during the period, they will have no effect until the transition to the next period.

It is probable that Ohlin here refers to something like a multiplier, and he actually mentions Kahn's article from 1931 for the first time in any Swedish work (Ohlin 1934:103n. 2). But in a period analysis, changes in expectations during the period can have no effects in the same period.[9] Hence, if the income expectations are correct, they include the effects of the multiplier, or the multiplier will have a lagged character, à la Dennis Robertson, where the difference between the realized income for the previous period and the current period is saved. However, there exists a further problem in grafting the multiplier onto Ohlin's analysis, namely whether Ohlin thought of these equilibrating changes as leading to an equilibrium situation, as in Keynes's application of the multiplier (cf. Hansson 1982:app. I), or just to positions in an ongoing disequilibrium process.

Equilibrating Mechanism or Ex post Identities

Last I will discuss the character of Ohlin's equilibrium notion and compare it with Myrdal's.

Ohlin often seems to confuse an equilibrating mechanism leading to an equilibrium situation of one sort or another with an ex post identity during a dynamic process at the end of the period. This is well exemplified by the following quotation:

> The new savings are produced by those, who for the time being have an increased cash holding. (Ohlin 1934:110; cf. p. 39)

Hence increased cash holding of a temporary character is looked upon as savings. This is in line with his use of the latter term as income that has not been spent, without taking into consideration saving plans or saving propensities, like (*s*) in Lindahl's price formula (Ohlin 1934:37; Hansson 1982:IV:1:3).

This is an offshoot to Ohlin's view of equilibrium as being just the ex post identity between bought and sold quantities. But it shows that he has not properly understood the capabilities of an ex ante analysis as developed by Myrdal, which would define equilibrium as a conditional ex ante equality among specific plans. From this point of view, the definitional ex post equality would only represent a confirmation of equilibrium if the ex ante anticipations have been fulfilled. Otherwise, it would serve as a basis for change of plans, which may or may not lead to equilibrium for the coming period. Therefore Ohlin's main mistake seems to be a mix-up of ex ante and ex post notions.[10]

I would therefore argue that Ohlin is not determining an equilibrium position via the principle of effective demand, even if his analysis of the process leading up to the ex post equalities has certain traits in common with Keynes's mechanism, for example, changes in real income.

From my point of view, it is more natural to look upon Ohlin's analysis as geared toward business cycle theory, which explains the ex post equality between savings and investment via changes in prices and quantities. But it does not determine any particular equilibrium level, and certainly not long-run equilibrium of aggregate income and employment (Ohlin 1933d:379).[11] Most business cycle theories do treat physical output as a variable, but that does not necessarily imply the principle of effective demand. The latter principle does not only say that output is changing but also that these changes are a mechanism determining the equilibrium level of output and employment.

As regards Ohlin's position on this problem, we can rely on his own comments to his report to the Unemployment Committee:

> [T]he very assignment given by the Unemployment Committee referred to the quantity of employment, and it would have been downright impossible not to consider the latter a variable and with it national income in terms of quantity side by side with the price level and income in terms of value. (Letter from Ohlin to Brems, 2 December 1977, as quoted in Brems 1978:410)[12]

In a business cycle analysis a situation characterized as "a deep depression in which everything price and cost relations is temporarily 'frozen'", could also be described as *a matter of fact* (Ohlin 1933d:362). This temporary situation might then be explained as follows:

> [W]hen prices have been falling for a while, investment demand and consumption demand may stop falling and the price fall come to an end. The reason may be that consumption demand cannot easily contract beyond a certain point, and its resilience will check the tendency to declining investment demand (Ohlin to Brems, as quoted in Brems 1978:379).

In fact both the situation and the explanation of its existence are identical to Myrdal's analysis in *Monetary Equilibrium* (Hansson 1982:144–48). Hence *Ohlin's analysis, like Myrdal's, amounts to an explanation of the bottom of a business cycle rather than of an underemployment equilibrium*. It must be remembered, however, that the bottom of a business cycle is a temporary situation, to be followed by an upturn, and it is not the same as a Keynesian underemployment equilibrium.

Conclusion

I conclude that Ohlin made no significant contribution to the development of a dynamic method. On the contrary, he shows a certain lack of understanding of the ex ante approach. Although emphasis on "what happens first," which means that the character of a sequence will depend on the speed of reaction of the different factors, leads him to adopt the "case-by-case" approach, and this is akin to Lundberg's model sequences from 1937.

Ohlin's main contribution instead lies within macroeconomic theory, where he pointed to the possibilities of autonomous changes in the demand for consumption goods. This was a step forward from Myrdal's and Lindahl's concentration on the relation between saving and investment. Ohlin's analysis of the equilibrating mechanism is partly superior to Myrdal and Lindahl's analyses in the sense that he explicitly incorporates quantity changes. At the same time, it is inferior, due to this lack of understanding of the difference between equilibrium conditions and ex post identities.

Notes

1. Cassel's *Theoretische Sozialökonomie* from 1917 had already been translated as *The Theory of Social Economy* in 1923 and his writings had a certain influence on Dennis Robertson (cf. Robertson 1926:5). Furthermore it is not unlikely that it was through Cassel's work that Keynes learned of Wicksell's ideas on the normal rate of interest.

2. "Dynamic methods" refer to notions such as temporary equilibrium and disequilibrium sequence analysis (cf. Hansson 1982:ch. II). Hicks has used the term in a similar way in classifying models according to how they deal with the dynamic character of reality (cf. Hicks 1965:28–29). The discussion of dynamic method is not a methodological discussion in any philosophical sense, such as, for example the advantages of a deductive or an inductive method.

3. Keynes makes the same extension of the fundamental equations of the *Treatise*, and looks only at I versus S:

The essence of the monetary theory of production ... can be expressed quite briefly, starting from the equation $dQ = dI - dS$ or, as it may also be written $dQ = dI + dF - dE$ or $dQ = dD - dE$ where Q stands for profit, I for investment, S for saving, F for spending, and D for disbursement [and E for income]. For these equations mean that profit (for entrepreneurs as a whole) is increasing or decreasing as the excess of investment over saving or (which amounts to the same thing) of disbursement over earnings is increasing or decreasing. (Drafts of chapters 7–10 of *General Theory* from 1931 or 1932; Keynes 1973a:381)

4. Steiger is basically correct in the following proposition:

Ohlin to a certain extent held a pioneering position [in relation to Myrdal and Lindahl] by his early development of the aggregate demand approach in the 1920's. (Steiger 1976:364)

However, unlike Steiger, we can find no sign of this approach until Ohlin's article "Den danska kronan efter 1914" (The Danish kronor after 1914) from 1927. In this article he speaks of disequilibrium in the capital market as increasing the purchasing power, and he denotes this idea as a generally accepted theory (cf. Ohlin 1927:122). It is only in 1932 that Ohlin mentions the possibility of extending the analysis to the market for consumption goods, but he does not explicitly develop this approach (cf. Ohlin 1932b:16). Later in 1932 Ohlin writes:

[T]he main push to an improvement *can* come from increased demand for consumption goods, whose producer will thereby order more capital goods. (Ohlin 1932d:23)

But the explicit analysis is still centered around a balance or imbalance in the capital market (cf. Ohlin 1932d:24). Therefore I would argue that Ohlin does not make an explicit analysis of autonomous changes in consumption until the draft of *On the Formulation* in the fall of 1932.

5. Ohlin's *Monetary Policy* has the following explicit aim:

[A]n investigation of the effects of certain instruments of business cycle and labor market policy that occur during times of widespread unemployment. (Ohlin 1934:3)

Hence the full title of this book is *Monetary Policy, Public Works, Subsidies, and Tariffs as Remedies for Unemployment.*

6. A similar idea is already mentioned by Ohlin in his article "*Prisstegringens problem*" (The problem of rising prices) of August 1932. In a situation with unused capacity in capital goods industries:

[T]he real saving that is necessary for increased production arises from a better utilization of the productive machinery so that production starts growing more than consumption. (Ohlin 1932d:28)

However, the explanation is not really theoretical. As happens so often with Ohlin, it is based on an empirical generalization:

[A]ll the facts support the idea that net saving is low during depressions and grows in parallel with the upswing. (Ohlin 1932d:28)

7. This pamphlet of March 1933 is a reprint of Myrdal's appendix to the budget for 1933. The budget is always presented at the first session of the Parliament in the beginning of January.

8. This mode of analysis is similar to Kahn's analysis of the fundamental equations in his multiplier article (cf. Kahn 1931:9–10). Kahn shows that for a closed economy, the increase in the cost of investment (I' in the *Treatise*) is exactly balanced by an increase in saving, if the supply of consumption goods is perfectly elastic. However, he assumes that $(I' - S)/R$ stays the same after the increase in investment and that I' is therefore much smaller than S. Hence the new situation is not an equilibrium situation, since the price level is different from the cost of production in the long-run equilibrium, $P \neq (E/0)$, (cf. Keynes 1930a:122, 137).

9. It is possible that already at this stage Ohlin is thinking in terms of a unit period shorter than the period it takes for the multiplier "to work itself out." During the latter period, *endogenous* changes will therefore take place (cf. Hansson 1982:244–47).

10. In August 1933 Hammarskjöld wrote a critical note on Ohlin's draft of the report to the commission where Hammarskjöld was secretary (cf. Steiger 1976:362). Among other things, the note contains an obscure critique of Ohlin's notion of savings (cf. Hammarskjöld 1933:4–5, 14). But Hammarskjöld's points were actually due to Ohlin's confusing use of ex ante and ex post notions without any proper equilibrium concept.

Hammarskjöld could not resolve the problem, but I cannot support Steiger's view of Hammarskjöld's critique:

[W]hat Hammarskjöld attacks as a "contradiction" was one of the most fruitful insights Lindahl, Myrdal, and Ohlin had developed—the *ex ante/ex post* perspective of macroeconomic variables—above all, that of saving and investment. (Steiger 1976:362)

It seems more likely that at this time, Ohlin did not fully understand or accept some of Lindahl's and Myrdal's "most fruitful insights."

11. This seems to be close to Yohe's characterization of Ohlin's analysis:

[I]t is in the broad sense of the term that Ohlin's 1933 paper may be classed at all as "monetary theory," i.e., a synonym for business-cycle theory. (Yohe 1978:451)

12. The same opinion had already been put forward by Lindahl in 1939:

It is very natural that the Commission should have devoted its attention principally to cyclical unemployment, since its work was necessarily influenced by the depression which came on during the time of its investigation. (Lindahl 1939c:351)

References

Brems, H. 1978. What was new in Ohlin's 1933–34 macroeconomics? *History of Political Economy* 10 (Fall): 398–412.

Cassel, Gustav. 1923. *The Theory of Social Economy*, vols. 1–2. London: Fisher Unwin.

Hammarskjöld, Dag. 1932. Utkast till en algebraisk metod för dynamisk prisanalys. *Ekonomisk Tidskrift*.

Hammarskjöld, Dag. 1933. Memorandum on a manuscript by Ohlin (1934). Circulated among the members of the Unemployment Committee. Dated August 17.

Hansson, Björn. 1982. *The Stockholm School and the Development of Dynamic Method*. London: Croom Helm.

Hicks, J. R. 1965. *Capital and Growth*. Oxford: Clarendon Press.

Kahn, R. F. 1931. The relation of home investment to unemployment. *Economic Journal* 41 (June). Reprinted in R. F. Kahn, *Selected Esssays on Employment and Growth*. Cambridge: Cambridge University Press, 1972, pp. 1–34.

Keynes, John Maynard. 1930. *A Treatise on Money*, vols. 1–2. First edition 1930. Reprinted in vols. 5–6 in *The Collected Writings*, London: Macmillan, 1971.

Keynes, John Maynard. 1973. *The General Theory and After. Parts I–II. The Collected Writings*, vols. 13–14. London: Macmillan, 1973.

Lindahl, Erik. 1929. Prisbildningsproblemet från kapitalteoretisk synpunkt. *Ekonomisk Tidskrift*: 31–81.

Lindahl, Erik. 1930. *Penningpolitikens medel*. Malmö: Förlagsaktiebolaget.

Lindahl, Erik. 1932. Offentliga arbeten i depressionstider. *Ekonomisk Tidskrift*.

Lindahl, Erik. 1934. A note on the dynamic pricing problem. Stencil dated Gothenburg, October 23. As reprinted in Steiger (1971) and in Keynes (1979).

Lindahl, Erik. 1935. Introduction to the theory of price movements in a closed community. Chapter 1, and the only surviving chapter, of *Monetary Policy and its Theoretical Basis*. Unpublished manuscript from the beginning of 1935.

Lindahl, Erik. 1939. *Studies in the Theory of Money and Capital*. London: George Allen and Unwin.

Lindahl, Erik. 1939a. The rate of interest and the price level. Translation of Lindahl (1930). Part two of Lindahl (1939).

Lindahl, Erik. 1939b. The place of capital in the theory of price. Translation of Lindahl (1929). Part three of Lindahl (1939).

Lindahl, Erik. 1939c. The problem of balancing the budget. *Ekonomisk Tidskrift*: 1–36. Appendix to Lindahl (1939).

Lindahl, Erik. 1941. Professor Ohlin om dynamisk teori. *Ekonomisk Tidskrift*: 236–47.

Lindahl, Erik. 1942. Metodfrågor inom den dynamiska teorien. *Ekonomisk Tidskrift*: 41–51.

Lundberg, Erik. 1937. *Studies in the Theory of Economic Expansion*. Reprinted New York: Kelley and Millman, 1955.

Myrdal, Gunnar. 1927. *Prisbildningsproblemet och föränderligheten*. Stockholm: Almquist and Wicksell.

Myrdal, Gunnar. 1931. Om penningteoretisk jämvikt. En studie över den "normala räntan" i Wicksells penninglära. *Ekonomisk Tidskrift*: 191–302.

Myrdal, Gunnar. 1933a. Der Gleichgewichtsbegriff als Instrument in der geldtheoretischen Analyze. In F. V. Hayek, ed., *Beiträge zur Geldtheorie*. Vienna: Julius Springer, 1933.

Myrdal, Gunnar. 1933c. *Konjunktur och offentlig hushållning*. Stockholm: Nordisk Rotogravyr.

Myrdal, Gunnar. 1939. *Monetary Equilibrium*. London: W. Hodge. Reprinted New York: Kelley, 1965.

Ohlin, Bertil. 1927. Den danska kronan efter 1914. *Nationaløkonomisk Tidskrift* 65:121–42.

Ohlin, Bertil. 1931. Den internationella penningpolitiken och dess inverkan på konjunkturutvecklingen. *Ekonomisk Tidskrift*: 12–31.

Ohlin, Bertil. 1932a. Ungelöste Probleme der gegenwärtigen Krisis. *Weltwirtschaftliches Archiv* 36:1–23.

Ohlin, Bertil. 1932b. Now or Never: Action to Combat the World Depression. *Svenska Handelsbankens Index*. May.

Ohlin, Bertil. 1932c. Prisstegringens problem. *Det Ekonomiska Läget*. August.

Ohlin, Bertil. 1933a. Ohlin's report to "Recent Periodicals and New Books." *Economic Journal* 43.

Ohlin, Bertil. 1933b. A note on price theory with special reference to interdependence and time. In *Economic Essays in Honour of Gustav Cassel*. London: George Allen and Unwin.

Ohlin, Bertil. 1933c. Draft to Ohlin (1933d). As translated in *History of Political Economy* 10 (Fall): 396–97.

Ohlin, Bertil. 1933d. On the formulation of monetary theory. A translation of Ohlin (1933e) in *History of Political Economy* 10 (Fall): 353–88.

Ohlin, Bertil. 1933e. Till frågan om penningteoriens uppläggning. *Ekonomisk Tidskrift*: 46–81.

Ohlin, Bertil. 1934. *Penningpolitik, offentliga arbeten, subventioner och tullar som medel mot arbetslösheten: Bidrag till expansionens teori.* Stockholm: Norstedt.

Ohlin, Bertil. 1937a–b. Some notes on the Stockholm theory of savings and investments. I–II. *Economic Journal* 47 (March, June): 53–69; 221–40.

Ohlin, Bertil. 1941a. Professor Lindahl om dynamisk teori. *Ekonomisk Tidskrift*: 170–81.

Ohlin, Bertil. 1941b. Metodfrågor inom den dynamiska teorien. *Ekonomisk Tidskrift*: 327–36.

Ohlin, Bertil. 1949. *The Problem of Employment Stabilization.* New York: Columbia University Press.

Robertson, Dennis. 1926. *Banking Policy and the Price Level.* London: King.

Steiger, Otto. 1971. *Studien zur Entstehung der Neuen Wirtschaftslehre in Schweden. Eine Anti-Kritik.* Berlin: Duncker and Humblot.

Steiger, Otto. 1976. Bertil Ohlin and the origins of the Keynesian revolution. *History of Political Economy* 8 (Fall): 341–66.

Steiger, Otto. 1978. Prelude to the theory of a monetary economy: Origins and significance of Ohlin's 1933 approach. *History of Political Economy* 10 (Fall): 420–46.

Wicksell, Knut. 1925. The monetary problems of the Scandinavian countries. *Ekonomisk Tidskrift*: 205–22. As translated in Wicksell (1936).

Wicksell, Knut. 1928–1929. *Lectures on Political Economy*, vols. 1–2. Translated from the third Swedish edition (1928–1929). London: Routledge, 1934–1935.

Wicksell, Knut. 1936. *Interest and Prices.* Translation of Wicksell (1968). London: Macmillan.

Wicksell, Knut. 1898. *Geldzins und Güterpreise*. Jena: Gustav Fischer. Reprinted Aalen: Scientia Verlag, 1968.

Yohe, W. P. 1978. Ohlin's 1933 reformation of monetary theory. *History of Political Economy* 10 (Fall): 447–53.

15 Bertil Ohlin and the Committee on Unemployment, 1927 to 1935

Eskil Wadensjö

In 1919, at the age of 20, Bertil Ohlin was engaged in a governmental committee for the first time—the Committee on Tariffs and Trade Agreements (*Tull- och Traktatkommittén*). He became assistant secretary of the committee, writing three separate reports on the development of the structure of three branches of the Swedish manufacturing industry. From the fall of 1920 he was assistant secretary of another committee, the newly founded Economic Council (*Ekonomiska rådet*), for one year. It was (and still is) common for Swedish economists to take part in the work of governmental committees, both for economists outside the universities often serving as experts or secretaries, and for university professors, serving as experts or members of committees.

At the end of the 1920s Ohlin was once again engaged by a governmental committee. It turned into one of the most important committees ever in Sweden on economic issues—the Committee on Unemployment (*Arbetslöshetsutredningen*). It was instrumental in developing the business cycle theory of the Stockholm School and also the monetary and fiscal policy in Sweden in the 1930s.[1] The Committee, active for more than seven years (1927 to 1935), engaged many economists. Several of them, Dag Hammarskjöld, Alf Johansson, Karin Kock, Erik Lindahl, Gunnar Myrdal, Bertil Ohlin and Ingvar Svennilson, are regarded today as members of the Stockholm School. Bertil Ohlin was one of the economists who worked most for the Committee. His supplement to the final report was one of the most important contributions to it.

This study deals with Ohlin's work for the Committee. It builds mainly on material from the Committee, filed in the National Archives (*Riksarkivet*). The file of the Unemployment Committee contains letters, many unpublished memoranda, minutes from meetings, and the like, as well as earlier versions of the whole or parts of the supplement. The papers of the Committee and the different versions of the supplement make it possible to follow the development of Ohlin's ideas. A second major source is the Bertil Ohlin Archives at the National Archives. Other material is also used like letters from Bertil Ohlin in other archives and other publications of his.[2]

The Committee on Unemployment

The Committee on Unemployment was appointed in April 1927, several years before the depression of the 1930s. The starting point was thus not the mass unemployment of the 1930s but the considerably lower unemployment rate of the second half of the 1920s.

The impetus for appointing a committee came from another committee, the Unemployment Committee of 1926 (*1926 års arbetslöshetssakkunniga*) which dealt with unemployment insurance and measures for helping the unemployed. This committee proposed (and the government later accepted) that the new committee should investigate "the nature and causes of unemployment." The main argument in support of the new committee was that despite a period of prosperity (including the year of 1927), unemployment was still much higher than before World War I. The indications of permanent unemployment and also of high youth unemployment were particular sources of concern. "Permanent unemployment" was defined as unemployment still being high despite a long period of economic recovery and economic expansion. Using present terminology, the persistence or hysteresis of unemployment was a matter of concern.

Gunnar Huss, head of the National Social Welfare Board (*Socialstyrelsen*), was appointed chairman of the committee. One of the five other members was Gösta Bagge, professor at *Stockholms Högskola* (now Stockholm University) and a specialist in labor economics. Elis Boseaus, Conrad Carlesson, Ernst Wigforss, and Anders Örne were the other members. Four of the six members were nonsocialists. Bagge was a member of the Conservative Party (and later its chairman), Carlesson and Huss were members of the Liberal Party, and Boseaus was an industrialist. Wigforss and Örne, on the other hand, were both members of the *Riksdag* for the Social Democratic Party. Wigforss had previously been Minister of Finance and was to take on this post once more when the Social Democratic Party formed its government after the election in September 1932. Appointed minister, he left the committee and was replaced by another Social Democrat, Frans Severin. Örne left the committee in April 1932 and was succeeded by Richard Lindström, also a Social Democrat. The majority of the committee was firmly market-oriented, and wage reductions were the expected recommendation from the committee.

Secretaries in Swedish governmental committees often play a crucial role, since they are usually the only ones working on them full time for an extended period. Sven Skogh was First Secretary from March 1928. Dag Hammarskjöld, Assistant Secretary from August 1930, succeeded Skogh in April 1932. Skogh and Hammarskjöld were both economists.

The Committee engaged several economists, most of them as experts for specific studies. Bagge, head of the Social Science Institute at *Stockholms Högskola*, played an important part in the Committee. Many of the economists who were engaged as experts to the Committee, for example, Johansson, Lindahl, Myrdal, and Svennilson, worked at the Social Science Institute at *Stockholms Högskola*, and were probably recruited by Bagge, as was Ohlin who was professor in Copenhagen at that time.[3]

Work in the Committee was intense. The minutes of the meetings for the period March 1928 to April 1932 are preserved. They show that the Committee had meetings on 150 days during this period. Bagge, Huss, and Wigforss had the highest rates of attendance. Bagge was only absent two days, and Huss and Wigforss were present at every meeting. The experts were present when their reports were discussed. Ohlin attended meetings on March 11, 13, and 17, 1930, when his memorandum on "Tariffs as a remedy for unemployment" was on the agenda.

According to the Committee's directives, a first report dealing with the current unemployment situation was expected to be completed by 1927. Thereafter the Committee would continue with analyses of the causes of unemployment and the effects of various measures to reduce it. However, the Committee's first report was delayed and not published until 1931 (SOU 1931:20). It contained an extensive account of the size and structure of unemployment in the 1920s and also an analysis of the causes of noncyclical unemployment (called "permanent" unemployment). Three separately published supplements to the report by Bagge (1931), Huss (1931), and Gustaf Åkerman (1931) dealt with various aspects of the causes of unemployment. Only a fraction of the material produced by the

Committee was published. In total, 102 memoranda were completed in the period before the publication of the first report. Some of these, however, were preparations for the second report, which was to deal with measures to reduce "permanent" unemployment.

The first report had lost some of its immediate interest when it was published. The labor market situation had deteriorated drastically in 1931. The report was concerned with unemployment in a period of prosperity, but the public debate now dealt with unemployment on a higher level and of a different character. The depression had reached Sweden. The first report (dated June 11, 1931) and also the preparations for the next report originated while Sweden was still on a gold standard. However, Sweden left the gold standard on September 27, 1931, and the Swedish krona was substantially depreciated. As a consequence the number of economic policy measures available against unemployment increased.

Work on the second report—on measures to prevent unemployment—was begun long before the publication of the first. Bagge presented an outline of the plan of the second report as early as 1929 and a proposal for special studies for "book two" in October the same year (Ohlin's study on tariffs was included in that proposal). The outline of the second report as well as the plan for special studies was revised on several occasions.

The first report, however, dealt with the causes of noncyclical unemployment. Now studies on the causes of cyclical unemployment were demanded. The further work of the Committee was therefore devoted both to the study of business cycle theory and the effects of measures against "permanent" as well as cyclical unemployment. Prior to the completion of the second report, several new studies were initiated by the Committee, among these the four later well-known supplements to the final report written by Dag Hammarskjöld (1933a), Alf Johansson (1934), Gunnar Myrdal (1934), and Bertil Ohlin (1934). In this period approximately 35 unpublished memoranda were also prepared.

The second and final report was published in 1935 (SOU 1935:6). Like the first one, this report was written in a cautious manner. As in the case of the first report, it was superseded by political and economic developments. The political debate and the declared policy were both more interventionist than the report. Nevertheless, the Committee was very influential in a more indirect way. Many economists and politicians took part in its work. It initiated research on monetary and fiscal theory among economists. At the same time as they wrote memoranda and supplements for the Committee, they published books and articles in journals and newspapers on the same issues (e.g., see Wadensjö 1991). In this way the Committee on Unemployment affected the theoretical development of macroeconomics and economic policy in Sweden.

The documents of the Committee on Unemployment reveal that three persons were the main authors of the second report, namely the secretary of the committee, Dag Hammarskjöld, the chairman, Gunnar Huss, and Gösta Bagge. Hammarskjöld wrote the main theoretical parts of the report and Bagge the chapter on public works.

Bertil Ohlin's Reports for the Committee on Unemployment

When the Unemployment Committee of 1926 proposed the founding of a new Committee on the Causes of Unemployment in February 1927, Ohlin wrote an article strongly supporting the proposal in the newspaper *Stockholms-Tidningen* (Ohlin 1927). Two years later he himself was commissioned to write a report for the Committee. Through Bagge's initiative, Bertil Ohlin was recruited for a study of the effects of tariffs on unemployment in April 1929. According to a letter to the Committee dated March 4, 1929, he thought it would take 2 to 3 months and that the report should be 60 to 80 pages long.

He delivered a 76-page memorandum in January 1930, dealing with the effects of both tariffs and public works (Ohlin 1930). The memorandum is sceptical of tariffs and public works as measures against noncyclical unemployment but in favor of them as measures against cyclical unemployment. Ohlin's study on tariffs (and public works) was initially to be published as a supplement to the first report, but instead, the assignment was expanded to include monetary policy.

Ohlin submitted a memorandum on monetary policy and unemployment in April 1931 (Ohlin 1931). The study gradually expanded and eventually resulted in the well-known *Monetary Policy, Public Works, Subsidies, and Tariff Policy as Remedies for Unemployment* (Ohlin 1934). Between the two memoranda from 1930 and 1931 and the published version of the supplement in 1934, Ohlin wrote a number of other memoranda. One of these is the preliminary version of the theoretical part of the supplement, which appeared in *Ekonomisk Tidskrift* in a revised version, and has previously been commented on

Table 15.1
Ohlin's memoranda and his supplement to the Committee on Unemployment

1. *Tullar som medel mot arbetslöshet* (Tariffs as a remedy for unemployment), 76 pages, January 13, 1930.
2. *PM rörande penningpolitiska åtgärder mot arbetslöshet* (Memorandum on monetary policy to prevent unemployment), 12 pages, April 16, 1931.
3. *PM rörande den konjunkturpolitiska diskussionen med särskild hänsyn till kostnadssänknings- och konsumtioninskränkningsteorin* (Memorandum on the debate on business cycle theory with special regard to cost-reduction and consumption-reduction theories), 50 pages, December 21, 1932.
4. *PM rörande penningpolitik och arbetslöshet* (Memorandum on monetary policy and unemployment), 13 pages, no date (1932).
5. *Till penningteorins centralproblem* (On the central problem of monetary theory), 49 pages, no date (1932).
6. *Penningpolitik, offentliga arbeten, subventioner och tullar som medel mot arbetslöshet* (Monetary policy, public works, subsidies and tariff policy as remedies for unemployment), Supplement 7 to the Reports of the Committee. 176 pages, SOU 1934:12.

by Otto Steiger.[4] There is also a short memorandum (13 pages) on norms for monetary policy and a memorandum containing a long, critical presentation of the Austrian business cycle school, to which I will return later. These memoranda and various versions of the supplement make it easier to date Ohlin's theoretical development. The supplement contains much of the material from the memoranda but many ideas are only found in the memoranda and not in the supplement. Table 15.1 lists Ohlin's contributions to the Committee.

The Founding of the Stockholm School

Two interrelated issues in the debate are when the Stockholm School was first considered a school, and the relationship between the Stockholm School and British economists.

A memorandum written in the fall of 1932 is of interest in this context.[5] At a conference held earlier that year, Ohlin had debated monetary policy and theory with Johan Åkerman, whose business cycle theory was close to that of the Austrians. This was one of several exchanges on business cycle theory between Ohlin and Åkerman.[6] After that debate Ohlin wrote a 50-page critical analysis of what he called the Vienna School for the Committee on Unemployment.

Ohlin argued that it was possible to divide business cycle theorists into two main groups:

[One English] represented by authors such as Keynes, Robertson, and Hawtrey. Most American and Scandinavian economists largely adopt the same line. In decided opposition to this group of economists, who recommend price increases and public works, there are a few French economists and the so-called Vienna School, which has lately also won followers in London. This school includes Mieses [sic], Hayek, Haberler, Strigl, Robbins, Benham, and probably also Gregory. (Ohlin 1932a:2)

Ohlin included also Johan Åkerman in this Vienna School.[7] He emphasized that it was important that the Committee take a stand on which theoretical school they would adopt:

Since the memoranda, prepared by Myrdal, Johansson, Hammarskjöld, and myself, will be closely associated with [the Anglo-Saxon School], it appears to be of some importance that in its assessment of the views presented in these memoranda, the Committee should also have access to an account of the opposite point of view. If the Committee should concur with [the Vienna School], it follows that all these memoranda cannot provide a basis for the Committee's standpoint in public works, wage policy, monetary policy, and fiscal policy. I will give an account [of the Vienna School] below. (Ohlin 1932a:3)

It is evident that Ohlin meant that the authors of the four supplements had the same basic theoretical view and belonged to the same theoretical school. However, Ohlin's colleagues in the Stockholm School were not necessarily of the same opinion.

In a letter to Huss of January 10, 1933, Ohlin complained about Bagge and Hammarskjöld's critical views of his memorandum. Ohlin mentioned two possible responses, either an enlargement of the treatment of the two schools to 500–600 pages or a reduction. He followed the second line. Part of the discussion on the two schools, however, was published in *Weltwirtschaftliches Archiv* (Ohlin 1932e). In his letter to Huss, Ohlin also stresses that an article published in *Index* (Ohlin 1932) is a first version of part of his supplement. The article is a summary of "The Newmarch Lectures" that Ohlin gave at London University in May 1932.

It is also evident that in 1932 Ohlin did not see the Stockholm economists and Keynes as two separate schools. On the contrary, he stressed that the Swedish economists (with the exception of Johan Åkerman) belonged to the same tradition as most British economists.

Minimization of Unemployment as the Norm for Stabilization Policy

Price stabilization was Knut Wicksell's norm for monetary policy first presented at the turn of the century. Leading Swedish economists—Cassel, Davidson, and Lindahl—also shared this view in the 1930's (Jonung 1979). Ohlin, however, did not adopt price stabilization as the norm for monetary policy in his analysis. In an early document, probably written in 1932, he declared that "the norm for monetary policy, on which the following study is based, is another, that is, the minimization of unemployment" (Ohlin 1932b:2). He stressed that it is not possible to eliminate all unemployment. Normal (frictional) and seasonal unemployment are mentioned as the two exceptions. Ohlin suggested that in practice "minimization of unemployment" is equivalent to maximization of production. This discussion of the choice of norm for monetary policy is not included in his supplement to the Committee, however.

The Supplement

The supplement consists of three different parts. The first, a theoretical analysis, is made up of three chapters. Its first chapter presents the foundations of monetary theory. The second chapter is an analysis of the processes leading to economic expansion and/or contraction, and the third chapter is an analysis of the factors that might influence an economy in the state of depression (the initial situation is an international depression that has lasted one year and an economy with underutilized capacity). In the second part, various policy measures are analyzed and proposed: monetary policy, public works, subsidies of private firms, and tariffs. In the third part, policies against unemployment caused by structural changes are analyzed.

Ohlin's supplement to the second report has been praised. However, within the Committee, this study was controversial. As already pointed out, Ohlin started his work on the effects of tariffs and public works on unemployment as early as 1929. His study was gradually extended but also delayed. In the late spring of 1933 he presented the first full-length version of his book to the Committee and received a very critical 16-page examination in return (dated August

16, 1933). Huss signed the critical assessment, but it was quite obvious that it had been written by Hammarskjöld (Hammarskjöld 1933b). Besides the criticism of the concepts in the theoretical part of the study, which Ohlin mentions in his memoirs, the detailed examination contained many other critical remarks. The criticism was divided into six general admonitions (*allmänna erinringar*) and nine special problems (*särskilda spörsmål*).

The six admonitions were (1) some parts of the study are too elementary and not always consistent, (2) some parts are repetitions of what was contained in the first report of the Committee, (3) some parts are mainly statements of political views, (4) some chapters are too short to be readable, (5) some statements are simply common knowledge, and (6) in some cases the discussion is too general and should be more specific. Examples were given under each heading. The nine special problems were mainly comments regarding the scientific analysis.

The tone of the examination was negative, especially toward Ohlin's analysis of the expansionary effects of public works. In this part, Ohlin described the multiplier effect of public works, which was labeled as unrealistic. Ohlin was also criticized for drawing his own political conclusions from his analysis (a privilege open to the Committee, rather than to the writers of supplements) and dealing with material that was the subject of other reports.

Ohlin did not respond to the criticism until December 1934. He did so indirectly by way of a letter to Lindahl (December 7, 1934; KB), with copies to members of the Economic Club including Hammarskjöld.[8] Hammarskjöld responded to the criticism in a letter of December 22, 1934 (Committee on Unemployment, National Archives). The response is in the form of an official letter from Hammarskjöld as the secretary of the Committee and registered as a letter sent from the Committee. The main content of the letter is that Hammarskjöld stands firm behind the criticism. In the copy of the letter in the Ohlin archives, there is an addition in handwriting by Hammarskjöld. He refers to a telephone conversation that had taken place after the letter was written but before it was sent and continues by praising Ohlin as an economist. "Despite our differences, and despite my remaining critical, of all leading economists in this country, it is with your method of observing and approaching a problem that I agree most. These abilities are also reflections of your personal traits, and you have my sincere admiration."

Ohlin was not placated and answered by sending a letter to the Committee (January 25, 1935; Committee on Unemployment, National Archives). In that letter he stated that he did not accept the arguments of the criticism and emphasized that his terminology differed from that of the secretary of the Committee [Hammarskjöld] and also from that of Keynes.

This criticism explains why a great deal of the material in the memoranda was not included in the published version of Ohlin's book. The galley proofs of the Supplement in the Committee's file in the National Archives are dated November 27, 1933, November 29, 1933, December 2, 1933, January 24, 1934, and January 29, 1934. Many changes were made, compared to the earlier version.[9] This version was also criticized.

It is not possible to follow the discussion in the correspondence, although there are some indications of the art and the tone of the criticism. In the copy of the galley proofs delivered from the Committee to the National Archives there are quite a few comments in the margins,[10] some of which are trivial such as indicating misspellings while others show relations to be tense. Especially critical are the comments against the analysis of the capital market based on Wicksell and his theory of the natural rate of interest. A suitable translation is not easily found for the exclamations in the margin (Fy f-n, Verkligen! sic! Å.H.G. [Å Herre Gud], *Polemik*! Klent). But the wording indicates that the relations between Ohlin and the Committee were not the best at that time. It is not possible to say who has written the comments. A comparison of the galley proofs and the final text shows that there are many changes, some of which have quite likely been initiated by Ohlin himself, some by the criticism of Hammarskjöld, Huss, or others. The multiplier effect is changed but is still more or less present. Ohlin calculated the first three rounds of the multiplier effect of public works.

Conclusions

The Committee on Unemployment engaged several economists, especially from the younger generation. In this way, it contributed to the interest taken by numerous Swedish economists in monetary and fiscal theory and policy. In supplements and especially in memoranda, the authors were able to write relatively freely. On the other hand, they had to be prepared to meet harsh criticism, and the Committee's own two reports were cautious products characterized by compromise.

From the memoranda and earlier versions of the supplements, it is possible to more accurately date the development of Ohlin's ideas and thereby the development of the ideas of the Stockholm School. The memoranda show that Ohlin was in favor of expansionist measures (public works, tariffs) as early as 1930. In practice, he used the multiplier to analyze the effects of public works in 1933. As early as 1932 he also based his analysis of economic policy on the norm of minimization of unemployment.

The Committee also fostered lasting conflict. Relations between Ohlin and Hammarskjöld never became friendly again. This conflict had also second-round effects. When Bagge and Ohlin clashed later in 1940 for various reasons, part of Ohlin's criticism against Bagge was that he did not defend him against Hammarskjöld's attacks.[11] In a letter to Bagge of March 23, 1940, Ohlin wrote as follows:

> PS. In the interests of candor in this "resolving of our differences," I should probably inform you that I am still quite surprised that a scientist—who possesses a sense of honor as I know you do—can
>
> 1. allow a committee, on which you serve as an expert, to nullify a scientific work on 18 counts,
> 2. try to show that 16 or 17 of these are due to an interpretation other than that which the author has intended,
> 3. state that the author's terminology is probably unusable (or something to that effect),
> 4. maintain that that terminology—or similar of the same kind—is used by a number of economists (Keynes, etc.) in a way that no one has claimed to be other than productive,
>
> and then omit giving the said author redress for *unjustifiable criticism*.
>
> I have long been of the view that in this matter, it is best to "call it quits and go on," considering that you have been so busy with important work—since the obvious invalidity of the criticism of my terminology is apparent to anyone who has read Keynes's *General Theory*. Perhaps a moment's reflection on your own behavior in this matter would be appropriate. It is, despite its insignificance, also a "matter of honor!"

Ohlin wrote a critical three-article review of the Second Report of the Committee on Unemployment in *Stockholms-Tidningen* (Ohlin 1935, 1935a, 1935b). In the first of the articles, Ohlin criticized the Committee for not taking into account that public works could lead to an expansion of private production. The Committee had not "utilized the new ground gained by economic science."

Dag Hammarskjöld, for his part, gave Ingvar Svennilson advice and comments when Svennilson wrote a five-article overview of the Report for LO's journal *Fackföreningsrörelsen* (Svennilson 1935).[12]

Acknowledgments

I would like to thank Helena Orrje for her assistance in finding the documents on which this study relies in various archives and Jean Parr for translating the quotations from Ohlin's letters.

Notes

1. See Wadensjö (1991).

2. Ohlin published extensively already from 1919. Like several other Swedish economists, he did not only write scientific papers but also contributed an impressive number of articles to newspapers. A recent bibliography of his articles in Scandinavian newspapers and journals contains no less than 2,315 articles. See Carlson, Orrje, and Wadensjö (2000). Since the publication of this bibliography, 68 additional articles have been found.

3. See the letter from Bagge to Ohlin dated February 15, 1929 (Ohlin Archives, National Archives).

4. See Ohlin (no date; 1932c), (1933), and (1978). Steiger's comments and analysis of the development of Ohlin's article are found in Steiger (1971) and (1978).

5. A letter from Ohlin to Huss of January 10, 1933 (Committee on Unemployment; National Archives) makes it possible to date the Memorandum to December 21, 1932.

6. See *Industriförbundets meddelanden* (1932) and also Ohlin (1932d) and Åkerman (1932a, 1932b).

7. Åkerman's conclusions are summarised in Åkerman (1933). Johan Åkerman wrote a memorandum for the committee; see Åkerman (1929). It was intended as a supplement to the first report from the committee but was not accepted. Bagge was very critical of Åkerman's memorandum; see, for example, his letter to Ohlin of August 3, 1929 (Ohlin Archives, National Archives).

8. It was made in the form of comments on a paper that Erik Lindahl had presented at the Political Economy Club. The paper by Lindahl was later published as Lindahl (1935).

9. The title was also changed from "Monetary Policy, Tariffs, and Public Works" in the galley proof of November to "Monetary Policy, Public Works, Subsidies, and Tariff Policy as Remedies for Unemployment."

10. In the Ohlin Archives, there is a copy of most pages (86 of 126) of the same galley proofs. The comments in this version of the galley proofs, which is signed Lundberg on the first page, are friendlier and constructive. Lundberg together with Bagge, Hammarskjöld, Lindahl, Myrdal, and Palander are thanked for their comments on

earlier versions of the text. In the Ohlin Archives there is also a copy of later galley proofs of the first chapter. On the first page it is stated that it is Svennilson's copy. It only contains a few minor comments.

11. See letters from Ohlin to Bagge March 20, 1940, and March 27, 1940 (National Archives). See also Bagge's letter to Ohlin of March 23, 1940. In that letter Bagge strongly criticized Ohlin for his commitment to *Stockholms-Tidningen*.

12. See the letter from Svennilson to Hammarskjöld of February 15, 1935 (Committee on Unemployment, National Archives).

References

Åkerman, Gustaf. 1931. *Om den industriella rationaliseringen och dess verkningar* (Industrial rationalization and its effects). Bilaga 3 till Arbetslöshetsutredningens betänkande I. *SOU* 1931:42.

Åkerman, Johan. 1929. De ekonomiska konjunkturerna i Sverige efter kriget (Business cycles in Sweden in the postwar period). Arbetslöshetsutredningens PM nr 78, February 1.

Åkerman, Johan. 1932a. Prisstegringens problem (The problem of the rise in prices). *Det ekonomiska läget* 3:1–34.

Åkerman, Johan. 1932b. Prisstegringens problem. Svar till prof. Bertil Ohlin (The problem of the rise in prices. A reply to Professor Bertil Ohlin). *Det ekonomiska läget* (4):33–50.

Åkerman, Johan. 1933. Saving in the depression. In *Economic Essays in Honour of Gustav Cassel*. London: Allen and Unwin.

Bagge, Gösta. 1928. PM angående arbetslöshetsproblemet ur teoretiska synpunkter (Memorandum on theoretical aspects of the unemployment problem). Arbetslöshetsutredningen PM nr 60.

Bagge, Gösta. 1931. *Orsaker till arbetslöshet* (Causes of unemployment). Arbetslöshetsutredningensbetänkande I, Bilagor, vol. 1. *SOU* 1931:21.

Carlson, Benny, Orrje, Helena, and Wadensjö, Eskil. 2000. *Ohlins artiklar. Register över Bertil Ohlins artiklar i skandinaviska tidningar och tidskrifter 1919–1979*. Swedish Institute for Social Research, Stockholm University.

"Direktiv för arbetslöshetsutredningen" (Terms of reference for the Committee on Unemployment). *Post- och inrikestidningar*, March 12.

Hammarskjöld, Dag. 1933a. *Konjunkturspridningen. En teoretisk och historisk undersökning* (Business cycles: A theoretical and historical study). Bilaga 4 till Arbetslöshetsutredningens betänkanden. *SOU* 1933:29.

Hammarskjöld, Dag. 1933b. PM till professor Ohlins bilaga (Memorandum to Professor Ohlin's supplement). Arbetslöshetsutredningen, August 16.

Huss, Gunnar. 1931. PM angående arbetsmarknaden och de faktorer som bestämma dess utveckling (Memorandum on the labor market and factors determining its development). Arbetslöshetsutredningens betänkande I, Bilagor, vol. 1. *SOU* 1931:21.

Industriförbundets Meddelanden. 1932. Sveriges industri och världskrisen. *Diskussion vid Sveriges Industriförbundets årsmöte den 19 april 1932* (Swedish industry and the world economic crisis. Proceedings of annual meeting of the Federation of Swedish Industries), vol. 2, pp. 66–101. Among other participants were Bertil Ohlin and Johan Åkerman.

Johansson, Alf. 1934. *Löneutvecklingen och arbetslösheten* (Wage formation and unemployment). Bilaga 6 till Arbetslöshetsutredningens betänkanden. *SOU* 1934:2.

Jonung, Lars. 1979. Knut Wicksell's norm of price stabilization and Swedish monetary policy in the 1930s. *Journal of Monetary Economics* 5:459–96.

Lindahl, Erik. 1935. Arbetslöshet och finanspolitik (Unemployment and fiscal policy). *Ekonomisk Tidskrift* 37:1–36.

Myrdal, Gunnar. 1934. *Finanspolitikens ekonomiska verkningar* (The economic effects of fiscal policy). Bilaga 5 till Arbetslöshetsutredningens betänkanden. *SOU* 1934:1.

Ohlin, Bertil. 1927. Bör arbetslöshetens orsaker undersökas? (Should the Causes of Unemployment be Investigated?). *Stockholms-Tidningen*, February 27.

Ohlin, Bertil. 1930. Tullar som medel mot arbetslöshet (Tariffs as a remedy for unemployment). Arbetslöshetsutredningens PM nr 93, January 13.

Ohlin, Bertil. 1931. PM rörande penningpolitiska åtgärder mot arbetslöshet (Memorandum on monetary policy to prevent unemployment). Arbetslöshetsutredningens PM nr 101.

Ohlin, Bertil. 1932. Nu eller aldrig (Now or never). *Index* 7:123–53.

Ohlin, Bertil. 1932a. PM rörande den konjunkturpolitiska diskussionen med särskild hänsyn till kostnadssänknings- och konsumtionsinskränkningsteorin (Memorandum on the debate on business cycle theory with special regard to the cost reduction or consumption reduction theory). Bilaga 4b till Betänkande II. Arbetslöshetsutredningen, December 21.

Ohlin, Bertil. [no date] 1932b. PM rörande penningpolitik och arbetslöshet (Memorandum on monetary policy and unemployment). Arbetslöshetsutredningen.

Ohlin, Bertil. [no date] 1932c. Till penningteorins centralproblem (On the central problem of monetary theory). PM, Arbetslöshetsutredningen.

Ohlin, Bertil. 1932d. Prisstegringens problem. Replik till fil. dr. Johan Åkerman (The problem of the rise of prices. Rejoinder to Dr. J. Åkerman). *Det Ekonomiska Läget*, no. 4.

Ohlin, Bertil. 1932e. Ungelöste Probleme der gegenwärtigen Krisis. *Weltwirtschaftliches Archiv* 36(2):1–23.

Ohlin, Bertil. 1933. Till frågan om penningteorins uppläggning (translated as Ohlin 1978). *Ekonomisk Tidskrift* 35:45–81.

Ohlin, Bertil. 1934. *Penningpolitik, offentliga arbeten, subventioner och tullar som medel mot arbetslöshet* (Monetary Policy, Public Works, Subsidies, and Tariff Policy as Remedies for Unemployment). Bilaga 7 till Arbetslöshetsutredningens betänkanden. *SOU* 1934:12.

Ohlin, Bertil. 1935. Hur arbetslöshet botas och förebyggas (How unemployment is remedied and prevented). *Stockholms-Tidningen*, March 13.

Ohlin, Bertil. 1935a. Socialdemokratisk arbetslöshetspolitik (Social democratic unemployment policy). *Stockholms-Tidningen*, March 16.

Ohlin, Bertil. 1935b. Sveriges sysselsättningsproblem (Sweden's unemployment problem). *Stockholms-Tidningen*, March 19.

Ohlin, Bertil. 1978. On the formulation of monetary theory. *History of Political Economy* 10:353–88.

Sociala Meddelanden. 1927. Utredning om arbetslöshetens karaktär och orsaker (Committee on the Characteristics and Causes of Unemployment), no. 3.

SOU 1931:20. Arbetslöshetsutredningens betänkande I. *Arbetslöshetens omfattning, karaktär och orsaker* (The extent, character, and causes of unemployment).

SOU 1935:6. Arbetslöshetsutredningens betänkande II. *Åtgärder mot arbetslöshet* (Policies for dealing with unemployment).

Steiger, Otto. 1971. *Studier zur Entstehung der Neuen Wirtschaftslehre in Schweden*. Berlin: Duncker and Humblot.

Steiger, Otto. 1978. Substantive changes in the final version of Ohlin's 1933 paper. *History of Political Economy* 10:389–97.

Svennilson, Ingvar. 1935. Den stora arbetslöshetsutredningen (The great Committee on Unemployment). *Fackföreningsrörelsen* 15:247–51, 311–18, 343–50, 396–401.

Wadensjö, Eskil. 1991. The Committee on Unemployment and the Stockholm School. In Lars Jonung, ed., *The Stockholm School of Economics Revisited*. Cambridge: Cambridge University Press.

IV The Heckscher-Ohlin Theory of Trade

16 Heckscher-Ohlin Trade Models for the New Century

Ronald W. Jones

A hallmark of economic models in the pure theory of international trade is their long half-life. This is certainly true of the Ricardian trade model, dating back to his 1817 Principles, and not just because of its illustration of the doctrine of comparative advantage. The simplicity of having outputs linked directly to inputs of a single composite productive factor (labor in David Ricardo's treatment) has encouraged the use of the Ricardian framework in analyzing questions in which the international distribution of income instead of the internal distribution of income is the focus, such as the consequences of changes in technology in a setting comprising many countries and commodities. So also the pioneering work of Eli Heckscher (1919) and Bertil Ohlin (1924, 1933) has spawned literally hundreds of articles and treatises that build upon their emphasis on the asymmetries exhibited both by countries in their endowments of productive factors and by commodities in the intensities with which these productive factors are utilized. If the Ricardian model serves as an appropriate analogy, Heckscher-Ohlin models of trade, starting scarcely a hundred years later, can be expected to survive and confirm their usefulness well into the new century.

In the title of this chapter, as well as in the preceding sentence, note the plural of the noun, models. The basic set of ideas spelled out by Heckscher and Ohlin is sufficiently rich to support a variety of settings in which the roles of relative factor endowments and relative factor intensities are paramount in describing the rationale for international trade and the consequences of such trade on the domestic economies. The most familiar of these is the two-factor, two-commodity, two-country case explored by Paul Samuelson, Abba Lerner, and followers, and now found in any textbook on international economics. This core version was explicitly treated neither by Heckscher nor Ohlin, but its development was essential in understanding the richness and subtleties of trade relationships in more complex settings. I leave to Paul Krugman in a later chapter to detail Ohlin's concern with the importance of increasing returns to scale and to Donald Davis a discussion of the empirical tests that have served to cast doubts on the relevance of the simple Heckscher-Ohlin model since the publication of Wassily Leontief's surprising paper in 1953. Thus I focus only on that part of the Ohlin vision that puts factor endowments and factor intensities at center stage.

The 2 × 2 × 2 Heckscher-Ohlin Core

Although it would be tedious to go through the details of the popular version of Heckscher-Ohlin that assumes that two countries are capable of producing the same pair of commodities with two inputs, each of the same quality in the two countries and utilizing the identical technology, a few words are appropriate. First, there are even other assumptions typically made, such as that taste patterns are identical between countries, production functions are nonjoint and exhibit constant returns to scale (with no factor intensity reversals), and perfectly competitive conditions characterize commodity markets. There are no natural transport costs so that in free trade the prices of commodities are the same in both countries (although commercial policy can introduce wedges), but factor markets are separate and factor quantities supplied completely inelastic. Wilfred Ethier (1974) has assembled the various parts of the 2 × 2 × 2 results into four core propositions:

1. The Heckscher-Ohlin theorem. The relatively capital abundant country exports the relatively capital-intensive commodity.

2. The factor-price equalization theorem. Free trade in commodities brings about an equalization of factor prices between countries even though such factors are not mobile in the world market (see Samuelson 1948, 1949).

3. The Stolper-Samuelson theorem. An increase in the relative price of the labor-intensive commodity, for example, as brought about by a tariff, unambiguously causes the real wage to increase (see Stolper and Samuelson 1941).

4. The Rybczynski theorem. If commodity prices are constant, an increase in the endowment of one factor causes an actual contraction in the commodity intensive in its use of the other factor (see Rybczynski 1955).

Even with the backing of the extensive set of assumptions outlined above, not all of these propositions hold of necessity. Much depends on the extent to which the composition of factor endowments differs between countries. The reason is that there is a crucial distinction between two divergent strands of Heckscher-Ohlin theory. The Heckscher-Ohlin theorem, which served as the focus for Ohlin's work, states that factor endowment differences are important in explaining trade patterns. Therefore the greater is that difference, the more likely is the relatively capital-abundant country to export its capital-intensive commodity. By contrast, the factor-price equalization theorem states that factor-endowment differences are *not* important, in the sense that factor prices can be brought to equality as a consequence of free trade in commodities despite the difference in endowment proportions. However, if endowments are sufficiently different, at least one country must specialize, and the factor-price equalization theorem no longer holds—but the Heckscher-Ohlin theorem must in such a case be valid. At the other extreme suppose that the capital-abundant country exports the labor-intensive commodity because although tastes are equivalent, they are not homothetic, and higher per-capita incomes in the capital-abundant country spill over primarily to greater local demand for the capital-intensive commodity. In such a case the factor-price equalization result must hold because both countries must be incompletely specialized (Minabe 1966). I suggest that some of the difficulty that students of trade theory have with the Heckscher-Ohlin model, even in its core form, stems from the fact that the H-O theorem must hold if the factor-price equalization result does not, and if the H-O theorem is invalidated by demand conditions, factor prices must be equalized. Of course the more neutral result that is discussed in most textbook treatment also may hold: the capital abundant country exports the capital-intensive commodity and free trade in goods equalizes factor prices.

The set of assumptions stated above can be extended in such a manner that all four propositions listed by Ethier are valid. Demand factors are neutralized if tastes are also assumed to be homothetic.

The other required assumption is that neither country is completely specialized. However, such an assumption is fundamentally different from the others because the question of specialization is an endogenous one, dependent in large part on the differences in factor endowments, and these differences provide the basic key to Heckscher-Ohlin theory.

More Relaxed 2 × 2 × 2 Heckscher-Ohlin Models

As I will argue throughout, one of the real strengths of Heckscher-Ohlin models is that the strict set of assumptions on which the core propositions are based can be relaxed in a number of ways that serve to enrich the model. And this can be done without losing the focus provided by the scenario in which production requires inputs in different proportions from one commodity to the other and countries differ in their factor endowments. One of the important ways to relax the model is in terms of dimensionality—allowing more than two factors of production, two commodities, and two countries. But I hold off on this in order briefly to survey a few other assumptions that can be modified while retaining small dimensionality.

Different Technologies

The rationale for the assumption adopted by Heckscher and Ohlin that countries share the same technology is that it, along with other assumptions, makes it possible to isolate the important role of factor endowment differences. Ohlin, in particular, was anxious to cast his model in opposition to the classical Ricardian view wherein trade was the result of countries possessing different technologies. As emphasized in the recent book by Andrea Maneschi (1998), this assumption served to preclude Ohlin from describing the case that highlights the significance of the doctrine of comparative advantage, namely that one country has an absolute advantage in both commodities and yet imports one of them. And the assertion that countries share the same technology includes not only a sharing of blueprints and similarity in "climate" but implicitly an assumption that factors of production, such as labor, possess the same level of skills and education from country to country. (Also implicit is an assumption that "history" does not matter, since this must be admitted to differ from place to place.)

How important is the assumption of identical technologies? For the Heckscher-Ohlin theorem, relaxation of this assumption implies that factor endowment differences still influence trade patterns in the manner suggested by the theorem. However, they no longer are the only influence, since differences in technology and factor skills have a role to play as well. As for the factor-price equalization result, this is a razor's-edge kind of theorem, and not surprisingly will be invalidated by any difference in technology. However, I would argue that a variation of this theorem is nonetheless valid: it states that a country's internal distribution of income is affected by its production pattern of traded commodities, and that if it produces a sufficient array of such commodities (at least as many as the number of factors), the country's internal factor prices are completely determined by its technology and the constellation of world prices of traded goods. Such a strong degree of dependence might be considered too heavy a cost to pay to obtain the gains from free trade (see Jones 1995). As for the Stolper-Samuelson theorem and Rybczynski theorem, neither of them depends on an assumption of technological equivalence. Indeed, although developed in the context of trade issues, each result is independent of trade patterns or foreign technology.

Factor-Intensity Reversals

Technology may not exhibit the property that one of the commodities is relatively capital-intensive at all sets of factor prices. The possibility that the intensity ranking could be reversed led to a challenge to the Heckscher-Ohlin theorem. Suppose that food in one country is capital-intensive and in the other is labor-intensive, although production functions are the same between countries. Whatever the pattern of trade, both countries would be exporting goods that are capital-intensive, on the one hand, or labor-intensive, on the other. This would make it impossible to infer the relative factor abundance of countries from the intensity of exports (Jones 1956). The damage such a possibility has for Heckscher-Ohlin theory is limited. For example, regardless of the trade pattern, the relatively capital-abundant country exports a commodity that is produced by more capital-intensive techniques than utilized by the other country's exports. Although it is fashionable in recent decades to dismiss concerns about factor-intensity reversals, there is a similar phenomenon that arises very generally in the case where more than two commodities are producible. I discuss this case below.

Nonjointness of Production

It is easy to slip into the habit of assuming that production processes always combine an array of inputs to produce a single output. Instead, they may yield more than one output (like raising sheep to obtain mutton and wool or the multiple products that emerge in the petroleum industry). Joint production is capable of doing significant damage to the Stolper-Samuelson and Rybczynski theorems, depending on a comparison of the degree to which output proportions differ as compared with input proportions (see Chang, Ethier, and Kemp 1980; Samuelson 1992; Jones 1992). However, the factor-price equalization result need not be disturbed, while the Heckscher-Ohlin theorem can be re-interpreted to link a country's relative factor endowments to the location of productive activities instead of the details of commodity trade.

Tastes

As already suggested, differences in tastes between countries, or nonhomotheticity even when taste patterns are assumed identical, open up the possibility that demand differences can overwhelm supply differences in determining trade patterns. In the development of Heckscher-Ohlin theory this potential difficulty was often resolved by stating factor endowment rankings in terms of pre-trade factor prices instead of physical factor endowments. Because factor prices already consolidate information about demand, a physically capital-abundant country with a strong taste bias in favor of the capital-intensive commodity will, in terms of pre-trade factor prices, be deemed a labor-abundant (low-wage) economy, exporting labor-intensive products.

Some decades ago Staffan Burenstam Linder (1961) pointed out that similarity in taste patterns could promote trade. Countries that have achieved comparable levels of real income may have tastes biased toward similar commodities, different from tastes found in much poorer or richer countries. And local production may have adjusted to these taste patterns so that, assuming commodities are somewhat differentiated, each such country has items to export that will be demanded by residents in other countries with similar standards of living. This work antedated and anticipated some of the writing in the "new trade theory."

Inelastic and Immobile Factor Supplies

There is no doubt that the simple $2 \times 2 \times 2$ version of Heckscher-Ohlin is made more simple by postulating that factor supplies are neither capable of moving between countries nor of adjusting to changes in factor prices. Relaxing these assumptions allows for a richer set of models that still can be labeled Heckscher-Ohlin. The recent published Ohlin lectures by Ronald Findlay (1995) establishes how capital accumulation, education of work forces, development of land and raw materials, and movement of factors among countries all can be analyzed within a framework that maintains that different commodities require different input proportions. Perhaps in the very long run all countries will look the same in terms of relative factor availabilities, but short of that, supply differences can prevail in a more relaxed scenario in which some are endogenous in the growth process. Furthermore much of the received literature on trade with some degree of factor mobility has explicitly ruled out the strong assumption that countries share the same technology (e.g., Kemp 1966; Jones 1967, 2000).

Higher-Dimensional Heckscher-Ohlin Models

To many trade economists the literature on Heckscher-Ohlin models in higher dimensions conjures up fancy restrictions on technology in order to get strong versions of Stolper-Samuelson or (the dual) Rybczynski types of results. This view, I would argue, does great disservice to the power of Heckscher-Ohlin thinking, especially in a world of many commodities and many countries. I leave until later a discussion of the many-factor extensions, so I will continue to assume that each country has endowments of two factors, called capital and labor or, in some circumstances, skilled labor and unskilled labor.

Consider the case of a single country embedded in a world economy consisting of many other countries, some of them sharing the same technology, others utilizing different technologies or having factors with different skills. One common exercise is to consider a preexisting world equilibrium that is then disturbed by the addition of this single economy. If this is a small country, world commodity prices will not be disturbed. If it is a large economy, the entire array of commodity prices can be expected to change. Trade economists are familiar with the techniques whereby changes in world supplies and demands can be analyzed for their impact on commodity markets. Here just assume that this country's impact on world markets has already been taken into account and there exists a set of prices for all traded items. What does such an economy produce and trade? The concept of a Hicksian composite unit-value isoquant proves to be highly useful for the question. Such an isoquant blends a knowledge of the country's own technology and factor skills with the array of commodity prices to yield a convex locus of minimal possible input bundles that will produce one or more commodities with total value of $1 on world markets. If there is enough variety in technologies throughout the world, and a sufficient number of countries, such a locus will be made up of strictly bowed-in sections (indicating complete specialization to a single commodity) as well as linear sections in which a pair of commodities is produced. The actual pattern of production for this economy depends on where the factor endowment ray cuts the Hicksian locus. Perhaps the most fundamental proposition in the whole of international trade theory is immediately revealed: with trade a country can concentrate its resources into a few or only a single commodity and, through exchanges with other countries, consume a large variety of commodities. How many need it produce? If world prices do not correspond with relative technology at home, the answer is no more than the number of factors. (A large country may have flats on the Hicksian isoquant that allow production of several commodities because world prices have adjusted to the technology of this country).

The trade pattern for a country embedded in this world economy with many commodities and countries needs to be expressed slightly differently than it is in the $2 \times 2 \times 2$ core version. A country tends to produce commodities for the world market that require factor proportions roughly similar to those found in the endowment bundle and to import other commodities that have both higher and lower capital–labor ratios than those produced at home. Furthermore a comparison of the capital–labor ratio required in a country's export good and those in the import-competing good (if it produces two commodities and if it indeed does import one of these) gives little information about the country's relative endowment bundle. Because the factor intensities of both produced commodities will be found within the cone of diversification, slight variations of the endowment bundle within that cone can change which of the two commodities produced is exported (or perhaps both are). Therefore in this expanded version of Heckscher-Ohlin the appropriate theorem links patterns of production to factor endowments, with the expectation that most commodities will be imported because they are not produced at home. To get more realistic cases in which the number of goods produced is expanded requires either that there exist natural or contrived barriers to trade (e.g., tariffs) or that the endowment base is richer than suggested by just two homogeneous factors. I return to the latter possibility below.

This multicommodity variant of the Heckscher-Ohlin model has two more important consequences. First, it allows a country that is growing, accumulating capital per unit of the labor force, to alter its production pattern over time. This has been an important feature of the growth experience of many of the Asian developing countries, including Japan, as well as the earlier experience of European countries such as Sweden. What the model outlined above suggests is that such a systematic growth in capital–labor ratios will result in strong heterogeneous behavior at the micro level, with the production of some commodity (in which the country is losing its comparative advantage) falling and with the growth rate of another commodity higher than the average for the whole economy (see Findlay and Jones 2001). Second, consider the situation of two countries trading in such a world and sharing identical technologies but having different factor endowments. If these endowments are very close, these countries might be producing the same two commodities. On the other hand, if endowments are a bit farther apart, they may be producing one commodity in common, and differ in the identity of the other commodity produced. This leads to the different kind of factor-intensity reversal that I referred to above. If the world price of the commonly produced commodity should rise, the real wage would fall in one country and rise in the other. Alternatively, suppose that one country imports the commonly produced commodity from the other and that country has protected the good with a tariff. Then a lowering of the tariff barrier would result in a change in factor prices in both countries in the same direction. Suppose that the two factors are skilled and unskilled labor. A move in the free-trade direction might then cause skilled wages to rise and unskilled wages to fall in both importing and exporting country. Furthermore these two countries need not share exactly the same technology. Although different technologies generally imply a different pattern of production, endowment differences might compensate to bring these patterns closer together so that a pair of such countries might produce a commodity in common, but with a different other commodity produced.

The assumption that there are only two factors of production limits the growth story above to a situation in which a country produces either two commodities for the world market or is completely specialized to one. Increases in capital–labor endowment ratios lead to fluctuations between being in one cone of diversification or being completely specialized en route to the next cone of diversification. With more factors of production somewhat similar remarks can be made. The number of traded goods produced could be as high as the number of productive factors or as low as one, with growth leading to changes in the pattern of production. Ed Leamer (1984) describes in considerable detail alternative paths of growth and development in a three-factor setting. The variety of possible results in even higher-dimensional cases may be staggering, but the principles outlined above nonetheless hold. If there are more commodities that can be produced than the number of factors, international trade allows a country to specialize, perhaps to a great extent, and the Heckscher-Ohlin insight is that its production (and therefore exports) will exhibit factor proportions somewhat similar to its endowment composition, and as the latter changes, so will its patterns of production and trade.

It is true that rather detailed restrictions on technology are required in order to generalize the Stolper-Samuelson or Rybczynski theorems in their strong version. For example, conditions under which a single commodity price increase will raise the real return to one factor and lower that for all others are set out in Jones, Marjit, and Mitra (1993), building on earlier work by Kemp and Wegge (1969), and, for a less restrictive version, by Chipman (1969). A much weaker set of conditions is supplied in Jones (1985) for a result that is, in my opinion, a more robust version of the Stolper-Samuelson theorem. Pick any factor of production and ask what government policy can be used so that the return to that factor is unambiguously raised. Although direct contributions or subsidies would do the trick, ask about the indirect route of affecting commodity prices. What conditions would be required in order that some change in relative commodity prices would raise that factor's real return? Only two conditions are required. First, that there is no joint production, or that if there is it is relatively "weak." Second, that there are sufficient numbers of commodities—at least equal to the number of productive factors. In my view, this result serves to underscore the general message of the Stolper-Samuelson result: the distribution of income among productive factors can be significantly altered by the indirect route of changing relative commodity prices.

Much of the literature on higher-dimensional versions of Heckscher-Ohlin theory has been concentrated on the case where the number of commodities exactly matches the number of factors. A rationale for this interest can be found in the fact that a country need not produce more goods for the world market than it has factors. Furthermore, from a mathematical point of view, the $n \times n$ case leads to a square matrix of distributive factor shares from the competitive profit conditions, and this raises the question of whether commodity prices determine factor prices uniquely (e.g., see Gale and Nikaido 1965; Mas-Colell 1979). And the inverse of this share matrix bears upon the strong version of the Stolper-Samuelson theorem (e.g., see Ethier 1984). However, the huge array of possible comparative statics results in the general $n \times n$ case has done much to dampen the enthusiasm of some for possible generalizations of Heckscher-Ohlin to higher dimensions. Clearly, more structure in production details is required in order to elicit detailed compositional answers to comparative statics questions. Several such structures have been forthcoming in the literature. Gruen and Corden (1970) introduced a special version of the 3×3 model in which one sector of the economy (agriculture) consisted of two activities (wool and grain) that used a pair of productive factors (labor and land) and the other sector consisted of a single activity (textiles) that used labor and a specific factor, capital, used nowhere else. This structure was utilized by Findlay (1993) to discuss international trade in services, and was generalized to the $n \times n$ case by Jones and Marjit (1992). In this generalization a single sector of the economy (the "nugget") consists of two industries and uses a common pair of factors, just as in the 2×2 core Heckscher-Ohlin model. All other industries follow the specific factors model, making common use of a single mobile factor (also used in the nugget) and another factor used only in that industry.

Another structure that proves easy to analyze has been called the "produced mobile factor" model (see Jones and Marjit 1991). Suppose that there exist n sectors in the economy, each using a factor specific to that sector as well as a mobile factor used in all. This is the $(n+1) \times n$ specific-factors model (discussed below). However, suppose that the mobile factor is itself produced in some fashion by all the "specific" factors. This reduces the model to a version of an $n \times n$ Heckscher-Ohlin model. Not only is this version easy to handle, it exhibits the properties associated with the strong versions of Stolper-Samuelson and Rybczynski. Finally, there is the "neighborhood" model introduced by Jones and Kierzkowski (1986) in which factors have extremely limited possibilities of employment (to only two sectors, those in the immediate "neighborhood") and each industry employs only two factors. This model exhibits the feature that a commodity price rise leads roughly half the factors to gain and the other half to lose.

With any of these models it is not difficult to obtain analytical results to detailed comparative statics questions. What all the models have in common is the even matching of numbers of commodities and factors. Although this corresponds to such a match in the $2 \times 2 \times 2$ core model, there is no compelling reason to limit the Heckscher-Ohlin type of reasoning to the even case. As earlier stated, international trade (unless modified by the appropriate set of "scientific" tariffs) generally does not require a country to produce more goods than factors. It is the reverse case, where factors exceed commodities in number, that is of particular interest. And here the specific-factors model, so labeled in early discussions by Haberler (1936) and developed formally by Jones (1971, 1975) and Samuelson (1971), provides an example that is exceedingly easy to analyze. Furthermore it is a model in which the higher-dimensional version retains all the major properties of the more simple three-factor, two-commodity version. In this latter version it is often portrayed as an alternative to the core Heckscher-Ohlin model. However, in my view, it can be thought of as a consistent variant of Heckscher-Ohlin models in which many of the higher-dimensional properties of the specific-factors model are mirrored as well in strong versions of the $n \times n$ Heckscher-Ohlin model. Characteristics of factor intensities and factor abundance carry over, perhaps in extreme form. Thus in every industry it is clear which factor is most intensively used there—it is the specific factor used nowhere else. And the real return to such a factor unambiguously rises if the price of the commodity in which it is used goes up, and the returns to all other specific factors fall. This is Stolper-Samuelson in its strong form. The difference is that the mobile factor has the relative change in its return trapped between relative commodity price changes. This latter phenomenon could easily be shared by a number of productive factors in more general versions of $n \times n$ Heckscher-Ohlin models. Furthermore countries differ in the relative endowments of specific factors, and this strongly influences their trade patterns, precisely as suggested by the Heckscher-Ohlin theorem.

The international trade literature has emphasized two ways in which the specific-factors model can be said to converge to the Heckscher-Ohlin model. In one, it is time that accomplishes the transformation (Neary 1978) by allowing capital goods that are crafted specifically for particular industries to depreciate and be replaced by capital goods used in other industries. In the other, it is trade that removes specificity (Sanyal and Jones 1982). Inputs that can be utilized only by specific sectors may nonetheless be converted to other specific inputs by exchanging them with other countries.

The specific-factors model is suited to the political economy question of the means by which government can reward certain factors of production. If governmental regulations have been devised to restrict entry of a factor to a particular industry (e.g., by licensing provisions), any induced price rises for that industry create greater rents for the specific factor. However, consider the following two alternatives that are illustrated by comparing the core version of the Heckscher-Ohlin model with the simple 3×2 specific factors model. Both industries use capital and labor, and the industry to be favored by a rise in price is capital-intensive. In the first instance, suppose that capital used in the favored industry can keep out entry from any capital used in the other industry. This entry prevention is what creates extra rents for capital in the favored sector. Now suppose that such entry is made possible, converting the specific-factors model into the core Heckscher-Ohlin model. The result is that the return to the previously specific capital used in the favored industry rises even further! Although more capital comes in to compete with the previously specific capital, more labor also enters the favored industry. The end result is a further increase in the labor–capital proportions used in the favored sector. Thus entry-prevention devices might indeed create rents, but there is no guarantee that these rents are greater than might be achieved without regulation.

Challenges to Heckscher-Ohlin Theory

For decades Heckscher-Ohlin models have attracted their naysayers. Already alluded to are criticisms that the core model does not generalize to higher dimensions. In addition the work of Posner (1961) and Vernon (1966) on technology gap theories of trade and the product cycle suggested to some that these were explanations of trade that would replace the Heckscher-Ohlin emphasis on factor endowments and factor proportions. And, of course, there is the challenge posed more recently by "new trade theory," with its emphasis on the prevalence of imperfectly competitive markets and the existence of intraindustry trade.

Of the literature in the 1960s Ray Vernon's scenario of the product cycle perhaps posed the most significant challenge to Heckscher-Ohlin explanations of trade patterns. According to Vernon an advanced country such as the United States possessed a comparative (and absolute) advantage in producing new products requiring new technology. At earlier stages there would exist some uncertainty about what technology to use, but eventually convergence would be obtained on a more simple, unskilled labor-intensive range of techniques. At this point the advanced country would lose its comparative advantage, and production would relocate in less advanced countries. With new products coming on line, an advanced country would continually change its pattern of production, exporting the new products. Does such a view suggest scrapping the Heckscher-Ohlin mode of thinking about trade? Not in my view. Instead, it enriches the Heckscher-Ohlin explanation. If technology is uncertain at early stages of a new product's development, the country that will have a comparative advantage in production will be the country that has relatively ample supplies of skilled labor and heterogeneous capital. That represents the "factor intensity" appropriate at this stage. Indeed, it is now fashionable to treat "technology" as an output in and of itself, requiring relatively heavy use of skilled labor in the input bundle for R&D. As technology develops, new, more unskilled labor-intensive techniques emerge, and this, in standard

Heckscher-Ohlin fashion, calls for the Vernon-predicted change in locale of production (see Jones 1970).

The "new trade theory" was motivated in part by the existence of intraindustry trade. It was thought that Heckscher-Ohlin theory was incapable of explaining such trade patterns, a view that has more recently been challenged by John Chipman (1988, 1992) and Donald Davis (1995). The model popularized by Helpman (1981) and Helpman and Krugman (1985) stipulated an industry in which commodities were horizontally differentiated products and the market was populated by monopolistically competitive producers each operating at a declining part of the average cost curve. When trade was opened up to a group of countries characterized in this fashion, each country would produce a separate subset of the differentiated goods. But these commodities were assumed all to share an identical technology so that within a country all factor intensities in the industry were the same. That being the case, it of course would be impossible to ascribe Heckscher-Ohlin reasoning linking factor endowment differences to factor intensity differences among products to explanations of trade patterns.

A perhaps more interesting variation on the theme of product differentiation would allow products to be vertically distinguished by consumers because they are of different quality. If higher qualities were produced by more capital-intensive techniques, then once again a factor endowment explanation of trade patterns à la Heckscher-Ohlin would be suggested (see Falvey and Kierzkowski 1987). Furthermore, with intraindustry trade of the vertically differentiated type highlighted, a new role for demand is introduced, one that links it to factor endowments. Suppose that there are a number of sectors in the economy, and in each sector there are numbers of vertically differentiated industries potentially capable of production, and differing in the intensity with which they use a type of capital specific to that sector. Consider the case of a relatively labor-abundant economy. In a free-trade world it may concentrate its efforts in sectors that are labor-intensive in a comparison with other sectors. Within such sectors, however, it may produce for export varieties that are more capital-intensive than the varieties it chooses to produce for itself. The link is that local demand differs from demand from the more capital-abundant countries in that capital abundance leads to higher per-capita income and therefore demand for more capital-intensive differentiated products. The variation in Heckscher-Ohlin theory suggested here is that a labor-abundant country may export commodities that are labor-intensive in an intersectoral comparison, but more capital-intensive intrasectorally when compared not to its imports but to local production for local demand (see Jones, Beladi, and Marjit 1999).

Neoclassical models of trade are based on the assumption that product markets are perfectly competitive, and therefore that commodity prices reflect unit costs. Models in the new trade theory emphasize that markets are imperfectly competitive, prices may differ from unit costs, and therefore unit costs (and a comparison of their component labor and capital costs) provide a poor guideline to trading patterns. But suppose that the world economy exhibits a fair degree of capital mobility and opportunities for foreign investment. In searching for the best locale in which to produce a commodity, or a fragment of a commodity, a firm will pay close attention to comparisons of cost and seek lower-cost areas. Prices may not accurately reflect costs, but costs may guide trade patterns.

Concluding Remarks

Heckscher-Ohlin models cannot help but prove useful well into the new century. Their focus on the importance of heterogeneity both in the manner in which commodities are produced and the composition of nations' factor supplies is well founded. It is difficult to argue that such compositional details are irrelevant in understanding trade patterns and the consequences of trade on a nation's internal distribution of income. This is not to say that variations in endowments and factor intensities are the only characteristics determining trade patterns. One reason that Ricardian type models have stayed the course is that their emphasis on differences in technologies, climate, and factor skills among countries provides clues to trade flows even if these models tend to ignore the compositional base of factors within a country.

Specific-factors models can be considered variations in the Heckscher-Ohlin constellation of trade models in which factor endowments and intensities matter. Furthermore the "rents" that specific factors earn in such a model could be interpreted as "profits" earned by firms or factors in an industry in which government licensing or regulations succeed in preventing entry. And the emphasis placed in new trade theory on analyzing the consequences of having imperfect markets for the theory of trade needs to be balanced by the analysis of the consequences of having freer international trade on the nature of markets. Trade encourages competition, and competition is what is assumed in Heckscher-Ohlin trade models.

Although it proved necessary in past decades to spend much time and effort exploring the sometimes rather subtle properties of the $2 \times 2 \times 2$ core version of Heckscher-Ohlin, the vision they provided transcends the limitations imposed by the restrictive assumptions of the core model. World markets are highly complex and dynamic, and enriched versions of the Heckscher and Ohlin view of trade will for years to come prove valuable in understanding these evolving markets.

References

Chang, Winston, W. Ethier, and M. Kemp. 1980. The theorems of international trade with joint production. *Journal of International Economics* 10:377–94.

Chipman, John S. 1969. Factor price equalization and the Stolper-Samuelson theorem. *International Economic Review* 10:399–406.

Chipman, John S. 1988. Intra-industry trade in the Heckscher-Ohlin-Lerner-Samuelson model. Mimeo. University of Minnesota.

Chipman, John S. 1992. Intra-industry trade, factor proportions and aggregation. In W. Neuefeind and R. Riezman, eds., *Economic Theory and International Trade: Essays in Memoriam J. Trout Rader*. New York: Springer.

Davis, Donald R. 1995. Intraindustry trade: A Heckscher-Ohlin-Ricardo approach. *Journal of International Economics* 39:201–26.

Ethier, Wilfred. 1974. Some of the theorems of international trade with many goods and factors. *Journal of International Economics* 4:199–206.

Ethier, Wilfred. 1984. Higher dimensional issues in trade theory. In R. Jones and P. Kenen, eds., *Handbook of International Economics*, vol. 1. Amsterdam: North-Holland, ch. 3.

Falvey, Rodney, and Henryk Kierzkowski. 1987. Product quality, intraindustry trade and (im)perfect competition. In H. Kierzkowski, ed., *Protection and Competition in International Trade*. Oxford: Blackwell, ch. 11.

Findlay, Ronald. 1993. Wage dispersion, international trade and the services sector. In G. Hansson, ed., *Trade, Growth and Development: The Role of Politics and Institutions*. London: Routledge.

Findlay, Ronald. 1995. *Factor Proportions, Trade, and Growth*. Cambridge: MIT Press.

Findlay, Ronald, and Ronald W. Jones. 2001. Economic development from an open economy perspective. In D. Lal and R. Snape, eds., *Trade, Development and Political Economy*. New York: Palgrave.

Gale, David, and Hukukane Nikaido. 1965. The Jacobian matrix and the global univalence of mappings. *Mathematische Annalen* 159:81–93.

Gruen, Fred H., and W. Max Corden. 1970. A tariff that worsens the terms of trade. In I. McDougall and R. Snape, eds., *Studies in International Economics: Monash Conference Papers*. Amsterdam: North-Holland, pp. 55–58.

Haberler, Gottfried. 1936. *The Theory of International Trade*. Edinburgh: William Hodge.

Heckscher, Eli. 1919. The effect of foreign trade on the distribution of income. *Ekonomisk Tidskrift*, pp. 497–512. Translated in H. Flam and M. J. Flanders, eds., *Heckscher-Ohlin Trade Theory*. Cambridge: MIT Press, 1991.

Helpman, Elhanan. 1981. International trade in the presence of product differentiation, economies of scale and monopolistic competition: A Chamberlin–Heckscher-Ohlin approach. *Journal of International Economics* 11:305–40.

Helpman, Elhanan, and Paul Krugman. 1985. *Market Structure and Foreign Trade*. Cambridge: MIT Press.

Jones, Ronald W. 1956. Factor proportions and the Heckscher-Ohlin theorem. *Review of Economic Studies* 24:1–10.

Jones, Ronald W. 1967. International capital movements and the theory of tariffs and trade. *Quarterly Journal of Economics* 81:1–38.

Jones, Ronald W. 1970. The role of technology in the theory of international trade. In R. Vernon, ed., *The Technology Factor in International Trade*. New York: NBER, pp. 73–92.

Jones, Ronald W. 1971. A three-factor model in theory, trade and history. In J. Bhagwati et al., eds., *Trade, Balance of Payments and Growth*. Amsterdam: North-Holland, ch. 1.

Jones, Ronald W. 1975. Income distribution and effective protection in a multicommodity trade model. *Journal of Economic Theory* 11:1–15.

Jones, Ronald W. 1985. Relative prices and real factor rewards: A re-interpretation. *Economics Letters* 26(3):47–49.

Jones, Ronald W. 1992. Jointness in production and factor-price equalization. *Review of International Economics* 1:10–18.

Jones, Ronald W. 1995. The discipline of international trade. *Swiss Journal of Economics and Statistics* 131:273–88.

Jones, Ronald W. 2000. *Globalization and the Theory of Input Trade*. Cambridge: MIT Press.

Jones, Ronald W., H. Beladi, and S. Marjit. 1999. The three faces of factor intensities. *Journal of International Economics* 48:413–20.

Jones, Ronald W., and Henryk Kierzkowski. 1986. Neighborhood production structures with an application to the theory of international trade. *Oxford Economic Papers* 38:59–76.

Jones, Ronald W., and Sugata Marjit. 1991. The Stolper-Samuelson theorem, the Leamer triangle, and the produced mobile factor structure. In A. Takayama, M. Ohyama, and H. Ohta, eds., *Trade, Policy and International Adjustments*. San Diego, CA: Academic Press, pp. 95–107.

Jones, Ronald W. 1992. International trade and endogenous production structures. In W. Neuefeind and R. Riezman, eds., *Economic Theory and International Trade: Essays in Memoriam J. Trout Rader*. New York: Springer.

Jones, Ronald W., and Tapan Mitra. 1993. The Stolper-Samuelson theorem: Links to dominant diagonals. In R. Becker et al., eds., *General Equilibrium, Growth and Trade II*. San Diego, CA: Academic Press.

Kemp, Murray C. 1966. The gain from international trade and investment: A neo-Heckscher-Ohlin approach. *American Economic Review* 56:788–809.

Kemp, Murray C., and Leon Wegge. 1969. On the relation between commodity prices and factor rewards. *International Economic Review* 10:407–13.

Leamer, Ed. 1984. *Sources of International Comparative Advantage: Theory and Evidence*. Cambridge: MIT Press.

Leontief, W. W. 1953. Domestic production and foreign trade: The American capital position re-examined. *Proceedings of the American Philosophical Society* 97:331–49.

Lerner, Abba P. 1952. Factor prices and international trade. *Economica* 19:1–15.

Linder, Staffan Burenstam. 1961. *An Essay on Trade and Transformation*. New York: Wiley.

Maneschi, Andrea. 1998. *Comparative Advantage in International Trade: A Historical Perspective*. Cheltenham, U.K.: Edward Elgar.

Mas-Colell, Andreu. 1979. Two propositions on the global univalence of systems of cost functions. In J. Green and J. Scheinkman, eds., *General Equilibrium, Growth and Trade*. New York: Academic Press.

Minabe, Nobuo. 1966. The Heckscher-Ohlin theorem, the Leontief paradox and patterns of economic growth. *American Economic Review* 56:1193–1211.

Neary, J. Peter. 1978. Short-run capital specificity and the pure theory of international trade. *Economic Journal* 88:488–510.

Ohlin, Bertil. 1924. The theory of trade. Translated in H. Flam and M. J. Flanders, eds., *Heckscher-Ohlin Trade Theory*. Cambridge: MIT Press, 1991.

Ohlin, Bertil. 1933. *Interregional and International Trade*. Cambridge: Harvard University Press.

Posner, M. V. 1961. Technical change and international trade. *Oxford Economic Papers* 13:323–41.

Ricardo, David. [1817] 1981. *On the Principles of Political Economy and Taxation*. Cambridge: Cambridge University Press.

Rybczynski, T. M. 1955. Factor endowment and relative commodity prices. *Economica* 22:336–41.

Samuelson, Paul A. 1948. International trade and the equalisation of factor prices. *Economic Journal* 58:163–84.

Samuelson, Paul A. 1949. International factor price equalisation once again. *Economic Journal* 59:181–97.

Samuelson, Paul A. 1971. Ohlin was right. *Swedish Journal of Economics* 73:365–84.

Samuelson, Paul A. 1992. Factor-price equalization by trade in joint and non-joint production. *Review of International Economics* 1:1–9.

Sanyal, Kalyan, and Ronald W. Jones. 1982. The theory of trade in middle products. *American Economic Review* 72:16–31.

Stolper, Wolfgang, and Paul A. Samuelson. 1941. Protection and real wages. *Review of Economic Studies* 19:58–73.

Vernon, Ray. 1966. International investment and international trade in the product cycle. *Quarterly Journal of Economics* 80:190–207.

17 What Role for Empirics in International Trade?

Donald R. Davis and David E. Weinstein

Introduction

The centennial of Bertil Ohlin's birth is an outstanding opportunity to reflect on his work. One must acknowledge that much of what has come to be known as the Heckscher-Ohlin theory of trade has been mediated by the contributions of others, including some contributors to this volume. But none would gainsay that even for a specialist in the field, there is great delight and inspiration to be found in reading the original texts. Deep economic intuition and breadth of vision grace each page. It would not be far off the mark to observe that a great deal of the theoretical work in positive trade in the last half-century—including some of the most recent—has involved elaboration of ideas for which Ohlin already provided interesting treatments.

The centennial of Ohlin's birth also provides stimulus to take the long view of our own field of international trade. Others will be discussing theoretical developments. Our charge is to consider empirical developments, addressing the role of theory only as it has helped to shape this enterprise. The existence of outstanding recent surveys of empirical trade, by some of the world's leading empirical and theoretical researchers (cf. Leamer 1990; Helpman 1999), allows us to forgo any attempt at a comprehensive survey. Instead, we will ask how our field has approached empirical research, how data findings have interacted with the development of theory, and how we can strengthen the useful interaction of the two.

Our chapter draws a few conclusions. Theory has been the heart of international trade research for the past half-century. And a glorious half-century of theorizing it has been! Yet this research program has been extraordinarily imbalanced. Moreover we believe that this imbalance is a serious problem for progress in the field as a whole.

We take the primary objective of our field to be an understanding of the determinants of trade patterns in the world we actually inhabit. Yet empirical analysis of actual trade relations plays a diminutive role in the field. Our field shows little of the two-way interplay between theory and data that is the very life of many fields of economics, such as macro, labor, and others. We believe it is possible to maintain what is beautiful and distinctive about our own field while enriching it in this dimension.

One response to this may be: Write interesting data analysis, and we will read it! Leamer and Levinsohn (1995) took this perspective as an implicit starting point, looking inward to understand why empirical research has failed to materially affect the views of most trade economists. Such introspection for empirical researchers is both important and necessary.

Yet we believe that such inward looking by empirical researchers addresses only one part of our field's problem. We believe that there needs to be a substantial change in the way that theorists think about data analysis. Theoreticians need to move beyond only working with a few stylized facts to a broader encounter with the empirical work. If there is anything that has been learned on the empirical side of trade in the last decade, it should surely be that spectacular failures of our theories, anomalies, and inconvenient facts are our most precious resources. Failure points the way to success—but only if we learn to embrace and understand facts that are inconvenient for our theories.

Our summary judgment is that at a deep level, the field has a quite limited empirical understanding of international trade patterns. We can say little about the relative importance of distinct fundamental determinants of trade. Some correlates of trade and production patterns have been established. Some work has been done on international patterns of absorption. But such efforts remain in their infancy. Grappling with the deeper problem of how the pieces really fit together within a world general equilibrium has barely begun.

One might read this and view us as relentless pessimists. This would be a mistake. We believe that skepticism about the state of our knowledge is a very healthy stance for researchers. But, lest we be misunderstood, let us add a few caveats. We are great admirers of what the field has achieved in theory over this half-century and more. To those who have written the beautiful and elegant models that constitute the very language or our field—and you know who you are—we send our cheers! Likewise the empirical side of trade has a number of researchers—you also know who you are—who have pioneered methods that provide the foundation on which others will build.

Moreover we see signs of hope, both in the interests of younger researchers and in the reception these have encountered among the leaders of our field. To give only one example, a simple survey, such as that by Helpman (1999), can be extremely important in focusing the profession's attention both on the achievements of the recent research and on the outstanding questions that remain.

Indeed, our belief is that an acknowledgment that the truly fundamental questions remain to be resolved is, for researchers, itself a hopeful stance. We believe that international trade economists will rise to the occasion to make our field richer and more complete.

Interaction of Theory and Empirics

The folklore of international economics holds that there is a simple difference between the subfields of international finance and international trade. In international finance, every theory ever proposed is decisively rejected by the data. In international trade, no theory ever proposed has ever been touched by data. This is of course a parody. But like many parodies it contains a grain of truth.

Data analysis has traditionally played a very marginal role in the field of trade. While macro and labor economics, for example, have the interaction of data analysis and theory as the lifeblood of the field, this has not been so in trade. This is what Trefler (1995) had in mind when he wrote: "In other fields of economics, the poor performance of a major theory leads to more careful consideration of the data and to new theories that can accommodate the anomalies." By contrast, he argued, the work in trade had by and large only produced conjectures, but no alternatives shown to do better. Leamer and Levinsohn (1995) argue that only two empirical results have materially affected the way international economists think about trade.[1]

The marginal role of empirics in trade is easily discerned in other fora. Graduate reading lists typically feature only a minute selection of empirical papers relative to the body of theory to be mastered.

Theorists are vastly more likely to say that their work is inspired by other theoretical work or by a few stylized facts than by any more resolute data analysis. Perhaps the ultimate metric of the extent of the marginalization of empirics within the field is the fact that with the last change of editorship, the *Journal of International Economics* felt it necessary to institute an affirmative action plan for empirical articles.

Why has empirical work in trade, in contrast to other fields, had so little influence on the evolution of the field? There is no single answer. One part of the answer is surely that over much of the last half-century, articulation of the theory has proved very fertile ground. Elaboration of the neoclassical theory, the great advances in commercial policy, increasing returns, imperfect competition, trade and growth, and more recently economic geography—these have been tremendous contributions to our understanding of international economic relations. One certainly can't say that the field has been sterile.

Yet the field has nonetheless been extraordinarily unbalanced. A second reason for this is that the project itself is rather daunting: to provide a parsimonious characterization of the principal determinants of the structure and evolution of production and absorption, hence trade, across countries. Of course, to say that the project is daunting is also to say that the returns to success should likewise be high. Certainly the limitations of the data, both in availability and quality, have been an issue. But with improved data collection by a variety of international agencies, and their systematization by various researchers, including Leamer and Feenstra, these constraints are declining.

Finally, Leamer and Levinsohn (1995) make the point that the work has failed to be persuasive because the experiments themselves were often not well formulated. This is no doubt true, but it begs the prior question of why the self-correcting mechanisms that lead other fields to concentrate intellectual firepower on relating the theory to the data had relatively little effect in the field of international trade.

Solid Empirics, Low Impact

Leamer has criticized many empirical papers as not having put enough intellectual capital on the line. But this is only part of the story of the limited influence of data analysis in our field. Many excellent empirical papers, including some by Leamer himself, have put a lot of intellectual capital on the line, found an important tenet of international trade theory wanting, and ended up off the radar screens of most trade economists. In this section we will explore some results that are well established in empirical trade, which should be part of the empirical toolkit of every trade economist but which have had very limited impact on the way we think about international trade.

The Failure of FPE and the Role of Comparative Advantage in the OECD

Let us start with an important fact. It is well known that FPE fails. Wages differ strongly across regions within countries and enormously across countries. International economists tend to hold two stylized facts in their heads with regard to this. The first is that wage differences are small across developed countries, and the second is that they are large between developed and developing countries. These facts are true, but one must also consider the magnitudes. It is not uncommon for wage differentials between developed and developing countries to be on the order of thirty or more. However, even in the OECD, wages vary by a factor of five. These are big numbers. Figure 17.1 portrays average compensation within the OECD. Even when considering relatively wealthy countries like Australia, Italy, and the United States, wages vary by a factor of two or more. The most likely explanations for this wage disparity in the OECD are differences in labor quality, productivity, and differences in endowments. Regardless of which of these stories one finds most plausible, it is hard to escape the conclusion that classical comparative advantage is likely to be quite important in the North.

One Cone or Many?

Leamer (1987) was the first to provide solid evidence that one reason for the failure of FPE was the fact that there are multiple cones of diversification. This paper made a clear contribution by putting some important intellectual capital on the line. If FPE were true or if FPE failures were due to factor quality or productivity differences, one would expect to see a linear, and not quadratic, relationship between country capital–labor ratios and output per worker in any

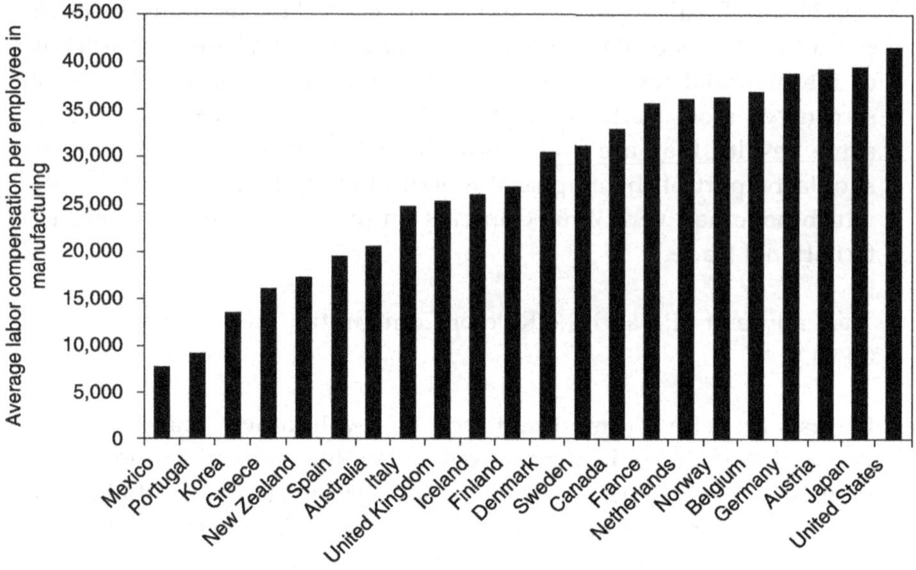

Figure 17.1
World wages in manufacturing (in 1993 U.S.$).

given sector. His finding of a quadratic relationship seems to us to be strong evidence against a single-cone world. It is interesting to ask why a paper like this is typically not a required reading for graduate students. We teach both the FPE and no-FPE models but spend essentially no time worrying about which world we occupy.

This is especially surprising considering that other studies tend to confirm Leamer's (1987) basic result. Dollar, Wolff, and Baumol (1989) make the search for multiple cones a centerpiece of their analysis. Using a somewhat different methodology than Leamer, they find that both industry output per worker and industry capital-to-labor ratios are highly correlated with country endowments. Indeed, the median correlation between industry capital-to-labor ratios and country ratios is 0.62. Over the course of the next decade, Davis and Weinstein (1998) and Schott (1999) confirmed this basic result using complementary methodologies.

A generous interpretation of why papers like Leamer (1987) don't enter the canon is concern with robustness. However, if this is so, one must ask why no one published a critique. A more likely reason for the silence is that Leamer's result is inconvenient for trade theory. Both CRS and IRS enthusiasts love the beauty and simplicity of FPE models. Multi-cone models are messy. It is a testament to the power of elegant theory that few seized on the importance of these results. Even though there was strong evidence that a particular cause for the failure of FPE is evident in international data, the general response of trade economists, both empirical and theoretical, has been to continue thinking in terms of FPE models.[2]

Ironically, when Ohlin wrote "complete equality of factor prices is ... almost unthinkable and certainly highly improbable," he got it half wrong. Despite being completely improbable, factor price equalization was far too easily thinkable. The fate of Leamer (1987) illustrates a problem that empirical researchers face. Studies that put intellectual capital on the line and confirm our preferred view of the world tend to do much better than studies that contradict our priors.

Industry-Level Technical Differences in the OECD

Another robust empirical result that tends to get pushed to the side is the role played by Ricardian differences. There have been innumerable studies that have demonstrated that industry-level technical differences in the OECD are large. Within this literature Jorgenson, Kuroda, and Nishimizu (1987) are notable in finding that even after matching the international data as carefully as is possible, enormous technological differences remain. They found that in 1985 in over two-thirds of the tradable goods sectors they examined, productivity in Japan was either 20 percent below or 20 percent above the U.S. level. In perhaps the only trade paper to take both the theory and the data in this area seriously, Harrigan (1997) found that these industry technological differences matter for international specialization. Despite the plethora of studies showing that industry-level technological differences are big even within the OECD, most trade economists abstract from this when thinking about determinants of trade within the OECD.[3] Again the profession seems fairly timid about engaging the data.

What Is Intraindustry Trade, Anyway?

The evolution of our understanding of intraindustry trade illustrates the successes and failures that occur as theorists and empirical economists communicate. Kojima (1964) was the first economist to note the large amount of intraindustry trade. Grubel and Lloyd (1975) expanded and greatly enhanced this early analysis and laid the foundation for much of our thinking about the empirical importance of intraindustry trade. Ultimately two popular theories of intraindustry trade arose. The first, based on Krugman (1979) and Lancaster (1980), held that intraindustry trade is the exchange of horizontally differentiated goods produced with identical factor intensities. The second, based on Falvey (1981) suggested, that intraindustry trade represents vertically differentiated products of different factor intensity. In the end the Krugman-Lancaster approach to intraindustry trade became the prevailing view because it could be presented in an elegant, comprehensive, and compelling framework that tied together what were viewed as key stylized facts.

Interestingly data analysis did not play much of a role in the success of the theory. The debate revolved around two easily observable issues. First, did exports in a sector to a country differ significantly in quality from imports from that country, and second, were they produced using differing factor intensities? A simple test of the first issue is straightforward. Are unit values in bilateral trade similar for exports and imports? Interestingly the first careful study that put this intellectual capital on the line was not written until over a decade after the original theory. Defining goods to be vertically differentiated if unit values at the five-digit level differ by more than ± 15 percent Greenaway, Hine, and Milner (1994) find that 70 percent of U.K. intraindustry trade is vertical. A similar study by Aturupane, Djankov, and Hoekman (1998) found even higher shares for vertical intraindustry trade for other European countries.

Of course, a major worry with this sort of empirical work is whether a mechanical cut off of ± 15 percent is really separating vertical and horizontal and vertical specialization. Obviously, as the bands expand, more trade will be classified as horizontal, and one is left wondering whether this type of study is really informing us about the world. To get a better sense of the meaning of these results, it makes sense to take a closer look at the data. The most detailed Harmonized Tariff System data is at the ten-digit level. At this level of aggregation there are 11,297 different agricultural, mining, and manufacturing product categories. Unfortunately, a quick look at these categories suggests that this is a tremendous underestimate of the true level of heterogeneity in the world.

Table 17.1 presents some sample categories that reflect products that we know something about. What is striking about each category

Table 17.1
Sample ten-digit data

HTS Code	Description
0201306000	Meat bovine animals, boneless ex processed, fresh or chilled
0403100000	Yogurt, sweetened, flavored or containing fruit/coco
0406904520	Cheese, swiss or emmenthaler with eye formation
0702002000	Tomatoes, fresh or chilled
0709510000	Mushrooms, fresh or chilled
0711201500	Olives, not pitted
0808100000	Apples, fresh
0901210030	Coffee roasted not decaffeinated for retail under 2 kg
1604142020	Tuna, albacore, no oil airtight container under 7 kg
1806900075	Chocolate confectionery put up for retail sale
2007991000	Strawberry jams
2204214005	Red wine grape under 14% alcohol
2208303030	Whiskies, scotch & irish, container not over 4 liters
3004906075	Cough and cold preparations
3004906020	Cardiovascular medicaments
3004400050	Dermatological agents and local anesthetics
3002200000	Vaccines for human medicine
3004400020	Anticonvulsants, hypnotics and sedatives
3004400030	Antidepressants, tranquilizers and other psychiatric agents
3926301000	Handles and knobs
4202219000	Handbags, outer surface of leather, value over $20 each
4901990050	Technical, scientific and professional books
6103110000	Men's or boys' suits of wool, knit
6104531000	W/g skirts of synthetic fibers cont 23% more wool, knit
6104622010	Women's trousers of cotton, knitted
7103910010	Rubies cut but not set for jewelry
8411919080	Parts of turbojet or turbopropeller a/c engines
8703240032	Passenger motor vehicle, 4 cylinder & under
9004100000	Sunglasses
9006530040	Camera, 35 mm with built-in electronic flash
9202100000	String musical instruments played with a bow
9306900040	Bombs, grenades, torpedoes, & similar munitions of war
9503411000	Stuffed toys
9506512000	tennis rackets, strung

is how much scope for both vertical and horizontal product differentiation there is even at the ten-digit level. Would you feel comfortable entering a good restaurant and asking simply for a bottle of red wine? How much should one pay for a four-cylinder passenger car, and what would one expect to receive? Would you order generic Swiss cheese on the internet and feel confident about what would arrive? Clearly, quality differences within these ten-digit categories may support tremendous price differences even when the varieties are sold side by side.

Consider a typical category: men's and boys knit wool suit-type jackets and blazers. Even at this level of disaggregation there is still substantial intraindustry trade. In 1994 Japan exported these jackets to 19 different countries and imported them from 31 countries. Overall, Japan's Grubel-Lloyd index of intraindustry trade, even at this tremendously fine division of the data, is 0.20. Interestingly, the two largest suppliers of men's wool suit jackets to Japan in terms of value are Italy and China. These two countries account for almost one-quarter of total Japanese imports in this sector. This fact alone strongly suggests that even at the ten-digit level, very different types of goods are being aggregated together. Unit values confirm this. The typical unit value for an Italian wool suit jacket is almost seven times higher than that of a Chinese wool suit jacket. The unit values for Japanese exports of suit jackets are triple those of Chinese imports. Clearly, there is a lot of vertical differentiation here.

This ad hoc analysis is easy to attack. We only picked a tiny subset of sectors and clearly have an agenda. What if we had picked a sector that we "know" to be homogeneous, like nondurum wheat meant for human consumption?[4] Even here we find Canadian wheat pellets entering Japan with unit values that are 23 percent above Australian pellets. And this is wheat! If we move downstream slightly to wheat flours, unit values skyrocket to factors of eight or more. This tends to confirm a problem with our tendency to group products we know nothing about as being differentiated only horizontally. Perhaps there is less quality variation in polyacetals, manure spreaders, or bovine semen, but we think there is cause for alarm.

What is worse is that Italian and Chinese suits are likely to be produced with very different factor mixes. This point was made early in the debates over intraindustry trade by Finger (1975) and Chipman (1992). More recently Davis and Weinstein (1999) examine the implications of this for our measures of net factor trade. If matched intraindustry trade was the exchange of goods produced with identical technologies, the net factor content of such trade would be zero. In fact we find that for many OECD countries over half of their net factor trade is accomplished through intraindustry trade. The United States is a particularly striking example. Over two-thirds of its net factor trade is accomplished by intraindustry exchange of goods of differing factor intensity. Much of what we call intraindustry trade is simply a data problem that reflects the failure of our industrial classification system to capture the fact that very different goods are being lumped together.

To say that these studies have made little impact on the day-to-day thinking of most trade economists is a gross understatement. A typical graduate student at a top department is likely to believe that intraindustry trade being the exchange of goods of similar factor intensity is true simply as a matter of definition. That this bears little relation to measured intraindustry trade does not even present itself as a problem. Such gross errors would be inconsequential if not for the fact that they form the core around which a great deal of theorizing occurs. And our beautiful models hold a tenacious grip on the way we view the world.

How Similar Are Endowments in the OECD?

A final stylized fact often ignored concerns endowment similarity. It is often asserted that OECD countries have endowments of factors that are similar. While it is true that there has been substantial income convergence in the OECD, enormous differences in factor abundance remain. A natural way to measure factor abundance is to divide each country's endowment of a factor by its share of world GDP multiplied by the world endowment of that factor. This produces a unitless measure of abundance that indicates what share of a factor should be exported in a frictionless FPE Heckscher-Ohlin-Vanek world. (Note the sleight of hand—even we feel compelled to appeal to the frictionless HOV model as a baseline! But see Davis and Weinstein 1998.)

Table 17.2 reports the results of this exercise for four factors: aggregate labor, capital, college-educated labor, and labor with less than a college education. For OECD countries, moving one standard deviation from the median often makes the difference between a country being a predicted exporter or importer of a factor's services.

Table 17.2
Distribution of country measured factor abundances in 1990

Country	Total labor	Capital	College educated labor	High school and below educated labor
World average	2.23	0.76	1.00	2.90
World standard deviation	2.37	0.37	0.87	3.21
World median	1.16	0.76	0.76	1.43
G10 average	0.33	1.12	0.84	0.54
G10 standard deviation	0.07	0.19	0.32	0.15
G10 median	0.31	1.12	0.80	0.52
OECD average	0.45	1.12	0.90	0.75
OECD standard deviation	0.25	0.21	0.46	0.41
OECD median	0.35	1.14	0.79	0.58

Sources: Education data are averaged for 1985 to 1990 from Barro and Lee. Total labor and capital data are from the Penn World Tables Mark 5.6. G10 corresponds to the 10 countries in Davis and Weinstein (1998).

This suggests a prima facie case in favor of endowment differences mattering even for trade within the OECD. It is not uncommon to find countries that are in the lowest quartile have abundances that are less than half of those in the upper quartile.

One possible criticism of this is that countries like Mexico, Korea, and Turkey may be driving the results. To see if this were true, we also considered a subset of ten wealthy and large countries in the OECD (Australia, Canada, Denmark, Germany, France, Japan, Italy, Netherlands, Britain, and the United States). The data reveal substantial differences in endowments even among these countries. The standardized U.S. endowment of college-educated labor is almost five times that of Italy. The United Kingdom's standardized endowment of noncollege labor is almost double that of the United States. And Japan's standardized endowment of capital is almost double that of the United Kingdom. Clearly, factor endowment differences are alive and well in the North, although this fact is largely ignored by the profession.

How Should We Respond to Uncomfortable Facts?

Ideally economic theory serves in part as a way to organize key facts about the world. Strategic simplification is essential. A consequence is that our theories are always wrong in some dimensions—this is a necessary fact of life. But we expect them to be right about the key facts around which they are organized. We have presented what we view as important examples in which empirical research has had something substantive to say about the theory, but these facts have had little influence on the way economists think about trade. In certain cases the romance of the models has had the upper hand on the facts.

We all recognize the fact that anomalies play an important role in the advance of knowledge. But it is always more convenient for the anomalies to grow in someone else's garden. We think that there are important examples—such as the work of Trefler (1995) discussed below—where the characterization of an anomaly has played an absolutely crucial role in advancing our understanding of trade patterns. Perhaps the best we can do is to all take a pledge to work harder to embrace our anomalies as the start of richer theories.

Virtually All of the Key Questions Remain Open

One of the great joys of academic economics is to encounter an area in which the most important questions have yet to be resolved. Surely there must have been great excitement as it became evident that a tremendous body of industrial organization theory could usefully be applied to problems of international trade. The same excitement no doubt existed for an earlier generation in consideration of the neoclassical theory of commercial policy, or more recently in work on trade and growth, political economy, or economic geography. Often the simple recognition that an important area and its major problems are open terrain is among the largest steps in finding answers.

Empirical international trade, in our view, is just such a field. Virtually all of the major questions remain quite open. Some are almost untouched. What is the role of increasing returns versus comparative advantage in determining international trade patterns? What role do endowments play in trade patterns beyond North–South trade? How do technological differences at the industry or firm level interact with other determinants of cost in shaping trade patterns? In a world of imperfect integration, how do absorption and production patterns interact? These are absolutely fundamental questions. They are also quite open.

We do not mean in the least to say that the existing empirical literature has taught us nothing about trade patterns. But it is important to understand the limitations either of the questions asked or the answers received. We will consider a few examples.

One of the signal successes of empirical trade is the so-called gravity model. It relates bilateral trade volumes to a parsimonious set of determinants. It fits well whether we look at aggregate trade volumes or instead at industry trade volumes. The fits of the estimating equations really are impressive, with typical R^2s in the range of 0.7. The gravity model, once considered a theoretical orphan, now has several sets of parents in waiting, with new ones arriving almost daily.[5] Yet the meaning of the gravity equation's success for our understanding of international trade is worth closer examination.

The core of international trade theory has always focused on the determinants of the pattern of production as the key fact to be explained in understanding trade patterns.[6] Yet the gravity model, such as in its industry-level approach, takes the level of production as given and then seeks to explain the distribution of imports across partner countries. Thus, even if one is willing to be surprised at how well the gravity model fits, the deeper question is what we can infer from these good fits. The fact that the empirical model takes the distribution of production as given should make clear that it would be very hard to use the good fit of the gravity model as evidence for one theory of the determinants of production patterns over any other.

The recent literature focusing on the near-universality of gravity has instead focused on the fact that it might provide evidence of a high degree of specialization, whatever its source. Yet Feenstra et al. (1999) have shown that gravity can arise even in a homogeneous goods model without a high degree of specialization. For all their good fits, the thousands of gravity models that have been run have done relatively little to inform our understanding of the deep determinants of trade patterns. Papers such as Feenstra et al. that actively seek to distinguish alternative models based on their performance in the gravity framework are an important contribution. But this work is still far from complete.

The literature also features important papers establishing robust correlates of international trade and production. Stellar contributions in this genre include Leamer (1984) and Harrigan (1997). Yet, as Leamer cautions, these represent incomplete tests of the theory. They do not try to get the pieces to fit together. The estimated parameters do not correspond to the structural parameters suggested by the theory.

The interested reader is encouraged to consult the surveys by Leamer and Levinsohn (1995) or Helpman (1999). We think our assertion will stand: virtually all of the most important questions in empirical trade remain to be resolved.

The Costs of Failing to Distinguish Models Empirically

Our understanding of the determinants of actual trade patterns is not deep. This is a problem in its own right. It becomes a yet larger problem when we turn to normative and policy analysis. This has been quite evident in the very extended discussion in the United States in recent years over the reasons for the rising relative wage of skilled workers and the role that trade may have played in this.

Among the many leading trade economists who contributed to this discussion were Jagdish Bhagwati and Paul Krugman. One of them wrote: "Unusually, serious economists have not by and large argued about theory: with few exceptions they have agreed that a more or less classical Heckscher-Ohlin-Samuelson model is the best framework to use." The other titled a section of a paper "Why FPE and [Stolper-Samuelson] Theorems Are Inadequate Guides to Reality," with a first subsection noting the potential gains from exploitation of scale economies as a counterweight to concerns about wage losses. For those who have not followed the debate closely, it might not have been evident that the first quote comes from Krugman, the second from Bhagwati (co-authored by Vivek Dehejia).[7]

A skeptic could argue that this apparent plasticity of belief about the appropriate underlying framework confirms that policy analysis is just ideology in fancy garb. Or, as a Columbia economics department Christmas skit once averred, it is a case of the assumptions following straight from the conclusions.

Such a skeptic would miss the central point: honest disagreement about which model should be applied in any given context, and even shifting from one to another in different settings, is at present not only respectable but entirely necessary. One reason for this is our reliance on MIT-style theory. This approach asks a model to be crisp and to the point; it does not ask the model to be a picture of reality. The deep beauty and great value of MIT-style theory is unassailable. But, as we have seen, it carries a price when it is not accompanied by a serious effort to distinguish alternative frameworks on empirical grounds. When turning to policy issues, it is a matter of judgment which simple model to apply. Serious economists can have honest disagreements. And these disagreements can make all the difference for the conclusions.[8]

What Can We Expect of Empirical Work?

We have argued that there would be great value to arriving at a stronger consensus about appropriate models of trade. But at least some prominent voices have expressed skepticism about whether this is a feasible project. This raises a series of questions. What should empirical analysis of positive trade be doing? What interaction should there be with theory? What is the role of estimation? What is the role of testing? What does theory have to learn from empirical work? What is the objective of this entire enterprise? These are among the most basic questions of our field, and we spend too little energy grappling with them.

Leamer (1990) argues that a great deal of empirical analysis fails to be persuasive because it tests propositions that we know to be false. Models in this view are not literally right or wrong; instead, they are useful or not. While holding fast to the idea that a persuasive data analysis must be developed in the context of a well-articulated theory, Leamer issues the injunction: "Estimate, don't test!"[9] This is of course a stricture that Leamer himself has violated—even in some of his most influential work. This should provide a hint that the injunction is too strong and, for a less accomplished empiricist, could be seriously misleading about the project of empirical trade.

The central object of empirical work in trade is narrowing the range of plausible belief. If all ex ante plausible views are untouched as a result of an empirical analysis, then it will strike earth with a resounding nothing. How does one place intellectual capital on the line? Sometimes we are simply looking for a number. We are willing to take as given, for the exercise, the underpinnings. We want to know a plausible value for an elasticity. We want to know a speed of adjustment. This is Leamer's "estimation." Such estimation is a thoroughly important part of the enterprise. The accumulation of studies that provide stylized facts about the economy does successively narrow the range of plausible belief.

Some caution, though, is warranted with a subset of such studies. It has become a too-frequent practice to use a framework as the basis for a study, estimate parameters, and if they are in (very gross) accord with the predictions of the theory, to pronounce it as being "consistent" with theory *xyz*. Strictly this is not incorrect, but it is often seriously misleading. This is so particularly when virtually any theory that might be in the least interesting is likely to yield the same or similar predictions. Why not take the extra step and seek to identify predictions that might usefully distinguish the models?

We also believe that the prospects for persuasive testing are more hopeful than are indicated by Leamer. He is quite right that there is no point in testing and rejecting propositions that we know beforehand to be false. But there is no reason to allow the existence of pointless exercises to define our attitude to testing more generally. We are strongly convinced that researchers can identify hypotheses in which two well-defined theories have contrasting implications, hence in which it is possible to test. The criterion for whether or not this is interesting has to be whether some real intellectual capital is placed on the line via the test. Will we look differently at the world depending on the results of the test? That there are many cases for which the answer is no should not discourage us from identifying cases where the answer is yes. We believe that such well-designed tests can be a crucial part of a research program that successively narrows the range of plausible belief.

In physics there has long been discussion of a "theory of everything." Its counterpart in international trade is to give a parsimonious account of the world general equilibrium.[10] Is there a way to specify the nature of differences in technology, endowments, tastes, plus the underlying parameters of trade costs that makes sense of world patterns of production, absorption, and trade? That should be our aim. We believe that the field is open for a great deal of progress.

Heckscher-Ohlin-Vanek Is Dead; Long Live HOV!

We believe that the project of successively narrowing the range of plausible belief by testing is not only a hypothetical possibility but a process already under way in a number of areas of trade. While a number of areas of inquiry could equally well have served as a model, the focus of this conference on Ohlin and our own research proclivities lead us to focus on recent work considering the Heckscher-Ohlin-Vanek (HOV) theory.

The work of Bowen, Leamer, and Sveikauskas (1987) is, in our opinion and that of the larger profession, a monumental contribution to the empirics of international trade. Very likely this is the single most widely read empirical paper on trade. We believe that an important reason for the influence of this paper is its substantive conclusion that the Heckscher-Ohlin-Vanek model has little predictive power for the measured factor content of trade. Perhaps oddly, our opinion of the paper's importance has little to do with its substantive conclusions; or rather, we think highly of the paper despite the fact that its substantive conclusions are unconvincing.

The major contributions of the BLS paper are several. This was the first paper to report results on HOV for a large number of countries, based on a wide array of endowments, trade, and technology. The sign and rank tests employed to measure the model's performance have become standard in the literature. Moreover the hypothesis testing developed in the later sections of the paper also proved to be very important in later research, such as that of Trefler (1995).

By far, though, the most important contribution of BLS is its conceptual grandeur: it dares rise to the challenge of assembling all of the empirical pieces to describe a world general equilibrium. In Leamer's terms, it provides a "complete" test of the HOV theory, employing data on endowments, technology, and trade. That it fails utterly to assemble the pieces in a coherent way is wholly secondary. The attempt itself changed the field.

The results of BLS, on their face, were devastating for the HOV theory. In their implementation, factor abundance provides no more information than a coin flip about which country will be measured to export services of a particular factor. What could be more damning? Despite their best efforts, they were unable to identify a model that performed better.

Faced with such results, what was the reaction of the profession? On one hand, the results were likely difficult to accept; trade economists receive the HOV theory with mother's milk. It may have seemed very hard to believe that observed differences in endowments really have no influence on net factor trade. On the other hand, the results seemed to lend greater credibility to an emerging consensus that however important relative factor endowments may have been in the past, they no longer matter much in determining trade patterns. Trade of jute for aircraft may be explained by Heckscher-Ohlin, but the bulk of trade is among countries that hardly differ in endowments, so the dramatic failure of HOV really presents no puzzle.

The next real landmarks in this literature are the papers by Trefler (1993, 1995). What is most remarkable in Trefler's papers is that they were written at all. In the wake of BLS, it would have been easy to conclude that the HOV theory was a deadend, perhaps something for historians to contemplate, but not a path for new research. Trefler's sound judgment was that it could not be satisfying to declare the theory dead when we really had no idea why it was failing.

Trefler asked two key questions. The first follows up directly on the work of BLS: Are there simple amendments in the spirit of HOV that allow the theory to work? The second is more novel (at least within empirical trade): Are the failures systematic? The latter, in particular, proved to be an extraordinarily fruitful question. And the answers Trefler provides are striking. The most memorable regularity he identifies in the data is what he terms the "mystery of the missing trade." In simple terms, the measured factor content of trade is an order of magnitude smaller than that predicted based on national incomes and endowments. This characterization of the data has been extraordinarily useful in focusing subsequent research on the types of amendments that might be needed to fit the pieces of the puzzle together.[11]

It seemed clear in the wake of BLS that the pure factor price equalization version of HOV would be a dismal failure if applied to a broad cross section of countries. This left two paths open. One approach to this is to look for ways to sidestep the problem while continuing to work broadly within the HOV framework. This is pursued in Davis, Weinstein, Bradford and Shimpo (DWBS 1997). The starting point for that paper is to ask what HOV predicts if only a subset of the world shares FPE—an FPE club. This has a definite answer and provides the basis for tests provided a suitable FPE club can be identified. Importantly, the focus on general equilibrium prohibits discarding information on the rest of the world (ROW). However, the ROW must be incorporated appropriately.

We chose regions of Japan as our FPE club. This has a number of advantages, including the high quality and comparability of the data, and the heightened plausibility of FPE for regions of a single country. A second important characteristic of DWBS is that while prior work focused solely on the factor content of trade, we were able to examine separately the HOV theories of absorption and production. This allowed us to see directly where the failures in predicting factor contents might arise, rather than needing to rely on indirect inferences.

The DWBS paper replicates the failures of the theory identified in prior work for the case in which it assumes that the whole world shares FPE. The mystery of the missing trade is then very evident. However, it also shows that when you drop the assumption of universal FPE, restricting this to the FPE club of Japanese regions, the results improve dramatically. The regions export the services of their abundant factors, and they do so in approximately the right magnitude. The mystery of the missing trade is in large measure eliminated for the regions of Japan. Both the production and consumption theory of HOV fare reasonably well in the Japanese data. This provides a first case of HOV working, while considering the problem within a full world general equilibrium.

The problem of getting HOV to work while directly confronting the failure of FPE internationally is addressed in Davis and Weinstein (1998). Prior work on an international sample had focused on two key reasons for the failure of HOV: (1) Countries use different techniques of production, possible reasons being efficiency differences or a breakdown of relative FPE; and (2) the absorption theory based on identical and homothetic preferences may be at fault. Our starting point was to note that while the key hypotheses for the failure of HOV-concerned technology and absorption, the prior work employed only a single observation on technology (that of the United States) and no data on absorption. An obvious strategy was to assemble more data to explore the nature of these failures directly, which should help in selecting which among the competing hypotheses really matters in trying to get an amended HOV to work.

For details of implementation, consult Davis and Weinstein (1998). We focus here just on the conclusions. In line with the literature on cross-country productivity (e.g., see Jorgenson and Kuroda 1990), efficiency differences matter. The failure of factor price equalization matters, even within the OECD: more capital abundant countries use more capital intensive techniques within each industry. Nontraded goods play an unexpectedly important role. They allow us to make inferences about the failure of FPE, and when FPE fails, they tend to absorb a great deal of the "excess" factor supplies that otherwise might have been available for factor service exports. Finally, trade costs matter, by reducing the opportunities to arbitrage the factor price differences.

Having directly estimated the nature of efficiency differences, the failure of FPE and its implications for production techniques, and the role of trade costs in reducing trade flows, how well does the model predict net factor trade? In considering the answer, it is well to keep in mind that due to the "mystery of the missing trade," the answer in the prior literature is that the model correctly predicts almost nothing. Here, having taken advantage of the new and richer data set, measured factor trade is approximately 60 to 80 percent of predicted factor trade. The mystery of the missing trade is, in large measure, solved. Countries export their abundant factors, and they do so in approximately the right magnitude. Suitably amended, HOV works.

At this point, it is tempting to append a fairy-tale ending. There was a moment in which all appeared lost for the HOV theory; now the theory has been rescued and provides a beautiful description of the workings of international trade. However, as devoted researchers, we do not believe in endings, fairy-tale or otherwise.

We do, though, believe that the profession's experience with the path of research on HOV holds important lessons. Some of these are substantive. We do believe that HOV, or Heckscher-Ohlin more broadly, will have to be an important component of any empirically based attempt to understand the pattern of trade.

Perhaps, though, the most important lessons have to do with the future approach to research in the field of international trade. There is no reason that this should be a field of very slight empirical content. It can preserve the traditional commitment of the field to elegant general equilibrium modeling and at the same time make progress in terms of matching theory and data in a coherent way. The models that emerge will surely be composites of the various approaches in the literature to trade patterns. However, if we use enough imagination, we can develop these hybrids so that they are both elegant in theory and robust when confronted with data. At least that is how we conceive of the project of future empirical research into trade patterns.

Conclusion

The field of international trade is falling short in its central mission. That mission is to understand the causes and consequences of trade in the world we actually inhabit. Trade economists can justly take pride in the theoretical achievements of our field. But these have not been matched with equally illustrious progress on the empirical side. Indeed, data analysis has long played a marginal role in the professional life of our field. Notable individual contributions notwithstanding, virtually all of the most important empirical questions remain open and at times nearly untouched.

The failure of our field to grapple seriously with empirics bears a cost. Our failure to identify a positive model adequate to describe the principal empirical features of trade leaves us in serious straits when we turn to policy analysis. Such analysis requires that we specify a positive model as a foundation. It is easy to appreciate that with empirical analysis having done so little to constrain the model that we select, such policy analysis is likely to be highly sensitive to the analyst's priors of which model is appropriate.

Empirical researchers must shoulder part of the responsibility for this state of affairs. They must ensure that their exercises truly place intellectual capital at risk in order for their analyses to be persuasive. But the field more broadly also needs to accept part of the responsibility. For long stretches it has operated from small collections of stylized facts that at times seem impervious to the intrusion of actual facts. Empirical analysis with substantive insights about the features of the world we inhabit, but which are at times inconvenient for theory, languish in obscurity.

We do believe that there are positive models of what the field can achieve when it is able to concentrate a larger share of its intellectual resources to investigate well-defined empirical projects. While several ongoing research dialogues could usefully serve as exemplars, the focus of this conference and our own research interests leads us to focus on verification of the Heckscher-Ohlin-Vanek model. This is truly a case where the contributions of many economists, including failures and successes for the models, played a crucial role in shaping our view of the problem.

The approach we suggest involves a reconception of the collective project of our field or, at the very least, a strong shift in priorities.

Crisp, lucid theory will always play a central role in the field. But this needs to be complemented by a serious encounter with data. Grappling with facts revealed by the data, pressing the limits of what our models can predict, and identifying the contours of the world should be viewed as a central part of the program of our leading empiricists and theorists.

This is a clarion call to a project that we see at least partly in progress. There is a relatively small, but influential, group of well-established empiricists and theorists who have actively undertaken research in this area or considered it at length in their own writings. There is a larger group of younger economists who have made it a key element of their work. It is time for each international economist to accept the challenge to make empirical analysis a central feature of our work and dialogue. We have a world to discover.

Notes

1. The exceptions are the Leontief paradox and the demonstration by Grubel and Lloyd (1975) that a great deal of trade is intraindustry trade. The fact that Leamer (1980) has strongly challenged Leontief's finding, and that we believe there is serious reason to question the meaning of the Grubel-Lloyd results (see below), indicates the limited reach of the empirical side of trade.

2. An interesting contrast is the strong professional interest accorded Trefler (1993).

3. Eaton and Kortum (1999) are a notable exception.

4. This category is drawn from the Commodity Classification for Japanese Tariff Statistics, which is actually more disaggregated than the HTS system.

5. See, for example, Deardorff (1998) on gravity in a neoclassical world and Feenstra, Markusen, and Rose (1999) on gravity with oligopolistic competition.

6. Noteworthy exceptions exist. The Linder theory is one example, as would be the recent work on economic geography, in which market segmentation leads to a more intimate interaction between demand and production patterns.

7. The quotes are from Krugman (1996) and Bhagwati and Dehejia (1994).

8. It is worth noting, though, that on this issue both Bhagwati and Krugman arrived at the same substantive conclusion.

9. See, for example, Bowen, Leamer, and Sveikauskas (1987).

10. Partial equilibrium, of course, is why a dog chases its tail; general equilibrium is why the dog's chase is in vain.

11. For a more complete discussion of Trefler's methodology and conclusions, see the survey by Helpman (1999) and the references therein.

References

Aturupane, Chonira, Simeon Djankov, and Bernard Hoekman. 1998. Horizontal and vertical intra-industry trade between Eastern Europe and the European Union. *Weltwirtschaftliches-Archiv/Review of World Economics* 135(1):62–81.

Bhagwati, J., and V. Dehejia. 1994. Free trade and wages of the unskilled: Is Marx striking again? In J. Bhagwati and M. Kosters, eds., *Trade and Wages: Leveling Wages Down?* Washington, DC: AEI Press.

Bowen, H., et al. 1987. Multicountry, multifactor tests of the factor abundance theory. *American Economic Review* 77:791–809.

Chipman, John S. 1992. Intra-industry trade, factor proportions and aggregation. In James Melvin, James Moore, and Ray Riezman, eds., *Economic Theory and International Trade: Essays in Memoriam, J. Trout Rader*. New York: Springer.

Davis, Donald, and David Weinstein. 1998. An account of global factor trade. *American Economic Review* 91:1423–53.

Davis, Donald R., and David E. Weinstein. 1999. Trade in a non-integrated world: Insights from a factor content study. Mimeo. Columbia University.

Davis, Donald, David Weinstein, Scott Bradford, and Kazushige Shimpo. 1997. Using international and Japanese regional data to determine when the factor abundance of theory of trade works. *American Economic Review* 87:421–46.

Deardorff, A. 1998. Determinants of bilateral trade: Does gravity work in a neoclassical world? In J. Frankel, ed., *The Regionalization of the World Economy*. Chicago: University of Chicago Press.

Dollar, D., E. Wolff, and W. Baumol. 1989. The factor-price equalization model and industry labor productivity: An empirical test across countries. In R. Feenstra, ed., *Empirical Methods for International Trade*. Cambridge: MIT Press, pp. 23–48.

Eaton, J., and S. Kortum. 1999. International technology diffusion: Theory and measurement. *International Economic Review* 40(3):537–70.

Falvey, R. 1981. Commercial policy and intra-industry trade. *Journal of International Economics* 11:495–511.

Feenstra, Robert, James Markusen, and Andrew Rose. 1999. Understanding the home market effect and the gravity equation: The role of differentiating goods. NBER Working Paper.

Finger, J. M. 1975. Trade overlap and intra-industry trade. *Economic Inquiry* 13(4):581–89.

Greenaway, David, Robert Hine, and Chris Milner. 1994. Country-specific factors and the pattern of horizontal and vertical intra-industry trade in the UK. *Weltwirtschaftliches-Archiv* 130(1):77–100.

Grubel, P., and P. Lloyd. 1975. *Intra-industry Trade: The Theory and Measurement of International Trade in Differentiated Products*. London: Macmillan.

Harrigan, J. 1997. Technology, factor supplies, and international specialization: Estimating the neoclassical model. *American Economic Review* 87:475–94.

Helpman, Elhanan. 1998. Explaining the structure of foreign trade: Where do we stand? *Weltwirtschaftliches-Archiv/Review of World Economics* 134(4):573–89.

Helpman, Elhanan. 1999. The structure of foreign trade. *Journal of Economic Perspectives* 13(2):121–44.

Jorgenson, D., and M. Kuroda. 1990. Productivity and international competitiveness in Japan and the United States, 1960–1985. In C. Hulton, ed., *Productivity Growth in Japan and the United States*. Chicago: Chicago University Press.

Jorgenson, D., M. Kuroda, and M. Nishimizu. 1987. Japan–US industry-level productivity comparisons, 1960–1979. *Journal of the Japanese and International Economies* 1(1):1–30.

Kojima, K. 1964. The pattern of international trade among advanced countries. *Hitotsubashi Journal of Economics* (June): 16–34.

Krugman, P. 1979. Increasing returns, monopolistic competition, and international trade. *Journal of International Economics* 9(4):469–79.

Krugman, P. 1996. But for, as if, and so what? Thought experiments on trade and factor prices. Mimeo. Massachusetts Institute of Technology.

Lancaster, Kelvin. 1980. Intra-industry trade under perfect monopolistic competition. *Journal of International Economics* 10(2):151–75.

Leamer, E. 1980. The Leontief paradox, reconsidered. *Journal of Political Economy* 88(3):495–503.

Leamer, E. 1984. *Sources of International Comparative Advantage: Theory and Evidence*. Cambridge: MIT Press.

Leamer E. 1987. Paths of development in the three-factor, *n*-good general equilibrium model. *Journal of Political Economy* 95:961–99.

Leamer, E. 1990. Testing trade theory. NBER Working Paper 3957.

Leamer, E., and J. Levinsohn. 1995. International trade theory: The evidence. In G. Grossman and K. Rogoff, eds., *Handbook of International Economics*, vol. 3. Amsterdam: Elsevier, North-Holland, pp. 1339–94.

Schott, P. 1999. One size fits all? Specialization, trade and income inequality. Mimeo. Yale University. October.

Trefler, D. 1993. International factor price differences: Leontief was right! *Journal of Political Economy* 101:961–987.

Trefler, D. 1995. The case of the missing trade and other HOV mysteries. *American Economic Review* 85:1029–47.

18 Was It All in Ohlin?

Paul Krugman

Let me begin with an embarrassing admission: until I began working on this chapter, I had never actually read Ohlin's *Interregional and International Trade*. I suppose that my case was not that unusual: modern economists, trained to think in terms of crisp formal models, typically have little patience with the sprawling verbal expositions of a more leisurely epoch. To the extent that we care about intellectual history at all, we tend to rely on translators—on transitional figures like Paul Samuelson, who extracted models from the literary efforts of their predecessors. And let me also admit that reading Ohlin in the original is still not much fun: the MIT-trained economist in me keeps fidgeting impatiently, wondering when he will get to the point—that is, to the kernel of insight that ended up being grist for the mills of later modelers.

Moreover one can argue that Ohlin actually gains something in the translation: Samuelson famously found implications in Ohlin's own view of trade that the great thinker himself, due to his "diplomatic style" (in Tjalling Koopmans's phrase), had missed. Ohlin seemed to say that while trade shifts the distribution of income against scarce factors, it nonetheless probably improves their lot in absolute terms; Stolper and Samuelson showed that in a simple model the stark fact is that scarce factors lose by any measure. Ohlin definitely viewed factor-price equalization as only a tendency, surely incomplete; Samuelson showed that under the assumptions of Ohlin's chapter I, "Interregional Trade Simplified," it was quite possible that trade will fully equalize factor prices. So just as a modern student of evolution might be forgiven for preferring to get his Darwin courtesy of John Maynard Smith, a modern economics student might be forgiven for preferring to get his Ohlin via Samuelson, and indeed via Krugman-Obstfeld.

And yet what Ohlin disparagingly called "model mania" can lead to a narrowing of vision. Samuelson himself entitled his 1971 article expounding what has since come to be known as the specific-factors model "Ohlin was right," conceding that in a multifactor model some of Ohlin's skepticism about the full factor-price equalization and strong Stolper-Samuelson effects that arise in a two-by-two model turns out to be justified after all. What else might Ohlin have been right about?

Some years back I gave a short series of lectures (the Ohlin lectures, as it happens, written up in my book *Development, Geography, and Economic Theory*) on the way that a growing emphasis on formal modeling led economists to "forget" insights about the role of increasing returns in industrialization and economic location, only to rediscover those insights when modeling techniques became sufficiently advanced. Was the same true in international trade theory? In particular, did Ohlin's informal exposition of a theory of interregional and international trade contain the essence of what later came to be known as the "new trade theory" and the "new economic geography"?

The answer, it turns out, is yes and no. Ohlin did indeed have a view of international trade that not only gave a surprisingly important role to increasing returns (surprising because in Samuelsonian translation that role disappeared), but also one that suggested a sort of "unified field theory" of factor-based and scale-based trade that is a clear antecedent of the "integrated economy" approach that ended up playing a central role in post-1980 trade theory. On the other hand, despite Ohlin's title and his repeated suggestion that he was offering a unification of trade and location theory, there is little in *Interregional and International Trade* that seems to point the way to the distinctive features of "new economic geography." And there were a number of insights in modern trade theory that Ohlin did not, as far as I can tell, anticipate at all.

But let me start with my startling discovery: the extent to which Ohlin in the original anticipates a view of trade that the "new trade" theorists had to rediscover some fifty years later.

Increasing Returns as a Cause of Trade

What did international economists know and think about increasing returns in trade circa, say, 1975? Certainly they were aware of the issue: R. C. O. Matthews's 1950 integration of external economies and offer-curve analysis showed up as a supplemental reading in graduate courses, as did later papers such as Chacoliades (1970). But I think my description in an essay of a few years ago (Krugman 1996) still captures pretty accurately the state of general understanding:

> The observation that increasing returns could be a reason for trade between seemingly similar countries was by no means a well-understood proposition: certainly it was never covered in most textbooks or courses, undergraduate or graduate. The idea that trade might reflect an overlay of increasing-returns specialization on comparative advantage was not there at all: instead, the ruling idea was that increasing returns would simply alter the pattern of comparative advantage. Indeed, as late as 1984 many trade theorists still regarded the main possible contribution of scale economies to the story as being a tendency for large countries to export scale-sensitive goods. The essential arbitrariness of scale-economy specialization, its dependence on history and accident, was hardly ever mentioned. To the extent that welfare analysis was carried out, it focused on the concern that small countries might lose out because of their scale disadvantages.

Now it turns out that while this description is, I submit, a good characterization of what the typical trade theorist thought before the rise of the new trade theory, it is not at all what Ohlin said in 1933. But let me maintain the suspense a bit, and next describe how one might model increasing returns in trade today.

The particular model I want to exposit is not the monopolistic competition, intraindustry-versus-interindustry story that has become emblematic of the new trade theory; you will see why shortly. Rather, it is the integration of external economies with factor proportions first suggested in Helpman and Krugman (1985), and subsequently presented in too many survey papers, including my recent survey in the *Handbook of International Economics* (1998).

The starting point for that model is an economy without trade, or more accurately one without borders—that is, one in which factors of production can work freely with each other, regardless of national origin. In the simplest case we think of a world with two factors of production, and (at least) three goods: *X*, *Y*, and *Z*, ranked in order of capital intensity. Of these, one of the goods—say *X*—is subject to external economies in production.

This "integrated economy" will have an equilibrium, with goods prices, factor prices, and resource allocation (assume away the possibility of multiple equilibria). In figure 18.1—a rather cluttered

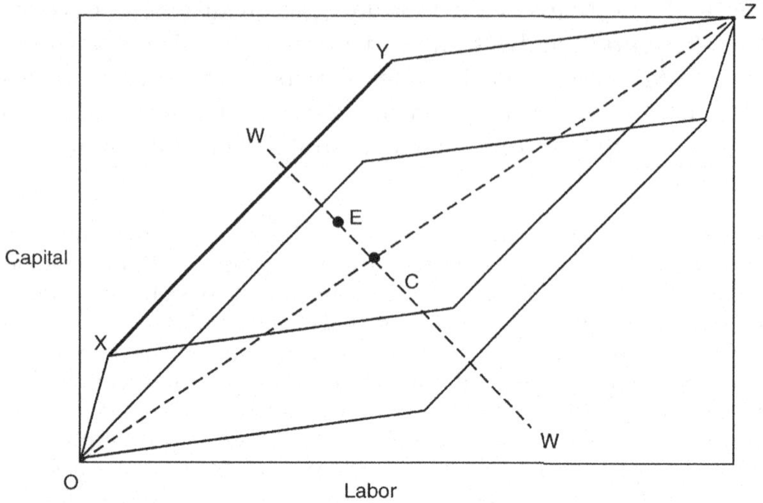

Figure 18.1
In a three-good model, in which one good is produced with increasing returns, trade can still reproduce the integrated economy.

picture, but the clutter has a purpose—I show the resources allocated to the three industries as the vectors *OX*, *XY*, and *YZ*; *OZ* is, given full employment, the resource endowment of the economy as a whole.

To turn this into a trade model, we now invoke Samuelson's angel, a character who appears in his "International factor price equalization once again" (1949). The angel—presumably the same one who stopped work on the Tower of Babel—divides up the world's factors of production into different nationalities, unable to work with each other. The angel's handiwork can be represented graphically by letting *O* be the origin for measuring the factor endowment of one country, *Z* the origin for the other; then the division of the world is indicated by a single point like *E*.

Can this divided world still reproduce the economic outcome of the integrated economy? Yes, if it is possible to figure out an international allocation of the pre-angel industries that uses all of each country's resources while meeting two criteria: nonnegative production of each good in each country (Samuelson's criterion) together with *concentration* of the *X* industry in only one country (so as not to dissipate the external economies). To do this, one must be able to put all of the factors originally producing *X* in one country, together with some of the factors producing *Y* and *Z*. Geometrically the integrated economy can be reproduced as long as E lies within either of the two parallelograms in figure 18.1. If E lies inside *both* parallelograms—as it does in this picture—there are *two* trading equilibria that reproduce the integrated economy, one in which X is concentrated in the country whose origin is at O, one with X concentrated in the other. (There might also be other equilibria that do not reproduce the integrated economy—but let us leave that possibility on one side.) This immediately implies that the pattern of production and trade may be indeterminate—but not that one cannot say quite interesting things about it.

For one thing, we know right away that whichever country gets the increasing-returns industry X will export that good. For another, we can surmise that whichever country has a higher capital–labor ratio will tend on average to export capital-intensive goods. This surmise can be made precise if we assume identical homothetic preferences, which means that each country's consumption of embodied factor services will lie along the diagonal OZ. Draw a line with slope equal to the wage–rental ratio (WW) through the endowment point E; then the division of the world's consumption of factor services will be indicated by C, and EC will be the net trade in such embodied factor services: the capital-abundant country will on average export capital-intensive goods. Of course, even if the countries have identical capital–labor ratios they will still trade because one will produce X and one will not. In the general case, however, trade will reflect both increasing returns and differences in resources.

Finally, this integrated-economy approach suggests that trade will almost surely increase the purchasing power of both countries. As in the causes of trade, there are two reasons, indicated in figure 18.2. The figure shows the unit isoquant II for some good before trade, with OA the resources used in producing that unit before trade and ww the factor prices. After trade the factor prices change, say to $w'w'$. If the industry has constant returns, that means that only OT resources are now needed to purchase a unit of the good, so that the country's resources are clearly able to purchase more after trade than before. If the industry has increasing returns, then as long as world production after trade (wherever it takes place) is larger than the country's own production would have been in the absence of trade, this comparative-advantage source of gains from trade is reinforced by an inward shift of the relevant unit isoquant to $I'I''$, further reducing the resouces needed to purchase that unit to T'.

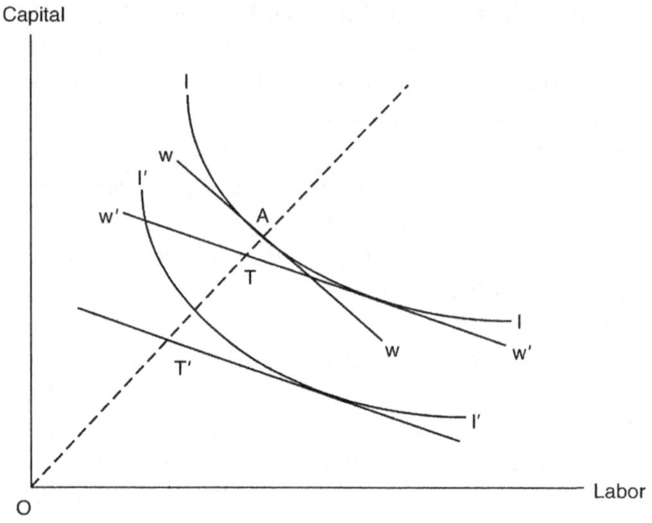

Figure 18.2
The presumption of gains from trade is strong, as long as trade reproduces the integrated economy—both increasing returns and comparative advantage produce gains.

The end result is a view of trade in which both differences in factor endowments and increasing returns are sources of trade—where in each case, what trade does is to allow the world economy to overcome the problem created by the dispersion of resources across countries. And both the embodied trade in resources—which allows countries in effect to trade abundant resources for scarce—and the ability, through trade, to concentrate industries (possibly arbitrarily) to achieve larger-scale lead to higher purchasing power than countries would otherwise have.

For me, at least, this integration of increasing returns and comparative advantage was not easily arrived at—it was, as already suggested, not at all a view one heard in the profession circa 1977, and it took me something like five years (from 1978 to 1983) and a lot of help from my colleagues and friends to get it down to the simplicity you see here. So it is quite amazing, and a bit humbling, to read Ohlin. Here are some selected quotations from chapter III of *Interregional and International Trade*, "Another Condition of Interregional Trade":

[T]he advantages of producing a large quantity of a single commodity instead of a little of all commodities must lead to interregional trade.... To

> demonstrate the importance of this, assume that a number of regions are isolated from each other, and that their factor endowments and their demand are so balanced that the relative prices of factors and commodities are everywhere the same. Under the [constant returns] assumptions of chapter I, no trade is then possible. As a matter of fact, insofar as the market for some articles within each region is not large enough to permit the most efficient scale of production, division of trade and labor will be profitable. Each region will specialize on some of these articles and exchange them for the rest.... The tendency toward specialization because of differences in factor endowments is reinforced by the advantages of large-scale production. The location of an industry in one region and not in another might simply be due to chance.... The conclusion that interregional trade reduces the disadvantages of indivisibility corresponds to the previous conclusion that trade mitigates the disadvantages of an unequal geographical distribution of productive agents.... Thus all interregional trade, whether due to the one cause or the other, might be regarded as a substitute for geographical mobility of productive factors.[1]

Now it is always tricky to reread old texts in the light of subsequent information; knowing what actually happened, you can probably find a prophecy of Nostradamus that fits the event, and knowing subsequent developments in economic theory, you can probably find most of it hinted at in Ibn Khaldun. Still I think that it is pretty clear that Ohlin in 1933 had a view of the role of increasing returns in trade that corresponds fairly well to the story told by figures 18.1 and 18.2. And yet that view remained hidden in plain sight for nearly fifty years: in the late 1970s, as I have already suggested, few trade theorists thought of increasing returns as a potential independent source of trade, and they tended to think of its welfare implications as a threat to rather than a reinforcement of the argument for gains from trade.

How did so many people miss what Ohlin not only knew but said reasonably clearly in a classic monograph?

How Increasing Returns Got Lost

The proximate answer to how Ohlin's insights about increasing returns as a cause of international trade got misplaced is surely that from the 1940s on few people actually read Ohlin in the original. Oh, many people may have skimmed the book—but they approached it with a mind already conditioned by Paul Samuelson's interpretation, and so they more or less failed to register the other things in there. In effect, they assumed that Samuelson had extracted all the juice.

And what about Samuelson? He was quite aware that Ohlin stressed increasing returns as a subsidiary cause of international trade, but understandably chose in his models to focus on the primary argument. The trouble was that those models were so successful—successful not only in distilling a long verbal argument into a few diagrams but in finding implications in those diagrams that the verbal exposition had missed—that they took over the whole discourse, and whatever was not in the simplest models got forgotten.

It is also worth pointing out that while Ohlin does give significant amounts of space to the discussion of increasing returns, he simultaneously downplays it. For one thing, he underestimates the extent to which increasing returns represent a break from the comparative-advantage tradition, possibly because he overstates the extent to which his factor proportions approach is a repudiation of Ricardian insights. In a modern graduate course, Heckscher-Ohlin seems to follow naturally from Ricardo—both models build on the basic idea of differences in production possibilities, with Heckscher-Ohlin simply shifting the explanation of these differences to one that stresses differences in resources rather than in technology; increasing returns stories about trade, in which differences are the result rather than the cause of trade, represent a major departure. In *Interregional and International Trade*, by contrast, resource-based explanations of trade are treated as a fundamental break with the Ricardian labor theory of value, and increasing returns as a sort of uncontroversial add-on.

At the same time Ohlin strongly discounts the practical importance of increasing returns: "[I]t is certainly the differences in factor supplies that determine the course of interregional trade—unless regions are small—whereas the advantages of large-scale production are more in the nature of a subsidiary cause, carrying the division of labor and trade a little further than it would otherwise go, but not changing their characteristics." This may well have been true at the time he was writing (some critics of the "new trade theory" insist, indeed, that it is still true today). In the 1920s world trade was still dominated by North–South exchanges of manufactures for raw materials rather than two-way trade in manufactures among advanced countries, and the striking examples of industry agglomerations leading to international trade tended to be old-fashioned craft sectors like jewelry. The great rise in intraindustry trade among advanced countries, and of huge exporting agglomerations like Silicon Valley (or, for that matter, the City of London) still lay in the future. (Actually Ohlin was not completely consistent: after disparaging the practical importance of increasing returns in Part One, he seemed in Part Two to suggest that increasing returns would play a growing role over time, and thereby ensure that trade did not decline even as industry spread across the world. At least that's what I think he said: the discussion of the "trend of international trade" in chapter VII is one of the murkiest passages in a book that is not exactly a model of crystalline clarity in any case). The point, however, is that by playing down half of his original contribution, Ohlin in effect encouraged subsequent modelers to omit that part of his insight entirely, and the next generation of trade theorists, who read Ohlin-as-modeled rather than the original, never heard about it.

But even if Ohlin had stressed increasing returns more forcefully than he did, there were some inherent reasons why the translation of his work into more formal models probably was fated to drop his insight.

First is the generic problem of market structure—the same problem that led to a temporary forgetting of insights in location theory and development economics. Ohlin, writing in a Marshallian tradition (and before the work of Chamberlin and Robinson), is cheerfully blurry about the distinction among types of increasing returns—he is aware that there is an important distinction between external and internal economies but is not careful to separate the cases. Once more formal modeling became the norm, however, any practicing economist was bound to come to a sudden stop over that issue. When Ohlin said "increasing returns," did he mean internal economies of scale? In that case we are in the realm of imperfect competition, and as Harry Johnson (1967) almost triumphantly declared, during the heyday of Heckscher-Ohlin-Samuelson theory imperfect competition seemed impossible to model in a general-equilibrium framework. Or did he mean external economies? In that case, as any postwar theorist was bound to realize, we were in a world of market failure, with the case for free markets in general open to question; on first thought one might expect that any theory that stressed external economies would also be a theory that challenged the case for free trade. (After all, that was the apparent implication of Frank Graham's 1923 discussion of protection under increasing returns.) At the time the natural inclination might well have been to forget about the whole thing. It was only with the development of tractable models of monopolistic competition that it became easy to think of increasing-returns trade as a beneficial overlay on comparative advantage; and only with those monopolistic competition models in hand that it also became natural to revisit external-economy models, as in the model above, and realize that they could tell a similar story.

There was also a more specific misconception that arose in trade modeling: the confusion that arose from the habit of thinking in terms of two-good models. The two-by-two version of Heckscher-Ohlin is, of course, a thing of beauty and a source of much insight when used properly. If one tries, however, to squeeze increasing returns into that same two-good framework, one ends up with a seriously misplaced view. First, you tend to think that increasing returns can give rise to arbitrary, accidental specialization only if they are sufficiently strong—specifically, strong enough to turn the production possibilities frontier concave instead of convex. Second, you find yourself thinking that absent that reversal of curvature, the only remaining effect of increasing returns is to modify comparative advantage, giving large countries an advantage in scale-intensive goods. All it takes to clear the air is a three-good model; indeed, you have to wonder why it took fifty years for someone to propose figure 18.1. But such was the focus on two-good models that somehow it never happened.

From my point of view, this is all a happy story. Since figure 18.1 requires none of the monopolistic competition modeling technology that became available only in the 1970s, there is no good reason why someone might not have read Ohlin carefully, been a bit more flexible about modeling strategy, and created much of what later became known as the new trade theory when I was still in grade school. In practice, a mixture of misplaced intellectual anxieties and modeling prejudices delayed that development until the late 1970s, and some of us were in a position to get a lot of professional mileage out of what in retrospect seems a fairly obvious set of ideas.

Economic Geography

It is obvious—in retrospect—that something special happens when factor mobility interacts with increasing returns. Suppose that there are strong advantages to concentration of factors—where these advantages may take the form of true external economies but may also be due to "linkage" effects arising from the effect of concentration on the size of markets and the availability of inputs. And suppose also that some factors are more mobile than others. Then factor mobility will tend to increase differences among regions rather than reducing them, and instead of substituting for regional specialization will promote it. Start with an exceptional concentration of nerds in the vicinity of Stanford University; the resulting industry specialization will attract more nerds, reinforcing the nerd-friendliness of the local environment, and you end up with Silicon Valley. Similar processes lead to concentrations of ambitious people in London, beautiful people in Hollywood, and so on; and more broadly, they lead most of the population of sparsely populated North America to live in a few densely populated metropolitan corridors.

This observation is, as I suggested, obvious in retrospect; but it certainly took me a while to see it. Why exactly I spent a decade between showing how the interaction of transport costs and increasing returns at the level of the plant could lead to the "home market effect" (Krugman 1980) and realizing that the techniques developed there led naturally to simple models of regional divergence (Krugman 1991) remains a mystery to me. The only good news was that nobody else picked up that $100 bill lying on the sidewalk in the interim.

But did Ohlin already know all about this, in the way that he more or less anticipated the new trade theory?

He certainly touched on all the elements. Here as in his treatment of increasing returns, Ohlin was in a way at an advantage over later economists because it was still possible to write in the Marshallian tradition: he did not need to describe carefully worked-out models—which meant that he could simply hand-wave his way past the nasty bits, like how to describe market structure, or how to integrate transportation costs into general equilibrium. (It is the process of taming those nasty bits that accounts for most of the algebra in the monograph by Fujita, Krugman, and Venables 1999.) So he could and did mention almost in passing many of the key insights that modelers would confirm some sixty years later. In the new economic geography a central theme is the tension between "centripetal" forces that pull factors together, and "centrifugal" forces that push them apart; well, Ohlin describes a tension between agglomerating and "deglomerating" tendencies. (Hey, economic jargon has not entirely changed for the worse.) The new economic geography stresses the role of historical accident in determining the location of industries; Ohlin writes that "Inventions may by chance lead to manufacture in one country or place when others would do just as well; yet the industry tends to remain where it was first located, for the quality of the labor factors adapt themselves and so do capital investments in production, transportation, and trade connections."

And yet it seems to me that while much of what the new economic geography says can be found in Ohlin, the case for a missed opportunity—for asserting that Ohlin had the right vision, but that subsequent readers or, perhaps more accurately, nonreaders failed to appreciate it—is much less striking than in the case of the new trade theory. For while Ohlin may have had many of the elements, he was far less sure-footed than he was with increasing returns as a cause of trade, and underplayed the implications to an even greater extent. Let me in particular note three ways in which Ohlin's vision seems to have gotten a bit blurry when it came to the ideas that make up the new economic geography.

First, Ohlin's Marshallian sloppiness about internal versus external economies may have caught up with him here, in the sense that he does not seem to make a clear distinction between individual and collective rationality. In chapter XII one encounters a section entitled "Arbitrary elements in location," which begins with this sentence: "The historical influence can lead to an uneconomical location of industry." Aha! one thinks; he is about to talk about how early decisions can be locked in by external economies. But no: what follows is a brief discussion of the likelihood that location decisions will be mistaken. Surely the point is that an industry can be in the wrong place even if nobody is making a mistake, that it might be individually rational to stay even though it is collectively irrational not to move, but somehow this point got missed.

Second, Ohlin downplayed the endogeneity of factor location, declaring that "even small and nearby districts show substantial and lasting differences in natural resources, transfer resources and facilities, and labor supply. Such differences are to a large extent causes rather than effects of location of industry." Now this may have been true in Europe at the time of writing, though it seems doubtful even there. If one considers the United States, however—and Ohlin often uses American examples of interregional trade—the location of activity in the 1920s was already largely driven by the logic of self-reinforcing concentration. After all, America was sharply divided between manufacturing belt and farm belt, with most of the manufacturing belt owing its dominance to an early start rather than inherent resource advantages; the auto industry in Detroit, the financial and garment industries in New York, the tire industry in Akron, and so forth, were already famous examples of industrial concentration. Indeed, one could argue that the "economic geography" forces of concentration played a larger role in interregional trade in America when Ohlin was writing than they do now.

But perhaps Ohlin underemphasized what we now think of as new economic geography issues for the same reason that a casual reader, trying to extract a key message from his book, would probably overlook his discussion of these issues: unlike the integration of increasing returns with comparative advantage, which in effect reinforced his basic vision, the interaction of increasing returns with factor mobility actually tended to run counter to that vision. For despite its Victorian sprawl and (by post-Samuelsonian standards) untidiness, *Interregional and International Trade* is in the main a tract animated by a single idea: the movement of goods and factors is the way the world economy tries to overcome the limitations placed upon it by the fragmentation of its resources, and the effect of that movement is one of convergence in prices. The logic of modern economic geography models, in which trade and factor mobility are often complements, and factor movements often lead to divergence in factor and even goods prices, is something that Ohlin realized could happen, but it ran counter to his main theme.

What Isn't in Ohlin (at all)

It is a bit humbling to realize that much of what would in the 1980s come to be called the new trade theory, and some of what would in the 1990s be called the new economic geography, is already present in a widely cited 1933 book. One might argue that the ability of economists to miss all those insights itself makes the case for formal models, if only for their tendency to concentrate the reader's mind. But have modern trade and geography theorists been doing more than making old ideas precise? What isn't in Ohlin, at all?

Well, I think that there are three main areas that are distinctive to late-twentieth-century models, and are truly absent from older writing—Ohlin, for all his perceptiveness, included.

The first is the appreciation of the importance and distinctiveness of imperfect competition. As I suggested above, Ohlin had a Marshallian tendency to fuzz over the distinction between internal economies of scale and external increasing returns, and was certainly not much worried about how firms with market power would behave. Yet when increasing returns finally did begin to play a central role in international trade theory, it was precisely because theorists finally managed to "tame" imperfect competition and hence to feel comfortable talking about internal scale economies.

As a practical matter, the focus on imperfect competition, and on monopolistic competition in particular, gave the new trade theory an immediate empirical focus: the rise of intraindustry trade among advanced countries, which meshed perfectly (at least in terms of casual empiricism) with the monopolistic-competition-cum-comparative advantage models developed by Dixit and Norman, Helpman, and myself. As a theoretical matter, once one realized that internal economies of scale necessarily implied imperfect competition, it became possible to consider stories in which imperfect competition—as opposed to the increasing returns per se—were the main source of action. One example was the theory of reciprocal dumping—trade driven neither by comparative advantage nor by increasing returns but rather as a result of the efforts of firms to raid each others' inframarginal customers. Another was the theory of strategic trade policy, in which the gap between price and marginal cost rather than the advantages of scale itself offered the potential scope for neo-mercantilist arguments.

A second aspect of modern trade theory that seems to me to be absent from Ohlin—though it might be worth a more careful reading—is the distinction between equilibria and optima. In constant-returns trade theory this is not a big issue (except when one is considering domestic distortions arguments for trade and industrial policy). But in the presence of increasing returns, either internal or external, it can be deeply misleading to confuse what is with what should be. I have already noted that Ohlin seems to have gotten confused over the nature of what we would now call lock-in to the wrong location, attributing it to mistakes by individuals rather than the difference between collective and individual rationality. He also seems to be far too blase about the way in which trade-offs involving the tension between agglomerative and "deglomerative" forces would be resolved. While that tension implies both that there is some appropriate size of industrial clusters and their market areas, and (probably) that some typical size of cluster and market area will arise in practice, there is no good reason to suppose—as Ohlin does—that the actual and appropriate sizes will be the same.

Why did Ohlin fail to make this distinction? Partly this was, no doubt, because Marshall and his followers had been more or less deliberately confused about such issues, preferring a diplomatic writing style that emphasized broad themes over presumably nit-picking details. Beyond this, Ohlin was attempting to offer a unified vision of trade as a way of overcoming the dispersion of factors; since in what has come to be known as "Hecksher-Ohlin" trade there is no important distinction between equilibrium and optimum, it would have spoiled the symmetry to make much of that distinction when it came to increasing returns.

Finally, I cannot find in Ohlin one of the central things that attracted me to the kinds of models used in the new economic geography: the idea of qualitative, discontinuous change. It is typical in the models now used to think about regional differentiation that small changes in underlying parameters—say, in transportation costs—sometimes bring about large changes in behavior. For example, when transport costs drop below some critical level a symmetric division of industry among regions may become unstable, and a cumulative process of concentration may begin. This is, to be sure, hardly a new idea. But it is an idea whose time has, in a way, come. New models of geography, which derive the agglomerative or centripetal forces from an underlying interaction among more basic determinants, are better suited to considering how the whole geographical logic of an economy might change than older accounts—like Ohlin's—that simply assumed agglomerative tendencies. And the availability of easy computation, letting us explore nonlinear dynamics quickly and cheaply, also probably encourages the exploration of such themes. Anyway, whatever the reason, the sorts of dramatic stories that I like in geography—the way that railroads could have precipitated the division of Italy into industrial north and depressed Mezzogiorno, or the discovery of oil could have pushed California over a critical threshold and started a self-reinforcing process of industrial development—are more or less new, at least to trade theorists.

So there is a reasonable amount of modern theory that is not in Ohlin, even in rough form. But it is still amazing how much is in there, if you really look.

What Do Trade Theorists Know, and When Do They Know It?

At the risk of offending many people living and dead, I think it might be fair to say that there have been no more than, say, five big ideas in international trade theory. They might include:

- Comparative advantage
- Determination of the terms of trade by reciprocal demand
- Interaction between factor abundance and factor intensity
- Interaction between domestic distortions and trade policy
- Arbitrary specialization driven by increasing returns

(I am open to suggestions about other big ideas that might belong on the list.)

We know both from intellectual historians (Douglas Irwin, in particular) and from the personal experience of many people at this conference that getting each of these big ideas into mainstream thinking required a major intellectual struggle, in general involving new techniques (offer curves, Edgeworth boxes, Dixit-Stiglitz) and a painful process of changing not only the way one answered questions but the questions themselves. And yet the funny thing is that once the intellectual struggle had reached a certain point, the central idea came to seem obvious—the sort of thing one could summarize in a paragraph or two, and make comprehensible to any reasonably bright congressional staffer (though probably not the congressman himself).[2] What is more, once the idea was clearly expressed, it generally turned out to be an idea that had been expressed not quite so clearly by a number of older economists.

The moral, surely, is that the next big idea in international economics—the idea that will transform the field—is often something simple, something already out there, something that all of us will later claim to have known all along. And that idea is…

Notes

1. Ohlin also stated, more or less clearly, the idea that if the increasing returns industry is capital-intensive, the country that gets it will shift to a labor-intensive mix of

constant-returns goods, and conversely. True, he argues in terms of factor prices, missing the Samuelsonian point about factor price equalization. But it is still amazingly close to what I regarded as a fresh discovery when I finally worked it out.

2. Richard Feynman once told a reporter who wanted a five-minute summary of his work that if it could have been summarized in five minutes, it wouldn't have warranted a Nobel. Yet the big ideas in trade theory probably *can* be summarized in not much more than five minutes.

References

Chacoliades, M. 1970. Increasing returns and the theory of comparative advantage. *Southern Economic Journal* 37:157–62.

Fujita, M., P. Krugman, and A. Venables. 1999. *The Spatial Economy*. Cambridge: MIT Press.

Graham, F. 1923. Some aspects of protection further considered. *Quarterly Journal of Economics* 37:199–227.

Grossman, G., and K. Rogoff. 1998. *Handbook of International Economics*, vol. 3. Amsterdam: North-Holland.

Helpman, E., and P. Krugman. 1985. *Market Structure and Foreign Trade*. Cambridge: MIT Press.

Johnson, H. 1967. International trade theory and monopolistic competition theory. In R. Kuenne, ed., *Monopolistic Competition Theory: Studies in Impact*. New York: Wiley.

Krugman, P. 1980. Scale economies, product differentiation, and the pattern of trade. *American Economic Review* 70:950–59.

Krugman, P. 1991. Increasing returns and economic geography. *Journal of Political Economy* 99:483–99.

Krugman, P. 1995. *Development, Geography, and Economic Theory*. Cambridge: MIT Press.

Krugman, P. 1996. How to be a crazy economist. In S. Medema and W. Samuels, eds., *Foundations of Research in Economics: How do Economists do Economics*? Aldershot, England: Edward Elgar.

Matthews, R. C. O. 1950. Reciprocal demand and increasing returns. *Review of Economic Studies* 17:149–58.

Ohlin, B. 1933. *Interregional and International Trade*. Cambridge: Harvard University Press.

Samuelson, P. 1949. International factor price equalization once again.

Samuelson, P. 1971. Ohlin was right. *Scandinavian Journal of Economics* 59:181–97.

19 Ohlin versus Stolper-Samuelson?

Douglas A. Irwin

Introduction

Anyone who has dipped into *Interregional and International Trade* (1933) knows that Bertil Ohlin's theoretical vision was much broader than the standard two-factor, two-good model that has been handed down to us as the textbook Heckscher-Ohlin-Samuelson model of international trade. Ohlin not only set out a theory of trade based on factor proportions but also investigated trade in relation to increasing returns to scale, economic geography, international factor movements, and a host of other topics that continue to be active areas of economic research.

While Ohlin's principal contribution will always be the sharp focus on relative factor abundance as a force driving international trade, his broad and eclectic approach is evident even here. An example of this is his treatment of the effects of product price changes, including those induced by trade policy interventions, on relative factor prices and factor incomes. At the time Ohlin wrote, the prevailing view of Frank Taussig (1927) and others was that while specific factors may be harmed as a result of free trade, mobile factors (e.g., labor) would be insulated from any potential losses precisely because of their mobility across sectors. In his analysis Ohlin advanced the contrary notion that the scarce factor of production might benefit from protection, regardless of its ability to move between sectors. This conflict between the then prevailing view and Ohlin's novel approach, which he did not fully spell out, spawned the classic paper by Wolfgang Stolper and Paul Samuelson (1941), who used a two-factor, two-good model to develop what we now know as the Stolper-Samuelson theorem.[1]

Yet it is not clear that Ohlin would have endorsed the Stolper-Samuelson framework as the most appropriate one in which to analyze the question of trade policy and factor returns. Ohlin himself analyzed the effects of trade policy on factor prices in a broader three-factor framework that included land, labor, and capital. Samuelson (1971) also recognized the important differences between Ohlin's implicit model and that of the two-factor, two-good model, but more in the context of factor price equalization rather than the Stolper-Samuelson theorem.

The first question posed by this chapter is whether Ohlin's own theory of the factor price response to tariff intervention is consistent with the Stolper-Samuelson theorem. This question is addressed first by setting out Ohlin's theory and then selecting among the multitude of extant three-factor models the one that seems most congruent with his framework. That model turns out to be the one described by Fred Gruen and Max Corden (1970), which blends elements of the specific-factor model and the standard Heckscher-Ohlin-Samuelson model. This model was also the basis for Anne Krueger's (1977) analysis of trade and development and has been further explored by Alan Deardorff (1984) and Edward Leamer (1987).

At the time when Ohlin was writing, the issue of whether labor could benefit from protection was a burning controversy among international economists, particularly in the context of the United States and Australia.[2] This question is now a live one for economic historians. Therefore the second question posed by this chapter is whether Ohlin's theory was in fact correct in predicting that labor could have benefited from protection. The major political justification for the high U.S. import tariffs during the late-nineteenth and early twentieth century was that it protected high American wages against the low wages paid by European producers. Was this rationale justified? While this chapter will not provide a definitive answer to this question, it will explore some of the empirical evidence for and against that proposition.

Ohlin on Trade Policy and Factor Prices

Ohlin (1933:306n. 2) opens his discussion of trade policy and factor prices by observing that "[i]nternational trade theory has, in my opinion, given far too much attention to the effects of certain variations, for example, in duties, on the national incomes, and too little to the effects on individual incomes. In many cases, changes in the sums count for very little, while changes in the individual incomes are distinctly relevant." This statement marks his break with the "real costs" approach which focused on labor as the only factor of production and thus tended to ignore any income distributional consequences of trade.[3]

Ohlin (1933:307) then considered the effect of tariff policy on labor income. "It seems beyond doubt that the tariff policy pursued during the last half-century has not raised the standard of living of the labouring classes. It is doubtful if agricultural duties increase the relative scarcity of manual labour compared with other factors, and they certainly raise the cost of living for the working classes." That may have been true for agricultural-importing countries in Europe, but what about the United States where tariff protection for manufacturers was the issue? "It is, however, true that manufacturing duties tend to depress the rent of farm land.... It is on the whole not at all unlikely that the sum total of rent is reduced in countries with high manufacturing duties.... In most countries, however, the sum of rents is small compared with the sum of wages to manual workers. Even a substantial reduction of the former brings only a slight increase in the latter."

Ohlin continued by adding capital to the analysis: "The effect of manufacturing duties upon the relative scarcity of labour and capital is rather to the advantage of the latter, although lack of statistical material prevents reliable conclusions. It seems probable that manufacturing industries in Europe require a greater amount of capital per labourer than agriculture; in the United States, where agriculture is more industrialised, it seemed before the War to require as much capital per worker as other industries."

Ohlin (1933:308) summed up in this way: "We must conclude that there is no reason for assuming that the share of the labouring class in the national income has been so much increased by the tariff policy pursued in the last half-century that the depressing effect of this policy on the size of the national income has been more than offset." Therefore Ohlin generally subscribed to the standard view that labor would not benefit from the tariff. Ohlin, however, then added this crucial caveat: "The situation would be different if manufacturing duties were placed specially upon products from industries using little capital and much manual labor. But such is not the case, at least in the countries for which statistical material is available." Yet Ohlin was soon to conclude that this caveat may indeed apply in the case of the United States.

Ohlin (1933:316–17) later turned to the issue of how free trade would affect the United States. Agriculture, he thought, would clearly expand: "Farm land would be more in demand, and the utilisation of forests, mines, etc., would be extended." On the other hand, he continued, "industries using large quantities of labour, particularly of the skilled type, would be reduced. The distribution of income would thus change in favour of natural resources, while the relative position of labour would be less advantageous. Whether demand for capital would rise or fall is difficult to say. A superficial study of American industries gives the impression that those dependent upon protection use more labour and less capital than those in export industries. If that is correct, an expansion of the latter would mean a tendency to a higher rate of interest."[4] In the case of the United States, therefore, Ohlin concluded that labor would benefit from protection and be harmed by free trade.[5]

Factor Prices in a Three-Factor Model

The previous section's brief review of Ohlin's writings makes it clear that he did not have a simple two-factor (capital and labor) model in mind when analyzing the impact of trade policy on factor rewards. Rather, Ohlin worked with a three-factor model consisting of land, labor, and capital.[6] The three-factor, three-good model of Gruen and Corden (1970) appears to be the most appropriate for illuminating Ohlin's approach and examining the impact of U.S. trade policy on factor rewards during this period.[7]

To adopt this model to an Ohlin-style analysis of the United States, we look to his description of an agricultural sector that produces with labor and land and a manufacturing sector that produces several goods with differing proportions of capital and labor. In this vein, consider the following simple framework: an agricultural sector produces a single output with a combination of labor and sector-specific land and manufacturing sector produces two-goods, one labor-intensive and the other capital-intensive, with both labor and sector-specific capital. Labor is homogeneous and perfectly mobile within manufacturing and between the two sectors.

Such an arrangement is shown geometrically using the dual of the production function in figure 19.1. This figure extends Michael

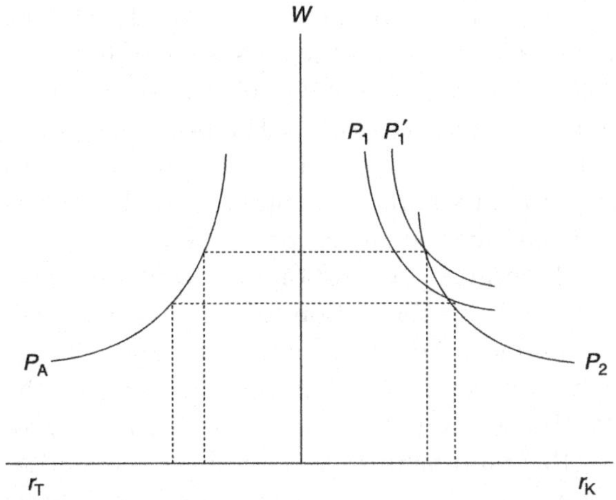

Figure 19.1
The geometric dual of the three-factor, three-good general equilibrium model.

Mussa's (1979) dual exposition for the two-sector model by depicting the isoprice contours for the three goods. The quadrants for the agriculture and manufacturing sector share the wage axis because the two sectors compete for labor, while the respective land and capital axes are independent. The absolute value of the slope of the isoprice contour indicates the capital–labor ratio used in production. The contour is convex to the origin, reflecting the fact that the capital–labor ratio is an increasing function of the wage–rental ratio. The elasticity of substitution between the two factors is represented by the curvature of the contour. Because land is sector-specific and assumed to be fixed in inelastic supply, substitutions reflected in the labor–land ratio in agriculture are made solely through adjustments in the amount of labor employed.

The right quadrant displays the isoprice contours of the two manufacturing goods, $P_1(w,r)$ and $P_2(w,r)$. Good 1 is assumed to be more labor-intensive than good 2 for all factor prices. Mussa's (1979) exposition explores this quadrant in detail and should be referred to for details. The left quadrant shows the isoprice contour for the agricultural sector, $P_A(w,r_A)$, which produces output from labor and the immobile factor land, which earns the return r_A. With the prices of all goods determined exogenously, the equilibrium wage rate is set by the intersection of the isoprice contours in the manufacturing sector.

Because another sector with a specific factor is grafted onto the two-sector model, the Gruen-Corden model retains some of the comparative static properties of the two-sector model. Consider an increase in the price of the labor-intensive good 1. The isoprice contour P_1 shifts out to P_1', leading to a new factor price equilibrium with higher wages and lower returns to land and capital. As with Stolper-Samuelson, these are real changes in factor prices. Wages rise by more than the increase in P_1 because, in addition to the outward shift of P_1 that boosts wages, there is a substitution toward more capital-intensive production techniques. The real return to land and to capital fall, and there is a reallocation of labor between sectors. The agricultural sector sheds labor and adopts a more land-intensive production method, whereas the manufacturing sector absorbs the additional labor, sees its overall capital–labor ratio fall, and yet adopts more capital-intensive production methods (a seemingly paradoxical result). An increase in the manufactured sector's labor endowment also gives rise to a Rybczynski effect on the manufactured outputs, with an increase in the output of the labor intensive good 1 and a fall in the output of the capital-intensive good 2 (above and beyond that induced by the increase in P_1 alone). Similarly an increase in the price of the capital-intensive good decreases the real wage and increases the real return to capital. The effect on the real return to land is ambiguous, although it increases in nominal terms.

If the price of the agricultural good increases, its isoprice contour shifts out. The return to land will increase, but if the economy remains diversified neither the wage nor the return to capital changes. Hence the real wage and return to capital fall in terms of the agricultural good while the return to land increases in a proportion greater to the increase in P_A.[8] Like the examples above, labor is reallocated in the economy. The agricultural sector attracts labor and switches to more labor-intensive methods. The capital–labor ratio in manufacturing rises as labor migrates to agriculture, leading to a Rybczynski effect on manufacturing output with no changes in the prices of those outputs.

Thus changes in the price of the manufactured goods and the agricultural good are not symmetric: a change in the price of a manufactured good affects all factor prices, while a change in the price of the agricultural good only alters the return to land if the manufacturing sector remains diversified.

Thus, in the context of his model, Ohlin was "right" in that a tariff that protected labor-intensive manufactured goods would raise the real return to labor and reduce the real return to capital and land.[9] Note that there is no basic conflict between the Ohlin and the Stolper-Samuelson prediction because in the Gruen-Corden model the diversified manufacturing sector (what Ronald Jones calls the two-by-two tradable "nugget") pins down factor prices for other sectors.

Tariffs and Income Distribution: United States Evidence circa 1909

In his stylized model of the U.S. economy, Ohlin showed that labor as a class could benefit from import protection. Is there evidence that this could have been the case?

The model sketched out in the previous section provides a useful stylized framework in which to think about the U.S. economy during this period. The United States had a comparative advantage in agricultural products (e.g., raw cotton and grains), a comparative disadvantage in labor-intensive manufactured goods (e.g., cotton and woollen textiles), and a changing comparative advantage in capital-intensive manufactured goods (e.g., iron and steel products and machinery). Before the mid-1890s the United States was a net importer of these capital-intensive manufactures. Then an export surge dating from that period quickly turned the United States into a net exporter of such goods (see Irwin 2002).

The rhetoric of U.S. trade policy was that high tariffs were necessary to protect the high wages of American workers. Economists then were justifiably skeptical of this extreme view. Taussig and others did not believe that the wages depended on tariffs and frequently countered that high U.S. wages reflected not protection but the high productivity of U.S. workers. Of course, average real wages and average labor productivity proved to be highly correlated then as now. Figure 19.2 plots labor productivity and real wages for the United States from 1889 to 1929. This relationship is frequently depicted today with recent data to counter the charge that the sluggish wage growth in the United States and in other industrialized countries is due to increasing trade with developing countries. Although this chart clearly shows that real wage growth is correlated with labor productivity, Taussig and Ohlin were grappling with the different issue of labor's share in national income.

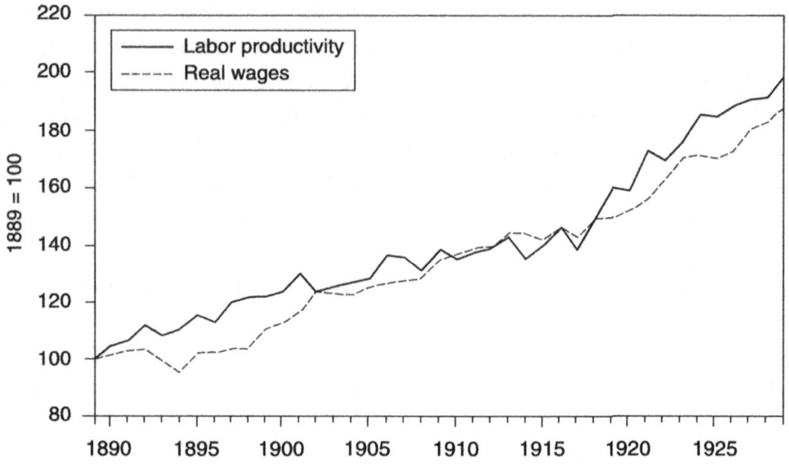

Figure 19.2
U.S. labor productivity and real wages, 1889 to 1929. Sources: U.S. Bureau of the Census, *Historical Statistics of the United States, Colonial Times to 1970* (Washington, DC: GPO, 1975), series D736, D726, W4.

J. Bradford De Long (1998:351) has recently came down on Taussig's side in examining the effect of protection on wages and growth during this period: "Economists's standard tools suggest that the tariff reduced the living standard of Americans—the real wage of American workers—by about 0.7 percent of national product in the short run." Assuming that the elasticity of demand for imports is one, De Long states that a 30 percent tariff would then reduce the import share of national demand from a counterfactual level of 9 percent to the actual level of 7 percent. Taking forgone producer and consumer surplus as 15 percent of the value of imports, De Long concludes that U.S. tariffs resulted in "a reduction in real incomes of 0.3 percent of national product, with little reason to think that this reduction in real incomes fell disproportionately on capital rather than on labor."

Yet Ohlin's theory suggests that the burden of the tariff could have fallen disproportionately on land and capital to the benefit of labor. Such a result hinges on whether import tariffs were skewed toward protecting labor-intensive industries, as Ohlin suspected in his "superficial study" of the matter. The validity of this assumption can be assessed by examining the structure of the U.S. tariff in 1909 using data from the Census of Manufactures of that year and tariff data available in the *Statistical Abstract of the United States*. The Census of Manufactures provides data that allow two measures of an industry's factor intensity to be calculated: the capital–labor ratio (k_i), and the wage share in industry value-added (θ_{Li}).

Table 19.1 reports regression results of the nominal tariff on the two measures of factor intensity for a sample of 17 manufacturing industries.[10] Using either measure, the nominal tariff is lower for industries with a higher capital–labor ratio and higher for industries with a high labor share in industry value added. (The statistical significance of these coefficients is marginal except in column 2.) The Spearman rank correlation between tariffs and the capital–labor ratio (−0.22) and the industry wage share (0.40) give us the same conclusion, although again neither of these correlations is statistically significant.

This evidence suggests, somewhat weakly, that Ohlin was correct in his impression that the tariff tended to be higher on labor-intensive goods. The next step is to determine the magnitude of the tariff's effect on wages.

Calibrated Evidence

How much could the tariff have helped labor? There is no "natural experiment" in which tariffs were significantly reduced so that we can observe the resulting wage effects.[11] Nor is there much variation in the tariff level or structure that would enable us to estimate a relationship between tariffs, product prices, and wages. While a full examination of the wage effects of import tariffs is beyond the scope

Table 19.1
Industry tariffs and factor proportions

Dependent variable: nominal tariff (by industry)	OLS (1)	WLS (2)	OLS (3)	WLS (4)
Capital–labor ratio (k_i)	−3.6	−7.9	—	—
	(2.5)	(1.7)		
Labor share in value added (θ_{Li})	—	—	42.6	51.8
			(29.7)	(31.6)
Adjusted R^2	0.06	0.56	0.07	0.10
Weights	None	Value added	None	Employment

Source: *Statistical Abstract of the United States, 1916* (Washington, DC: GPO, 1917).
Note: Number of observations were 17 manufacturing industries for year 1909.

of this chapter, there are two simple methodologies for calculating the effects of changes in trade on wages—a simple general equilibrium calculation and a factor content of trade calculation. Both of these methods rely on the calculation of a counterfactual rather than on direct estimation techniques, and unfortunately, both methods give radically different assessments of the potential wage impact of (in this case) trade liberalization.

An extreme upper bound can be generated by use of a "Jones algebra" (1971) version of the Gruen-Corden model in figure 19.1.[12] Three linear equations describe the impact of changing product prices on factor prices:

$$\hat{w} = \frac{\theta_{2K}}{\theta_{1L} - \theta_{2L}} \hat{p}_1,$$

$$\hat{r}_K = \frac{-\theta_{2L}}{\theta_{1L} - \theta_{2L}} \hat{p}_1,$$

$$\hat{r}_T = \frac{-\theta_{AL}}{\theta_{AT}} \hat{w},$$

where the "hat" refers to proportion change (i.e., $\hat{p}_1 = dp_1/p_1$) and θ is the factor shares (i.e., θ_{1L} is the share of labor in the cost of producing good 1), w is the wage of labor, r_K and r_T are the returns to capital and land, respectively.

We can parameterize these equations with the 1909 census data used above in table 19.1. In this sample the average wage share in the labor-intensive sector (defined as those industries with a capital–labor ratio above the median) is 0.5 and in capital-intensive sector is 0.3; namely $\theta_{1L} = 0.5$ and $\theta_{2L} = 0.3$. D. Gale Johnson (1948) calculates factor shares in agriculture in 1910 and finds that the labor share in agricultural income was about 0.55 to 0.60.

How do we measure the impact of free trade on product prices? The average tariff on labor-intensive goods was 47 percent, while the average tariff on capital-intensive goods was 38 percent. This means that ignoring a host of issues (intermediate goods and effective protection, terms of trade effects, etc.), we find that the structure of the tariff increased the price of labor-intensive goods (relative to capital-intensive goods) by about 10 percent. The impact of free trade on the United States can be considered as a 10 percent fall in the price of the labor-intensive good 1 ($\hat{p}_1 = -0.1$).

Using the three equations above, a 10 percent decline in the price of the labor-intensive good implies that $\hat{w} = -0.35$, $\hat{r}_K = 0.15$, and $\hat{r}_T = 0.5$. If we modify the shares slightly, so that $\theta_{1L} = 0.6$ and $\theta_{2L} = 0.4$ (yielding an unweighted average of 0.5, close to the U.S. average in 1909), and take $\theta_{AL} = 0.55$, then $\hat{w} = -0.3$, $\hat{r}_K = 0.2$, and $\hat{r}_T = 0.37$. The "magnification effect" implicit in this model implies large factor price changes as a result of product price changes. The magnification is enormous: the 10 percent price shock translates into a 30 decline in wages, a 15 to 20 percent increase in the return to capital, and a 40 to 50 percent increase in the return to land. The real factor price changes are, of course, larger than these nominal changes.

These figures strike one as implausibly large, and there are several reasons for discounting them. The linear structure of the model means that product price changes bring about large impact on factor prices, whereas a more conventional computable general equilibrium model would have greater curvature and imperfect substitutability that would mute the impact of such price changes.[13] Capital and land are owned by labor, so the distribution of ownership is a key determinant of the true impact of the prices changes on labor's income. There is no separation of skilled and unskilled workers, so we ignore the distribution of labor income as well as the role of human capital.[14] In this simple model we also ignore other nontraded sectors such as services and distribution, often thought by labor economists to play an important role in wage determination, that loom large in the actual economy.

These omissions may seriously jeopardize the credibility of the results. For example, we observe improvements in the U.S. terms of trade (consistent with a decline in the price of imported goods) during the 1920s that are orders of magnitude larger than the 10 percent price shock considered here, and yet figure 19.2 shows that any effect on real wages is difficult to discern.[15]

An alternative method of calculating the wage effects is to consider trade as an exchange of bundles of factors and calculate the factor content of trade. The factor content of trade method focuses on changes in the volume of trade flows rather than on product prices directly and gives a distinctly different result. In 1909, U.S. imports of manufactures amounted to $525 million, or about 2 percent of GDP. The average tariff on labor-intensive goods, calculated above, was about 40 percent. Consider an extreme case: assume that all of the manufactured imports are labor-intensive and abolish the tariff. This results in a 40 percent reduction in the price of labor-intensive goods, a substantially larger shock than considered previously. If we take the price elasticity of import demand as about −2.6 (as estimated over 1869 to 1913 by Irwin 1998), then such a tariff reduction will more than double the amount of imports to $1,071 million, an increase of $546 million. How much labor will be displaced by this surge of imports of labor-intensive manufactured imports? To be specific, consider the textile industry, the prototypical labor-intensive industry with large employment that was protected through high tariffs during this period. In 1909, 1,000 textile workers produced $2.13 million in products. If imports of labor-intensive goods were all textiles products and increased by the magnitude suggested above, then about 256,600 workers would be displaced. This amounts to 17 percent of all textile workers, 1.3 percent of all workers in tradable goods (agriculture and manufacturing), and 0.3 percent of total U.S. employment in 1909.

Is it really plausible that the displacement of 1.3 percent of workers in the tradable good sector could generate such enormous wage effects as calculated above? Not according to the factor content of trade calculations, which—though popular with labor economists (and controversial among trade economists; see Leamer 1998, 2000)—have recently been resurrected by Krugman (2000). In our notation, Krugman assesses the change in the wage–rental ratio as

$$\hat{\omega} = \frac{\Delta(w/r)}{(w/r)} = -(\lambda_{L1} - \lambda_{K1}) \frac{\hat{M}(M_1/y_1) + \hat{X}(X_2/y_2)}{\sigma_{KL}},$$

where

λ_{L1} is the share of labor in sector 1,

$\hat{M}$ is the proportionate change in imports,

$\hat{X}$ is the proportionate change in exports (to maintain balanced trade),

M_1/y_1 and X_2/y_2 are the trade to output ratios,

σ_{KL} is the elasticity of substitution between capital and labor.

There is no direct evidence on λ_{K1} and λ_{L1} because of our arbitrary delineation between capital- and labor-intensive industries, but assume that $\lambda_{K1} = 0.4$ and $\lambda_{L1} = 0.5$, $\hat{M} = 1.04$ and $\hat{X} = 0.8$ from above, and $(M_1/y_1) = 0.05$ and $(X_2/y_2) = 0.1$ (which were roughly the case for the textile and the iron and steel industry during this period).

Schmitz (1981) estimates that the late-nineteenth century elasticity of substitution between capital and labor (σ_{KL}) was around 0.5. In the end, a doubling of imports of labor-intensive manufactures implies that $\hat{\omega} = -0.026$, or that the wage–rental ratio falls by about 2.6 percent. This is a trivial reduction that does not change significantly when the underlying parameters are altered around the chosen values.

The lack of a strong conclusion about the magnitude of the tariff's effect on wages mirrors the unresolved current debate over the role of international trade in generating wage inequality. Those who champion the Stolper-Samuelson theorem (e.g., Leamer 1998) find it difficult to believe that wage inequality is not in some way related to international trade developments, while those who champion the factor content approach insist that the magnitude of such an effect is incredibly small. It will be difficult to resolve the turn-of-the-century debate until there is a greater consensus on how to evaluate empirically the impact of international trade on the domestic wage structure.

Indirect Evidence

While a full examination of the wage effects of import tariffs is beyond the scope of this chapter, does some corroborating evidence exists that would support the implication that labor had an economic interest in supporting tariffs? One tact would be to employ Magee's (1980) ingeniously simple test of the Stolper-Samuelson theorem when he examined the lobbying position of capital and labor representatives in Congressional testimony concerning the 1974 Trade Act. Unfortunately, it is difficult to construct a comparable test for the period under question here. While tariff hearings were held in conjunction with the 1909 tariff revision (the Payne-Aldrich act) among others, the question faced by the lobbying groups was quite different. The Trade Act of 1974 was not about any specific tariff rate but dealt with the possibility of an across-the-board reduction in import tariffs. The 1909 Payne-Aldrich act, by contrast, considered adjusting tariffs (either up or down) on each and every individual product in the tariff code.

As a result virtually all those testifying—either labor or management (capital)—supported maintaining or raising the tariff levied on the particular product they were producing. An examination of the

30 labor groups that testified before the House Ways and Means Committee in 1909 reveals that 23 groups took this position, while the other 7 argued for lower tariffs, not on their products but on important intermediate goods.[16]

Another avenue to consider is the popular support for protection as revealed in the votes for the political parties. The U.S. presidential election of 1888 provides an interesting test case because the tariff was the most important issue in that campaign.[17] Viewing this election as a referendum on the issue of trade policy, examining the role of factor endowments in cross-state voting patterns would be a test in the spirit of Wolfgang Mayer's (1984) model of direct democratic voting on trade policy. Such a test is, at least, plausible. The tariff ranked among the most important issues in American politics during the late-nineteenth century, and the two main political parties were sharply differentiated over the issue. Republicans rallied around the cause of high tariffs, which, they argued, promoted national prosperity by protecting workers and home industries from foreign competition, while the Democrats called for a tariff for "revenue only" and sought lower tariffs to ease the tax burden on farmers and consumers. With few interruptions, the electorate consistently returned the presidency and the Congress to the Republicans who, in turn, maintained high tariffs. Since the United States was also a competitive political democracy (for white males at any rate), the tariff probably had broad political support for it to have been sustained.[18] Unless one wishes to explain the Republican political dominance either in terms of a bamboozled electorate that unwittingly bought the "high tariffs–high wages" rhetoric or an electorate that voted for the Republicans for non-tariff-related reasons, then perhaps there may be some truth to the idea that if the electorate was voting based on their economic interests, labor supported protection on self-interested grounds.

The tariff became the principal topic of political debate after President Grover Cleveland, a Democrat, devoted his entire State of the Union message to Congress to a call for tariff reform in December 1887. In the 1888 election, the two main presidential candidates offered the electorate faced a clear choice about the future of U.S. tariff policy—continued protection or tariff reform—depending on which was elected to office. Cleveland won the popular vote with 48.6 percent of the popular vote, while his Republican rival Benjamin Harrison captured 47.8 percent of the vote. However, Harrison easily won the electoral college by 233 to 168 and thus became president.[19] The extremely close popular vote could be interpreted as suggesting that the electorate was equally divided over the question, with half standing to gain from tariff reform and another half standing to lose. As Mayer (1984) points out, voting on tariffs in a direct democracy hinges crucially on the distribution of factor endowments among voters (as well as the economic structure of production). In the context of Ohlin's theory, this line of reasoning suggests that at least half of the electorate owned sufficient land and capital such that their factor incomes would rise as a result of lower tariffs.

The cross-state pattern of voting may help identify the underlying sources of support for and opposition to protection in terms of factor endowments. This will be a far from perfect test because the United States was a net importer of labor- and capital-intensive manufactures during this period. Hence there was not likely to be seen a sharp impact of the capital–labor ratio in manufacturing on the voting pattern; indeed, it was shortly after 1888 that the United States became a net exporter of capital-intensive manufactured goods. The results, however, could be suggestive.

The following equation enables us to study state-level voting patterns:

$$\log\left[\frac{r_i}{1 - r_i}\right] = \gamma_0 + \gamma_1 x_i + \varepsilon_i,$$

where r_i is the proportion of votes cast in state i for Republicans (total votes only include Republicans and Democrats), the column vector x_i consists of economic attributes of each state. The equation can be estimated by weighted logit (on grouped data) where the weights are $n_i r_i(1 - r_i)$.

Table 19.2 considers the results from several specifications. The first column considers the raw quantities of the factors in each state (the logit is weighted by the number of votes in a state). The signs on the coefficients indicate that states with greater amounts of capital tended to vote Republican while states with greater amounts of land tended to vote Democratic. This is consistent with land being an abundant factor of production and capital being a scarce factor. The next column includes labor (employment), which carries a negative coefficient and switches the sign on land. The next two columns consider factor proportions with one measure of the capital–labor ratio (capital–employment) and two measures of the land–labor ratio (the

Table 19.2
Voting patterns in the presidential election of 1888: Weighted logit regression on grouped economic data

	Factor quantities (1)	Factor quantities (2)	Factor proportions (3)	Factor proportions (4)	Employment shares (5)
Value of capital	0.04 (0.03)	0.28 (0.17)	—	—	—
Acres of improved land	−0.09 (0.06)	0.01 (0.09)	—	—	—
Employment	—	−0.28 (0.20)	—		
Acres of improved land/employment	—	—	0.04 (0.05)	—	—
Value of land/employment	—	—	—	0.14 (0.05)	—
Value of capital/employment	—	—	0.15 (0.08)	0.22 (0.05)	—
Share of employment in agriculture	—	—	—	—	−0.70 (0.40)
Share of employment in manufacturing	—	—	—	—	0.03 (0.09)
F-statistic	2.05	2.02	1.98	8.80	4.39
Adjusted R^2	0.10	0.07	0.10	0.29	0.15

Sources: U.S. Census Office, Department of the Interior, Report on Manufacturing Industries in the United States at the 11th Census: 1890, Part 1, Totals for States and Industries (Washington, DC: GPO, 1895), pp. 67–69. U.S. Census Office, Department of the Interior, Report on Agriculture in the United States at the 11th Census: 1890, Totals for States (Washington, DC: GPO, 1895).
Note: The dependent variable is the log of the odds ratio of the Republican vote in the 38 U.S. states. The independent variables have been standardized (mean zero, variance one) to facilitate comparisons across coefficients. Standard errors in parentheses.

acreage–employment ratio and the value of land–labor ratio). Both measures are positively correlated with votes for the Republicans, yet neither coefficient is statistically significant. As with the other regressions the overall explanatory power of the regression is poor. The last column, which examines employment shares, finds that states with a higher fraction of employment in agriculture tended to vote Democratic, while those with a higher fraction in manufacturing tended to vote Republican.

At best the results can be viewed as conditional correlations, but the results are so weak and hard to interpret—partly because of the difficulty of defining and measuring factor intensity, and finding the data to match what theory suggests (see Jones, Beladi, and Marjit 1999)—that they fail to shed much light on the economic interests of labor vis-à-vis the tariff. Ohlin's hypothesis regarding labor's economic interests must remain a hypothesis for now.

Conclusions

This chapter has considered Bertil Ohlin's analysis of trade policy and factor rewards in the context of the late-nineteenth and early twentieth century United States. Although he examined international trade through the lens of a three-factor model, Ohlin's findings are closely related to the Stolper-Samuelson result because the two-by-two "nugget" in his framework preserves the basic predictions from the two-sector model. Ohlin raised the issue of factor prices in the context of the controversial question of whether labor could benefit from import protection. Ohlin correctly pointed out that, in principle, this could be the case. Unfortunately, whether this was actually the case is unclear because the evidence from the turn of the twentieth century United States is decidedly mixed on the issue. Though this particular debate remains unresolved, it is a tribute to Ohlin that his ideas have formed the basis for an enduring and lasting framework in which these questions can be analyzed.

Notes

1. Samuelson (1994:343) relates that Stolper asked him, "How can Haberler and Taussig be right about the necessary harm to a versatile factor like labor from America's tariff, when the Ohlin theory entails that free trade must hurt the factor of production that is scarce relative to land?" Precisely that question prompted the fruitful collaboration.

2. Indeed, the "Australian" case for protection hinged on exactly this issue; see chapter 11 of Irwin (1996).

3. It is somewhat ironic that the "real labor costs" approach championed by Taussig (1927), and others, is associated with David Ricardo when Ricardo himself explicitly sought to examine income distributional effects of trade policy; see Findlay (1974).

4. Ohlin also introduced another complication: the possible favorable effect of U.S. tariffs on its terms of trade. He (1933:317) concludes: "it is not entirely unthinkable that the terms of exchange in international trade should be somewhat less favourable under free trade than now.... It is not certain, therefore, that the national income in the United States would be increased by a free trade policy, still less that the standard of living of manufacturing workers would rise. But the farming population would benefit."

5. At one point, Ohlin (1933:44) seems to deny Stolper-Samuelson reasoning and conclude that all factors would benefit from trade: "we are satisfied to know that the total value of all productive factors in terms of goods will rise in all regions as a result of trade ... a relative decline in the price of one of them, say labour, compared to another, land, does not necessarily mean that the wage level is lowered in terms of goods. Should Australian labour be worse off because of international trade? Of course not."

6. Or possibly land, skilled, and unskilled labor. Ohlin (1933:308–309) noted that "Skilled workers in the United States, for instance, may profit from protection. The gap between skilled and unskilled workers in this country is unusually large.... The relatively high expenses incurred as soon as skilled labour is employed would tend to keep back industries which use much of this factor, if protection did not prevent competition from foreign industries with lower costs of production.... If skilled workers are favoured by the American tariff, the owners of natural resources are, on the other hand, almost certainly put in a less favourable position."

7. The Gruen-Corden stylized model of Australia consists of a Heckscher-Ohlin agricultural sector that produces wool and grain with land and labor (grain is assumed to be labor intensive); appended to that is a manufacturing sector that produces textiles with labor and capital. Capital is specific to the manufacturing sector, land is specific to the two-good agricultural sector, and labor is mobile between the sectors. Variations on this model have been examined by Krueger (1977), Deardorff (1984), and Leamer (1987).

8. Deardorff (1984) was in error with regard to the change in the real return to land.

9. Samuelson (1971) also thought Ohlin was "right" in the context of a similar model on the issue of partial versus full factor price equalization.

10. The industries include chemicals, clocks, cotton manufactures, furs, glass, jewelry, hats and bonnets, iron and steel manufactures, leather, metals, paints, paper, silk, tobacco, toys, wood, and wool.

11. The Underwood tariff of 1913 reduced tariffs considerably, but the start of World War I shortly after its enactment confounds any attempt to isolate the tariff's impact on U.S. trade or wages.

12. Williamson (1974) constructs an elaborate Jones-styled general equilibrium model of the late-nineteenth century United States, but does not consider trade policy in detail.

13. Such imperfect substitution is not imposed, but rather is based on econometric evidence that indicate such a relationship. Incidentally, Siriwardana (1996) develops a computable general equilibrium model of Australia in the 1930s to evaluate the "Australian case for protection," referred to in note 2. Unfortunately, this model is only able to evaluate intersectoral resource flows and terms of trade effects of tariffs and gives no insight into the effect on real wages.

14. On wage inequality during this period, see Margo (1999).

15. The actual impact of the terms of trade improvement, however, depends on the underlying source of the shock that generates it.

16. For example, the Chair Makers' Union testified in favor of moving chair cane imports to the free list, and the International Stereotypers' and Electrotypers' Union argued in favor of moving paper and pulp imports to the free list (U.S. House of Representatives 1909).

17. "There is no question that the tariff was the central issue of the election of 1888," Reitano (1994:108) argues. "If local or cultural concerns were important, it was still the tariff that determined the nominations and dominated the campaign."

18. For a strong, if not wholly convincing, argument that public policy would reflect voter preferences in this way, see Whittman (1996).

19. This demonstrates the importance of the regional distribution of voting in the electoral college system. As president, Harrison raised tariffs considerably by signing the McKinley tariff of 1890.

References

De Long, J. Bradford. 1998. Trade policy and America's standard of living: A historical perspective. In Susan Collins, ed., *Imports, Exports, and the American Worker*. Washington, DC: Brookings Institution.

Deardorff, Alan V. 1984. An exposition and exploration of Krueger's trade model. *Canadian Journal of Economics* 17:731–46.

Findlay, Ronald. 1974. Relative prices, growth and trade in a simple Ricardian system. *Economica* 41:1–13. Reprinted in Ronald Findlay, *Trade, Development and Political Economy*. Aldershot, U.K.: Edward Elgar, 1993.

Findlay, Ronald. 1995. *Factor Proportions, Trade, and Growth*. Cambridge: MIT Press.

Gruen, Fred H., and W. Max Corden. 1970. A tariff that worsens the terms of trade. In I. A. MacDougall and R. H. Snape, eds., *Studies in International Economics*. Amsterdam: North-Holland.

Irwin, Douglas A. 1996. *Against the Tide: An Intellectual History of Free Trade*. Princeton: Princeton University Press.

Irwin, Douglas A. 1998. Higher tariffs, lower revenues? Analyzing the fiscal aspects of the "Great Tariff Debate of 1888." *Journal of Economic History* 58:59–72.

Irwin, Douglas A. 2002. Explaining America's surge in manufactured exports, 1880–1913. *Review of Economics and Statistics*, in press.

Johnson, D. Gale. 1948. Allocation of agricultural income. *Journal of Farm Economics* 30:724–49. Reprinted in J. M. Antle and D. A. Sumner, eds., *Selected Papers of D. Gale Johnson: The Economics of Agriculture*, vol. 1. Chicago: University of Chicago Press, 1996.

Jones, Ronald. 1971. A three-factor model in theory, trade, and history. In J. Bhagwati et al., eds., *Trade, Balance of Payments, and Growth*. Amsterdam: North-Holland.

Jones, Ronald, Hamid Beladi, and Sugata Marjit. 1999. The three faces of factor intensity. *Journal of International Economics* 48:413–20.

Krueger, Anne O. 1977. Growth, distortions, and pattern of trade among many countries. Princeton Studies in International Finance, no. 40. International Finance Section, Princeton University, 1977. Reprinted in Anne O. Krueger, *Perspectives on Trade and Development*. Chicago: University of Chicago Press, 1990.

Krugman, Paul. 2000. Technology, trade, and factor prices. NBER Working Paper 5355. November. Revised version published in *Journal of International Economics* 50:51–72.

Leamer, Edward E. 1987. Paths of development in the three-factor, *n*-good general equilibrium model. *Journal of Political Economy* 95:961–99.

Leamer, Edward E. 1998. In search of Stolper-Samuelson linkages between international trade and lower wages. In Susan Collins, ed., *Imports, Exports, and the American Worker*. Washington, DC: Brookings Institution.

Leamer, Edward E. 2000. What's the use of factor content? *Journal of International Economics* 50:17–50.

Mayer, Wolfgang. 1984. Endogenous tariff formation. *American Economic Review* 74:970–85.

Magee, Stephen P. 1980. Three simple tests of the Stolper-Samuelson theorem. In Peter Oppenheimer, ed., *Issues in International Economics*. London: Oriel Press.

Margo, Robert A. 1999. The history of wage inequality in America, 1820–1970. Unpublished paper. Vanderbilt University. August.

Mussa, Michael L. 1979. The two sector model in terms of its dual: A geometric exposition. *Journal of International Economics* 9:513–26.

Ohlin, Bertil. 1933. *Interregional and International Trade*. Cambridge: Harvard University Press.

Reitano, Joanne. 1994. *The Tariff in the Gilded Age: The Great Debate of 1888*. University Park: Pennsylvania State University Press.

Samuelson, Paul A. 1994. Tribute to Wolfgang Stolper on the fiftieth anniversary of the Stolper-Samuelson theorem. In Alan V. Deardorff and Robert M. Stern, eds., *The Stolper-Sameulson Theorem: A Golden Jubilee*. Ann Arbor: University of Michigan Press.

Samuelson, Paul A. 1971. Ohlin was right. *Scandinavian Journal of Economics* 73:365–84.

Schmitz, Mark. 1981. The elasticity of substitution in 19th-century manufacturing. *Explorations in Economic History* 18:290–303.

Siriwardana, Mahinda. 1996. The economic impact of tariffs in the 1930s in Australia: The Brigden report re-examined. *Australian Economic Papers* 35:370–89.

Stolper, Wolfgang F., and Paul A. Samuelson. 1941. Protection and real wages. *Review of Economic Studies* 9:58–73.

Taussig, Frank W. 1927. *International Trade*. New York: Macmillan.

U.S. House of Representatives. Committee on Ways and Means. 1909. *Tariff Hearings*. 60th Congress, 2nd Session. 9 vols. Washington, DC: GPO.

Williamson, Jeffrey G. 1974. *Late Nineteenth-Century American Development: A General Equilibrium History*. Cambridge: Cambridge University Press.

Whittman, Donald A. 1996. *The Myth of Democratic Failure: Why Political Institutions Are Efficient*. Chicago: University of Chicago Press.

V

The Heckscher-Ohlin Theory and Economic History

20 The Heckscher-Ohlin Model between 1400 and 2000: When It Explained Factor Price Convergence, When It Did Not, and Why

Kevin H. O'Rourke and
Jeffrey G. Williamson

Global Trade and Global History

This chapter is about intercontinental trade, since factor proportions differ far more between continents than within them. Long-distance intercontinental trade was also the economic event that motivated the theoretical work of Bertil Ohlin. Indeed, the first and most frequent example offered by Ohlin to illustrate his argument is land-abundant Australia trading with land-scarce Europe (Flam and Flanders 1991:90–92), while Eli Heckscher spoke of trade between land-abundant America and labor-abundant Europe to illustrate his (Flam and Flanders 1991:56–60).

The key insights of Heckscher and Ohlin were that factor endowment differences could be a basis for trade, and that trade could lead to factor price convergence between trading partners (or, Heckscher argued, even factor price equalization). These Swedish economists, one a theorist and one a historian, were motivated by late-nineteenth-century intercontinental trade, when the regions of recent settlement (as the League of Nations would later call them) shipped ever-increasing quantities of food and raw materials to the capital- and labor-abundant European continent. We have argued in previous work that Heckscher and Ohlin were right insofar as the late nineteenth century was concerned since commodity price convergence did induce some factor price convergence in what we now call the OECD (O'Rourke and Williamson 1994; O'Rourke, Taylor and Williamson 1996; O'Rourke and Williamson 1999a:ch. 4),[1] as well as in what we now call the Third World (although there it involved relative, not absolute, convergence). But was the Heckscher-Ohlin model only relevant to that period of history that motivated its

Swedish founders in the first place, or can it help us understand the evolution of factor prices in other periods as well?

In order for trade to influence factor prices, two things have to be true. First, trade-creating forces have to change domestic commodity prices. Second, the changes in domestic commodity prices have to induce a reshuffling of resources between sectors. This chapter offers powerful evidence that these conditions were not always satisfied. Indeed, they only began to be satisfied less than two centuries ago. Like most economic paradigms, the Heckscher-Ohlin model can only help us understand some phases of world history, not all.

After about 1800, long-distance trade between continents developed as transport costs, monopoly, government intervention, and international conflicts declined. Prior to the 19th century, only goods with very high value to bulk ratios were shipped, like silk, exotic spices, and precious metals. The range of goods traded extended over time. It was *not* a gradual evolution but rather a history punctuated by abruptly changing trade regimes. In fact the six centuries from 1400 to the present trace out three very distinct eras of commodity exchange and specialization. Long-distance trade in the pre-eighteenth century period was strictly limited to what might be called noncompeting goods: Europe imported spices, silk, sugar, and gold, which were not found there at all, or were in very scarce supply; Asia imported silver, linens and woolens, which were not found there at all (with the important exception of Japanese silver before 1668). Ronald Findlay (1996:53–54) reports that Dutch exports of precious metals to Asia accounted for between a half and two-thirds of the value of Asian products imported into Europe by the Dutch East India Company (hereafter, VOC: Vereenigde Oostindische Compagnie, established 1602). Almost by definition, these noncompeting goods were very expensive in importing markets, and thus could bear the very high cost of transportation from their (cheap) sources.

There are two contrasting views on this pre-eighteenth century trade in the literature. First, there are the world history scholars like Andre Gunder Frank (1998) who attach globalization "big bang" significance to the dates 1492 (Christopher Colombus stumbles on the Americas in search of spices) and 1498 (Vasco da Gama makes an end run around Africa and snatches monopoly rents away from the Arab and Venetian spice traders). Such scholars are on the side of Adam Smith who believed that these were "the two most important events in recorded history" (Tracy 1990:3), although Smith was writing those words before the industrial and transport revolutions of the nineteenth century. One well-known scholar of the early modern world, James Tracy, expressed his skepticism with the 1490s big bang theory this way: "What remains . . . in doubt is the *contemporary impact or significance* of these new configurations of long-distance trade," and "it is far less clear what meaning the new connections had for those who lived in the sixteenth or even the seventeenth century" (Tracy 1990:2–3, emphasis added). Second, there is the contrasting view of the economic historians who now "argue that long-distance trade has been overemphasized by students of the early modern period, [that] the international economy was poorly integrated before 1800, [and] that if there was a transport revolution . . . it happened then in the nineteenth century" (Menard 1991:228, 272).

This chapter offers, we think for the first time, a way to discriminate between these two competing views, and we will use it to conclude that there is precious little evidence that the age of discovery, and the age of commerce that followed, had the immediate economic impact on the global economy that world historians seem to assign to it, while there is plenty of evidence of a very big bang in the nineteenth century. Although it is commodity price convergence that matters, historians rarely look for evidence of such convergence or its absence. They look instead at shipping technologies, port histories, the evolution of trading monopolies, the rise and fall of trade routes, and so on. Such evidence may or may not correlate with commodity price convergence, but we see no evidence documenting significant pre-nineteenth century global price convergence for the (competing) commodities that really mattered to the economic lives of the vast majority. Nor do we see any evidence of significant commodity price convergence even for those (noncompeting) commodities that mattered little to the vast majority. And trade theory tells us that if a country's relative commodity prices are little affected by such external events, then its consumption, production, and factor income distribution will also be little affected. This inference follows regardless of how colorful are the tales of explorers, discoverers, sea battles, plunder, pirates, flows of gold, flows of silver, and the immense spice trade profits that fill our history books. However colorful, those are tales about rent-seeking, not about the integration of global commodity markets.

The second era starts in the early nineteenth century with the rise of trade in "basic" competing goods such as wheat and textiles, preceded by an eighteenth-century transitional phase sprinkled with trade in furs, tobacco, and cotton. The nineteenth century is the classic Heckscher-Ohlin era of spectacular transport cost declines, commodity price convergence, and a big income distribution impact on long-distance trading partners. The third era contains the present, decades that have seen trade in both basic and highly differentiated manufactured commodities. The power of the Heckscher-Ohlin model is more difficult to identify in this period, characterized as it is by the rising dominance of skills and new technologies, than it is in the previous era of more stable technologies during which endowments of land, labor, and capital mattered most. Since other chapters in this book show better than we how well the Heckscher-Ohlin model has performed in the second half of the twentieth century, this chapter will dwell instead on the experience between 1400 and 1940. We will generously part with 60 years while keeping 540 years to ourselves.

World historians don't view these 540 years the way we do, perhaps because they rarely offer an explicit economic model that can be used to organize global history, and because they rarely offer any systematic evidence supporting their view that "there was a single global world economy with a worldwide division of labor and multilateral trade from 1500 onward" (Frank 1998:52) and that, even before 1500, "trade networks reached almost all regions of Eurasia and sub-Saharan Africa and large volumes of commerce encouraged specialization of agricultural and industrial production" (Bentley 1999:7). Heckscher-Ohlin theory offers an elegant model for organizing global history, and it shows what happens when we put some empirical content into world history rhetoric.

Heckscher-Ohlin-Samuelson Economics versus the Economics of Ohlin

In his introduction to the Flam and Flanders edition of Heckscher's and Ohlin's original contributions, Paul Samuelson graciously regretted that Ohlin had left to Samuelson's own generation the "easy pickings" of such low-dimensional models as the 2×2 Heckscher-Ohlin-Samuelson model. As the title of Samuelson's (1971) article, "Ohlin was right," suggests, had Ohlin chosen to formulate such a model, it would more likely have been the specific factors model than the 2 × 2 model that bears his name today. Although we are not historians of economic thought, it seems clear to us that Ohlin's insistence that trade would lead to factor price convergence across countries (but not equalization) can be explained by the features of the late-nineteenth-century economy which he was trying to describe. In this economy, trade could and did influence income distribution, but factor price differences continued to provide an incentive for intercontinental factor mobility, which in turn led to further factor price convergence.

The late-nineteenth-century Atlantic economy saw unprecedented levels of international migration and capital transfers: 60 million Europeans sailed to the New World in the century following 1820 (Hatton and Williamson 1998), while as a percentage of GDP, international capital flows in the years before the Great War attained levels never matched before or since. Moreover the trade flows that characterized the era largely took the form of the New World exchanging agricultural products for European manufactured goods: land was a crucial factor of production then, in addition to labor and capital. Both of these stylized facts are more easily captured in a 3 × 2 model, than in a 2 × 2 model. More than thirty years ago, Peter Temin wrote a paper on the antebellum American economy in which he assumed that manufactured goods were produced with labor and capital, while food was produced with labor and land (Temin 1966). This specific factors model was fully developed shortly thereafter by Ronald Jones (1971), who thanks Robert Fogel in a footnote for bringing Temin's article to his attention. We draw attention to the cliometric antecedents of this model, not just out of team spirit, but in order to highlight a theme of the present paper: the "correct" trade model may vary with the period being studied.

Within the context of this model, what are the determinants of factor prices, and in particular, of the wage-rental ratio? First, take the Heckscher-Ohlin open economy case, in which commodity prices are determined in world markets and thus are exogenous to the individual (small) economy. Endowments matter: increases in either the capital–labor or land–labor ratio will push up wages, lower land rents, and increase the wage–rental ratio. Commodity prices matter too: when the ratio of agricultural prices to manufactured goods prices rises, wage-rental ratios fall. The specific factors model is quite explicit about which factor price should do the most adjusting: the magnification effect identified in the 2 × 2 model will apply to sector-specific factors, but not to the mobile factor (Jones 1971:9). Thus returns to specific factors such as land rents should change proportionately by more than returns to mobile factors such as labor. Finally, technological progress may change the wage–rental ratio. Many economic historians have argued that technological change in the Old World was labor-using and land-saving during the late nineteenth century, whereas technological change in the New World was labor-saving and land-using (O'Rourke, Taylor, and Williamson 1996), implying that technological progress should have raised wage–rental ratios in Europe but lowered them in the New World.

Second, take the closed economy case, in which commodity prices are determined in local markets. An increase in the land–labor ratio will increase the relative supply of food and lower its relative price, while it will still increase the wage–rental ratio. As in the open economy there should be a negative correlation between the wage–rental ratio and the relative price of food. But in the closed economy, the correlation is not causal. Rather, both price ratios are determined by factor endowments. Is this the better description of historical reality until the nineteenth century, or was the open economy Heckscher-Ohlin model relevant from 1490s onward?

The First Era: Noncompeting Goods and the Absence of Commodity Price Convergence

Long time series documenting early modern intercontinental commodity price convergence, or the presumed sharp fall in transport costs, are very scarce. This section summarizes some of the available evidence, but none of it reported here or elsewhere (O'Rourke and Williamson 2000) supports the view that trade between continents became dramatically cheaper during the three centuries after the 1490s and prior to the 1820s when the French wars had ended.

Was There an International Transport Revolution before 1800?

The best summary we have seen dealing with the evolution of transport costs in the North Atlantic prior to the early nineteenth century is by Russell Menard (1991),[2] and he finds very little evidence favoring a transport revolution. Peacetime real freight charges on sugar were stable between the 1650s and the 1760s, while the rice trade shows no fall in real freight rates between the 1690s and the 1760s, although it did undergo an impressive decline thereafter (Menard 1991:264, 268–69). The best case for a North Atlantic pre-nineteenth century transport revolution lies with the tobacco trade. Between 1618 and 1775, freight charges on tobacco shipments from the Chesapeake to London fell consistently, and by a lot. Adjusted by the Brown-Hopkins CPI, real freight rates fell by 1.6 percent per annum over the entire colonial period (Menard 1991:255). Menard is unimpressed by this fall, since it had nothing to do with transport revolutions. Almost all of the gains were due to the introduction of standard containers and the more efficient use of cargo space. In any case it is the only evidence suggesting significant pre-nineteenth century commodity price convergence in the North Atlantic.

Unfortunately, there is not much evidence documenting what happened to transport costs along the Euro-Asian route in the centuries following 1498. Nor is there even a scholarly tradition of seeking that evidence. One impressive exception, however, is a paper by Niels Steensgaard (1965) on Dutch and English freight costs on southeast Asian trade routes between 1601 and 1657. The cost declines documented by him were due to a reduced turnaround time in Southeast Asia rather than to improved shipping technology. Prior to 1640, these ships were also required to perform protective duties in Asian waters—to put down local revolts, build forts, show the flag, negotiate agreements, and so on. After 1640, chartered ships did not perform these functions, but rather a permanent Asian fleet of smaller VOC ships did. The cost per ton per trip does not include the cost of the permanent fleet, borne by the East India Company as before, but not directly included as part of the charter cost per ton. When these costs are added back in, our guess is that most of the decline in transport costs over the half-century would evaporate.[3] Ralph Davis (1962:262–64) and Bal Krishna (1924:321–23) extend the freight cost evidence from the 1650s to the 1730s. They find that freight costs "were higher in the 1720s and 1730s than they had been in the 1660s and 1660s and they took another step upward in the 1760s, when they return to the levels prevailing in the early seventeenth century" (Menard 1991:250).

All of this evidence suggests that there was no transport revolution along Euro-Asian routes during the age of commerce. What evidence we have on Euro-Asian price spreads confirms this impression (O'Rourke and Williamson 1999b, 2000). There is no evidence of commodity price convergence between Amsterdam and Southeast Asia for cloves, pepper, and coffee, noncompeting commodities that together accounted for 68 percent of Dutch homeward cargoes in the midseventeenth century (Reid 1993:288–89). Of course, the price spread on pepper, cloves, and coffee was not driven solely, or even mainly, by the costs of shipping but rather, and most important, by monopoly,[4] international conflict, and government tariff and nontariff restrictions. But we are indifferent about the sources of commodity price convergence. Anything that impedes price convergence suppresses globalization, and there is no evidence of significant globalization before the 1820s. Is there any reason to expect the price spread on competing goods between Europe and Asia to have behaved differently? We think not.

The Second Era: Nineteenth Century Transport Revolutions and Commodity Price Convergence

The Amazing Worldwide Decline in International Transport Costs[5]

In the nineteenth century, international freight rates collapsed. Steamships and the Suez Canal linked continents, and railroads penetrated their interiors. It is important to stress that this nineteenth century transport revolution was not limited to the Atlantic economy. Certainly the Black Sea and the eastern Mediterranean were part of it. Gelina Harlaftis and Vassilis Kardasis (2000) have shown that the declines in freight rates between 1870 and 1914 were just as dramatic on routes involving Black Sea and Egyptian ports as on those involving Atlantic ports, and perhaps even more so. Asia was a part of it too. The tramp charter rate for shipping rice from Rangoon to Europe, for example, fell from 73.8 to 18.1 percent of the Rangoon price between 1882 and 1914.[6] China and Japan were also involved in this Asian transport revolution. The freight rate on coal (relative to its export price) between Nagasaki and Shanghai fell by 76 percent between 1880 and 1910, and total factor productivity on Japan's tramp freighter routes serving Asia advanced at 2.5 percent per annum in the thirty years between 1879 and 1909 (Yasuba 1978: tables 1 and 5).

Perhaps the greatest nineteenth century "globalization shock" in Asia did not involve transport revolutions at all. Under the persuasion of Commodore Perry's American gun ships, Japan switched from virtual autarky to free trade in 1858. It is hard to imagine a more dramatic switch from closed to open trade policy, even by the standards of the recent Asian miracle. In the fifteen years following 1858, Japan's foreign trade rose from nil to 7 percent of national income (Huber 1971). The prices of (labor-intensive) exportables soared, rising toward world market levels; the prices of (land- and machine-intensive) importables slumped, falling toward world market levels. One researcher estimates that Japan's terms of trade rose by a factor of 3.5 between 1858 and the early 1870s (Huber 1971); another thinks it rose even more, by a factor of 4.9 (Yasuba 1996:548). This combination of declining transport costs and the dramatic switch to free trade unleashed powerful globalization forces in Japan. Other Asian nations—China, Siam, Korea, India, and Indonesia—followed this liberal path, most forced to do so by colonial dominance or gunboat diplomacy. This shift had largely taken place from the 1860s; from then on, commodity price convergence was driven entirely by sharply declining transport costs in Asia without much change in tariffs one way or the other. Asia's commitment to globalization, forced or not, started more than a century ago.

Figure 20.1 offers a summary of the impact of these productivity improvements on transport costs in the Atlantic economy. What is

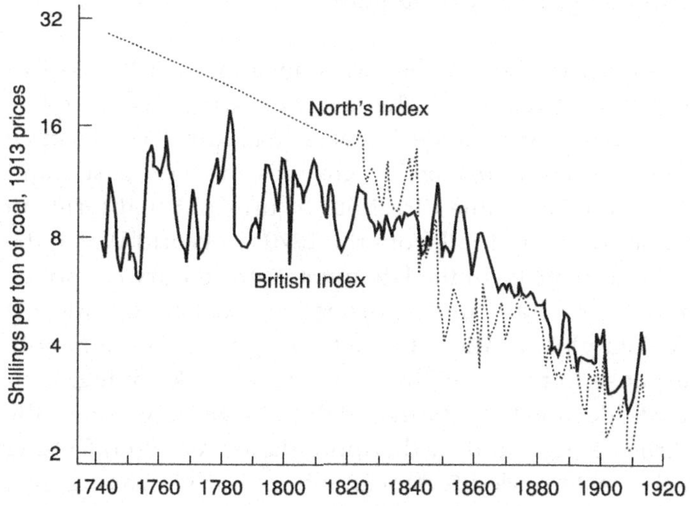

Figure 20.1
Real freight rate indexes, 1741 to 1913. Nominal rates are deflated by a UK GNP deflator. Source: Harley (1988).

labeled the North index (North 1958) accelerates its fall after the 1830s, and what is labeled the British index (Harley 1988) is fairly stable up to midcentury before undergoing the same, big fall. The North freight rate index dropped by more than 41 percent, in real terms, between 1870 and 1910, while the British index fell by about 70 percent between 1840 and 1910. These two indexes imply a steady decline in Atlantic economy transport costs of about 1.5 percent per annum, for a total of 45 percentage points up to 1913, a big number indeed. There is another way to get a comparative feel for the magnitude of this decline. The World Bank reports that tariffs on manufactures entering developed country markets fell from 40 percent in the late 1940s to 7 percent in the late 1970s, a 33 percentage point decline over thirty years (Wood 1994:173). This spectacular postwar reclamation of "free trade" from interwar autarky was still smaller than the 45 percentage point fall in pre-1914 trade barriers due to transport improvements.

Figure 20.1 makes another point. The nineteenth-century transport revolution was a spectacular regime switch, occurring some time between 1820 and 1850. If world historians are looking for a globalization big bang, they should switch their gaze from the 1490s to the 1820s.

Worldwide Commodity Price Convergence

What was the impact of these transport innovations on the cost of moving goods between markets? The cost has two parts, that due to transport and that due to trade barriers (e.g., tariffs). The price spread between markets is driven by changes in these costs, and they need not move in the same direction. It turns out that tariffs in the Atlantic economy did not fall from the 1870s to World War I; the globalization that took place in the late nineteenth century cannot be assigned to more liberal trade policy. Instead, it was falling transport costs that provoked globalization. Indeed, rising tariffs were mainly a defensive response to the competitive winds of market integration as transport costs declined (O'Rourke 1997). As we have seen, the opposite was true of Asia, and furthermore there were no offsetting tariff hikes in the eastern Mediterranean either. But we have gotten ahead of the story. What about commodity price convergence?

Trend estimates based on Knick Harley's (1980) annual data show that Liverpool wheat prices exceeded Chicago prices by 57.6 percent

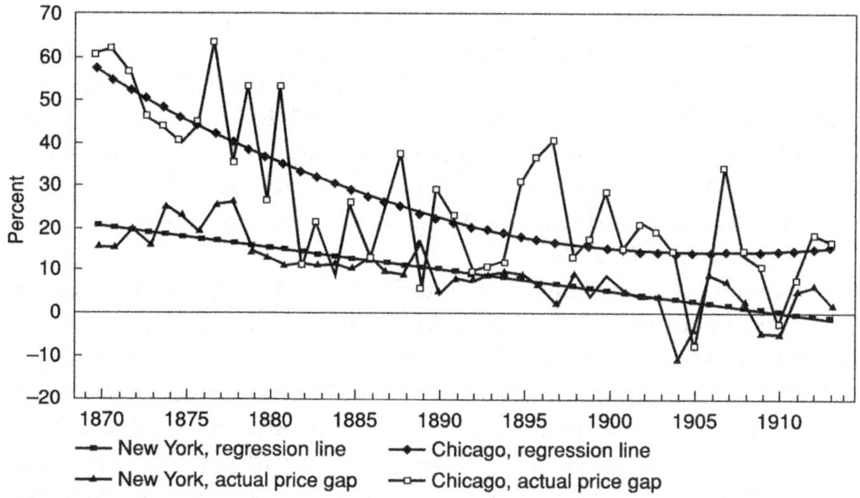

Figure 20.2
Wheat price differentials: Britain as percent of the United States, 1870 to 1914. Source: O'Rourke and Williamson (1999a).

in 1870, by 17.8 percent in 1895, and by 15.6 percent in 1912. Both the Liverpool–New York and New York–Chicago price gaps declined steeply (figure 20.2), which is consistent with the evidence on freight rates offered earlier. Moreover these estimates *understate* the size of the price convergence because they ignore the collapse in price gaps between Midwestern farm-gates and Chicago markets. This price convergence experience in Anglo-American wheat markets was repeated for other foodstuffs. The second biggest tradable foodstuff consisted of meat and animal fats such as beef, pork, mutton, and butter. While there was no convergence in London–Cincinnati price differentials for bacon across the 1870s, there was convergence after 1879–80. Indeed, the price convergence after 1895 was even more dramatic for meat than it was for wheat: price gaps were 92.5 percent in 1870, over 100 in 1880, 92.3 in 1895, and 17.9 in 1913. The delay in price convergence for meat, butter, and cheese has an easy explanation: it required the advances in refrigeration made toward the end of the century.

Anglo-American price data are also available for many other nonagricultural commodities (O'Rourke and Williamson 1994). The Boston–Manchester cotton textile price gap fell from 13.7 percent in 1870 to about zero in 1913; the Philadelphia–London iron bar price gap fell from 75 to 20.6 percent, while the pig iron price gap fell from 85.2 to 19.3 percent, and the copper price gap fell from 32.7 to almost zero; the Boston–London hides price gap fell from 27.7 to 8.7 percent, while the wool price gap fell from 59.1 to 27.9 percent. Commodity price convergence can also be documented for coal, tin and coffee. Furthermore similar trends can be documented for price gaps between London and Buenos Aires, Montevideo, and Rio de Janeiro (Williamson 1999b, 2000).

Transport cost declines from interior to port and from port to Europe also ensured that Asian economies became more integrated into world markets. Price gaps between Britain and Asia were driven down by the completion of the Suez Canal in November 1869, by the switch from sail to steam, and by other productivity advances on long distance sea lanes. The cotton price spread between Liverpool and Bombay fell from 57 percent in 1873 to 20 percent in 1913, and the jute price spread between London and Calcutta fell from 35 to 4 percent (Collins 1996:table 4). The same events were taking place even farther east, involving Burma and the rest of Southeast Asia. Indeed, the rice price spread between London and Rangoon fell from 93 to 26 percent in the four decades prior to 1913 (Collins 1996:table 4). These events had a profound impact on the creation of an Asian market for wheat and rice, and, even more, on the creation of a truly global market for grains (Latham and Neal 1983; Brandt 1985; Kang and Cha 1996). Finally, the impact of transport revolutions on commodity price convergence involving the eastern Mediterranean was just as powerful. The price spread on Egyptian cotton in Liverpool and Alexandria markets plunged off a high plateau after the 1860s. The average percent by which Liverpool exceeded Alexandria price quotes was 1824–1832, 42.1; 1837–1846, 63.2; 1863–1867, 40.8; 1882–1889, 14.7; and 1890–1899, 5.3 (Issawi 1966:447–48).

Documenting the Regime Switch: English Wage–Rental Ratios and the Intersectoral Terms of Trade, 1565 to 1936

If the first great globalization shock hit the world economy in the early nineteenth century rather than in the late fifteenth century, then it follows that European prices should have been determined primarily by domestic supply and demand prior to the early nineteenth century, while they should have been determined by global supply and demand afterwards. Moreover the distributional implications of international trade, central to the economics of Bertil Ohlin, should only have begun to manifest themselves some time between Waterloo and the Great War. Here we test this intuition for one economy, Great Britain, which was at the heart of the nineteenth-century global economy and which was thus fully exposed to the effects of growing international trade. Previous work has shown that international commodity price convergence can explain a large proportion of British distributional trends between 1870 and 1914 (O'Rourke and Williamson 1994; O'Rourke, Taylor and Williamson 1996), and that British grain markets were well integrated with those on the European Continent as early as the 1830s (Williamson 1990; O'Rourke 1994). Was this also true of earlier centuries, or does the Heckscher-Ohlin model only apply to British experience after Waterloo?

To answer these questions, we gathered data on British endowments, commodity prices, and factor prices from 1565 to 1936. For these four centuries, we were able to construct: the ratio of agricultural land to the economywide labor supply (LANDLAB), the ratio of agricultural prices to industrial prices (PAPM), and the ratio of wage rates to farm land rents (WR1 and WR2, corresponding to two alternative rent series).[7] All variables are expressed in natural logarithms. To repeat, increases in land–labor ratios should in a closed economy lead to a decline in relative agricultural prices and to an increase in the wage–rental ratio: commodity prices and factor prices should both be determined by endowments (and demand). Moreover, if Malthus was right, then a technology-induced rise in the real wage should induce an increase in the labor force, and a reduction in the land–labor ratio. Thus we might also observe factor and commodity prices having an impact on endowments in a closed economy. As commodity prices become increasingly exogenous in an open economy (i.e., determined by world market conditions rather than by domestic factor endowments), factor prices should be determined more and more by commodity prices and less and less by endowments (or even by commodity prices alone, in the historically unrealistic 2×2 case). Land–labor ratios might still depend on wages and prices through some sluggish Malthusian mechanism, or through more responsive international migration flows.

To see if these predictions hold, we split the data into two parts: 1565 to 1828 and 1828 to 1936. We chose 1828 as the break point, since that year saw a radical liberalization of British commercial policy, and Britain stuck to that liberal policy up to the 1846 Repeal

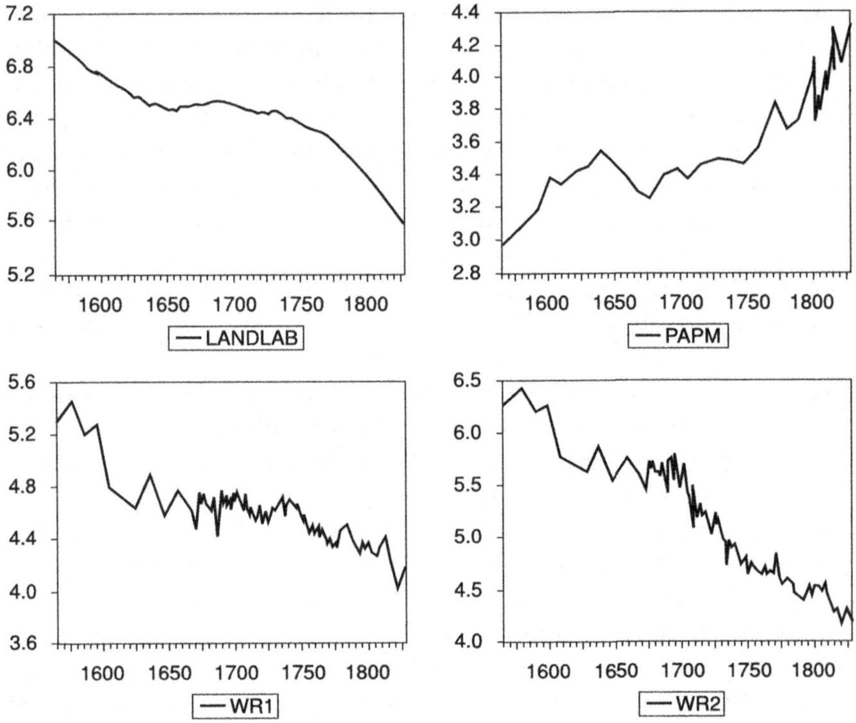

Figure 20.3
(a) Trends in land–labor ratios, wage–rental ratios, and relative prices of agricultural goods: England, 1565 to 1828. (b) Trends in land–labor ratios, wage–rental ratios, and relative prices of agricultural goods: England, 1828 to 1936.

and beyond. Prior to 1828, grain imports were prohibited if domestic prices fell below a certain "port-closing" level, and during the early postwar years grain imports were effectively excluded much of the time. In 1828, the Duke of Wellington's government replaced these import restrictions with tariffs that varied with the domestic price. This not only lowered British grain prices but increased the integration of British and Continental grain markets (Williamson 1990). Moreover the adoption of the sliding scale tariff came at the end of a decade that had seen several other moves toward freer trade: a reform of the Navigation Acts in 1822, tariff reductions across the board, and the repeal of more than 1,100 tariff acts in 1825, the year in which the emigration of skilled workers was once again authorized. Of course, prior to 1815, the French wars effectively served to block commodity trade and factor mobility.

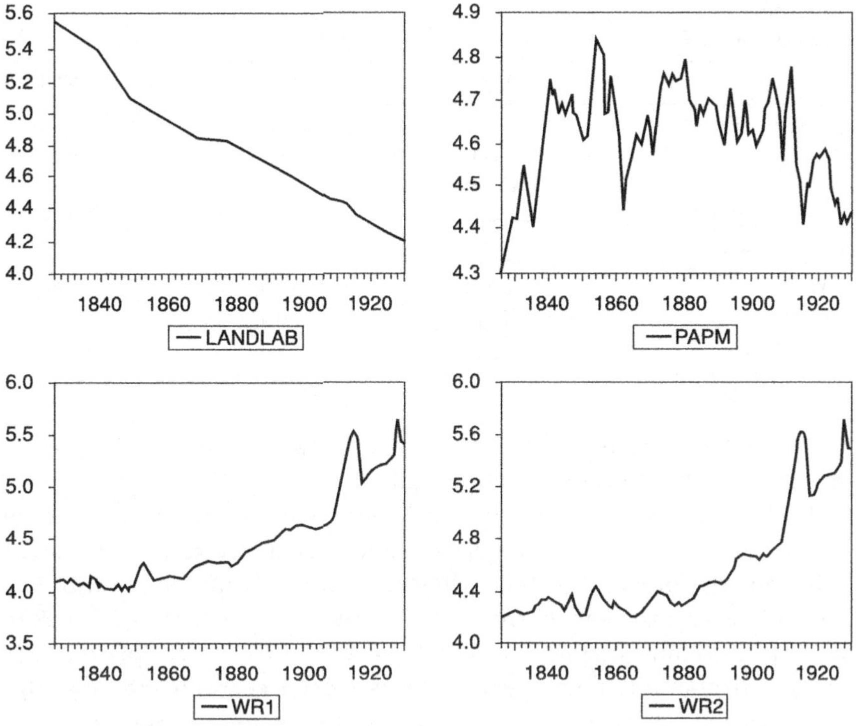

Figure 20.3 (continued)

Figure 20.3 shows plots of the raw data. The data indicate that the 1820s do indeed mark a watershed in British economic history. Prior to the 1820s, the relative price of agricultural commodities (PAPM) rose steadily, while the wage–rental ratio (WR) fell steadily. After the 1820s, the wage–rental ratio rose steadily, while from the 1840s onwards the relative price of agricultural goods stopped increasing and, eventually, started falling in response to cheap food imports from Russia and the New World. It is the striking reversal in distributional trends that is most suggestive: it looks like a regime switch in which wage–rental ratios were first determined primarily by domestic endowments (and thus declined as land–labor ratios fell) to one in which they were determined primarily by booming trade with more land-abundant economies (and thus rose despite the fact that land–labor ratios at home kept falling). But can we show with econometrics that the closed economy model fits the facts prior to the 1820s, and that it is the open economy model associated with

Table 20.1
Correlation coefficients, 1565 to 1936

	PAPM	WR	LANDLAB
Panel A: 1565–1828			
PAPM	1.000	−0.829	−0.956
WR	−0.829	1.000	0.889
LANDLAB	−0.956	0.889	1.000
Panel B: 1828–1936			
PAPM	1.000	−0.340	0.058
WR	−0.340	1.000	−0.859
LANDLAB	0.058	−0.859	1.000

Bertil Ohlin's name that becomes relevant after the introduction of the Duke of Wellington's sliding scale?

Table 20.1 reports correlation coefficients between our three variables in each of the two periods, and they are certainly consistent with our hypotheses. In the earlier period the land–labor ratio was strongly and positively correlated with the wage–rental ratio (0.889), and strongly and negatively correlated with the relative price of agricultural goods (−0.956), precisely as closed economy theory suggests. In the later period, prices and endowments are uncorrelated, as they should be in an open economy; what is now a negative correlation between endowments and wage–rental ratios (−0.859) seems puzzling, a bit of unexpected overkill in favor of our hypothesis, driven, we suppose, by omitted factors.[8]

In a background paper we estimate VARs incorporating these three variables, as well as a time trend, for each of the two subperiods.[9] The results were consistent with the closed economy prediction that endowments were driving commodity and factor prices prior to the early nineteenth century. In the later period none of these variables were significantly related to each other, indicating that the earlier relationships had broken down. These VARs were then used to perform Granger causality tests among the variables. The most important hypothesis tested concerned the impact of endowments on prices, and it was confirmed. Endowments Granger-caused prices in the earlier period, but not in the later, regardless of the number of lags used.

All variables appeared to be integrated of order one, and we next proceeded to see if there were cointegrating relationships link-

Table 20.2
Closed-economy theory: Determinants of commodity and factor prices, 1565 to 1936

LHS variable Time period	PAPM 1565–1828 (1)	PAPM 1565–1800 (2)	WR1 1565–1828 (3)	PAPM 1828–1936 (4)	WR1 1828–1936 (5)
C	9.152	9.048	−1.153	4.545	9.148
	(85.722)	(59.158)	(−6.234)	(33.606)	(33.857)
LANDLAB	−0.882	−0.866	0.907	0.017	−0.973
	(−52.921)	(−36.680)	(31.422)	(0.598)	(−17.390)
R^2	0.914	0.852	0.790	0.003	0.739
Adjusted R^2	0.914	0.851	0.789	−0.006	0.736
Standard error of regression	0.081	0.076	0.140	0.111	0.222
Sum squared residual	1.708	1.335	5.128	1.327	5.295
Loglikelihood	290.753	275.775	145.631	85.615	10.172
Durbin-Watson statistic	0.268	0.022	0.116	0.267	0.103
Mean dependent variable	3.508	3.441	4.653	4.625	4.464
Standard deviation dependent variable	0.276	0.196	0.305	0.111	0.433
Akaike info criterion	−2.188	−2.320	−1.088	−1.534	−0.150
Schwarz criterion	−2.160	−2.291	−1.061	−1.485	−0.101
F-statistic	2800.645	1345.412	987.336	0.358	302.421
Prob(*F*-statistic)	0.000	0.000	0.000	0.551	0.000
Included observations	264	236	264	109	109

ing them. We first estimated these relationships directly, using OLS methods. Table 20.2 reports the estimates that would obtain in a closed economy, in which both commodity and factor prices were driven by endowments. The results for the pre-1828 period indicate an elasticity of prices w.r.t. endowments of −0.882 (equation 1), and an elasticity of wage-rental ratios w.r.t. endowments of 0.907 (equation 3). Unfortunately, when the residuals from these equations were inspected, the hypothesis that the series contained a unit root could not be rejected (albeit by a narrow margin). In the case of prices, this failure may have been due to the impact of the Napoleonic wars; when the relationship was re-estimated for the subperiod 1565 to 1800, the elasticity of prices w.r.t. endowments was −0.866 (table

20.2, equation 2), and the Engle-Granger procedure shows PAPM and LANDLAB to have been cointegrated. For the 1828 to 1936 period, simple OLS regressions show no relationship at all between prices and endowments, consistent with our predictions (equation 4), while wage–rental ratios are now negatively related to endowments (equation 5). Clearly, the structure of the economy was very different after 1828 than before. While the closed economy model fit the facts very well prior to 1828, it fit them very badly thereafter.

The wage–rental ratio should be a function of endowments, technology and prices in an open economy, with prices being exogenous. In the sixteenth, seventeenth, and even eighteenth centuries, land and labor were the most important factors of production, but by the nineteenth century, capital was also having an important impact on economywide wages. Any post-1828 equation expressing wage–rental ratios as a function of land–labor ratios and commodity prices without in addition including capital–labor ratios and technology would be misspecified, as suggested earlier.[10] Since capital-intensity and total factor productivity were both trending up during the nineteenth and twentieth centuries, we estimated the following equation (as before, all variables are in logarithms):

$$WR = a_1 + a_2\text{LANDLAB} + a_3\text{PAPM} + a_4\text{trend}, \tag{1}$$

where the trend term is a proxy for the combined impact of capital deepening and technological change. The results for both periods are given in table 20.3. They show that the open economy model fits the post-1828 facts extremely well, but that it fits the pre-1828 facts extremely poorly (prices have the wrong sign in the regression). Table 20.3 also shows that there was a dramatic switch in the impact of capital-deepening and technical change on the wage–rental ratio after 1828. Moreover, when the residuals from the post-1828 regression were examined, the null hypothesis of a unit root in the series was rejected at the 1 percent confidence level, indicating that the estimated equation constituted a cointegrating relationship between the variables.[11]

We conclude that there is strong evidence for our contention that the closed economy model fits the facts before 1828 but not afterward, while the open economy model fits the facts after 1828 but not before. A world historian looking for a big globalization bang will find it in the 1820s, and not in the 1490s.

Table 20.3
Open-economy theory: Determinants of the wage–rental ratio, 1565 to 1936

	1565–1828 (1)	1828–1936 (2)
C	0.053	−4.500
	(0.047)	(−1.691)
LANDLAB	0.666	1.013
	(5.481)	(3.706)
PAPM	0.158	−0.770
	(1.560)	(−5.496)
@TREND(1565)	−0.002	0.024
	(−6.092)	(7.268)
R^2	0.821	0.882
Adjusted R^2	0.819	0.879
Standard error of regression	0.130	0.151
Sum squared residual	4.372	2.384
Loglikelihood	166.686	53.659
Durbin-Watson statistic	0.134	0.321
Mean dependent variable	4.653	4.464
Standard deviation dependent variable	0.305	0.433
Akaike info criterion	−1.232	−0.911
Schwarz criterion	−1.178	−0.812
F-statistic	398.067	262.437
Prob(*F*-statistic)	0.000	0.000
Included observations	264	109

The Impact of Commodity Price Convergence on Factor Price Convergence: Wage–Rental Ratios Worldwide, 1870 to 1940[12]

If there was truly a globalization big bang in the century prior to 1914, the Heckscher-Ohlin model tells us that we should see unambiguous evidence of factor price convergence. We should see it worldwide. And since agriculture was still such a large sector, and since farmland was still such an important asset, we should see it in the behavior of the wage–rental ratio. The previous section argued that these predictions hold up well in the British case. Can we extend the evidence to other parts of the world as well?

With the collaboration of Alan Taylor, the present authors have already shown how factor price convergence took place in the Atlantic economy over the four decades or so following 1870 (O'Rourke,

Taylor, and Williamson 1996). These factor price convergence trends are reproduced in table 20.4, where new evidence for the interwar period join revisions of the rest, yielding for the decades prior to about 1940 data for three land-abundant overseas settlements—Australia, Canada, and the United States; four land-scarce European countries that pretty much stuck to free trade—Denmark (data only to 1913), Great Britain, Ireland, and Sweden; and three land-scarce European countries that raised tariffs to help fend off the winds of competition—France, Germany (data only to 1913), and Spain. The wage–rental ratio collapsed in the land-abundant New World, and it surged in the land-scarce Old World. Land-scarce European countries that were less committed to the globalization game—raising tariffs to fend off foreign competition—underwent a less dramatic increase in their wage–rental ratio, just as Ohlin would have predicted. While there is certainly no evidence of factor price *equalization* anywhere in the Atlantic economy during this century of globalization, table 20.4 offers overwhelming evidence of factor price *convergence*, at least up to the eve of World War I and prior to interwar de-globalization.

What happened outside of the Atlantic economy? And what happened during the interwar years? As we have seen, the move to free trade in much of Asia and the eastern Mediterranean, plus the revolutionary decline in transport costs everywhere in the Third World, dramatically eroded commodity price gaps between the European core and the periphery in the century before 1914. It eroded them even more *within* the periphery, since there was far less globalization backlash there. Prices of exportables boomed in the exporting countries. Price trends reversed after World War I, but on either side of that great divide one would have thought that the relative rewards to land and labor should have been dramatically affected. Exactly how they were affected should have depended, of course, on whether the abundant factor was land—as in the Southern Cone, Egypt, Southeast Asia, and the Punjab—or labor—as in Japan, Korea, and Taiwan.

Consider again the canonical land-scarce and labor-abundant case, Japan. As we noted above, when Japan emerged from isolation after 1858, prices of its labor-intensive exportables soared, rising toward world market levels, while prices of its land- and machine-intensive importables slumped, falling toward world market levels. The Heckscher-Ohlin model predicts that the abundant factor, labor, should have flourished while the scarce (and sector-specific) factor,

Table 20.4
Wage–rental ratio trends in Europe and the New World, 1870 to 1939 (1911 = 100)

	Land abundant					Land scarce				
Period	Australia	Canada	United States	Britain	Denmark	France	Germany	Ireland	Spain	Sweden
1870–1874	416.2		233.6	56.6	44.8	63.5	84.4		51.3	42.7
1875–1879	253.0		195.0	61.4	43.5	62.9	80.0	62.2	55.8	43.7
1880–1884	239.1		188.3	64.9	44.8	67.3	82.3	72.7	58.6	50.7
1885–1889	216.3		182.1	73.1	56.6	73.8	86.0	86.4	73.0	57.8
1890–1894	136.2		173.5	79.1	66.7	80.4	98.0	102.7	81.8	65.3
1895–1899	147.7		175.0	87.3	87.9	91.8	108.2	122.1	85.5	78.6
1900–1904	130.0	81.4	172.4	91.4	103.8	103.2	107.6	111.2	74.9	87.9
1905–1909	97.9	93.4	132.7	98.1	99.7	106.4	104.6	101.7	85.7	92.5
1910–1914	100.6	95.6	101.1	102.7	100.0	99.8	100.2	94.1	86.4	99.1
1915–1919	111.0	134.3	124.7	153.1		123.7		79.7	52.5	143.4
1920–1924	137.2	146.5	122.4	197.6		156.5		105.7	38.8	136.5
1925–1929	115.1	236.4	160.1	167.6		117.1		168.6	38.7	116.3
1930–1934	98.3	219.2	165.2	190.3		133.1		192.3	39.1	135.1
1935–1939	110.5	225.1	240.1	206.5		168.2		227.8		

Source: Williamson (2000: table 3).

land, should have languished over the fifteen years or so following 1858. Did they? Land rent evidence is not available until 1885, long after Japan's leap to openness had taken place. We do have some crude pre-1885 evidence, however, and it seems to confirm the Heckscher and Ohlin hypothesis: namely that the wage–rental rose 3.3 times. To repeat, this is exactly what one would have predicted when a technologically quiescent economy is hit with a huge price shock that favors the exportable and disfavors the importable: in a land-scarce economy like pre-industrial Japan, the wage–rental ratio *should* have soared, with obvious distributional (and, one supposes, political) consequences.

For pre-industrial Japan, these are only informed guesses, but table 20.5 reports the real thing for subsequent decades. East Asian wage–rental ratio trends can be constructed for Japan starting in the late 1880s, Korea starting in the late 1900s, and Taiwan starting in the early 1900s. In contrast with the Punjab in the four decades after 1873 or Japan in the two or three decades after 1858, the early twentieth century was not a period of technological quiescence for East Asian agriculture. Instead, the region was undergoing land-saving and labor-using innovation (Hayami and Ruttan 1971), forces that should have served by themselves to raise the wage–rental ratio. It was also a period of dramatic industrialization, at least in Japan, which served to pull labor off the farms, another force serving to raise the wage–rental ratio. The period after 1910 to 1914 was also one of unfavorable farm price shocks (Kang and Cha 1996), yet another force serving to raise the wage–rental ratio. In short, we might expect those wage–rental ratio trends initiated by globalization forces in midnineteenth century East Asia, as illustrated by Huber's data for Japan, to have continued well into the twentieth century. That is exactly what table 20.5 reveals: East Asian wage–rental ratios surged up to the 1920s and 1930s. Indeed, land-scarce Europe experienced the same surge in wage–rental ratios during its export-led industrialization and the so-called grain invasion after the 1870s, at least where trade policy remained liberal (O'Rourke, Taylor, and Williamson 1996). Furthermore the magnitudes were not so different. Between 1910–14 and 1925–1929, the wage-rental ratio rose by 88 percent in Japan, by 72 percent in Korea, and by 40 percent in Taiwan (table 20.5). The average increase in the wage–rental ratio for Britain, Ireland, Denmark, and Sweden was 27 percent between 1890–04 and 1910–14, and 50 percent between 1875–79 and 1890–94

Table 20.5
Wage–rental ratio trends in the third world, 1870 to 1939 (1911 = 100)

	Land abundant						Land scarce		
Period	Argentina	Uruguay	Burma	Siam	Egypt	Punjab	Japan	Korea	Taiwan
1870–1874		1112.5		4699.1		196.7			
1875–1879		891.3		3908.7	174.3	198.5			
1880–1884	580.4	728.3		3108.1	276.6	147.2			
1885–1889	337.1	400.2		2331.6	541.9	150.8	79.9		
1890–1894	364.7	377.2	190.9	1350.8	407.5	108.7	68.6		
1895–1899	311.1	303.6	189.9	301.3	160.1	92.0	91.3		
1900–1904	289.8	233.0	186.8	173.0	166.7	99.8	96.1		68.1
1905–1909	135.2	167.8	139.4	57.2	64.4	92.4	110.4	102.8	85.2
1910–1914	84.0	117.9	106.9	109.8	79.8	80.1	107.5	121.9	96.6
1915–1919	53.6	120.8	164.7	202.1	83.5	82.5	104.9	109.4	111.2
1920–1924	53.1	150.3	113.6	157.9	124.3	81.1	166.1	217.4	140.0
1925–1929	51.0	150.2		114.9	120.8	72.6	202.4	209.2	134.8
1930–1934	58.4	174.3		113.1	116.2	50.4	229.5	194.0	130.7
1935–1939	59.5	213.5		121.6	91.0	33.2	149.9	215.4	123.6

Source: Williamson (2000: table 4).

(table 20.4). It might also be relevant to add that politically powerful landed interests were able to secure some protection from these globalization forces in continental Europe with tariffs on wheat (O'Rourke 1997) so that the wage–rental rose only about a third as fast in the average of France, Germany, and Spain compared with the open four of Britain, Ireland, Denmark, and Sweden. Japan achieved much the same with import restrictions on rice.

In contrast with East Asia and Europe, we take the Punjab to have been relatively land-abundant, an assumption that seems to be confirmed by the fact that agricultural exports from that Indian region to Europe boomed after the 1860s and early 1870s. Compared with land-scarce Japan, globalization should have had the opposite effect on the wage–rental ratio in the land-abundant Punjab: it should have fallen, and fall it did. Between 1870–74 and 1910–14 the wage–rental ratio in the Punjab fell by 60 percent. The Punjab's wage–rental ratio experience was not so different from that of the Southern Cone and other parts of the New World. Between 1870–74 and 1910–14 the wage-rental ratio fell by 69 percent in the combined pair of Australia and the United States, and between 1880–84 and 1910–14 it fell by 85 percent in the combined pair of Argentina and Uruguay. Egypt, riding a cotton boom, conformed to these Asian and Latin American trends: from the late 1870s to 1910–14, the Egyptian wage–rental ratio fell by 54 percent, and from the late 1880s it fell by 85 percent.

However, perhaps the best examples of factor price convergence in land-abundant and labor-scarce economies can be found in rice-exporting Southeast Asia. Table 20.5 documents wage–rental ratio trends there for two countries, Burma and Siam. Pre-1914 globalization shocks served to lower the wage–rental ratio in both places, and the decline was huge. The Burmese ratio fell by 44 percent over the twenty years between 1890–94 and 1910–14, while the Siamese ratio fell by 92 percent over the same period, and by 98 percent between 1870–74 and 1910–14! These are even bigger wage–rental ratio declines than those recorded in the Southern Cone, Australia, or North America.

What happened after 1914 when so many countries in the Atlantic economy retreated behind tariff walls, underwent competitive devaluations, restricted migrations, and used other devices to try to move back towards their pre-1800 autarkic roots? Factor price convergence ceased, and in many cases divergence set in, but that story will have to wait for another paper.[13]

The factor price convergence theorem seems to have been alive and well before 1940 the world round—in the Atlantic economy, in Asia, in Latin America, and in the Middle East.

Concluding Remarks

Eli Heckscher and Bertil Ohlin developed a theory of international trade that was motivated by the late-nineteenth-century experience. While their theory does a very good job in accounting for that nineteenth-century experience, this fact does not necessarily imply that Heckscher-Ohlin forces were also important in accounting for distributional trends in earlier periods. Commodity price convergence was not nearly strong enough to have had a big impact on domestic commodity prices and, by extension, on factor prices. Furthermore most intercontinental trade was in noncompeting goods which by definition did not displace domestic production.

None of this should come as a surprise: Why should any economic model be equally relevant for all periods and places? One key difference between today's developed economies and those of a century ago is that agriculture plays a much smaller role today. The specific factors model suggests that trade should have had a much greater impact on land rents than on wages, and the evidence bears that prediction out. European wages grew more rapidly than they did in the New World during the late nineteenth century, but on average the margin was slim. In any event, most of the international real wage convergence experienced then can be attributed to international migration, rather than to commodity market integration (Taylor and Williamson 1997). By contrast, while real land values rose by over 400 percent in Australia between 1870 and 1910, and by over 250 percent in the United States, they fell in European countries such as Britain, France, and Sweden (in Britain by more than 50 percent). Commodity prices do a very good job explaining land price movements during this period (O'Rourke 1997), but they seem to have had a less systematic impact on real wages, just as theory suggests: the strong correlation between relative commodity prices and the wage–rental ratio was driven more by movements in the latter's denominator than by movements in its numerator.

Specific factors were more affected by trade, and they also had a greater incentive to lobby for protection. Unlike farm labor, land could not exit from agriculture, and so it exercised considerable voice. This was particularly true in Europe where restrictions on agricultural produce were erected that remain in place to this day. Trade had a large impact on domestic politics in the nineteenth century, and the divisions to which it gave rise can largely be understood by Heckscher-Ohlin thinking, as Ronald Rogowski (1989) and others have shown so convincingly. Thus free-trading slave and land owners in the antebellum cotton South opposed northern industrial capitalists in the United States, free-trading labor and capital opposed protectionist landowners in midcentury Britain, and protectionist coalitions of land and capital opposed labor in Germany after 1879. The fact that trade policy frequently gave rise to major political debates, and that those debates seemed to evolve along class lines, is in itself powerful evidence that the Heckscher-Ohlin model describes the nineteenth century well. Their model suggests that trade produces losers as well as winners, and by the end of the nineteenth century many of those losers were able to gain protection from accommodating legislators. This globalization backlash was sometimes quite significant.[14]

The politics of trade were very different before 1800 when conflicts were far more likely to erupt between nations than within nations. The evidence summarized here can help us understand why. If trade had no large distributional effects on domestic economies, then the various classes in society had no great incentive to lobby for protection or free trade. If trade was still largely characterized by monopoly rents, then the key political question for (mercantilist) statesmen was who would get those rents—their own monopolists or those of other nations.[15]

We hope that this chapter has demonstrated why Heckscher-Ohlin trade theory is not very helpful in understanding the mercantilist era but very helpful in understanding the global era that followed. There was no big global bang in the 1490s, but there was a very big global bang in the 1820s.

Acknowledgments

The authors acknowledge with pleasure the excellent research assistance of Andrea Cid, Matt Rosenberg, and especially Ximena Clark.

We thank Vincent Hogan, Anthony Murphy, and especially Rodney Thom for their invaluable econometric advice, and Greg Clark for providing us with data on British land rents. The revised version of this chapter was improved by comments from Arne Bigsten, Don Davis, Ron Findlay, Elhanan Helpman, Doug Irwin, Ron Jones, Lars Jonung, Paul Krugman, Bob Mundell, and participants at the Ohlin Conference. Williamson also acknowledges generous research support from the National Science Foundation SBR-9505656.

Notes

1. We also found, but did not emphasize, that Knut Wicksell was wrong. Wicksell argued that trade would lead to a decline in the demand for Swedish labor and thus, we take it, in the real wage (Flam and Flanders 1991:7). In fact CGE models suggest that commodity price convergence vis-à-vis America would have led to a *rise* in Swedish real wages (O'Rourke and Williamson 1995).

2. Much of Menard's evidence is taken from Shepherd and Walton (1972), but these scholars did not deflate their nominal indexes as has Menard.

3. We say "most" but do not assert "all." Presumably the VOC saved on costs by switching to a permanent Asian fleet. In Steengaard's words, "The extra expense involved in setting up this permanent Asian trading fleet must have been slight compared with the saving achieved by employing the big return ships solely for the purpose for which they were intended" (Steengaard 1965:156).

4. A reading of Irwin (1991:1297) suggests that pretty much *all* of the intercontinental trade at this time was by state-chartered monopolies. Like most monopolies, they raised prices paid by consumers (in Europe), lowered prices paid to suppliers (in Asia), restricted output, and limited trade. These are hardly the ingredients that make globalization flourish!

5. This and the next subsection draw heavily on chapter 3 of our recent book (O'Rourke and Williamson 1999a:33–54).

6. The Asian material that follows is taken from Williamson (1999a, 2000).

7. We emphasize the results obtained with WR1 in the text. The results using WR2 were similar, and are reported in subsequent notes.

8. As we will see, this result is driven primarily by time trends in the data, and by the increasing impact of capital–labor ratios on income distribution. Table 20.1 reports results using the WR1 wage–rental estimate. Its replacement by WR2, however, does not seem to matter to our results. In the earlier period the correlation between WR2 and LANDLAB is 0.907, while in the later period it is −0.799. The correlation between PAPM and WR2 is −0.864 in the earlier period, and −0.361 in the later period.

9. O'Rourke and Williamson (1999b). All econometric exercises described below were performed using Eviews 3.

10. O'Rourke, Taylor, and Williamson (1996). Technology, as proxied by the Solow residual, was found in our 1996 paper to be positively related to the wage–rental ratio

in Europe, suggesting that technological change was indeed labor-using as economic historians had previously suggested.

11. When WR2 is used, the coefficients are very similar to those in table 20.3, equation (2); however, the residuals from this equation narrowly fail the Engle-Granger cointegration test.

12. This section draws heavily on two papers by one of the authors (Williamson 1999c, 2000).

13. All of these issues are pursued in greater depth elsewhere (Williamson 2000), where the econometric connections among relative factor prices, relative commodity prices, and endowments in the pre-1940 world economy are estimated and attention is paid to cointegration and causality.

14. See, for example, O'Rourke (1997) on European grain tariffs and Williamson (1997) on New World manufacturing protection and immigration restrictions.

15. This topic—mercantilism—was, of course, explored at length by Heckscher (1931). More recently its monopolistic and rent-seeking attributes have been explored by Irwin (1991).

References

Bentley, J. H. 1999. Asia in world history. *Education about Asia* 4:5–9.

Brandt, L. 1985. Chinese agriculture and the international economy 1870–1913: A reassessment. *Explorations in Economic History* 22:168–80.

Brown, H. Phelps, and S. V. Hopkins. 1981. *A Perspective of Wages and Prices*. London: Methuen.

Bulbeck, D., A. Reid, L. C. Tan, and Y. Wu. 1998. *Southeast Asian Exports since the 14th Century: Cloves, Pepper, Coffee, and Sugar*. Leiden: KITLV Press.

Collins, W. J. 1996. Regional labor markets in British India. Mimeo. Department of Economics, Harvard University. November.

Davis, R. 1962. *The Rise of the English Shipping Industry in the Seventeenth and Eighteenth Centuries*. London: Macmillan.

Findlay, R. 1996. The emergence of the world economy. Columbia University Department of Economics Discussion Paper 9596-08. April.

Flam, H., and M. J. Flanders. 1991. *Heckscher-Ohlin Trade Theory*. Cambridge: MIT Press.

Frank, A. G. 1998. *ReOrient: Global Economy in the Asian Age*. Berkeley, CA: University of California Press.

Harlaftis, G., and V. Kardasis. 2000. International shipping in the eastern Mediterranean and the Black Sea: Istanbul as a maritime center. In S. Pamuk and J. G. Williamson, eds., *Globalization Challenge and Economic Response in the Mediterranean before 1950*. London: Routledge, pp. 233–65.

Harley, C. K. 1980. Transportation, the world wheat trade, and the Kuznets cycle, 1850–1913. *Explorations in Economic History* 17:218–50.

Harley, C. K. 1988. Ocean freight rates and productivity, 1740–1913: The primacy of mechanical invention reaffirmed. *Journal of Economic History* 48:851–76.

Hatton, T. J., and J. G. Williamson. 1998. *The Age of Mass Migration*. New York: Oxford University Press.

Hayami, Y., and V. W. Ruttan. 1971. *Agricultural Development*. Baltimore: Johns Hopkins University Press.

Heckscher, E. 1931. *Merkantilismen*. Stockholm: Norstedt.

Huber, J. R. 1971. Effect on prices of Japan's entry into world commerce after 1858. *Journal of Political Economy* 79:614–28.

Irwin, D. A. 1991. Mercantilism as strategic trade policy: The Anglo-Dutch rivalry for the East India trade. *Journal of Political Economy* 99:1296–1314.

Issawi, C. 1966. *The Economy of the Middle East 1800–1914*. Chicago: University of Chicago Press.

Jones, R. W. 1971. A three-factor model in theory, trade, and history. In J. N. Bhagwati et al., eds., *Trade, Balance of Payments, and Growth*. Amsterdam: North-Holland, pp. 3–21.

Kang, K. H., and M. S. Cha. 1996. Imperial policy or world price shocks? Explaining interwar Korean living standards. Paper presented to the Conference on East and Southeast Asian Economic Change in the Long Run, Honolulu, April 11.

Krishna, B. 1924. *Commercial Relations between India and England (1601–1757)*. London: Routledge.

Latham, A. J. H., and L. Neal. 1983. The international market in rice and wheat 1868–1914. *Economic History Review* 36:260–75.

McCusker, J. J., and R. Menard. 1991. *The Economy of British America, 1607–1789*. Chapel Hill: University of North Carolina Press.

Mechner, E. 1999. *Pirates and Planters: Trade and Development in the Caribbean, 1492–1680*, Ph.D. dissertation. Department of Economics, Harvard University.

Menard, R. 1991. Transport costs and long-range trade, 1300–1800: Was there a European "transport revolution" in the early modern era? In J. D. Tracy, ed., *Political Economy of Merchant Empires*. Cambridge: Cambridge University Press, pp. 228–75.

North, D. C. 1958. Ocean freight rates and economic development 1750–1913. *Journal of Economic History* 18:538–55.

O'Rourke, K. H. 1994. The repeal of the Corn Laws and Irish emigration. *Explorations in Economic History* 31:120–38.

O'Rourke, K. H. 1997. The European grain invasion, 1870–1913. *Journal of Economic History* 57:775–801.

O'Rourke, K. H., A. M. Taylor, and J. G. Williamson. 1996. Factor price convergence in the late nineteenth century. *International Economic Review* 37:499–530.

O'Rourke, K. H., and J. G. Williamson. 1994. Late 19th century Anglo-American factor price convergence: Were Heckscher and Ohlin right? *Journal of Economic History* 54:892–916.

O'Rourke, K. H., and J. G. Williamson. 1995. Open economy forces and late 19th century Swedish catch-up: A quantitative accounting. *Scandinavian Economic History Review* 43(2):171–203.

O'Rourke, K. H., and J. G. Williamson. 1999a. *Globalization and History.* Cambridge: MIT Press.

O'Rourke, K. H., and J. G. Williamson. 1999b. The Heckscher-Ohlin model between 1400 and 2000: When it explained factor price convergence, when it did not, and why. NBER Working Paper 7411. National Bureau of Economic Research, Cambridge, MA. November.

O'Rourke, K. H., and J. G. Williamson. 2000. When did globalization begin? NBER Working Paper 7632. National Bureau of Economic Research, Cambridge, MA. April.

Reid, A. 1993. *Southeast Asia in the Age of Commerce 1450–1680: Expansion and Crisis,* vol. 2. New Haven: Yale University Press.

Rogowski, R. 1989. *Commerce and Coalitions: How Trade Effects Domestic Political Arrangements.* Princeton: Princeton University Press.

Samuelson, P. A. 1971. Ohlin was right. *Swedish Journal of Economics* 73:365–84.

Shepherd, J. F., and G. M. Walton. 1972. *Shipping, Maritime Trade, and the Economic Development of Colonial North America.* Cambridge: Cambridge University Press.

Slaughter, M. J. 1995. The antebellum transportation revolution and factor-price convergence. NBER Working Paper 5303. National Bureau of Economic Research, Cambridge, MA. October.

Steensgaard, N. 1965. Freight costs in the English East India trade 1601–1657. *Scandinavian Economic History Review* 13:143–62.

Taylor, A. M., and J. G. Williamson. 1997. Convergence in the age of mass migration. *European Review of Economic History* 1:27–63.

Temin, P. 1966. Labor scarcity and the problem of American industrial efficiency in the 1850s. *Journal of Economic History* 26:277–98.

Tracy, J. D. 1990. Introduction. In J. D. Tracy, ed., *The Rise of Merchant Empires.* Cambridge: Cambridge University Press.

Williamson, J. G. 1990. The impact of the Corn Laws just prior to repeal. *Explorations in Economic History* 27:123–56.

Williamson, J. G. 1997. Globalization and inequality, past and present. *World Bank Research Observer* 12:117–35.

Williamson, J. G. 1999a. Globalization, factor prices and living standards in Asia before 1940. In A. J. Latham and H. Kawakatsu, eds., *Asia Pacific Dynamism 1550–2000.* London: Routledge.

Williamson, J. G. 1999b. Real wages, inequality, and globalization in Latin America before 1940. *Revista de Historia Economica* 17:101–42.

Williamson, J. G. 1999c. The impact of globalization on pre-industrial, technologically quiescent economies: Real wages, relative factor prices, and commodity price convergence in the third world before 1940. NBER Working Paper 7146. National Bureau of Economic Research, Cambridge, MA. May.

Williamson, J. G. 2000. Land, labor and globalization in the pre-industrial third world. NBER Working Paper 7784. National Bureau of Economics Research, Cambridge, MA. July.

Williamson, J. G., and P. H. Lindert. 1980. *American Inequality: A Macroeconomic History*. New York: Academic Press.

Wood, A. 1994. *North–South Trade, Employment and Inequality: Changing Fortunes in a Skill-Driven World*. Oxford: Clarendon Press.

Yasuba, Y. 1978. Freight rates and productivity in ocean transportation for Japan, 1875–1943. *Explorations in Economic History* 15:11–39.

Yasuba, Y. 1996. Did Japan ever suffer from a shortage of natural resources before World War II? *Journal of Economic History* 56:543–60.

21 Testing Trade Theory in Ohlin's Time

Antoni Estevadeordal and
Alan M. Taylor

Factor Abundance Theory in Historical Context

Some years ago, scholars in the field of international trade, and perhaps especially the empiricists, might have viewed an invitation to the Ohlin centennial with a sense of unease. Most of us saw factor abundance trade theory as possibly unparalleled in the realm of economic science in its elegance of form and powerful statements on the sources of comparative advantage. At the same time the theory was viewed as having been confounded by empirical contradictions in a series of studies dating back to the paradox unearthed by Leontief.[1] Given such an environment, what kind of conference paper could one offer that would not mar the spirit of celebration?

Happily, at least for the legacy of Ohlin, perspectives do change. In recent years new approaches and extensions to this landmark theory and its empirical testing have attested to its durability and relevance for explaining modern-day trade patterns.[2] In one tradition of empirical research, following Leamer (1984), scholars have constructed large datasets on national endowments and trade patterns so as to measure the link between factors and trade. This is predicted by the theory to be a linear relationship depending on technical coefficients, suggesting that, say, an increase in capital endowment should spill over into trade as an increase in the net export of capital-intensive goods. In another strand of work, following the notation and methodology of Vanek (1968), scholars have focused on the implicit factor trade alone and its relationship to factor abundance (Leamer 1980; Bowen, Leamer, and Sveikauskas 1987). This approach seeks to establish a pass through—in principle, a unit coefficient—relating increments in relative factor endowment directly to net exports of the same factor, as production shifts relative to a stable consumption pattern. Most of the very recent empirical contributions (e.g., Trefler 1993, 1995; Davis and Weinstein 2001) have used the Vanek representation.

These recent works point to a compromise position where the Heckscher-Ohlin theory, augmented in various ways, might better account for the contemporary pattern of factor trade. To deal with the Leontief paradox, one can allow for differences in cross-country productivities, as suggested by Leontief, and implemented empirically by Trefler (1993, 1995). Still, this modification alone doesn't get us very far toward narrowing the huge gap between measured and predicted factor trade. Trefler (1995) coined the term "missing trade" to depict the extent to which measured trade is still negligible compared to the prediction of the pure theory.[3] To get an even closer fit, other modifications have been suggested by Trefler (1995) and Davis and Weinstein (2001) such as home bias in consumption, an allowance for nontraded goods, and models without factor price equalization. However, before basking in fresh optimism over how the factor abundance theory has been thoroughly rehabilitated by these various devices, we should note that lurking here is a danger. After so much ornamentation has been added to the model, the skeptics might reasonably ask what is left of Heckscher and Ohlin's original design.

One wonders what Ohlin would make of all these developments and modifications to his theory given his original standpoint. Here was an economist working in the early twentieth century who was inspired to explain the international trade patterns previously witnessed in a largely free-trade regime—the trade of mostly commodity goods and manufactures in the Greater Atlantic economy during the first era of globalization before World War I.[4] And when Heckscher and Ohlin made their seminal contributions, most observers still hoped that this regime would soon be restored for the long run in the 1920s, though that was not to be.

Heckscher and Ohlin would not necessarily condone the use of their theory in today's very different global economic environment. Today we see numerous barriers to trade (especially in agricultural commodities and simple manufactures), trade in differentiated products and services, and significant intraindustry trade.[5] However, the duo still might be impressed by the substantial technical apparatus that we have developed to evaluate their theory, even as they might regret that they never had easy access to the kinds of large datasets we now take for granted as we implement our sophisticated tests. Given all this, we can imagine one possible reaction from the fathers of factor abundance trade theory. Might they not call on us to take our considerably refined empirical skills back in time and at least give the theory—and its authors—some kind of a break by testing the model in the historical context for which it was first designed?

Imagining that we heard such a call at the time of Ohlin's centennial, and having a taste for economic history, we thought it would only be fair to him to do just that. Not only does this idea appeal for sentimental reasons, but also, we will argue, it helps resolve questions stimulated by the research on contemporary global factor trade. Testing the model in an earlier historical epoch might help us see the sources of difficulty in applying the model in the present. By bringing to the discussion new datasets from a different economic and political era, we can gain a new perspective. And in some ways, the pre-1914 period offers a better testing ground for the pure Heckscher-Ohlin trade model, as economic historians love to remind us. Indeed, a strand of the economic history literature has already found strong support in that era for several features of standard theory, including predictions of factor price convergence and the pattern of goods trade.[6]

What are the features of the pre-1914 era that make it a better laboratory for testing pure trade theory compared to today? And are there other aspects that favor the present? We know, first, that there were much lower trade barriers then than now, and this could be why the theory fails in the present. In figure 21.1 we plot the dispersion of the average applied tariff levels for 1913 and for the post–Uruguay Round period (mid-1990s) for several country samples.[7] Although the 1913 levels are slightly higher than those for the recent period, we must remember that market access negotiations under the Uruguay Round brought tariffs to the lowest point in all postwar period, and the theory has usually been tested for earlier periods (the mid-1960s, mid-1970s, or mid-1980s). In addition postwar tariff reductions have been offset, in part or in whole, by an increasing presence of NTMs (nontariff measures) and other distortionary trade instruments that were practically nonexistent during the pre-WWI period. In the last three boxplots of figure 21.1 we include a measure of the incidence of NTMs based on the percentage of tariff lines (in the tariff schedules) affected by any type of NTM for each country in the sample. It is not a direct measure of the level of protection but

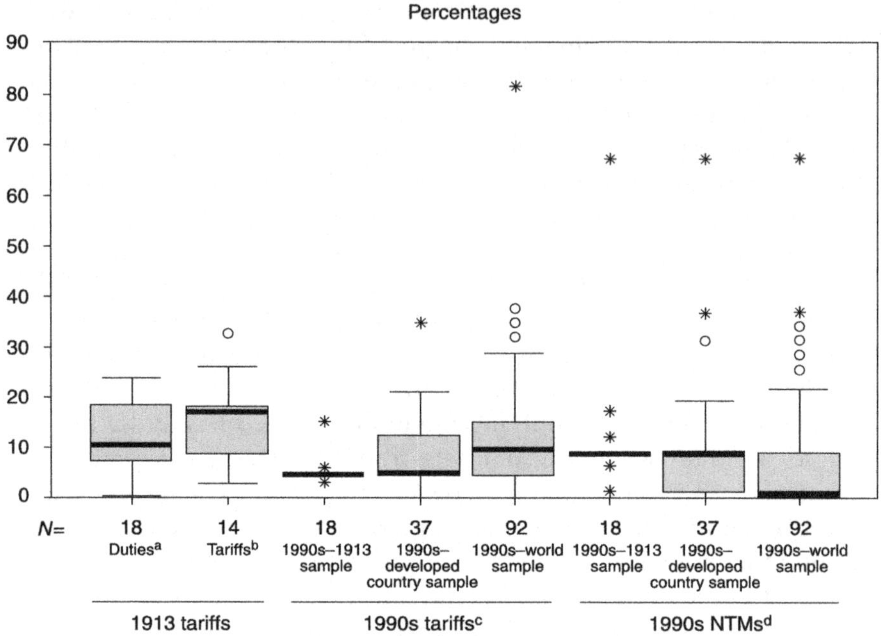

Figure 21.1
Tariffs and nontariff indexes, 1913 and mid-1990s. Notes: (a) Duties as a percentage oftotal imports as reported in Estevadeordal (1997); (b) League of Nations tariff level indexes as reported in Estevadeordal (1997); (c) total charges from UNCTAD/TRAINS database; (d) nontariff incidence measure from UNCTAD/TRAINS database.

highlights the degree of importance of this new type of protectionism. Thus the past epoch might more closely match the free-trade assumptions of the theory.

Second, in the last century certain endowments were very skewed in their distribution, most famously the agricultural land that differentiated the endowments of the New World from the Old. Today, in contrast, many of the countries in the samples studied have very similar endowment patterns, and this leaves little data variation from which to get a strong fit.[8] In the context of standard econometric tests of predicted-versus-measured factor content of trade such variation would strengthen the test enormously by offering a wide range in the independent variable. In figure 21.2 we plot the relative shares of the endowments of the three classical factors—capital, labor, and land—for 1913 and for the late-1980s. Comparing the relative dispersion of the 1913 data with the same sample of

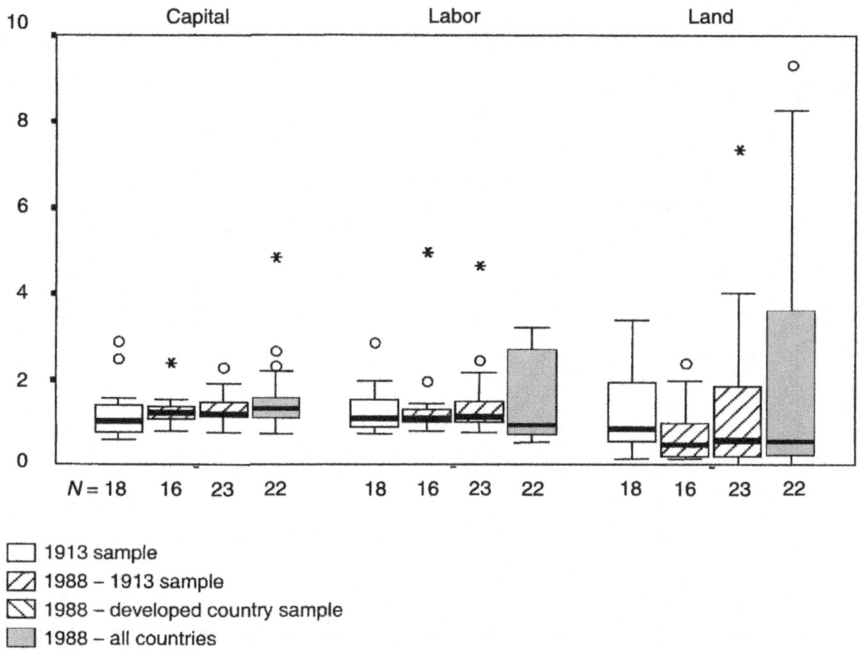

Figure 21.2
Relative shares of endowments, 1913 and 1988, measured as $(V_n/V_{fw})/(Y_i/Y_w)$. Notes: The samples do not include Argentina and Australia; V_{fi} is country i's endowment of factor f; V_{wi} is the world endowment of factor f; Y_i is country i's GNP; Y_w is world GNP. "World" is defined by the sample size. Sources: 1913 data from Estevadeordal (1997), and 1988 data from Trefler (1995).

countries, or even with a developed country sample, for 1988 (representing then and now most of the world trade), we observe a higher degree of dispersion and skewness in the earlier period. This could be another weak point in tests using modern data.

Third, we note that there was considerable divergence in productivity across countries circa 1913, just as there is today. Over the course of the twentieth century we have seen dramatic productivity convergence within a narrow club of countries—mostly the OECD, and thus much of the Greater Atlantic economy. Yet it is equally true that outside this subset, productivity convergence of the unconditional variety has been weak or nonexistent.[9] In figure 21.3, again using boxplots for different country samples, we report the relative levels of productivity measured as real GDP per capita relative to the

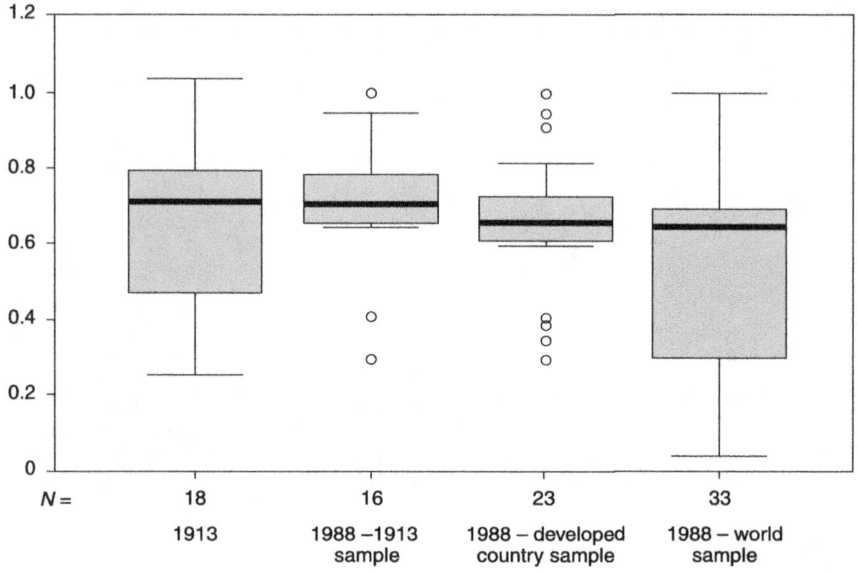

Figure 21.3
Relative productivity, 1913 and 1988, measured as real GDP per capita, U.S. = 1. Note: The samples do not include Argentina and Australia. Sources: 1913 data from Maddison (1995), and 1988 data from Trefler (1995).

United States. The data for 1913 show a high variance of productivity levels when compared with a similar group of countries in 1988 and not much difference if a larger sample is considered. Thus, by doing our tests circa 1913, we are in no way making the problem simpler for ourselves by avoiding an essential ingredient in the "missing trade" puzzle: the possibility of international productivity differences.

Raw differences in factor productivity were postulated by Leontief (1953a) as a possible solution to his paradox for the United States, and his idea was supported in international samples by Trefler (1993, 1995) and Davis and Weinstein (2001). However, as Helpman (1999) notes, this way out just creates another disturbing puzzle: namely, where do these differences in productivity originate? In historical work, this same disturbing idea was brought to the fore by the controversial work of Clark (1987). He found no comfort in any economic explanation of international variations in the productivity of cotton mills in various countries circa 1913. There seemed to be no compelling economic reason why one New England cotton textile

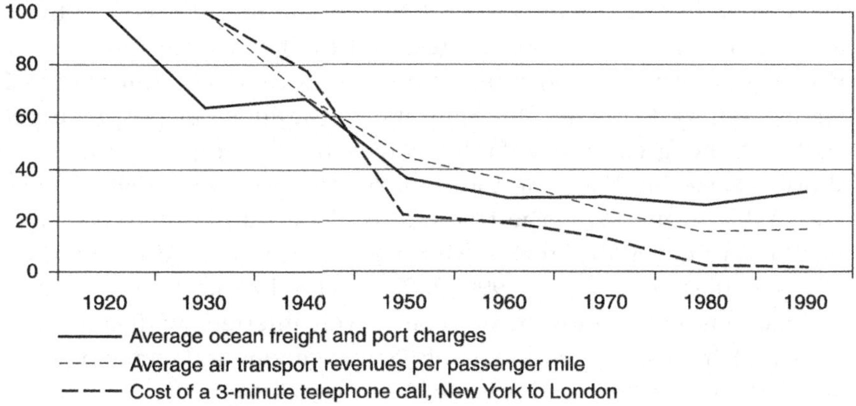

Figure 21.4
Transport and communication costs, 1920 to 1990. Source: Hufbauer (1991).

operative performed as much work as 1.5 British, 2.3 German, and nearly 6 Greek, Japanese, Indian, or Chinese workers. After controlling for capital intensities, breakdowns, human capital, learning, and other effects, Clark was forced to admit the possibility of a purely cultural origin of the differences, quite possibly exogenous to the economic system. If Clark's idea holds in a wide range of sectors circa 1913, then, just as output would have been affected by these raw productivity differences, so too would the levels of trade and the factor content therein, with direct implications for our proposed tests.

Finally, we should note a couple of characteristics that work against the earlier period as a good testing ground. First, we must consider the higher transport costs of the past. Like measuring true tariffs from actual import data, measuring true transport costs from trade data is problematic. Comparing CIF and FOB prices then and now might not lead to a big difference in the measured transport cost premium *on goods actually shipped*: goods too expensive to ship never make it into the sample, creating a serious selection problem.[10] Data are scarce here, but it is a reasonable conjecture that many bulk goods shipped today move at a fraction of their cost a hundred years ago, and surely many exotic goods and services can now move more cheaply than they did in the past. Figure 21.4 illustrates the dramatic declines in transportation and communication costs that have occurred throughout this century. The second problem for the earlier period—though it is by no means absent in the present—concerns factor mobility. It is well known that the theory predicts that trade and factor mobility are substitutes, and the late nineteenth century was a time of very fluid international factor markets. International labor mobility facilitated the migration of millions of people, especially in the great transatlantic waves from Europe to the New World (Easterlin 1961; Hatton and Williamson 1994, 1998; Taylor and Williamson 1997). The first era of global capital markets functioned very efficiently, reallocating vast sums of capital internationally (Obstfeld and Taylor 1998, 2002; Taylor 1996). The presence of endogenous factor movements could well interfere with empirical tests that treat factor endowments as exogenous independent variables. We will return to this issue in our conclusion.

The rest of this chapter is organized around the steps we took to mount such an attack. We focus on the two types of tests used, those based on goods trade and those based on factor trade. We describe the historical data and their manipulation for the test at hand. Results are presented in the usual form for each test and the implications are discussed. A brief conclusion offers some broader interpretations and directions for future research.

Factor Endowments and Product Trade circa 1913

Tests

Consider the standard Heckscher-Ohlin theory, in a world of C countries, I industries, and F factors. Let the output in country c be $\mathbf{X}^c(I \times 1)$. The factor content of $\mathbf{X}^c$ is $\mathbf{B}\mathbf{X}^c$, where $\mathbf{B}$ is a matrix $(F \times I)$ of factor content coefficients.[11] Full employment implies that $\mathbf{B}\mathbf{X}^c = \mathbf{V}^c$, where $\mathbf{V}^c$ is the factor endowment of country c. Consumption $\mathbf{C}^c(I \times 1)$ in country c equals the country share of world expenditure s^c (assumed equal to world output in this study) times world consumption $\mathbf{C}^W$. The latter, by world market clearing, equals world output, $\mathbf{C}^W = \mathbf{X}^W = \Sigma_c \mathbf{X}^c$. Hence $\mathbf{C}^c = s^c\mathbf{X}^W$, and the net goods trade $\mathbf{T}^c$ of country c equals $\mathbf{T}^c = \mathbf{X}^c - \mathbf{C}^c = \mathbf{X}^c - s^c\mathbf{X}^W$. If we denote world factor endowment by $\mathbf{V}^W = \mathbf{B}\mathbf{X}^W$, then

$$\mathbf{T}^c = \mathbf{B}^{-1}(\mathbf{V}^c - s^c\mathbf{V}^W). \tag{1}$$

This equation says that trade in each industry is linearly related to factor endowments. We assume that $\mathbf{B}$ is invertible (i.e., square, with $I = F$). Leamer (1984) argued that the equation need not be restricted to the square case and he proposed that it be tested by regressions for each industry i. Evaluation centers on the fit and reasonableness of these equations, allowing for both statistical and quantitative significance.[12]

This methodology was used to study trade circa 1913 by Estevadeordal (1993). The challenge was to construct new datasets on net trades (the left-hand side) and endowments (the right-hand side) for the econometric study. A detailed explanation of the data, coding, and aggregation is found in the appendix to Estevadeordal (1997). We provide a brief overview here.

Data, Coding, and Aggregation

Data on net trade for the period circa 1913 was collected for $C = 18$ countries: Argentina, Australia, Austria-Hungary, Belgium, Canada, Denmark, Finland, France, Germany, Italy, Netherlands, Norway, Portugal, Spain, Sweden, Switzerland, United Kingdom, and United States. The sources used were official national reports of trade statistics, originating from such agencies as the Board of Trade (U.K.) or the Department of Commerce (U.S). The principal problem in ensuring consistency across countries was to set up a universal classification scheme for industries, since, prior to World War II, no standards had been developed and each country used its own classification. The solution was to laboriously construct country-specific concordances that would map each country's sectors into selected sectors of the Standard International Trade Classification (SITC, Revised 1961) at the two-digit level. In this way the trade data $\mathbf{T}^c$ was rationalized into a database for $C = 18$ countries and $I = 55$ sectors expressed in U.S. dollars at market exchange rates.[13]

National product estimates were taken from Mitchell (1980, 1983) and Maddison (1995) and expressed in U.S. dollars at market exchange rates, providing the basis for expenditure shares s^c.[14]

Endowment data $\mathbf{V}^c$ for all countries were collected for $F = 5$ types of factor: capital stock, skilled and unskilled labor force, agricultural land, and mineral resources. In Estevadeordal (1993) a proxy for capital stock based on energy consumption of solid fuels was used. The data on energy consumption refer to apparent consumption of primary sources, including net imports of secondary as well as primary energy forms. Because of data availability only solid fuels had been considered (hard coal, brown coal, lignite, and coke). In order to permit aggregation and comparison, data were expressed in thousands of hard-coal equivalents. In this section of the chapter we report results based on those of Estevadeordal (1993) which use the original capital measure. However, in order to carry out the subsequent factor content analysis in the next section, we made new capital stock estimates for 1913 using a perpetual-inventory method applied to pre-1913 annual investment rates and real outputs. The results gave capital-output ratios for the terminal year 1913, and multiplying by national products yielded capital stocks in U.S. dollars at market exchange rates. The labor force figures originate in Maddison (1982) and Mitchell (1980, 1983), and we use interpolation between census years as necessary. Agricultural land is measured in hectares, and the data are largely from a study by the League of Nations (1927). Mineral resources are estimated using as a proxy the U.S. dollar value of the annual production of petroleum plus twelve other minerals and ores; quantities are drawn principally from Mitchell (1980, 1983) and prices from Potter and Christy (1962).[15]

Results

The Heckscher-Ohlin equation (1) expresses trade in terms of excess endowments $\mathbf{V}^c - s^c\mathbf{V}^W$. For empirical purposes, following Leamer (1984), we can regress trade on endowment supplies alone.[16] We report results at two different levels of aggregation (six and forty-six commodity groups).

Table 21.1, panel (a), reports the estimates for the following six commodity groups: agricultural products, raw materials, capital-intensive goods, labor-intensive goods, machinery, and chemicals. The R^2 measures of fit are typically very high and most of the estimated coefficients are correctly signed and statistically significant. The coefficients still depend on the units of the explanatory variables. Since we are not only interested in the statistical significance of a coefficient but also in knowing how important each of the variables is in explaining the trade pattern, panel (b) reports β values for each of the five explanatory variables for each trade aggregate considered.[17] If we select arbitrarily, as in Leamer (1984), 1.0 to define a significant β value, then capital is significant five times, land four times, and labor-skilled and minerals three times.

Generally speaking, in the estimates of table 21.1, comparative advantage in agricultural products is associated with abundance of land and mineral resources and is negatively related to capital. Trade in raw materials owes comparative advantage to the avail-

Table 21.1
Tests of factor endowments and product trade

	Capital	Labor—skilled	Labor—unskilled	Agricultural land	Minerals	R^2	Adjusted R^2
a. OLS estimates							
Agricultural products	−7.6***	−26.3	−31.9	8.5**	4.5***	0.81	0.73
	(−5.22)	(−1.74)	(−0.55)	(2.38)	(4.50)		
Raw materials	2.7***	−20.6***	41.6*	−3.0***	0.4	0.78	0.69
	(5.22)	(−4.61)	(2.14)	(−4.91)	(1.67)		
Capital-intensive goods	2.1***	18.4***	13.3	−6.5***	−0.7*	0.83	0.77
	(5.98)	(4.21)	(0.66)	(−4.98)	(−2.08)		
Labor-intensive goods	−0.9***	17.8***	−9.8	−4.0***	0.8**	0.65	0.51
	(3.20)	(8.89)	(−1.24)	(−3.79)	(2.59)		
Machinery	1.1***	5.0*	−9.6	−3.1***	0.08	0.91	0.88
	(4.73)	(2.12)	(−1.05)	(−5.87)	(0.54)		
Chemicals	−0.1	6.7***	−6.3	−2.3***	0.38	0.69	0.56
	(−1.08)	(5.87)	(−1.62)	(−2.53)	(1.72)		
b. β values							
Agricultural products	−1.83	−0.51	−0.11	0.72	1.64		
Raw materials	2.36	−1.45	0.50	−0.92	0.53		
Capital-intensive goods	1.30	0.92	0.11	−1.42	−0.65		
Labor-intensive goods	−1.10	1.76	−0.17	−1.73	1.48		
Machinery	1.22	0.45	−0.15	−1.22	0.13		
Chemicals	−0.24	1.29	−0.21	−1.93	1.37		

Source: Estevadeordal (1993).

Notes: *t*-ratios in parentheses. (***) denotes significant at the 1% level. (**) denotes significant at the 5% level. (*) denotes significant at the 10% level. Commodity groups based on SITC Rev.1, 2-digit codes: agricultural products (groups 0, 1, 2 except 27 and 28, 4), raw materials (groups 27, 28, 3 and 68), capital-intensive goods (groups 61, 62, 63, 64, 651–655, 67 and 69), labor-intensive goods (groups 656, 66 and 8), machinery (group 7), and chemicals (group 5).

Table 21.2
Tests of factor endowments and product trade (disaggregated data)

	Capital	Labor—skilled	Labor—unskilled	Agricultural land	Minerals	R^2	Adjusted R^2	$F(6, 11)$
a. OLS estimates								
SITC group 0: Food and live animals								
00	0.06*	−0.67**	−0.25	0.80**	−0.21**	0.66	0.48	2.52
01	−1.34**	0.60	−12.12*	1.88**	0.54**	0.79	0.69	7.30**
02	−1.03**	0.18	−8.37	1.79**	0.20*	0.75	0.62	5.62**
03	0.10**	−1.13**	−1.41**	0.33**	−0.10*	0.39	0.06	1.17
04	−1.16**	−8.52**	−17.8*	5.2**	0.18	0.90	0.85	17.53**
05	−0.42**	−0.74	7.21*	1.26	−0.20	0.68	0.50	3.90**
06	−0.64**	1.11	−4.02	−0.29	0.45**	0.58	0.35	2.55
07	−0.28**	−2.13**	1.50*	0.08**	0.06**	0.98	0.97	137.11**
08	−0.00	0.09	0.07	0.43**	−0.06**	0.70	0.54	4.36**
09	−0.28**	0.51*	−2.33*	0.16**	0.12**	0.73	0.59	5.08**
SITC group 1: Beverages and tobacco								
11	0.06*	−1.22**	6.45**	−0.24**	0.039*	0.70	0.54	4.41**
12	−0.06**	−0.43**	−0.16	0.07	0.06**	0.78	0.66	6.70**
SITC group 2: Crude materials, inedible (except fuels)								
21	0.20**	−0.40*	−0.56	0.88**	−0.22**	0.96	0.94	46.34**
22	0.13*	−5.80**	3.72	1.27**	−0.15	0.74	0.61	5.48**
23	−0.59**	1.44**	−3.28**	0.08	0.16**	0.96	0.94	49.54**
24	0.06	−3.83**	−3.0*	1.76**	−0.21**	0.72	0.57	4.83**
25	−0.16**	0.27	−2.80**	0.16**	0.06**	0.58	0.35	2.55
26	−1.27**	−17.24**	−4.11	5.64**	0.66*	0.79	0.68	7.25**

27	0.00	−1.04**	2.02**	0.07	0.01	0.22	0.10	0.53
28	−0.46**	−0.28	−4.29**	1.46**	−0.08	0.84	0.76	10.06**
29	−0.02	−2.27**	2.87	0.66**	−0.06**	0.62	0.41	3.04
SITC group 3: Mineral fuels, lubricants, and related materials								
32	2.02**	−8.33**	22.71**	−2.64**	−0.21**	0.89	0.83	15.04**
33	0.17**	−4.13**	2.15	0.88**	0.04	0.86	0.78	11.42**
SITC group 4: Animal and vegetable oils and fats								
41	−0.03	−0.44	−1.43	0.68**	−0.11**	0.70	0.53	4.31**
42	−0.20**	0.73**	−0.46	−0.11*	0.12**	0.80	0.69	7.35**
43	−0.03**	0.03	−0.21	0.02**	0.01**	0.74	0.60	5.40**
SITC group 5: Chemicals								
51 + 52 + 53 + 55 + 59	0.04	0.82*	−0.17	−0.54**	0.03*	0.74	0.59	5.23**
54 + 56 + 57 + 58	0.03**	−0.04	0.45	−0.24**	0.05**	0.66	0.47	3.58**
SITC group 6: Manufactured goods classified chiefly by material								
61	−0.42**	2.49**	−5.08**	−0.20*	0.25**	0.82	0.73	8.71**
62	−0.06**	1.04**	−0.61*	−0.19**	0.05**	0.80	0.69	7.35**
63	−0.90**	2.24**	−6.96*	0.23	0.41**	0.77	0.64	6.14**
64	−0.21**	1.08**	−2.18**	−0.39**	0.21**	0.70	0.54	4.42**
65	2.25**	10.86**	17.1	−3.74**	−1.23**	0.86	0.79	12.22**
66	−0.11	1.31	−8.69**	−0.80**	0.18**	0.69	0.52	4.12**
67	0.73**	0.80	10.93	−3.28**	0.37**	0.83	0.74	9.15**
68	−0.15**	−3.98**	1.60	0.94**	0.11	0.77	0.65	6.35**
69	0.21**	1.16*	2.61	−1.95**	0.38**	0.84	0.76	10.23**
SITC group 7: Machinery and transport equipment								
71	0.84**	−2.82**	5.18**	−1.50**	0.17**	0.94	0.91	29.85**
72	0.08**	0.30	0.44	−0.75**	0.16**	0.87	0.80	12.49**
73	0.24**	2.21**	−0.12	−0.48**	−0.06**	0.94	0.91	31.32**

Table 21.2 (continued)

	Capital	Labor—skilled	Labor—unskilled	Agricultural land	Minerals	R^2	Adjusted R^2	$F(6, 11)$
SITC group 8: Miscellaneous manufactured articles								
81 + 83 + 85	0.11**	−0.08	1.19*	−0.40**	0.06**	0.88	0.82	14.65**
82	0.02**	−0.04	0.52**	−0.05**	−0.00	0.59	0.38	2.72
84	−0.04	4.29**	0.79	−1.17**	0.10*	0.80	0.69	7.39**
86	−0.15**	0.73**	−3.26**	0.10	0.06**	0.49	0.22	1.82
89	−0.41**	4.74**	−7.66*	−1.23**	0.24**	0.34	0.01	0.99
SITC group 9: Commodities not classified according to kind								
95	0.08**	0.16	0.35	−0.06**	−0.04**	0.83	0.73	8.96**
b. β values								
SITC group 0: Food and live animals								
00	0.46	−0.41	−0.03	2.14	−2.41			
01	−2.26	0.08	−0.24	1.13	1.38			
02	−2.29	0.03	−0.25	1.4	0.67			
03	1.04	−0.95	−0.2	1.21	−1.57			
04	−1.19	−0.68	−0.18	1.87	0.28			
05	−0.79	−0.11	0.22	0.83	−0.57			
06	−2.25	0.31	−0.2	−0.36	2.39			
07	−0.86	−0.53	0.06	0.09	0.28			
08	0	0.09	0.01	1.82	−1.09			
09	−2.72	0.4	−0.3	0.55	1.76			

SITC group 1: Beverages and tobacco					
11	0.7	−1.15	1.03	−0.98	0.68
12	−1.13	−0.65	−0.04	0.46	1.71
SITC group 2: Crude materials, inedible (except fuels)					
21	0.62	−0.1	−0.02	0.96	−1.03
22	0.47	−1.68	0.19	1.63	−0.82
23	−2.32	0.46	−0.16	0.11	0.95
24	0.23	−1.19	−0.15	2.38	−1.22
25	−2.31	0.32	−0.56	0.82	1.31
26	−0.84	−0.86	−0.04	1.3	0.66
27	0	−1.01	0.34	0.3	0.18
28	−1.56	−0.08	−0.21	1.75	−0.41
29	−0.11	−1.04	0.23	1.32	−0.51
SITC group 3: Mineral fuels, lubricants, and related materials					
32	3.37	−1.08	0.45	−1.56	−0.53
33	0.57	−1.12	0.11	1.03	0.2
SITC group 4: Animal and vegetable oils and fats					
41	−0.28	−0.33	−0.19	2.26	−1.57
42	−3.02	0.89	−0.1	−0.59	2.74
43	−2.35	0.19	−0.23	0.55	1.18
SITC group 5: Chemicals					
51 + 52 + 53 + 55 + 59	0.43	0.71	−0.03	−2.06	0.49
54 + 56 + 57 + 58	0.55	−0.06	0.11	−1.54	1.38
SITC group 6: Manufactured goods, classified chiefly by material					
61	−2.81	1.34	−0.46	−0.47	2.52
62	−1.09	1.53	−0.15	−1.22	1.38

Table 21.2 (continued)

	Capital	Labor—skilled	Labor—unskilled	Agricultural land	Minerals	R^2	Adjusted R^2	$F(6, 11)$
63	−3.04	0.6	−0.35	0.27	2.09			
64	−1.62	0.67	−0.24	−1.06	2.45			
65	1.73	0.65	0.17	−1.01	−1.43			
66	−0.52	0.5	−0.52	−1.34	1.29			
67	1.36	0.12	0.33	−2.16	1.04			
68	−0.6	−1.27	0.08	1.33	0.66			
69	0.58	0.26	0.1	−1.91	1.59			
SITC group 7: Machinery and transport equipment								
71	1.75	−0.48	0.16	−1.1	0.53			
72	0.56	0.17	0.04	−1.87	1.7			
73	1.1	0.82	−0.01	−0.78	−0.42			
SITC group 8: Miscellaneous manufactured articles								
81 + 83 + 85	1.2	−0.07	0.18	−1.54	0.99			
82	1.26	−0.2	0.45	−1.11	0			
84	−0.18	1.54	0.05	−1.85	0.68			
86	−2.09	0.82	−0.62	0.49	1.26			
89	−0.87	0.81	−0.23	−0.92	0.77			
SITC group 9: Commodities not classified according to kind								
95	1.93	0.31	0.12	−0.51	−1.46			

Source: Estevadeordal (1997).

Notes: *t*-ratios not reported. (***) denotes significant at the 1% level. (**) denotes significant at the 5% level. (*) denotes significant at the 10% level.

ability of capital and unskilled labor; land and skilled labor contribute to comparative disadvantage. The sources of comparative advantage in manufacturing are, in general, as expected. Capital is a source of comparative advantage for capital-intensive goods and machinery. Mineral resources are important for labor-intensive and chemicals groups. Skilled labor also contributes to comparative advantage in all manufacturing groups. The β values indicate, again, that the contribution is most important in labor-intensive and chemicals products, followed by capital-intensive goods and machinery. Net exports of all manufacturing groups are negatively associated with the supply of land.[18] We also performed some sensitivity analysis on these results.[19]

Table 21.2, panel (a), reports results from Estevadeordal (1997) where a more disaggregated Heckscher-Ohlin model was estimated with the goal of obtaining measures of trade protection by sector. Based on the reported F-statistics, thirty-seven out of the forty-six net trade regressions are significant. Moreover, most of the R^2 measures of fit are very high. For individual factor endowments, out of forty-six estimated equations, capital has significant coefficients (at the 10% confidence level) in twenty-six cases, skilled labor in fourteen, unskilled labor in only seven, land in twenty-nine, and mineral resources in twenty-seven. The β values are reproduced in panel (b).

In general, capital and skilled labor are sources of comparative disadvantage for primary product trade. Capital is a source of comparative advantage in most capital-intensive goods; it is a source of disadvantage in labor-intensive commodities, where skilled labor contributes to comparative advantage. Agricultural land is consistently a source of advantage for primary products and creates comparative disadvantage in manufacturing. Interestingly, mineral resources are a source of comparative advantage in the processed agricultural products group and in almost all manufactures. Using the conventional 0.5 level to define a significant β value, capital is significant in thirty-six out of forty-six net trade equations.[20] Skilled labor is significant twenty-four times, unskilled labor only four times, agricultural land thirty-eight times, and mineral resources thirty-six times.

Summary

In this section we have shown how it is possible to implement a test circa 1913 of the Heckscher-Ohlin prediction that there exists a linear relationship between factor endowments and the net trade of goods. The results are very favorable to the hypothesis. For most goods the fit is acceptably good and many coefficients have statistical significance. Moreover, once we compare the signs of the coefficients for each type of good with what we expect—based on whether certain goods are intensive in certain types of factor—we also find a reassuring correspondence between the econometric results and our intuition. Finally, using the technique of β coefficients to see how much the variation in factor endowments explains the variation in net trade, we find that the quantitative significance of the model is also very high. In short, having appealed to the 1980s vintage of empirical trade tests of the form pioneered by Leamer (1984), we have found a good deal of correspondence between the empirical results of the past and present. In both cases the fit of the model is good, and it is quite a bit stronger in the historical data from Ohlin's time. Thus, viewed from a 1980s empirical perspective, the factor abundance theory seems to work very well in its own time. We now ask whether the same holds true from a 1990s perspective, where attention has shifted to tests based on factor content.[21]

Factor Endowments and Factor Trade circa 1913

Tests

The factor content test is based on the immediate precursor of Equation (1) that does not depend on any assumptions about the dimensions or invertibility of the matrix **B**, namely

$$\mathbf{BT}^c = \mathbf{V}^c - s^c\mathbf{V}^W. \tag{2}$$

Here the left-hand side vector is the measured factor content of trade (denoted MFCT_f) and the right-hand side is the predicted factor content of trade (denoted PFCT_f). In this methodology all parameters in equation (2) are measured, none are estimated econometrically, and the test centers on whether the equation holds. Thus the method is harder to implement since its data requirements are considerably larger, which might explain why cross-country tests of this type have only appeared relatively recently.

Testing equation (2) can take a variety of forms, as outlined by Davis and Weinstein (2001). Four tests have been deployed, usually one factor at a time and using the set of countries c as the sample:

- The *sign test* focuses on whether, the direction of MFCT_f matches that of PFCT_f. In equation (2) this amounts to asking whether the sign of the left- and right-hand sides are equal. The results are displayed in terms of the fraction of correct predictions.
- The *variance ratio test* asks whether the variance of MFCT is as large as PFCT. Of course, if the theory were a perfect fit, the ratio of the variances of the left- and right-hand sides of equation (2) would be unity.
- The *slope test* depends on a regression of MFCT on PFCT. One can calculate the slope coefficient and its significance level from a regression of the left-hand side of equation (2) on the right-hand side. Again, if the theory were a perfect fit, the slope would be unity.
- The *t-test* reports the *t*-statistic for the slope test where the null is a zero slope. This test can detect a positive and significant relationship of endowments to trade, although the relationship need not be one for one.

Data, Coding, and Aggregation

As in the previous tests, we will still need each country's trade and factor endowment data ($\mathbf{T}^c$ and $\mathbf{V}^c$), and for these we draw on the data described in the previous section for $C = 18$ countries, $I = 55$ sectors, and $F = 4$ factors.

We also need a factor use matrix $\mathbf{B}$. In general, when there are intermediate goods, $\mathbf{B}$ depends on the direct factor use matrix $\mathbf{B}^d$ and the input-output matrix $\mathbf{A}$. Calculating $\mathbf{B} = \mathbf{B}^d(\mathbf{I} - \mathbf{A})^{-1}$ is straightforward if data on technology can be found to construct $\mathbf{B}^d$ and $\mathbf{A}$. In the pure version of the theory and empirics, it is assumed that $\mathbf{B}$ is constant across countries. The objective can then be easily met if we can construct $\mathbf{B}$ for just one country and, like Trefler (1993, 1995), we pick the United States as the source of the $\mathbf{B}$ data.

The direct factor use matrix $\mathbf{B}^d$ for the United States is taken from the study of Eysenbach (1976), as employed by Wright (1990). She used the BLS-Leontief 1947 input-output table and a 165-industry classification. Her capital and labor coefficients came from the census of 1899, and her natural resource coefficients, via Vanek (1963), from the 1947 input-output table. Capital input is a stock measure in U.S. dollars that we take as corresponding to our endowment definition, up to a deflator. She measures nonrenewable resource inputs in the same units (dollars) as our endowment measure of mineral resources, up to a deflator.[22] However, her renewable resources measure is not the same (neither in definition nor in units) as our endowment category of agricultural land. This will invalidate some of our tests for this case: consistent units are needed for a meaningful benchmark of unity in the slope coefficient and variance ratio tests. Thus in the construction of $\mathbf{B}$ from $\mathbf{B}^d$ we will have four factors, but not an exact match to the structure of the endowment data.

Our final data collection task was to find a suitable input-output matrix $\mathbf{A}$. We used Leontief's input-output table for 1919 (Leontief 1953b), built around a classification scheme of only 41 industries. Considering the extent of the overlap and consistency between the various classifications, it was decided to settle finally on a 25-industry aggregation scheme for the present exercise. Thus two sets of concordance mappings were constructed, one from the 165-industry classification to the new 25-industry classes, and one from the 41-industry classification to the 25 new classes. Our previously constructed vectors and matrices $\mathbf{T}^c$ and $\mathbf{B}^d$ were converted to this $I = 25$ classification by some simple arithmetic aggregation, and $\mathbf{B} = \mathbf{B}^d(\mathbf{I} - \mathbf{A})^{-1}$ was calculated.

Results

Table 21.3, upper panel, and figure 21.5 show the results of applying the four basic tests (sign, t, variance ratio, and slope) to the raw data for eighteen countries, for four individual factor types plus a set of pooled factor types. In cases where the factors are pooled, we need to worry about the commensurability not only on each side of the equation but also from one type of factor to the next. Units of, say, labor and capital, will never be commensurate in a physical sense, but econometric adjustments are needed to permit valid estimation, specifically to ensure homoskedasticity. Following Trefler (1995), we weight each observation by $\omega_{fc} = 1/(\sigma_f {s_c}^{1/2})$, where the σ_f are the standard deviations of the pure Heckscher-Ohlin-Vanek error $\mathrm{MFCT}_{fc}-\mathrm{PFCT}_{fc}$ for each factor f, and where s_c is an adjustment for country size.[23]

Table 21.3
Tests of measured versus predicted factor content of trade

Factors in the sample		Sign	t	VR	Slope
Productivity correction: None					
K	Capital	0.50	1.4	0.01	0.03
L	Labor	0.44	−1.1	0.00	−0.02
R_r	Resources—renewable	0.67	2.6	—	—
R_n	Resources—nonrenewable	0.78	2.4	0.38	0.35
K, L, R_n	Pooled	0.57	2.7	0.21	0.17
Productivity correction: GDP per capita					
K	Capital	0.72	2.4	0.01	0.06
L	Labor	0.44	0.2	0.18	0.02
R_r	Resources—renewable	0.83	3.0	—	—
R_n	Resources—nonrenewable	0.78	3.6	0.51	0.52
K, L, R_n	Pooled	0.65	4.9	0.39	0.37

Source: Estevadeordal and Taylor (2002).
Notes: For description of tests, see text; sign = sign test; t = t-test; VR = variance ratio test; slope = slope test.

The results are, at best, mixed, and perhaps a little disappointing. They are, in this regard, comparable with the mid-1990s empirical findings of Trefler (1993, 1995) and Gabaix (1997). For capital and labor all the tests offer almost no support for the theory. The sign test reveals a predictive power no better than a coin flip. The t-tests are insignificant and often of the wrong sign. The variance ratio and slope tests confirm that the fit is very poor, the slope is almost a horizontal line, and overall the model can explain maybe 1 percent of the overall variance of the dependent variable.

So far so bad, but our hopes pick up a little bit when resources are considered. For renewable resources, the noncommensurability problem confines us to the sign test and the t-test, but the results are more favorable. The sign test rises to 67 percent, and the slope is significant and positive. For nonrenewable resources, we can run the full battery of tests, and we find the best fit of all. The sign test shows that we get the direction of trade right for this factor in almost 4 out of every 5 cases, the t-ratio is a respectable 2.4, the variance ratio is 38 percent, and the slope is 0.35. Finally, what the regressions are telling us can also be shown graphically, and figure 21.5 depicts the scatter plots for the five cases . The poor fit for labor and capital is immediately apparent given the diffuse cloud of dots seen in each

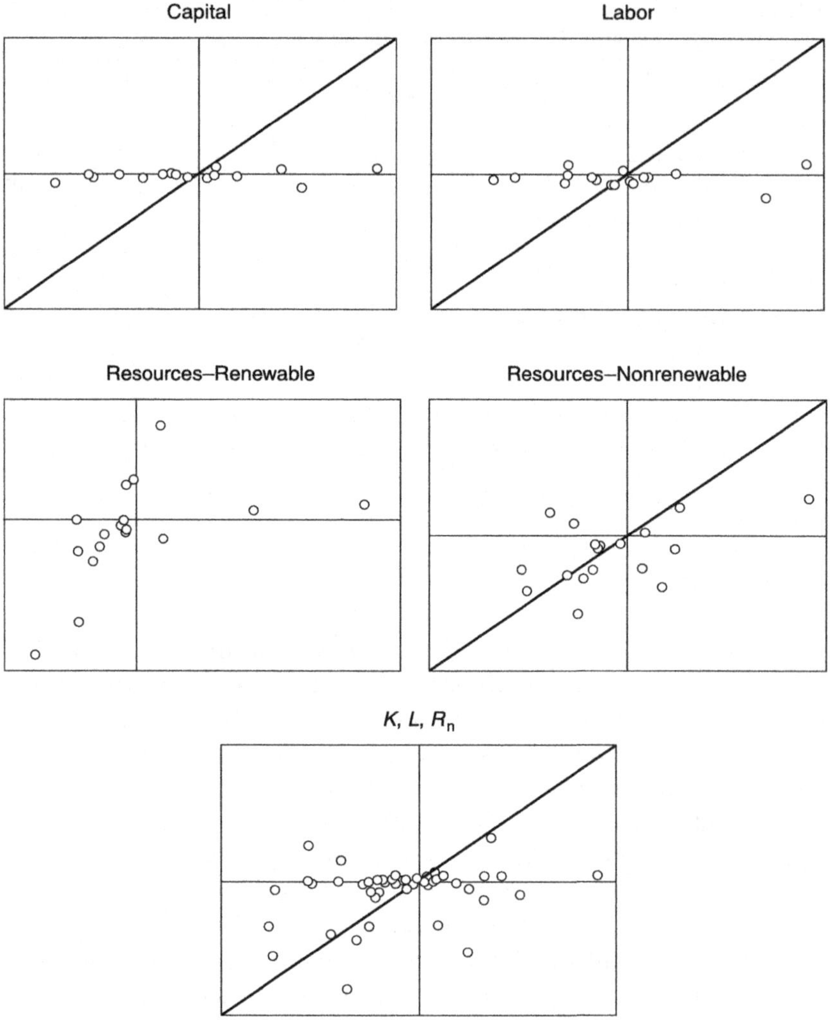

Figure 21.5
Measured versus predicted factor content of trade. Notes: MFCT on vertical axis, PFCT on horizontal. Trefler weights, no productivity correction. See table 21.3. Units on each axis are incommensurate for renewable resources, hence the 45-degree line is omitted. Source: Estevadeordal and Taylor (2002).

case. For resources, the basis for a tighter fit is also clearly visible, and the pooling is a mélange of the two.

Such results, though disappointing, are not too surprising given the equally weak findings of the recent literature using the basic, unadorned specification of the Heckscher-Ohlin-Vanek hypothesis. Accordingly, various enhancements of the basic specification have been proposed. These looser specifications appeal to theory as a basis for adding additional parameters that allow for a better fit: for example, adjustments for factor productivity differences and home bias in consumption. We applied each of these refinements to the historical data (Estevadeordal and Taylor 2002). Our research indicates that the home bias adjustment makes no more sense in the historical context than it does in the recent data, and we find very perverse parameters (like Trefler 1995). The Leontief-style productivity adjustment does find support, though, as we can see from the lower panel of table 21.3, it does not eliminate the missing trade problem for capital and labor.[24]

By our reading, these productivity adjustments do help the model fit better, confirming the findings on contemporary data (Trefler 1993, 1995; Davis and Weinstein 2001). The sign tests starts to rise well above the coin-flip level for capital, and improves somewhat for renewable resources. The slope for nonrenewable resources also rises, doubling to the level of about 0.6, and the variance ratio rises to a favorable 0.51. However, the joy is short-lived, since the slope and variance ratio tests are still demoralizingly low for both capital and labor. The pooling of the results does not add a great deal to the analysis. With pooling the tests come out somewhere in between the good results for nonrenewable resources and the poor results for labor and capital, as expected.[25] All in all, productivity adjustment appears to be a useful and necessary step, but it is not a solution to the missing trade problem.

Summary

In this section we have shown how it is possible to implement a test circa 1913 of the Heckscher-Ohlin-Vanek prediction that there exists a linear relationship between factor endowments and the net factor content of trade. The results are not very favorable to the hypothesis. For labor and capital, the fit of the model is close to nonexistent. For resources, there is evidence that the model fits—though we are hampered by a units problem that prevents us from fully testing the predictions for renewable resources. For all factors, the fit of the model is improved by a Leontief-style productivity correction. In short, having appealed to the 1990s vintage of empirical trade tests of the form pioneered by Trefler (1993, 1995), we have found a good deal of correspondence between the empirical results of the past and present. Missing trade is everywhere, though it is less absent in the case of resources than in the cases of labor and capital (Gabaix 1997). It is also less absent than in the present. Thus the simple factor-content approach seems to work not much better in its own time than it does today—that is, not very well at all. Our study brings us to a point that corresponds to the year 1995 in the contemporary empirical literature—the year Trefler announced the mystery of the "missing trade." In the conclusion we ponder where we can go from here.

Conclusion: Give Heckscher and Ohlin a Break!

This work has looked very broadly at the applicability of modern tests of the Heckscher-Ohlin trade theory to the historical data for 1913, an earlier period of relatively well-integrated goods markets, and a time in history that inspired the creators of the factor-abundance model. The results of this exercise have been mixed. The relationship between factor endowments and goods trade appears strong, even stronger than that found in contemporary data. But the factor content tests perform as poorly as they do on recent data, although a Leontief-style productivity correction can go some way toward correcting the problem. Even then, the best fit in 1913 seems to be for resource endowments, rather than for capital and labor.

Though we are disappointed to find such weak evidence, is this cause to dismiss the Heckscher-Ohlin model? We think not. First, on empirical grounds, we are not fully satisfied with the methodology adopted here, and compared to the most recent advances in the field that have attained a close match between theory and data, we have many gaps in our data. The Davis and Weinstein (2001) analysis goes further than any previous work in achieving a satisfactory fit, but their OECD data allow them to investigate different factor-use matrices **B** for each country. In contrast, we have been limited to only one factor-use matrix **B** for the United States in 1913. It would be a very difficult, almost impossible, data collection exercise to build full set of input-output tables and production-consumption accounts for even just these 18 countries at a 25-sector level circa 1913. Still, such an effort would be necessary to advance beyond the circa 1995 econometric approaches that we have employed here.

Notwithstanding these methodological constraints, what can we say about the interpretation of our results when they are taken at face value? Gabaix (1997) protested that the good fit of the Heckscher-Ohlin-Vanek model on natural resources today was cold comfort, since such endowments constitute such a paltry share of world output in the modern, service-oriented, knowledge-based economy. In today's world the bulk of factor rewards accrue to capital and labor (mostly skilled, i.e., human capital). Such objections are clearly less relevant in 1913, when much of the basis of world trade, and still significant portions of world output, were based on primary-producing activities.

The role of resources, and the good fit of the model there, also brings us back to the point made in the introduction: the Heckscher-Ohlin theory supposes that factors are not mobile and endowments are exogenous. Only then would estimation be valid. Note that these shortcomings are econometric problems, not a failure of the theory itself: indeed, the theory very usefully predicts that trade and factor migration can be substitutes. This brings us back to the nature of the world economy in 1913: it was not just a world of relatively free trade, it was also a world with a high degree of factor mobility. Capital mobility is potentially a problem today for factor content tests, but in 1913 we have an even bigger problem, for both labor and capital were highly mobile then. These are the factors for which the fit of the Heckscher-Ohlin-Vanek model is weakest in our data—a coincidence? We think not. The fit of our model is strongest for the immobile factors that have long been considered the key source of comparative advantage in the late-nineteenth and early-twentieth centuries.[26]

In summing up, we urge caution before interpreting poor static regression results as providing evidence against the theory for this historical period. A large literature in economic history has drawn attention to capital and labor flows in the Greater Atlantic economy of that era (Taylor and Williamson 1994, 1997; Hatton and Williamson 1994, 1998; O'Rourke and Williamson 1999; Williamson 1995; Edelstein 1982; Obstfeld and Taylor 2002). Until an econometric strategy can be found that adapts the factor-content tests to cope with this simultaneity problem we should, perhaps, give Heckscher and Ohlin a break.

Notes

For helpful comments we thank the conference participants, especially our discussant Rikard Forslid, and workshop participants at the Inter-American Development Bank and the University of California at Davis. For superb research assistance we are indebted to Brian Frantz.

1. Leontief (1953a) shocked everyone when he computed a U.S. input-output table for 1947 and discovered that the seemingly capital-abundant and labor-scarce United States was actually engaging in net labor export via trade, with a capital-labor ratio in imports 60 percent higher than exports.

2. We need not review the whole literature here, but direct the reader to the excellent survey by Helpman (1999) on which we have drawn extensively in what follows.

3. The same point has been forcefully repeated by Gabaix (1997).

4. For a study of the era, encompassing trade and factor flows, see O'Rourke and Williamson (1999).

5. Still, in theories of differentiated products and intra-industry trade, the concepts of Heckscher-Ohlin trade theory endure in basic textbook formulations (Dixit and Norman 1980; Helpman and Krugman 1985).

6. On factor price equalization, see O'Rourke, Taylor, and Williamson (1996) and O'Rourke and Williamson (1994). On goods trade and factor endowments see Estevadeordal (1993). We review the latter in the next section.

7. As a measure of relative dispersion we use boxplots representing the interquartile ranges. The line in the middle of the box represents the median or 50th percentile of the data. The box extends from the 25th percentile ($x_{[25]}$) to the 75th percentile ($x_{[75]}$), the so-called interquartile range (IQR). The lines emerging from the box are called the whiskers, and they extend to the upper and lower adjacent values. The upper adjacent value is defined as the largest data point less than or equal to $x_{[75]} + 1.5$ IQR. The lower adjacent value is defined as the smallest data point greater than or equal to $x_{[25]} + 1.5$ IQR. Observed points more extreme than the adjacent values are individually plotted.

8. For example, Davis and Weinstein (2001) find inevitably that OECD countries are clustered together with similar capital–labor ratios, a feature arising from those countries' similar levels of development and industrial structures. Their rest-of-the-world data point lies far away from the OECD group, but this gives a great deal of leverage to one point, so much so that it is thought prudent to exclude it from the tests as a sensitivity check. And in terms of data quality, the rest-of-the-world point uses less consistent data, and the required measures have to be constructed by a more fragile procedure.

9. The first studies of long-run convergence (Abramovitz 1986; Baumol 1986) used the 16-country data of Maddison (1982). Baumol was the first to note the postwar failure of unconditional convergence in wider samples that included less-developed countries. The origin of this failure was first identified by Dowrick and Nguyen (1989); they found conditional convergence controlling for investment and population growth, narrowing the problem to a determination of these factor accumulation processes.

10. This caveat must be kept in mind, even though plenty of evidence attests to the fact that on a wide range of goods shipped before 1914 transport costs in the Atlantic

were collapsing over a span of several decades, both on primary products and manufactures. See O'Rourke and Willamson (1994); see also North (1958) and Harley (1988).

11. In detail, B_{fi} is the direct and indirect use of factor f per unit output of industry i. Direct use refers to factors used as inputs in the given industry; indirect use refers to the factors embodied in the intermediate products used as inputs in the given industry.

12. A potential weakness here is that we do not measure the matrix $\mathbf{B}^{-1}$ but rather estimate it. The specification is loose, and the estimated matrix has totally free parameters that may be unrelated to the true technological coefficients. This weakness is avoided in the factor-content approach we use later.

13. For all the data described in this section, figures were collected for the year closest to 1913. Exchange rates were taken from international compendia of exchange rates, where available, or from national sources.

14. We do not calculate consumption or expenditure shares directly, but rather assume that they are equal to income or output shares. That is, we set $s^c = \mathrm{GDP}^c/\mathrm{GDP}^w$, and not, following the trade-balance correction of Trefler (1995), as $s^c = C^c/C^w$. This correction makes no material difference to our results.

15. The twelve ores are bauxite, copper, iron, lead, manganese, nickel, phosphate, potash, pyrites, sulphur, tin, and zinc. Some data were also drawn from Rothwell (various issues) and national sources of mineral production for various countries.

16. The Heckscher-Ohlin model of trade can express trade in terms of endowment supplies or in terms of excess endowment supplies. In a 2×2 version the equations of the model are

$$T_1 = \beta_{1L}(L - YL^w/Y^w) + \beta_{1K}(K - YK^w/Y^w),$$

$$T_2 = \beta_{2L}(L - YL^w/Y^w) + \beta_{2K}(K - YK^w/Y^w),$$

$$Y = w_L L + w_K K,$$

where T_1 and T_2 are net exports of the two commodities, Y is GNP, L is labor, K is capital, w_L and w_K are factor returns, the w superscripts refer to the world, and the β are Rybczynski coefficients. This form of the model expresses net trade as a linear function of excess supplies of factors. However, excess factor endowments are a linear function of all factor supplies: that is, $L - YL^w/Y^w = L - (w_L L + w_K K)L^w/Y^w$. Thus, for almost all distributions of K and L, these excess supplies are correlated, and a regression of trade on a subset of the excess supplies will yield biased and inconsistent estimates. This problem will be compounded if there are measurement errors. Because of this problem a reduced form of the model is preferred in empirical studies. This reduced form is found inserting the GNP equation into the net exports equations:

$$T_1 = \beta_{1L}L + \beta_{1K}K,$$

$$T_2 = \beta_{2L}L + \beta_{2K}K,$$

$$Y = w_L L + w_K K.$$

17. A β value is equal to the estimated coefficient times the ratio of the standard deviation of the explanatory variable divided by the standard error of the dependent variable (Maddala 1977; Leamer 1978). These β values are directly proportional to the contribution that each variable makes to a prediction of net trade. These values indicate the amount of change in standard deviation units of the net trade variable induced by a change of one standard deviation in the factor endowment. A β value of

0.1 is small, since a change of one standard deviation in the resource would have a hardly perceptible effect on net exports, but a value of one can be regarded as large.

18. Results such that agricultural land have a negative impact on the comparative advantage of all manufacturing groups should not be surprising. Although the model used here appears to require that all factors be used in all industries, this is not the case. The existence of industry-specific factors implies that particular elements of the factor requirements matrix **B** may be zero. For example, in a model with two inputs, labor (L) and land (M), and two goods, agricultural (X_1) and industrial (X_2), if land is not used to produce the industrial commodity, the B_{M2} element of matrix **B** will be zero. It can be easily shown that even though both labor and land are used to produce the agricultural good, the output of agricultural goods depends only on the endowment of land. And although land is not used to produce industrial goods, the level of output of industrial goods depends on both the endowment of labor and the endowment of land. This apparently paradoxical result stems from the fact that full employment requires that land must be fully utilized in the agricultural sector. This fact, together with the fixed input requirement B_{M1}, determines the level of agricultural output M/B_{M1}. Since the labor residual left over for industrial production is then dependent on the endowment of land (i.e., $L - X_1 B_{L1} = L - MB_{L1}/B_{M1}$), it becomes obvious that the level of industrial output is also dependent upon the endowment of land.

19. To test for the robustness of these estimates a sensitivity analysis was performed. Influential observations were identified using the extreme t-statistics of dummy variables that select a single country and that are included in the equation one at a time. In general, however, the coefficients in table 21.1 with high t-statistics are insensitive to the omission of those observations.

20. In this highly disaggregated studies, 0.5 is usually used as a threshold for a β value to be considered significant (see Leamer 1984; Saxonhouse 1986).

21. The next section draws on Estevadeordal and Taylor (2002).

22. Here we are careful to modify our endowment measures $\mathbf{V}^c$ to include coal, so as to match Eysenbach's data, a slight change from the original Estevadeordal data as used in the previous section, where coal was a proxy for capital.

23. We also tried the Gabaix (1997) weights $\omega_{fc} = 1/s_c$ and the Davis-Weinstein (2001) weights $\omega_{fc} = 1/V^W{}_f$ and found little difference. See Estevadeordal and Taylor (2002).

24. Trefler (1993, 1995) showed that a way to correct for this problem is to rescale the endowment vector V_{fc} by some measure of relative productivity. If such a productivity correction δ_c is common to all factors in one country, then we would arrive at a productivity-corrected endowment vector of the form $\tilde{V}_{fc} = \delta_c V_{fc}$, and the analysis can then proceed as before. We use two proxies for δ_c, the relative GDP per capita (like Trefler) and the relative real wage. In each case we set U.S. equal to 1, since we are using the U.S. factor-use coefficients on the left side. GDP per capita measures were taken from Maddison (1995) and real wages from Williamson (1995). See Estevadeordal and Taylor (2002).

25. We have also repeated the exercise by estimating, rather than imposing, the implied technology shift parameters. In this method, the parameters δ_c are chosen to maximize the fit of modified Heckscher-Ohlin-Vanek equation, subject to the normalization that $\delta_{US} = 1$. See Estevadeordal and Taylor (2002).

26. In a paper entitled "Give Heckscher and Ohlin a Chance!" Wood (1994a) raised this concern in connection with contemporary tests of the theory that ignore the fact of considerable international capital mobility that can equate rates of return across countries. Instead, he argues, we must restrict attention only to the factors that are basically immobile, resting his case on the theoretical work of Ethier and Svennson (1986). Land being problematic to measure, Wood's research agenda has focused on skilled and unskilled labor as the key contrast in his "North–South" view of the global economy (1994b). The same thrust of argument can be found in the study of the United States by Wright (1990), but the recent analysis of Estevadeordal (1999) generalizes the point to a much broader sample of countries using Wood's approach applied to same 18-country dataset we have used here.

References

Abramovitz, M. 1986. Catching up, forging ahead, and falling behind. *Journal of Economic History* 46 (June):385–406.

Baumol, W. 1986. Productivity growth, convergence and welfare: What the long-run data show. *American Economic Review* 76 (December):1072–85.

Bowen, H. P., E. E. Leamer, and L. Sveikauskas. 1987. Multicountry, multifactor tests of the factor abundance theory. *American Economic Review* 77 (December):791–809.

Clark, G. 1987. Why isn't the whole world developed? Lessons from the cotton mills. *Journal of Economic History* 47 (March):141–73.

Davis, D. R., and D. Weinstein. 2001. An account of global factor trade. *American Economic Review* 91 (December):1423–53.

Dowrick, S., and D.-T. Nguyen. 1989. OECD comparative economic growth 1950–85: Catch-up and convergence. *American Economic Review* 79 (December):1010–30.

Dixit, A. K., and V. Norman. 1980. *Theory of International Trade.* Cambridge: Cambridge University Press.

Easterlin, R. 1961. Influences in European Overseas Emigration before World War One. *Economic Development and Cultural Change* 9:331–51.

Edelstein, M. 1982. *Overseas Investment in the Age of High Imperialism.* New York: Columbia University Press.

Estevadeordal, A. 1993. Historical essays on comparative advantage, 1913–1938. Ph.D. dissertation. Harvard University.

Estevadeordal, A. 1997. Measuring protection in the early twentieth century. *European Review of Economic History* 1 (April): 89–125.

Estevadeordal, A. 1999. A note on comparative advantage and natural resources in the early twentieth century. In A. Carreras et al., eds., *Doctor Jordi Nadal: La industrialización y el desarrollo económico de España.* Barcelona: University of Barcelona Press.

Estevadeordal, A., and A. M. Taylor. 2002. A century of missing trade? *American Economic Review* 92 (March), forthcoming.

Ethier, W. J., and L. E. O. Svennson. 1986. The theorems of international trade when factors are mobile. *Journal of International Economics* 20:21–42.

Eysenbach, M. L. 1976. *American Manufactured Exports, 1879–1914: A Study of Growth and Comparative Advantage*. New York: Arno Press.

Gabaix, X. 1997. The factor-content of trade: A rejection of the Heckscher-Ohlin-Vanek-Leontief hypothesis. Harvard University (May). Photocopy.

Harley, C. K. 1988. Ocean freight rates and productivity, 1740–1913: The primacy of mechanical invention reaffirmed. *Journal of Economic History* 48 (December):851–76.

Hatton, T. J., and J. G. Williamson, eds. 1994. *Migration and the International Labor Market, 1850–1939*. London: Routledge.

Hatton, T. J., and J. G. Williamson. 1998. *The Age of Mass Migration*. New York: Oxford University Press.

Helpman, E. 1999. The structure of foreign trade. *Journal of Economic Perspectives* 13 (Spring):121–44.

Helpman, E., and P. R. Krugman. 1985. *Market Structure and Foreign Trade*. Cambridge: MIT Press.

Hufbauer, Gary. 1991. World economic integration: The long view. *International Economic Insights* 2(3):23–27.

League of Nations. 1927. *Population and Natural Resources*. Geneva: League of Nations.

Leamer, E. E. 1978. *Specification Searches: Ad hoc inference with Nonexperimental Data*. New York: Wiley.

Leamer, E. E. 1980. The Leontief paradox reconsidered. *Journal of Political Economy* 88 (June): 495–503.

Leamer, E. E. 1984. *Sources of International Comparative Advantage*. Cambridge: MIT Press.

Leontief, W. W. 1953a. Domestic production and foreign trade: The American capital position re-examined. *Proceedings of the American Philosophical Society* 97 (September): 332–49.

Leontief, W. W. 1953b. *The Structure of the American Economy 1919–1939*. Oxford: Oxford University Press.

Maddala, G. S. *Econometrics*. New York: McGraw-Hill, 1977.

Maddison, A. 1982. *Phases of Capitalist Development*. Oxford: Oxford University Press.

Maddison, A. 1995. *Monitoring the World Economy*. Paris: OECD.

Mitchell, B. R. 1980. *European Historical Statistics, 1750–1975*, 2nd ed. New York: Facts on File.

Mitchell, B. R. 1983. *International Historical Statistics: The Americas and Australasia*. Detroit: Gale Research.

North, D. C. 1958. Ocean freight rates and economic development, 1750–1913. *Journal of Economic History* 18 (December):537–55.

O'Rourke, K. H., and J. G. Williamson. 1994. Late-nineteenth century Anglo-American factor-price convergence: Were Heckscher and Ohlin right? *Journal of Economic History* 54 (December):892–916.

O'Rourke, K. H., and J. G. Williamson. 1999. *Globalization and History: The Evolution of a Nineteenth-Century Atlantic Economy*. Cambridge: MIT Press.

O'Rourke, K. H., A. M. Taylor, and J. G. Williamson. 1996. Factor price convergence in the late nineteenth century. *International Economic Review* 37 (August): 499–530.

Obstfeld, M., and A. M. Taylor. 1998. The Great Depression as a watershed: International capital mobility in the long run. In M. D. Bordo, C. D. Goldin and E. N. White, ed., *The Defining Moment: The Great Depression and the American Economy in the Twentieth Century*. Chicago: University of Chicago Press.

Obstfeld, M., and A. M. Taylor. 2002a. Globalization and capital markets. In M. D. Bordo, A. M. Taylor, and J. G. Williamson, eds., *Globalization in Historical Perspective*. Chicago: University of Chicago Press.

Obstfeld, M., and A. M. Taylor. 2002b. *Global Capital Markets: Integration, Crisis, and Growth*. Japan–U.S. Center Sanwa Monographs on International Financial Markets. Cambridge: Cambridge University Press, forthcoming.

Potter, N., and F. T. Christy Jr. 1962. *Trends in Natural Resource Commodities*. Baltimore, Md.: Johns Hopkins University Press.

Rothwell, R. P. Various issues. *The Mineral Industry, Its Statistics, Technology, and Trade*. New York: Scientific Publishing Company.

Saxonhouse, G. R. 1986. What's Wrong with Japanese Trade Structure? *Pacific Economic Papers* 137:1–36.

Taylor, A. M. 1996. International capital mobility in history: The saving-investment relationship. Working paper series 5743. National Bureau of Economic Research (September).

Taylor, A. M., and J. G. Williamson. 1994. Capital flows to the New World as an intergenerational transfer. *Journal of Political Economy* 102 (April): 348–71.

Taylor, A. M., and J. G. Williamson. 1997. Convergence in the age of mass migration. *European Review of Economic History* 1 (April): 27–63.

Trefler, D. 1993. International factor price differences: Leontief was right! *Journal of Political Economy* 101 (December): 961–87.

Trefler, D. 1995. The case of the missing trade and other mysteries. *American Economic Review* 85 (December): 1029–46.

Vanek, J. 1963. *The Natural Resource Content of United States Foreign Trade 1870–1955*. Cambridge: MIT Press.

Vanek, J. 1968. Factor proportions theory: The *N*-factor case. *Kyklos* 21 (October): 749–55.

Williamson, J. G. 1995. The evolution of global labor markets since 1830: Background evidence and hypotheses. *Explorations in Economic History* 32 (April): 141–96.

Wood, A. 1994a. Give Heckscher and Ohlin a chance! *Weltwirtschaftliches Archiv* 130:20–49.

Wood, A. 1994b. *North–South Trade, Employment, and Inequality: Changing Fortunes in a Skill-Driven World*. Oxford: Clarendon Press.

Wright, G. 1990. The origins of American industrial success, 1879–1940. *American Economic Review* 80 (September): 651–68.

22

Toward a Factor Proportions Approach to Economic History: Population, Precious Metals, and Prices from the Black Death to the Price Revolution

Ronald Findlay and Mats Lundahl

In the history of economic doctrine the name of Bertil Ohlin is inseparable from that of Eli Heckscher. The origin of the famous Heckscher-Ohlin theorem is the pathbreaking article by Heckscher (1919) in the special 1919 David Davidson *Festschrift* issue of *Ekonomisk Tidskrift*, later developed by Ohlin in his doctoral dissertation (1924) and his monumental *Interregional and International Trade* (1933). Together, these three works established the factor proportions approach to international trade.

Heckscher, History, and Theory

When it came to economic history, Ohlin and Heckscher differed completely. There are historical examples in both *Handelns teori* and *Interregional and International Trade*, but Ohlin was mainly concerned with theory and contemporary economic problems in his work. Heckscher was different. Despite his original contributions to trade theory and his numerous pieces on the empirical economic problems of his day he was first and foremost an economic historian—"the sole creator of economic history in Sweden as an institutionalized field" (Henriksson 1991:142)—with such works as *Mercantilism* (1931a) and a four-volume (uncompleted) economic history of Sweden from the early sixteenth century to 1815 (1935–49) to his credit. It was the writing of the latter that he conceived of as his "real task" (Henriksson 1991:148).

Even so, it would be unfair not to conclude that Heckscher had one foot in history and another in economic theory. What is more, he was a pioneer when it came to linking the two. Heckscher dealt with the principles of connection between economic theory and economic history on at least nine occasions: 1904, 1920, 1922, 1929, 1930 (1933, 1936), 1937 (1944), 1942, 1947, and 1951. The main credo was laid down already in the first of these (1904), when the inductive method was rejected and the use of deductive economic theory was (implicitly) held out as the method to be applied in the gathering and interpretation of historical facts. This part of Heckscher's research program was to stay with him for the rest of his life. Both the early 1904 article and his subsequent publications on method foreshadow the development of the modern analytical approach by the New Economic History movement that began in the late 1950s. This is true not least of his 1920 article and 1922 book chapter (which overlap to some extent). The latter headed a volume intended to demonstrate the connection between the study of economics and of history, the importance of knowledge of general economic relations and of insight into the historical development for understanding economic relations (Heckscher 1922:9).

For Heckscher, the fundamental characteristic of economics is that it deals with problems of scarcity, and since scarcity is a feature that has accompanied mankind since the beginning of history, "the economic problem must be *fundamentally* the same in all ages" (Heckscher 1929:527). It then follows that economic theory should have some contribution to make not only when we deal with recent times but also to the study of more remote historical periods (Heckscher 1922:29, 1929:526). Already in 1904, quoting the dedication to Gustav Schmoller of a book of essays by William J. Ashley (1900:v), he wrote that for the economic historian it was "an imperative duty" to "be an economist without ceasing to be an historian" (Heckscher 1904:198). To be sure, Heckscher never argued that all of history could be explained by economic factors (Heckscher 1944), and he was also quite adamant in his opinion that the use of economic theory had its limitations. Theory was useful in the analysis of events during a given period or epoch with more or less given characteristics, but when it came to questions such as how one epoch evolved into another he argued that economic theory had little to offer (Heckscher 1920:20). The causes had to be sought elsewhere, "since the changes in the conditions of economic life have sprung mainly from other areas of society and hence must be considered as inaccessible for economic theory" (Heckscher 1951:54; cf. Henriksson 1991:165).

Heckscher was also cautious to point out that in the historical perspective the institutional framework matters (Heckscher 1922:24–25):

[I]t is very dangerous to regard economic history only from the point of view of material for comparison with the theories that aim to explain present-day economic relations, since to a large extent, the kind of theory required to explain the circumstances of earlier times must be one that *differs* from the one valid for today. The economic theory that has been developed above all during the last century and a half takes as its point of departure a host of assumptions both with respect to the organization of society—rule of law, regular transportation possibilities, market organization, etc.—and with respect to the state of mind—the ability to calculate, procure information, take care of one's interests, etc., which in no way have always been present in previous times or, for that matter, today.

Still he argued that "for most periods of known Economic History the changes necessary in the usual theory are not fundamental, however" (Heckscher 1929:528). Furthermore Heckscher (1922:29) claims:

[N]othing could bear more witness of less insight into the ways of science than believing that a theory would be completely useless because something, no matter what, in the surrounding reality has changed.... Sometimes, it seems the reasoning criticized here more or less explicitly takes as its point of departure the notion that it is impossible to apply modern economic theory to times when it did not exist. The absurd character of such an idea, however, immediately stands out.

What was fundamental for Heckscher was that when it came to the "*choice* of facts and the *explanation* of them" (Heckscher 1929:529, cf. 1951:45–54), the use of economic theory was indispensable, since "only when the pure theory of economic relations has been made clear has a heuristic principle has been found, and insight obtained about the questions to be posed in the area of economic history" (Heckscher 1936:10). At the end of the day, the "plea for theory" had to be made, "since central parts of the course of economic history cannot be studied successfully without access to or, rather, familiarity with the body of ideas of the economic science" (Heckscher 1951:45).

Strangely, however, in his empirical historical work Heckscher does not appear to have made much use of the basic theoretical construct he himself originated: the factor proportions approach. His 1919 paper receives a passing mention in a footnote in *Mercantilism* (Heckscher 1931a, vol. 2:110), and in the discussion of labor as a factor of production in the mercantilist system, he notes that the policy of keeping labor costs down would lead to increased exports of labor-intensive goods (Heckscher 1931a:135). No use of the approach is made either in his work on the history of industrialism (Heckscher 1931b), or in his two major surveys of Swedish economic history (Heckscher 1942:1935–49).

What was it then that inspired Heckscher to produce his 1919 theoretical breakthrough? If we are to believe the introduction of Flam and Flanders (1991) to their translations of Heckscher's 1919 article and Ohlin's 1924 dissertation, it was his desire to defend free trade from the charge by Knut Wicksell, that it might induce extensive emigration, as happened in Sweden at the end of the nineteenth century under the stimulus of cheap grain imports from across the Atlantic. If it was possible, even if not empirically likely, that trade alone could equalize factor prices, then it would not be necessary for any adjustment through factor movements to occur at all.

In this chapter we will attempt to demonstrate the power of the factor proportions approach not just as a pure theoretical construct but as a tool of economic history. To some extent the point has already been made by the literature that emanated from the "sector-specific" version of the factor proportions model of Ronald Jones (1971). The connection of this theoretical contribution with the explicitly historical concerns of Habbakuk (1967), Temin (1966, 1971), and Fogel (1967) is examined in Findlay (1998).

A major historical episode, to which the factor proportions approach must be applicable if indeed it is applicable at all, is the Black Death, the catastrophic plague epidemic that reduced the population of Europe in the middle of the fourteenth century by a third, possibly even more. We will propose in what follows a suitably extended factor proportions model that can account for the most important facts of this momentous event.

An Extended Factor Proportions Model

The model that we are going to sketch is an extended version of the Jones model with sector-specific inputs. One sector produces "goods," considered as a generalized commodity à la Solow, with a specific factor "capital" that is a stock of the same "stuff" as the output that it produces together with labor. The only other sector of the economy produces a commodity, "silver," with inputs of a specific stock of natural resources (which we can think of as an essentially limitless deposit of silver), obtainable with the input of labor but with diminishing returns at the margin. Thus far the model has exactly the same structure as the original Jones (1971) article.

The relevant equations are

$$G = G(L_g, K), \tag{1}$$

$$S = S(L_s, \bar{N}), \tag{2}$$

$$L_g + L_s = L, \tag{3}$$

where G and S are the flow outputs of goods and silver, L_g and L_s the labor allocated to each sector, K the specific input to G, and N the specific input to S. The labor allocations to each sector add up to the total labor force L available. Both production functions have constant returns to scale and positive but diminishing marginal products for all the inputs. Of the three inputs only natural resources, the specific input N to the silver sector, are fixed as in the original Jones model.

The supply of labor is determined endogenously by a Malthusian mechanism of the type proposed by the economic demographer Ronald Lee (1973). Denoting the real wage in terms of goods as w, we have fertility f and mortality m as increasing and decreasing functions respectively of the real wage, as stated in equations (4) and (5) and figure 22.1:

$$f = f(w), \quad f'(w) > 0, \tag{4}$$

$$m = m(w), \quad m'(w) < 0. \tag{5}$$

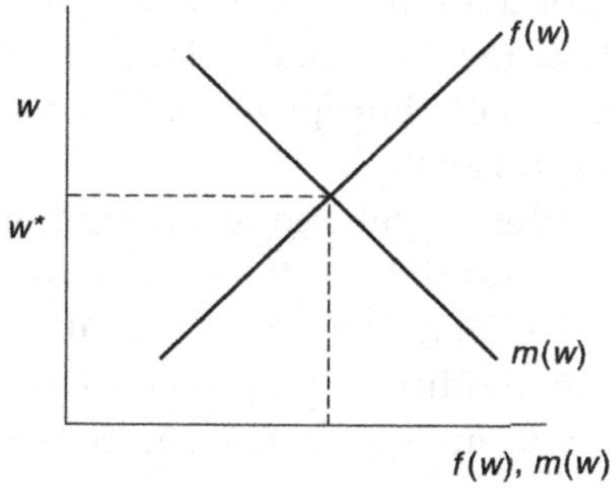

Figure 22.1
The Malthusian mechanism

Population is stationary at a real wage w^* in terms of goods where

$$f(w^*) = m(w^*). \tag{6}$$

The *size* of the population and labor force at this equilibrium real wage w^* will depend upon the endowment of capital and natural resources that the economy has. Assuming, for the moment, that the capital stock K and the relative price of goods and silver is given, the equilibrium level of employment in goods and silver, and thus the size of the total labor force, will be given by

$$\frac{\partial S}{\partial L_s}\left(\frac{\bar{N}}{L_s}\right) = pw^* = p\left(\frac{\partial G}{\partial L_g}\right)\left(\frac{K}{L_g}\right), \tag{7}$$

where $p = P_g/P_s$ is the price of a unit of goods in terms of silver. The equilibrium allocations L_s and L_g are determined from the values specified for p and K by equating the marginal value products of labor in the two sectors.

Suppose now that the Black Death occurs, carrying off a third of the labor force. With fixed stocks of natural resources and capital, and holding the relative prices constant, the effect will be a substantial rise in the real wage, a fall in the outputs of both sectors, and reduced total incomes of the specific factors. This follows directly from Jones (1971).

With higher real wages and per capita incomes, the Malthusian mechanism will lead to a fall in natural mortality after the "one-shot" decline in population due to the plague and a rise in fertility. Population and the labor force will therefore slowly recover, driving down real wages and per capita income until the economy gradually returns to its initial position with the equilibrium values of all variables unchanged. This initial drop in population, and the sharp rise in real wages, followed by a population recovery and a long slow fall in real wages is broadly consistent with European experience over the century and a half after the Black Death.

We now turn to the full extension of the model endogenizing the relative price of goods in terms of silver and the capital stock. If we take silver as the unit of account, so that one "ducat" has a silver content of one ounce in a system of commodity money such as we are going to specify, the national income in the model can be expressed as

$$Y = pG + S. \tag{8}$$

Since p is defined as P_g/P_s, where P_g and P_s are the "nominal" prices of goods and silver in terms of "ducats," it can be thought of not only as the relative price of goods in terms of silver but also as the price level of goods in terms of silver. With silver and goods transformable into one another at increasing marginal cost, a price level of, say, five "ducats" per unit of goods will also be equal to a relative price and a marginal rate of transformation of five ounces of silver for one unit of goods.

The flow supplies of goods and silver are functions of p so that we have

$$G = G(p), \quad G'(p) > 0, \tag{9}$$

$$S = S(p), \quad S'(p) < 0. \tag{10}$$

As the reader can readily verify, we also have

$$Y'(p) > 0, \quad Y'\left(\frac{1}{p}\right) < 0. \tag{11}$$

The national income in terms of silver is an increasing function of the relative price of goods in terms of silver, and a decreasing function of its reciprocal, the relative price of silver in terms of goods.

For any given values of the capital stock K, the natural resource N, and the total labor force L the production possibility frontier showing the trade-off between the flow supplies of goods and silver, will be determined as depicted in figure 22.2. Changing the slope of the tangent to the production possibility frontier, that is, the relative

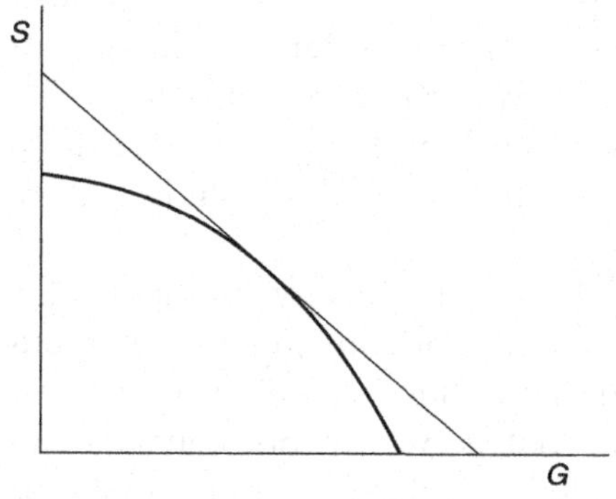

Figure 22.2
The production possibility frontier

price of the two goods, depicts the effects on national income Y of these changes in terms of the vertical intercept, the axis for silver in figure 22.2.

It also follows from the familiar properties of the specific-factor model that the real wage w and the real return to capital r in the goods sector are determined as

$$w = w(p), \quad w'(p) < 0, \tag{12}$$

$$r = r(p), \quad r'(p) > 0. \tag{13}$$

Raising the relative price of goods in terms of silver increases employment in the goods sector with K unchanged and so reduces the marginal physical product of labor in this sector and hence also the "real wage" w in terms of goods, while raising the marginal physical product of capital and hence the real return on capital r in terms of goods. In the silver sector the marginal product of labor increases and the marginal product of the natural resource decreases. The wage in terms of goods and the wage in terms of silver thus move in opposite directions in response to a relative price change, the familiar "neoclassical ambiguity" in the specific-factor model, as opposed to the Stolper-Samuelson or Heckscher-Ohlin-Samuelson model where the real wage changes in the same direction in both sectors when there is a shift in relative product prices.

We now turn to the monetary side of the model. Paper or "fiat" money has become universal only since the twentieth century. In the medieval and early modern periods of western history, and for the Middle East and Asia up to quite recently, movements of the precious metals and their impact on price levels have been of utmost significance. While commodity money is mostly ignored in current modern works on monetary theory it was the focus of detailed attention by the early writers of the subject, from Hume and Ricardo to Wicksell, Marshall, and Irving Fisher. It is an indispensable feature of the story we wish to tell here.[1]

The money supply in our model consists, at any moment, of a stock of coins with a given silver content. For convenience we maintain the convention that each coin has a "face value" of one ducat and a silver content of one ounce, that is, we do not consider debasement and other related issues although these could be analyzed as comparative static exercises within the context of the model. The commodity silver can be costlessly minted into coins. The coins in circulation "depreciate" at a given rate due to "wear and tear," so that we assume that a fraction μ of the coins simply disappears per unit of time.

The demand for money in our model for transactions purposes is given by the familiar Fisher quantity theory in its Marshallian or "Cambridge" version

$$M_{\mathrm{d}} = \alpha Y\left(\frac{1}{p}; K, L\right) \tag{14}$$

where α, the Cambridge "k," is the reciprocal of the income-velocity of circulation of money. Thus M_{d} is a "stock" demand, related to the flow of national income, Y, through the desired ratio, α.

Denoting the supply of money at any moment by M, and requiring demand and supply to be balanced at every moment, we obtain the "momentary" equilibrium condition

$$M = \alpha Y\left(\frac{1}{p}; K, L\right) \tag{15}$$

Taking K and L, together with M, as state variables initially given by history, (15) is one equation in one unknown, the reciprocal of the price level of goods in terms of silver $1/p$. Figure 22.3 depicts the momentary equilibrium specified in (15) by showing how the value of $1/p$ that prevails will equate M to M_{d} when M, K, and L are given. The demand for money curve is negatively sloped because Y varies inversely with $1/p$, as specified in (11), and M is vertical because it is determined by past history at any given point in time.

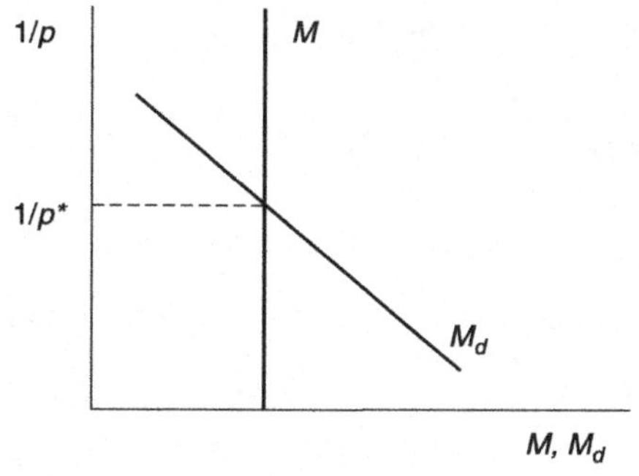

Figure 22.3
Money market equilibrium

With the relative price of goods and silver determined at any instant by equating the stock demand for money to the given stock of money in circulation, the relative price $1/p$ thus emerges as an "asset price" instead of in its more familiar role as equating the flow demands to flow supplies in standard Walrasian general equilibrium fashion of which the specific-factor model is a particular case. What we therefore have is an instance of what André Burgstaller (1994) calls the "asset market approach to the theory of value."

The relative price p determined by (15) determines the flow supplies of goods and silver as specified in (9) and (10). These flow supplies have now to be reconciled with flow demands, which will be specified below.

The consumer budget constraint is given by the national income Y, which is determined at any moment by the historically determined values of M, K, and L, which also determine p through (15). With this income consumers can either purchase domestically produced goods or what we will term "Eastern luxuries," such as spices, silk, and other exotic wares that were not produced within Europe at all. We assume, with historical justification, that all these goods had to be paid for in silver. We also assume that the prices of all these goods are fixed in terms of silver irrespective of the level of Western demand. Thus, by suitable choice of units, we can set the price of a "bundle" of these Eastern luxuries at one unit of silver so that p, the relative price of a unit of goods in terms of silver, is also the relative price of a unit of goods in terms of Eastern luxuries, and its reciprocal is the relative price of Eastern luxuries in terms of goods.

Additional flow demands for silver and goods will be the "depreciation" of the stock of silver coins, equal to μM, and the depreciation of the capital stock, δK, where δ is also a constant.

The budget constraint can be written as

$$Y = pG + S = p(G_c + \delta K) + (E + \mu M), \tag{16}$$

where

$$G_c = G_c(p, Y), \quad \frac{\partial G_c}{\partial p} < 0, \quad \frac{\partial G_c}{\partial Y} > 0 \tag{17}$$

and

$$E = E\left(\frac{1}{p}, Y\right), \quad \frac{\partial E}{\partial(1/p)} < 0, \quad \frac{\partial E}{\partial Y} > 0 \tag{18}$$

are the consumption demands for goods and Eastern luxuries, respectively. The total flow demands for goods and silver are obtained by adding the depreciation of the capital stock δK and of the money supply μM to the respective consumption demands. There is no guarantee that flow demand will equal flow supply, since

$$G_{\mathrm{d}} \equiv G_{\mathrm{c}} + \delta K \gtreqless G, \tag{19}$$

$$S_{\mathrm{d}} \equiv E + \mu M \gtreqless S. \tag{20}$$

Walras's law and equation (16), however, imply that

$$(S_{\mathrm{d}} - S) \equiv p(G - G_{\mathrm{d}}), \tag{21}$$

that is, the excess flow demand for silver equals the value of the excess flow supply of goods. Our model implies that the excess flow demand (supply) reduces (increases) the corresponding stock of either money or goods, so that we have

$$\dot{K} = (G - G_{\mathrm{d}}), \tag{22}$$

$$\dot{M} = (S - S_{\mathrm{d}}). \tag{23}$$

From (21) it follows that $\dot{K}$ and $\dot{M}$ are either both equal to zero, when flow demands equal flow supplies, or of opposite sign. For the economy to be in a long-run steady state equilibrium it is of course necessary for all the state variables, L, K, and M, to be constant, that is,

$$\dot{L} = \dot{K} = \dot{M} = 0. \tag{24}$$

We now turn to the determination of this long-run steady state equilibrium of the model. For population and the labor force to be stationary, we know from (6) that the real wage in the goods sector must be equal to w^*. From (7) this determines uniquely the ratio of capital K to employment L_{g} in the goods sector that makes the marginal physical product of labor in this sector equal to w^*. Also from (7) it follows that for each value of p there is a unique employment level L_{s} in the silver sector that equates the marginal physical product of labor in that sector to pw^*, the wage in terms of silver. The lower is p, the higher is $1/p$, the greater is L_{s} and hence the output of silver $S(1/p)$, which equates the marginal physical product of labor in the silver sector to the lower wage in terms of that commodity. Thus, given the size of the stock of natural resource deposits N,

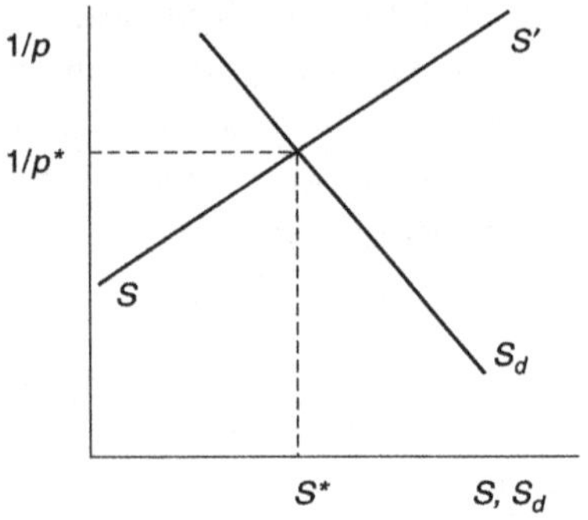

Figure 22.4
Flow equilibrium in the silver market

equation (7) determines the long-run steady state flow supply curve of silver

$$S = S\left(\frac{1}{p}; w^*, \overline{N}\right), \tag{25}$$

which is depicted in figure 22.4 as the positively sloped curve SS'. The long-run flow demand for silver, S_d in figure 22.4, at each price $1/p$ will depend only on K, since L_s is determined by $1/p$. L_g is proportional to K, as determined by w^*, and so the labor force L and national income Y are determined for each value of K. By (14) the stock demand for money M_d is determined by $1/p$ and Y, and so the money supply M and its "depreciation" μM are determined as well. The expenditure on Eastern luxuries E is also determined by $1/p$ and Y from (18). The total flow demand for silver, equal to E plus μM, is thus an increasing function of Y, and hence K, for each value of $1/p$. By (20) we can therefore find the unique value of K, and hence L, Y, and M, that equates the flow demand S_d for silver to the flow supply $S(1/p)$ for each value of $1/p$, as illustrated in figure 22.4. It also follows that steady state L, K, and M are all increasing functions of $1/p$.

We therefore see that there is a continuum of steady state equilibria (L, K, M), each corresponding to a particular value of $1/p$ and varying positively with changes in this relative price.

To determine a unique steady state, we now introduce the final behavioral equation of the model. This is a long-run "portfolio balance" equation that makes the desired ratio of physical capital K to the money supply M an increasing function of the relative rate of

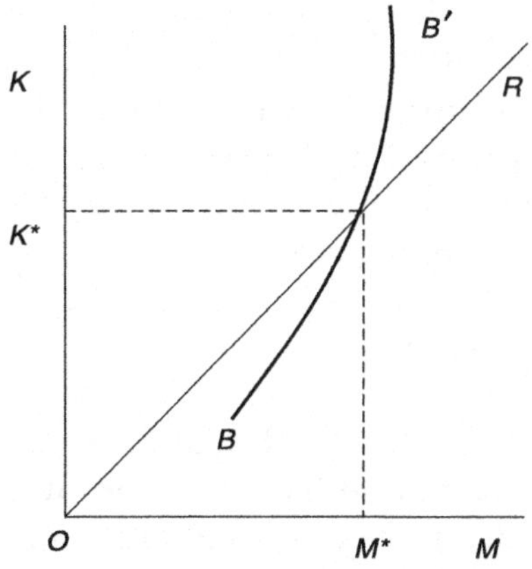

Figure 22.5
The portfolio balance

return to holding capital instead of commodity money as an asset, so that we have

$$\frac{K}{M} = h(\rho), \quad h'(\rho) > 0, \tag{26}$$

where

$$\rho \equiv (r - \delta) + \mu. \tag{27}$$

The higher the net rate of return $(r - \delta)$ on capital itself, the more attractive it clearly is to hold capital. Commodity money "depreciates" at the rate μ, so holding capital instead of commodity money as an asset brings an additional return of μ, as stated in (27).

In every steady state the real wage must be equal to w^*, and hence the marginal product of capital must be equal to $r(w^*)$ by the "factor-price frontier" in the goods sector. Whatever the price level p may be in the steady state, its future values are stationary at that level, so there is no Fisherian "capital gain" component to add to the relative rate of return ρ as defined in (27). Thus ρ is uniquely determined by w^*, and consequently the *ratio* of K to M in all steady states is a ray through the origin OR as in figure 22.5.

The other curve BB' in figure 22.5 shows the *values* of K and M corresponding to each other in a segment of the continuum of steady states (L, K, M), one value for each value of $1/p$, as determined above.

We assume that "diminishing returns" in the natural resource-based silver sector are so strong that the curve BB' cuts OR from below. In other words, the capital accumulation proceeds faster than the increase of the money stock as $1/p$ increases. The intersection of BB' and OR determines K^* and M^*, and consequently L^* and $1/p^*$, as the unique long-run steady state equilibrium of the model.

Economic Consequences of the Black Death

To model the impact and consequences of the Black Death, we assume that the European economy of the midfourteenth century was initially in the long-run demographic, monetary, and economic equilibrium corresponding to the steady state depicted in the last section. The Black Death itself is conceived of as a one-time, instantaneous shock that reduces population and the labor force substantially. (The exact proportion does not matter since our analysis will be qualitative rather than using or providing numerical estimates.) We begin by deducing the consequences from the model in the first section below. The second section briefly examines the historical record to check whether the analytical consequences derived from the model broadly conform to the facts established in the voluminous historical literature on this demographic catastrophe.

Model Analysis

The instantaneous decline of the labor force has some obvious immediate consequences. Wage rates rise in terms of both goods and silver, and the output of both commodities falls. Silver deposits and the capital stock (at first) are unchanged but the decline in the labor force means that the production possibility frontier shifts inward. The outputs of both sectors decline, if relative prices are held constant, because each sector will employ less labor due to the rise in the real wage.

The relative price of goods and silver, as we have seen, is determined in the asset market; that is, it depends on what happens to the stock demand for money since the stock of silver coins is at its initial level. The stock demand for money falls, since national income declines because of the reduction in the labor force. The result is an instantaneous fall in the relative price of silver in terms of goods, that is, a jump in the price level of goods in terms of silver. All of this follows from quantity theory reasoning. In terms of the famous Fisher equation, MV is constant and Q falls, so p must rise.

This shift in relative prices implies that the fall in the output of silver induced by the reduction of the labor force is accentuated by the fact that goods production is now relatively more attractive. The flow supply curve of silver has shifted to the left, so production falls at constant relative prices, and the fall in the relative price induces a movement down the supply curve as well. In the goods sector, on the other hand, the rise in relative prices moves production up the supply curve, mitigating the reduction in output caused by the decline in the labor force.

Real wealth and income per capita of the surviving population are both considerably higher than before the catastrophe. The demand for Eastern luxuries, in particular, will then rise. The combination of the reduction of the population and the shift in relative prices that this creates on impact thus produces an excess demand for silver and an excess supply of goods. The stock of silver coins in circulation therefore starts to shrink, while the capital stock increases. The rise in the real wage makes fertility exceed mortality, so population begins to increase slowly from its level in the immediate aftermath of the Black Death. With labor and capital both increasing the production possibility frontier begins to expand, making it possible for production in both sectors to recover. The increase in national income means that the stock demand for money also starts shifting back toward its original level. Together with the ongoing decline in the money supply (silver in circulation) due to depreciation and purchases of Eastern luxuries, this makes the relative price of silver rise again; that is, the jump in the price level of goods that was the consequence of the negative population shock begins to be reversed. This encourages the recovery in the production of silver relative to that of goods.

The picture we have of the postcatastrophe scenario is that population and production are expanding from the depressed levels in the immediate aftermath of the arrival of the plague, while the price level and real wages decline from their initially inflated levels. Real wages fall as population recovers, although they remain well above their pre-plague level for a long time. The price level of goods in terms of silver continues to fall since production is recovering while the stock of silver is shrinking, because the output of silver is insufficient to cover "depreciation" and the expenditure on Eastern luxuries induced by the rise in per capita wealth and income.

However, the deflation of the price level itself stimulates the output of silver. Together with falling real wealth and per capita incomes due to the rise in population, it also reduces the demand for Eastern luxuries while at the same time the "depreciation" component of the flow demand for silver itself shrinks since its base is reduced. Eventually the excess demand for silver must therefore reverse itself into an excess supply, and the amount of silver in circulation begins to rise again. The mirror image of the excess demand for silver, the excess supply of goods, must also be reversed and the capital stock, which is above its pre-plague level, is reduced.

The relative price of silver l/p must continue to rise as long as the money supply is contracting, since the stock demand for money must be rising because of the increasing labor force and capital stock. If the money supply continues to fall when the price of silver rises to its initial pre-plague level $1/p$ will "overshoot" its initial level; that is, the price of goods in terms of silver must fall below the pre-plague level. Eventually, however, the excess flow demand for silver that is contracting the money supply must be reversed and the money supply will begin to increase again. The relative price of silver $1/p$ will continue to rise if the demand for money rises faster than the supply. The long deflation of the price level must, however, eventually be reversed to an inflation as the labor force and the capital stock converge back towards their initial levels. The initial pre-plague price level is returned to from below rather than from above. The price level of goods in terms of silver will thus display an initial upward spike on the impact of the plague, followed by a long deflationary phase that takes the price level below its initial value (i.e., "overshooting"), followed by a gradual inflation as the supply of money increases faster than demand, converging asymptotically back to the pre-plague level when the full adjustment is completed and the values of all variables have returned to their initial levels.

It is conceivable, however, that the money supply will begin to expand before the rise in the relative price of silver $1/p$ has reached its initial pre-plague level. At this turning point the demand for money always increases faster than the rising supply. Otherwise, $1/p$ would fall and the system would not get back to the initial equilibrium. Then the possibility arises that $1/p$ continues to rise until the

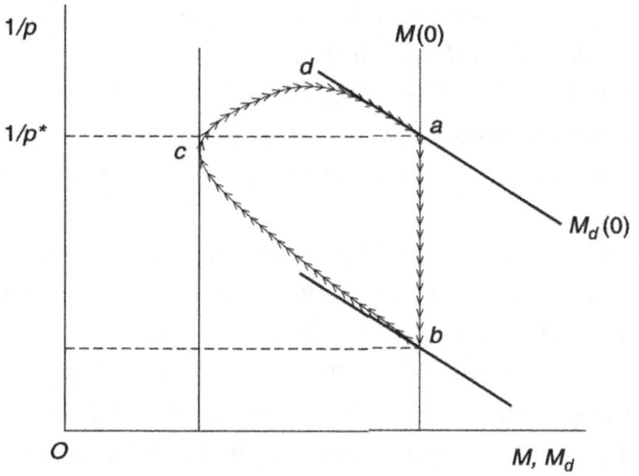

Figure 22.6
The long swing in the price level due to the Black Death

initial level is attained and the labor force and capital stock will converge to their long-run steady state values, without any "overshooting" of the price level. The initial inflationary spike is followed by slow deflation back to the original pre-plague level. It is, however, also possible for $1/p$ to rise above the initial level before the long-run equilibrium is attained; that is, there is "overshooting." In this case, again, the deflation of the price level must eventually be reversed and followed by an inflationary phase as the initial pre-plague price level is approached from below rather than above.

Thus "overshooting" will not occur in one of the three cases considered. However, the two cases in which it does occur both appear to be more consistent with the historical record, as we will argue below.

The process that we have described is depicted graphically in figure 22.6. The initial position is that of point *a*, with money supply $M(0)$, money demand $M_d(0)$, and the price of silver in terms of goods at $1/p^*$. The Black Death instantaneously shifts the money demand function downward on the vertical supply curve $M(0)$ to point *b*, producing a fall in the relative price of silver in terms of goods $1/p$. In quantity theory terms, MV is constant while Q falls, so p must rise; that is, $1/p$ must fall. For the reasons that we have given above, there is now an excess flow demand for silver, which means that the money supply shrinks, shifting the vertical supply curve of the money stock leftward. The recovery of population and the labor force, and the increase of the capital stock due to the excess flow supply of goods, means that the stock demand curve for money starts to shift back upward again. The relative price of silver $1/p$ therefore starts to rise above the level to which it initially fell at point b, since the demand for the money stock of silver is rising while the supply is falling.

Eventually, however, the excess flow demand for silver that is draining the stock must be reversed as the rising price of silver and the falling real wage in terms of goods increase the flow supply while the demand for Eastern luxuries is reduced and the "depreciation" component μM is also falling as M itself declines. At point c in figure 22.6, the money supply stops contracting and begins to increase back toward its initial level. (As noted above, point c could be above point a, without affecting the essentials of the process described here.)

The stock demand for money continues to rise because of the increasing labor force. Despite the beginnings of the increase of the money supply, the increase in the demand for money keeps on raising $1/p$, the relative price of silver. The rise in $1/p$ can "overshoot" the original level of $1/p$, corresponding to point a, if the increase in the stock demand for money at that price is larger than the increase in the amount of silver in circulation. The price of silver $1/p$ then rises to point d in figure 22.6, after which the increase in money demand, which is being dampened as the original size of the labor force and capital stock are being approached, falls short of the increase in money supply, causing $1/p$ to fall thereafter toward the original level at point a. At this point the recovery from the effects of the Black Death is complete. With all parameters, technology and behavioral relations unchanged the system returns to the original position.

The time path of the price level p over the entire sequence is depicted in figure 22.7 for the "overshooting" case. At the onset of the Black Death, at time $T(0)$, the price level jumps instantaneously from p^* to p' and then descends slowly from that level, falling below p^* itself and reaching a floor at p'' at time T. After that it rises back toward the original equilibrium level p^*, with all other variables unchanged as well.

The next section examines the historical record to assess the extent to which the predictions of the model are consistent with historical facts and interpretations.

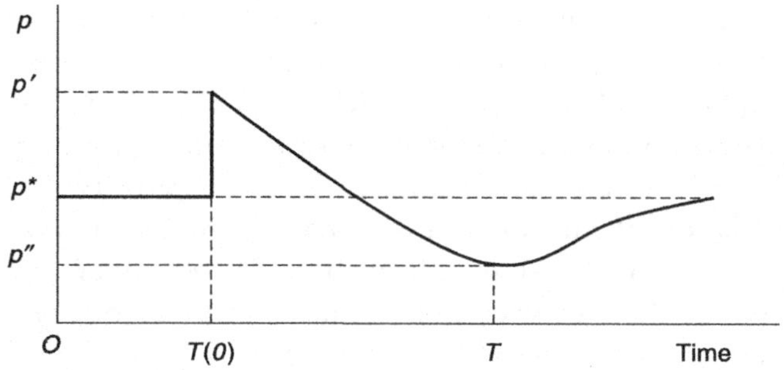

Figure 22.7
The price level pattern following the Black Death

History

The bubonic plague, *Yersinia pestis*, that struck Europe in 1347 was, ironically, a consequence of the increased trade and commercial activity between East and West stimulated by the unification of the Eurasian continent under the Pax Mongolica. According to McNeill (1977) the plague bacillus was transmitted to Central Asia by Mongol troops who were infected by it on a punitive expedition to the Burma-Yunnan border in 1253. It crossed Central Asia to the port of Caffa on the Black Sea, a major Genoese trading station. From there it was apparently carried by Genoese vessels to Messina in Sicily and eventually to the whole of Europe. The death rate during the initial outbreak was devastating. Cipolla (1964:131) gives an estimate of 25 million killed out of a total population of approximately 80 million between 1348 and 1351. The plague recurred in several waves of diminishing average intensity, before disappearing from Europe by the end of the seventeenth century. There has been a prolonged debate on the extent of the mortality but no disagreement on the fact that it was substantial.

The way we have modeled this demographic disaster, as an instantaneous one-shot catastrophe, is thus not strictly accurate but it corresponds quite well to the estimates of Cipolla for the 1348 to 1351 period. Our treatment of the plague as an exogenous shock is also supported by demographic evidence. Livi-Bacci (1997:53) says: "The plague constitutes a population check largely exogenous, or external, to the sociodemographic system." He also notes the tendency of endogenous economic and social forces to reduce mortality and increase fertility, just as in the present model. A reduction in the age of females at marriage is an important adjustment stressed by many demographers and historians, which can plausibly be explained by the better economic circumstances of the surviving population. Under the influence of the induced effects on fertility and mortality the population of Europe seems to have regained its pre-plague level by the end of the sixteenth century. It took over two centuries for the shock that we give to our model to peter out and long-run Malthusian equilibrium to be restored.

There is also considerable scattered evidence on the consequent rise in real wages. England provides the best data, partly because of the famous index of real wages calculated for a period of seven centuries by Phelps-Brown and Hopkins (1956). This index is effectively combined by Hatcher (1977:71, fig. 2) with estimates of population from 1250 to 1750. Population falls from a peak of close to 6 million around 1300 to about 3 million in 1350, continuing to decline to barely 2 million around 1450. It then slowly climbs back to reach the 1300 level of 6 million only as late as 1750. The real wage index (of building craftsmen) rises from a level of 60 in 1300 to 105 in 1450, that is, 75 percent. The 1450 to 1460 decade sees the trough of the population curve coinciding with the peak of the real wage index. Real wages decline after the 1450 peak to a trough with the index at 40 in the first half of the seventeenth century. It then rises slowly back to the 1300 level of 60 only as late as 1750. In other words, real wages were unchanged at the beginning and end of half a millennium! The 1460 peak of 105 was not attained until the second half of the *nineteenth* century. The swing in real wages that our model predicts is thus dramatically borne out by the English data. Goldthwaite (1980:334) presents evidence on the construction industry in Florence, showing that real wages were about 50 percent higher than the 1360 level in the period from 1420 to 1470, after which they fall back to pre-plague levels by 1600.

Economic historians have conducted an intense debate about whether the two centuries after the Black Death, which coincide with the conventional periodization of the Renaissance, could be characterized as a boom or a depression. Lopez (1953) tries to account for the paradox of cultural efflorescence during an economic contraction by arguing that "hard times" with low rates of return on investment induce rational businessmen and bankers such as the Medici to "invest in culture" instead. Cipolla (1964) criticizes this and a related paper by Lopez and Miskimin (1962), pointing to evidence of prosperity. The controversy can be reconciled by distinguishing between total and per capita magnitudes. Total production and trade would fall in response to the decline in numbers but much less than proportionately, so per capita wealth and incomes go up. The point is made with a macabre sense of humor by Bridbury (1962:91) when he remarks that the Black Death corresponded to a "sort of Marshall Plan on a stupendous scale."

From simple two-sector general equilibrium reasoning we can expect that labor-intensive goods would decline in production while land-intensive or capital-intensive goods would expand, if relative product prices are held constant (the Rybczynski 1955 theorem). Furthermore, since per capita income is now higher, the relative prices of labor-intensive goods would rise and the prices of land or capital-intensive goods would fall. There is considerable evidence of this sort of shift in the composition of total production, with livestock-raising and viticulture expanding relative to food crops, for example. Luxury consumption of all kinds would also rise because of the higher per capita incomes. Examples abound. Indeed the primacy of Italy during the Renaissance can partly be explained by her comparative advantage within Europe in luxury products, such as silk-weaving and other high-quality textiles, expensive arms and armor, and especially the Venetian and Genoese grip on the supply of Eastern spices and other goods.

One sector of production to which we have paid particular attention in our theoretical analysis is the mining of precious metals, "silver" as we have called it. A strong prediction was that this sector would be particularly hard hit, since it would suffer not only from the general labor shortage and rise in wages but also because the sharp fall in the demand for money would lower the price of silver relative to goods in general. This prediction is strongly confirmed in the historical record. Nef (1987:721) states that in the aftermath of the Black Death "the production of gold and silver in Europe as a whole actually declined," and he also speaks (1987:722) of a "long slump which lasted for several generations." Recovery only came with the revival of population and total real incomes.

Combining this reduction in the supply of silver with the rise in demand for Eastern luxuries, also amply documented in the historical record, makes for an excess demand for silver that must result in a contraction of the stock of silver coins in circulation. This is exactly what happened, for so long and to such an extent that it led the monetary historian John Day to speak of "The Great Bullion Famine of the Fifteenth Century" (Day 1987:ch.1). The shortage of silver and the precious metals generally in Europe in the century or so after the Black Death is well attested and analyzed in this work and other authoritative treatments, such as Miskimin (1975) and Spufford (1988:ch.14–16).

Our model predicts first a rise in the relative price of goods in terms of silver, when real income drops and the money supply is constant, followed by a fall in this relative price as the demand for money begins to rise back to its initial position and the money supply contracts. The scanty data on industrial and agricultural prices expressed in terms of silver exhibit exactly this pattern. Day (1987:100) presents two industrial price indexes rising from 100 to 125 and 100 to 133–200 from 1330 to 1370, and falling from 125 to 72 in 1410 and 43 in 1470, and from 133–200 in 1370 to 83–100 in 1410, and 104–125 in 1470. Indexes of agricultural prices in Northern France go from 100 for the 1331 to 1340 decade to 107 in 1361 to 1370, then fall to 78 in 1401 to 1410 and 42 in 1461 to 1470. In England the pattern for the same periods is from 100 to 127, then falling to 102 and 69. Some other evidence and discussion is also provided in the recent book on price history by Fischer (1996).

The demand for Eastern luxuries, to which we have assigned major weight in connection with the reduction in silver output as the cause of "the great bullion famine," is extensively documented, although numerical estimates are relatively scarce. We should first note that "Eastern" does not necessarily mean "Southern," the familiar exotic products of the Islamic world, the East Indies, and China. Russia, Finland, and the eastern shores of the Baltic also provided a major luxury import for Western Europe, namely the rich furs of ermine, sable, and marten, so familiar to us from the Renaissance portraits not only of nobility but also of the merchant princes of the age. Miskimin (1975:138) reports that 450,000 furs were shipped from Riga to Bruges in one year, 1405, alone, and Riga was not the sole outlet for the fur supply. This fur trade particularly enriched the merchants of the Hanseatic League. Wax for candles was also a luxury import of a rather morbid kind, since one of the main sources of demand was the lighting of candles at the masses for the dead.

More than matching the drain of silver to the northeast through the Baltic for furs, wax, and amber was the drain to the southeast through Italy, especially Venice and Genoa, and then to Egypt, where the spices and silks of Asia were acquired by European merchants. A particularly fascinating account of the drain of silver eastward in exchange for luxuries is given in an article by Lopez, Miskimin, and Udovich (1970). The article has three sections, one by each author. The first, by Miskimin, tells how silver was drained out of England and France to Italy, in exchange for luxuries of various kinds. The next section, by Lopez on Italy, explains how all this northern silver did not stay in Italy but was transferred to Cairo and Alexandria by Venetian and Genoese merchants in exchange for spices, silks, and other Eastern luxuries. The third section, by Udovich on Egypt, explains how all this Italian silver did not remain in Egypt but was drained eastward to the region of the Caspian Sea for slaves and furs and through the Red Sea to India and the East Indies for spices and silks. All three regions meanwhile were devastated about equally by the plague. The authors report that they were looking for expert co-authors on India and China to explain what finally happened to the silver but could not find anyone suitable in time for the conference at which they had to present the paper.

Our model predicts that this persistent drain of silver was destined to end and be reversed. This again is exactly what happened. From about 1460 the stock of silver in circulation appears to start rising again, the excess (flow) demand for silver now being converted into an excess supply. On the demand side the "depreciation" as a constant fraction of a declining stock was becoming a smaller proportion of a rising flow supply in response to the rising relative prices of silver in terms of goods. Per capita wealth and income were shrinking as population rose, reducing the demand for Eastern luxuries. The rising relative price of silver encouraged the re-opening of old mines, stimulated the search for new ones and also the search for better methods of extracting metal from the ore. Nef (1987:735) speaks of a "boom in mining and metallurgy" from 1460 to 1530, reporting that: "[b]etween 1460 and 1530 the annual output of silver in Central Europe increased several times over, perhaps more than fivefold," reaching a maximum during the 1526 to 1535 decade.

It is vitally important to note that all the events that we are describing have nothing to do as yet with the voyages of discovery in the last decade of the fifteenth century. As we will see in the next section the fact that prices in terms of silver were rising in Europe *before* the great influx of silver from the New World in the middle of the sixteenth century has been taken in some quarters to refute the monetary view of the Price Revolution of the sixteenth century, and even the quantity theory itself.

American Silver and the Price Revolution

Few ideas have been more famous or controversial in economic history than the celebrated thesis of Earl Hamilton (1934) about the impact of the influx of silver from the New World on European prices in the sixteenth century and its implications for the future course of economic development. Despite an enormous outpouring of theoretical, statistical, and historical research, the subject does not appear to have found a resolution, more than sixty-five years later. While a full discussion of even the most basic of the issues involved will require more space than is available for the present chapter, it may be useful to put the model presented here through the paces of another exercise. As we will see, the results could be illuminating, particularly if taken in conjunction with those of our analysis of the consequences of the Black Death. For other interesting approaches to this problem of American silver and the Price Revolution, the reader is referred to Niehans (1993) and Flynn (1996).

As in the previous exercise we assume that the system begins in full long-run equilibrium with population, money supply, and capital stock all stationary. The "discovery of America," for purposes of the model, will simply be an exogenous increase in the stock of silver deposits available. The initial effect is therefore to shift out the production possibility frontier on the silver axis. The rise in real income that this represents shifts the demand for money function to the right, with the initial supply of money (stock of silver coins in circulation) remaining constant. The immediate impact of the discovery is therefore to raise the relative price of silver in terms of goods; that is, there is a *deflationary* spike in the price level of goods in terms of silver at the moment of the discovery. The flow supply curve shifts to the right, so the flow output will increase because the relative price of silver in terms of goods has risen as well. Although the demand for Eastern luxuries will rise because of the higher real income, this increased expenditure will be less than the increase in the flow supply of silver. There is then an excess supply of silver leading to an increase in the stock of silver coins in circulation. Thus the fabled influx of "American treasure" into Europe begins.

The rise in real income and the increase in silver output pull labor out of the goods sector, raising the real wage in terms of goods. This, under the demographic regime that we have postulated, leads to an increase in population and the labor force. That in turn shifts out the production possibility frontier even further for both commodities and implies increasing real income, shifting the demand for money outward as well. On the basis of the historical evidence, it is clear, however, that the increase in the net supply of new silver, added to the money stock, must have exceeded the increase in the demand for money due to the higher real income. The discovery of American silver led to huge additions to world silver stocks, about 50 percent during the sixteenth century and 85 percent during the seventeenth. Out of these additions 74 and 71 percent respectively reached Europe, and 40 percent was passed on to Asia. Production in the Americas amounted to 74 percent of world output from 1493 to 1600 and 85 percent from 1601 to 1700 (Barrett 1990). When the addition to the money stock exceeds the increase in the transactions demand for money, the price of silver in terms of goods will fall; that is, there will be inflation of the price level of goods in terms of silver. It is this outcome and its continuation that constitutes the celebrated Price Revolution of the sixteenth century.

The falling relative price of silver in terms of goods will tend increasingly to reduce the flow supply of silver, despite the increases in the labor force induced by a real wage above the Malthusian equilibrium level. The "depreciation" component of the flow demand will rise steadily, proportionately to the increasing base of the total stock of silver in circulation. The expansion of real incomes also means that the expenditure on Eastern luxuries is rising. Thus, eventually, the rate of growth of the money supply will slow down, below the rate of expansion of the demand for money, caused by increasing real incomes, and the relative price of silver $1/p$ will begin to rise. Deflation will follow inflation, creating another "long wave" in the price level. In the end the excess flow supply of silver must turn into an excess flow demand, so the stock of silver in circulation within the extended European economy will start to shrink. The falling real wage will also eventually lead to a stationary population.

The final long-run equilibrium will therefore have the same real wage that preceded the discovery of the silver deposits of the New World that set the whole "long wave" in motion. Population will be stationary, but at a higher level than previously, because of the augmented stock of silver deposits. The capital stock first declines because there must be an excess demand for goods corresponding to the excess flow supply of silver during the inflationary phase of the "long wave." It begins to increase when the money supply starts to shrink because of the logic of the model. The final capital stock will be larger, supporting the increased population and augmented natural resources created by the discovery. This, in turn, means that the price level must "overshoot." To the increase of the capital stock through the excess supply of goods corresponds an excess flow demand for silver and a reduction of the monetary stock. Deflation must follow inflation and lower the price level of goods in terms of silver back toward its initial value.

The final long-run steady state to which the system tends can now be briefly described. The three state variables, the labor force L the capital stock K, and the supply of money M, will all increase in proportion to the increase in the stock of natural resource deposits N due to the "discovery of America." The real wage w^* and price level p^* will remain constant at their original levels. Thus the stock demand and supply of money in figure 22.3 will both shift proportionately to the right leaving the relative prices of silver, $1/p^*$, and hence the price level, p^*, unchanged. In figure 22.4 the flow supply and demand for silver will also be shifted to the right at unchanged $1/p^*$, in proportion to the increase in N. In figure 22.5 the desired proportion of capital stock to money stock remains unchanged, since $r(w^*)$ is unaffected by the increase in natural resource depicts. The BB' curve shifts to the right as a result of the increase in N, leading to an increase in the same proportion of K and M at the point where the new BB' curve intersects the ray OR from the origin.

The transition to the new equilibrium and the time path of the price level are depicted in figures 22.8 and 22.9.

We begin in figure 22.8 at the initial steady state equilibrium at point a. The discovery of the additional natural resource deposits shifts out the production possibility frontier and raises real income and the stock demand for money. With the initial money supply given, this implies a jump in the relative price of silver $1/p$ from point a to point e. The additional resource deposits and the higher relative price stimulate the output of silver, leading to an excess flow supply and hence an expansion of the money supply. The demand curve for money shifts steadily to the right, because the higher real wage induced by the expansion in silver production stimulates the

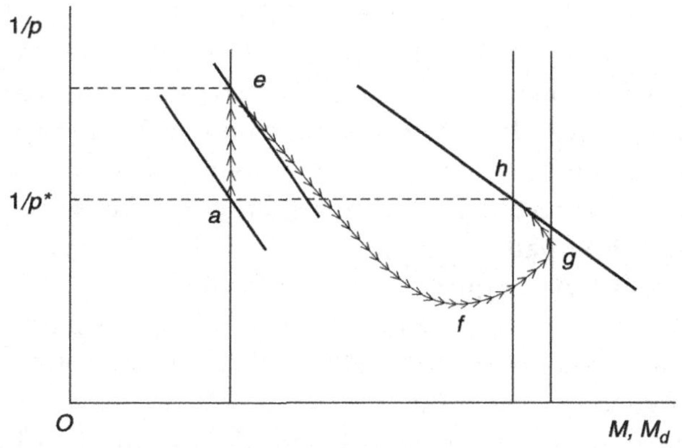

Figure 22.8
The long swing in the price level due to American silver

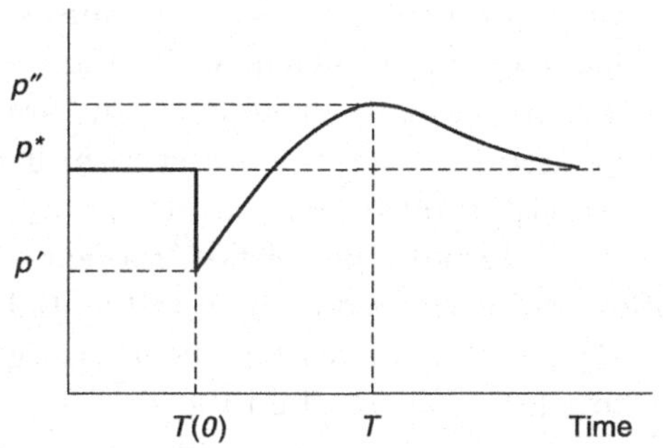

Figure 22.9
The price level pattern following the silver discoveries

growth of population and the labor force. The rate of expansion of the money supply exceeds the growth of money demand, leading to a falling relative price of silver $1/p$ or an inflation of the price level of goods in terms of silver.

The fall in $1/p$ continues to point f, falling below the initial relative price $1/p^*$. The growth of the money supply begins to slow down and is exceeded by the expansion of money demand, leading to a rising relative price $1/p$ from point f to point g. At point g the excess flow supply of silver finally becomes zero, after which it turns negative; that is, the money supply starts to contract while the relative price $1/p$ continues to rise in response to the continuing rise in money demand. Equilibrium is finally restored at point h, where $1/p$

returns to the original level $1/p^*$ the real wage falls back to w^*, and the capital stock, labor force, and the money supply all have increased in the same proportion as the increase in the natural resource deposits. Since the money supply is contracting from g to h, the capital stock now rises, recovering its losses in the transition from e to g and increasing in proportion to the money supply and the labor force.

Figure 22.9 plots the time path of the price level p that is a reciprocal of the movement of $1/p$ in figure 22.8. At $T(0)$ there is an initial deflationary spike from p^* to p', after which there is a long inflationary phase from $T(0)$ to a peak of p'' at T, followed by an asymptotic decline of the price level back toward p^*.

To confront the implications of our model with the actual historical experience is a task that we will not attempt here. There is no doubt that the price level of goods throughout Europe rose in terms of silver throughout the sixteenth century, although there is much disagreement about the extent and pattern of the rise. The causes, however, continue to be fiercely debated. Hamilton's quantity theory explanation was criticized by historians on many grounds. Some are mutually contradictory, such as the assertion that the Fisher formula is "only a truism" and that it is "based on unrealistic assumptions." Stronger than these criticisms of the internal logic of the "monetarist" explanation was the contention, pointedly made in an influential article by Ingrid Hammarström (1957), that prices had been rising well before the influx of American silver ever reached the shores of Europe.

This is where our consideration of the long-run adjustment to the shock of the Black Death can be useful. That shock was deflationary for a long time, during the "bullion famine" of the fifteenth century, but was eventually self-correcting since the rise in the relative price of silver would stimulate an expansion of silver output. This rise in European silver output has been well established by the work of Nef (1987) on the 1460 to 1530 mining boom. The two "thought experiments" that we conduct for our model, on the Black Death and the discovery of New World silver, are not fully separated in historical time. The *Niña*, *Pinta*, and *Santa María* sailed before the full adjustment to the Black Death, a century and a half earlier, had been worked out. The American silver started to arrive at Seville before the inflationary final phase of the Black Death "long wave" had ended. Thus it is no valid criticism of Hamilton's thesis to say that inflation was already occurring in Europe. The inflation was undoubtedly greatly amplified and prolonged by the American silver.

In their disillusionment with "monetary" explanations several historians have looked for "real" explanations, with population changes as the most favored among these. Much of the underlying logic of these arguments appears spurious and exasperating to economists. The pressure of population on scarce land, making food more expensive and thereby causing "inflation," is only one of the more egregious examples. Nevertheless, the controversies between "Monetarists" and "Malthusians" among economic historians (e.g., see the exchange between Robinson 1959 and Postan 1959) have the merit of trying to do justice to what is undoubtedly two fundamental factors involved in all these episodes, factors that economists have for the most part kept in separate compartments. Our model, however, embraces both population and commodity money as endogenous variables along with production in a general equilibrium framework. In this model the price level of goods in terms of silver is a *relative* price of goods and silver, and so the distinction between "real" and "monetary" factors loses its relevance.

The model requires the Price Revolution to recede and be followed by a deflationary phase. Here again it conforms to reality. While the sixteenth century was a booming inflationary period with an initial rise in real wages and expanding population under the stimulus of the discoveries, the seventeenth century was a century of stagnation and falling prices, as emphasized in a famous article by Eric Hobsbawm (1954) on the "seventeenth-century crisis," which is still the subject of a debate that shows no signs of ending. In that century real wages had fallen toward the Malthusian equilibrium level, making population stagnate, while the drain of silver to the East through the activities of the Dutch and English East India Companies lowered the price level. The model thus has the merit of pointing to a necessary connection between two historical episodes that have been considered as quite distinct. The explanation for the "seventeenth-century crisis" has been sought in such exogenous factors as for example, climatic change, when a good part of the story can be traced to the consequences of the preceding epoch.

Concluding Observations

We began this essay by invoking Heckscher on the relation between theory and history. Our intention was to respond to his "plea for theory" in the practice of economic history. In 1929 his plea was a cry in the wilderness, not heeded until about a generation later, by the emergence of the New Economic History school. The main emphasis of that school, however, on the application of econometric techniques to historical data and less on theory per se. Almost as a by-product of this work a number of contributions emerged that specifically applied or developed appropriate economic models to investigate historical problems. Whenever possible it is sufficient to simply take a well-known model or conceptual tool "off the shelf," as it were, and apply it directly to economic history. Frequently, however, the historical circumstances are such that no standard model applies directly. One then needs to be sufficiently resourceful and opportunistic to "do it yourself." What we have presented here is just such a do-it-yourself model.

The core of our model is the Jones (1971) specific-factors construct, which was itself inspired by the historical problem of Anglo-American productivity differences in the nineteenth century. What we have added is the endogenization of the labor supply by appending a neo-Malthusian demographic regime, combined with a model of commodity money, requiring stock-flow adjustments through the application of the asset market approach. The best modern treatment of commodity money is Barro (1979). His paper also uses the stock-flow adjustment mechanism but takes real national income and the flow supply curve of "gold" as exogenously given. In our system real national income and the flow supply of silver are both endogenously determined along with the supplies of labor, capital, and money in a full general equilibrium framework. What we have done therefore is to start with one of the standard variants of the "factor proportions" approach, endogenizing the supplies of factors and money, in the spirit of the Findlay (1995) Ohlin Lectures. It is interesting to note that Heckscher himself briefly considered the implications of making factor supplies respond positively to increases in their own real rewards in his 1919 article.

The application of this analytical apparatus to history takes the form of "thought experiments," investigating the effect on the long-run equilibrium of the model and the transition to that state of some "shock" that corresponds to a significant historical event. The two experiments that we have conducted are the Black Death, in which one-third of the population and labor force disappears practically overnight, and the effect of the discovering of rich silver deposits in the New World. The first is a demographic shock that has subtle and complex monetary consequences, since we show that the phenomena associated with the great bullion famine of the fifteenth century can be derived as consequences of the demographic disaster of the previous century. The other is a monetary shock that has demographic consequences. Together, the two experiments show that it would be misguided to take an exclusively "Malthusian" or "Monetarist" view of history, for the demographic and monetary regimes are both embedded in a wider system of general interdependence.

We also saw that despite his plea for the application of theory to the analysis of historical epochs, Heckscher did not consider it applicable to shifts from one epoch to another, since the determinants of such shifts generally lie outside the realm of economics. Thus the plague outbreak in Europe in the midfourteenth century and the discovery of silver mines in the New World are both examples of Heckscher's point. Each of these events had momentous economic consequences but were largely, though not entirely, brought about by circumstances independent of economic conditions.

The spirit of our model is entirely "classical." What we call long-run equilibrium is nothing but the "stationary state" of Malthus, Ricardo, and Mill. (Why else did Paul Samuelson 1971 talk about the Ricardo-Viner model?) The system returns to its original state, as in the case of the adjustment to the Black Death. But can it really be that the Europe of, say, 1547, was the same as the Europe of 1347 even if population, real wages, money supply, and so on, were all the same? Not really. What is missing is "hysteresis," the alteration to the underlying parameters of the system when it is subjected to a shock, so that it does not return to the original starting point but to some other position determined by the changes during the transition.

This is the idea underlying the brilliant little book by the late Harvard medievalist David Herlihy (1997) entitled *The Black Death and the Transformation of the West*. Herlihy argues persuasively that the experience of affluence in the aftermath of the Black Death fundamentally altered cultural and social values in a direction conducive to material advancement and economic growth. To take but one example, the age at marriage of females could have increased, shifting the fertility curve of our figure 22.1 to the left, resulting in a higher equilibrium wage and per capita income, with a smaller equilibrium population. Such changes could ultimately have led to the Industrial Revolution, in which the "Unbound Prometheus" of technological change altered the world forever and made our "preindustrial" classical model no longer applicable.

Notes

We are indebted to Rolf Henriksson for letting us dip into his immense knowledge of Eli Heckscher's ideas and to André Burgstaller, Stan Engerman, Duncan Foley, Paul Krugman, David Laidler, Lars Magnusson, and Alan Taylor for constructive comments. Carin Blomkvist and Lilian Öberg typed the manuscript. The essay was financed by a SAREC research grant, which is gratefully acknowledged.

1. We are grateful to David Laidler for drawing our attention to the exposition by Marshall in a volume of his early writings edited by Whitaker (1975), in which the money commodity is the shells of an extinct fish that can be dredged for at increasing marginal cost in terms of goods.

References

Ashley, William J. 1900. *Surveys Historic and Economic.* London: Longmans.

Barrett, Ward. 1990. World bullion flows, 1450–1800. In James D. Tracy, ed., *The Rise of the Merchant Empires: Long-Distance Trade in the Early Modern World, 1350–1750.* Cambridge: Cambridge University Press.

Barro, Robert J. 1979. Money and the price level under the gold standard. *Economic Journal* 89:13–33.

Bridbury, A. R. 1962. *Economic Growth: England in the Later Middle Ages.* London: Allen & Unwin.

Burgstaller, André. 1994. *Property and Prices.* Cambridge: Cambridge University Press.

Cipolla, Carlo M. 1964. Economic Depression of the Renaissance? *Economic History Review* 16:519–24.

Day, John. 1987. *The Medieval Market Economy.* Oxford: Basil Blackwell.

Findlay, Ronald. 1995. *Factor Proportions, Trade, and Growth.* Cambridge: MIT Press.

Findlay, Ronald. 1998. A Plea for Trade Theory in Economic History. *Economic and Social Review* 29:313–21.

Fischer, David Hackett. 1996. *The Great Wave: Price Revolutions and the Rhythm of History.* Oxford: Oxford University Press.

Flam, Harry, and Flanders, June M. 1991. Introduction. In Harry Flam and June M. Flanders, eds., *Heckscher-Ohlin Trade Theory.* Cambridge: MIT Press.

Flynn, Dennis O. 1996. *World Silver and Monetary History in the 16th and 17th Centuries.* Aldershot: Variorum Collected Series, Ashgate.

Fogel, Robert. 1967. The Specification Problem in Economic History. *Journal of Economic History* 27:283–308.

Goldthwaite, Richard A. 1980. *The Building of Renaissance Florence.* Baltimore: Johns Hopkins University Press.

Habakkuk, H. J. 1967. *American and British Technology in the Nineteenth Century.* Cambridge: Cambridge University Press.

Hamilton, Earl J. 1934. *American Treasure and the Price Revolution in Spain.* Cambridge: Harvard University Press.

Hammarström, Ingrid. 1957. The price revolution of the sixteenth century: Some Swedish evidence. *Scandinavian Economic History Review* 5:118–54.

Hatcher, John. 1977. *Plague, Population and the English Economy 1348–1530*. London: Macmillan.

Heckscher, Eli F. 1904. Ekonomisk historia: några antydningar. *Historisk Tidskrift* 24:167–98.

Heckscher, Eli F. 1919. Utrikeshandelns verkan på inkomstfördelningen. *Ekonomisk Tidskrift* 21:1–32.

Heckscher, Eli F. 1920. Historia och nationalekonomi. *Historisk Tidskrift* 40:1–22.

Heckscher, Eli F. 1922. *Ekonomi och historia*. Stockholm: Bonniers.

Heckscher, Eli F. 1929. A Plea for Theory in Economic History. *Economic History* (suppl. to *Economic Journal*) 1:525–34.

Heckscher, Eli F. 1930. Den ekonomiska historiens aspekter. *Historisk Tidskrift* 50:1–85.

Heckscher, Eli F. 1931a. *Merkantilismen: ett led i den ekonomiska politikens historia*, 2 vols. Stockholm: Nordstedt och Söner.

Heckscher, Eli F. 1931b. *Industrialismen: Den ekonomiska utvecklingen 1750–1914*. Stockholm: Nordstedt och Söner.

Heckscher, Eli F. 1933. The Aspects of Economic History. In *Economic Essays in Honour of Gustav Cassel*. London: Allen & Unwin.

Heckscher, Eli F. 1935–49. *Sveriges ekonomiska historia från Gustav Vasa*, 4 vols. Stockholm: Bonniers.

Heckscher, Eli F. 1936. Den ekonomiska historiens aspekter. In *Ekonomisk-historiska studier*. Stockholm: Bonniers.

Heckscher, Eli F. 1937. Materialistisk och annan historieuppfattning. *Svensk Tidskrift* 27:109–20.

Heckscher, Eli F. 1942. *Svenskt arbete och liv: från medeltiden till nutiden*. Stockholm: Bonniers.

Heckscher, Eli F. 1944. Materialistisk och annan historieuppfattning. In *Historieuppfattning: materialistisk och annan*. Stockholm: Bonniers.

Heckscher, Eli F. 1947. Ekonomisk historia och dess gränsvetenskaper. *Historisk Tidskrift* 67:1–17.

Heckscher, Eli F. 1951. *Studium och undervisning i ekonomisk historia*. Lund: Gleerups.

Henriksson, Rolf G. H. 1991. Eli F. Heckscher: The economic historian as economist. In Bo Sandelin, ed., *The History of Swedish Economic Thought*. London: Routledge.

Herlihy, David. 1997. *The Black Death and the Transformation of the West*. Cambridge: Harvard University Press.

Hobsbawm, Eric J. 1954. The crisis of the seventeenth century. *Past and Present*, nos. 5–6. Reprinted in Trevor Aston, ed., *Crisis in Europe 1560–1660*. New York: Doubleday Anchor Books, 1967.

Jones, Ronald. 1971. A three-factor model in theory, trade and history. In Jagdish N. Bhagwati et al., eds., *Trade, Balance of Payments and Growth: Papers in International Economics in Honor of Charles P. Kindleberger*. Amsterdam: North Holland.

Lee, Ronald. 1973. Population in pre-industrial England: An econometric analysis. *Quarterly Journal of Economics* 87:581–607.

Livi-Bacci, Massimo. 1997. *A Concise History of World Population*, 2nd ed. Oxford: Basil Blackwell.

Lopez, Robert S. 1953. Hard times and investment in culture. In Wallace K. Ferguson et al., eds., *The Renaissance: Six Essays*. New York: Harper.

Lopez, Robert S., and Miskimin, Harry A. 1962. The economic depression of the Renaissance. *Economic History Review* 14:408–26.

Lopez, Robert S., Miskimin, Harry A., and Udovich, Abraham L. 1970. England to Egypt, 1350–1500: Long-term trends and long-distance trade. In Michael A. Cook, ed., *Studies in the Economic History of the Middle East*. London: School of Oriental and African Studies.

McNeill, William H. 1977. *Plagues and Peoples*. New York: Anchor Books.

Miskimin, Harry A. 1975. *The Economy of Early Renaissance Europe, 1300–1460*. Cambridge: Cambridge University Press.

Nef, John U. 1987. Mining and metallurgy in medieval civilisation. In M. M. Postan and Edward Miller, eds., *Cambridge Economic History of Europe: Trade and Industry in the Middle Ages*, vol. 2, 2nd ed. Cambridge: Cambridge University Press.

Niehans, Jurg. 1993. A reassessment of scholastic monetary theory. *Journal of the History of Economic Thought* 15:229–48.

Ohlin, Bertil. 1924. *Handelns teori*. Stockholm: Nordiska Bokhandeln.

Ohlin, Bertil. 1933. *Interregional and International Trade*. Cambridge: Harvard University Press.

Phelps-Brown, E. H. and Hopkins, Sheila V. 1956. Seven centuries of the prices of consumables, compared with builders' wage rates. *Economica*, n.s., 23:296–314.

Postan, M. M. 1959. Note. *Economic History Review* 12:77–82.

Robinson, W. C. 1959. Money, population and economic change in late medieval Europe. *Economic History Review* 12:63–76.

Rybczynski, T. M. 1955. Factor endowment and relative commodity prices. *Economica*, n.s., 22:336–41.

Samuelson, Paul A. 1971. Ohlin was right. *Swedish Journal of Economics* 73:365–84.

Spufford, Peter. 1988. *Money and Its Use in Medieval Europe*. Cambridge: Cambridge University Press.

Temin, Peter. 1966. Labor scarcity and the problem of American industrial efficiency in the 1850s. *Journal of Economic History* 26:361–79.

Temin, Peter. 1971. Labor scarcity in America. *Journal of Interdisciplinary History* 1:251–64.

Whitaker, J. K., ed. 1975. *The Early Economic Writings of Alfred Marshall, 1867–1890*, vol. 1. London: Macmillan.

Index

Made in United States
North Haven, CT
04 November 2026

21772746R00313